A GRAMMAR OF NEW TESTAMENT GREEK

A GRAMMAR OF NEW TESTAMENT GREEK J. H. MOULTON

VOLUME II

ACCIDENCE AND WORD-FORMATION

WITH AN APPENDIX ON

SEMITISMS IN THE NEW TESTAMENT

J. H. MOULTON
W. F. HOWARD

T&T CLARK
EDINBURGH

T&T CLARK LTD
59 GEORGE STREET
EDINBURGH EH2 2LQ
SCOTLAND

Latest impression 1996

ISBN 0 567 01012 0

British Library Cataloguing-in-Publication Data
A catalogue record for this book is available from the British Library

Printed and bound in Great Britain by Hartnolls Ltd, Bodmin

PREFACE TO VOLUME II.

At last, with the publication of Part iii., the second volume of Moulton's *Grammar of New Testament Greek* is brought to a close. The reader may be reminded that before sailing for India in October 1915 Dr. Moulton had finished the MS of Parts i. and ii., and had already written the important chapter upon Word-Composition for Part iii. His intention was to complete Part iii. with a chapter on Word-Formation by Suffixes, and to enrich the volume with an introductory chapter on New Testament Greek, which would lead up to an Appendix on Semitisms in the Greek Testament. In writing this Appendix he counted on the collaboration of his colleague the Rev. C. L. Bedale, a Semitic scholar of real distinction and great promise. Dr. Moulton died in the Mediterranean in April 1917, a victim of the ruthless submarine campaign. Mr. Bedale died in a military hospital at Cambridge on 8th March 1919.

The editor, a former pupil of Dr. Moulton at Didsbury College, who had also worked under his guidance as a research student in Hellenistic Greek at Manchester University, was entrusted with the responsible duty of completing this volume and seeing it through the press. Part i. appeared in 1919, Part ii. in 1921. Meanwhile death had removed another worker whose tireless industry and unslumbering vigilance were well known to other toilers in this field. How sorely the editor has missed the help of Mr. Henry Scott may be gauged by comparing the number of misprints in Part ii. with the few corrections to be made in Part i., which owed so much to his careful reading of the proofs. Beyond writing the last thirteen pages of the Introduction, the editor's responsibility in preparing the first two parts for publication was limited to the verification or insertion of numerous references and the less important though exacting labours of proof-correction.

It is in the third part which now appears that the reader will recognise the immeasurable loss which this Grammar has suffered through the death of its brilliant author. Happily the chapter on Word-Composition can be printed almost exactly as it left the writer's hands. Every student of New Testament lexicography will be grateful for this last gift of a great philologist. In passing to the chapter on Suffixes, the reader cannot fail to notice an abrupt change. No one is more acutely conscious of the reader's loss than the editor himself. In all matters of comparative philology, Dr. Moulton wrote with the authority of a master. The editor can only claim to have exercised the diligence of the scribe. He gladly acknowledges his debt to two writers in particular where many might be named. The late Karl Brugmann's compendious *Vergleichende Grammatik* has been in constant use, and his *Griechische Grammatik* (edited by Albert Thumb in Iwan Müller's *Handbuch der klassischen Altertumswissenschaft*) has been a close companion for years past. Grateful acknowledgment is also made to Professor Albert Debrunner, formerly of Bern, now of Jena, for his useful manual in Max Niedermann's *Sprachwissenschaftliche Gymnasialbibliothek*, as well as for his contributions to the *Indogermanische Forschungen*. Other debts are freely acknowledged throughout the chapter.

The discussion about the Semitic element in the Greek of the New Testament has passed into a new phase since Dr. Moulton projected his Appendix in conjunction with Mr. Bedale. This is chiefly due to three great Semitic scholars who have challenged the accepted theory regarding the original language in which the Acts, the Apocalypse, and the Fourth Gospel were written. Professor Torrey's brilliant work on the Composition and Date of Acts appeared in 1916, but the editor first met with it while on a visit to America shortly after the war, when the first part of the Grammar had already passed through the press. Archdeacon Charles had already impressed Dr. Moulton by some of his arguments in *Studies in the Apocalypse*, but the exhaustive examination of the grammar of Revelation came before the public with the issue of the International Critical Commentary upon that book in the autumn of 1920. The lamented Professor Burney's *Aramaic Origin of the Fourth Gospel* appeared in the summer of 1922. These books have aroused learned discussion among both Hellenists and Semitists, and the time has come for a critical survey of this entire field in its bearing upon the Grammar of New Testament Greek. If some readers are disposed to lament the long delay in completing the publication of this volume, others will be thankful that it has been possible to take full account of the most important literature since Wellhausen's *Einleitung*, including the revised edition of Radermacher's *Neutestamentliche Grammatik* and the valuable linguistic studies by the eminent Semitist Père Lagrange, in his Commentaries on Luke (1921), Matthew (1923), and John (1925).

Another feature in the Appendix deserves special mention. When the MS had already gone to the publisher in the spring of 1927 the editor had the good fortune to read a thesis by Dr. R. McKinlay, dealing with Semitisms in the New Testament in the light of later popular Greek. It is to be hoped that this valuable work will soon find a publisher. Meanwhile, by the kindness of the author, the editor has been allowed to insert within square brackets an allusion to this work wherever Dr. McKinlay has proved that an alleged Semitism is an established construction in either Medieval or Modern Greek. The actual evidence will be forthcoming when the thesis is published.

A word may be permitted with regard to the Indices. Limits of space forbid the registering of every Greek word that occurs in this volume. But prepositional compounds will generally be found by consulting the index under the prepositions, and most other words can be traced under the suffix heading. Words about which special information is given and those which occur more than once in the book are included to facilitate cross-reference. The index of papyrus citations has been prepared with special care. Almost without exception these quotations have been made from the original collections. For the benefit, however, of those students who have not access to the principal collections, the editor has provided a list of all the citations which can be consulted in the well-known selections edited by Wilcken, Mitteis, Milligan, and Witkowski.

It now remains to acknowledge with warmest gratitude the help so generously given by friends. From the first Professor Milligan has put his great knowledge and experience at the editor's disposal, and has encouraged him in many ways. The late Mr. Henry Scott read the proofs of Part i. with minute care. Mr. E. E. Genner, Fellow of Oriel, was kind enough to read the first proofs of Part iii. Numerous footnotes testify to his learned suggestions, but it would be impossible to indicate the extent of his ungrudging kindness. He not only discovered many misprints that might have escaped the editor's eye, but he also saved him from careless blunders of a more serious kind. Only those who have had experience of the unselfish help so freely given by this most accurate of scholars can guess how deep is the obligation under which both editor and reader stand to Mr. Genner. Three Handsworth colleagues, the Rev. Dr. W. F. Lofthouse, the Rev. Henry Bett, and the Rev. C. R. North, with all their customary kindness, have read through the page proofs and ensured greater accuracy, and Mr. North has also helped where the pointing of Aramaic words was in doubt. It is a special delight to record this assistance given by one who laid the foundations of his wide Semitic scholarship under the inspiring teaching of Charles Bedale.

No words can express the editor's grateful sense of the generous encouragement and the patient forbearance shown by the publishers, Messrs. T. & T. Clark whose disinterested service to the cause of biblical scholarship has long been a tradition throughout the theological world. Gratitude is also due to Messrs. Morrison & Gibb, for their skill and care, as well as for their patience, in setting and resetting the type at all the tedious stages by which this volume has passed through the press.

Whatever be the imperfections in the pages for which the editor himself is solely responsible (*i.e.* pp. 22–34 and 332–543), he desires to express his humble gratitude for the privilege that has fallen to him of preparing this legacy of his beloved teacher for the press, and of making it available by means of cross-references and indices as a standard work of reference for all students of the Greek Testament.

W. F. HOWARD.

HANDSWORTH COLLEGE,
July 1928.

CONTENTS.

PART iii. WORD-FORMATION.

ABBREVIATIONS.

The abbreviations for papyri and inscriptions are given in Index I (*e*) and (*f*), pp. 503–512 below, with the full titles of the collections quoted.

References are to pages, unless otherwise stated.

Abbott *JV*=*Johannine Vocabulary*, by E. A. Abbott. London, 1905.
AJP=*American Journal of Philology*. Baltimore, 1880 ff.
AJT=*American Journal of Theology*. Chicago, 1897 ff.
Allen *Comm. Matt.*=*A Critical and Exegetical Commentary on the Gospel acc. to St Matthew*, by Willoughby C. Allen. 3rd ed. Edinburgh, 1912. (See *ICC*.)
Allen *Comm. Mark*=*The Gospel acc. to St Mark, with Introduction and Notes*, by Willoughby C. Allen. (The Oxford Church Biblical Commentary), London, 1915.
Archiv—see Index I (*e*).
Audollent—see Index I (*e*).
Bauer *HNT*=*Das Johannesevangelium* erklärt von Walter Bauer. 2te Aufl. Tübingen, 1925. (See *HNT*.)
Bauer *Lex.*=*Griechisch-Deutsches Wörterbuch zu den Schriften des Neuen Testaments und der übrigen urchristlichen Literatur*, von Walter Bauer. Giessen, 1924–28.
Beginnings of Christianity=*The Beginnings of Christianity*, Pt. I., *The Acts of the Apostles*. Edited by F. J. Foakes Jackson and Kirsopp Lake. London, vol. i, 1920; vol. ii, 1922; vol. iii, 1926.
Berl. Phil. Woch.=*Berliner Philologische Wochenschrift*.
Bl-D, or Blass-Debrunner=*Friedrich Blass' Grammatik des neutestamentlichen Griechisch*, bearbeitet von A. Debrunner. Göttingen, 4te Aufl. 1913, 5te 1921.
Blass *Gr.*=*Grammar of NT Greek*, by F. Blass. English tr. by H. St J. Thackeray. 2nd ed. London, 1905.
Blass *Philology*=*Philology of the Gospels*, by F. Blass. London, 1898.
Blass *Pron.*=*Pronunciation of Ancient Greek*. English tr. by Parton, 1890.
Boisacq=*Dictionaire Étymologique de la Langue Grecque*, par Émile Boisacq. Heidelberg and Paris, 1907–16.
Bonhöffer=*Epiktet und das Neue Testament*, von Adolf Bonhöffer. Giessen, 1911.
Bornhäuser=*Die Bergpredigt*. Versuch einer zeitgenössischen Auslegung, von Karl Bornhäuser. Gütersloh, 1923.
Bousset—see *SNT*.

Brugmann *Dem.*=*Die Demonstrativpronomina der indogerm. Sprachen* von K. Brugmann. Leipzig, 1904.

Brugmann *Dist.*=*Die distributiven u. d. kollektiven Numeralia der idg. Sprachen*, von K. Brugmann. Leipzig, 1907.

Brugmann *Gr.*[4] or Brugmann-Thumb=*Griechische Grammatik*, von Karl Brugmann. 4te vermehrte Aufl., von Albert Thumb. München, 1913.

Brugmann *Grd.*[2]=*Grundriss der vergleichenden Grammatik der indogerm. Sprachen*, von K. Brugmann u. B. Delbrück. Strassburg. 2te Aufl. I., 1897; II. i, 1906; ii, 1911; iii, 1913–16. (For Syntax see under Delbrück.)

Brugmann *KVG*=*Kurze vergleichende Grammatik der idg. Sprachen*, von Karl Brugmann. Strassburg, 1904.

Buck *Gr. Dial.*=*Introduction to the Study of the Greek Dialects*, by C. D. Buck. Boston, 1910.

Burkitt *Ev. d. M.*=*Evangelion da-Mepharreshe*, collected and arranged by F. C. Burkitt. Cambridge, 1904.

Burkitt *Gosp. Hist.*=*The Gospel History and its Transmission*, by F. C. Burkitt. 3rd ed. Edinburgh, 1911.

Burkitt *Syr. Forms*=*Syriac Forms of NT Proper Names*, by F. C. Burkitt. London, 1912.

Burney *Aram. Orig.*=*The Aramaic Origin of the Fourth Gospel*, by C. F. Burney. Oxford, 1922.

Burney *Poetry*=*The Poetry of our Lord.* An Examination of the Formal Elements of Hebrew Poetry in the Discourses of Jesus Christ, by C. F. Burney. Oxford, 1925.

Burton *Gal.*=*A Critical and Exegetical Commentary on the Epistle to the Galatians*, by E. De Witt Burton. Edinburgh, 1921. (See *ICC.*)

Cadbury *AJT*=*Luke—Translator or Author?* by H. J. Cadbury. (Reprint from *AJT* (see above), xxiv, No. 3, July 1920.)

Cagnat—see Index I (*e*).

Capes *Ach. L.*=*The History of the Achaean League as contained in the remains of Polybius*, edited with introduction and notes by W. W. Capes. London, 1888.

CBE=*Cambridge Biblical Essays*, ed. H. B. Swete. London, 1909.

CGT=*Cambridge Greek Testament.*

Chandler=*A Practical Introduction to Greek Accentuation*, by H. Chandler. 2nd ed. Oxford, 1881.

Charles *Asc. Isai.*=*The Ascension of Isaiah*, translated from the Ethiopic Version, by R. H. Charles. London, 1900.

Charles *Enoch*=*The Book of Enoch*, ed. by R. H. Charles. Oxford, 1893.

Charles *Revelation*=*A Critical and Exegetical Commentary on the Revelation of St John*, by R. H. Charles. 2 vols. Edinburgh, 1920. (See *ICC.*)

Charles *Studies*=*Studies in the Apocalypse*, by R. H. Charles. Edinburgh, 1913.

Charles *Test. XII Patr.*=*The Greek Versions of the Testaments of the Twelve Patriarchs*, ed. by R. H. Charles. Oxford, 1908.

Charles—see also under *OA*.

Chrest.—see Index I (*f*).

Cl. Phil.=*Classical Philology*. Chicago.

Cobet *NT Vatic.*=*Novum Testamentum Graece ad fidem codicis Vaticani restitutum*, ab A. Kueno et C. G. Cobeto, cum praefatione Cobeti. Leiden, 1860.

Conybeare and Stock *Sel.*=*Selections from the Septuagint*, by F. C. Conybeare and St G. Stock. Boston, 1905.

CQ=*Classical Quarterly*. London, 1907 ff.

CR=*Classical Review* (London, 1887 ff.). Especially reference is made to J. H. Moulton's collection of forms and examples from the papyri in *CR* xv, 31–38 and 434–442 (Feb. and Dec. 1901), and xviii, 106–112 and 151–155 (March and April 1904).

Crönert *Mem.*=*Memoria Graeca Herculanensis*, by W. Crönert. Leipzig, 1903.

DAC=*Dictionary of the Apostolic Church*, ed. by J. Hastings. 2 vols. Edinburgh, 1915, 1918.

Dalman *Gr.*^{2}=*Grammatik des Jüdisch-Palästinischen Aramäisch*, von Gustaf Dalman. 2te Aufl. Leipzig, 1905.

Dalman *WJ*=*The Words of Jesus*, by G. Dalman. Eng. ed. tr. D. M. Kay. Edinburgh, 1902.

Dalman *Wörterbuch*=*Aramäische-neuhebräisches Handwörterbuch zu Targum, Talmud und Midrasch*, von Gustaf H. Dalman. 2te Aufl. Frankfurt a. Main, 1922.

DB=*Dictionary of the Bible*, ed. by J. Hastings. 5 vols. Edinburgh, 1898–1904.

Debrunner-Blass—see Bl-D.

Debrunner *Wortb.*=*Griechische Wortbildungslehre*, von Albert Debrunner. Heidelberg, 1917.

Deissmann *BS*=*Bible Studies*, by G. A. Deissmann. Eng. ed., including *Bibelstudien* and *Neue Bibelstudien*, tr. by A. Grieve. Edinburgh, 1901.

Deissmann *In Christo*=*Die neutestamentliche Formel "in Christo Jesu,"* von G. A. Deissmann. Marburg, 1892.

Deissmann *LAE*=*Light from the Ancient East*. Eng. tr. by L. R. M. Strachan. London, 1910. 2nd ed. (4th Germ. ed.), 1927.

Deissmann *Paul*=*St Paul, A Study in Social and Religious History*. Eng. tr. by L. R. M. Strachan. London, 1912. 2nd ed., Eng. tr. (of 4th Germ. ed.) by W. E. Wilson, 1926.

Delbrück=*Vergleichende Grammatik der indogermanischen Sprachen*, von K. Brugmann und B. Delbrück. Bde III–V, *Syntax*, von B. Delbrück. Strassburg (i) 1893, (ii) 1897, (iii) 1900. (Large Roman numerals indicate the volume number in the whole Grammar; small Roman numerals in brackets give the volume in Delbrück's *Syntax*.)

DLZ=*Deutsche Literaturzeitung*. Leipzig.

G. R. Driver *Orig. Lang.*=*The Original Language of the Fourth Gospel*. A criticism of Dr Burney's thesis, by G. R. Driver. (Reprinted from the *Jewish Guardian*, Jan. 5 and 12, 1923.)

S. R. Driver *Tenses*=*A Treatise on the Use of the Tenses in Hebrew*, by S. R. Driver. 3rd ed. Oxford, 1892.

EBi=*Encyclopædia Biblica*, ed. by T. K. Cheyne and J. S. Black. 4 vols. London, 1899–1903.

EGT=*Expositor's Greek Testament*, ed. by W. Robertson Nicoll. 5 vols. London, 1897–1910.

Eranos=*Eranos. Acta philologica Suecana.* Upsala.

Expos=*The Expositor*, ed. by W. R. Nicoll, afterwards by James Moffatt. London, 1875–1925. (Cited by series, volume and page.)

Exp T=*The Expository Times*, ed. by J. Hastings, afterwards by A. W. and E. Hastings. Edinburgh, 1889 ff.

Field *Notes*=*Notes on the Translation of the New Testament*, by Frederic Field. Cambridge, 1899.

Fraenkel *Geschichte d. Nom. Ag.*=*Geschichte der griechischen Nomina agentis auf -τήρ, -τωρ, -της(-τ-)*, von Ernst Fraenkel. Strassburg, 1910, 1912.

Fraenkel *ZVS*=(1) Zur Geschichte der Verbalnomina auf -σιο-, -σία. (2) Beiträge zur Geschichte der Adjectiva auf -τικός. Göttingen, 1913. (For *ZVS* see below.)

G and H—see P Oxy in Index I (*f*).

Ges-K (or G-K)=*Gesenius' Hebrew Grammar*, ed. by E. Kautzsch. Eng. tr. by Collins and Cowley. Oxford, 1910.

Gildersleeve Studies=*Studies in Honor of Basil L. Gildersleeve.* Boston, 1902.

Giles *Manual*²=*A Short Manual of Comparative Philology for Classical Students*, by P. Giles. 2nd ed. London, 1901.

Goodwin *Gr. Gr*²=*A Greek Grammar*, by W. W. Goodwin. 2nd ed. London, 1894.

Goodwin *MT*=*Syntax of the Moods and Tenses of the Greek Verb*, by W. W. Goodwin. 3rd ed. London, 1889.

Gregory *Prol.*—see under Ti.

Guillemard=*Hebraisms in the Greek Testament*, by W. H. Guillemard. Cambridge, 1879.

Harnack *Luke*=*Luke the Physician*, by A. Harnack. Eng. tr. by J. R. Wilkinson. London, 1907.

Harnack *Sprüche*=*Sprüche und Reden Jesu*, von A. Harnack. Leipzig, 1907.

Harnack *Sayings*=*The Sayings of Jesus.* Eng. tr. by J. R. Wilkinson. London, 1908.

Harris *Codex Bezae*=*A Study of Codex Bezae*, by J. Rendel Harris. Cambridge, 1891.

Harris *OPJ*=*The Origin of the Prologue to St John's Gospel*, by Rendel Harris. Cambridge, 1917.

Harris *Testimonies*=*Testimonies*, by Rendel Harris, with the assistance of Vacher Burch. Cambridge, pt. i, 1916; pt. ii, 1920.

Harsing=*De Optativi in Chartis Aegyptiis Usu*, by Carl Harsing. Bonn, 1910.

Hatzidakis=*Einleitung in die neugriechische Grammatik*, von G. N. Hatzidakis. Leipzig, 1892.

Haupt=*Die Gefangenschaftsbriefe* (Meyers Kommentar ü. d. NT), von Erich Haupt. Göttingen, 1902.

Hawkins *HS*=*Horæ Synopticæ*, by J. C. Hawkins. 2nd ed. London, 1909.

Heinrici=*Die Korintherbriefe* (Meyers Kommentar), von G. Heinrici. Göttingen, 1896.

Heinrici Studien=*Neutestamentliche Studien Georg Heinrici dargebracht*. Leipzig, 1914.

Helbing *Gr.*=*Grammatik der Septuaginta*: Laut- und Wortlehre, von R. Helbing. Göttingen, 1907.

Herwerden *Lex.*=*Lexicon Graecum suppletorium et dialecticum*. 2nd ed., 2 vols. Leiden, 1910.

Hirt *Gram.* or *Hbd.*=*Handbuch der Griechischen Laut- und Formenlehre*, von Herman Hirt. Heidelberg, 1902.

Hobart=*The Medical Language of St Luke*, by W. K. Hobart. Dublin, 1882.

HNT=*Handbuch zum Neuen Testament*, herausgegeben von Hans Leitzmann. Tübingen, 1907.

H-R=*A Concordance to the Septuagint*, by E. Hatch and H. A. Redpath. Oxford, 1897.

HTR=*Harvard Theological Review*. Cambridge, Mass., 1908 ff.

ICC=*The International Critical Commentary*. Edinburgh.

IF or *Idg F*=*Indogermanische Forschungen*, ed. formerly by K. Brugmann and W. Streitberg. Strassburg, 1892 ff.

IG, *IGSI*, *IMAe*—see Index I (*e*).

James *Lang. of Pal.*=*The Language of Palestine and Adjacent Regions*, by J. Courtney James. Edinburgh, 1920.

Jannaris *Gr.*=*A Historical Greek Grammar*, by A. N. Jannaris. London, 1897.

JBL=*Journal of Biblical Literature*. New Haven, Conn.

JHS—see Index I (*e*).

Johannessohn *Kasus u. Präp.*=*Der Gebrauch der Kasus und der Präpositionen in der Septuaginta*, von Martin Johannessohn. Teil i. Berlin, 1910.

JTS=*Journal of Theological Studies*. Oxford, 1900 ff.

Kaibel—see Index I (*e*).

Kautzsch *Gr.*=*Grammatik des Biblisch-Aramäischen*, von E. Kautzsch. Leipzig, 1884.

K.Bl. and K-G—see Kühner.

Kennedy *EGT*=The Epistle to the Philippians, ed. by H. A. A. Kennedy in the *Exp. Greek Testament*, vol. iii. London, 1903.

Kennedy *Sources*=*Sources of NT Greek*, by H. A. A. Kennedy. Edinburgh, 1895.

Kieckers—see p. 9 n.[1].

Knowling=The Acts of the Apostles, ed. by R. J. Knowling in the *Exp. Greek Testament*, vol. ii. London, 1900.

Kretschmer *Einl.*=*Die Einleitung in die Geschichte der griechischen Sprache*, von P. Kretschmer. Göttingen, 1896.
Kretschmer *Entstehung*=*Die Entstehung der Koine* (Sitzungsberichte d. Wien. Akad., 1900).
Kretschmer *Vaseninschriften*=*Die griech. Vaseninschriften ihrer Sprache nach untersucht.* Gütersloh, 1894.
Kühner or K.Bl., K-G=*Ausführliche Grammatik der griechischen Sprache*, von R. Kühner. 3te Aufl., Elementar- und Formenlehre, von F. Blass, i, ii. Hannover, 1890–92. Satzlehre, von B. Gerth, i, ii, 1898, 1904.
Kuhring=*De Praepositionum Graec. in Chartis Aegyptiis Usu*, by W. Kuhring. Bonn, 1906.
KZ=*Kuhns Zeitschrift für vergleichende Sprachforschung.* Berlin and Gütersloh, 1852 ff.
Lagrange *S. Matt.*=*Évangile selon Saint Matthieu* (Études Bibliques), par Le P. M.-J. Lagrange. Paris, 1923.
Lagrange *S. Marc*=*Évangile selon Saint Marc* (Ét. Bibl.). Paris, 1920.
Lagrange *S. Luc*=*Évangile selon Saint Luc* (Ét. Bibl.). Paris, 1921.
Lagrange *S. Jean*=*Évangile selon Saint Jean* (Ét. Bibl.). Paris, 1925.
Lake *Cod. Sin.*=*Codex Sinaiticus Petropolitanus.* With Introduction by Kirsopp Lake. Oxford, 1911.
Law=*The Tests of Life.* A Study of the First Epistle of St John, by R. Law. Edinburgh, 1909.
Lewy *Fremdwörter*=*Die Semitischen Fremdwörter im Griechischen*, von H. Lewy. Berlin, 1895.
Lietzmann *HNT*=*Handbuch zum NT*, iii. 1. Römerbrief, I. u. II. Korinther-, Galaterbrief, erklärt von Hans Lietzmann. Tübingen, 1906 ff.
J. Lightfoot *Hor. Hebr.*=*Horae Hebraicae et Talmudicae*, by John Lightfoot (1658). Oxford, 1859.
J. B. Lightfoot *Ep. Ign. ad Polyc.*=*The Apostolic Fathers*, by J. B. Lightfoot, part ii, 3 vols. 2nd ed. London, 1889.
Lightfoot *Fresh Revision*=*On a Fresh Revision of the English New Testament*, by J. B. Lightfoot. London, 1891.
Lightfoot *Notes*=*Notes on Epistles of St Paul from Unpublished Commentaries*, by J. B. Lightfoot. London, 1895.
Lindsay=*The Latin Language*, by W. M. Lindsay. Oxford, 1894.
Lipsius *Gr. Unt.*=*Grammatische Untersuchungen über die bibl. Gräcität*, von K. H. A. Lipsius. Leipzig, 1863.
Lob. *Paral.*=*Paralipomena Grammaticae Graecae*, by C. A. Lobeck. Leipzig, 1837.
Lob. *Phryn.*=*Phrynichi Ecloga*, ed. C. A. Lobeck. Leipzig, 1820.
Lohmeyer *HNT*=*Handbuch z. NT*, iv. 1. Die Offenbarung des Johannes, erklärt von Ernst Lohmeyer. Tübingen, 1926.
LS=*A Greek-English Lexicon*, by H. G. Liddell and R. Scott. 8th ed. Oxford, 1901. (The new LS=a new edition, revised and augmented throughout by Henry Stuart Jones. Oxford, 1925.)

Margolis *Gr.*=*A Manual of the Aramaic Language of the Babylonian Talmud*. Grammar, Chrestomathy and Glossaries, by Max L. Margolis. München, 1910.

Marti *Gr.* (or *K. Gr.*)=*Kurzgefasste Grammatik der Biblisch-Aramäischen Sprache*, von Karl Marti. 4te Aufl. Berlin, 1911.

Mayor *Comm. James*=*The Epistle of St James*. The Greek text with introduction, notes and comments, by J. B. Mayor. 3rd ed. London, 1910.

Mayor *Comm. Jude and 2 Pet.*=*The Epistle of St Jude and the Second Epistle of St Peter*. Greek text with introduction, notes and comments, by J. B. Mayor. London, 1907.

Mayser *Gr.*=*Grammatik der gr. Papyri aus der Ptolemäerzeit*, von E. Mayser. Leipzig, i. 1906; ii. 1. Berlin u. Leipzig, 1926.

McKinlay=*Semitisms in the New Testament in the Light of Later Popular Greek*. Unpublished thesis by R. McKinlay.

McNeile *Comm. Matt.*=*The Gospel acc. to St Matthew*. The Greek text with introduction, notes and indices by A. H. McNeile. London, 1915.

Meisterhans[3]=*Grammatik der attischen Inschriften*, von K. Meisterhans. 3te Aufl. von E. Schwyzer. Berlin, 1900.

Mélanges Nicole—see Index I (*e*).

Melcher=*De Sermone Epicteteo quibus rebus ab Attica regula discedat*, by P. Melcher. Halle, 1906.

Merx=*Die vier kanonischen Evangelien nach ihrem ältesten bekannten Texte*, von Adalbert Merx. Berlin, 1902–11.

Meyer *Gr.*=*Griechische Grammatik*, von Gustav Meyer. 3te Aufl. Leipzig, 1896.

Milligan *Selections*—see Index I (*f*).

Milligan *Thess.*=*St Paul's Epistles to the Thessalonians*, the Greek text, with introduction and notes, by G. Milligan. London, 1908.

Mitteis *Papyruskunde.*=*Grundzüge und Chrestomathie der Papyruskunde*, II. i., ed. L. Mitteis. See under Wilcken, also Index I (*f*).

Moeris=*Moeridis Lexicon Atticum*, ed. J. Pierson. Leiden, 1759.

Moffatt *ICC*=*A Critical and Exegetical Commentary on the Epistle to the Hebrews*, by James Moffatt. Edinburgh, 1924.

Moffatt *Introd.*=*Introduction to the Literature of the NT*. Edinburgh, ed.[2] 1912, ed.[3] 1918.

Moffatt *NT*=*A New Translation of the NT*. 3rd ed. London, 1914.

Monro *Hom. Gr.*=*A Grammar of the Homeric Dialect*, by D. B. Monro. 2nd ed. Oxford, 1891.

Moulton *Christian Religion*=*The Christian Religion in the Study and the Street*, by J. H. Moulton. London, 1918.

Moulton *Einl.*=*Einleitung in die Sprache des Neuen Testaments*. (Translated, with additions, from *Proleg.*[3]) Heidelberg, 1911.

Moulton *Prol.* or *Proleg.*[3]=*A Grammar of NT Greek*, by James Hope Moulton. Vol. i, Prolegomena. 3rd ed. Edinburgh, 1908.

Nachmanson *Beitr.*=*Beiträge zur Kenntnis der altgriechischen Volkssprache*, von E. Nachmanson. Upsala, 1910.

Nachmanson *Magn.*=*Laute und Formen der Magnetischen Inschriften*, von E. Nachmanson. Upsala, 1903.

Nägeli=*Der Wortschatz des Apostels Paulus*. Beitrag zur sprachgeschichtlichen Erforschung des Neuen Testaments, von Theodor Nägeli. Göttingen, 1905.

Nöldeke *Beitr.*=*Beiträge z. semit. Sprachwissenschaft*, von Theodor Nöldeke. Strassburg, 1904.

Nöldeke *Syr. Gr.*[2]=*Kurzgefasste syrische Grammatik*, von Theodor Nöldeke. 2te Aufl. Leipzig, 1898.

Norden *Agnostos Theos*=*Untersuchungen zur Formengschichte religiöser Rede*, von Eduard Norden. Leipzig, 1913.

Norden *Ant. Kunstprosa*=*Die antike Kunstprosa vom VI Jahrhundert v. Chr. bis in die Zeit der Renaissance*, von E. Norden. 2 Bde. Leipzig, 1915.

O(xford) A(pocrypha)=*The Apocrypha and Pseudipigrapha of the Old Testament in English*, ed., in conjunction with many scholars, by R. H. Charles. 2 vols. Oxford, 1913.

OCT (Oxford Classical Texts)=*Scriptorum Classicorum Bibliotheca Oxoniensis*.

OGIS—see Index I (*e*).

OHL (or *Oxf. Heb. Lex.*)=*Hebrew and English Lexicon of the OT*, ed. by F. Brown, S. R. Driver, and C. A. Briggs. Oxford, 1906.

Ottley *Isaiah*=*The Book of Isaiah acc. to the Septuagint*, trans. and ed. by R. R. Ottley. 2 vols. 2nd ed. Cambridge, 1909.

Oxford Studies=*Oxford Studies in the Synoptic Problem*, ed. by W. Sanday. Oxford, 1911.

Parry=*The Pastoral Epistles*, with introduction, text and commentary, by R. St J. Parry. Cambridge, 1920.

Peake's Commentary=*A Commentary on the Bible*, ed. by Arthur S. Peake. Edinburgh, 1919.

Pelagia=*Legenden der heiligen Pelagia*, ed. H. Usener. Bonn, 1879.

Petersen *Gr. Dim.*=*Greek Diminutives in -ION*. A Study in Semantics, by Walter Petersen. Weimar, 1910.

v. d. Pfordten=*Zur Geschichte der griechischen Denominativa*, von H. F. von der Pfordten. Leipzig, 1886.

Preisigke *Ostr.* and *Sammelb.*—see Index I (*e*).

Prellwitz=*Etymologisches Wörterbuch der griechischen Sprache*, von Walther Prellwitz. Göttingen, 1892.

Psichari=*Essai sur le Grec de la Septante*, par Jean Psichari. (Extrait de la *Revue des Études juives*, Avril 1908.) Paris, 1908.

Radermacher *Gr.*=*Neutestamentliche Grammatik* (*HNT* i. 1), von L. Radermacher. Tübingen, 1911. 2te Aufl., 1925.

Ramsay *C. and B.*—see Index I (*e*).

Ramsay *Paul*=*Paul the Traveller and Roman Citizen*, by W. M. Ramsay. 3rd ed. London, 1897.

Ramsay *Teaching of Paul*=*The Teaching of Paul in the Terms of the Present Day*. London, 1913.

REGr=*Revue des Études grecques*. Paris, 1888 ff.

Reinhold=*De Graecitate Patrum*, by H. Reinhold. Halle, 1898.

Riddell=*A Digest of Platonic Idioms*, by J. Riddell (in his edition of the *Apology*). Oxford, 1867.

R. McK.—see under McKinlay.

Roberts=*Introduction to Greek Epigraphy*, by E. S. Roberts. Cambridge, 1887.

Robertson *Gr.*=*Grammar of the Greek Testament in the Light of Historical Research*, by A. T. Robertson. New York, 1914. 3rd ed., 1919.

Rossberg=*De Praepositionum Graecarum in Chartis Aegyptiis Ptolemaeorum Aetatis Usu.* C. Rossberg. Jena, 1909.

Rouffiac=*Recherches sur les charactères du grec dans le Nouveau Testament d'après les inscriptions de Priène*, par Jean Rouffiac. Paris, 1911.

Rudberg=*Neutestamentliche Text und Nomina Sacra.* Upsala, 1915.

Rutherford, *Gram.*=*First Greek Grammar*, by W. G. Rutherford. London, 1907.

Rutherford *NP*=*The New Phrynichus*, by W. G. Rutherford. London, 1881.

Sanders=*Facsimile of the Washington Manuscript of the Four Gospels in the Freer Collection*, with an introduction by H. A. Sanders. Michigan, 1912.

Sandys and Paley=*Select Private Orations of Demosthenes.* Cambridge, 1875. 3rd ed., 1898.

Scham=*Der Optativgebrauch bei Clemens von Alexandrien*, von Jakob Scham. Paderborn, 1913.

Schmid *Attic.*=*Der Atticismus in seinen Hauptvertretern von Dionysius von Halikarnass bis auf den zweiten Philostratus*, von W. Schmid. 4 Bde und Register. Stuttgart, 1887–97.

Schmidt *Jos.*=*De Flavii Josephi Elocutione*, by W. Schmidt. Leipzig, 1893.

Schrade=*Reallexikon der indogermanischen Altertumskunde*, von O. Schrade. Strassburg, 1901.

Schubart=*Einführung in die Papyruskunde*, von W. Schubart. Berlin, 1918.

Schulthess *Das Problem*=*Das Problem der Sprache Jesu*, von F. Schulthess. Zürich, 1917.

Schulthess *ZNTW* (see below)=*Zur Sprache der Evangelien.* Giessen, 1922.

Schwyzer=*Grammatik der pergamenischen Inschriften*, von E. Schweizer (since Schwyzer). Berlin, 1898.

Scrivener *Codex Bez.*=*Bezae Codex Cantabrigiensis*, ed., with a critical introduction, annotations and facsimiles, by F. H. Scrivener. Cambridge, 1864.

Scrivener *Collation*=*A full Collation of the Codex Sinaiticus with the Received Text of the NT*, by F. H. Scrivener. Cambridge, 1864. 2nd ed., 1867.

SH=*A Critical and Exegetical Commentary on the Epistle to the Romans* (*ICC*), by W. Sanday and A. C. Headlam. 5th ed. Edinburgh, 1902.

Sharp *Epict.*=*Epictetus and the New Testament*, by D. S. Sharp. London, 1914.

Simcox—*The Writers of the New Testament*, by W. H. Simcox. 2nd ed. London, 1902.

Smith *L and L of Paul*=*The Life and Letters of St Paul*, by David Smith. London, 1919.

SNT=*Die Schriften des Neuen Testaments*, herausgegeben von Johannes Weiss. 3te Aufl. Göttingen, 1917. (Gal. 1 u. 2 Kor. erkl. von W. Bousset.)

v. Soden, *Die Schriften*=*Die Schriften d. Neuen Testaments in ihre ältesten erreichbaren Textgestalt*, hergestellt von Hermann Freiherr von Soden. 4 Bde. Berlin, 1902–13.

Solmsen *Gr. Wortf.*=*Beiträge zur Griechischen Wortforschung*, von Felix Solmsen. 1te Teil. Strassburg, 1909.

Sophocles *Lex.*=*Greek Lexicon of the Roman and Byzantine Periods*, by E. A. Sophocles. Boston, 1870.

Souter *Lex.*=*A Pocket Lexicon to the Greek New Testament*, by Alexander Souter. Oxford, 1917.

Stahl *Synt.*=*Kritisch-historische Syntax des griechischen Verbums der klassischen Zeit*, von J. M. Stahl. Heidelberg, 1907.

Stephanus *Thes.*=*Thesaurus Graecae Linguae*, ab Henrico Stephano constructus. 5 vols. Paris, 1572.

Stevenson *Gr.*=*Grammar of Palestinian Jewish Aramaic*, by W. B. Stevenson. Oxford, 1924.

Sütterlin=*Zur Geschichte der Verba Denominativa im Altgriechischen*, 1te Teil: die Verba Denominativa auf -άω -έω -όω, von Ludwig Sütterlin. Strassburg, 1891.

Syll.—see Index I (*e*).

Thackeray *Gr.*=*A Grammar of the OT in Greek*, i, by H. St J. Thackeray. Cambridge, 1909.

Thackeray *Schweich Lectures*=*The Septuagint and Jewish Worship*. London, 1922.

ThLZ=*Theologische Literaturzeitung*. Leipzig, 1876 ff.

Thompson *Palaeography*=*Handbook to Greek and Latin Palaeography*, by E. Maunde Thompson. 2nd ed. London, 1894; 3rd ed., 1913.

Thumb—see Brugmann *Gr.*[4]

Thumb *Dial.*=*Handbuch der griechischen Dialekte*, von A. Thumb. Heidelberg, 1909.

Thumb *Handb.*=*Handbook of the Modern Greek Vernacular*, by A. Thumb. Translated from the second German ed. by S. Angus. Edinburgh, 1912.

Thumb *Hellen.*=*Die griechische Sprache im Zeitalter des Hellenismus*, von A. Thumb. Strassburg, 1901.

Thumb *Sp. Asper*=*Untersuchungen über d. Spiritus Asper im Griechischen*, von A. Thumb, Strassburg, 1889.

Ti=*Novum Testamentum Graece*, by C. Tischendorf. Editio octava critica maior. 2 vols. Leipzig, 1869–72. Also vol. iii, by C. R. Gregory, containing *Prolegomena*, 1884.

Torrey *CDA*=*The Composition and Date of Acts*, by C. C. Torrey. Camb. Mass., 1916.

Torrey, *C. H. Toy Studies*=*The Translations made from the original Aramaic Gospels*, by C. C. Torrey. (See *C. H. Toy Studies.*)

Torrey *HTR*=*The Aramaic Origin of the Gospel of John.* (See *HTR.*)

C. H. Toy Studies=*Studies in the History of Religions presented to Crawford Howell Toy.* New York, 1912.

Valaori=*Der delphische Dialekt*, von J. Valaori. Göttingen, 1901.

Veitch=*Verbs Irregular and Defective*, by W. Veitch. Oxford, 1887.

Viereck *SG*—see Index I (*e*).

Viteau *Étude sur le grec du Nouveau Testament*, par J. Viteau. i, Paris, 1893; ii, 1896.

Vocab.=*The Vocabulary of the Greek Testament illustrated from the Papyri and other non-literary sources*, by J. H. Moulton and G. Milligan. London, 1914– .

Vogeser=*Zur Sprache der griechischen Heiligenlegenden*, von J. Vogeser. München, 1907.

Völker=*Papyrorum gr. Syntaxis Specimen*, von F. Völker. Bonn, 1900.

W^1, W^2—see Wellhausen.

Wackernagel *Hellen.*=*Hellenistica* (Einladung zur akadem. Preisverkündigung), von Jacob Wackernagel. Göttingen, 1907.

Wackernagel *Vorlesungen*=*Vorlesungen über Syntax.* Erste Reihe. 2te Aufl. Basel, 1926; zweite Reihe, 1924.

Walde *Lat. Etym. Wort.*=*Lateinisches etymologisches Wörterbuch*, von A. Walde. Heidelberg, 1906. 2te Aufl., 1910.

J. Weiss=*Der erste Korintherbrief* (Meyers Kommentar), von Johannes Weiss. Göttingen, 1910.

Wellhausen=*Einleitung in die drei ersten Evangelien*, von J. Wellhausen. Berlin, 1te Aufl. (W^1), 1905; 2te Aufl. (W^2), 1911.

Wellhausen *Das Evangelium Matthaei.* Berlin, 1904.

Wellhausen *Das Evangelium Marci.* Berlin, 1903.

Wellhausen *Das Evangelium Lucae.* Berlin, 1904.

Wellhausen *Das Evangelium Johannis.* Berlin, 1908.

Wendland=*Die urchristlichen Literaturformen*, von Paul Wendland. (*HNT* I. 3.) 2te Aufl. Tübingen, 1912.

Wernle=*Die synoptische Frage*, von Paul Wernle. Freiburg i. B., 1899.

Wessely *Studien*=*Studien zur Palaeographie und Papyruskunde*, herausgeg. von C. Wessely. Leipzig, 1901.

Wessely *Zauberpap.*=C. Wessely, *Griechische Zauberpapyri von Paris und London.* See Index I (*f*), under P Par 574.

Wetstein=*Novum Testamentum Graecum*, by J. J. Wetstein. 2 vols. Amsterdam, 1751.

WH=*The New Testament in the Original Greek*, by B. F. Westcott and F. J. A. Hort. Vol. i, Text (also ed. minor); vol. ii, Introduction. Cambridge and London, 1881; 2nd ed. of vol. ii, 1896.

WH *App*=Appendix to WH, in vol. ii, containing Notes on Select Readings and on Orthography, etc.

Wilamowitz *Lesebuch*=*Griechisches Lesebuch*, von U. von Wilamowitz-Moellendorff. i. Text; ii. Erläuterungen. 3te unveränd. Aufl., 1903; 7te unveränd. Aufl., 1920. Berlin.

Wilcken *Papyruskunde.*=*Grundzüge und Chrestomathie der Papyruskunde*, I. i, ed. U. Wilcken. See under Mitteis, also Index I (*f*).

Wilcken—see *Archiv* and *UPZ* in Index I (*e*) and (*f*.)

Windisch=*Der zweite Korintherbrief* (Meyers Kommentar), von H. Windisch. Göttingen, 1924.

Witk.—see Index I (*f*).

WM=*A Treatise on the Grammar of New Testament Greek, regarded as a sure basis for NT Exegesis*, by G. B. Winer. Translated from the German, with large additions and full indices, by W. F. Moulton. 3rd ed. Edinburgh, 1882.

Wright *Comp. Gr. Gram.*=*Comparative Grammar of the Greek Language*, by Joseph Wright. Oxford, 1912.

WS=*G. B. Winers Grammatik des neutestamentlichen Sprachidioms*. 8te Aufl. neu bearbeitet von P. W. Schmiedel. Göttingen, i. Teil, 1894; ii. Teil, erstes Heft, 1897; zweites Heft, 1898.

Zahn=*Introduction to the NT*, by Theodor Zahn. Eng. tr. of 3rd ed. Edinburgh, 3 vols., 1909.

Zahn *Matthäus*=*Das Evangelium des Matthäus*, ausgelegt von Theodor Zahn. Leipzig. 1te Aufl. 1903, 4te Aufl. 1922.

ZNTW=*Zeitschrift für die neutestamentliche Wissenschaft*. Giessen, 1900 ff.

ZVS=*Zeitschrift für vergleichende Sprachforschung* auf dem Gebiete der indogermanischen Sprachen. Begrundet von A. Kuhn. Göttingen.

Signs:

For † see pp. 225 and 334.

For *, †, ‡ see p. 292.

ADDENDA ET CORRIGENDA.

Page 10, line 11, *after* Luke, *insert* (12^{28}).
„ 16, line 14, *read* Aramaic.
„ 19, n.[2] line 3 *ab imo*, *read* Lietzmann.
„ 22, line 4, *read* 1 Co 15^{55}.
„ 22, line 17, *after* Ephesians *read* (4^{29}, 5^{5}).
„ 44, § 25, inset title, *under* Consonants, *insert* Mutes.
„ 57, line 8, *before* Moeris *insert* See p. 209 n.[1] ;
„ 70, line 20, *after* WS 47 f., *insert* also Charles *Rev.* (*ICC*) i. 216.
„ 82, line 2 *ab imo*, for *indicio* read *iudicio*.
„ 91, line 10, *for* § 53 *read* § 52.
„ 99, n.[1] line 2 *ab imo*, first word, *read* that.
„ 100, line 6, *for* § 76 *read* § 77.
„ 103, line 13, *read* *Grd.*[2] I. 827.
„ 103, line 18, *after* λήμψομαι *insert* (p. 106), after σφυδρόν (p. 112).
„ 121 *C.* (*b*), *read* Ἵλεως survives in NT only in the nom. sing (but see Clem *ad Cor.* passim).
„ 130, line 5 *ab imo*, *for* (=i. 109–88) *read* (=i. 166–88).
„ 131, line 10 *for* -ὺς *read* -ύς.
„ 131, (3) (*b*) line 2, *read* association.
„ 135 (*b*) line 4, *read* (=-ῃ- σι).
„ 135, line 10 *ab imo*, *read* ὠδῖν.
„ 172 (*b*) **Arrangement** should be in italics.
„ 173 (4) line 2, *for* χιδιάδες *read* χιλιάδες.
„ 175, line 11, *for* τέσσαρις *read* τέσσερις.
„ 176, line 3, *after* Appendix, *insert* p. 439.
„ 176, line 8 *ab imo*, **Fractions** should be in italics.
„ 177 (*b*) last line, *read* Tob 10^{10} B.
„ 192 7. line 6, *insert* comma after (ἀπόλογος).
„ 192 8. line 2, *insert* bracket) after *ulcus*.
„ 192 n.[6], line 2, *read* Jer $43(36)^{30}$.
„ 193 9. line 3, *read* ἐρρ.
„ 198, line 8, *read* Hermas *Vis.* iii. 10^{7}.

Page 199, line 3 *ab imo*, *read* **φιλώμεθα**.
„ 204, line 8, *insert* 3 under 1 and 2.
„ 207, line 18, for τιθῇ *read* τιθῆ.
„ 210. Subjunctive. In 2 sg. *read* **δῷς, δοῖς**.
„ 219, line 16, *after* see *insert* p. 216.
„ 223, line 22, *after* Hermas *insert* *Mand.* xii. 5[3].
„ 225, line 10 *ab imo*, for -οσα *read* -υσα.
„ 226 **αἱρέω**, 3rd col. *read* **ἡρέθην**.
„ 231 **βούλομαι**, *for* (II. *a*) *read* (I. *a*).
„ 232, *after* **δέομαι** *insert* (I. *a*).
„ 234, *Fειδ, last col., *for* **ᾔδειν** *read* **ᾕδειν**.
„ 235, *Fεικ *for* present *read* perfect.
„ 235, **ἐλαύνω** Comp., *for* **ἀπ-** read **ἀπ-**.
„ 238, line 4, *for* **ἐρωτήθω** *read* **ἐρωτήσω**.
„ 239, *after* **ζωγρέω** *insert* (VII.).
„ 241, between lines 7 and 8 *insert* **ἰάομαι** *heal*.
„ 241, line 21, delete hyphen *before* **ἵστημι**.
„ 242, line 15, *after* κάθημαι *insert* (For flexion see § 87.).
„ 242, between lines 19 and 20 *insert* **κάθημαι** *sit* (*be seated*).
„ 242, line 20, *after* **καθίζω** *insert* (VII.).
„ 243, line 10 *ab imo*, *after* κεράννυμι *for* (I. *β*) *read* (II. *β*).
„ 243, foot, *insert* **κηρύσσω** *proclaim*.
„ 244, between lines 21 and 22 *insert* **κλέπτω** *steal*.
„ 246, line 3 *ab imo*, *read* **-λημπτός** †.
„ 247, **λείπω** 3rd col., *read* **ἐλείφθην**
„ 249, line 14, delete hyphen *before* **μίγνυμι**.
„ 254, transfer **πίμπρημι** to between lines 22 and 23.
„ 254, transfer **-πιπλάω** to between lines 27 and 28.
„ 255, between lines 9 and 10 *insert* **πληθύνω** *increase*.
„ 257, line 6, *for* **ῥήζω** *read* **ῥήξω**.
„ 259, line 12 *ab imo*, read *turn*.
„ 260, line 7, **σχίζω**. Comp. **δια-** *not confirmed*.
„ 260, line 27, **τάσσω**. Comp. **ἐν-** *not confirmed*.
„ 262, line 5 *ab imo*, *for* **ἔφᾱνα** *read* **ἔφᾱνα**.
„ 263, lines 20, 21, transfer **φείδομαι** to between lines 10 and 11.
„ 266, line 3 *ab imo*, *for* **-έωσα** *read* **-ἕωσα**.
„ 276. Good examples of K.D. cpds. are πρωτοπολίτης P Oxy i. 41[4], and προβατοκτηνοτρόφοι P Ryl ii. 73[6] (33–30 B.C.) and note.
„ 470, line 9. Possibly we should add a third class (*c*) ἵνα for ὅτι (=ה). So Archd. Allen attempts to explain the hard saying in Mk 4[12] (*Comm. Mark*, p. 80). But it is simpler, with Lagrange, to take ἵνα as equivalent to ἵνα πληρωθῇ in introducing the citation.

A GRAMMAR OF NEW TESTAMENT GREEK.

VOLUME II.

INTRODUCTION.

§ 1. A BOOK which has already offered Prolegomena at considerable length and furnished with plenty of detail does not seem to need an Introduction when the systematic presentation of grammatical material is at last about to begin. But there are very cogent reasons for procedure which may fairly enough be charged with cumbrousness. To begin with, my *Prolegomena* appeared in 1906, and much has to be added from the accumulations of a decade. The papyri and other sources have provided abundance of fresh material from which I could now enlarge the book much beyond the scale of the latest English or German edition. We have now the advantage of discussion upon the views of New Testament Greek grammar which Deissmann's pioneer studies in the vocabulary prompted. Without repeating what has been examined at length in the first volume, I may now apply the results to subjects which must be placed in their right light before we can fill up the outline of Hellenistic grammar as it appears in the New Testament. I shall not tarry to repeat from Winer the history of earlier research in the subject: there is enough to do in delineating the conditions as we read them to-day.[1]

1. New Testament Greek as a Unity.

§ 2. That NT Greek is in general the colloquial *lingua franca* of the early Roman Empire has been made clear by the facts presented already, and we need not even summarise

[1] Many of the subjects discussed in this Introduction were sketched in the paper on "NT Greek in the light of modern discovery," in *Cambridge Biblical Essays* (ed. Swete, 1909).

the case. With all the difference that there is between the writers of the NT, we can say of them collectively that they stand apart from literary Hellenistic monuments, the LXX excepted, in eschewing vocabulary, grammar and style which belonged to the artificial dialect of books, and applying to literary use the spoken Greek of the day. Their differences are comparable with those we notice between English speakers of varying degrees of education. Except for literal, and to some extent conventional translations, the NT contains no element which would strike contemporary Greeks as the archaic English of AV or RV strikes us to-day.

§ 3. The first impulse to this use of the *lingua cottidiana* comes from the LXX. The Pentateuch, earliest and most important section of the Greek OT, quoted in NT so frequently as to show us at once how commanding was its influence, consists generally of good and easy vernacular Greek. In the day when it was made the tendency to Atticism had hardly begun to taint Greek literature. Literary Hellenistic was not colloquial in style, but it was no artificial dialect. Despite Aristeas, the LXX was not produced for learned consumption. The Greek OT, like the NT, was meant from the first to be the people's book. When, therefore, evangelists began to write down their story, or Christian preachers to compose informal pastorals for their Churches when far away, there was a precedent ready for their use of the popular speech. It was vital that they should write in language which would enable them to reach the widest audience at once. They could have used the literary dialect, some of them, at any rate. But Paul used the tongue of the unlearned for the same reason as John Wesley did: simple language is very easy for men whose one desire is to be clear and get their message home. Two centuries later Clement of Alexandria was Atticising for the same motive that made Paul Hellenise. Cultured people then would not read a book written in the vulgar tongue, and Clement was eager "by all means to gain some." In the same spirit the apostles wrote as they spoke, that all might hear and understand. Their Greek represents, from the literary historian's point of view, the greatest of those revolts against artificialism which have recurred through the ages and kept true literature alive. Just because Attic was the finest instrument human thought has ever played upon, the Epigoni tried to honour it by destroying the reality that gave it tone. The living daughter-speech was with them, tuneful and rich in all resources of expressiveness, though the foreign strain in her parentage had brought in some new intonations and lessened the delicate refinement of the mother-tongue. The taste of an age that could not understand refused to listen to the fresh young voice, and preferred to grind out ancient records on a grammophone. The Greeks are doing it still to-day, garnishing the mummy of the past instead of cultivating the rich resources of the present. Against this and every other such outrage on the spirit of literature the New Testament makes its protest. Only nature can give the touch which stamps the highest literature, and every book of the New Testament bears this mark beyond cavil. The Apocalypse is perhaps the extreme case. Its grammar is perpetually stumbling, its idiom is that of a foreign language, its whole style that of a writer who neither knows nor cares for literary form. But just because the weird dialect is the native speech of its author, if he must use Greek, we accept it without apology; and no anthology of the rarest gems in human literature could be complete without contributions from its pages.

§ 4. We shall have to differentiate presently between writers of very unlike culture and style, but a few summary words must be ventured as to the fitness of the Hellenistic vernacular as a medium for expressing what evangelists and apostles had to say. How does it compare with the languages which lie nearest, by nature or by circumstance? Take first Semitic, in a dialect of which the NT might so easily have been written, since all its authors (except probably Luke and the author of *Hebrews*) counted Aramaic as their mother-tongue. The narrative parts, and such a book as the Apocalypse, would have suffered little. Lost Aramaic originals lie behind a fair proportion of these documents; and if these treasures had survived, those familiar with the language might well have found them no less simple, forceful and vivid than the Greek which has supplanted them. It is in the hortatory and doctrinal parts that the special advantage of Greek appears. Equally capable of simplicity, it is capable of subtlety and precision beyond any Semitic dialect, and has a far wider range. We cannot imagine the foundation documents of Christian doctrine expressed in Old Testament Hebrew. Comparing Hellenistic with classical Greek, we may fairly say that the greater simplicity of the former gives it a decided advantage over even Attic for pure narrative, although the Ionic of Herodotus may claim equality. And it is fair to assert that what the *Κοινή* has lost of subtlety and grace, as compared with the Attic of the golden age, has been of little moment for the uses of the Christian writers. These elements are comparable with the more elaborate vocabulary which we find so highly cultured a man as Paul deliberately avoiding, as over the heads of simple people whom he wanted to reach. The characteristic strength of Greek was unimpaired—its wealth of significant differentiation in verbal tense system, its simple but adequate cases, made clear by prepositional resources which are no longer over-complex as in the earlier language.

I might repeat here some words written in *Cambridge Biblical Essays* (500 f.) upon one significant instance:—

The delicate precision of the use of the optative commands our admiration as we see it in the great writers of Athens. And yet we may remember that, except to express a wish, the optative has really no function which other moods cannot express equally well, so that by practically dropping the rest of its uses, Hellenistic has lost no real necessity of language. Indeed the fact that all the Indo-European dialects have either fused these two moods into one (as Latin) or let one of them go (as post-Vedic-Sanskrit), is evidence enough that classical Greek was preserving a more superfluity, developing the same after its manner into a thing of beauty which added to the resources of the most delicate and graceful idiom the world has ever seen. But we are not belittling the masterpieces of Hellas when we say that their language was far less fitted than Hellenistic for the work that awaited the missionaries of the new world-faith. The delicacies of Attic would have been thrown away on the barbarians whom

Paul did not disdain to seek for the Kingdom of Christ. If much of the old grace was gone, the strength and suppleness, the lucidity and expressiveness of that matchless tongue were there in undimmed perfection. They are recognised still when travellers master the unschooled "jargon" of the peasants in modern Hellas, the direct descendant of the Greek of Mark and Paul. As one of the most accomplished of them, Dr. W. H. D. Rouse, well says: "The most abstruse and abstract ideas are capable of clear expression in the popular speech. The book-learned will often hesitate for an expression, the peasant never. He spends all his days in talking, and has plenty of practice; and his vernacular is not only vivid and racy, it is capable of expressing any thought. . . . His language has the further advantage of being able to form new words by composition." Assuredly a language which had all these characteristics three thousand years ago, and has them to-day, is scarcely likely to have lost them awhile during the great period when Greek was spoken and understood by a far larger proportion of civilised mankind than it had ever been in the period of its greatest glory, or has ever been again since East and West parted asunder and let the dark ages in.

2. Contacts with Literary Language.

§ 5. The general rule that NT writers do not make use of the artificial literary dialect has one partial exception to prove it; and there are naturally degrees of approximation towards this dialect according to the extent of the writer's education. We may take the exception first. It is a book which stands apart in many ways, by general consent decidedly the latest in the Canon, and the solitary NT example of pseudepigraphic writing. *2 Peter* is written in Greek which seems to have been learnt mainly from books. Greek proverbs,[1] Greek inscriptions,[2] and Greek books which we can no longer handle, contributed to the writer's vocabulary, and moulded the fine sense of rhythm to which Mayor bears effective testimony. It is to literature rather than to vernacular inscriptions and papyri that we go when we

[1] See J. B. Mayor on 2^{22}.

[2] Deissmann, *Bible Studies*, 360 ff.

seek to illustrate rare words in this little book; and the general style is far removed from the language of daily life, as any tiro can see. These traces of elaboration are as much in keeping with the character of the book as the well-understood convention by which the writer shelters under a great name from the past. Only a shallow judgement could find in either the justification of disparaging views as to the Epistle's value. The presence of a fair crop of solecisms is natural in a book so composed. If it was written, as generally supposed, early in the second century, we may note that the development of a language proper to books had advanced greatly since the age whence most of the NT writings come. As has been remarked already with reference to Clement of Alexandria, at the close of the same century,[1] the motive of this artificial language may well be that at the time of writing it commended a book to readers whose taste was no longer satisfied with a simple and natural style.[2]

§ 6. It is a long step from *2 Peter* to the Lucan writings, but we take them next because they and *Hebrews* alone show any consciousness of style. *Hebrews,* indeed, may be summarily dealt with as a composition into which admittedly[3] nothing artificial has entered, though the writer's culture prompts a style decidedly removed from the colloquial.

---

[1] For Clement's Atticising see the monograph on his use of the optative by Jakob Scham, and my review in *Deutsche Literaturzeitung*, 1914, 1503-6.

[2] On Atticism as a literary phenomenon, reaching its climax in the second century A.D. and almost justifying itself in the hands of the brilliant Syrian Lucian, see especially Schmid's *Atticismus* (Stuttgart, 1887-96). Its theory is seen best in Phrynichus (fl. A.D. 180), with his fine scorn of ἀμαθεῖς who (for example) could use γλωσσόκομον instead of γλωττοκομεῖον, and applied it to a box for books or clothes instead of restricting it to the mouthpieces of flutes. W. G. Rutherford's *New Phrynichus* (London, 1881) edits the old pedant for us, and adds thereto many like words.

[3] Blass, indeed (*Brief an die Hebräer, Text mit Angabe der Rhythmen*, Göttingen, 1903; cf. *Grammatik der Neutestamentlichen Griechisch*[2], 304 f.), argued for an elaborate system of rhythm in *Hebrews*, which would have transferred the Epistle into the literary category very decisively. It may be very seriously questioned whether prose rhythm was *consciously* elaborated even by the Attic orators, from the study of whom Blass derived his theories: it is probable that instinct alone trained the ear to rhythm, even when analysis can formulate rules. That Blass could discover orthodox rhythms even in Paul might fairly count as a *reductio ad absurdum* of his theory for *Hebrews*.

The absence of the potential optative is a primary test of freedom from artificialism, and this is complete in the Epistle. The best analogue will be the pulpit style of a cultured extempore preacher, or that of his letters to the religious press. The test just mentioned needs further inspection for Luke, the only NT writer to use the potential optative, in indirect questions and conditional with ἄν. The latter is still used in the epistolary formulæ of Ptolemaic times, when the writers are well educated, and it can hardly be called artificial, though in i/A.D. it must have been almost confined to book language. Since the growth of the Atticising movement was bringing the optative into greater prominence as a literary usage, it may be safely said that the presence of this survival was by this time essential for any claim to style. We are left then with Luke as the only *littérateur* among the authors of NT books. (I make no apology for speaking of "Luke": those who prefer "Lk_1," "Lk_2," . . . "Lk_n," are, of course, welcome to their opinion. I would only observe that in grammar and vocabulary and phraseology $Lk_{1,2} \ldots {}_n$ have an astonishing resemblance to one another.) In using the term we are not suggesting that Luke capitulated to the growing fashion of going back to archaic models as alone suitable for literary composition. A page of Josephus would disabuse our minds of any such idea. It is only that Luke as a Greek fell by a native instinct into the habit of style which would make his narrative tell. It would be hard to find ancient parallels for the variation of style he shows as his story changes its scene. A modern novelist will see to it that his country yokel and his professor do not talk the same dialect; and he will often try to make a Lancashire weaver or a Cornish miner approximate to the speech actually current in those areas. Similarly, Aristophanes makes a Megarian, a Bœotian, a Spartan woman speak their own dialect fairly correctly. But this is only partial illustration: it suits Luke's accurate reproduction of the reported dialogues that came to him in rough translations like that we postulate for Q. But it is not going as far as Luke when he steeps his style in Biblical phraseology, drawn from the Greek Old Testament, so long as his narrative moves in Palestinian circles, where the speakers use Greek that obviously represents a foreign idiom—like Shakespeare's Fluellen with his Welsh English. That Luke should do this fits in well with his presumed history. A proselyte who made his first acquaintance with the Old Testament in its Greek version was likely to feel for that version as no Hebrew could feel, accustomed to keep all his reverence for the original. His imitation of the translation-Greek of his model—*e.g.* in the construction καὶ ἐγένετο καί with a finite verb, which yields to the *acc. et infin.* in Ac[1]—reminds us of the Biblical style of John Bunyan, and other English writers whose education it was to be *homo unius libri.* That Luke instinctively departs from that style when his subject takes him away from the Biblical land and people, is equally natural. It is mostly in these parts of his work that he makes what concessions he does make to the book style. We are sometimes able to distinguish between the Greek of his sources. Compare the masterpiece of Lk 15 with the parable that follows. There is absolutely nothing in the story of the Two Sons which suggests translation from a Semitic original: the conjecture rises to one's thought that it never was translated, but spoken in Greek to an audience that knew no Aramaic—a point to which we shall return.

§ 7. There is only one other writer whom we might expect to show contacts with the literary Greek. A highly educated man like Paul,[2] who spent his early years in a great centre of Hellenistic culture, might have used the book Greek as to the manner born. It is very obvious that he did not. The exordium of an address to Athenian philosophers survives to show us that he could use the language of the higher culture when occasion required.[3] But his letters,

[1] See *Proleg.*, 16 f.

[2] Professor Deissmann's brilliant work, *St. Paul*, seems to miss the mark altogether in describing Paul as a working man, largely on the strength of his big clumsy writing inferred from Gal 6^{11}. If this interpretation of πηλίκοις γράμμασιν be conceded, such writing does not nowadays imply illiteracy, and we have no evidence that it did in Paul's day. The Apostle's tent-making is completely explained by a well-known precept of the Rabbis, and his exercise of the art by Ramsay's most reasonable supposition that a bigoted Jewish father had cut him off.

[3] Of course Luke is usually credited with Paul's *Areopagitica*, and it may be difficult to prove completely that he wrote his report from full notes, given

addressed to churches into which "not many wise were called," are studiously kept within the range of popular vocabularly and colloquial grammar. Nägeli's monograph[1] shows this conclusively for the vocabulary. As to the grammar, it may be noted that Paul uses the highly colloquial types *γέγοναν*, and perhaps *παρελάβοσαν*[2] (the former also Luke), also *καυχᾶσαι, ζηλοῦτε* and *φυσιοῦσθε* as subj., *νοΐ, ἐφ' ἐλπίδι*, etc. In the use of popular forms he and Luke go as far, with rare exceptions, as the least cultured of NT writers. These facts are the strongest possible disproof for both Paul and Luke of any charge of using book Greek: no author who could favour the Atticist rules would fail to purge his pages of vernacular inflexions. If, however, the two friends keep company in their inflexions, they part again in vocabulary and in so typical a matter as the use of the optative, and in both Paul leans away from the literary style. What Paul might have done had he been writing "treatises" (λόγοι—Ac 1[1]) like Luke, we cannot say. What has come down to us from him is all of a casual character, open letters to communities, for which permanence was never contemplated. There is a good modern parallel in Wesley's Sermons, addressed to plain folks in simple language: even when the Fellow of Lincoln preached before his University, he took care, in republishing the sermons in a volume destined to be an informal manual of doctrine, to keep their language within popular range. In them as in the Pauline Epistles "ignorant and unstable men" might find *δυσνόητά τινα*, but it would not be because of their dialect.

---

him not long after by his master. But when we find the Lukan Paul quoting Epimenides (Ac 17[28a]), and the Paul of the Pastorals citing the very same context (Tit 1[12]), with the Aratus-Cleanthes quotation (*ib.*[28b]) to match the Menander (1 Co 15[33]), we may at least remark that the speech is very subtly concocted. Paul was, moreover, much more likely than Luke to know the tenets of Stoics and Epicureans so as to make such delicately suited allusions to them. Luke's knowledge of Greek literature does not seem to have gone far beyond the medical writers who so profoundly influenced his diction. He no doubt shared with all educated Greeks some familiarity with Homer: the obsolete word *ναῦς* in Ac 27[41] was acutely traced to Homer by Blass (*Philology of the Gospels*, 186).

[1] *Das Wortschatz des Apostels Paulus* (Göttingen, 1905).

[2] *Proleg.* 52: I have modified my view with the accumulation of evidence.

§ 8. The remarkably good Greek of *James* and *First Peter* will engage our attention under another heading, but we may add here one or two points which suggest themselves in another Palestinian writer, the author of the First Gospel. In spite of Harnack, there seems little doubt that he alters the language of his sources very much more than Luke does, so as to make the style of his work decidedly more uniform. He shows the artist in his genius for compression,[1] and in his fondness for Hebraic parallelism;[2] while he frequently substitutes literary flexions for popular. Thus where Q *ap.* Luke has *ἀμφιάζει*, Mt 6^{30} shows the obsolete *ἀμφιέννυσιν*, where it has *συνάξαι* (Lk 3^{17} ℵ^{a}), Mt 3^{12} dexterously brings in the future *συνάξει*,[3] as in *ἐπισυνάξαι*, Lk 13^{34}, mended to *ἐπισυναγαγεῖν* in Mt 23^{37}.

The degree of literary flavour attained in all these amounts to very little. It may be compared, on the one side, to our literary avoidance of colloquialisms like *don't* and *can't*, which everybody uses almost exclusively in conversation, but instinctively replaces by the *lento* forms in written style, except in private letters. On the other side, we have a whole vocabulary which has its perfectly natural place in written English, with the same exception, and in the higher spoken style of serious oratory, but strikes us instantly as pedantic or affected when brought into conversation. Greek words of a similar type are avoided by Paul, but used by Luke and the *auctor ad Hebræos*. The mere fact that no NT writer thinks of avoiding the flexions which conspicuously distinguish Hellenistic from Attic,[4] or of using the dual, the final optative, or other Atticist hall-marks, is enough by itself to show that even though NT writers might sometimes take some pains with their style, the better to achieve their purpose, they would never allow themselves an archaism or affectation

---

[1] Cf. 3^{11} where *βαστάσαι*, *take off*, expresses the full content of four words in Mk 1^{7} and 11^{27} where *ἐπιγινώσκει* exactly represents *γινώσκει τίς ἐστιν* of Q, etc.

[2] See my paper in *Expositor*, VII. ii. 97 f. (reprinted in J. H. Moulton, *The Christian Religion in the Study and the Street*, 47 ff.; cf. *ib.* 79).

[3] See *Camb. Bibl. Essays*, 485.

[4] Such as the types *σπείρης*, *νοός νοΐ*, *ἡμίσους*, *ἀπεκατεστάθη*, *ἐλελύκεισαν*, *γένοναν*, *δοῖ*, *δδυνᾶσαι*, *φάγεσαι*, *λυέτωσαν*, *οἶδας οἴδαμεν*, *ἤμην*, *ἐλήμφθην*, etc. There are, of course, some which only Mark or the Apocalyptist would admit, such as *λέλυκες* or *ἔλυσες*.

which might endanger their being "understanded of the people."

§ 9. One further point needs to be guarded. There are some tests of literary Greek which have been applied in misapprehension of the facts and have produced results that are wholly misleading. Such is especially the assumption—treated as axiomatic by Harnack—that compound verbs are an evidence of cultured Greek. Harnack[1] builds upon it one of his working principles in reconstructing Q out of Mt and Lk: where either of them (which usually means Mt) shows the simplex, it goes back to Q, which is assumed to be written in rude vernacular. The axiom fails to survive so elementary a test as the counting of compound verbs in Mk and Lk. It is found that the two evangelists have an identical percentage per page, while their Greek notoriously differs more widely than anything else within the limits of the NT. Mark has actually 5·7 compound verbs per page (of WH), while *Acts* has 6·25, *Hebrews* 8·0, and Paul only 3·8. Reference may be made to the statistical investigation in *Camb. Bibl. Essays*, 492 f., where it is shown that illiterate private letters among the papyri employ compound verbs as conspicuously as Mark. A fondness for compounds is fairly enough noted as a characteristic of an individual style: for example, the contrast between the figures for Paul and for *Hebrews* (3·8 per page and 8·0) is enough to discredit the Pauline authorship of the Epistle, were there further need of witnesses. But Harnack's test must clearly disappear from our critical tool-box. The real history of the matter is that the increased use of compounds was one of the features of the **Κοινή** as compared with classical Greek,[2] and applied to literary and vernacular language alike. Writers like the First[3] and Fourth Evangelists, who markedly prefer simplicia, are in this regard aloof from a prevailing tendency.

---

[1] *Sayings*, 150 ; see the German *Sprüche*, 106.

[2] Compare the fact that *βαίνω* simplex is very nearly extinct in Hellenistic: see *Vocabulary*, *s.v.* Mark uses compounds of *πορεύομαι*, the simplex never.

[3] Note as a typical example Mark's *ἀνεμνήσθη* in 14^{72}, which Mt 26^{75} reduces to *ἐμνήσθη*, while Lk 22^{61} varies it to *ὑπεμνήσθη*.

3. Semitic Colouring.

(1) *Language Conditions of Palestine.*

§ 10. There is a large bibliography on the problem of "the mother-tongue of Jesus." We cannot discuss the problem here, but summary statements of results are demanded. It seems to me highly probable that some of the contradictory data may be reconciled by making more of the difference between Jerusalem and Galilee. The Holy City was in our Lord's time a metropolis of aggressive nationalism. The Hellenising high priests, who had filled the city with Greek customs and speech, were no more; and a fanatical hatred of all things foreign was limited only by the hard fact of a Roman Procurator and soldiers at his command, within striking distance of the Temple. Under such conditions it is easy to see that a knowledge of Greek would be reduced to a minimum demanded by the necessities of intercourse with pilgrims from the Dispersion and officials of the Roman government. Galilee, on the other hand, was notoriously "of the Gentiles." There were towns there, such as Tiberias, where Jews and Judaism were invisible. Two centuries before, there had been a general clearance of Jews, and the consequences were sufficiently lasting to give a cue to modern paradoxists like Herr Houston Stewart Chamberlain, who would fain convince us that as a Galilean Jesus must have been of Aryan blood.[1] The swine of Gerasa (Mk 5^{11}), when all is said, do not approve themselves as belonging to Jewish masters. The question really is what language or languages did the Gentile majority in Galilee speak in the first century, which the Jewish minority were compelled to use if they had any dealings with them. Now Aramaic was not only the special language of the Jews: it was in rapidly growing use as a *lingua franca* in Western Asia, its rival, of course, being Greek. The realm of Greek as a world-language extended far beyond Palestine at the time of its greatest influence. Greek inscriptions are found all over Asia Minor and eastward up to the borders of India

---

[1] *Foundations of the Nineteenth Century*, i. 210; cf. Paul Haupt, *Transactions of the Third International Congress for the History of Religions*, i. 304.

—as far, in fact, as Alexander's arms had penetrated.[1] Two parchments have been published lately[2] which came from Avroman in Media, dated respectively B.C. 88 and 22–1. They are the title-deeds of a vineyard, and are written in good *Κοινή* Greek: with them, however, is a third in a dialect unknown, the document being still undeciphered. In his notes Mr. Minns calls attention to the fact that the tide of Greek language supremacy began to ebb from Western Asia about the beginning of the Christian era. Aramaic or Syriac would be the natural tongue of Gentiles as well as Jews in Galilee a very few generations later. But it does not appear that Greek was expelled, or near expulsion, in the early part of i/A.D. We are at liberty then to reflect on the notable fact that three NT books are traditionally assigned to Galilean writers, viz. 1 Pet, Jas and Jude, and that their Greek—especially that of the first two—is of a remarkably free and idiomatic kind. On the other hand, Mark was a Jerusalemite, and his Greek equipment is very meagre. The John of the Fourth Gospel and the Epistles is also on very strong grounds claimed as a Jerusalemite, and his Greek, while correct enough, is very bald and destitute of idiom. May we not infer that Galileans might be expected to use Greek freely, as having been accustomed to it by living among Greek-speaking people? This does not mean that we should question the usual assumption that the bulk of our Lord's teaching, public and private, was in Aramaic, the language from which Palestinian Jews were not likely to deviate except when speaking to people who only knew Greek. But that He and His disciples were thoroughly familiar with Greek seems altogether probable. It is evident that if Mark's indifferent Greek may be credited to his Jerusalem upbringing, we have a contributory item which may be useful for some critical questions.

---

[1] See Dittenberger's two volumes, *Orientis Græci Inscriptiones Selectæ* (Leipzig, 1903, 1905).

[2] Ellis H. Minns, "Parchment of the Parthian Period from Avroman in Kurdistan" (*JHS*, 1915, 22 ff.).

(2) *Aramaisms and Hebraisms.*

§ 11. The past decade has produced much helpful discussion on the burning question of Semitism in the Greek Bible. Nothing has emerged, I believe, to shake the general position taken by Deissmann, adopted with some developments in *Prolegomena*, but there are some applications of the principle which I should myself admit to be too rigorous. It will be advisable therefore to restate the central thesis of "Deissmannism," albeit, alas! without the advantage of Professor Deissmann's own judgement, to seek which was in happier days as much a pleasure as a duty.

Semitism in the NT will be defined as a deviation from genuine Greek idiom due to too literal rendering of the language of a Semitic original. "Semitic" for this purpose means either Hebrew, as the language of the Old Testament, or Aramaic, as the mother-tongue of many NT writers. The definition omits intentionally the case in which literal rendering of Semitic produces Greek which is perfectly idiomatic.

The resulting sense may be (1) identical. In that case it might have seemed that we were spared the trouble of discussing Semitism, unless we felt ourselves bound to find "Latinism" in the sentence "Balbus built a wall," which is an undeniably literal rendering of *Balbus murum ædificauit.* E. Nestle, however, a first-rate authority on Semitic subjects, stoutly claimed ἕως πότε; as a Hebraism, "even if it is still used by Pallis in his MGr translation," and though it "may be quotable from early Greek, and have spread in later times." To this declaration, put forth in a review of my *Prolegomena*, I replied with the question whether the Emperor Hadrian's ἐκ πότε; and our own *till when?* were likewise to be branded as Hebraism.[1] Of course, all languages when we compare them show multitudes of idioms in which two or more of them exactly agree. The generally similar structure of the human mind secures this mitigation of the translator's otherwise intolerable lot. But beside this case, which really does not deserve detailed investigation, there is the more difficult case of approximation not amounting to identity. A literal or nearly

[1] *Camb. Bibl. Essays*, 473 f.; *Proleg.*[3] 107.

literal rendering may give us a phrase which is moderately idiomatic, but of decidedly restricted use in the language of the translation. The result may be a very marked *over-use* of a rare locution, as representing exactly what is common in the language from which the translation is made. Thus the very rare preposition ἐνώπιον—the adverbial neuter of an adjective found in Greek literature, though seldom enough—figures in legal Greek papyri to represent *coram*, without a case expressed, and in some NT writers to render לִפְנֵי. It is quite genuine Greek, but it is fair to call it a Latinism in the papyri and a Hebraism in Luke, since it is most unlikely that either would have used it except in reference to its original. So again the relative frequency of ἰδού in *James*—compared (*Proleg.* 11 n.) with the Welshman's "look you" in Shakespeare—may be reasonably enough called Hebraism if we only mean that its prominence is to be connected with the writer's familiarity with a language in which an interjection with this meaning was used much more frequently than it was in native Greek. While, however, we are justified in considering all such cases of "over-use" when we are estimating the language of a particular writer, it would be well to restrict the term Semitism (Hebraism, Aramaism) to cases where Greek idiom is violated or at least seriously strained. We will add the adjective "secondary" when Semitisms of the milder kind are in question.

Then (2) the resultant meaning, when literal translation has produced idiomatic Greek, may be something different from that of the original. In this case, of course, the translator must have misunderstood his original, or else failed to realise in what sense ordinary Greek readers would understand his phrase. A good example of the former was pointed out by Thackeray[1] in Lk 14[32]. It is clear that when we meet in a NT book a phrase which makes good sense as Greek, we shall have to treat it as Greek: we may sometimes suspect that the writer was really thinking of something different, and we may have evidence from his lapses elsewhere

[1] *JTS* xiv. 389 f. Here the reading of B preserves the recognised translation-Greek of the later LXX for the familiar Hebrew phrase for salutation, which where royalty was concerned acquired the special connotation of tendering allegiance, or, as in this passage, of making unconditional surrender.

which makes the suspicions plausible, but obviously the Greek readers for whom the book was intended never suspected anything of the kind. Except in the Apocalypse, where we have a writer who simply did not know the grammar of Greek except in shreds and patches, we shall hardly care to allow that the readers of the book on its first appearance had no adequate equipment for understanding what the author meant; and even in that book we shall only admit the assumption very sparingly. We may take as an example Wellhausen's treatment of Mk 2^7:[1] *λαλεῖ βλασφημεῖ* are to be taken together as a blundering attempt to represent an Aramaic construction which would be accurately rendered by *λαλεῖ βλασφημίας* (Lk 5^{21}).[2] Whether this is the most probable Aramiac original we need not inquire: it is enough to reply that no Greek reader could possibly suspect any other sense than that which the RV represents, and that Luke's paraphrase is no warrant for making Mark guilty of a wildly impossible Greek combination, with no second offence to create a presumption against him. The fascinating pursuit of Aramaic originals may lead to a good percentage of successful guesses; but they are mere guesses still, except when a decided failure in the Greek can be cleared up by an Aramaic which explains the error, and this acts as corroboration.

§ 12. True Semitisms in the NT are of two kinds. First come imitations, conscious or unconscious, of the Greek OT, where the translators had perpetrated "translation Greek." Secondly, there are similarly slavish renderings of Semitic sources, oral or written, which lie behind the NT documents: we may here stretch the term "sources" to include a writer's native Semitic in which he frames his sentences in his own mind, and then more or less successfully translates them into Greek. Of course, in the OT the Semitisms only differ from the second class just named in that they are Hebraisms, while those in the NT are Aramaisms—Aramaic originals in OT and Hebrew possible originals in NT may be left out of account. Perhaps we should add the difference due to the

---

[1] See his *Einl.*[1] 22.

[2] Matthew characteristically abbreviates: *οὗτος βλασφημεῖ* (9^3) practically contains the sense of *τί οὗτος οὕτω λαλεῖ; βλασφημεῖ*—see above.

fact that the LXX is a definite translation of a series of books, long current and highly authoritative, while in the NT we have free composition in Greek, based frequently upon Semitic which had no fixed or authoritative form. The NT Aramaisms accordingly will be unconscious, and due to defective knowledge of Greek. The Hebraisms of the LXX were very often conscious sins against Greek idiom, due to a theory that words believed to be divinely inspired must be rendered so that every detail had its equivalent. It was this which gave birth to Aquila's ἐν κεφαλαίῳ ἔκτισεν ὁ θεὸς σὺν τὸν οὐρανὸν καὶ σὺν τὴν γῆν: no Greek could imagine what the σύν meant, but the Hebrew אֵת must not be left without an equivalent. It must be admitted that our own RV was as unhappily conscientious when it gave us "By hearing ye shall hear," or "who also have been in Christ before me" (Rom 16[7]). Translation of this kind is, of course, an outcome of conditions peculiar to canonical books. In the LXX we find very little of it in the Pentateuch, executed before this theory of a translator's duty was framed, and very little in a book like *Tobit*, which only became (semi)canonical in its Greek, or rather in one of its two Greek forms. In estimating the effect of the LXX upon NT language we have to note carefully the very different degree in which its various parts influenced NT thought.

If we count the separate verses cited in WH to make a rough test, we find that the Pentateuch accounts for a quarter of the New Testament quotations and allusions, the Prophets (and Daniel) for nearly a half, and the Psalms for a fifth, while all the rest only amount to 6 per cent.[1] It may be added that *Isaiah* claims two-fifths of the proportion credited to the Prophets. Putting aside, therefore, the relatively negligible historical and poetical books, we have two forces acting on the NT writers from the Greek OT. On the one side is the good *Κοινή* Greek of the Law, the work of men who understood their original thoroughly, and aimed at expressing its meaning in plain every-day speech. On the other, there is the often inferior Greek of the Psalms and the Prophets, where the much more difficult original was frequently

[1] *Camb. Bibl. Essays*, 475.

misunderstood, and the misunderstanding often veiled by slavish literalness, while the development of the more rigorous theory of translation introduced yet more of this Greek that was no Greek. Since quotations from Prophets and Psalms are between two and three times as numerous as those from the Pentateuch, we might expect to find the stylistic influence of the latter altogether counterbalanced by the linguistically mischievous effects of the former. But the NT writers, except probably Luke and the author(ess) of *Hebrews*, knew the Hebrew original too well to be at the mercy of a defective translation. We very rarely find quotations which seriously violate Greek idiom. The "Biblical style" which influenced pre-eminently Luke among NT writers was that of the Pentateuch. It came first in time, stood first in authority, and being very largely narrative was more calculated to affect narrative books than the other books, which mostly supplied isolated phrases for quotation.[1]

§ 13. We proceed to remark on the extent to which Semitisms and secondary Semitisms may be observed in the several writers.[2] Let us take **Luke** first, both as the largest individual contributor and as the one who exhibits specimens of Hebraism to an appreciable extent. The most typical of Luke's many imitations of OT Greek is the narrative "it came to pass"—to represent it by the Biblical English, the appearance of which in one of our own writers would produce almost exactly the same mental association. How far this locution approximated to vernacular Greek idiom has been discussed in *Proleg.* 16 f.; and the significant fact is noted that in *Acts* Luke reverts to the form which least diverges from that vernacular. Luke often goes further in imitation of the Hebrew by writing *καὶ ἐγένετο ἐν τῷ c. infin. καὶ* . . .: here, also, there are cases elsewhere, as in Mk 4[4], where both Mt and Lk agree in omitting. Apart from these imitations of the Greek Bible, Luke shares with others certain Aramaisms which arise from literal rendering of vernacular sources. Whether Luke himself or his own immediate

---

[1] For some further remarks on LXX Greek, see my already cited essay in *Camb. Bibl. Essays*, 475 f.

[2] The details will be reserved for the Appendix.

sources in Greek were responsible can hardly perhaps be decided dogmatically. Neither Aramaic specialists nor Hellenistic have the right to decide whether he had any knowledge of a Semitic tongue: what we really need is prolonged collaboration of both, till a joint impression is formed which may have elements of authoritativeness. Much depends upon our opinion as to Luke's antecedents. If he was an Antiochene, he might very well speak Aramaic, as a language already beginning to dispute with Greek the position of general medium of communication all over Western Asia.[1] If he was a Philippian, which seems to me very much more probable,[2] he would have to learn Aramaic in Palestine, which he seems to have visited first in 57 A.D. His "two years" (cf. Ac 24^{27}) in the country were doubtless the opportunity of collecting material for his Gospel and the earlier part of *Acts.* Did he trouble to acquire Aramaic for the purpose? It was in any case not essential, for in Galilee Greek-speaking people abounded, and even in Judæa—if Luke's researches were really pursued there, of which there is not much evidence—it would be very easy to find interpreters. If this is true, all Luke's Palestinian material could come to him in Greek, and any Aramaisms or other phenomena traceable to defective Greek may be transferred to the various informants whose contributions Luke scrupulously noted down and reproduced. When, on the other hand, we find evidence that Luke's text involves a misunderstanding of a Semitic original, such as would often occur when a foreigner with a fair but incomplete knowledge of the native dialect gathers information from people of varying degrees of education, it is obvious that such misunderstanding may as easily be credited to Luke's sources as to himself. To prove him responsible, we should at least have to show that they were very numerous and evenly distributed, and that the same kind of mistake occurred in different places. And even then it

---

[1] See § 10.

[2] The tradition of his connection with Antioch appears in Eusebius (*HE* iii. 4. 6), Jerome (*de Vir. Illustr.* vii.), and the *Monarchian Prologues* (*Kleine Texte* i., by H. Leitzmann, Bonn, 1902). See art. "Luke," by K. Lake, in *DAC.* For the view that Luke belonged to Philippi, see Ramsay, *St. Paul the Traveller*, 200 ff.; art. "Luke," by Souter, in *DCG.*

might only mean that Luke took about with him some Christian brother as his dragoman, a Greek who had been in the country longer than himself and had a passable knowledge of Aramaic.

That the two chief sources, used by Luke and by the First Evangelist, were Greek, is, of course, admitted. Mark's defective Greek supplied Luke with Aramaisms ready made; and sometimes a phrase of Mark's, by which an Aramaic idiom is rendered word for word, the corresponding Greek idiom being inaccessible to him, may produce misunderstanding on Luke's part. Equally assured is Luke's use of a Greek Q, one of the translations of the Apostle Matthew's Logia, as Papias's famous sentence prompts us to hold.[1] Here we are constantly finding that Luke faithfully preserved the rough Greek of his original, where Mt freely edits.[2] That Luke treats his other sources along similar lines does not even depend on the acceptance of this doctrine, which I do not pretend to state as an admitted fact, though it seems to me quite certain. The wide differences in Greek style between one section and another of Luke's peculiar matter can only be explained by assuming that he reproduced his sources generally as he received them. Probably this was mainly because in reporting discourses of Jesus he felt it was the safest procedure, since he had no materials for checking his sources. He had "revised them afresh" (1[3] *παρηκολουθηκότι ἄνωθεν*) with personal inquiry; but when he had no information enabling him to improve what he felt to be defective, it was better to copy his notes as they stood than to amend them by guesswork. It is the existence of these wide divergences between the discourses in Luke's peculiar sections which weighs most with me in

[1] We probably do not make enough of his very definite assertion that "every one translated the Logia as best he could." While "Matthew" and Luke certainly used the same version for a considerable number of the sayings, for which we are justified in using the common symbol Q, it is highly probable that they often had different versions, and that with this in mind we should spare our ingenuity superfluous exercise in places where Mt and Lk widely differ.

[2] For some argument in support of this thesis, against Harnack, I may refer to *Expositor*, VII. vii. 411 f. (or Moulton, *Christian Religion*, 71 f.). One or two typical minutiæ are repeated above, p. 10.

my own judgement that Luke knew no Aramaic. Had he been his own translator, we should have expected to find the same evenness in the distribution of Aramaisms as we find in those general features of grammar and style which so overwhelmingly vindicate the unity of the two books *ad Theophilum.*

§ 14. We pass on to **Paul**, the next largest contributor to the NT Canon. It is soon realised that we have no longer to do with effects of conscious style. Opinions may differ as to the proper description of *Romans*, his weightiest work: some insist upon its casual character as an open letter addressed to a church that needed doctrinal upbuilding, with no more elaboration than we should put into a letter to the press, while others would make it approximate to a set treatise. But even if the second alternative were adopted, there is no possibility of claiming any definitely literary form. Nägeli's study of a section of Paul's vocabulary shows that he kept himself to words in popular use. Similarly in grammar and style we look in vain for constructions or inflexions of an archaic or worked-up character. As to his Greek, it is obvious from all we know of him that he must have spoken Greek from the first as freely as Aramaic. He calls himself *Ἑβραῖος ἐξ Ἑβραίων*, "a Hebrew of Hebrew descent," and the term naturally implies the familiar use of the Semitic mother-tongue. But the most patriotic Jew of the Dispersion could not get on without Greek. It need not be added that for Paul's missionary work in the West, Greek had no possible alternative except Latin. A man thus accustomed to use the language of the West was not likely to import into it words or constructions that would have a foreign sound. The LXX had no such supreme authority for Paul that a copying of its language would strike him as natural. And if Greek was an alternative mother-tongue to him, he would use it too unconsciously to drop into Aramaisms, defective renderings of a language he could correct as well as any one. The *a priori* view thus sketched tallies satisfactorily with the observed facts. Paul very rarely uses phrases which come from a literal rendering of the Semitic. His Semitisms are secondary at most—defensible as Greek, and natural to a Greek ear.

How carefully he kept away from language which might seem archaic or remote to the ordinary people for whom he wrote is well seen in the case of ᾅδης.[1] Paul deliberately mars the rhetorical effect of the quotation from Hosea in 1 Co 15* by substituting *θάνατε* for ᾅδη. For Hades was a Greek divinity, not a place, and the name, though common enough in literature, had dropped out of the ordinary vernacular. Its occurrence elsewhere in the NT may be traced directly to the influence of the LXX, where it is freely used. The LXX translators appropriated it from the technical language of Greek religion because they found it to be an exact rendering of the Hebrew שְׁאֹל. For Paul, however, no such felicity in the commerce of tongues could stand against the plain fact that the word in question had no place in the vocabulary of every-day Greek. In turning from lexical to grammatical considerations of style we may look at one or two hall-marks of Semitism as they affect Paul.[2] Twice in Ephesians we find the collocation *πᾶς οὐ* or *μή* for *οὐδείς* or *μηδείς*, which has been quoted as "a sign that the Semitic influence passed from Paul's thought into his language." But this Hebraism never occurs elsewhere in Paul, and its occurrence twice in this one disputed Epistle must at least be put among the special features of its language which have to be explained.[3] In 5^5 there is another possible Hebraism, *ἴστε γινώσκοντες*, the coincidence of which with *πᾶς . . . οὐ* in the same sentence perhaps emphasises the presence of language moulded on Biblical phraseology. *Ephesians* keeps to itself almost as completely another noteworthy Semitism—"sons of disobedience," "sons of men," "children of wrath," "children of light." I can find no Pauline parallels except 1 Thess 5^5 "sons

---

[1] See *Vocabulary*, *s.v.*

* At this point Dr. Moulton's MS ends abruptly in the middle of a sentence.

[2] The rest of this section (§ 14) is taken from a paper read by Dr. Moulton before the Society of Historical Theology, Oxford, on January 24, 1913; it is partly a reply to a valuable critique of his *Prolegomena* by Mr. G. C. Richards in *JTS* x. 283 ff.

[3] See *Proleg.*[3] 246 and *Einl.* 127. A unique parallel for this "Hebraism" is provided by P. Ryl ii. 113^{12} (A.D. 133), where Hieracion of Letopolis, beekeeper, complains of unjust treatment from persons *μὴ ἔχοντας πᾶν πρᾶγμα πρὸς ἐμέ*: the document is very ungrammatical, but shows no marks of Semitic nationality in the writer.

of light and sons of day," and 2 Thess 2^3 "son of perdition." The first of these Deissmann regards as a quoted Logion, and the second as a quotation from the LXX. In Col 3^6 "sons of disobedience" is interpolated; and the phrase "the children of the promise" in Gal 4^{28}, Rom 9^8 is taken out of this category altogether by the context. Here, then, is another secondary Semitism from which Paul was quite free, except when he wrote *Ephesians*, or (if so preferred) unless he wrote *Ephesians*.[1] The same absence of Semitism comes out for Paul by other tests. *Οὐ μή* in the NT is characteristic of Logia and OT quotations, both, of course, admitting the suspicion of "translation Greek," with the consequence that the locution need no more be emphatic than when in the LXX it will alternate with *οὐ* in one verse as a rendering of לֹא. In Paul it occurs only four times (with two LXX quotations to be added), and in all four the emphasis is unmistakable, making his use identical with that of classical and Hellenistic Greek. Then *ἰδού* used freely is a natural product of Semitic thought. I have compared Fluellen's "look you" as a mark of a Welshman talking English. Even the excellent Greek of the Epistle of James may show relics of the writer's Semitic mother-tongue in the frequency of *ἰδού*, as in the isolated *προσευχῇ προσηύξατο*. Paul uses *ἰδού* only eight times (and once in a quotation), and never has a trace of James's other Semitism, unless Eph 5^5 is rightly thus read[2] and comes from Paul's hand. Both *ἰδού* and *ἴδε* (*semel*) are used by him with the classical *nuance* and with normal Greek frequency. The participle with *ἦν*, etc., is probably an Aramaism sometimes in translated books, however justifiable as Greek: when Paul uses it, we can trace the same force which it has in classical writings. One more example may be named—the curious *ἐν ῥάβδῳ ἔλθω πρὸς ὑμᾶς* (1 Cor 4^{21}), which even Deissmann had to explain away, until Ptolemaic papyri, linked with Lucian, showed that *ἐν*, meaning "armed with," was good vernacular Greek.[3]

---

[1] For an interesting conjecture as to the authorship of Ephesians and its relation to Colossians, see Dr. Moulton's popular lectures, *From Egyptian Rubbish-heaps*, 59 ff. (London: C. H. Kelly. 1916).

[2] See *Proleg.*[3] 245, *Einl.* 119.

[3] See *Vocab. s.v.* *ἐν*.

§ 15. When we pass from Paul to that noble work which came from the pen of some unknown member of his circle we are met by the striking paradox that a letter "to **Hebrews**" is written by some one who knew no Hebrew, and used the Greek Bible alone. It is hardly necessary for our present purpose to discuss the structure of this Epistle. Whether it was originally an epistle or a treatise,[1] it has a literary flavour that distinguishes it from any other book in the NT Canon. "Alike in form and contents this epistle strives to rise from the stratum in which Christianity had its origin towards the higher level of learning and culture."[2] We have already[3] referred to the author's sensitive ear for the rhythm of words, and have looked in that direction rather than to any elaborate system of rhetoric for the true explanation of what must strike even the casual reader as a distinctive feature of this book. Blass was on surer ground when he pointed out another characteristic,—viz. a general avoidance of the harsher kinds of hiatus between successive words. This would probably be almost instinctive in any one who had received a good Greek education, to whom *ἐλέγετο αὐτῷ* would have sounded harsh, much as a word like "idea" sounds harsh in English when followed by a vowel in rapid speech.[4] Familiarity with some of the niceties of classical syntax may be traced in the exact significance of the tenses, in the freer and more skilful use of particles and conjunctions, and in the more complex structure of the sentence as compared with the other NT writings. Yet his skilful mastery of language never betrays the writer into artificiality, nor is his sonorous vocabulary allowed to weary us with the excessive use of heavy compounds. Dr. Nairne[5] calls our attention to the "sudden touch of conversational audacity" which introduces such a word as *πηλίκος* into the majestic description of Melchizedek (7^4). So flexible a Greek style might seem to entitle its possessor to unconditional exemption from any examination into his Semitic connexions. There is no reason to suspect him of acquaintance with either Aramaic

---

[1] See Deissmann, *BS* 49 f., and Moffatt, *Introd.* 428 ff.

[2] Deissmann, *LAE* 237. [3] *Supra*, p. 6 n.[3] [4] *CBE* 482.

[5] *The Ep. to the Hebrews*, in *CGT*, cli. His chapter on *The Style of the Epistle* abounds in illustrations of the characteristics of the author's Greek.

or Hebrew. Nevertheless one fact necessitates the inquiry. This Epistle is steeped in the language of the LXX, and quotes from it even more copiously than does St. Paul. It is therefore not surprising to find a formidable list of Semitisms in the arraignment. Three of them [1]—the predicative use of *εἰς*, *οὐ μή*, and a violent use of the participle standing by itself in the genitive absolute—need not detain us, as they occur in a direct citation from the LXX in chap. 8. A similar defence might secure speedy acquittal on another count, for the phrase *ἐν αἵματι διαθήκης* (13^{20}) is certainly based on Zech 9^{11}. It should be counted to him for righteousness, however, that in his use of such a Hebraism the author transcends Semitic idiom.[2] The presence of a "secondary Semitism" must be acknowledged in *ἐν τῷ λέγεσθαι* (3^{15}). Dalman's claim was denied on the strength of the frequent occurrence of the locution in Thucydides, Plato and Xenophon; but in view of Dr. E. A. Abbott's acute criticism, that the instances cited must convey the sense of "during," we have transferred this "Hebraism" to the category of "possible but unidiomatic Greek."[3] The same chapter furnishes another instance of the pervasive influence of the phraseology of the LXX. *Καρδία πονηρὰ ἀπιστίας* (3^{12}) can be easily paralleled from Sophocles, as was shown in *Proleg.* 74. But its subject-matter leaves us in little doubt that Biblical associations prompted this rather overstrained use in prose of the poetical genitive of definition.

§ 16. In the linguistic conditions of Palestine we have already found a clue to the remarkably free Greek of a group of writings traditionally ascribed to three members of our Lord's own circle, **1 Peter, James and Jude**. When, therefore, the question is asked [4] about the first, "Is it credible that a Galilean fisherman who left out his H's (Mt 26^{73}) should after middle life, and in the midst of absorbing occupa-

[1] See, further, *Proleg.* 72, 74, 187.

[2] Cf. Nairne, *ib.* cxlvii, "He will adopt a rude Hebraic use of the preposition *ἐν*, and by careful context fill it with significance, as in 1^{1} *ἐν τ. προφήταις* . . . *ἐν υἱῷ*, 10^{10} *ἐν ᾧ θελήματι*, $13^{20f.}$, where notice how *ἐν αἵματι* and *ἐν ἡμῖν* explain one another."

[3] *Proleg.*[3] 249, *Einl.* 341.

[4] Simcox, *The Writers of the New Testament*, 68.

tion, have learnt to write scholarly Greek like this?" the answer is by no means a foregone conclusion. Without denying the possibility that this "open letter" owes its mastery of idiom to the practised pen of Silvanus, we can yet argue that Peter's Greek may well have been better than his Aramaic. A provincial brogue of Aramaic that attracted attention in the metropolis of Judaism does not necessarily imply defective culture.[1] Moreover, in the thirty-five years that lie between the Crucifixion and the probable date of this letter, Greek rather than Aramaic would be the tongue in which Peter conversed with the Hellenist Jews of Jerusalem and Antioch, and the LXX would of necessity be the Bible used in all his missionary work abroad. Now it is evident that the author of *1 Peter* was steeped in the language of the LXX. This appears in the number of direct quotations, still more in the reminiscences of LXX phraseology which are woven into the fabric of his style. In view of the rhythm and balance of sentence, the copiousness of vocabulary, and the management of tenses and prepositions to which Bp. Chase[2] has drawn attention, it is interesting to notice points of contact which the same scholar has indicated between this Epistle and the non-Hebraic and literary books of the Apocrypha, such as *Wisdom*, *2 Mac* and *4 Mac*. From Semitisms this Epistle is singularly free, if we exclude from consideration the plentiful sprinkling of phrases and citations from the LXX. A secondary Semitism may be allowed in 1^{14} (τέκνα ὑπακοῆς),[3] and no doubt the OT is responsible for such a word as ἀπροσωπολήμπτως (1^{17}). The influence of the LXX may be traced in such words as ἀναστροφή, ἀναστρέφομαι and παρεπίδημος, but the evidence from papyri and inscriptions removes them from the old class of "Hebraisms of Vocabulary."[4]

The bilingual birthright of the Galilean may also account for the paradox that "the letter of that specially Jewish

[1] See Dalman, *Words*, 80.

[2] Hastings, *DB* iii. 781 f. Mayor (*Comm. on Jude and 2 Pet.*) even says, "Perhaps no other book of the NT has such a sustained stateliness of rhythm as *1 Pet.*"

[3] *Supra*, pp. 22 f. Cf. also Deissmann, *BS* 163 f.

[4] Deissmann, *BS* 88, 149, 194. *Vocabulary*, *s.vv.*

apostle, St. James, is perhaps the best Greek in the New Testament."[1] We need not linger over the theory of an Aramaic original.[2] The writer's fondness for paronomasia and alliteration do not suggest the hand of a translator; and whilst the crisp vivacity of James offers a striking contrast to the rather long and well-balanced sentences of *1 Peter*, such constructions as ἄγε νῦν, ἔοικεν, χρή, ἀπαρχή τις, are evidence that his style takes high rank in the Greek of the NT. Two traces of the author's Semitic mother-tongue have already been mentioned (p. 23). We must also notice an overstrain in the use of the genitive of definition in such phrases as τὸ πρόσωπον τῆς γενέσεως αὐτοῦ and ἀκροατὴς ἐπιλησμονῆς. Instrumental ἐν in 3^9 was formerly counted a Hebraism, so were the aorists in 1^{11}. But the publication of the *Tebtunis Papyri* closed the controversy about the former (cf. *supra*, p. 23), as the weighty judgement of Hort[3] may be held to have settled the other question in favour of the gnomic aorist.

The little letter that bears the name of Jude is chiefly remarkable for the wealth of its vocabulary, derived in part from the LXX, the pseudepigrapha and the Pauline Epistles. Its fondness for sonorous words might seem to suggest a wider acquaintance with literature. But writers of the **Κοινή**, "embodying older strata of the language, would suffice to supply him with his vocabulary."[4] Less flexible than *1 Peter* in syntactical structure, Jude also lacks the epigrammatic succinctness of James. Vigorous and descriptive he certainly is; and the tendency to triple expression is a well-marked feature of his style. Mayor's exhaustive analysis of his grammar shows that the author was quite at home in Hellenistic idiom. Indeed the critical microscope fails to detect a genuine Semitism in the 24 verses.

Another writer calls for brief mention with this Palestinian group on the ground of literary indebtedness rather than from considerations of style. The "Atticism" of **2 Peter** has been mentioned in an earlier section (§ 5),

---

[1] Salmon, *Introd.*[3] 139.

[2] Bp. John Wordsworth's *a priori* arguments have been fully answered by Mayor (*Comm.*[3] ccxxxii ff.).

[3] *Comm. on 1 Pet.* 96.

[4] Chase, Hastings' *DB* ii. 801.

which explained the unique character of its Greek as an artificial dialect of high-sounding words learnt from rhetoricians or books and employed with the uneasy touch of one who acquired the language in later life. It is significant that this Epistle has not a single quotation from the OT and but five uncertain allusions. This absence of the phraseology of the LXX may account for its freedom from the slightly Semitic colouring that we have noticed in the admirable Greek of the other Epistles in this group. In only two places is there any real approach to Semitism. *Ἐν ἐμπαιγμονῇ ἐμπαῖκται* may belong to the same class as James's *προσευχῇ προσηύξατο.* But in view of the slight impression which the LXX has left on his diction, and bearing in mind Dalman's caution,[1] it seems more reasonable to explain this locution as an instance of the author's tendency to reduplication. *Κατάρας τέκνα* claims kinship with that familiar genitive of definition, though a quasi-classical turn is given to the phrase by the inverted order of the words.

§ 17. Starting from Luke we have fetched a wide compass and must now return to the other three Gospels. There can, of course, be no question that translation-Greek occurs in Mark and those parts of the Synoptic Gospels which reproduce "Q." Enough has already been said to indicate that real Aramaism may be allowed ungrudgingly in those parts of the NT which are virtually translated from Aramaic oral or written sources. Wellhausen's brilliant investigation serves to remind us of the need of keeping in view the distinction made above between secondary Semitisms and Semitisms pure and simple. For like other Semitic specialists, that lamented scholar was perhaps sometimes in danger of recognising foreign idiom where a Greek reader of the book would never suspect anything wrong. Thus in Lk 14[18] *ἀπὸ μιᾶς* is said to be the Aramaic *min ch'da*, which he calls "a thumping Aramaism." But why call it an Aramaism when the phrase was a very idiomatic expression in Luke's own language? It is merely a case of coincidence between the

[1] *Words*, 34. "The Hebrew mode of emphasising the finite verb by adding its infinitive or cognate substantive . . . is in the Palestine Aramaic of the Jews—apart from the Targums—quite unknown."

idioms of two languages; and while Mark perhaps might have been ignorant of it as Greek, and was capable of employing it as a literal translation of the Aramaic, Luke simply could not have used it as other than a normal Greek term. Although the same instinct for Greek style cannot be claimed for **Matthew**, the First Gospel betrays Semitic authorship only in its range of ideas and its sympathetic understanding of the Jewish-Christian point of view. The language, on the other hand, is a correct if rather colourless Greek which avoids the vulgar forms without displaying a mastery of the literary syntax. The Hebraisms which in Luke express a literary feeling that formed itself on ancient models are noticeably wanting from Matthew's narrative. Instances have already been given of his editorial revision where Luke preferred to sacrifice style in favour of fidelity to the original source. The same freedom is shown in his treatment of Mark,[1] so much so indeed that it has been said[2] that "Matthew græcises Mark." One or two exceptions, however, may be noticed because of their bearing on the question of Semitisms. The phrase *πέμψας διά* is unquestionably the right reading in 11², and Wellhausen points out that שלח ביד in Aramaic as in Hebrew is a regular phrase for sending a message. In the Lucan parallel *διά* has become *δύο τινάς*, from which it seems to follow that Luke misread[3] the literal *διά* of his source, which is preserved in Matthew. Incidentally we have here strong evidence in favour of the Greek basis in the common source. Similar testimony is borne by the notable logion in Mt 10²⁶⁻³³ where, in addition to the sequence of words in v.²⁷ and the whole of v.³¹, the Lucan parallel gives us also Matthew's *ἐπὶ τῶν δωμάτων*, a good Hellenistic phrase; *φοβηθῆναι ἀπό*, a very marked piece of translation-Greek; and *ὁμολογεῖν ἐν ἐμοί*. Deissmann[4] describes this last as a translation made "with a painful scrupulousness coming near to a pedantry of interpretation." Even the author of the Apocalypse gives this logion in a better Greek form (cf.

[1] For instances see W. C. Allen, *ExpT* xiii. 328 f., and *Comm. on Matt.* xix f.

[2] This is Wellhausen's summary (*Einl.*¹ 35) of Zahn's argument as quoted by Wernle, *Die synoptische Frage* (1899, vii, viii and 120). But see Zahn, *Introd.* (E.T.) ii. 576, 591–2.

[3] See § 13.

[4] *In Christo*, 60, quoted in *Proleg.* 104.

Rev 3[5]). Turning to Matthew's treatment of his other chief source we note another apparent exception to the general rule. In the lawyer's question (Mt 22[36]) ποία ἐντολὴ μεγάλη ἐν τῷ νόμῳ; Mark has not μεγάλη but πρώτη πάντων, a thoroughly vernacular phrase. Matthew's form is quite clearly a much less idiomatic translation of the Aramaic (which has no degrees of comparison), and it falls in with various indications that he is here drawing upon other material, quite possibly derived from Q. This literal translation of the Aramaic would be very natural when we bear in mind the obsolescence of μέγιστος.[1] Another instance of translation-Greek which Wellhausen notices is the impersonal use of the 3 plur. active in place of the passive. This is common to all the Synoptists, but may be mentioned here because of two occurrences in Matthew which raise points of interest in Synoptic criticism. In 1[23] καλέσουσιν replaces the more natural καλέσεις of the LXX and suggests an Aramaic translation from the Hebrew current in Matthew's time as part of a collection of *testimonia*.[2] Once again in 5[15] the Matthæan οὐδὲ καίουσιν καὶ τιθέασιν preserves an Aramaism where Luke employs the more idiomatic οὐδεὶς ἅψας τίθησιν. The fact that this logion is a doublet in Luke and that in the Marcan passage the Aramaism is absent, seems to show that the saying was current in more than one form, which would account for the divergence without crediting it, with Harnack, to Luke's stylistic improvement of Q. In many of these instances given by Wellhausen,[3] although the active use of the verb is quite permissible Greek,[4] it must be allowed that the passive would probably have been used but for the influence of a Semitic original.

The language of our Second Gospel shows a very marked deficiency in culture on the part of the Jerusalemite **Mark**, who seems to have a foreign idiom perpetually behind his Greek. "Peter's former interpreter"—for so we must render Papias's phrase[5]—had been a ὑπηρέτης or "minister of the

---

[1] See *Proleg.* 78, and cf. the frequent introduction of μέγας μέγας in early papyri (as P Tebt i. 63[5] (ii/B.C.)); so *Einl.* 122, 124.

[2] So A. H. McNeile, *Comm. in loc.*

[3] *Ibid.* 25 f.

[4] Cf. *Proleg.*[3] 58 f., also *Einl.* 87.

[5] Μᾶρκος μὲν ἑρμηνευτὴς Πέτρου γενόμενος (or "having been Peter's interpreter"); cf. *Vocabulary, s.v.* γίνομαι.

word," that is, a teacher or catechist who accompanied an apostle on his missionary tour for the purpose of instructing inquirers in the outlines of the life and teaching of that Jesus whom they preached. We may repeat here what has been said elsewhere:[1] "There can be no question that the catechetical lessons on which the written Gospel was ultimately based, were given first in Aramaic; and they may well have become so fixed in that form that when their author transferred them to Greek they retained ubiquitous marks of too literal translation. It is of great critical importance to observe how these Aramaisms of translation were progressively smoothed away. Wellhausen shows that D has most of them and B distinctly less. Unless this is due (as Bishop Chase argued) to a Syriac infection in D, we have here a most important source of evidence as to the origin of the Western Text, of which in this respect the 'Neutral' becomes a revision. As has been noted already, there is plenty of revision of Mark's Aramaism to be seen in Matthew and Luke. In a considerable number of little points these Evangelists coincide in their amendments, a fact well explained by Dr. Sanday's suggestion[2] that the text of Mark had been polished by a cultured scribe before it reached them: our Mark descends from the unrevised form. Mark's Semitisms . . . are hardly ever really barbarous Greek, though his extremely vernacular language often makes us think so, until we read the less educated papyri. Generally we recognise them by their over-use of a possible though uncommon idiom which happens to agree with Aramaic."

A singularly neat instance came to light in a Berlin papyrus[3] to confute those who would describe *βλέπειν ἀπό* (Mk 8^{15} etc.) as a rank Hebraism: *ὡς ἂν πάντες καὶ σὺ βλέπε σατὸν ἀπὸ τῶν Ἰουδαίων.* Surely it was no Jew who gave this warning to his friend!

§ 18. The **Fourth Gospel** and the **Johannine Epistles** (which, on every consideration of style, form with it a literary unity) are the work of a writer to whom Greek was

[1] *Camb. Bibl. Essays*, 491. [2] *Oxford Studies*, 21.
[3] BGU iv. 1079^{24} (A.D. 41) (=*Selections*, p. 40).

evidently no mother-tongue. We infer this from the excessive simplicity of the style and its poverty of idiom, not from any grammatical aberrations. The conditions lend support to the theory that the author was brought up in Jerusalem (see p. 13). But in spite of certain superficial indications that point that way the style is not Semitic. Two such indications in the Gospel may be briefly noticed,—the prevailing use of parataxis and the priority of the verb in the sentence. As for the former, parataxis predominates to such an extent that we instinctively recognise an editorial hand in the flowing periods that form the prologue to the Passion narrative (13^{1-4}). Yet it is impossible to claim that the incessant co-ordination of simple sentences by *καί* is a hall-mark of Semitism after studying Deissmann's parallel[1] between the narrative in John 9^{7-11} and a Roman inscription of the time of the Antonines giving an account of the marvellous cures wrought by Asclepios. A stronger argument can be based on the arrangement of words, for, as a rule, in the Johannine writings the verb stands first and the subject follows, and it is tempting to trace the Semitic genius of language in such an order. Even upon this subject it is well to suspend judgement until careful statistical investigation on the lines of Kieckers's important monograph[2] has provided us with material for a wider induction. Meanwhile we do well to observe other significant features in the order of words. Wellhausen[3] attributes the precedence given to the verb to imitation of the Biblical style as best fitted to the subject-matter. He even discovers in the solemn rhythm a self-conscious, sacerdotal language, to be compared with the pedantry of the Priestly Code in the Pentateuch. Whatever we may think of this judgement we must accept his verdict that the position of words in general is unSemitic. This can be seen best in the tendency to remove the subject to the very end of the sentence (cf. 2^{9}, 6^{3}, 18^{33}, 19^{38}), and in the position of the dependent genitive in phrases like *αὐτοῦ οι μαθηταί, δύο ἀνθρώπων ἡ μαρτυρία*, etc. The great Semitist discovers no trace of the construct state in John, and stays

---

[1] *LAE* 131.
[2] *Die Stellung des Verbs im Griechischen* (Strassburg, 1911).
[3] *Das Evangelium Johannis*, 133–146.

his hand when he finds an occasional *casus pendens* followed by a resumptive pronoun. The linguistic evidence all goes to show that the author of the Fourth Gospel was a man who, while cultured to the last degree, wrote Greek after the fashion of men of quite elementary attainment. His uneasy movement in the region of unfamiliar idiom is never suffered to betray him into a breach of the laws of grammar.

§ 19. Very different are the phenomena that meet us in that marvellous book which so fittingly closes the canon of the NT. The Greek of the **Apocalypse** differs in an extraordinary degree from that of the Fourth Gospel. Not only does it display a greater freedom in copiousness of vocabulary and elaborate phraseology; it is simply defiant of the restraints of grammar. Various attempts have been made to secure the traditional unity of authorship with the Gospel. But even Hort's strong argument for an early date, leaving thirty years in which the author could improve his Greek before writing the Gospel, falls short of a solution. Modern criticism has little to add to the penetrating analysis which Dionysius of Alexandria furnished in the middle of the third century. Speaking with the authority of one to whom Greek was a native tongue, this critic discerned a difference not of degree but of kind. Even if the decision against an early date were not fairly unanimous, it would still tax our ingenuity to bridge the chasm between the unchartered liberty of *Revelation* and the austere simplicity of the Gospel according to St. John. The Apocalypse, in the contrast it affords between wealth of diction and grammatical solecisms, suggests an author who had used Greek all his life as a second language and never from choice. His seeming indifference to the rules of concord can be readily understood by Englishmen who stumble over the genders of French and German after speaking a language unburdened with this useless survival. A fresh impetus has been given to the study of this strange dialect by Dr. R. H. Charles, who has shown in his *Studies in the Apocalypse* [1] that many of its

[1] And with greater fulness of detail in his two-volume commentary in the *Int. Crit. Com.* from which Canon Charles has kindly shown me extracts in the proof stage.

mannerisms are due to the literal transference of Semitic idioms. A striking illustration (found seven times in Rev) is the co-ordination of the participle in one of the oblique cases and the finite verb, *e.g.* 2^2 τοὺς λέγοντας ἑαυτοὺς ἀποστόλους καὶ οὐκ εἰσίν. But while the book abounds in translation-Greek and bears constantly the imprint of the author's Semitic mind, it is easy to go too far in attributing all its peculiarities of grammar and idiom to the influence of the LXX when a Hebrew or Aramaic source is not in question. Thus Moffatt's treatment of the subject[1] finds a useful counterpoise in Radermacher's[2] judgement. After all the author was capable of writing a vigorous though irregular Greek with a very free pen and, as Dean Armitage Robinson has pointed out,[3] "the Greek in which he expressed himself was more like the Greek of the Egyptian papyri and of inscriptions found in various parts of the Graeco-Roman world." The very blunders in concord do not imply ignorance in the ordinary sense; "it is familiarity with a relaxed standard of speech, such as we find often enough in the professional letter-writers who indited the petitions and private correspondence of the peasants of the Fayûm." Perhaps it was but fitting that the weird melodies and daring harmonies in which the seer of Patmos gave utterance to the things which he had seen "which must shortly come to pass," should speak to us now in the haunting cadences of Jewish apocalyptic, and again in the popular idiom of the Graeco-Roman world.

---

[1] *Introd.* 501.

[2] *Neutestamentliche Grammatik*, 87: "Was die Apokalypse, und zwar sie allein unter den Schriften des Neuen Testaments, an entsprechenden Fällen zeigt, hat also nicht mehr als Solöcismus zu gelten und darf schwerlich als sklavische Nachbildung eines hebräischen Originaltextes erklärt werden."

[3] *JTS* x. 9.

PART I.

SOUNDS AND WRITING.

PART I.

PHONOLOGY AND WRITING.

§ 20. The Greek Alphabet in the Hellenistic period had twenty-four letters :—

Form.			Translitera-tion.	Name.	
1	2	3		In Greek.	In English.
Α	ⲁ	α	a	ἄλφα	Alpha
Β	Β	β	b	βῆτα	Bēta
Γ	Γ	γ	g	γάμμα	Gamma
Δ	Δ	δ	d	δέλτα	Delta
Ε	ϵ	ϵ, ε	ĕ	εἶ, later ἐ̆	Epsīlon
Ζ	Ζ	ζ	z	ζῆτα	Zēta
Η	Η	η	ē	ἦτα	Ēta
Θ	Θ	θ, ϑ	th	θῆτα	Thēta
Ι	Ι	ι	i	ἰῶτα	Iōta
Κ	Κ	κ	k (c)	κάππα	Kappa
Λ	Λ	λ	l	λά(μ)βδα	Lambda
Μ	Μ	μ	m	μῦ	Mu
Ν	Ν	ν	n	νῦ	Nu
Ξ	Ξ	ξ	x	ξεῖ	Xi
Ο	Ο	ο	ŏ	οὖ, later ὀ̆	Omīcron
Π	Π	π	p	πεῖ	Pi
Ρ	Ρ	ρ	r	ῥῶ	Rho
Σ	C	σ, ς	s	σίγμα	Sigma
Τ	Τ	τ	t	ταῦ	Tau
Υ	Υ	υ	u (y)	ὖ	Upsīlon
Φ	Φ	φ	ph	φεῖ	Phi
Χ	Χ	χ	kh (ch)	χεῖ	Chi
Ψ	Ψ	ψ	ps	ψεῖ	Psi
Ω	ω	ω	ō	ὦ	Omega

Notes.

1. The first column represents the printed form of the capital letters, based on the alphabet (*τὰ Ἰωνικὰ γράμματα*) which from iv/B.C. was generally used in inscriptions. For the history of the forms see §§ 21 f.

2. In the second column stands the alphabet of the oldest uncial MSS, as printed by WH in citations from the OT. The third column is the ordinary alphabet of modern printed books, based on that which the early printers derived from "cursive" or "minuscule" MSS. The alternative forms here given are indifferent except in the case of *σ*, *ς*, the latter of which is used at the end of words only. Some print it also at the end of a preposition or adverb compounded with another word (*προςφέρω* etc.); but the historical justification of this form does not apply to any position other than the actual end of a word.[1]

3. The transliteration column shows the value of the letters as evidenced by the form they take in contemporary Latin: an exception is made with *κ*, *υ*, *χ*, which in Latin take the bracketed form only. The pronunciation of the letters will be treated summarily below §§ 23 ff., and in detail under the Orthography.

4. The names of the letters are given in English according to their conventional forms, many of which, however, are unwarranted by early usage. The addition of *ψιλόν* to the names *ἒ* and *ὖ* is a late misunderstanding: Byzantine grammarians, giving rules for writing *αι* or *ε*, *οι* or *υ* (which were not distinguished in sound), would say that a particular word was written *διὰ τὸ ε ψιλοῦ*, "with a simple *ε*," as distinguished from a diphthong *αι*. "Little *ο*" and "big *ο*" are names dating from the Byzantine period, when the two letters were pronounced alike. The name for λ is better attested as *Labda* than as *Lambda*.

History of the Alphabet.

§ 21. For the history of the alphabet, a long and complex subject, reference may be made to special works: see literature in art. "Writing," *Enc. Brit.* (P. Giles). It must only be mentioned here that the alphabet (in Greek *γράμματα*, of the forms of the letters, *στοιχεῖα*, of the sounds) came in prehistoric times[2] into Greece from Phoenicia. The date

[1] In the earlier printed books we find the compendia ϛ = στ, ȣ = ου.

[2] The event is already covered with a myth, Cadmus, the "eastern" (קדם), being credited with the *καδμήϊα γράμματα* (Herod. v. 58), which are, however, *Φοινικήϊα* in the same context and elsewhere. Nöldeke (*Beitr. z. semit. Sprachwiss.*, 1904, 124–136) rejects the suggestion that Aramaic influence is traceable in the names *ἄλφα* and others: the forms are only due to Greek modification. (I owe the reference to Prof. Hogg.) Nestle (*Philologus*, 1900, 476 f.) says the theory is as old as the sixteenth century. Dr. A. J. Evans has shown that the Phoenicians themselves derived the alphabet from the prehistoric Cretan script of the newly discovered Minoan inscriptions; see his *Scripta Minoa* (1909), 86 ff.

may possibly be prior to the composition of the oldest parts of the *Iliad*, but certainty on this famous question can hardly be expected. It is a very striking fact that contact with the Semites should have occurred before the dawn, and after the sunset of classical Greek literature, and hardly at all in the interval. The letters seem to have been adapted to some extent independently by different Greek communities. But we find in all alike the central principle which betrays Greek genius at work even when, for once, it was borrowing and not inventing. An alphabet without vowels would have been peculiarly useless for expressing Greek words. Accordingly superfluous consonants were adapted to new uses: א became *ἀλφα*, ה supplied *εἶ*, ח *ἦτα* (in earlier times *h*, as in the local alphabet with which Latin was ultimately written), י was *ἰῶτα*, ע was *οὖ*. Later invention produced *ὖ* and *ὦ*. In several Greek dialects ו survived as *F* (*βαῦ*, or *δίγαμμα*, from its form); but this sound disappeared in Attic before the birth of its literature, and there is no trace of it left in the ***Κοινή***. Its sign was still used in numeration: see § 70. So also with ק (*κόππα*) and שׁ (*σάν*),[1] the former of which (preserved in the Latin alphabet) still survives in the earlier period inscriptions to represent the *k*-sound before *o* and *u*. The other equations may be summarily stated: ב $=\beta$, ג $=\gamma$, ד $=\delta$, ז $=\zeta$, ט $=\theta$, כ $=\kappa$, ל $=\lambda$, מ $=\mu$, נ $=\nu$, פ $=\pi$, ר $=\rho$, צ(?) $=\sigma$, ת $=\tau$. In ס adapted as *ξ* we have an application of a useless letter which was at first confined to the Asiatic Ionians; but it was their alphabet which ultimately established itself in universal use. The last five letters of the Greek alphabet are later additions, and of these *υ* alone is found in all parts of Greece alike. The different value attaching to **X** in Latin, which owed its letters to Chalcis in Euboea, through its colony of Cumae, illustrates the independence with which these non-Phoenician signs were used in different localities.

§ 22. We must not tarry here to show how the forms and names of the Semitic letters are related to the Greek derivatives, nor how in Greece itself these letters and their names varied from place to place and

---

[1] There is considerable doubt as to the history of the sibilants: see Roberts, *Greek Epigraphy*, i. 9 f., where צ is identified with *σάν*.

generation to generation, till the final victory of the Ionic alphabet in which alone the Common Greek was ever written. Two points only may be selected from the history of Greek writing, the development of the Breathings, and the change of direction from the retrograde Semitic to that which we inherit now. In the pre-Ionic alphabets H was used for *h*; but when it was requisitioned to express *ē*, the first half of it, ⊢, was used as an aspirate sign, perhaps as early as iv/B.C. (Blass). The Alexandrian grammarians introduced the corresponding ⊣ to represent the voiced sound answering to the breathed *h*, the glottal catch which Semitic languages wrote with א : it is a sound with which every vowel-initial opens, if not aspirated. From ⊢ and ⊣ respectively are derived the ʽ and ʼ which we call rough and smooth breathing (πνεῦμα δασύ and πνεῦμα ψιλόν). The other matter, the direction of writing, need only be mentioned here because the relation of the Greek to the Hebrew writing specially interests students of the Greek Bible. It it enough to say that in the earliest Greek inscriptions the writing is from right to left; that this develops into what was called βουστροφηδόν, because it "turns" at the end of each line in the opposite direction as the "ox" does in ploughing; and that out of this in v/B.C. developed the left-to-right style which Greece passed on to Rome, and Rome to modern Europe. The three stages may be illustrated by short examples. (1) ƎƧOΓƎ ἐποίε(ι) (Thera, vii/B.C.). (2) ΕΝ ΓΟΛΕΜΟΙ ΜΟΜƎΜΙΦΘ ἐν πολέμῳ φθίμενον (Attica, vii/B.C.). (3) ΡΑΗ ΔΗΟΜ παῖ Διός (Thera, vii/B.C.).

On the whole subject see Roberts, *Introduction to Greek Epigraphy*, vol. i. (Cambridge, 1887).

Classification of Sounds.

Sounds. § 23. Greek sounds are thus classified for the Hellenistic period.

(*a*) *Vowels*:—α, ι, υ, long or short; ε, ο, (short only); η, ω, (long only).

(*b*) *Diphthongs*:—αι, ει, οι, υι (short); ᾳ, ῃ, ῳ (long); αυ, ευ, ου (short); ηυ (long). For the vowels and diphthongs see §§ 33 ff.

(*c*) *Mutes.*—These sounds are divided in two ways: (1) according to the point of articulation, (2) according to the presence or absence of *voice*, *i.e.* the tension of the vocal chords, and of *aspiration*, *i.e.* the accompaniment of an *h*-sound. By the first, sounds are classed as *labials*, made with the lips, *dentals*, made with the tip of the tongue against the teeth, and *gutturals* or *palatals*, made with the back of the tongue against the palate. By the second, they are *breathed* or *hard*, *voiced* or *soft*, and *aspirate*, the last class being breathed (hard) as well. The classification is as follows:—

	Breathed.	*Voiced.*	*Aspirate.*
Labial	π	β	φ
Dental	τ	δ	θ
Guttural	κ	γ	χ

There are other names used for *breathed* and *voiced*, such as *surd* and *sonant*, *tenues* and *mediae*, *smooth* and *middle*: Goodwin, who employs the last-named pair, calls the aspirates *rough*.

(*d*) *Continuous*, or *Semivocalic* consonants. These sounds differ from the Mutes, or stopped sounds, in that they are capable of prolongation, and may even become vowels. They are classed thus. *Spirants* result from relaxing slightly the contact which produces a mute. Thus the position of *t*, if the tongue is held loosely to allow breath to pass, produces our English *th*. Nearly the same position, with a groove along the tongue, results in σ, the only spirant represented in the Greek alphabet (see however § 43): the breathings ᾿ and ῾ belong to the same class. The labial spirant Ϝ, our *w*, is obsolete in Hellenistic Greek. *Nasals* are characterised by the opening of the nasal passage. They are three in Greek, μ (labial), ν (dental), and that which is written γ before gutturals (κ, γ, χ, ξ), the guttural nasal *ng* (as in *sing*). *Liquids* are ρ and λ: the same rather elastic term is often used to include μ and ν. Both ρ and λ are made with the tip of the tongue against the front palate: in λ it is at rest there, while voice passes on both sides; in ρ it vibrates, while the two sides are stopped. Initial ρ in earlier Greek was breathed, as also is the second element in the doubled ρρ: it may be questioned whether this was really true for i/A.D.

This classification does not include the digraphs ψ, ζ, ξ, which are mere combinations of labial, dental and guttural mutes with the sibilant, like our superfluous letter *x*. The pronunciation of ζ however fluctuated considerably: see § 43.

Pronunciation.

Summary of Pronunciation. § 24. The pronunciation of Greek in the Hellenistic period raises a great many difficult questions which cannot be discussed here. It is probable that considerable differences existed between the Greek of Rome and Asia, Hellas and Egypt. The pronunciation of i/–iv/A.D. is a matter of great importance from its bearing on textual criticism. If we could delimit the localities affected by certain variations, we should have important evidence for the localising of textual types. Unhappily our information is too scanty to make this a really useful resource. Pronunciation had greatly changed since the classical period. As shown already (*Prol.* 34), Hellenistic Greek, though written with Attic orthography, sounded much more like Boeotian than Attic. Many of the processes had already started which reach their full effects in MGr. It does not follow that to pronounce Hellenistic as if it were MGr would compensate in accuracy for the inconvenience it would cause. For pronouncing Attic of the classical period, the MGr system is almost as wide of the mark as our English system of reading Greek as if it were English—a system which pretends to no advantage but convenience. For Hellenistic, it is much closer, but still far from exact, as we shall see; and the practical awkwardness of blotting out the difference between *ει*, *ι*, *η*, *ῃ*, *οι* and *υ* would be too great a price to pay for the approximation gained.

Vowels and Diphthongs. Under the head of *Vowels*, we have first the distinction between long and short. In classical Greek this is felt throughout the language. It is the basis of all metrical composition, when combined with the rules by which a short vowel before groups of consonants counted as long. Its influence upon accentuation will be seen in § 29. The essence of the distinction is that a long vowel took the time of two shorts: in technical language a short vowel had one *mora*, a long vowel two. The progressive disappearance of this distinction is one of the most important changes in the language. It established itself very gradually, and localities differed widely in their treatment of the several sounds concerned. Perhaps Asia Minor was its earliest home: Greece proper was the latest to accept it. The main cause of this levelling was the change in the character of the *accent* (see § 29): when stress replaced pitch accent, the accented syllable tended to be long, and the unaccented inevitably was shortened. We may take the process to have been complete before the date of our oldest uncials, though many quantity-distinctions were still operative in i/A.D.

The other general tendency needing mention at this stage is that by which the diphthongs as such were destroyed, being replaced by simple sounds. This was a tendency which Hellenistic owed to Boeotian phonology: see *Prol.* 33. The only exceptions were found in *αυ* and *ευ*, which tended to consonantise the second element, so that the MGr pronunciation is *av*, *ev* (or *af*, *ef*, before breathed consonants). Even these last changes were incipient already in our period, and were complete before the mass of our MSS were written.

On the vowel *a*, long and short, it need only be said that its pronunciation was the same as in nearly every I.E. language except our own. The *ā* was sounded as in *father*, and the *ă*, so far as it was still distinguished, was the same sound pronounced in half the time. Our characteristic *ᵉa* (in *man*, only short) was unknown in Greek. From *a*, in which both lips and throat are wide open, the vowels bifurcate along two lines, according as the throat is narrowed or the lips rounded and contracted. The former class includes the *e–i* vowels, the latter the *o–u*.

In classical Greek of early times the progressive narrowing of the throat aperture produced the series *η* (long, open), *ε* (short or long, close), *ι* (short or long). When *ε* was long it was written *ει* in the Ionic alphabet: it must be carefully distinguished from the genuine diphthongal *ει*, which was never written with simple E.[1] Open *e* is the sound of French *è*, our *e* in *there*; close *e* is French *é*, which we do not possess—our common *a* in *day*, *daisy*, *date*, is the same sound with an *i* "glide" making it diphthongal. In the Hellenistic period there were many changes going on, and in different directions according to locality. H in many places is still open *e*, especially in the area once occupied by Ionic. In inscriptions of Asia Minor we very often find *η* confused with *ε* (short), which was by this time probably not as close as it was in Attic: *ε* is a medium *e* now. But in the Greek of Hellas itself it would seem that *η* had become closer than *ε*, as in the Boeotian of the earlier age; and the difference is reflected to-day. In the Pontic-Cappadocian MGr *η* is frequently *ε*, as *πεγάδι* from *πηγή*; and such general MGr words as *στέκω*, from Hellenistic *στήκω*, may have originated in districts where this pronunciation was the rule. But in continental MGr *η* is now a simple *i*: this change was complete before vi/A.D. Finally *ι*, with which *ει* was now wholly convertible even when short, was the closest vowel of all: note that in transliterating Latin, where *ĭ* was open like our *ĭ* in *kin*, *ε* was often used instead of *ι*.

By rounding the lips and progressively contracting the aperture there came in early Greek the corresponding series *ω* (long, open), *o* (short or long, close), and in one or two dialects, as Boeotian, *υ* short or long (as in *full*, *fool*). In Attic however, and most dialects, *υ* had become *ü* (German, like the French *u*), which is pronounced by simultaneously rounding and contracting the lips and narrowing the throat aperture. This was still the sound generally in our period. Meanwhile the close long *o*, written *ου*—as in the case of *ει*, to be distinguished from the

[1] Thus *εἶμι* *ibo*, where *ι* is radical, was always EIMI; *εἰμί* *sum*, where *ει* is simply *ε* lengthened by compensation for the loss of *σ*, was written EMI in Attic before the archonship of Euclides (403 B.C.).

genuine diphthong *ου*—had become so close as to answer entirely to our own *oo*. In Hellenistic *ο* no longer seems to differ from *ω* in the original way, as the *o* in *mote* differs from that in *more*. The original open vowel, as in the case of *η*, has become closer: as *η* approximates to *i*, so *ω* ultimately does to *u*. In i/A.D., in many parts of the Greek-speaking world, there was little perceptible difference between *ο*, *ω* and *ου*, a fact which leaves its traces on our texts.

The *Diphthongs* were largely monophthongs by the time with which we are concerned. Αι seems to have become entirely equivalent to *ε*, (but see § 36). Ει and *ι*, even *ῐ*, are constantly confused; and in both these diphthongs the MS tradition is valuable only in so far as it may preserve a historical difference affecting the sense—if an unlettered scribe supplied a link in the chain, its value for us is gone, and we can write *αι* or *ε*, *ει* or *ι*, according to our own preference. Οι was in classical Attic not very different from our *oi*; but it passed through *ö* (German, as French *eu*) to *ü*, like *υ*, with which it ultimately coalesced. Illiterate papyri of i/A.D. and even earlier show this confusion; but outside Egypt the sounds were distinct for generations after this time. Υι, in *υἱός*, *ὀργυιά* and perfect participles feminine, maintains itself against the literary *υ*: it was presumably still *üy*. The *ι*-diphthongs with long vowels as their first element—in which *ι* has since xii/A.D. been *subscript*—completely lost their diphthongal character at an early date. Ηι was fused with *ει* in Attic; but the indifference with which *ι* is added, especially in i/B.C. and i/A.D., to long vowels without justification,[1] shows that in the Κοινή *ῃ* was nearer to *η* than to *ει*, while *ᾳ* and *ῳ* were identical with *ᾱ* and *ω*. See further § 36.

In the *υ*-diphthongs (*αυ*, *ευ*, *ου*, *ηυ*) the *υ* had from the first the sound of simple *u*. The tendency to consonantise this *u* in the case of *αυ* and *ευ* has been already mentioned. Apart from this, the pronunciation of *αυ* and *ευ*, *ηυ* was normally what we should get by running together *ah-oo*, *eh-oo* respectively. Ου had been for long simply *ū*, sometimes representing even *ŭ* (in *full*). In the case of *αυ* there was a separate tendency to slur and finally drop the *υ* when it came before a consonant: a similar tendency is observable in the later vernacular Latin. For NT exx. of this see *Prol.* 47.

Consonants; § 25. We pass on to the *Consonants*, and take first the nine *Mutes* or "stopped" sounds. The *breathed* *π*, *τ*, *κ* call for no remark, as they were pronounced very nearly as in English. The *voiced* *β*, *δ*, *γ*, had changed considerably from the sounds they had in Attic, which were virtually *b*, *d* and *g*. Γ was clearly (as partially in MGr) the voiced form of *ch* (Scotch or German), a guttural spirant like the German *g* between vowels (*Tage*), not far from the English *y*. Similarly *β* and *δ* came to be our *v* (nearly) and *th* (as in *thou*), but the change was not completed so early, and it seems to have varied in different districts. The fact that ϝ consonantal is still *υ* in Δαυείδ (all uncials

[1] Thus in BGU iii. 883[2] (ii/A.D.) . . . ὀκτώι, οὐλῆι δακτύλω πρώτωι.

which do not use exclusively the abbreviation), and the Latin consonantal *u* in *Siluanus* is ου (see § 37), shows that the interlabial *v* sound of β was not established in the Greek of the NT writers; otherwise the sound was so near the *w* that we should have had a certain amount of inconsistency in our documents. (At a later time Δαβίδ and Δαυείδ would be pronounced alike.) The *aspirates* were during the classical period mutes followed by *h*: our *shepherd*, *hothouse*, *packhorse* give the sounds fairly, except that the mute has to be pronounced in the same syllable as the *h* (*she-pherd* etc.). In Laconian however θ was apparently our *th* (in *thin*) at an early date, as is shown by the frequent spelling σ, which may represent a further development. In other dialects likewise the tendency to make θ a spirant seems to have worked fairly early. In the Hellenistic period we may probably assume that the spirant pronunciation (φ=*f*, θ=*th*, χ=Scotch or German *ch*) was fully developed in most parts of the Greek-speaking world, though it may have lagged in some. After σ, or another aspirate, the spirant never developed: φθάνω is in MGr *ftáno*, αἰσθάνομαι is *estánome*. This only partially applies to φ. The MGr spirant pronunciation of κ and π before τ (ἑπτά = *eftá*, ὀκτώ = *ochtó*), shows its earliest indications in the period to which our uncial MSS belong.

Liquids, The *Liquids* λ and ρ, and the nasal liquids γ (before κ, γ, χ, ξ), μ and ν, being practically identical with the modern sounds, need no detailed description. As in nearly all European languages except (southern) English, the ρ is trilled: when initial, or following an aspirate or another ρ, it was breathed (Welsh *rh*), but in our period the breath in initial ρ was feeble.

Sibilants. The *Sibilant* σ was always breathed (our *hiss*), though the voiced sound (as *his*) was heard before voiced consonants, as in σβέσαι, Σμύρνα. For this *z* sound ζ was often written. This symbol, which in the classical period seems to represent sometimes *dz*, sometimes *zd*, was already tending towards the simple *z*, as in MGr. The pronunciation of the closely related combinations σσ and ττ is very difficult to determine. There is some reason for assigning the value *ts* to the former, and *tth* (as *that thing* pronounced in one word) to the latter; but this is conjectural. The combinations ξ and ψ are always breathed.

Breathings. There remain the *Breathings*, ʼ and ʽ. The former, which the Hebrew alphabet represented by א (initial) is heard at the beginning of every English word with vowel initial in normal pronunciation: it is the glottal catch which, except in singing, we can hardly avoid sounding before the vowel. The corresponding breathed sound, our *h*, was already obsolete in some of the Greek dialects of classical times, and must have been faintly heard in many districts in the Hellenistic period, apart from those which inherited the early *psilosis*. In Palestine we may fairly assume that the aspirate survived intact, as was natural in a country where the native speech retained this element so clearly. A native name like חלפי was represented by Ἁλφαῖος: the Vulgate transliteration *Alphaeus* illustrates the enfeeblement of *h* in other regions and at a later time. The fact that effects of initial aspirate like καθ' ἡμέραν not only survived but even produced analogic forms like καθ' ἔτος (see § 40), is evidence as far as it goes that the complete *psilosis* of MGr was only local in the earlier centuries of Hellenistic.

The above *resumé* of results will be enough to show how complex the subject is. A history of Greek pronunciation in the Hellenistic period is greatly needed, showing both when and where the various developments first appeared which issue in the system, or rather systems, of MGr. Such a history would have an important bearing on textual questions. The pronunciation of Greek in Palestine can be ascertained with considerable accuracy from the very numerous Greek words borrowed by Aramaic and Aramaic words transliterated into Greek. Since, however, the bulk of the NT was written outside Palestine, there seems no reason for taking up one part of a complicated investigation, to complete which would be impossible within our limits. The sections which follow on Orthography will raise a number of points bearing on pronunciation, supplying some of the evidence for summary statements already made, and discussing the relations of these facts to the phenomena of our MS tradition.

Modern Printed Greek.

Punctuation.

Punctuation; § 26. Ancient writing knew very little of so obvious a help to reading as punctuation. As early as iv/B.C. we find the mark : in the "Artemisia" papyrus at the end of some sentences. The great grammarian Aristophanes (iii/B.C.) invented the stops (˙) and (.), to which he gave the reverse values to those for which we use them; also a comma (·), placed half-way between the position of the colon and the full stop. Literary papyri, especially those of lyric poets, who needed such helps to reading more than others, show these punctuation marks earliest. Thus the Bacchylides papyrus (i/B.C.) shows the colon freely at the end of sentences, and "generally, it would seem, correctly," says Kenyon (*Bacchylides*, xxi). See further E. Maunde Thompson *Palaeography*, 60.

in Earlier Uncials, The oldest NT uncials have none of these adjuncts. "In אB the first hand very rarely shows any points, and the words are not divided except sometimes when a change of subject brings in א a new line or in B a small blank. Later we find a single dot, as in the second hand of אB and the first in ACIN[b]PQZΞ; sometimes as in A a comma and a double dot. In NR 0115 the dot is placed at the top, the middle or the bottom of the letter without distinction. The dot is most freely used in F[p] and G[p]" So Gregory (Ti[8] iii. 111), who gives a specimen from F in 1 Tim 3^{16}, with each word divided from the next by a dot. He goes on to observe that obviously no argument towards a right punctuation can be drawn from the barrenness of the earlier or the abundance of the later signs.

in Later Uncials. A fuller system is observed by the later uncials, including ELM[p], and they are here as in some other features anticipated by W: though its punctuation is scanty, it goes decidedly beyond אB. The single dot occurs on the average less than three times per page, being most frequent in the first part of Lk, and least so in Mk. "The double dot (:) occurs 12 times in Mt, 6 in Jn (excluding the first quire), 23 in Lk, and 11 in Mk (7 are in the first four chapters)." Sanders (*The Washington Manuscript* 12) goes on to observe that (:) was "a decidedly strong punctuation," used generally at the ends of paragraphs. There is also "a substitute for punctuation formed by leaving small blank spaces between the phrases. These occur frequently and regularly in all parts of the MS," and are said to correspond fairly well with the number of *στίχοι* (see below), and more closely still to the *ῥήματα*. "They doubtless coincided with the sense-divisions used in reading." Sanders compares these phrase-lengths in W, and the *στίχοι* in D, with the introduction of each phrase by a capital in Δ, so as to deduce "an ancient system of phrasing, used in reading the Scriptures in church service." It may have originated as early as ii/A.D.

Paragraphs. Paragraphs are found even in the earliest uncials: an account of those in W, as compared with א, B and D, may be seen in Sanders 15 ff. On the *στίχοι*, so conspicuous in D, where the text looks like poetry in very short uneven lines, and *ῥήματα* or *ῥήσεις* "sentences," a very similar but independent division, see J. R. Harris *Origin of Ferrar-Group* (Cambridge, 1893), 8 ff.

It will be clear that there is little probability that any punctuation worth counting such was present in the NT autographs. If they had any of Aristophanes' points—never found in papyri dated B.C.—or those of different systems which are known to have existed in Aristotle's time,[1] we have no proof that they underlie the meagre punctuation of W and later MSS.

Modern Punctuation. Passing to our modern system, we should begin with a full recognition that it is purely modern. Apart from the use of (;) for the query, and (·) for colon and semicolon alike, the punctuation of our printed Greek Testaments is on exactly the same footing as that of their English versions. It is simply in essence a form of commentary; and the modern editor is on every page compelled to choose between alternative punctuations, involving different interpretation, where the only ancient authority is that of patristic comments or early versions. Since these go back to periods considerably antedating our best uncials, they have naturally the weight in many cases of a primitive tradition, which no wise exegete would ignore. But as little would he consent to be bound hand and foot by interpretations which do not depend on the autographs, and may be no more than guesses by readers who were not by any means better qualified from all sides than ourselves. When therefore we use an extremely careful edition like that of WH, where punctuations in text and in margin are constantly determining the meaning for us, we must always be careful to realise our freedom to take our own line on sufficient reason. Rarely—as when in Jn 1^3f. W punctuates *εγενετο ουδε εν· ο γεγονεν εν | αυτω ζωη·*—their interpretation may have behind it the punctuation of the oldest MSS in which such marks appear at all. But even

[1] On these see Kühner-Blass i. 351–3, Mayser 48–50. Mayser notes that an instance of the *παράγραφος*, a stroke which points to the end of a sentence, is found in v/B.C. in a Laconian inscr. More rarely still in papyri appears the double point, which may also be seen on inscrr.

there, if exegetes insist on the reading of AV and RV, we cannot oppose them successfully on the authority of W: our arguments must be exegetical, and the traditional punctuation seen in W will count for little.

It is not the function of a Greek Grammar under these circumstances to lay down principles for punctuation. Our system being purely modern, we insert commas just where we should insert them in a corresponding sentence of English. Since any kind of editing in modern form involves in many places the editor's decision between rival interpretations, it is well frankly to recognise this, and insert these helps to reading freely. At the best they will not be equal to those we employ. Quotation marks—which many uncials use for OT citations—might be multiplied to advantage. There is one further difference between ancient and modern writing which we might well reduce. The absence of facility for indicating parentheses introduces complications into our understanding of a great many passages. Often we should simplify a passage considerably by taking out a parenthesis and putting it underneath as a footnote. Thus in Jn 4[9] the last sentence is taken as the author's comment in RV, and in a modern work would naturally become a footnote: still more clearly Ac 1[18f.], which interrupts the speech with matter extraneous to it. Further instances may be Heb 3[4], 1 Co 7[21] ἀλλ' εἰ καὶ . . . χρῆσαι, *ib.* 15[27b]. Illustrations, of course, could be multiplied indefinitely, and those given already do not pretend to be indisputable.[1]

Other modern accessories. § 27. Very few of our modern accessories existed in the early periods of the NT, or appear in our oldest MSS. *Breathings* begin to appear in v/A.D., as we shall see in § 40. *Accents* had been invented long before, but seem only to have been used in poetical texts, such as the Bacchylides papyrus (i/B.C.): see § 36. It was a long time before MSS even began to divide words—a point in which Greek was curiously behind Latin, where words are separated in early inscrr. The use of

[1] An attempt is made in *The Modern Reader's Bible*, by R. G. Moulton (New York and London, 1907), to present the English RV text with these accessories of modern printing.

"*iota* subscript," convenient as distinguishing sundry flexions, but not answering to any living feature of speech, was discontinued some time before the NT began to be written, and only returned with Byzantine scholarship: indeed in the strict sense it is a practice of xii/A.D. and later, for not till then was the unpronounced ι written underneath. To complete the difference between a modern printed Greek Bible and an early MS thereof, we have the use of the small and convenient "minuscule" script, in place of the clumsy and space-filling "capital" letters, which though in early use for non-literary purposes, only in ix/A.D. began to be applied to books. Further details on most of these subjects will be given below.

Diaeresis. One of these accessories, however, stands on a different footing, the Diaeresis, which figures largely in our oldest MSS and in the papyri. It is used to distinguish vowels, especially ι and υ, which begin a syllable: thus we find ϊνα, ϋπο etc. Our use of it is a special application of the same principle—if we may call it a principle which is applied only in a minute proportion of the instances where on the above definition it should appear. We employ it to distinguish vowels which are to be pronounced separately, and keep them from being merged in the vowel before. Thus ΓΑΙΟϹ might be read *Γαῖος* (as WH actually print), had we not evidence that the Latin *Gaius* was trisyllabic, so that we should write *Γάϊος*: in this case the accentual difference makes the diaeresis less necessary. In MSS the diaeresis often preserves evidence of pronunciation, as when ℵ writes η|ϋδοκηϲα in Mt 3[17], even dividing the line after the first element in the diphthong. The diaeresis often affects transliterations of foreign words. Thus in Mt 11[21] = Lk 10[13] D has *χοροζαϊν* and *βεθσαειδα* (*βεδσαϊδα* in Lk), implying by two typical devices (diaeresis and *αει* for *αι*) the tetrasyllabic pronunciation of both names. On the other hand Jn 11[54] *'Εφρέμ* ℵL reinforces the absence of diaeresis in the uncials which write *'Εφραίμ*. Our uniform accent system spares us the necessity of using the diaeresis very often: *πρόιμος*, *πρωί*, *πρωινός*, *Πτολεμαίδα*, *Λωίς*, etc. might as well be left without, while *'Αχαΐα*, *'Ρωμαϊστί* and the like might be ambiguous.

SOUNDS AND ORTHOGRAPHY.

Spelling no longer Phonetic.

§ 28. Educated Greek writing in our period had practically lost the earlier phonetic character. Attic literature dominated the orthographic tradition, though Hellenistic pronunciation diverged widely from Attic. We have accordingly a great difference between the conventional spelling and that of less educated people, who tended in various points to write as they and others spoke. The great NT uncials present a considerable number of spellings thus depending on the pronunciation current in the period when they or their originals were written. How far we ought to follow them in their deviations from conventional spelling is an open question. There are some points in which the evidence of papyri and inscriptions shows that a particular spelling was widely current in i/A.D., and may reasonably be traced to the author. This is made especially plausible in the not infrequent cases where the said spelling was extinct before the actual period of the scribe. This point is well brought out for Codex Bezae by Rudberg, *Ntlicher Text u. Nomina Sacra* (Upsala, 1915). He notes that while D perpetually confuses *αι* and *ε*, *ει* and *ι*, it hardly ever confuses *η* and *ι*, and never (according to von Soden) *η* and *ει*, although in v/vi A.D. *ι*, *η* and *ει* were indistinguishable: he argues that we have here a proof that the orthography of D is that of ii/A.D. He proceeds on the same lines with sundry other orthographical peculiarities of the Bezan text.

The notes which follow are restricted to matters of spelling, and the questions of pronunciation affected. Where flexions are concerned, reference must be made to the Accidence.

Accentuation.

Accents, ancient and modern.

§ 29. The accents with which Greek has been written since the Hellenistic age are the invention of the great grammarians who tried to preserve a record of the classical language when it was in danger of obscuration. In their time the character of the accent was changing from pitch to stress. The MGr accent, which remains with few exceptions on the same syllable as in the ancient language, is just like our own; and, as in English, the stress affects the quality of all syllables, stressed or unstressed. Thus ἄθρωπος *man* has stress on the first syllable, and the second and third syllables in consequence have the same vowel: ω becomes long again in the plural, where the accent falls on the penult. In classical Greek there was a "musical" accent, the tone involving a higher note but no sort of stress. We have this musical accent in English, and it plays a very important part. But it is perfectly free, depending on the shade of meaning intended by a speaker, and differing very much with different individual speakers: in Greek the tone was tied to the word or word-group, and was capable of no variation. It was a fixed element, almost as much as a similar but more elaborated tone-system is in Chinese. We recall the well-known story of the actor Hegelochus, who in declaiming a line of Euripides ending with γαλήν' ὁρῶ ("I see a calm") pronounced a circumflex instead of an acute, and sent the audience into roars of laughter: γαλῆν ὁρῶ = "I see a weasel."

Acute. We need not pause to state in detail the rules of the Greek accents, which are fully given in the ordinary Greek grammars. The *acute* accent marks the rising inflexion of the voice: the second syllable of our interjection "*Really?*" (expressing surprise or incredulity) usually shows this intonation. The falling tone (heard in the same syllable of "*Really!*") is written only

Grave. when an acute falls on the last syllable of a word and is changed by rule to "*grave*": this happens when the word as it comes in a sentence does not precede an enclitic (see below), or a stop (comma, colon, full stop or query). The interrogative τίς however keeps its acute accent under all conditions. The falling inflexion belongs naturally to all syllables which are not marked with accents. In addition to the acute (´) and the grave (`) there

Circumflex. was the *circumflex* accent, which denoted the combination of the two (῀ = ´`): it was confined to long syllables, where the voice rose in pitch during the first half (technically *mora*) and fell in the second. We may represent the three accents in musical notation, premising that the notes would vary in pitch with different individuals, and that the intervals would not be constant:—

(The time of a *mora* is represented here by a crotchet.)

Rules of Accentuation. The following rules are a summary of the general principles governing Greek accentuation:—

(1) The limits of the position of an accent depend on the "three-syllable law," by which the rising inflexion cannot stand farther back than on the third syllable from the end of a word. Only in the case of a word ending with a trochee (¯˘) can the equivalent of three short syllables at the end of a word stand together unaccented.

Thus (*a*) if a word ends with a *short* syllable, the *acute* may fall on the ultima, as λεκτός, an "*oxytone*" word, or on the penult, as παρθένος, a "*paroxytone*," or on the antepenult, as λέγομεν, a "*proparoxytone*"; the *circumflex* may fall on the ultima, as τιμῶ, a "*perispomenon*" word, or on the penult, as τιμῶμεν, a "*properispomenon.*" (N.B.—If a word ends with ¯˘ and the penult has an accent, it must be a circumflex.)

(*b*) If a word ends with a *long* syllable, the *acute* may fall on the ultima, as τιμή (oxytone), or on the penult, as τιμώντων (paroxytone); the *circumflex* can fall only on the ultima, as τιμῶν (perispomenon).

The rationale of these restrictions appears as soon as the circumflex is resolved into acute + grave, and each *mora*—short syllable or half of a long one—has its accent supplied. Thus τίμὼντὼν and τιμὼντὼν are seen to be impossible, since in each case the rising inflexion is followed by more than two *morae* with falling tone. Τιμώντων, accented in full, would be τὶμὼντὼν, and is according to the rule.

(2) For purposes of accent, syllables are not long unless the vowel in them is a long vowel or diphthong. Thus in λαῖλᾰψ the second syllable is short, and the circumflex falls on the first syllable accordingly, although the word is a spondee for metrical purposes. Greek grammarians tell us that we must write κῆρυξ and φοῖνιξ: if this is correct, we must assume that the ῡ and ῑ were shortened in the nominative before ξ.

Final αι and -οι (not followed by a consonant) had only one *mora* each, except when they were *locative* terminations or *optatives*, and of course when they were contracted. Thus we have οἶκοι, χῶραι nom. pl., but οἴκοι, Ἰσθμοῖ, loc. sing.; τίμησαι imper mid., τιμῆσαι infin. act., but τιμήσαι opt. act.

(3) Since accents were in existence long before the contraction of vowels or other later modifications which arose in the historical period, the accentuation must follow the earlier conditions. Thus *τιμάομεν* (*i.e.* *τὶμάὸμὲν*) became *τιμῶμεν*, *ἑσταώς* (*ἓστὰώς*) *ἑστώς*, *πόληος* became *πόλεως* when the quantity of its last two vowels was inverted. When *τὰ ἄλλα* is contracted into one word we write *τἆλλα*, not *τἄλλα*, since the crasis joins grave + acute, and the rising inflexion comes on the second *mora*.

(4) Against these *orthotone* (*i.e.* accented) words may be set two classes of words which were without an accent under specific conditions.

Proclitics. *Proclitics* linked themselves to the word following, and took an accent only when that word threw its accent upon them. Thus *ἐκ τούτου*, *ἔκβηθι*, *οὐκ ἔστι*, *οὔποτε*. *Enclitics* (except when standing at the beginning of a sentence) threw their accent

Enclitics. back upon the last syllable of the preceding word, unless this would involve two acutes following. Thus *τινὲς μὲν . . .* (Phil 1[15]), *ἔκ τινος*, *εἴ τινων*, but *ἄλλα τινά* : *ὁποῖά τινα*, but *ὁποίων τινῶν*. *Proclitics* include the article forms *ὁ*, *ἡ*, *οἱ*, *αἱ*, the prepositions *εἰς*, *ἐξ* (*ἐκ*), *ἐν*, the conjunctions *εἰ* and *ὡς*, and the negative *οὐ* (*οὐκ*, *οὐχ*). But *οὐ* takes accent (*οὔ*) at end of sentence, or standing alone. In reality all prepositions are proclitic, for (*e.g.*) *ἀπὸ* has no rising inflexion, and its own accent is paroxytone when standing free or after its case. *Enclitics* include the pronoun forms *μοῦ*, *μοί*, *μέ* : *σοῦ*, *σοί*, *σὲ* (except when emphatic) : *τὶς* (indefinite) and the indefinite adverbs *πού*, *ποτέ*, *πώ*, *πώς* : the particles *γέ*, *τέ* : and the present indicative of *εἰμί* (except 2 sg. *εἶ*), and *φημί*, *φησί*. (*Ἐστί* at the beginning of a sentence becomes *ἔστι* : so after *οὐκ*, *μή*, *εἰ*, *ὡς*, *καί*, *ἀλλά*, and *τοῦτο*, and when it means "exists" or "is possible.")

A proparoxytone or properispomenon or a proclitic, followed by an enclitic, receives an acute accent on its ultima ; an oxytone keeps its acute without change to grave. A perispomenon is unchanged, as is a paroxytone, but if the enclitic has two syllables, the second is accented. If a series of enclitics follow one another, each throws an accent back on the preceding, as *εἴ τίς τί σοί φησιν*. But *μοῦ*, *σοῦ* throw an acute upon the preceding word and receive it from a following enclitic, *e.g.* *σύνδουλός σού εἰμι* (Rev 19[10] 22[9]). The rules for enclitics account for some combinations which seem to break the ordinary principles given above : thus *ᾧτινι*, *ὥστε*.

(5) The accent of nouns, adjectives and pronouns must generally be learnt from observation, and there are few general rules. Monosyllabic

Noun Accent. 3rd decl. nouns usually are oxytone in gen. dat. sing. and dat. pl., perispomenon in gen. pl. Other nouns keep the accent on the same syllable as in nom. sing. unless it is forced forward by the rules of accent, as *θάλασσα* gen. *θαλάσσης*. The gen. pl. in 1st decl. nouns (not adj. or pron.) is perispomenon (since *-ῶν* comes from *-έων*, and that from (*-ήων*), *ά-(σ)ων*). Vocatives sometimes retain their primitive *recessive* accent (*i.e.* accent as far as possible from the end of the word) : thus *πάτερ* from *πατήρ*, *ἄδελφε* from *ἀδελφός*. **(This arises from the original enclitic character of vocatives when not**

opening a clause.) It may be noted that (as in MGr) common nouns when taken to serve as proper names often suffered a change of accent.

Verb Accent. (6) Finite verb forms are recessively accented—a consequence of their primitive enclitic condition. Infinitives and participles, being nouns or adjectives, do not come under this rule. In compound verbs the accent cannot go behind the augment or reduplication. Apparent exceptions to the recessive rule are historically due to contraction: there is however the peculiar case of strong aorist imperatives, εἰπέ, εἰπόν, λαβέ, λαβοῦ, which (like the case of ἔστι above) are survivals of the primitive condition retaining the verb's original accent when standing first in a sentence, as imperatives naturally did.

Crasis. (7) In a few words which suffer *crasis*—the fusing of two words into one by contraction—the accent of the first word is ignored. See § 32.

Imperfection of accent record. § 30. The record of classical accentuation is in many respects seriously imperfect, and it is probable that our modern printed texts differ not infrequently from the genuine pronunciation of their authors. This is well seen when we study classical texts preserved for us in ancient papyri. Professor Wilamowitz goes so far as to say (*Sappho und Simonides*², 100 f., *ap.* Sonnenschein in *The Year's Work in Classical Studies,* 1913, p. 102):—

> We now possess so many remains of ancient books that we see clearly how late, how rare, and how incomplete is the indication of accents, and how far it departs from that which is customary among us at the present day. No one can any longer dispute the fact that our accentuation is a product of the time of Photius.

The statement is not intended to suggest that we must simply acquiesce in ignorance, for Wilamowitz declares that we are "well able to go behind the Byzantine period," and are bound, to do so. It must not be forgotten that the MGr accent, scientifically used, can help us a great deal in verifying our accentuation of ancient texts, going back as it does to the period of the *Κοινή*.

Accentuation of NT text. Our specific information for the accentuation of the NT text comes necessarily from later authorities. Sir E. Maunde Thompson states [1] that accentuation, only occasional even in literary texts

---

[1] *Introduction to Greek and Latin Palaeography* (Oxford, 1912), 61 f.

of the papyrus period, begins to become general in iii/A.D. The oldest literary texts showing accents at all regularly are the Bacchylides and the Alcman, both i/B.C.; Sir F. G. Kenyon observes that lyric poets seem to have needed helps to the reader more than other texts. The earlier uncial MSS on vellum have no accents at all: we have to wait till vii/A.D.[1] There are a few instances of the circumflex in D, perhaps in N, and in *Δ* and F_2G_3, but mostly alien from our modern use. The later uncials are accented on our system generally, and late correctors have equipped B and C; but the best of them are least accurate in this respect. Gregory's table (*Prol.* 100 ff.) may be consulted for the evidence of these MSS as to the accent of doubtful words.

Pitch accent becoming stress. Soon after the date A.D.—a period when the *Κοινή* began its first new period—the old musical accent developed into a pure stress; and we may assume that the NT documents were from the first pronounced with the accentual conditions familiar in MGr. If we read the words aloud with a stress upon the syllables written with an accent—all three accents being now equivalent—we shall be practically compelled to reduce to a minimum the difference between long and short vowels, imparting the quality of length to the stressed syllable alone (cf. *Prol.* 34 n.[2]). This is practically the pronunciation of the modern language. Quantitative levelling was not complete in i/A.D., but the distinction between *ο* and *ω*, *ă* and *ā*, was becoming very slight. It follows that when texts were transmitted to any extent orally, such distinctions as that of *ἔχομεν* and *ἔχωμεν* were very easily lost. The new stress accent began to affect the forms of words. The Hellenistic *νοσσίον* for *νεοσσ.* has been attributed to this cause; Thumb rejects this (Brugmann *Gr.*[4] 76). A clearer case is that of Kretschmer's Law, by which an unstressed vowel after a liquid or nasal dropped out when the same vowel stood in the previous syllable. Thus ***Βερνίκη*** answers to an older form ***Βερενίκη***: see Brugmann *Gr.*[4] 80, and § 33 below.

---

[1] Gregory ***Prol.*** **99.**

Specific accent questions in NT. Some points may be collected in which the accentuation of NT words is doubtful, or specially significant:—

(1) There are some words in which we have evidence of a change of pronunciation between classical and Hellenistic times:—

(*a*) Certain 2 aor. imper. forms—*ἰδέ, εἰπέ, λαβέ, εὑρέ*—which in Attic retained a primitive oxytone, have in Hellenistic succumbed to levelling. (Moeris, *s.v.* *ἴδε*, p. 193.)

(*b*) Shortening of quantity took place in the penult in many nouns in -*μα*. Thus in Hellenistic we find *ἀνάθεμα* (in poetry *ἄνθεμα*) in place of *ἀνάθημα*, and even words like *σύστεμα*, not *-*στᾰμα*, showing that the shortening is late. The wide extent of this phenomenon, which is probably due to the analogy of nouns in -*σις*, makes *κλίμα, κρίμα* (so MSS), *μίγμα* preferable to the class. properispomena. In the case of *χρίσμα* we have definite evidence that the *ι* was short: see W. M. Lindsay *The Latin Language*, 30. Possibly the case of *κῆρυξ* and *φοῖνιξ* may come here: for the grammarians who prescribe this accentuation see Chandler's reff., § 669. The ultimate shortening of *ι* and *υ* before *ξ* may perhaps have been Hellenistic, in which case we might accentuate *Φῆλιξ, κῆρυξ* and *κηρύξαι*[1] in Hellenistic, leaving the question open whether *κήρυξ* and *κηρῦξαι* should be retained for classical times. See Lobeck *Paral.* 411. In his *Phryn.* 107, Lobeck mentions a number of dissyllabic nouns which shortened their penult in later Greek. We may add *ψύχος*. Shortenings like *θλίψις* (so MSS) may be defended on the same lines, but we should need special evidence to justify *ρίψαν* (as several MSS), *συντετρίφθαι*. *Σπῖλος* is a mere mistake, for the *ι* is short from its first appearance, which is not early. See in general Lipsius, *Gr. Unt.* 31–46, summarised by W. F. Moulton, WM 57 n.

(*c*) A different class of shortening may arise in the nom. acc. sing. of nouns in -*ειᾰ* where confusion with those in (*ε*)*ία* is possible: the complete identity of *ει* and *ι* in popular speech helps the confusion by bringing -*εία* and -*ία* nouns together. *Ἐριθεία* and *ἀρεσκεία* are claimed for the -*ᾱ* class on the strength of derivation from verbs in -*εύω*. See on these nouns below under Word-formation.

(2) In the following NT words the accent is questioned, or accentuation distinguishes different words or forms:—

ἀγόραιος and *ἀγοραῖος* are differently distinguished by grammarians. Zonaras has *ἀγοραῖοι* for *οἱ ἐν ἀγορᾷ ἀναστρεφόμενοι ἄνθρωποι*, and *ἀγόραιος* as *ἡ ἡμέρα ἐν ᾗ ἡ ἀγορὰ τελεῖται*. If that is correct, we must write *ἀγόραιοι* in Ac 19[38], and make *ἀγοραῖοι* the nom. of the noun in 17[5]; but Ammonius, who is eight centuries older than Zonaras, gives an entirely different distinction. HLP have *ἀγοραῖοι* in Ac 19[38].

---

[1] So FHKMUΓΔ in Lk 4[19], and HL 61 in Ac 10[42]: the MSS for *κήρυξ* and *κηρῦξαι* seem to be few (Gregory *Prol.* 101).

ἄγων from *ἄγω* : *ἀγών* a noun.

ἀδελφός has the old voc. *ἄδελφε*, as seems proved by the survival of *ἄδεφλε* in Pontic MGr (beside *ἀδερφέ*).

αἱ from art. : *αἵ* relative.

ἄλλα is neut. pl. of *ἄλλος*: *ἀλλά* *but* is the same become proclitic for a conjunction.

ἄνω=*up* : *ἀνῶ* 2 aor. subj. of *ἀνίημι*.

ἀπόδεκτος, as a compound verbal assumed to be of two terminations, will retract accent : see however Kühner-Blass i. 538, WS 69.

ἀρά=*curse* : *ἄρα* *then*, *ἆρα* asks question.

ἀχρεῖος said by gramm. to be non-Attic for *ἄχρειος*.

γλωσσοκόμον is defended by Schmiedel (WS 140), on the ground that the second element is active : WH print *γλωσσόκομον*.

δεινά *terrible things* : *δεῖνα* *so-and-so*.

διά *through* : *Δία* acc. of *Ζεύς*.

εἰ *if* : *εἶ* *thou art*, or in *εἶ μήν* (also written *εἰ μήν*) *verily*.

εἰπόν imper. : *εἶπον* indic. The grammarian Charax tells us that the former was Syracusan Greek ; the latter appears to be Attic (Lobeck *Phryn.* 348). Which belongs to the *Κοινή* is not very certain, but editors in Ac 28[26] print *εἰπόν* (so B^3—*contra* L_1HL_2 1, 61).

ἐκλεκτός has three terminations and is oxytone : Kühner-Blass i. 538, Chandler 199.

ἔρημος, *ἕτοιμος*, *ὅμοιος* are said by gramm. to be Attic, while properisp. is Homeric or Ionic. Supposing this true, it would not be proof that we should not write *ἐρῆμος* etc. in NT. But MGr has *ἔρημος*, *ἕτοιμος*, *ὅμοιος*, which is better evidence.

ἔχθρα *enmity* : *ἐχθρά* fem. of *ἐχθρός* *hostile*.

ἡ def. art. : *ἥ* rel.

ἴσος is doubtless the *Κοινή* form (Attic), though the Epic *ἶσος* occurs in late poetry.

καθαίρω *purge* : *καθαιρῶ* *pull down*.

κλείς *key* : *κλεῖς* *keys*.

μωρός is generally preferred, but gramm. give *μῶρος* also as Attic. MGr seems to speak for *μωρός*, but an interj. *μῶρε* survives in Pontus : there was presumably dialectic variation.

Νύμφαν *Nympha* (acc. fem.) : *Νυμφᾶν* *Nymphas* (masc.).

ὁ, *οἱ* nom. masc. sing. and pl. def. art. : *ὅ*, *οἵ* neut. sing. and masc. pl. relative.

ὅμοιος see *s.v.* *ἔρημος*.

ὄργυια and *ὀργυιά* alternate in our authorities.

πότε, *ποῦ*, *πῶς* interrog. : *ποτέ*, *που*, *πως* indef.

πρωτότοκος *first-born* : *πρωτοτόκος* *first-bearing*. See on this general distinction under Word-formation.

σκῦλον and *στῦλος* should be left unchanged : see WS 68.

τεσσαρακονταέτης (and the like) of time :— *-ετής* elsewhere—thus in Ac 7[23] 13[18] (so 81) parox., but *ἑκατονταετής* Rom 4[19] (not D^cL). But the evidence is insufficient : see Lobeck *Phryn.* 406.

τίς τί etc. interrog. : τις τι etc. indef.
τροχός *wheel* : τρόχος *course* has no real claim in Jas 3[6].
φάγος is printed as a paroxytone, on the ground that it is a substantive, the adjective being φαγός. MGr φαγᾶς, fem. φαγοῦ, "gourmand," are some evidence against this.

(3) When oxytones or paroxytones were adapted as proper names, the accent was drawn back. This is perhaps due to the strong influence of the vocative in personal names, and the survival of the old rule by which the vocative took recessive accent: cf. πάτερ, ἄδελφε, and note how the predominance of the vocative changed the accent of μήτηρ (Skt *mātá*, with same accent evidenced by O.E. *mōder*). In NT we have Τύχικος, Φίλητος, Ἐπαίνετος, Ἔραστος, Πύρρος, Βλάστος, Κάρπος, Ὀνησίφορος (for parox.), Σωσθένης, Ἑρμογένης, Διοτρέφης : cf. WS 70. The name Χριστός was not changed, since it was never in the first age treated as a real proper name. Ἀχαϊκός, not having been a common noun to start with, was not altered. The rule does not seem to be conditioned by convenience of differentiation, for names like Ὑμέναιος, Τρόφιμος, Ἀσύγκριτος retain their accent unchanged. The principle survives in MGr: see Thumb *Handbook*, § 38. 1.

Recession of accent.

(4) Oxytone adjectives retract the accent when they become nouns: thus κρύπτη from κρυπτός. This is also MGr (Thumb *l.c.*).

(5) Latin words were sometimes accented in a manner which reminds us that Latin and Greek accentuation differed altogether in quality. (Thus we get the place-name *St. Heléna* ultimately from the Greek Ἑλένη, but the personal name *Hélen* from Latin *Hélena*, where the accent was changed by the short penult.) The Latin *Christiánus* became Χριστιανός, as it is still in MGr: similarly other adj. in *-ānus*. Words in *-īnus*, but not those in *-ēnus* or *-ūnus*, retain accent on penult, as Ἀλεξανδρῖνος, λιβερτῖνος. The analogy of genuine Greek words in -ανός, -ηνός presumably worked here. Generally however we accent Latin words in accordance with their original form: thus Λίνος, Τίτος, Πειλᾶτος, Γάιος (trisyll.), Κουάρτος, Σεκοῦνδος, Πρισκίλλα, etc.

Accent of Latin words,

(6) The current accentuation of Semitic words is, as Schmiedel notes (WS 76), often governed by pure caprice. The only intelligible principle would be to set the accent always on the tone-syllable of the original Semitic. Our difficulties in that case would arise only where words had been partially Hellenised; and even here, unless popular etymology had produced a really new form, or the word could be shown to have taken an independent place in Greek—as in our treatment of the place names *Paris* and *Vienna*—it would be safe to keep the tone-syllable unaltered if possible. When Hebrew names were inflected in Greek declension the variations of case naturally affected the accent in places. It is needless to discuss the application of these principles, as the number of words affected is extremely large.

and of Semitic.

Differentiation by accent.

(7) WS (71) gives a selection of passages in which (except in those marked *) a different accentuation would involve a change of sense. The forms are quoted here as they stand in WH, the alternative, whether probable or not, being added in brackets :—μενεῖ 1 Co 3^{14} (μένει), κρινοῦσιν 6^{2} (WH *mg.* κρίνουσιν), ἴαται Mk 5^{29} (ἰᾶται—as Ac 9^{34}), καθῆσθε Lk 22^{30} (κάθησθε indic.), βαθέα Rev 2^{24} (βάθεα ! an uncontr. pl. from βάθος), ἅγια Heb 9^{2} (ἁγία), ἢ before πόρνος 1 Co 5^{11} (ἦ), ὅμως 14^{7} (ὁμῶς = ὁμοίως), φώτων Jas 1^{17} (φωτῶν *men* !), τίνες Heb 3^{16} (τινές, as in AV), τίσιν $3^{17\text{f.}}$ (τισίν), τῷ 1 Co 15^{8} 16^{16}, 1 Th 4^{6}, Mt 24^{41} (τῳ, Attic for τινί, and obsolete), *συνίων Rom 3^{11} (συνιῶν—see § 86*n* 1 (β)), *συνίουσιν Mt 13^{13} (συνιοῦσιν), ἆρα Gal 2^{17} (ἄρα), οὐκοῦν Jn 18^{37} (οὔκουν), αὕτη Mt 22^{39} (WH *mg.* αὐτῇ), Lk 2^{2} (αὐτή), Rom 7^{10} (αὐτή), 1 Co 7^{12} (αὐτή), αὐτή Lk 2^{37} 7^{12} 8^{42}, Rom 16^{2} (αὕτη), εἰμί Jn $7^{34.\,36}$ 14^{3} 17^{24} (εἶμι !—obsolete), Ἐλαιῶν Lk 19^{29} 21^{37} (Ἐλαιών—see § 61 (*b*), *Prol.* 49, 69, 235), μακρά Mk 12^{40} (μακρᾷ), ΠΟΡΝΩΝ Rev 17^{5} (indeterminate between πόρνων m. and πορνῶν f.), κερδανῶ 1 Co 9^{21} (κερδάνω subj.—see § 95), *πίμπρασθαι Ac 28^{6} (πιμπρᾶσθαι—see § 95), ἐκφύῃ act. Mt 24^{32}, Mk 13^{28} (ἐκφυῇ pass.—see § 95), *ἀποκυεῖ Jas 1^{15} (ἀποκύει—§ 95), μένει Jn 14^{17} (μενεῖ), φάνῃ Rev 8^{12} 18^{23} (φανῇ—§ 95), ἐγχρῖσαι Rev 3^{18} (ἔγχρισαι imper. mid.), ἐπιβλέψαι Lk 9^{38} (ἐπίβλεψαι imper. mid.), τινά 1 Pet 5^{8} in WH *mg.* (τίνα), Heb 5^{12} (τίνα), ἦ τίς Mt 7^{9} (ἤ τις), ἀλλὰ Jn 6^{23} (ἄλλα), ἐν Mk 4^{8}, ^{20} (WH *mg.* ἕν).

Syllabification.

Word-division and Syllabification.

§ 31. The Greek rules for word-division, carefully laid down by grammarians, and normally observed in MSS and papyri, are important because of the light they throw on the syllabification of Greek speech. The most general rule is that the new line must begin with the largest consonant group which is capable of beginning a word. In addition to γρ, δρ, θρ, κλ, κμ, κρ, κτ, μν, πλ, πρ, πτ, τρ, φθ, χθ, which are found initially, we have γμ, θμ, τν and χμ. A liquid (except in the case of μν) is taken to end the preceding syllable. On the same principle σ is often thus abstracted, but here there were differences of usage: the verbal suffixes with σθ tended to bring the σ over to the next line. Before a vowel σ stood at the head of the new syllable. Proclitics were counted as belonging to the next word, and divided accordingly, except in the case of the prepositions εἰς, πρός, σύν and ὑπέρ. Similarly, if there was elision the two words ran into one. Thus we have κα|τ' ἔτος P Oxy i. 101 *ter* (A.D. 142), ὦ]|ς ἂν *ib.* ii. 270^{32} (A.D. 94), πα|ρ' αὐτοῦ *ib.* ^{36}, ἐ|κ τοῦ P Lond 22^{18} (=i. p. 7—B.C. 164), οὐ|κ ἐφρόντισας P Petr ii. 23 $(3)^{11}$ (iii/B.C.), μη|δ' ἄλλον P Reinach 11^{12} (B.C. 111), ἐ|ξοῦ = ἐκ σοῦ Mt 2^{6} ℵ, etc.

The rationale of this may be seen in English. If we used the same general principle of word-division, we should print "not a-t all," for the syllables are divided exactly as in "not a tall man." For further illustration see Mayser 44 ff., also WH *Intr.*^{2} 315.

There is a tendency to make continuous sounds, especially σ and the nasals, divide themselves between both syllables. The effect is sometimes to double the letter, as ἐν|ναντίος, θαλ|λάσσῃ (Mt 8^{26} ℵ), προστάγ|γμασιν, κατέσ|σπαρκεν, μνησ|στευθίσης (Mt 1^{18} ℵ), sometimes to omit one of a genuine double, as τῆ|σωτηρίας, ἄφε|σαυτόν, ἐά|νῦν. The practice should be borne in mind as one calculated to generate various readings. Thus it might be applied to the reading πλήρης σῖτον Mk 4^{28} C* cu^2, which seems to be the oldest accessible: the alternative (see § 65) is to regard the adj. as indeclinable.

Elision.

Elision § 32. In the Hellenistic period the practice of writing elided final vowels (as in Latin) considerably advanced. In 1 Co 15^{33} the iambic line from Menander is written φθείρουσιν ἤθη χρηστὰ ὁμιλίαι κακαί, and there is no authority at all for χρήσθ'. This is a common practice in metrical inscriptions and papyri of our period. In prose the rules observable in the best NT uncials are set forth by WH (*App.*[2] 153) thus :—

in NT uncials, Elision takes place habitually and without variation before pronouns and particles; also before nouns in combinations of frequent occurrence, as ἀπ' ἀρχῆς, κατ' οἶκον. In other cases there is much diversity, and occasional variation.

In ἀλλά elision takes place usually before articles, pronouns and particles, but with many exceptions and much variation. [In W the full form is normal (Sanders 25).] The passage Rom 6^{14}–8^{32} is remarkable as having consecutively (with a single exception 7^{15} ἀλλ' ὃ) 9 non-elisions attested by 3 or more primary MSS: in the six following cases (to 10^{16}) there is no evidence for any non-elision. Elision is commonest before words (of all kinds) beginning with ε, rarest before those that begin with α.

Δέ is never elided except in ὃς δ'ἄν, once or perhaps twice in τὸ δ' αὐτό (not Phil 2^{18}), and perhaps in ἡνίκα δ' ἄν 2 Co 3^{16} (see margin); οὐδ' occurs a few times.

The places where WH regard the reading as open to some doubt may be tabulated thus: the figures represent the totals for the text, non-elisions standing first—the same figures reversed would accordingly represent their margin :

ἀπὸ ἀ.	0 : 2	διὰ ἀ.	0 : 3	ἐπὶ ἐ.	1 : 2	ἀλλά	28 : 38
ὑπὸ ἀ.	2 : 0	κατὰ ἀ.	1 : 0	ἐπὶ ὀ.	1 : 0	δέ	1 : 0
ὑπὸ ἁ.	1 : 1	κατὰ ἑ.	1 : 0	ἐπὶ ὑ.	1 : 0	οὐδέ	1 : 1
		μετὰ ἐ.	0 : 1	ἐπὶ ἰ.	0 : 1		
		μετὰ ὁ.	1 : 1				

Thus, in places where MS evidence is evenly balanced, WH prefer non-elision 39 times and elision 50 times.

in papyri. A comparison may be instituted with some representative papyri. For this purpose nos. 1–41 in Milligan's *Selections* are examined, dating from B.C. 311 to the end of ii/A.D.

(1) *Prepositions.*—Here elision preponderates greatly. Ἐπί occurs once unelided, and ἀπό three times, and all of these are with nouns. On the other hand we find elision with ἀπό (2–1 noun), διά (5–1 δι' ὀλίων, 1 δι' ἐγγύου), ἐπί (7–1 ἐφ' ὕβρει, 1 ἐπ' ἄχυρον 1 ἐπ' ἀληθείας), κατά (10–3 καθ' ἡμέραν, 1 κατ' ὄνομα, 1 κατ' ἀρχάς, 1 κατ' οἰκίαν), μετά (3), παρά (8–1 a name), ὑπό (5). The exx. not stated above are all with pronouns, and so suit WH's rule. Nearly all the nouns are also in combinations answering to the requirement of "frequent occurrence." These statistics may be supported by the totals in Witkowski's collection of Ptolemaic private correspondence.[1] Here elision takes place 16 times where prepositions stand with pronouns, and twice with nouns (καθ' ἡμέραν, παρ' Ἰουδαίου). There is not one example of non-elision.

(2) Ἀλλά has elision 3 times, and never non-elision; δέ 7 and 13 respectively; οὐδέ and μηδέ 4 and 4; τε and ὥστε are never elided, nor are με and σε. Ἵνα has elision in the formula ἵν' ὑγιαίνῃς (so in Witkowski 8 times), but never elsewhere. In Witkowski ἀλλά is always elided (6 times), and δέ 14 times to 10; μηδέ 1 : 1, ὥστε 2 : 0, τε 2 : 0 (unless τοῖς τ [ἄλλοις] in no. 24 must count). Με and σε are not elided, except ἅ σ' οὐ in no. 46 (illiterate).

(3) Rarely other words suffer elision: viz. ἠναγκάσμεθ' ὑ., ἐποεῖσθ' ἐ., ἐνοφιλόμεν' ἀ., μηδέν' ἀ.: add ὁπηνίκ' ἄν from Witkowski. Ὅσας δ' ἐάν might equally be read ὅσας δὲ ἄν, and is therefore not counted. The occurrence of μηδέν' ἀπολελύσθαι in BGU i. 27^{14} (=Milligan p. 101—ii/A.D.) might be cited in support of μηδέν' ἀπελπίζοντες in Lk 6^{35}, thus making ABL etc. agree in sense with the μηδένα of ℵW (cf. syr $^{vt. pesh.}$).

Allegro utterance. The bearing of these facts on the enunciation of sentences in the Common Greek is not unimportant. Elision is due to *allegro* utterance; and the uniform absence of elision shows us under what conditions this was avoided. Δέ and the enclitics τε, με, σε, attached naturally to the preceding word, were not linked with the following word enough to produce elision. The prepositions and ἀλλά, being proclitic, suffered elision as naturally as the former did when compounded with verbs (with initial vowel): exceptions seem to occur almost only where nouns which are not parts of a formula may prompt *lento* pronunciation to produce a kind of emphasis.

Hiatus. The subject is closely connected with one which figures largely in discussions of literary Greek, viz. the avoidance of hiatus which became an instinct with prose writers. Definitions may be found in Blass *Grammar*, 296 f., together with a detailed attempt to show that a partial observance of the hiatus rule can be seen in Heb. The attempt does not seem very successful, and no other NT book is accused of attention to this refinement. Dr. Rendel

---

[1] Documents also included in Milligan are omitted.

Harris calls my attention to the avoidance of hiatus as a motive present in literary revisers of the text of NT, who would change the order of words for the purpose. This applies especially to the class of variants which Hort called "Alexandrian." But in genuine vernacular this disposition to avoid hiatus was almost wholly absent. The well-marked tendency by which in vernacular Hellenistic hiatus is permitted in compounds at the juncture—as in τετραάρχης, ἀλλοτριοεπίσκοπος[1] etc.—may be set by the practice of writing elided vowels in verse, to create a presumption that the later language was indifferent to the confluence of vowels. In pronunciation no doubt the usage was to sound the vowels rapidly, except in the cases where elision was still the rule, which means as we have seen cases of proclisis. Thus τετραάρχης was a real quadrisyllable, produced by the influence of other compounds in τετρα-, and χρηστὰ ὁμιλίαι (1 Co 15[33]) had the α ο distinct, but pronounced in quick time so as not to disturb the rhythm of the verse. In this respect the difference between Hellenistic and classical usage is very much like that between modern and eighteenth century or older English: where poets used to write "th' action," we write and pronounce "the action," though the scansion is the same. English dialects of course use the *allegro* forms very largely (as *Irlams o' th' Height*, *in t'hoos = in the house*); and the analogy may prepare us for the probability that Hellenistic was not uniform. MGr implies as much by its free use of elision.

Crasis.

Crasis. As we should expect, this result of virtual proclisis is greatly restricted in later Greek. In NT, except for τοὔνομα in Mt 27[57], τοὐναντίον *ter*, and ταὐτά in Lk, crasis is confined to combinations with καί, which retains the same tendency in MGr more conspicuously. We find κἀγώ, κἀμέ etc., with which cf. κἀγώ, P Petr iii. 53 n.[3] (iii./B.C.)—but καὶ 'γώ in P Oxy ii. 294[13] (A.D. 22); also κἀκεῖ, κἀκεῖθεν, κἀκεῖνος, and the stereotyped κἄν (MGr), on which see § 29 (7). Papyri of culture low enough to admit phonetic spelling show us that crasis was practised sometimes when unaccented words were capable of being fused with the preceding word: thus P Oxy iv. 744[4] (B.C. 1) ἐν 'Αλεξανδρέᾳσμεν, as we might write—'σμεν with prodelision would suit our practice better, and means the same thing—, BGU iii. 975[11] (A.D. 45) οὐλὴ καστρογνημίῳ 'κξ ἀριστερῶ. Note κἀπεθύμει in D* (Lk 15[16]).

Combinations written as one word.

One word or more? There is no evidence earlier than the minuscules by which we may decide whether to print phrases like δέκα ἕξ, ἀπ' ἄρτι, ἐφ' ἅπαξ, ὑπὲρ ἐκ περισσοῦ etc. as one word or as two or three. The only case in which it matters

[1] ℵB have ἀλλοτριεπ., which may well be right, though papyri have parallel forms to support the other: see *Vocabulary*, *s.v.*

—for of course in the older uncials there is no division of words—is where the fusion involves assuming that the accent of one element was dropped. Sometimes MGr may give possible evidence, though we must not lay too much stress on it: fusion may easily be of late origin, and the evidence of MSS which divide or punctuate off the words may be of equal weight, since though in danger of being literary it is of higher antiquity. Thus MGr ἀνάμεσα disagrees with ἀνὰ μέσον which Ti prints, presumably on evidence of MSS.

Vowels.

Vowel System. § 33. The vowel system in the **Κοινή** has undergone more extensive change than is apparent from the spelling, which is still largely dominated by the literary tradition. The operative factor in change was the development of a stress accent out of a pitch accent (see § 30), which necessarily worked towards an ultimate levelling of quantity in vowels. In MGr long vowels and short are not distinguished: an accented syllable is half-long with an ο, an unaccented one short with an ω. The process which thus radically altered the whole sound of Greek speech was not complete for generations after the NT, but it had set in strongly, and must have done much of its work. In so far as accent was gathering stress character, it necessarily produced the *ablaut* effects which we may note in English, where also spelling fails to express many of the products of accentual conditions. Among those which find expression in writing we may instance "Kretschmer's Law" (see § 30) by which an unaccented short vowel after a liquid or nasal fell out when the neighbouring syllable had the same (or nearly the same) vowel. Thus **Βερενίκη** became **Βερνίκη**, σκόροδον σκόρδον, ἐπηκολούθηκα loses its first ο and ἀπελήλυθε its υ. Illiterate papyri and inscriptions show more of these syncopations than "correctly" written documents,[1] but doubtless ordinary speech showed them plentifully. They are like our own pronunciation of words like *láboratory*, where the first *o* is practically crushed out by the stress before it. The result is that Vowel-gradation (*Ablaut*), which ceased to work during the earlier period of Greek, when all

---

[1] But our uncials are not without instances: see a list in Thackeray 99 f. of such forms found in LXX.

syllables had equal weight and there was no force operating to produce disintegration, started afresh as it must whenever stress accent comes in. It will not be necessary to enlarge upon the later gradation developments, for they only produce visible results on a large scale when we come to the MGr: of course gradation in its prehistoric working belongs to the description of the earlier language, from which the *Κοινή* inherited the familiar series λέγω : λόγος, λείπω : λέλοιπα : λιπεῖν, πένθος : πέπονθα : παθεῖν, ἵστημι : ἵστᾰμεν, etc. Our only concern with *Ablaut* here is to observe that it is not simply a force acting in the period when the Indo-European languages were undivided, but a necessary and constant sequence of stress accent, only suspended when language takes the musical accent like French or ancient Greek.

Itacism. It need only be remarked further that in i/A.D. itacism was levelling the vowels considerably. *Αι* and ε were not far behind in their fusion, and οι and υ followed in time: see each development discussed below. These changes of pronunciation are of great importance in textual criticism. The extent of itacism in an early uncial may be well illustrated by a summary in Sanders's introduction to Codex W (p. 20):—

> In the first quire of John the itacisms are as follow: ι for ει, 193 times; ει for ι, 17; ε for αι, 82; αι for ε, 16; ο for ω, 3; ι for ε, 3; οι for ω, or οι for η, υ for οι, ι for η, and ε for υ occur once each.

Of course some of these are mere isolated freaks: the nature and significance of the rest will appear from the following pages.

We proceed to take the vowels *seriatim*, starting in each case from the classical form and chronicling variations.

1. *A.*

(*a*) *Short.*

A short. There are some cases of substitution of ε for ᾰ in contact with ρ. The possibility of phonetic origin must be considered, especially as it is accepted by Thackeray for some LXX phenomena of the kind. The Egyptian deity Serapis came into Greek first as Σαρᾶπις (Mayser 56 f.); but Mayser gives two Ptolemaic instances of Σεραπιεῖον, and suggests that the distance from the accent was responsible, coupled with the influence of ρ. Σερᾶπις does not appear till the Roman age. Ἐρσενικός also (Mayser 5) seems best explained by the two forces which produced Σεραπιεῖον: an isolated περά for παρά (P Tebt i. 110[4]—B.C. 92 or 59) may be thrown in. Τέσσερα is witnessed first by a British Museum inscr. from Egypt (B.C. 51–47), *OGIS* 193[11] τάλαν[τα τέσ]σερα;[1] next comes BGU i. 133[9] (A.D. 144)—there seem to be hardly any others till the Byzantine age.[2] Τέσσαρες as accus. belongs to an entirely different category: see the accidence, § 71 (*a*) (*γ*). The case for τεσσεράκοντα is distinctly better, but it is greatly outnumbered by the α form until the Byzantine period.[3] It is perhaps significant that the earliest instance we possess (see below) is of the ordinal, where the αρ syllable was further away from the accent than in the cardinal. When we note that *four* differed from *forty* in the fact that the accent preceded the αρ syllable instead of following it, we have a reason for presuming phonetic causes at work. Ionic influence[4] would not account for the unequal treatment of parts of the same numeral. It is significant that τεσσάρων maintained itself even in Byzantine, as in MGr; cf. P Flor i. 37 (v/vi A.D.), where τεσσάρων and τέσ[σ]ερα come in successive lines. That the order of development is seen in the chronological succession Σεραπιεῖον and ἐρσενικός and τεσσερακοστός, then Σερᾶπις and τεσσεράκοντα, and finally τέσσερα(ς) much later, encourages us to hold that the earliest change depended on the position of αρ well *before* the accent.[5] The evidence here given will suffice to make it

[1] Or δέκα [τέσ]σερα, as given by Strack, *Archiv* i. 209.

[2] See *CR* xv. 33*a*, also xviii. 107*a*, where I cite εἰκοσιτέσσερας *bis* from a ii/A.D. papyrus: CPR 242 (cited in the former paper) is apparently a mistake. Mr. Thackeray (in a letter) retracts his statement (p. 74) that "Σερᾶπις and τέσσερα appear to have come into general use together about i/A.D." Add P Oxy viii. 1142[4] τέσσερα (late iii/A.D.).

[3] For τεσσεράκοντα before ii/A.D. may be cited P Tebt ii. 388[8 10] (A.D. 98), P Gen 24[11] (A.D. 96), CPR 220[1] (i/A.D.), P Flor i. 61[62] (A.D. 86–8), *ib.* 86[9] (i/A.D.), BGU iii. 916[4] (Vespasian), P Lond 262[1] τεσσερακοστοῦ (A.D. 11 = ii. p. 177): the same document has τεσσαράκοντα *bis*. Mr. Thackeray's tables for papyri published before 1907, which he has kindly sent me, contain 25 instances of τεσσεράκοντα (-κοστός) from i/ to iii/A.D., and 46 + with α. In making my own tables I have ceased to enumerate instances of α for the early centuries. That there was a marked difference between cardinal and ordinal may be seen well in P Flor i. 1 (A.D. 153), where τέσσαρες [nom. and acc.] occurs twice and τεσσεράκοντα four times. See also *Prol.*[3] 243 f., and Mayser's reff., p. 57. I have one ex. of τέσσερας, a Tebtunis ostracon of B.C. 6/5 ?, in P Tebt ii. p. 337.

[4] Which accounts for τεσσεράκοντα in the ii/A.D. Homer, P Tebt ii. 265 (*Il.* ii. 545), and the Teos inscr. *Syll.* 177[45] (B.C. 303), although the latter is in Κοινή Greek.

[5] I can quote only one instance of *accented* α>ε, viz. BGU iv. 1013[8] (mid i/A.D.) θυγατρέσι, which is not a case of αρ but of ρα: moreover the case may be one of blundering declension, the -τερ- of the stem affecting the abnormal -τρα-. Mayser's instances (p. 58) are referred by him to Coptic influence. Κρέβαττος (twice in W), which has left its mark on MGr, is too late to be brought into the case.

certain that τέσσαρες etc. and τεσσαράκοντα (-κοστός) were the autograph forms for NT. Against these stand "Jn 19[23] τέσσερα ℵALM, Rev 4[6] A, 4[8] ℵA etc." (Debrunner), with τεσσεράκοντα regularly in the uncials: see Ti.-Gregory 80. Dissimilation, which WH (*App.*[2] 157) postulate as cause, is excluded by the fact that τέσσερας has no attestation except A once in Rev 4[4]. On τέσσερα it is only necessary to observe that sporadic instances meet us in documents contemporary with Jn and Rev. In proper names of foreign origin there is considerable variation, but it need not occupy us where Semitic is concerned. Δελματία 2 Ti 4[10] A (ερ) C 424** cu[12] is compared by Deissmann (*BS* 182) with δελματική in BGU i. 93[7] (ii/iii A.D.), against CPR 21[16] (A.D. 230): Radermacher 35 assigns it to Latin influence, which is likely enough. See *Vocab. s.v.* Δαλματία. Πάτερα, however, found in AC at Ac 21[1], has no European support. A different matter is the change of αρ to ερ in augmented and reduplicated forms of καθαρίζω.[1] In LXX (Thackeray 74) A has it 14/21 times, B once, while ℵ never shows it in LXX or NT. As we might expect, the evidence is scantier (and probably insufficient) for Luke and Heb, more satisfactory for Mt and Mk. Thus Mt 8[3] has ερ in B*ELXΠ*, Mk 1[42] in AB*CGLΔΠ**al.*; but Lk 4[27] ACLX, 17[14] AX,[17] ALΔ, Ac 10[15] ACLP 33 81, 11[9] AHL *al.*, Heb 10[2] AC. Thackeray attempts a phonetic account of the change, but the fact that in one case (ἐκαθέρισα) the vowel is accented makes it much more probable that the ε is a double augment; Schmiedel (WS 50) seems inclined to this. Of course it is abnormal, as a verb καθ-αρίζω, if a compound of κατά, would have made -ήρισα. But this does not seem a serious objection.

There are one or two other instances of ε substituted for an older α. Ἐγγαρεύω, derived from the early (Persian) loan word ἄγγαρος, appears in Mt 5[41] ℵ, Mk 15[21] ℵ*B*: the spelling is not infrequent in inscrr. and papyri—see *Vocabulary, s.v.* It did not however ultimately prevail, as MGr ἀγγαρεμένος shows; but its claim to a place in the autographs is strong, especially in Mk. Χλιερός stands in Rev 3[16] ℵ*; ὕελος in Rev 21[18] cu[21] (two have λλ) and so 21[21] 4[6] 15[2] *bis.* For LXX forms of this kind see Thackeray 75: the variation was said to be dialectic, ὕαλος and χλιαρός being Attic. See Lob. *Phryn.* 282 (Rutherford *NP* 364), Moeris 418, Thumb *Hellen.* 75 f., Schweizer *Perg.* 36 f. (where inscriptional evidence is cited). Thumb (*l.c.*) thinks that both α and ε forms had their place in Hellenistic. In NT χλιαρός, ὕαλος (ὑάλινος) and φιάλη seem certain, though WH admit χλιερός as alternative (*App.*[2] 157).

The variation between ἕνεκα and ἕνεκεν, εἵνεκεν is due to dialect mixture. The Attic ἕνεκα in Ac 26[21] is regarded by Blass as in keeping with a speech in the presence of royalty: it appears also in Ac 19[32] ℵAB, Lk 6[22] (exc. DW *al. pauc.*), Mt 19[5] (exc. CDW), Mk 13[9] B. Ἕνεκεν (partially Ionic in origin) is normal, but the still more Ionic εἵνεκεν figures in Lk 4[18] 18[29] ℵB, Ac. 28[20] ℵ*A, 2 Co 3[10] (exc. C *al.*). Ἕνεκεν is the normal form in later Attic and Κοινή: see Mayser 241 f., Crönert,

[1] Mr. H. Scott points out that in *Test XII Patr.* Charles (Oxford, 1908) gives following *v.ll.* Reuben iv. 8 ἐκαθάρισεν (his text) af, ἐκαθάρησεν c, ἐκαθαίρισεν b, ἐκαθέρισεν de.

Mem. 113 f.—the two other forms occur relatively much as in NT. The similar Ionic εἶτεν is only found in Mk 4[28] ℵB*LΔ: Phrynichus gives it and ἔπειτεν a specially bad mark (ἐσχάτως βάρβαρα), and a solitary appearance in the least cultured book of the NT is quite in keeping.

A has yielded to ο in 1 Ti 1[9] πατρολῴαις, μητρολῴαις, where only cursives have ρα (exc. K πατραλ.). The consciousness of origin (πατρ-αλοίας, cf. ἀλοιάω) has weakened, and analogy of πάτρο- and μητρο- compounds prevails. Βατταλογήσητε Mt 6[7] ℵB (W βατταλογεῖται) is replaced by βαττολ. in the other MSS (βλαττολ. in D*). See *Vocab. s.v.* and below § 105. Since the word is probably for βατταλο-λογ., by haplology, the α is original, and βαττολ. will be due to wrong association with βάττος. Mayser 60–62 gives a few exx. of α>ο and ο>α, but they are not enough to be significant.

(*b*) *Long.*

A long. Σίνᾱπι shows the Ionic η in Lk 17[6] W. This would have been the Attic form if Attic had used the word: at Athens they said νᾶπυ (Lob. *Phryn.* 288, where Κοινή citations for σίνηπι are given). The survival of ᾱ in λαός and ναός is noted in § 34. Mayser thinks λαός may be originally a poetic word, used primarily in plur.: see p. 29, but note also Thumb's comments on this section in *Archiv* iv. 490. The flexion of the -ήω verbs, with their tendency towards the -άω type, is discussed under verbal accidence. In two words apparently the Ionic η has secured a place in the Κοινή, διηνεκής (Att. διᾱν., but not consistently), and πρηνής (usually taken as = Att. πρᾱνής): if Chase's explanation of the latter is right, the root is *prē* 'burn.'[1] So also χορηγεῖν (Att. χορᾱγ.), which is not so much an Ionism as an effect of analogy (στρατηγός, ὁδηγός). It is needless to bring in proper names, which might of course start in Doric or other dialects as easily as in normal Κοινή.

2. *E.*

E and α. Two verbs in -άζω appear in NT where ε would be expected. Ἀμφιάζει replaces the literary ἀμφιέννυσιν (still in Mt 6[30]) in Lk 12[28] B, where the rest read ἀμφιέζει: so ἠμφιασμένον Mt 11[8] D, and predominantly in LXX (Thackeray 75). The outside evidence for -άζω is not early: see *Vocab. s.v.*, and add P Iand 62[14] (vi/A.D.). Radermacher 35 accepts the explanation of it as coming directly from ἀμφί, as ἀντιάζω from ἀντί. The fact that ἀμφί did not survive in the Κοινή is one of the difficulties in this view. I prefer the account which Schweizer, *Perg.* 37, takes from W. Schmid, that -άζω (said to be Doric) is the product of a very large class of -άζω verbs, which naturally exerted strong influence on the comparatively few verbs in -έζω. The new present ἀμφιέζω was of course a back-formation from the

---

[1] See *JTS* xiii. (1912) 278 ff., and J. R. Harris in *AJT* xviii. 128 f.

aor. in -εσα. Πιάζω may be similar in history, but it seems to have assumed a new meaning, which would encourage the supposition that it came into the Κοινή separately from some dialect: Theocritus 4^{35} πιάξας τᾶς ὁπλᾶς, "gripping it by the hoof," is warrant for the Doric provenance. The older form still survives with the meaning "press" in Lk 6^{38}. MGr πιάνω "take" joins several papyrus exx. in support of the Κοινή πιάζω with that meaning.

The interesting blunder ἔλαβον γυναῖκας in Heb 11^{35} p[13] ℵ*AD* is perhaps not phonetic in origin, though Thackeray 149 quotes three exx. of nom. in -ας from LXX; and the opposite, γυναῖκες for -ας, occurs in P Catt (*Chrest.* ii. $372^{ii. 2}$)—cf. § 55(4) on acc. pl. in -ες. The importance of the reading consists in the link it helps to establish between all the best MSS: the mistake was very probably in the autograph itself.

E and αι. The itacistic variation between ε and αι figures incessantly in the MSS, as in papyri and other witnesses. It was indeed hardly even a case of "shortening" (as WH *App.*[2] 157 f., where στύλος and κρίμα are put on the same footing): ε and αι were as completely identical as ι and ει in the uncial period. WH 309 f. give Gal 4^{18} as "one of the few instances in which B and ℵ have happened to fall into the same itacistic error," ζηλοῦσθε for -αι. Practically this means that where either would make sense we are allowed to choose for ourselves on other considerations than MS authority. When in 1 Tim 6^{20}, 2 Tim 2^{16} some δ-text authorities (FG and a few cursives) read καινοφωνίας for κεν., we recognise it as a legitimate interpretation of what when read aloud is an ambiguous word. But our acceptance of it is discounted by finding that the version which adopts it (lat [vt (vg semel)]) is one which has a close nexus with the δ-text uncials; while the Sahidic, Bohairic and Syriac vss. justify the spelling with ε. But in Mt 11^{16} the choice between ἑτέροις and ἑταίροις is not so easy, in spite of WH's description of the latter as a "perverse confusion" (p. 310). Ἑταίροις is read by poor uncials only, but the Old Syriac ([sin] and [cu]) and the Latin Vulgate support it; and that in many uncials (including CL) ἑτέροις means ἑταίροις, is shown by the addition of αὐτῶν. Indeed ℵ itself makes us uncertain as to its testimony, when just above τοῖς ἑτέροις we read τες ἀγορες, with αι in each case supplied by the corrector: can we say more than that the corrector saw nothing wrong with ἑτέροις, while he did with ἀγορες? The oldest tradition in vss. is here divided, the Old Latin being against the Old Syriac. The rendering of WH ("the other 'side' or party in the game") is very attractive; but I should accept it on its merits, and not because in such a matter ℵB are to be preferred to CL.

In one frequent category αι and ε involve different renderings, that of inf. -σθαι against imper. -σθε, as in Lk 14^{17}, 19^{13}. There is further the choice between ἐπάναγκες (most MSS) and ἐπ' ἀνάγκαις ℵAC in Ac 15^{28}: the second does not seem to have much of a case. Only one remark need be made as to words which through isolation may have lost their traditional spelling, such as κερέα, ἐξέφνης etc. (WH *App.*[2] 158).

The acceptance of ε here is justified if it is clearly understood that the preponderant spelling of the oldest uncials is taken simply as the best attested, and is not claimed for the autographs. For these the papyri of i/ or ii/A.D. are decidedly better evidence. Thus for φελόνης 2 Tim 4[13] ℵACDEFG I know only one papyrus parallel (P Fay 347, ii/A.D.) against twelve occurrences of φαιν. (φαιλ. *ter*) from papyri of i/–iii/.[1] Similarly αἰφνίδιος has one papyrus parallel (ἐφν. none—see *Vocab. s.v.*), while ἐξαίφνης is less clear.[2] Ἐπάναγκες (which Blass called *doctum vocabulum* !) is very common in papyri with this spelling, and there is nothing to suggest the alternative. So far then as the evidence of our vernacular documents goes, there is little encouragement for deserting the traditional orthography in words where the substitution of ε does not affect the sense : the variation appears to be purely casual, and probably nowhere became a habit as early as i/A D.[3] On the date of the development see below, § 36, under αι.

Schmiedel gives the following list of ambiguous places where we must decide between ε and αι on internal grounds. ἔγειρε Mt 9[5] *al.*, ἀνάπεσε Lk 14[10] 17[7], παρένεγκε Mk 14[36], Lk 22[42], ἔρχεσθε Lk 14[17], πραγματεύσασθε Lk 19[13], φυσιοῦσθαι 1 Co 4[6], ἀγνοεῖτε 1 Co 14[38]; also the choices in Mt 11[16] and Ac 15[28] mentioned above. (See WS 47 f.)

E and ει. It will be shown later (§ 36) that the contacts between ε and ει are of a special nature, and do not fall into the same category as those with ι proper. One conspicuous instance of the latter is the series of compounds in ἀρχι-, which becomes a very large one in Hellenistic. Forms like Ἀρχέλαος—to name one which survives as a proper name in NT — are older; but the change is not phonetic, but extended from the influence of a special category found in early Greek. Instances of ι for ε in Egypt may sometimes be due to the native language, where *e* and *i* were very close together. See Mayser 80 ff. That ἀποστείλω in Ac 7[34] is misspelt for ἀποστελῶ is wrongly assumed by WS 43 n.[27] : it is a matter of syntax, not orthography. See *Prol.* 185,[4] and additions in *Einl.* 292.

A special case is ἀνάγαιον, which in Attic presumably would have ended in -γειον : see Rutherford *NP* 357 f. The Hellenistic form was Doric or Ionic.

---

[1] P Oxy iv. 736 *ter* (*c.* A.D. 1); P Giss 10[21], 12[4], 79[iv. 2], P Oxy iii. 531[14], vi. 933[30], P Hamb 10[19] (ii/A.D.); BGU iii. 816[24] and P Oxy vi. 936 *bis* (iii/A.D.).

[2] Ἐξαί[φνης in P Par 51[8] (B.C. 160) and in P Flor ii. 175[7] (A.D. 255) ἐξεφνης (with αι written above ε), where the correction is significant. *Per contra* ἐξέφνης in P Giss 86[2] (early ii/A.D.), and ἐξεφάνης in *Cagnat* iii. 1145 (Syria).

[3] How little significance the variation has in the uncials may be seen from a random page of ℵ (Mt 9[33]–10[17]), where out of 23 occurrences of αι no less than 9 are wrong, while 6 times ε is wrongly written for αι. On the other hand, in Rom 3[5]–4[11] there is but one itacism (αἰνός) to 40 which are right.

[4] Add there P Ryl ii. 233[8] (ii/A.D.) ἀνενέγκω δὲ Ἡρακλείωι, "I will refer it to H."

E and η. The change of ε to η—for which see below, § 34—may be tentatively recognised in the special case of πλήρης for πλῆρες, which is not uncommon in papyri of the Roman age. Thackeray 176 f. thinks this may have arisen partly from the working of the ρ flanking two vowels that were approximating in sound. This would first assimilate πλῆρες and πλήρεις, and then πλήρη, with πλήρους following later, so that the adj. became indeclinable. The explanation is not without difficulties, but is perhaps the best yet offered. On the appearance of this indeclinable πλήρης in NT see under the flexion, § 65.

E and ο. E has been assimilated to ο in ὀλοθρευτοῦ 1 Co 10[10] (all but D*), ὀλοθρεύων Heb 11[28] (ℵω, against ADE), ἐξολοθρευθήσεται Ac 3[23] (ℵEPω, against AB*CD). Thackeray (p. 88) shows that it was rare in LXX uncials: it was a later development, due to the λ, and surviving in MGr ξολοθρεύω. He compares the much earlier development of ὀβολός in Attic out of ὀβελός, on which see Meisterhans[3] 22 n. In ὀχύρωμα (2 Co 10[4], P Petr ii. *ter*—see Mayser 96) we have a variation from Attic, which had ἐχυρός and ἐχυρόω; but ὀχυρός was older, and Attic seems to have assimilated to ἔχω.

3. *H.*

H. § 34. Attic η maintained itself in the Κοινή overwhelmingly, against the ᾱ of all dialects except Ionic. This, the most impressive evidence of the predominance of Attic as basis of the Κοινή, is confirmed by the reversion of η when "pure" to ᾱ, wherein Ionic differs from Attic (Ion. πρήσσω, ἀληθηΐη etc.). (The Κοινή naturally never changes pre-Greek η, as in τίθημι: Elean was the only dialect which did so.) Compound nouns in -ηγός (from ἄγω) not only show the η throughout (ἀρχηγός, ὁδηγός, στρατηγός), but their analogy changes the Attic χορᾱγός, so that in the Κοινή we have only χορηγέω. Λᾱός and νᾱός (contr. νεωκόρος) established themselves in Hellenistic from dialects outside Ionic-Attic. There are sporadic occurrences of ᾱ forms. For ὁδηγ. we find ὁδαγοί and ὁδαγῇ Mt 15[14] D, ὁδαγεῖν Lk 6[39] D, and ὁδαγήσει Ac 8[31] B*: B shows the ᾱ 1/8, D 3/7. In Mk 9[18] D 565 read ῥάσσει, which need not be equated with ῥήσσει—see below, § 95: the α is therefore short. The very attractive reading of B in Ac 27[27] προσαχεῖν (g *resonare*), which accounts for the variants, has the difficulty of being a Doric (etc.) form which disagrees with the common derivatives of the same root: κατηχεῖν and ἦχος are conspicuous in NT. Can it have been a term used by sailors from Crete, Cyprus, Lesbos, Corinth, or some other maritime country outside the Ionic-Attic area, appropriated as a *t.t.*? One other abnormal α is that in Νύμφαν Col 4[15]: in *Prol.* 48 it is argued that this was probably Νύμφᾰν, a woman's name, not Νυμφᾶν masc., which involves a less probable reading (αὐτῶν).

H and ει. In two words class. η is replaced by ει. The spelling εἶ μήν cannot be due to confusion with εἰ "if," as is shown by the quotation from a Doric inscr. in *Prol.* 46 n.[4]. Thackeray (83 f.) supplements the account there by observing that papyrus citations for εἶ μήν begin with B.C. 112: he also shows how

LXX usage is sometimes inconsistent with any connexion with εἰ, though there are many instances where אִם לֹא is rendered by εἶ μήν, and confusion with εἰ μή would be possible were it not for the plentiful papyrus exx.; cf. Mayser 78 n. To these may be added now some parallels. In *Archiv* v. 232, Wilcken quotes a papyrus of Wessely's, which he reads εἶ (=ἦ) οὐ [δί-]δοταί μοι κ.τ.λ. (reign of Augustus). BGU iv. 1141[6] (B.C. 13) ἢ ἔστιν ἦ οὐ gives us ἠ for εἰ: P Hamb 4[4] (A.D. 87) has εἶ μήν followed in [13] by εἶ (=ἦ) ἔνοχος εἴην τῷ ὅρκωι, and so P Lips 121[13] (A.D. 151). In P Oxy viii. 1148[2] (i/A.D.) Hunt takes εἶ βέλτιον as for ἦ, asking a question: may this be simply the interrogative εἰ common in NT, and could we regard this use as originating in ἦ? See *Vocab. s.v.* εἶ μήν for further instances. We may note that in 2 Co 2[9] we have to make this same choice with resulting difference of meaning—ει (*i.e.* εἰ) with ℵCDGω, or η (=ᾗ) with AB 33. We find one or two exx. of this itacism, earlier that our uncials, in two Oxyrhynchus MSS: P Oxy iv. 655[14] (uncanonical Gospel, not later than A.D. 250) εἰλικίαν, and 656[28, 43] (LXX of Gen 19[33, 35]—early iii/A.D.) εἴ]δη, εἴδη, for ᾔδει. See further Mayser 78 f. He puts under this heading the new perf. τέθεικα for τέθηκα: the latter stands alone in Attic inscrr. from 400 to 200 B.C. (Meisterhans[3] 189, Schweizer *Perg.* 184): τέθεικα begins to appear in ii/B.C., as *Perg.* 248[23] (B.C. 135/4). The old explanation of this from analogy—ἀφῆκα : ἀφεῖκα : : ἔθηκα : τέθεικα—seems however to be adequate. But no analogy is apparent for κηρίαις Jn 11[44] AX *al.*, nor for ἀνάπειρος Lk 14[13, 21] ABDE*LW (-πιρ. ℵPR) *al.*, which is further recommended to us by the stigma of ἀμαθία in Phrynichus (*ap.* Ti *in loc.*). His note mentions further that the Hellenistic spelling was ει and not ι.[1]

H and ι. In the same category stands ι for η. So Rev 18[12] σιρικοῦ (all uncials), for which WH quote *CIG* 5834; 1 Co 4[11] γυμνιτεύομεν (all exc. L— -νειτ. B*D*); σιμικίνθιον Ac 19[12]; Κυρήνιος Lk 2[2] (exc. BW)—Blass thinks that Κυρήνη provided the suggestion; οὐ μὶ [μνησθήσο]μαι Heb 10[17] ($\mathfrak{p}^{13}$); πλήρις Jn 1[14] (W). The name Μιτυλήνην Ac 20[14] ends with -ίνην in AEL. Under this heading comes also Lk 23[11] W ἐξουθενίσας, which however may be a deliberate correction, since it agrees with the form that seems to have been used by Plutarch: see below, § 46, and further on this verb § 119. The spelling Χρηστιανός ℵ* 3/3 (also 81 in Ac 11[26]) is not so much an itacism as a consequence of the common pagan misreading of the mysterious name Χριστός. Finally, we may preserve for the museum of exegetical curiosities the Byzantine invention of a κάμιλος "cable" to be an improvement on κάμηλος in the paradox of Mt 19[24] and ||s (Suidas and a scholiast). Instances of ι for η in LXX may be noted in Thackeray 85: they are "distinctly rare in B and not much commoner in ℵA." See above, § 28, for Rudberg's note on the rarity of a confusion of η and ι in D.

---

[1] WH compare ἄπειρος (*qs.* "unmaimed") in Hdt. i. 32: if the reading is sound, we might take the NT word to be Ionic. But cf. Stein *in loc.* It should be added that in Heb 11[37] WH mention with some approval the conjecture ἐπηρώθησαν for ἐπειράσθησαν, which would come by way of ἐπειρώθησαν.

Η and υ. The very common MS confusion of ἡμεῖς (and cases) with ὑμεῖς is discussed under υ in § 35, and a suggestion is made as to the phonetic cause. WH *Intr.* 310 urge that confusion of sound plays only a part: they recognise a "prevailing tendency . . . to introduce ἡμεῖς wrongly, doubtless owing to the natural substitution of a practical for a historical point of view." 1 Pet and 2 Co are specially mentioned as largely affected, and Ac 17[28] [B cu[6] boh] τινὲς τῶν καθ' ἡμᾶς ποιητῶν is noted as a reading they would much like to accept, but for "the limited range of attestation."

Η and ε. Nouns in -ημα are sometimes found with -εμα, through the strong association with the -σις class, in which the weakened root-vowel was primitive: εὕρεσις, θέσις etc. produced εὕρεμα, θέμα, just as κρίσις produced κρίμα. See § 30, and Thackeray's list, *Gr.* 79 f. On ἐρρέθην, ῥηθῆναι, see § 95 *s.v.* εἴρω. In verb-endings WS 48 gives στήκετε Mk 11[25], 1 Thess 3[8], θαυμάζετε Jn 5[20], ἐξομολογήσεται Phil 2[11], as instances of well-supported but grammatically dubious substitutions.

Η dropped. An apparent extrusion of η after οι is rather widely found in forms of ποιέω: cf. also βοιθοῦ for βο(ι)ηθοῦ in Wilcken *Ostr.* 1084[11] (B.C. 136), 1089[7] (B.C. 135). So ποῖσαι Lk 11[42] ℵ, ποίσας Jn 5[11] W. Mayser 83 cites four papyrus exx. from ii/B.C. See Blass *Pron.* 38 n.[5], and G. Meyer *Gr.*[3] 132 n.[2]; also Radermacher 34, who accepts Hatzidakis' postulate of a parallel stem ποίω, like νόω against νοέω.

4. *O*.

Ο and α. A replacing of ο by α is seen in μεσανύκτιον (-ου) Mk 13[35] B*W, Lk 11[5] D*. MGr μεσάνυχτα shows that it is not a mere accident: the adv. μέσα may suggest its origin. Αἱμαροοῦσα Mt 9[20] ℵ* is an obvious assimilation to the primary. Κολασσαεῖς in the title of Col in AB*K *al.* and in ℵ twice at the top of the page, is shown by Lightfoot (*Comm.*[7] 17n) to be a later spelling: Paul's own spelling in 1[2] is Κολοσσαῖς.

Ο and ω. The close approximation of ο and ω, which has plentiful evidence in ii/B.C. in Egypt, but in Attica not before ii/A.D. (Thackeray 89), accounts for some doubtful spellings, and for a few more important matters. WH mention the following:—Συκομορέα (Lk 19[4] DQ -μωρ.); χρεοφιλέτης (L 1/2, U 2/2 have the "correct" χρεωφ.); πρόιμος (from πρό, antithetic to ὄψιμος) but πρωινός (from πρωί), both as in LXX—see Thackeray 90; ἐνδώμησις, now confirmed by the inscr. *Syll.* 583[30] (i/A.D.)—ο is only due to false etymology; Στωϊκός, in Ac 17[18] B, is the original spelling (see Brugmann-Thumb 64), which in ℵADE *al.* is changed to Στο. by influence of στοά. Nouns in -ωσύνη and comparatives in -ώτερος may be taken as maintaining their place when the preceding syllable is short: such exceptions as there are explain themselves simply by levelling, which works easily when the two sounds are getting very near together.

The fact that the uncials generally preserve the historic spelling in cases like these where nothing turns upon it must count for something in their favour when it is urged that mere itacism accounts for the change of -ομεν into -ωμεν, or the like, which WH (309) call "probably the commonest permutation." It may be questioned whether the great uncials show instances of ω for ο, or ο for ω, in which the matter is one of mere orthography. Thackeray (91) remarks, "In the LXX at least we shall not expect ἔχομεν and ἔχωμεν to be confused in Cod. B": the rarity of this confusion in the principal LXX uncials comes out strikingly on p. 89 f. He is applying this to the crucial case in Rom 5¹. The only objection to following the uncials here is removed by syntactical considerations, which will be taken in their place: meanwhile see *Prol.* 110, 247. Here we find all the uncials (exc. ℵᵃGP) and all the vss. on the side of ἔχωμεν; so also patristic testimony from Marcion down, except Didymus, Epiphanius, Cyril (³|₄). If then Paul really meant ἔχομεν, we must assume a primitive error in the written text, due possibly to a mishearing on the part of his scribe. Nachmanson *Magn.* 64 f. gives inscriptional instances of confusion of ο and ω in Asia, especially Hierapolis. But it can hardly be called common in Asia Minor in i/A.D.; and the fact that in Egypt the fusion was practically complete before Paul's day proves nothing for our purpose, since Egypt was manifestly ahead of other countries in this change. Schweizer *Perg.* 95 gives further evidence for the Asia Province, but it is also indecisive. Champions of ἔχομεν must first examine the point of syntax, and then if dissatisfied claim the right to emend the text: their case cannot rest on authority, nor on the assumption of itacism.[1] A further important instance of the same confusion is 1 Co 15⁴⁹ φορέσωμεν, if we are to listen to the modern authorities who disapprove of the hortatory sense which Tertullian and Chrysostom attest. Here B and one cursive support ο: it is probably again a matter of syntax and not itacism. Jas 4¹⁵ ζήσωμεν is best taken as a genuine *v.l.* due to misunderstanding of the construction. To take exx. of another kind, we are justified in regarding καθαρίζων in Mk 7¹⁹ ℵABLΔW *al.*, μεῖζον in Jn 10²⁹ AB*X (μείζων in MSS reading ὅ being a compromise), and many other readings where the question is between ο and ω, as genuine *vv.ll.*, and not mere misspellings. Perhaps καυθήσωμαι 1 Co 13³ CK *al.* κερδηθήσωνται 1 Pet 3¹ cu, stand about alone as genuine exx. of the itacism which we are asked to recognise in Rom 5¹ and 1 Co 15⁴⁹. Schmiedel (WS 48) gives sundry other verb forms where ο is well attested for what he regards as a grammatically necessary ω: viz. Rom 14¹⁹ διώκομεν, Mt 13¹⁵ *al.* ἰάσομαι (LXX), 1 Jn 5²⁰ γινώσκομεν, Ac 21²⁴ ξυρήσονται, Rev 14¹³ ἀναπαήσονται (!), Gal 6¹² διώκονται, Rom 14⁸ ἀποθνήσκομεν, Lk 3¹⁴ ποιήσομεν, Jn 4¹⁵

---

[1] I modify, mainly on Thackeray's lead, the freedom I claimed for the modern editor in *Prol.* 36. I have H. A. A. Kennedy (cited *Prol.* 247), Rendel Harris (*Expositor*, VIII. viii. 527) and Deissmann (*Paul* 148) against me —a trio I am not likely to ignore. Nor do I object to their use of virtual conjecture; I only cannot see why it is necessary, when the sense is practically the same.

διέρχομαι, Rev 6[11] ἀναπαύσονται; also *vice versa* Lk 9[13] ἀγοράσωμεν, Mk 6[37] δώσωμεν. He mentions further two tempting conjectures, Rom 13[3] ἀγαθοεργῷ and 2 Pet 3[6] δι' ὅν. In 1 Co 9[27] Lk 18[5] ὑποπιάζειν is an unsuccessful attempt to explain an unusual word, and not an orthographic variant.

Corroboration of the general line here taken may be found in the fact that only two of the iv/A.D. and earlier Biblical texts in P Oxy i.–xi. (see § 36) show this itacism, viz. ii. 209, where in Rom 1[2, 5] we find πρωφητῶν and ὑπακωὸν πίστεος (GH call this document (iv/A.D.) a "schoolboy's exercise") and iv. 657[147] (=Heb 10[34], iv/A.D.) κρίσσωνα. In W I can see no instance, unless we count παιδίον for -ων in Mk 9[37], and even this is translatable and may be a genuine *v.l.* Scrivener (*Collation of Codex Sinaiticus* (1864), p. liii) says that ℵ interchanges ου and ω 20 times in the termination of verbs, and ο and ω 68 times. It soon appears that the question is one of syntax as much as of orthography—*e.g.* ἵνα with a fut. ind. instead of an aor. subj.—and must be examined on syntactical lines before we can confidently pronounce for itacism. Against the assumption that MSS commonly confused indic. and subj. may be set the round declaration (Blass-Debrunner 17) that in NT there are only a few traces of quantity-levelling. Rudberg[1] remarks that "D observes quantity-distinctions very well, and distinguishes indic. and subj."

5. *Ω*

Ω. § 35. In earlier Greek ω differed from ο as η from ε: it was the open ō to which we come nearest in the syllable *ore*, as to the open ē in *ere* (th*ere*). In Egypt ω becomes much closer in ii/B.C.: Mayser counts from that century 50 instances of ο for ω, and 20 more when accented, 37 and 33 respectively of ω for ο.

Ω and ου. We find ου for ω(ι) quite infrequently in Ptolemaic papyri: see Mayser 99 f., 138, where they are all explained as syntactical or orthographical confusions signifying nothing. Later exx. such as ἀγωνιοῦμεν, διαιτουμένων, ἀγαπουῦντες, ἀπαντούντων (see *CR* xviii. 110*b*), are late enough to be classed as due to mixture of classes in the Contracta. Θυρουρός in papp. and Mk 13[34] D*, Jn 10[3] D, is merely on the analogy of κηπουρός etc. Ζηλοῦτε Gal 4[17] and φυσιοῦσθε 1 Co 4[6] are doubtless subj. (see §§ 84, 85), but owe their form to the assimilation of indic. and subj. in Contracta which started naturally from the -άω class. Depending as before on his syntactical presuppositions, which will be examined in their place, Schmiedel gives the following well-attested *reicienda*: Mt 7[6] καταπατήσουσιν, Gal 2[4] καταδουλώσουσιν, Rev 6[4] σφάξουσιν, 9[20] προσκυνήσουσιν, 2[22] μετανοήσουσιν, Ac 7[7] δουλεύσουσιν (Gal 4[17] ζηλοῦτε, 1 Co 4[6] φυσιοῦσθε—see §§ 84–5), Mk 15[20] σταυρώσουσιν, Mt 18[19] συμφωνήσουσιν, Rev 13[15] προσκυνήσουσιν, Jn 17[3] γινώσκουσιν, Tit 2[4] σωφρονίζουσιν, Rev 12[6] τρέφουσιν. He bases his rejection of these, as of those in § 34, on the evidence of confusion of vowels in the Egyptian vernacular Greek.

---

[1] *Ntlicher Text* 15.

Ω and α. The perplexed forms of ἀνάγαιον (so WH) are noted under ε above: a form ἀνώγειον would account for the MGr, but ἀναγ. must have been the earlier—it is a choice between ἀνά and ἄνω for first element, and on the analogy of κατάγαιον we should expect the former, which is in the best MSS. WS 51 compares the alternative forms καταφαγᾶς and κατωφαγᾶς in Phrynichus (*NP* 497).

6. *I.*

I and ε. Dissimilation takes place in ἁλεεῖς, from ἁλιεύς, for which WH's Δεκελεεῖς is an illusory parallel, since the nom. sing. will be Δεκελε(ι)εύς.[1] Ἁλεεῖς is found in LXX (Thackeray 84), and can be illustrated from P Flor i. 127^{15} (A.D. 256): six papyrus citations must be set against this one. On the contraction which more commonly affects two concurrent *i*-sounds see below, § 38. The Latin *legio* is transliterated λεγιών, but λεγεών appears not only in ACω at Mt 26^{53}, Mk 5^{15}, Lk 8^{30}, but also in papyri—see *CR* xv. 33*b*, 434*b*, xviii. 107*b*. Among 31 occurrences of λ. and deriv. in papyri I find 6 with ε; but when only i/A.D. exx. are counted ε has 4 and ι has 7. The ε was probably older, and marks the fact that Latin *i* was more open than Greek ι. A similar case is λέντιον for *linteum* Jn 13^{4}, where in the second syllable we note the more open sound of ι before a vowel. Cf. Lindsay *Latin Language* 30, and note the transliteration Ποτίολοι from *Puteoli*. The late νηφάλεος, which is not an orthographic variant, appears in Tit 2^{2} D*E, and in later uncials in 1 Tim 3$^{2, 11}$.

I and ο. There is no relation whatever between ἱμείρομαι and the rare verb ὁμείρομαι, on which see § 95.

I and οι. Στοιβάδας Mk 11^{8} ACSVXΓ (στυβ. N) is probably a mistake of a period in which οι and υ were locally reduced altogether to the *i*-sound. It is not worth considering as a possible reading of the autographs. Jannaris *Gr* 52 f. would actually have us believe that οι was monophthongal in the age of Thucydides: that he can quote οἴκει as a phonetic equivalent of οἶκοι is sufficient illustration of his equipment in comparative philology.

I and ει. The most conspicuous and universal of all itacisms is the complete equivalence of ι and ει in uncials as in papyri and inscrr. of the Hellenistic period: whether ι is long or short it may always be replaced by ει. Scribes have their individual preferences. Thus Lake remarks (*Codex Sinaiticus*, p. xi) that scribe A of א prefers ι, while scribe D prefers ει. WH *App.*^{2} 159 f. give an elaborate analysis of the orthography as determined by the best uncials. They note (p. 306 f.) that "א shews a remarkable inclination to change ει into ι, and B to change ι into ει . . . the converse confusions being very rare in both, and particularly in B. Hence B has to be left virtually out of account as an authority against unclassical forms with ι, and א against unclassical forms with ει; while in the converse cases the value of their evidence remains unimpaired, or rather is enhanced, allow-

---

[1] Cf. Meisterhans^{3} 42.

ance being made for the possible contingency of irregular permutations here and there." Set by this Thackeray's account (p. 86 f.) of the ways of ℵB in LXX. An analysis of 𝔭[13] (before A.D. 350, perhaps before 325) shows 12 instances of ει for *short* ι, 8 for ῑ, while there are 16 of ι for ει, one of them corrected (λ^ε^ιτου[ργῶν). This summary, reinforced by the abundance of ει for ῐ in vernacular inscrr. and papyri, makes it futile to differentiate ῑ and ῐ for the uncial period. WH are struck by the good attestation of γεινώσκω and γείνομαι in the best NT uncials, but we may assume with safety that it is purely accidental. According to Mayser (87) the change of ẹ̄ (whether the old diphthong ει or the lengthened ε) to *i* dates in Egypt from *c.* 200 B.C., while in Attic, Pergamene and Magnesian inscrr. it is a century later. In Boeotian dialect the change was established in v/B.C. (cf. Thumb *Dial.* 223). Wackernagel acutely points out that the new future δανιῶ in LXX from δανείζω convicts the translators and not merely the MSS of itacism.[1] In agreement with this is the fact that in papyri of ii/i B.C., except in carefully written official papers, ει is constantly changed to ι, and ι to ει (half as often), without any appreciable difference between accented and unaccented syllables : the ει for ῐ is much commoner when unaccented. Attic does not begin to show ει for ῐ till ii/A.D., Pergamene still later, and Magnesian much the same.[2]

We may safely conclude that for the NT, of which probably no part was written in Egypt, there was complete equivalence of ει and ῑ, but that we have no adequate reason to expect from the autographs ει for ῐ. A practical inference is that it is perfectly futile to follow our best uncials in printing abnormal forms like ἴδον[3] for εἶδον and ἱστήκειν for εἱστήκειν. It would be quite reasonable to accept an unaugmented aor. indic. in the one case, and to suppose the analogy of ἵστημι operative in the other. But the MS evidence is not adequate proof that such forms really existed A still more practical inference is the futility of insisting upon εἰ δὲ for ἰδὲ in Jas 3[3] : see Mayor *in loc.*

(Ε)Ι and ε. Before vowels, which in practice means before ο and α, the ẹ̄-sound appears to have remained unmodified even in i/A.D. This is shown by the very frequent spelling with η in Attica, Asia and Egypt, especially during the Augustan period. This is essentially the same as the ε which appears *e.g.* in δωρεά and Ἀρεοπαγίτης, where ε = older ει : so also Αἰνέας, Ἀνδρέας, where the ε has the accent. This involves a sharp distinction between nouns in -ειᾰ and -ία̅, where the difference of accent persisted in nom. acc. sing. and nom. pl., the quality of the penultimate vowel and the quantity of the ultima retaining their difference also. Their coincidence in the other cases, together (perhaps) with Ionic influence, produced no doubt some confusion ; but it is very doubtful whether our MSS are good witnesses in

---

[1] Reviewing Helbing, *ThLZ*, 1908, p. 637. See Thackeray 85 ff.

[2] For these statements cf. G. Meyer *Gr*[3] 180 ff. ; Meisterhans[3] 48 ff. ; Schweizer *Perg.* 52 ff. ; Nachmanson *Magn.* 40 f.

[3] Wackernagel (in his review of Helbing just cited) calls ἴδον an "imbecile spelling."

any such cases. Since the accent is the only element concerned which normally remains unchanged, and documents of iv/A.D. and later[1] are admittedly affected by the complete equivalence of *ει* and *ι* prevailing in their own day, it seems best to spell according to the classical tradition, not because we can prove it for the autographs, but because the autographs are in this matter unattainable and no real difference is made. It may be worth while therefore to cite from the lists in Meisterhans[3] 50 55 the Attic spelling of words occurring in NT. (1) (*δοκιμεῖον*); *μείξω, ἔμειξα, μεικτός*; (*σειρά*); *τείσω, ἔτεισα*; *τρεισκαίδεκα*. (2) *ἐμπορία, ἐμπόριον*; *ἱμάτιον*; *κακοπαθία*; *ὀθόνιον*; *οἰκτίρω*; *πτερύγιον*; *σιρός*;[2] *ὠφελία*. (3) Inscrr. differ as to *στρατεία* and *στρατιά* for "expedition": "army" is always *στρατία*. For the rest, it will suffice to refer to WH for the words in which they think unclassical spellings attested. They include "*ἄστιος*" as an alternative for *ἀστεῖος*, which means shifting the accent: here again ℵ has *ι* in Ac 7[20], Heb 11[23], and its evidence may be disregarded. The only word that matters is -*ελειπον* (-*εν*) "in places . . . where the aorist would be the most natural tense": since ℵD with -*λιπ*. are faced by AC 33 *al.* with -*λειπ*., it is hard to see why the less appropriate aor. should be preferred. The syllable in question is unaccented, and the difference in sound between *ει* and *ι* would be infinitesimal. It is hard to set aside, even on small matters, judgements based on so unique a knowledge of the MSS. But since in this place (Heb 10[25]—*v. App.*[2] 162) B is not extant, and ℵD are to be deducted from the list of "the better MSS" on whose "constancy" WH depend for their reading, one feels blind obedience difficult. A little problem of spelling arises in 1 Co 2[4] *π(ε)ιθοῖς*: see WS 135 n[20]. A *ἅπ. εἰρ.* like this may be written indifferently, and analogies are mostly lacking—perhaps *πειθός*, as a new adj. straight from the verb-stem, is best. But Schmiedel's supposition, that ΠΕΙΘΟΙ ϹΟΦΙΑϹ has had an intrusive sigma put in, has great plausibility: we may follow FG and omit *λόγοις*. On the doubling of *σ* etc. at a line division see § 31: the denial of such a possibility in an archetype of ℵB etc. seems to involve a too childlike faith in Vatican and Sinaitic infallibility.

7. *Υ*.

Υ and *ου*. Some confusion with *ου* appears in the word *κολλύριον* Rev 3[18] ℵC 046 cu[30], where APω have *ου*. See Thackeray 92 for variations in LXX MSS. Blass *Gr.* 22 pronounces the *ου* "certainly" due to Latin influence: Debrunner 27 drops this, only noting (from Crönert *Mem.* 130) that *ου* is later. The papyri vary:

---

[1] In the cursive period a reversion to classical spelling as such may be seen everywhere.

[2] This word supplies a good test of WH's method. They declare *σειροῖς* "certain" in 2 Pet 2[4]. Here ℵ has *σιρ.* and B *σειρ.*, and on the principles quoted above from WH neither of these counts. The "certainty" of *σειρ.* seems to depend on AC, unless the witnesses for *σειραῖς* are to be counted. But this word had *ει* in Attic.

for υ stands P Oxy viii. 1088[42] (early i/A.D.); for ου P Flor ii. 177[20] (A.D. 257)—P Ryl i. 29(*a*)[46] (ii/A.D.) is ambiguous. An inscr. from Rome apparently from Caracalla's reign, *IGSI* 966[16] (=*Cagnat* i. 41) has υ. The corruption of λύσαντι Rev 1[5] ℵAC into λούσαντι P 046 is hardly a. case in point, for a supposedly easier sense accounts for the *v.l.* better.

Υ and ι. Changes between υ and ι are practically always due to assimilation or dissimilation. Βήριλλος Rev 21[20] A is a negligible exception. Assimilation changed βυβλίον to βιβλ., and (in reverse direction) ἥμισυς to ἥμυσυς. That βυβλίον is much commoner than its primary accounts for the equally regular spelling βίβλος (in Mk 12[26] and Lk 20[42] D has βυβλ.). Meisterhans[3] 28 cites Attic inscrr. down to ii/B.C. with βιβλίον and βίβλος: from i/B.C. the original υ comes in for a while, Kretschmer *Vaseninschriften* 119 f. showed that in Attic a short unaccented υ passed into ι if a neighbouring syllable contained ι. The Attic reversion to type in later inscrr. shows that there βύβλος never completely yielded to levelling: according to Moeris, Plato said βιβλία but Demosthenes βυβλία. See Schweizer *Perg.* 99 f. In the papyri βιβλ. predominates considerably: see *Vocabulary*, *s.v.* Ἥμισυ was in the papyri frequently assimilated ἥμυσυ: see Mayser 100, who says it was overwhelmingly predominant in iii/B.C. After this the ι came in again, by the influence of oblique cases. We find τὰ ἥμυσοι[1] (with -οι=-υ by itacism) in Lk 19[8] D*. See further § 73. The island Μυτιλήνη was so named in v/ii B.C. (Meisterhans[3] 29): from B.C. 100 it became progressively Μιτυλήνη by the same dissimilation which is illustrated above. So Ac 20[14], except for Μυτυλίνην L, like ἥμυσυ. The next verse has Τρωγυλίᾳ D, from which we may fairly presume Τρωγύλι(ον) was produced by later assimilation in MSS of Strabo and NT.

Ὑμεῖς and ἡμεῖς. The very common confusion of ὑμεῖς and ἡμεῖς in the MSS goes back as far as ii/B.C in papyri: see Mayser's instances, p. 86. The phenomenon is rather perplexing, for we have plenty of evidence that neither η nor υ had found their MGr goal, the *i*-sound, for centuries after ii/B.C., unless it was in strictly limited areas. Thumb, *Hellen.* 150, 193, thinks that approximations of υ to *i* were due to foreign influence, esp. in Asia Minor; but we can hardly apply this principle to Egypt in the Ptolemiac period. Is it possible to set down its origin to assimilation of the vowels in nom. and dat., the other cases following suit? The η and υ were in the weak position before the stress, and the difference between an unstressed *e* and *ü* would be easily slurred when the next syllable had an accented *ī*. It was the confusion in pronunciation between the pronouns which ultimately produced the new forms ἐμεῖς (from ἐμέ, but barely differing from ἡμεῖς) and ἐσεῖς.

---

[1] Robertson *Gr.* 199 wrongly reports D as reading ἥμυσον. The corrector has written H over the OI, so as to indicate τὰ ἡμίση. "The reading ἡμίση can be seen to be later by observing that the first stroke of the H is not straight, and the cross-bar was made from right to left, and not carried through to meet the other limb" (Dr. J. R. Harris, letter of Sept. 4, 1915).

῾Αλυκός (Jas 3^{12}) is really a different word from ἁλικός. Moeris makes υ Attic and ι Κοινή. See Mayser 102.

8. *Diphthongs with ι.*

§ 36. These were all monophthongal in pronunciation before the beginning of the Byzantine age. When our oldest MSS were written, the three short diphthongs were respectively *e*, *i*, and *ü*, the three long ones had lost the ι element altogether.

Αι, date of fusion with ε. (*a*) On ᾰι most of what need be said has been given under ε, where it is shown that the uncials confuse the two completely, the pronunciation having become identical. The date at which the change took place naturally differed locally. In Attica it become conspicuous from A.D. 150 on: a little earlier αι was sometimes written η,[1] as it was in Boeotian long before. In Egypt the itacism appears in ii/ and i/B.C., but very sparingly and in illiterate papyri.[2] Pergamum supplies only two late stones, badly spelt.[3] Magnesia has one instance of αι for ε as early as A.D. 50, and isolated cases a little later.[4] Nachmanson gives samples of the abundance available from Asia Minor everywhere in later times. Pompeii is specially instructive, since of course A.D. 79 is the latest possible date. When therefore we find (Diehl, no. 10) an iambic ἐ[νθ]άδαι κατοικεῖ· μηδὲν εἰσειαίτω κακόμ, with αι twice scanned short as an itacism for ε, we have adequate evidence that in Italy of i/A.D. the confusion was possible.[5] Blass however denies[6] that the fusion was generally complete till iii/iv A.D. While, therefore, Mark might have confused αι and ε if he wrote in Rome and used a liberty possible there outside cultured circles, there is no proof that books written in Asia Minor would show this licence. It was complete before our uncials, but probably the autographs showed very little of it.

Αι in Biblical papyri, Some materials for further inductions may be secured by studying the Biblical or quasi-Biblical papyri from Oxyrhynchus, coeval with or older than ℵ and B. Only four of these have any itacisms of this kind. P Oxy 657, a copy of Heb. covering about one-third of the Epistle and dated in the first half of iv/A.D., has ε 14 times among 61 places where αι should stand, as well as κέ once for καί, which is elsewhere universal and is not included in the enumeration following. It has also 3 cases of αι for ε. The close affinity between this strongly itacistic MS and B in some important readings may be remembered. The two Logia papyri, P Oxy 1 and 654 (iii/A.D.), have -αι twice for -ε, and 6 times rightly. The Hermas papyrus, P Oxy 1172 (iv/A.D.), shows ε 4/10 times. Finally we have in 1229 πλανᾶσθαι Jas 1^{16} (5 exx. of correct αι), and in 1230 ἔλεον

[1] Meisterhans[3] 34. His exx. for ε are all before vowels, until nearly the end of ii/A.D.

[2] Mayser 107.

[3] Schweizer 78.

[4] Nachmanson 37.

[5] Cf. Kretschmer *Entstehung* 7.

[6] *Pronunc.* 68.

Rev 6^6 (no αι): both fragments are iv/A.D. The other documents have αι 133 times in all, without a single instance of itacism.[1]

and in ℵB. In Egypt accordingly this itacism hardly ever appeared in Christian literary documents till iv/A.D. and most scribes avoided it even in that century, common though it was in non-literary writing. The extent to which ℵ and B show it becomes the more remarkable; but it does not affect their date, since the Hebrews papyrus is securely anchored in the same period, and is strongly itacistic. But the authority of ℵB as evidence between αι and ε is seriously shaken, just as it is for ει and ι, when we consider the strong claim that Egypt has to be the home of the β-text.

List of substitutions of ε in WH. It may be convenient to append Schmiedel's list of forms in which WH print ε for αι (not all of them invariably): — φελόνης, κερέα, κρεπάλη, ἐφνίδιος, ἐξέφνης, Λασέα, συκομορέα, ῥέδη. It will be noticed that they are all isolated words in which there is no analogy to preserve their older form: they were likely therefore to take on a new spelling earlier than words protected by association with a system. We have seen (p. 80) that even here the ε has a very precarious footing before iv/A.D.

Αι and α. A note may be added as to relations of αι and α. The archaic αἰεί is not uncommon in post-Ptolemaic papyri, but ἀεί predominates: the word itself survives mainly in formulae —see *Vocab. s.v.* There is no trace of this or of αἰετός in NT MSS; nor of ἐλάα (etc.), κάω, κλάω (unless ἔκλααν for ἔκλαιον in Rev 5^4 ℵ is to be counted), which Mayser 104 f. notes as occurring sporadically in papyri. He notes that early papyri not seldom show Ἄγυπτος (-ιστεί), under influence of Egyptian, as also final -α for -αι (unaccented) and in καί, even before consonants. If instances of this phenomenon were found in NT MSS, it might perhaps be taken as a sign—*valeat quantum*!—of Egyptian influence. But it does not occur in ℵ, nor in $\mathfrak{p}^{13}$, in the word Αἴγυπτος (-ιος): to assert the negative for the other matter would involve an endless search, even if the silence of Ti could be implicitly taken as evidence. Κά occurs seven times in W, and in L at Mk 11^8.

Αιϊ and αϊ. A special case is the passage of αιϊ into αϊ, as in the names Ἀχαϊκός and Πτολεμαΐς, both of them in accord with normal papyrus spelling. Phrynichus considered Ἀλκαιϊκός Attic: see Rutherford *NP* 111–3.

Ει and ε (η). (*b*) Ει in its relation to ι has been already discussed. Some instances of ει becoming ε remain to be noted. In a LXX quotation, Rom 3^{12}, we find ἠχρεώθησαν in ℵAB*D*G,

---

[1] The following are their numbers and volume references. All are iv/A.D., except those marked* (iii/) and † (iii/iv).

(1) LXX and OT Apocrypha: iv. 656*, vii. 1007*, 1010, viii. 1075*, ix. 1166*, 1167, 1168.

(2) NT: ii. 208†, 209, vi. 847, vii. 1008, 1009, viii. 1078, 1079†, 1080, ix. 1171*, x. 1228†.

(3) Hermas, Apocryphal Gospels and Acts: iii. 404†, 406*, iv. 655*, v. 840, vi. 849, 850, x. 1224, 1225, 1226†.

against ἀχρεῖος. This is attested by a i/A.D. Cilician inscr.: see *Vocab.* on ἀχρεῖος and ἀχρειόω Meisterhans[3] 47 f. argues that the very frequent spelling -ηα for -εια etc. (inscrr.—also papyri, esp. the Alexandrian collection of the reign of Augustus) proves the ει to have been still an *e*-sound before vowels. See exx. in Schweizer *Perg.* 55 ff., Mayser 67 f.: cf. Brugmann-Thumb 56. In *ib.* 247 the history of πλέον (πλεονάζω, πλεονέκτης) is described: the case is not parallel with those which arose in the Κοινή period. Levelling has naturally brought in πλεῖον in most places (18/21 according to WH *App.*[2] 158), but not in derivatives. Mayser 69 shows how the ει form progressively ousted the ε in B.C. papyri: it is clear therefore that our uncials here represent their originals. In the case of Ἀρεοπαγίτης as compared with Ἄρειος Πάγος we cannot be quite certain whether we are dealing with a Hellenistic or an older sound-change.[1] When Attic δωρειά (so till B.C. 403) became δωρεά (which was inherited by Hellenistic) it was a genuine loss of ἰ̯ between vowels, and so when τέλειος became τέλεος (as in Heb 10[1] D[c] and 3 Macc A *bis*—Thackeray 82); but when the late noun λογεία becomes λογέα in Ptolemaic papyri (Mayser 67), it means that ει retains an *e* sound before a vowel. The relations of ἔσω and εἰς belong to the earlier history of Greek. In the Κοινή, εἴσω did not survive, nor ἐς, but we have ἔσοπτρον.

Ει in infin. of Contracta. Hellenistic shows no trace of the double value of ει, the ancient diphthong (written ΕΙ in early alphabets) and the lengthened close *e* (written Ε): they had been completely fused before the Κοινή was born. One consequence remains, the infin. in -οῦν from verbs in -όω, the regular contraction of ο+ε̄: similarly -ᾶν from -άω (not -ᾷν). The incorrect -οῖν—found in our uncials (see § 84), but certainly not in the autographs—was not derived from a fresh fusion of ο+-ειν, since for that a re-forming of the uncontracted -όειν would be needed: it was only that in all other -ω verbs the pres. inf. differed from 3 sg. pres. indic. by adding -ν.

Οι and υ. (*c*) Οι had the same relation to υ that αι had to ε and ει to ι: as in those cases, the approximation began with the long simple vowel (η, ῑ, ῡ), and then the levelling of quantity brought in the short vowel. Apart from its early completion in Boeotian, this change appeared first in Egypt, before other Κοινή-speaking districts, as was the case with the change in αι. There are sporadic exx. in badly written papyri of ii/B.C.; and the fusion becomes evident after i/A.D. Meanwhile in Attica exx. are not found till A.D. 238–44; in Pergamum the common people of ii/A.D. seem to have lost the distinction which—as elsewhere—cultured men kept up generations longer; while in Magnesia no instances are forthcoming. Schweizer *Perg.* 80 and Nachmanson *Magn.* 44 f. give a number of exx. from Asia Minor generally, and by the time our uncials were written οι and υ must have been everywhere identical except in rather artificial speech. Among the Oxyrhynchus literary documents examined above (§ 36 (*a*))

---

[1] Tacitus (*Ann.* ii. 55, *Areo indicio*) transliterates with *e* in the primary, but this proves nothing for the Greek form before him.

there are no exx. at all except in 𝔭[13] (P Oxy 657), where we find ἐν]νυῶν and ἑτοιμ[πα]νίσθησαν (Heb 4^{12}, 11^{35}). It is not uncommon in the LXX uncials, especially in words where the papyri soonest and most freely show the itacism: ἀνοίγω is so marked an example that Radermacher proposed to recognise the analogy of ἀνύτω—see *Vocabulary*, *s.v.* So λοιμαίνομαι six times in B: Thackeray (94) thinks λοιμός responsible. See his LXX evidence. The verb ἀνοίγω will supply a fair sample of the prevalence of this itacism in NT uncials:—Mt 20^{33} ℵ, Mk 7^{34} D, Lk 12^{36} D, 24^{32} ℵBDΔ, Jn 9^{17} DE, ^{26} ℵDM, $^{30, 32}$ D, 11^{37} B*D, Ac 7^{56} B*, 9^8 ℵ*, 12^{10} ℵB*D, Rev 3^7 *bis* ℵ, 6^{12} ℵ*. In W the only instances of this itacism are forms of ἀνοίγω in Mt 7^7, Mk $7^{34, 35}$, Lk 11^9 (cf. ^{10} ἀνηχθ.); and σύ for σοί in Mk 1^{24}, Jn 2^4, σοί for σύ Jn 13^7. When we note that W simply swarms with the αι and ει itacisms, and that ἀνοίγω is a very common word and more affected by this itacism than any other word in LXX, inscrr. and papyri, we have evidence enough that the οι–υ confusion was much less conspicuous than either of the others, and still less likely to have figured in the autographs. One remarkable *v.l.* should be mentioned as involving the itacism, viz. Ἑτοιμᾶς for Ἐλύμας, Ac 13^8 D**d* (Lucifer and Ambrosiaster): see J. Rendel Harris, *Exp.* VI. V. 189–95 (1902). The loss of ι from οι before vowels (not the ο vowels) is very

Οι and ο (ω). conspicuous in early papyri: see Mayser's tables, 108 f. It is also frequent in Pergamum, but does not appear in Magnesia. It was very common in Attic. Its origin belongs to the time when οι was still a diphthong: it is significant that Thackeray can note only one LXX instance, ποῆσε Jer 39^{35} ℵ. Hellenistic sometimes uses οι forms where Attic had dropped the ι: thus ποία (*grass*) occurs in LXX 2/3 (Thackeray 93),[1] as in the Doric inscr. from the Asclepieum, *Syll.* 803^{121} (iii/B.C.)—P Lille 5^3 (B.C. 260) has πωολογ[ίαν. This substitution of ω for an older οι is seen also in δῴη (LXX and NT), in -ῴην from -έω verbs ("as early as Epicurus," says Radermacher 73), and in πατρολῴας and μητρολῴας; *per contra* δοῖς, δοῖ, γνοῖ and διδοῖ for the subj. in -ῷ(ς)—cf. ἔγνοιν = -ων Lk 16^4 D(*al.*—see Crönert *Mem.* 217), Ἀρισταρχοι dat. P Lille 17^{20} (iii/B.C.) and a few other exx. in Mayser 137. In all these cases ῳ would be written, but ῳ and ω were identical. It would be possible to explain πῴα, δῴη and πατρολῴας on the same lines as cases of ει > η before vowels ((*b*) above), assuming that before vowels οι was arrested in its passage towards *ü*, in the *ö* stage, where ω might be a graphic equivalent. The opposite change, δοῖ etc., is explicable always without phonetic considerations.

Οϊ and οι. Mayser 110 shows that οϊ tended towards οι, as αϊ to αι (above (*a*)): in NT we have however ἀγαθοποιΐα (A -εία) and εὐποιΐα (AC -εία).

Diphthongs and the diaeresis. Before leaving αι, ει, οι we should note that there are words in which the use of the diaeresis, or the substitution of ει for ι in the second part of the diphthong, shows that the two elements were still pronounced with their

[1] And quite conceivably in Jas 4^{14}.

own original value. Ἀχαΐα is transliterated *Achaia* in Latin, and Ἀχαιΐη in Herodotus shows that we have a tetrasyllabic word. The Latin praenomen *Gaius*, which was never spelt with *ae*, is found in vulgar Greek inscrr. with υ for *i*, at a date when υ was a pure *i* sound. While our uncials are by no means systematic in the use of diaeresis, their evidence is often important. Blass, for example (*Gr.* 17), notes that Ναιμάν and Ἰεσσαί have no diaeresis in MSS, and Νεμάν is therefore not surprising: Ναΐν and Κάϊν always in אB: Ἠσαΐας 10/19 in א, but αι in B except for four places; Βηθσαϊδά(ν) *ter* in א, but also αι *ter*, while B usually has αι.

Long ι diphthongs. (*d*) The *long* diphthongs, which we write ᾳ, ῃ, ῳ, have been briefly alluded to in § 27. The "silent ι" (ι ἀνεκφώνητον) is not regularly "subscript" till xii/A.D., though Blass (*Pronunciation* 50) notes a vii/A.D. papyrus where it is written a little higher or lower than the vowel to which it is attached. In the middle Hellenistic period it has become a mere matter of orthography; and it is only because our spelling normally conforms to the Attic that we trouble about it at all. It is omitted in the uncials till vii/A.D., and ranks accordingly with accents and punctuation as a device of Byzantine and mediaeval orthography, useful for distinguishing nom. and dat. sg. fem. etc. It preserves, like the accents, a feature of Attic pronunciation, which—unlike the accents—had been for centuries extinct.

(*a*) Classical usage decides for κᾆτα (=καὶ εἶτα), but κἀγώ etc., where the second element has no ι; ᾖρον impf., but ἦρα aor. etc., in verbs where ι appears in present stem because of the suffix -yω; ζῆν, τιμᾶν etc., where our rejection of δηλοῖν (see § 36 (*b*)) forbids our altering the classical spelling: πρᾶος, πρωΐ, ζῷον, ὑπερῷον, Ἡρῴδης, πρῷρα, Σαμοθρᾴκη, πατρῷος, ἀποθνῄσκω, σῴζω and σέσῳσμαι, but ἔσωσα, etc., Τρῳάς, ᾠόν, ἀθῷος, μιμνῄσκειν. See reff. in WS 41.

(*β*) Some forms which look like datives, but were in part primitive instrumentals, varied in their acceptance of the -ι: on their historical basis see Brugmann-Thumb 269. The Attic inscriptions are the only safe basis, for we cannot always dogmatise as to the datival or instrumental origin of the form. It seems best to write κρυφῆ, λάθρα, πάντη, εἰκῆ, but to allow the -ι in ἄλλῃ, πανταχῇ, ἰδίᾳ, δημοσίᾳ, etc.

Dropping of ι ("subscript")—its date. Mayser (132 f., 125) shows that the omission of ι in dative sing. is hardly found in iii/B.C.: in ii/B.C. ωι: ω in dat. is as five to one, though medial and initial it is only two to one. Against 250 exx. of correct ηι in iii/B.C. he finds only 2 of initial ι and 11 of final ι dropped. But while in ii/B.C. 414 datives and conjunctives in -ηι are noted, to 121 with -η, in a series of documents dated *c.* 100 B.C. (P Grenf) there are 27 of each. This prepares the way for the period in which ι is added or dropped indifferently, having ceased to affect the pronunciation. The disappearance of the ι from the long diphthong ᾱι presents the same chronology (Mayser 120 f.). The analysis of P Tebt i. (ii/i B.C.) is instructive :—

"The proportion of -ᾱι to -ᾱ final is in official documents [including petitions] (nos. 5–54) 25 : 14 ; in private letters and the land survey (nos. 55–103) 8 : 2 ; in contracts (nos. 104–111) 8 : 3 ; in private accounts (nos. 112–123) 0 : 11."

The next stage is the irrational addition of -ι, sporadically found even in iii/B.C., and visible in ii/i (once or twice even with -ᾰ), but not common.

Latin Evidence. These facts obviously show that before the second period of the Κοινή developed (*c.* A.D.—see § 30) these long ι-diphthongs had lost the glide. That this was not a peculiarity of Egyptian pronunciation may be seen, among other evidences, from Latin transliterations. Blass (*Pronunciation* 50) cites *Thraex* etc. from Cicero, later *Thracia; citharoedus, comoedia, tragoedia,* later *ode* and *melodia.* He also quotes Strabo († A.D. 24), who tells us that "many write datives without the ι, and reject the whole custom [of adding -ι] as having no reason grounded on nature" (xiv. p. 648).

Application in NT. It follows that in ambiguous passages of the NT we are as much at liberty to insert or drop ι *subscr.* as to alter accents or punctuation, since none of these can have been in the autographs. Early translations and patristic quotations, if unanimous, will attest a traditional interpretation which must not be ignored, but need not wholly bar our freedom.

Thus in Jn 5[2] Milligan and Moulton (*Comm. in loc.*) proposed to read κολυμβήθρᾳ (". . . by the sheep pool the (pool) that is called . . .").[1] In Heb 11[11] WH *mg* read αὐτῇ Σάρρᾳ, thus making Abraham the subject of ἔλαβεν. An instance of another kind is the convincing emendation ὃ ἂν (so D) ὠφελήθῃς for ὠφεληθῇς in Mk 7[11] : see Goodspeed in *ExpT* xx. 471 f.

In forms which are born in the Κοινή our orthography is necessarily guided only by analogy, there being no authority unless the word happens to occur in well-written papyri of iii/B.C., when the ι still represents a real sound. Whether Crönert's instances of δῴῃ (*Mem.* 215) are early enough for the purpose is doubtful : here however the classical τιμῴην encourages us. But πατρολῴας (μητρολ.) has no real reason behind it, nor πῳολογία in P Lille 5[3] (§ 36 (*c*)).

9. *Diphthongs with υ.*

Ευ, Αυ. § 37. Ευ and ᾰυ retain their full diphthongal character, and the υ necessarily resisted the tendency towards *ü*. Hence the spelling εου, found even in D_2 at 2 Ti 4[14] (χαλκεούς), as Debrunner notes, with ref. to Crönert *Mem.* 128 f. Later

[1] So Moffatt renders, "there is a bath beside the sheep-pool." The reading of W, τῇ ἐπιλεγομένῃ, points the same way ; and there is new evidence that it was so read in v/A.D. (?), from a Christian amulet P Oxy viii. 1151[7f.], which appeals to ὁ θ̅ς̅ τῆς προβατικῆς κολυμβήθρας.

we find even εβ ; and as an ultimate result there is the pronunciation *ev*, *av*, which gives us MGr *aftós* (αὐτός). So Hebrew לֵוִי becomes Λευεί, דָּוִד Δαυείδ : on the later use of β in Λεββαῖος, Δαβίδ, see § 45. Οὐ on the other hand became completely monophthongal. See Mayser 114 and reff.

Ευ has a peculiar tendency towards αυ in the derivatives of ἔρευνα. The αυ forms do not appear in Ptolemaic times (Mayser 113). The earliest known ex. is one supplied by Wackernagel [1]—ἐξεραυνησομένους in a psephism from Syros, one of the Cyclades, dated mid i/B.C. Then follow instances from the papyri, beginning with ἠραύνηται in P Oxy ii. $294^{9, 10}$ (A.D. 22) : see *Vocab. s.v.* ἐραυνάω. Only in CP Herm 102^{13} does ἐρευν[. . . appear in Roman age papyri.[2] Crönert *Mem.* 128 gives several instances from MSS of Philo and Josephus. Thumb *Hellen.* 176 f. cites two or three papyrus exx. of ε broadening to α, which he thinks might be due to native Egyptian (not Alexandrian) influence. But there are closer parallels from Greek dialects, in Delphian ἐλαυθέραν, and Theran Doric compounds of εὐ- as αὐ-.[3] In LXX Thackeray 79 cites κολοκαύει 1 Es 4^{31} B and πέταυρον Prov 9^{18} $B^{ab}ℵ^{c.a}$. (The converse ἐντεῦθα 1 Es 5^{66} A is clearly a mere confusion with ἐντεῦθεν.) These, so far as they go, might be taken as showing that there was some tendency towards such a pronunciation in Egypt. But in uncials of the NT we find it 7/8 in ℵ, 6/7 in B*, 4/7 in A, 2/4 in C, 1/1 in T, 1/2 in W, and 0/5 in D and D_2. It is rather difficult to reconcile such wide attestation with any very close association with Egypt, which is also discouraged by Wackernagel's Syros inscr. ; but it may be noteworthy that the δ-text authorities have no trace of it—unless the fact that in Jn 7^{52} W has a reading shared only with D lat^{vt} is to mark that passage as of δ character, and so neutralise the association of W with AB*T in ἐραυν. there. Schmiedel's observation (WS 51) that B prefers ευ in OT and αυ in NT would suit the evidence of papyri very neatly ; but it needs checking by Thackeray's figures (p. 79n), whence it appears that in OT B has 13 of each. Proportionally therefore the statement is true.

It is noteworthy however that it is only in the imperfect that there is authority worth counting for the ηυ in the conjugation of εὑρίσκω. The moods in the aorist would form a check upon a spelling in indic. that represented no practical difference of sound. That ηυ was still thoroughly diphthongal is well seen by a tendency, esp. in ℵ and A, to write ηϋ ; moreover ℵ can even divide η|ϋ between two lines—see § 27. The foreign word Μωυσῆς was trisyllabic, as the Latin transliteration helps to show.

Eυ and υ. Thackeray 97 gives four LXX passages where πρεσβύτης = *senex* is written for πρεσβευτής = *legatus*, and recalls Lightfoot's note on Phm [9], in which πρεσβύτης was rendered "ambassador." The evidence Lightfoot gives for believing in a confusion

---

[1] See Nachmanson in *Berl. Phil. Woch.*, 1911, 1184 : the ref. is *IG* XII. v. 653^{21}.

[2] Undated, but apparently Roman.

[3] Nachmanson, *Eranos* xi. (1912) 220 ff. ; Kretschmer, *DLZ* 1901, 1049.

consists of MS mistakes, dating necessarily centuries after our period. Both words can be freely quoted from vernacular sources in their distinct forms: on P Oxy vi. 933 (ii/A.D.), a letter to a πρεσβευτής, the edd. remark that an error for πρεσβύτῃ is unlikely. Thayer, however (Grimm, *s.v.* πρεσβύτης), cites πρεσβευτέροις from an inscr. from the great theatre at Ephesus, which may be set with Lightfoot's MS citations. Hort (WH, *App.*[2] 136) prefers to read πρεσβευτής in Phm[9], rather than take πρεσβύτης in that sense. Whether πρεσβύτης in its proper meaning is not tenable after all is quite open to debate: the unanimity of the great Cambridge triumvirate did not convince a bare majority of the Revisers, as appears from their unpublished first draft ("an aged man," with margin "an ambassador").

Ωυ. The long diphthongs, hysterogenous in Greek, (see Brugmann-Thumb 64), had a very limited place in the Κοινή. Ionic used ωυ, but it did not penetrate Hellenistic, except in the Egyptian names Θῶυθ and Μωύσης, where Thackeray 163 recognises an attempt to represent a Coptic pronunciation: in both words the ωυ passed later into ω. **Ᾱυ.** So also ᾱυ is distinguished from ᾰυ only by a rather doubtful phonetic principle (see below). **Ηυ.** Ηυ is found in the augment syllable of a few verbs, as αὐξάνω, εὑρίσκω. There are hardly any *vv.ll.* when ηυ comes from αυ—Ac 12[24] εὔξανε D*, ἤξανεν P—but from εὑρίσκω many exx. of εὗρον etc. show that the shortening here was merely levelling from the present stem.

Ᾱυ and ᾱ. The papyri show very largely the reduction of ᾱυ to ᾱ, scantily till i/B.C. (Mayser 114), but freely later, especially in less educated writing. It appears often in Attic inscr. after B.C. 74 (Meisterhans[3] 154) in the case of ἑαυτοῦ and αὐτοῦ. Radermacher 37 makes the length of the diphthong essential, in which case the common ἀτός must be analogical;[1] but Mayser's early citations (Γλακίου, and similarly Πολυδέκῃι: cf. ἐχαριστεῖ in a papyrus) do not encourage the limitation. In NT we have 'Αγούστου Lk 2[1] ℵC*Δ, but it is probably Latin which accounts for this: cf. Ital. *agosto*. (See *Vocab. s.v.*) A more certain instance is κλαθμός, six times in W (once also in L, and regularly in E, according to Wetstein: see Sanders *The Washington Manuscript* 21n). It is noteworthy that W never has ἑατοῦ or the like. There is very little of this phenomenon in LXX: see Thackeray 79, where one or two apparent instances are (perhaps needlessly) explained away. It was at first strictly limited in range. As in MGr αὐτός and (ἀ)τός exist side by side (Thumb *Handb.* 85), we may assume dialectic difference within the Κοινή. As noted in *Prol.* 47, ἀκαταπάστους 2 Pet 2[14] AB and ἀχμηρῷ 2 Pet 1[19] A (see Mayor, *Comm. in loc.*) are probably cases in point. They would be excluded if we allowed only ᾱυ to be thus affected.

Ου. Ου had become a simple ū sound in the classical period; as in the case of ει, there was no distinction between the inherited diphthong and the close ο lengthened by com-

---

[1] So also Thumb in Brugmann[4] 64.

pensation or contraction. As the quantity distinction weakened, ου could represent even ŭ, as it had done in Boeotian long before (*e.g.* τιούχα = Att. τῠ́χη). It is also used regularly to express consonantal *u̯* in Latin, as *Quartus* Κουάρτος, *Siluanus* Σιλουανός, or *vae* οὐαί.

Passing by analogy formations like δῶναι[1] Mt 26^{15} ℵ (often in papp., after γνῶναι), we note some relations between ου and ευ which descend partly from classical dialects. The Ionic contraction ευ from εο survives in the proper name Θευδᾶς (= Θεόδωρος or Θεόδοτος): see Mayser 114, 148, also 10, where he gives several other names in Θευ- against the usual Θεο-. Ionic forms in such cases would start with individuals hailing from Ionic country. An interesting question is raised by the transliteration of *Lucius* by Λεύκιος in P Tebt i. 33^{3} (B.C. 112) *al.*: contrast Λούκιος Ac 13^{1}, Rom 16^{21}. Nachmanson 61 gives several other exx. of Λεύκιος, and thinks a genuine Greek name (derived from λευκός) has affected the spelling. The fact that this common name appears with both these forms has naturally suggested the possibility of regarding Λουκᾶς as = *Lucius* rather than as *Lucanus*; but there does not seem to be any strong reason. A link between ου and ω is implied by the frequently asserted identity of Κλεόπας (for Κλεόπατρος) and Κλωπᾶς, since if the εο did contract it would normally make ου, as in Θουκυδίδης etc. The contraction is very abnormal, and can be made plausible only by the difficulty of otherwise explaining the name. Confusion of ου and ω in verb terminations is another matter: it may be questioned if we are ever to credit this to itacism. See above, under ω.

Ου and ω.

Ου and ο.

Ο and ου are not infrequently confused in early papyri: see Mayser 116 f., where the conclusion is drawn that in this period ο, ου and ω were pronounced close—cf. the same development with ε, ει, η. A case of a different kind is the fluctuation between Διόσκουροι (as Ac 28^{11}) and Διόσκοροι, with derivatives: Mayser 10 f. makes the latter normal in papyri for the divine name, the former for derived human names like Διοσκουρίδης. Here the difference depends simply on mixture of dialects, κόρος being Attic and κοῦρος Ionic (see *Vocab. s.v.*).

10. *ΥΙ.*

Υι.

This combination, not reckoned among the proper diphthongs because the elements could not truly combine, was sometimes written υει (as Mk 9^{1} ἐληλύθυειαν W), to show that the vowels were really distinct. Crönert *Mem.* 123 ff. shows with a mass of exx. that υι continued to be so written in the Κοινή, the Attic υ being rare. Radermacher's note (*Gr.* 32 n.[2]) that εἰδῦα εἰδύης had replaced the old εἰδυῖα εἰδυίας must accordingly be read in close connexion with the reference to "educated people" in the text to which it is appended.

---

[1] In ℵ the reading is δωνε [= δῶναι] which Scrivener marks as a scribe's error.—[Ed.]

How far the Attic εἰδυῖα survived in archaising speech need not be discussed here: there is no doubt about εἰδυῖα εἰδυίης in the vernacular and in NT. Similarly there is no sign of any form but υἱός, regularly declined: contrast Attic inscrr., where from vi/ to i/B.C. there are only 8 instances of υἱ. to 67 of ὑ. After this υἱ. becomes "much more frequent" than υ (Meisterhans^3 60). It should be added that Blass 10 and Radermacher argue that the flexion -υῖα -υίης in Hellenistic proves that the ι has no force, or even (Blass) was "not pronounced." But of course the change of η to ᾱ after ρ or ι in Attic was a phonetic process which ceased to work generations before Hellenistic arose, as such a word as Attic κόρη shows. We have to do with inherited forms, and the presence or absence of the ι has no concern with the appearance of the new flexion.

Prothesis.

Prothesis. § 38. Ἐχθές (Attic: see Rutherford *NP* 370–2) was the regular Hellenistic form, not the (Ionic) χθές: the two appear to be related as ἐκεῖνος (Attic and Κοινή) and κεῖνος (Ionic —*ib.* 4). The ἐ- is supposed to be a deictic pronominal element. On the other hand ἐθέλω, where the ἐ- has a different origin, is not Hellenistic: we have only θέλω, ἤθελον.

In certain districts of the Κοινή prothesis is very marked before σ and consonant, as ἰστήλη, εἰστρατιώτης, ἰστοργή. Thumb gives a table of them in *Hellen.* 145, where 25 instances are mentioned from Asia Minor, 13 of them being from Phrygia. He infers with reason that we should seek the centre of the infection in Phrygian influence, it being natural to suspect some foreign admixture where the language outside Asia shows no real sign. Where a similarly limited prothesis before "impure σ" occurs in other regions, it may, as Deissmann suggests, be traced on the same principle to vulgar Latin: cf. G. Meyer *Gr.*^{3} 166.

Contraction.

Contraction. Two ι-sounds. The most important and almost the only new rule of contraction observed in the Κοινή is that by which two ι-sounds were made into one. Thus πιεῖν, ταμιεῖον, ὑγίεια were in the NT period π(ε)ῖν, ταμ(ε)ῖον, ὑγ(ε)ῖα, and this spelling is reflected in our best uncials normally: in the later MSS there is reversion to the classical type. An independent anticipation of this contraction is found in Ionic πόλῑ from -ιι. Ἀφεῖς in Rev 2^{20} is probably for ἀφίεις (see § 86): cf. ἀνασῖ Lk 23^5 ℵ.[1] Ἐπιεικείᾳ loses ι in Ac 24^4 B*, but elsewhere it and the adj. retain it. Ταμεῖον is found only in L 33 at Mt 24^{26}. But πιεῖν (καταπ.) appears in Mt 20^{22} (exc. W), Mk 10^{38} (exc. D), Ac $23^{12, 21}$ (exc. B*), Rom 14^{21} (exc. D*), 1 Pet 5^8 (exc. ℵ*),

---

[1] *Prol.* 45, where the parallel διασεῖν (P Leid G^{19}—i/B.C.) must be cancelled, as Wilcken reads διασίειν there. It is too early for that contraction. Ἀνασεῖς occurs in Wessely *Zauberpap.* p. 116.

Rev 16[6] (exc. AC), as well as in Mt 27[34] ABN, Jn 4[7, 10] A, 1 Co 9[4] A, 10[7] AC. (WH rather unaccountably edit πεῖν in Ac 23[12, 21], following B* alone, but obey D* rather than ℵB when they go with the multitude in Rom 14[21]. Since they have no objection to πιεῖν in 5/14 places, it is hard to deduce any principle.) The fluctuations of the uncials are reflected in vernacular documents. Mayser (92) cites one papyrus of B.C. 111 for contraction (Σουχίωι, P Tebt i. 114[10]—not a striking instance), and one pre-Christian inscr., *OGIS* 194[22] (B.C. 37), while ιει is common to the end of the Ptolemaic age. Attic began to contract as early as B.C. 100 (Meisterhans[3] 49 f.). In Asia Minor it becomes abundant in the Roman period, but the date of the change is hard to fix: see instances in Schweizer *Perg.* 101, Nachmanson *Magn.* 69 f. In Egypt we note [ὑ]γῇ = ὑγιῇ BGU iii. 912[13] (A.D. 33), ἀποκλεῖν = -είειν P Oxy ii. 265[14] (A.D. 81/95); but ταμιεῖον once in A.D. 199, ἁλιεῖς twice in iii/A.D. Thackeray (63) gives ταμεῖον CPR 1[13, 30] (A.D. 83/4) as the earliest instance; and we put beside it ταμιε[ῖον in BGU iv. 1194[15] (B.C. 27)—the contraction falls anyhow somewhere between these limits. Ὑγεῖα begins in the papyri early in ii/A.D., and so does πεῖν (πιεῖν appearing twice in i/A.D.). Thackeray's analysis shows that in LXX the Bℵ text does not represent the spelling of the age when the LXX was written. It cannot be proved to agree even with NT autographs, as we cannot be sure of it till the end of i/A.D. The change would naturally affect some words sooner than others. Ταμιεῖον was not so obviously connected with ταμίας as πιεῖν was with πιών; and the softening of the γ in ὑγίεια would hasten the contraction of a word decidedly awkward in pronunciation. The MSS record for such words in NT probably reflects a state of inconsistency in the autographs. It is perhaps not without significance that πιεῖν is best attested in books written early, and πεῖν most certain in Jn, traditionally published at the end of i/A.D. If we follow the lead of the uncials, and edit ταμεῖον everywhere, πιεῖν in Mt, Mk, Ac, 1 Pet, πεῖν in Jn and Rev, we shall probably come as near the original as we can hope to do. Paul we must leave to be inconsistent, with πιεῖν in Rom but πεῖν in 1 Co: if the original copies had these, it only meant that Tertius and the amanuensis who wrote 1 Co differed in their practice at a period when πεῖν was just coming in. We must add a caveat against Radermacher's account (*Gr.* 36) of the genesis of this contraction. He would get it from the spirantising of the ι, just as σιωπᾶν became σωπᾶν sometimes, or σαρδιόνυξ in Rev 21[20] A became σαρδόνυξ. It is simply a contraction of identical vowels coming together, just as in Ionic πόλιι produced πόλῑ generations earlier.[1]

Reversion to uncontracted forms. The contractions which operated in classical Greek, and especially in Attic, were no longer demanded by phonetic necessity in the Κοινή, and only remained in being because they were inherited. It was therefore possible for levelling of flexion to bring back uncontracted forms like ἔρρεεν P Oxy vi. 850[24] (Acts of John—iv/A.D.), ἐδέετο Lk 8[38] (all except

[1] Cf. Nachmanson in *Berl. Phil. Woch.* 1911, 1183.

ℵaBLX33). Phrynichus and Thomas regarded these as Ionic, but it is more likely to be a new operation of analogy—ἔλυον : ἔλυε : : ἔρρεον : ἔρρεε etc.[1] The forms of χέω present problems which will be discussed in their place (§ 95) : here it is enough to say that while κατέχεεν Mk 14^{3} is an aorist, ἐκχέετε Rev 16^{1} and συνέχεον Ac 21^{27} need not be detached from the present stem unless syntactical considerations appear weighty. For further parallels cf. *Prol.* 54 f., and 234. Uncontracted noun forms such as χρυσέων and ὀστέων are more likely to be Ionic inasmuch as they are specially characteristic of the Eastern Κοινή : see below under noun-flexion, § 53 B (*b*). Occasional contraction of ὄγδοον to ὄγδουν in papyri is explicable by analogy, if uncontracted forms of other adjectives survived by the side of contracted. Words like νέος, where the uncontracted form was traditional, showed no tendency to contract, but see below on the forms of νεοσσός. An occasional form like νόῳ from νοῦς (BGU ii. 385^{5}–ii/iii A.D.) serves as a set-off for ὄγδουν. On open forms in 3rd decl. (ὀρέων, χειλέων) see § 58 (1) (*c*), and on πήχεων, § 59 (1) : ἄν for ἐάν is discussed in *Prol.* 43 n.

Ω and εο. The identification of Κλωπᾶς and Κλεόπας—on which see also § 44—raises some questions belonging properly to commentaries. Of course Κλωπᾶς could not be due to contraction : εο in Hellenistic as in earlier Greek would become ου, unless Ionic influence made it ευ—as in Θευδᾶς for Θεόδωρος or the like, Τεύφιλος or Θεύφιλος (papp.) for Θεόφιλος. But some analogy beyond our reach might account for the variant form. Κλεόπας is normally abbreviated for Κλεόπατρος. I should add that, while ready to leave the decision to the Semitists, I myself find the identification of Κλωπᾶς, Κλεόπας and Ἁλφαῖος an extremely hard saying.

New forms with hiatus. The Hellenistic indifference to the confluence of vowels, due to the slower pronunciation which has been already noted, is well seen in the levelling which assimilates τετρα-άρχης to other compounds of τέτρα-, and made even ἀρχι-ιερεύς possible (Mt 26^{14} B, P Petr iii. 53 (*p*)^{2}—iii/B.C.). See Ti on Ac 13^{1}. So with late cpds. like ἀγαθοεργεῖν (1 Tim 6^{18}—not Ac 14^{17}), against the inherited κακοῦργος and ἱερουργεῖν, and numeral forms like δεκαοκτώ, τεσσαρακονταετής. This feature of the Κοινή makes it very plain that classical scholars of the last generation were yielding to their besetting sin when they ruled out (*e.g.*) etymologies of ἐπιούσιος that broke the laws of "correctness" by allowing hiatus. We shall see in this example (see § 120), and many others, that Hellenistic must be held as subject to its own laws alone. Analogy, and the retention of local dialectic forms, may account for a few new contracted forms, as -ὄγδουν (see § 72), ἐλᾶν=ἐλαίαν P Ryl ii. 130^{11}, 231^{4} (A.D. 31 and 40), φρῆτος from φρέαρ *Letr.* 12 (ii/A.D.). On the other side is νεομηνίας Col 2^{16} BFG, Ionic for νουμην.: it is not quotable from papyri or inscrr. till ii/A.D.,[2] and is doubtless a *f.l.* Ἱερωσύνη for Attic ἱερεωσ. is Ionic, but need not

---

[1] Cf. the compromise form ἀποχείεται, P Ryl ii. 154^{14} (A.D. 66).

[2] Thackeray 98.

be contraction. Ἐάν for ἄν after ὅς etc. was selected in *Prol.* 42 f. as a test of the uncials' accuracy, and it was shown that their usage agrees with that of the papyri during i/ and ii/A.D., while the use of either ἄν or ἐάν in this construction was very rare in the century of our oldest uncials. My statistics may be compared with Thackeray's (*Gr.* 67 f.), which take in later material but do not alter the result.[1] As the cause of this variation cannot be phonetic, we may postpone further notice of it till the Syntax.

Syncope.

Syncope. The total loss of a vowel, reducing thus the number of syllables in a word, is a phenomenon obviously resembling the prehistoric effects of Gradation; and as we know a stress accent was developing in the Κοινή—especially, we may assume, in districts where the native dialect had stress, and people had difficulty in pronouncing without it—we may confidently trace it to an identic cause. Νοσσός (-ία, -ίον) is an established Hellenistic form exclusively found in NT: it arose from the slurring of ε into a *y* sound, just as βορέας much earlier produced (βορyᾶς) βορρᾶς. The phonetic principle is still active, as such MGr forms as παιδία (pron. *pedhyá*) show. Attic ἑορτή kept its ground, despite Ion. ὁρτή; but in ἐλεεινός we find the ε slurred once before ει, in Rev 3^{17} AC (contrast 1 Co 15^{19}, where only FG reads thus). Even here ἐλεϊνός, with ι for ει, may just as well be read: A actually has a diaeresis over the ι, if I read it rightly. The reading ἀλλοτριεπίσκοπος 1 Pet 4^{15} ℵB cu[1] is due to the same treatment of ο, which became a *w* and dropped out, just as in the other words ε vanished through the stage *y*. Note that in all these products of *allegro* pronunciation the sound affected lies well behind the accent. Ἔσθων Mk 1^{6} for ἐσθίων is not a case in point, for ἔσθω is an alternative conjugation.

A different application is that of "Kretschmer's Law," by which *e.g.* Βερενίκη became Βερνίκη. See §§ 30 and 33. Different again is καμμύειν, regular in LXX and NT (Thackeray 99), and warranted good Κοινή by the ban of Phrynichus (?) (cf. Rutherford *NP* 426). Forms involving κάτ for κατά, ἄν for ἀνά, πάρ for παρά, were abundant in poetry from the first, and easily if occasionally crept into popular language. It was forgotten that καμμύειν was a compound.

There are not a few instances in our MSS of a peculiar syncopation affecting prepositions, found largely in inscrr. Thus in D, Rendel Harris notes[2] κα(τα)φαγόντι Lk 15^{30}, πε(ρὶ) τοῦ Ἰ. Mk 5^{27}, ἀ(να)στάς Mk 10^{1}, ἀ(να)πτύξας Lk 4^{17}, κα(τα)λῦσαι Ac 5^{39}, and perhaps ἐ(πι)πλήσ(σ)οντι Lk 23^{43}: he observes that ℵ in Hermas is not free from such forms.

---

[1] It may be added that Jannaris *Gr.* 421 gives several instances of ὃς ἐάν etc. from MSS of classical authors. As he puts it, we should suppose Xenophon, Demosthenes etc. responsible for the form—*quod erat absurdum*!

[2] *A Study of Codex Bezae* (Cambridge, 1891), p. 147.

Words which always stand in the pretone are liable to changes of this kind when the accent has become stress; and we see the process complete in MGr μέ for μετά.

Pronunciation of the Vowels.

Pronunciation and Textual Criticism.

§ 39. Our survey of the vowel system in detail may now be focused into a general view, and its results brought into line with our whole purpose. Pronunciation might seem to have but little interest for us, to whom the written page of the NT must be everything. But the sounds as well as the signs have to be studied if we would have a clear conception of the value of our oldest MS tradition. Textual Criticism can restore to a large extent the text of the period after A.D. 150, but in matters of spelling it gives us no evidence that is not two centuries later than that epoch. How far can we regard the spelling of אB and their successors as faithfully representing that of the first century? Faithfulness in so trifling a department of a scribe's duty, especially if it is maintained where contemporary usage had diverged from that of the first century, creates a strong presumption that the transcript will faithfully represent its exemplar in more important matters. It becomes therefore a really serious duty to go behind our MSS and evaluate as far as we can the phonetic conditions of the language in which Paul dictated his letters and Mark and Luke wrote their chronicles. Only by such inquiry can we gauge the accuracy of the copies on which we depend.

Quantity-levelling:—its date.

We first ask as to the *quantity* of vowels. The classical language, where accent was purely "musical," and there was no stress to lengthen or reduce a vowel, is governed by strict rules of quantity which are necessarily familiar to all students of poetry. These rules were maintained in literary tradition, so that a cosmopolitan collection of epigrams like the Greek Anthology can show us poems from the Byzantine age in which mistakes of quantity are almost as rare as in the Greek verses of a Jebb or a Headlam. But when we take up copies of metrical epitaphs rudely inscribed on Anatolian tombs in the period from which our great Biblical MSS come, we find a great contrast. Short syllables are scanned long, and long as short, in odd disagreement with Homeric phrases and conventional terms of older poetry. When did the change in quantity fulfil itself, as a consequence of the change in accent?

Hatzidakis, in his monograph on the subject referred to in *Prol.* 34 n.[2], shows that quantity-levelling began outside Greece and established itself very gradually. The iambic quoted above (§ 36) from Pompeii shows that in i/A.D. both *ει* and *αι* could be written for short *ι* and *ε*. Philostratus (ii/iii A.D.) tells us[1] that in his time the Cappadocians "shortened the long and lengthened the short vowels." That an Athenian graduate like Philostratus noticed the difference tells us at once that the vowels were still long and short in educated Attic and that they had lost their quantity in the Eastern Κοινή. Meanwhile in Egypt, as Mayser shows (p. 138 ff.), from ii/B.C. down the long vowels and the diphthongs were free to change with short: it is clear however that there was in Egypt no relation between accented syllables and length, or *vice versa*—see Mayser's tables pp. 140 f. Crossing to Roman Asia, we have in Schweizer *Perg.* 94 ff. inscriptional evidence to show that *η* could stand for *ε* and *ι*, that the name Νικομήδεια could scan ⏑⏑–́⏑⏑, and that *ο* and *ω* were free to interchange: *ου* could represent Latin *ŭ*, and *αι* and *οι* were sometimes *ε* and *ῠ*. The evidence is not dated as narrowly as we should like. Nachmanson (*Magn.* 63) makes the levelling begin in Asia Minor and Egypt in ii/B.C.: his instances from Magnesia are not very numerous, but are more precise in date. In his elaborate review of Radermacher,[2] the Swedish scholar refutes R.'s inference from *αα* in Μάαρκος, Ἰσαάκ etc., that there was a sense of long vowels needing separate notation such as the additional sign supplied for *e* and *o*. Attic instances of levelling are given by Meisterhans[3], but can only be dated as "Kaiserzeit." It was natural that a phenomenon depending ultimately on the speaking of Greek by various peoples with native languages of their own, should develop earliest in foreign countries.

Changing quality in vowel system. From quantity we pass on to quality. It has become very clear already that the whole vowel system has taken a different aspect from that which it wears in the golden age of Athens. Any modern reconstruction by which we may attempt to pronounce Attic as the Athenians did will be almost as far from representing Hellenistic as the avowedly haphazard pronunciation we have hitherto used in England. The language is well on the way towards the pronunciation

---

[1] *Vit. Soph.* ii. 13

[2] *Berl. Phil. Woch.* 1911, Sept. 23, p. 1192.

of MGr, where *αι* and *ε* are *e*, *ο* and *ω* are *o*, and *ου u*, *α* is still *a*, and *η*, *ι*, *ει*, *οι*, *υ* and *ῃ* have all sunk into *i*. But we have already seen that it would be a serious mistake to suppose that even in the age of our uncials the process was complete. Not even the speech of the common people had in any country "etacised" *οι* and *υ*, or even *η*, in the century of the NT autographs, or for generations after. We must always be ready to take our proofs from the language of the common people, rather than from literary documents which are likely to be touched with artificiality; though of course we shall expect to find a considerable difference between NT writers due to geographical separation and to varying degrees of Greek culture. As knowledge of the varieties of dialect within the *Κοινή* grows, we may reasonably expect to discover traces in our best MSS of the minute distinctions by which higher criticism might argue towards a book's original home, or lower criticism claim some particular district for the place where a MS was written.

Causes of the change.

A word should be added as to the forces that produced a change of pronunciation at least as extensive as that which marks modern English against that of Chaucer's time. When it is recalled that the Boeotian dialect of v/B.C. was already pronouncing *αι* as *e*, *ει* as *i*, *οι* as *ü*, and *η* as a close *e*, it is natural to conjecture a historical connexion with the same pronunciation in a later time all over the new Greek-speaking world. To this it is replied that Boeotian never seems to have affected even its next-door neighbour Attic until—on the assumption that this development really was due to Boeotian—the infection had already passed through every other region where Greek was spoken. It is abundantly clear that Attic accounts for (say) seventy per cent. of the *Κοινή* in phonology, accidence and syntax, Ionic for perhaps twenty per cent., and the other dialects possibly for as much as ten. It becomes therefore very improbable *a priori* that Boeotian should affect Hellenistic pronunciation so profoundly without doing much more, and equally improbable that this very widespread charity should have failed to begin at home. To substitute some other single cause is beyond our power. In the change of the accent system we shall probably find a more powerful solvent of the vowels than any other influence at work. And this in its turn may well have been largely due to the fact that Hellenistic was everywhere (except in Greece itself) the language of bilingual people. Of course the influences of native dialects—discussed at length by Thumb in chap. iv. of *Hellenismus*—would affect Greek in very different ways. But they would mostly agree in possessing stress rather than pitch accent; and it would be natural for them to impart a stress to the Greek accent. This however is mere conjecture. We must mostly be content to recognise the fact of development without attempting to explain it, the conditions being largely outside our range of knowledge.

Itacism and Syntax. A summary of pronunciation was attempted above, but we must return to one problem more in detail. How does itacism affect questions of syntax? If *η*(*ι*) and *ει* were identical, and *ο* and *ω*, was there any real difference between the future indicative and the first aorist subjunctive, the present indicative and subjunctive of verbs like *λύω*? The answer has so much effect on our views of verb syntax that we must examine the history of the *e* vowels more closely. We may start with the Attic *ηι*, which in iii/ii B.C. was predominantly changed to *ει* (Meisterhans[3] 38 f.), but recovered itself in i/B.C., and afterwards dropped its *ι* like *ᾳ* and *ῳ*. One curious survival of this orthography is very general in Hellenistic (see Mayser 127 and the inscrr. cited in Dittenberger's index, *Syll.*[2] iii. 226 f.), viz. the perf. act. and mid. (not the other augmented tenses) of *αἱρέω* and cpds.[1] In *λῃστής* and *ἀποθνῄσκω* the older *η* survived, in *λειτουργός* the later *ει* or *ι* (perhaps through association with *λιτή* 'prayer'): so also *κλείς* and *κλείω*. The dative *τιμεῖ* was replaced by *τιμῇ* after a short period of prominence by levelling action: *χώρα* nom. and *χώρᾳ* dat. were only orthographically different in i/A.D., and *τιμή*, *τιμῇ* followed suit, except for the accent. This takes us to the relations of *ει* and *η*, already described in detail. H and *ει* have contacts especially in prevocalic position. Such a table as Dittenberger's in *Syll.*[2] iii. 226 will show how abundant was *η* for *ει* before vowels. The same may be said of the papyri, especially during the Augustan period. H had thus two values, one that of an open *ē*, as in earlier times, and the other close *ẹ̄*: the former drew *ϵ* to it and the latter *ει*. Ultimately *ϵ* remained an *e* sound, as it does to-day; and the old *η* which had this value was ultimately spelt *ϵ* (as *στήκω*, MGr *στέκω*). The other *η* passed at last into *i*: thus *Quirīnius* is transliterated Κυρ(ε)ῖνος in BW, but Κυρήνιος in the rest. Why *στήκω* kept an *e* sound while *πλῆθος* took an *i* we are hardly able to say.

---

[1] The NT has only one occurrence, 2 Co 9[7], but there FG 33 show *-ειρ*: in Ac 5[36] and 27[20] there is no variant upon *ἀνῃρέθη* and *περιῃρεῖτο*.

To return to the practical problem of indicative and subjunctive. It is clear that in the Attic of iii/ii B.C. the two spellings of the 2nd sing. pres. indic. mid., λύει and λύῃ, were wholly equivalent, and the indic. λύεις -ει, λύσεις -ει, identical with subj. λύῃς -ῃ, λύσῃς -ῃ. Restricting ourselves to Attic, we ask whether this identity continued. Differentiation could arise, as in the noun, by levelling: λύεις λύητε invited assimilation as strongly as τιμή -ήν -ῆς -εῖ. But the very levelling which brought back a new ῃ tended to keep it nearer to η than the old ηι that had passed into ει. Hence its readiness to lose ι and attach itself rather to η than to ει. Meanwhile η itself was becoming close, and in ii/A.D. had largely lost its difference from ει even in Attica.[1] Outside Attica, according to Brugmann-Thumb, final -ῃ never changed to -ει. In that case there was an additional force tending to differentiate indic. and subj. for a time. There was moreover a reason for the survival of the normal -ῃ (=-ε(σ)αι) in 2 sg. pres. ind. mid.: the three exceptions βούλει (still in NT), οἴει, ὄψει, may perhaps be treated as Attic forms surviving through the influence of idiomatic turns of speech in which they occurred.[2] We have thus a reason for the survival of a separate flexion for indic. and subj. until the time when η and its equivalent ῃ had sunk into *i*. By that time ο, ω and ου were very near each other,[3] and ο and ω in many parts were identical. Thus the 2nd pl. was the only person unaccounted for, and in an unaccented syllable *e* and *i* did not differ greatly. All this will account well for a partial fusion of indicative and subjunctive, such as we shall have to note in the Syntax: syntactical forces may have cooperated with phonetic in producing this. But it is extremely hazardous to assume that these conditions applied in i/A.D., except in districts which had little or nothing to do with the NT, and in an educational stratum lower than any represented there.

Aspiration.

Breathings in MSS. § 40. The early uncials have breathings marked as little as they have punctuation or accents; but literary documents have begun to insert them at a date not much later than that of ℵ and B. They appear in W, where Sanders (p. 18) says the rough breathing may be rarely seen on monosyllables, and on words liable to be confused: he counts "29 instances in Mt; none in Mk 1-5[30]; 3 in the rest of Mk; 44 in Lk; and 4 in Jn 5[12] to end. There are no mistakes in its use. In the first quire of Jn there are no breathings." This MS is accordingly the earliest to show them. We find breathings marked in some of the papyri edited in *Berliner Klassikertexte* vi. by Schmidt and Schubart (1910)—a v/A.D. codex of Ignatius, and an anthology of Basil's letters (same cent.): see *CR* xxvii. 176 f. (The sign ⊢ was used for *h* by grammarians perhaps as early as Aristotle; see Blass *Pron.* 92).

---

[1] See Brugmann-Thumb 62-4, Nachmanson *Beiträge* 37, Meisterhans[3] 19.
[2] But the history of this form is much disputed: see Brugmann-Thumb 405.
[3] Radermacher 37 dates this approximation in iii/A.D.

Interaspiration. A point of interest arises in these documents, where we find ἀόρατοι (p. 5) and ἀνθέστηκε (p. 26). The second of these does not represent classical pronunciation, since the *h* was absorbed in combination with the *τ*, while *ἀόρατος* certainly lost any aspiration centuries before this papyrus was written. But it may be assumed that while the aspirate lasted it was pronounced in medial position in such cases: cf. such Latin transliterations as *Euhemerus*, *Euhodius*. As *h* was not yet dead in i/A.D., we may safely infer that *εὑόδοῦν* and the like would represent pronunciation more accurately than our conventional spelling. Alexandrian grammarians wrote the "inter-aspiration" in the texts of the poets; but there is no doubt that the *h* was even weaker in this position than it was when initial. See Blass *Pron.* 96.

Misplacement of *h*. Initial *h* was weak, but still pronounced in our period, and (as in other dialects where it is weak) it is not infrequently misplaced. There is a series of wrongly aspirated words which obtained such a hold that a trace even survives in MGr, where an initial *h* has not been pronounced for many centuries. This is *ἐφέτο(ς)* "of this year," which takes us back to *ἐφ' ἔτος*, a very common combination in papyri and Κοινή inscriptions. So *καθ' ἔτος* etc. This form does not happen to occur in NT, for in Lk 2^{41} the newly discovered W alone reads *καθ'*. But "*ἐφ' ἑλπίδι*, accepted Rom 8^{20}, has some primary authority ($\aleph^{2}$. A^{1}. B^{1}. C^{1}. D^{4}. $D_{2}{}^{1}$. $G_{3}{}^{5}$) 8/9 times, besides *ἀφελπίζοντες* 1/1" (WH *App.*² 150). This last is read by DP in Lk 6^{35}. The occasional aspiration of *εἶδον* and its compounds, accepted by WH in Ph 2^{23} and Ac 2^{7}*mg*, is found in the best MSS; while *οὐχ ὀλίγος* appears 6/8 times in Ac ($\aleph^{4}$. A^{3}. B^{1}. D^{1}) as in LXX twice. *Καθ' ἰδίαν* occurs "9/16 times ($\aleph^{1}$. B^{8}. D^{3}. Δ^{1}"—add W^{1}). *Αὐθόπται* stands in Lk 1^{2} W, and *οὐχ ὄψεσθε* in Lk 17^{22} A. A series of such forms is noted from D by Rendel Harris in his monograph on the MS [1]—*ἡδύνατο*^{1}, *εἶδον*^{8}, *ἴδιος*^{3}, *ὀλίγος*^{1}, *ἐφίστασθε*^{1}, *ἐφαγαγεῖν*^{1}, *ἑμοῦ*^{1}, *ἑμέ*^{1}, *ἑλπίζω*^{1}, *ἑλπίς*^{4}.

Due to analogy. The causes of this phenomenon must be sought in the working of analogy. Thumb puts this concisely in Brugmann *Gr*⁴. 143, where he shows how in classical Greek *ἡμεῖς*, *ἧσται* and *ὀκτὼ ἑννέα* (in Heraclean Doric) followed respectively *ὑμεῖς*, *ἕζομαι* and *ἑπτά*, etc. "In the Κοινή this process went further, *e.g.* *ἔτος* after *ἡμέρα*, *ἵσος* after *ὅμοιος*, *ἐφιδεῖν* and *ἐφόπτης* after *ὁρῶ*: see Thumb *Spiritus Asper* 70 ff., Mayser 199 f." Common formulae like *καθ' ἡμέραν*, *ἐπ' ἴσῃ καὶ ὁμοίᾳ*, and the unifying effect of a paradigm like *ἐφορᾶν* : *ἐπιδεῖν* : *ἐπόψεσθαι*, help us to see how the analogy worked. *Καθ' ἰδίαν* may have followed *καθ' ἑαυτόν*. *Ἐφ' αὔριον* (as P Tebt i. 119^{17}, B.C. 105–1; P Ryl ii. 441^{4}, iii/A.D.) obviously follows *ἐφ' ἡμέραν*, and is itself an argument for a similar account of *ἐφ' ἔτος*. *Οὐχ ὀλίγος*

---

[1] Where (p. 138) he also notes a dropped aspirate, in *εὑρίσκω*^{4}, *κατεξῆς*^{3}, *οὗτος*^{1} and *ἑαυτῶν*^{1}. The explanations offered in this chapter (dated 1891) are antiquated by later developments of comparative philology. Some of the instances included are discounted by the special conditions affecting *οὐκ* and *οὐχ*: see below.

arose later than the rest, being rare in LXX, where other cases are frequent: see Thackeray 126, where an explanation is attempted, based on a (less probable) account of the common Hellenistic ἐφιορκεῖν (Mt 5[33] ℵ), ἐφίορκος (1 Tim 1[10] DP). Brugmann-Thumb 166 explains the latter as a mixture of ἐπιορκ. and ἐφορκ., which are *lento* and *allegro* forms respectively. Since it is only with οὐχ that these aspirated forms of ὀλίγος occur, we cannot safely draw any inference: see below, and cf. Crönert *Mem.* 152 n.[4], where one instance of μεθ' ὀλίγον is the only exception. It is less easy to suggest analogical cause for ἑλπίς, which (Prof. Souter tells me) is supported by proper names in Latin inscrr.—*Helpis*, *Helpidius*, *Helpidophorus*. Was ἑλεῖν in thought?

Not connected with long lost digamma. Since even Thackeray[1] still clings to the old idea that the lost *F* produced this *h*, it should be observed that a large proportion of forms already mentioned—add from papyri such types as μεθηνέχθη, καθ' ἐνιαυτόν, 'Εφ' 'Ασκληπιάδου, μήθ' ἄλλον, ἐφ' ὄνοις, ἐφαγαγεῖν—cannot be explained in this way. And there is this further objection, that the phenomena in question are late, whereas in Attic and Ionic *F* totally disappeared in prehistoric times. We should have to assume, for example, that *F*ελπίς generated ἑλπίς in some dialect which ultimately influenced the Κοινή, but left no trace of itself until the *h* outcropped in post-classical times. For this there is nowhere any evidence; and even if (as in the case of ἑλπίς) we have no complete explanation to offer, it is safer to assume some hidden analogy. Can we always account scientifically for our own cockney's sins of commission and omission in this matter? The analogy is the more instructive since contemporary Rome had "'Arry" similarly employed: cf. Catullus 84:

> *Chommoda* dicebat, si quando commoda uellet
> dicere, et insidias Arrius *hinsidias*.

It saves us a good deal of trouble to realise that when *h* is feeble it always tends to be misused in ways which cannot be wholly accounted for.

See on the whole subject Thumb's monograph on the *Spiritus Asper* in Greek (Trübner, 1889), also Crönert *Mem.* 148 ff.; Schweizer *Perg.* 116 ff.; Radermacher *Gr.* 38; Mayser 199 ff.

Miscellaneous irregularities. Miscellaneous problems involving the aspirate may be collected here (mostly from WH *App.*[2] 150 ff.).

'Επίσταται 1 Th 5[3] ℵBL 33 (Wisd 6[9] B) is an isolated slip, to be set beside ἀποκατιστάνει Mk 9[12] B* (where however the true read-

[1] And later still A. T. Robertson *Gram.* 209. It should be observed that he fails to represent the philologist's case against the digamma as a *vera caussa* for the Hellenistic aspiration. No one doubts that *h* sometimes represents *F*: it is found in three words beginning with *ves-*, as explained by Thumb in Brugmann *Gr.*[4] 52. But all this belongs to a period centuries earlier than hat in which καθ' ἔτος and the like began to appear, when *F* was absolutely dead except in a few corners where old dialects still struggled for life.

ing may be ἀποκαταστάνει ℵ*D—cf. MGr στάνω, a form thrice found in D). The converse is found in ἐφίστασθαι for ἐπίστασθε, Ac 10[28] D* WH and Schmiedel take both as "thoughtless confusion of the verbs ἐφίστ. and ἐπίστ." (WS 39).

Αὑτοῦ (etc.) is read by WH some twenty times: see the question discussed below, § 76.

Οὐχ appears in LXX and NT not infrequently where οὐκ is expected. Thus οὐχ ἠγάπησεν Rev 12[11] A, οὐχ Ἰουδαικῶς Gal 2[14] ℵ*ACP 33 (οὐχ Ἰούδα Sus [56] ABQ, according to WH p. 314), οὐχ ὀλίγος (see above), οὐχ ὄψεσθε Lk 17[22] A (see above), οὐχ ἰδού Ac 2[7] ℵDE 61; οὐχ ἐπόνεσαν, οὐχ εἰσακούσομαι, οὐχ ὠδῖνες, οὐχ ἰσχυρός in LXX (WS 39). Some of these cases may be specially explained: thus WH would make Ἰούδας the regular representative of יְהוּדָה. But there does not seem to be strong reason for our seeking to take them one by one. Moreover there are instances of οὐκ for οὐχ, as οὐκ ἕνεκεν 2 Co 7[12] ℵCDE 33, οὐκ ὑπάρχει Ac 3[6] ℵC, οὐκ εὗρον Lk 24[3] ℵC* ("etc.," says Schmiedel). We must apparently allow exegesis to decide between ἕστηκεν and the Hellenistic imperfect ἔστηκεν after οὐκ in Jn 8[44].

Metathesis of aspiration. An important class of variant forms due to metathesis of aspiration came into the Κοινή through Ionic influence, and are shown by MGr to have maintained their position: see *Prol.* 38. Χιτών κιθών, χύτρα κύθρα, ἐνταῦθα ἐνθαῦτα, βάτραχος βάθρακος, φάτνη πάθνη, are instances, and there are further complications due to mixture, such as χιθών and κιτών. See plentiful exx. from papyri for κιθών etc. and κύθρα in Crönert *Mem.* 82 n.[3], 83 n.[1]; also Mayser 16, 41 and 184, Thackeray 103. Traces in NT are not many: χειθῶνας Mt 10[10] D*, Lk 9[3] W, κιτῶνας Mk 14[63] B* ("ut alibi ℵ" Ti), πάτνης Lk 13[15] W. See Brugmann-Thumb 121 f. Rendel Harris (*Codex Bezae* 140) points out that in Lk 3[11] D has χιτῶνας, with a smooth breathing: this is by way of correcting his exemplar, which had χιθ. Dr. Harris gives other instances of this metathesis of aspiration from D (or its Latin), viz. Ac 16[16] *phytonem* (*i.e.* *φύτωνα), 16[11] *Samotrachiam* (*Σαμοτράχην), Mk 7[9] ἀτεθεῖτε.

Words beginning with a single ρ, with another ρ at the head of the second syllable, were according to the ancient grammarians (see WS 40) without the usual ʽ. Thus ῥεραντισμένοι etc. This is in accord with the rule which makes reduplication involve loss of aspirate (τίθημι etc.), if we may assume that the voiceless initial ῥ kept its quality when pushed into a second syllable. But it is not really certain that initial ρ was voiceless except when it came from *sr-*: see Brugmann-Thumb 145.

The breathing has been variously determined for ὁμείρεσθαι (see § 95), εἱλικρινής and -ία (§ 105), ἀλοᾶν (cf. ἀπαλοᾶν and καταλ.) and ἅλυσις.

In Semitic loan-words WH use ʽ for ה and ח, ʼ for א and ע. There is no reason for writing ὕσσωπος (אֵזוֹב) except that initial υ regularly has ʽ: apparently even English has only aspirated the word since the Genevan Version. There is difference between editors as to the breathing in the name *Jerusalem.* WH (*Intr.*[2] 313) refuse the ʽ to Ἱεροσόλυμα as coming from a "false association with ἱερός." But however "false," it may well be quite real as popular etymology. In Ἰερουσαλήμ Blass is right in giving Ἰ., since the association would not affect the indeclinable.

Single and Double Consonants.

Single and Double Consonants. § 41. Ambiguous cases under this heading are practically restricted to the continuous sounds, the Liquids and Nasals and σ. We find in papyri and inscriptions of the Hellenistic age, as in inscriptions of classical times, a tendency to double and a counter-tendency to drop one of the elements in a double: thus we have τᾶλα, ἀναβάλουσιν, παρησία, γραματῖς, γεναί(ου), ἔλασον etc. in early papyri (see Mayser 212–4), and again διάλλογον, ἐνναντίων, εἰσσαγγελέων, ἔλλαττον, Ὥρρου, λατομμίδα, ἀνναιεώσεις, ἐκπεσσεῖν (*ib.* 217–9). Instances with mutes are virtually negligible.

(*a*) Ἐννέα but ἔνατος ἐνενήκοντα must be kept as in earlier Greek. D shows ἔννατος, an obvious case of analogy.

Γένημα (from √γεν of γίνομαι) is a Κοινή word for "vegetable produce," and must be sharply distinguished from γέννημα (from γεννάω) "offspring."

Ἐνεός has ν as in cl. Gr.

Ἐκ- and συν-χύννω are supported by MGr (*Prol.* 45 n.[2]): cf. ἐκτίννω in BGU iii. 896[8] (ii/A.D.) and i. 282[40] (*ib.*), and ἀποτίννω in P Gen 74[21] (? iii/A.D.), and ἀποτιννυτω *Syll.* 737[81] (ii/A.D.).

Ἀρ(ρ)αβών with ρ and ρρ has about equal warrant in papyri (*Prol.* 45).

Παρ(ρ)ησία (-ιάζομαι) has ρ single in some of the best uncials in nearly one-third of its occurrences.

Πυρ(ρ)ός and πυρ(ρ)άζω drop an ρ in Mt 16[2] C and late uncials, Rev 6[4] AP 046, 12[3] C 046: in these last πυρός was sometimes mistaken for the gen. of πῦρ.

The proper names Μύρρα (Ac 27[5] B Hier) and Φύγελος have the single liquid better attested in inscriptions: see WS 58, and note Μύρα in Ac 21[1] D.

Πλημύρης Lk 6[48] DW *al.* is the older spelling: the doubled μ is due to a popular etymology connecting the first part with πλήν—see Boisacq, *s.v.* Of course it does not follow that we should edit the single μ, which may well be due to correction by literary hands in some ancestor.

(*b*) The older doubling of ρ after the augment or in composition is very imperfectly carried out, and in many forms vanishes entirely. Words which have an established existence as compounds, with the simplex no longer in conscious contact, tend to keep their ρρ: thus χειμάρρους, ἄρρητος (but ἀναντίρητος), ἔρρωσθε (ῥώννυμι being obsolete), ἄρρωστος, αἱμορροεῖν. But for words kept in contact with a paradigm the ρρ is in a minority: διαρρήξαντες Ac 14^{14} (but διαρήξας Mk 14^{63}, περιρήξαντες Ac 16^{22}), ἐρριζωμένοι, ἐρρέθη(σαν), ἔρριπται Lk 17^{2} (but ρ in other forms from ῥίπτω), against ἄραφος and various forms from ῥάπτω, ῥήσσω, ῥέω, ῥαπίζω, ῥαβδίζω, ῥύομαι, ῥαντίζω. The opposite tendency may be seen in sporadic spellings like παρρών in 2 Co 10^{2} DE 47.

(c) Semitic words (among which should be included the thoroughly naturalised ἀρραβών above) show some degree of uncertainty in their spelling. Ἰωάνης is accepted by WH except in two places, since B has it 121/130 times. But ℵ has νν except in one part, which Lake has now shown *not* to be "written by the scribe of B."[1] The inscriptional evidence WH quote is relatively late, but it is as good evidence as the *a priori* considerations in WS 57. The record of D is curiously divergent: it has νν in Mt, Mk and Jn at the beginning, but ν in Jn from 5^{33} to the end, and in Lk and Ac. See the discussion of the significance of this variation in G. Rudberg's *Ntlicher Text*, 14.[2] Ἐλισαῖος and μαμωνᾶς are clear, Ἰόπ(π)η, Γεν(ν)ησαρέτ, Βαρσαβ(β)ᾶς are regarded by Schmiedel as more doubtful, on the ground of their Semitic etymology. In Ac 7^{2} D has Χαράν after the Hebrew: *contr.* Κάρραι (Strabo), Lat. *Carrhae.*

(d) Κράβαττος, a word of foreign origin (said to be Macedonian), is spelt with single τ several times in B, which thus agrees with Latin *grabatus.* ACDW[3] have ττ always, as also ℵ 1/11: elsewhere ℵ reads κράβακτος, a form found elsewhere only in two papyri, dating respectively from the centuries before and after that in which ℵ was written: for the bearing of this on the provenance of ℵ see Lake's introduction to the facsimile of the MS, p. xi. The spelling κράβατος can be quoted from Egypt much earlier, viz. from a "probably Ptolemaic" ostracon in *Mélanges Nicole*, 184, which enables us, if we like, to associate B also with Egypt as far as the evidence of this word goes. But κράβαττος also can be quoted from Egypt: see P Lond 191^{16} (A.D. 103–17) (=ii. p. 265). Κράββατος appears in Ac 5^{15} E and in the mass of later MSS: it seems to be a dialectic variation in the Κοινή, which has left descendants in MGr dialects. Cf. my *Einleitung* 60, and *Vocabulary*, *s.v.*

(e) Doubled aspirates in Semitic words like Μαθθαῖος, ἐφφαθά, or the Phrygian Ἀφφία, are contributory evidence of the spirant pronunciation.

---

[1] WH *App.*[2] 166: see Lake, *Codex Sinaiticus* xii.

[2] Upsala University publications, 1915.

[3] W has κρέβαττος twice—a form which has parallels in MGr.

Intrusive Consonants.

Intrusive dental between σ and ρ, The combination σρ, which is not found in native Greek words, sometimes developed a transition sound τ in the name Ἰσραήλ and derivatives. So in Mt 19^{28}, Mk 12^{29} in W, with D in the latter, and sometimes in Ac in B. In ℵ there is a δ, which appears 8/9 times in the word Ἰσδραηλείτης. The occurrence of Ἰστραήλ in magic papyri and in one or two Egyptian inscrr. is noted by Lake (*Cod. Sin.* xi.) as nullifying the argument of WH[1] that the intrusive dental was a Latinism and therefore supported Western provenance for ℵ or B or both. The phonetic development was easy, as is shown by the fact that the root *sreu* "flow" (ῥέω) produced the original of our *stream* in Germanic and Στρυμών in Thracian, with the same thing in Albanian and Lithuanian: see Brugmann *Grd.*[2] i. 827.

and labial between μ and ρ or σ. Intrusive β between μ and ρ (as in ἄμβροτος, μεσημβρία) appears in the proper name Ἰαμβρῆς, if the usual Hebrew etymology is right. So Mamre becomes Μαμβρῆ, and Samson Σαμψών (Heb 11^{32}). Cases like the analogical λήμψομαι and the (unexplained) σφυδρόν are dealt with elsewhere.

Liquids and Nasals.

Variations of λ and ρ, § 42. Variation between λ and ρ appears in κλίβανος, for which Phrynichus (Rutherford *NP* 267 f.) claimed κρίβανος as Attic: the λ form probably entered the Κοινή from Ionic (as Herodotus has it) or Doric (Sophron). As Lat. *lībum* and our *loaf* (A.S. *hláf*) show, the *l* was original, and Attic was peculiar. The Latin word *flagellum* is dissimilated to φραγέλλιον (φραγελλόω): D keeps the λ, as does a papyrus written apparently by a Roman, in Trajan's reign—P Lond 191^{11} (=ii p. 265). The Hebrew בְּלִיַּעַל is transliterated Βελίαρ,[2] which again may be mere dissimilation; but some Semitic etymology need not be excluded—see *EBi s.v.* In D the ν in λύχνος is twice written λ, and in πνέω once: see J. R. Harris, *Codex Bezae* 143 f., where also μέγαρ in Lk 1^{15} is connected with the λ in μεγάλη. The form πλέοντα (Lk 12^{55}) is a happy accident, agreeing with a prehistoric ancestor of πνεύμων: see Walde, *Lat Etym. Wört. s.v pulmo.* So κάλφος Lk 6^{41} W, λεφέλη Lk 9^{34} W: also P Oxy ii. 242^{12} (A.D. 77) λαύλας.

ρρ and ρσ. The relations of ρρ and ρσ affect the NT forms of θαρσέω and ἄρσην. Θάρσει -εῖτε is used exclusively (Evv., Ac), while for the rest of the verb forms of θαρρέω occur 2 Co *quinquies* and Heb 13^{6}, without variant. Ἄρσην (a derivative) appears

---

[1] *Intr.*[2] 265.

[2] WS 58 cites *Berial* from *Asc. Isai.*, but see Charles's edition, p. 6.

unchallenged in Mk 10^6, Lk 2^{23}, 1 Co 6^9, 1 Tim 1^{10}; but ἄρρην has some warrant in Mt 19^4 E, Rev 12^5 ℵ 046, *ib*^{13} 046 cu^{pl}; and in Paul, Rom 1^{27} ℵ*AC 33 (*ter*, but C has ρσ 3°), Gal 3^{28} ℵ, where WH give ρρ as an alternative. Wackernagel (*Hellenistica*, Göttingen, 1907) shows that the sporadic appearance of Attic ρρ is parallel with that of ττ, and normally comes into the Κοινή with specifically Attic words that contained it. Whereas, however, "the Attic ττ was shared only with the dialects of Eretria, Oropus and Boeotia, numerous dialects agreed with it in the use of ρρ" (*op. cit.* p. 25). Ionian influence would be the only serious discouragement to the use of θαρρῶ and ἄρρην, so that mixture was easy. We might imagine, for instance, that θάρσει, θαρσεῖτε, "cheer up," was a favourite phrase in Ionic: if that were so—it is only offered as an illustrative speculation—we could understand how the rest of the verb came from θαρρεῖν, while the imperative phrase lived only in the ρσ form. This distinction is maintained in NT, and in LXX with only one or two exceptions; and it might easily arise from such cause as has been suggested. An interesting confirmation may be seen in W at Mk 10^{49}, where θαρρῶν ἔγειρε is read instead of θάρσει, ἔγ. The noun θάρρος was not really even Attic, and θάρσος accordingly stands alone. In the Ptolemaic papyri however we have ρσ only (Mayser 220): ρρ begins to appear later (cf. *CR* xv. 33), as it does even in Ionic territory on the inscrr. of Pergamum (Schweizer *Perg.* 125). MGr shows mixture still: see Thumb *Hellen.* 77 f. In NT ἄρσην is read throughout by WH (against ℵAC in Rom 1^{27} and ℵ in Gal 3^{28}); but the papyri show great variation—see *Vocabulary, s.v.* Δέρρις occurs in Mk 1^6 D: Wackernagel (p. 13) notes that δέρσις never existed.

Assimilation of ν in ἐν and σύν. Assimilation of the ν of ἐν and σύν takes place in composition according to the traditional spelling, which probably represents the pronunciation even in the Hellenistic age, to judge from the freedom with which assimilation takes place in inscriptions and papyri when proclitics are linked closely with the following word. Mayser's exhaustive presentation of the evidence from Ptolemaic papyri is summed up in tables on p. 231 (with which compare those of Thackeray 132–4, tending the same way). He shows that the words which most favour assimilation are τόν, τήν, τῶν; ὅν, ἥν, ὧν; ἄν, ἐάν, ἐν, ἐπάν, μέν, αὐτόν, τοσοῦτον, πλέον; πλήν, νῦν. There is moreover a marked difference between the effect of labial and guttural initial. For a large number of papyri from iii/ and ii/B.C. the proportion of assimilations to non-assimilations in separate words is for iii/ 1 : 4 before labials, 1 : 9 before gutturals; for ii/ 1 : 11 before labials, none before gutturals (80 exx.). The tables for ἐν and σύν in composition (p. 234) give for iii/ 7 : 1 for assimilation before labials, 4 : 3 for ii/; before gutturals 4 : 1 and 5 : 6 respectively. Even here therefore the progressive ousting of assimilation is very marked, and the difference between gutturals and labials.

In NT συγγενής (-εια) and σύγχυσις are the only forms with συγ- that find their way into WH's list of "certain and constant" assimilations: they print with an alternative συγκεκαλυμμένον and συγκυρίαν. Compounds of ἐν show 7 assim. to 7 non-assim. with ἐγ-, and 26 assim. to 1 non-assim. with ἐμ-. This means that assimilation remains decidedly more prominent in the semi-literary MSS of NT than it is in the non-literary papyri even of the early Ptolemaic age, but the difference between labials and gutturals is still well marked. According to WH (*App.*² 156 f.), non-assimilation is the usual practice in the best NT uncials before π, ψ, β, φ; κ, γ, χ; ζ, σ; λ, μ. But some words have assimilation regularly, the ἐν compounds showing it more freely than those of σύν. Details may be sought in their list, or more fully in that of Gregory, pp. 73 ff., where uncial evidence in each case is supplied. How far the oldest uncials in this matter represent the autographs must be left an open question. Note the frequency of ἐμ μέσῳ "in good MSS wherever ἐν μέσῳ occurs, but never in ℵ, B, D or D_2"; also ἐγ Κανά Jn 2^{11} AF, ἐγ γαστρί Lk 21^{23} A, ἐμ πραΰτητι Jas 1^{21} ℵ, ἐμ πολέμῳ Heb 11^{34} $\mathfrak{p}^{13}$, σὺμ Μαριάμ Lk 2^5 AE *al.* σὺμ πᾶσιν Lk 24^{21} EG *al.* (Debrunner 14). Thackeray 131 gives corresponding evidence from LXX, but remarks that such forms were probably more abundant in the autographs—which for the NT is hardly likely.

Causes of non-assimilation. The rationale of this tendency to drop assimilation may be sought partly in *lento* pronunciation: a nasal ending a syllable would naturally tend towards ν, the form of all final nasals *in pausa*. This is supported by the frequency of such spellings as ἄνγελος and πένπω (cf. Mayser 235 f., Nachmanson 106): NT exx. are Κενχρεαί Ac 18^{18} ℵADE, πένψω 13 times in D_2, ἔλανψεν 2 Co 4^6 D_2 (Debrunner 14), where the ν was not due to etymological association as in other NT words, παλινγενεσία, πανπληθεί, ἐξηρανμένην (Mk 11^{20} W), μεμιανμένοις (Tit 1^{15} D_2). We must note that nasals at the end of syllables were by this time becoming faint, and the distinction between their three classes (μ, ν, γ) was less easily heard. It should be added that in literary papyri of the period assimilation was decidedly more abundant: Mayser (p. 232) gives 12 : 8 before labials and 10 : 2 before gutturals in favour of assimilation for a series of classical papyri from the Ptolemaic age. The contrast emphasises the non-literary practice the more.

Βεεζεβούλ The form Βεεζεβούλ, which we must assume to be for Βεελζεβούλ (read by all the later Greek authorities), is found throughout in ℵB except in Mk 3^{22}, where ℵ joins the mass. No explanation of this reading is suggested which would justify its originality: we must perhaps assume a kind of assimilation based on the abnormality of the combination λζ in Greek. If so, the corruption must go to swell the list of small errors which ℵ and B share, proving their common origin. The word involves a further problem in the matter of λ, if we follow the Latin and Syriac vss. in the equation with OT *Ba'al zᵉbûb*. But this is unnecessary, and whatever interpretation is adopted, we may be quite sure that -λ is the original and -β a primitive guess by students acquainted with Hebrew.

Γολγοθά. Γολγοθά has also lost λ (by dissimilation ?), when compared with either Hebrew or Aramaic: see *EBi* *s.v.* In Mt 27^{33} Δ and syrhr have Γολγολθά.

Φαιλόνης. In 2 Tim 4^{13} φελόνην is read practically without variant. Its relation to Lat. *paenula* is difficult, for the latter can be quoted from a much earlier date. In papyri the form φαινόλης is commoner, but both are found. If it were not for the Latin, we might have regarded φαιν. as popular etymology (φαίνω). It is quite possible that both Latin and Greek go back to some unknown foreign word.

Insertion of Nasal. The word μογγιλαλος in Mk 7^{32} is found in W, in LNΔ *al.*, and the important cursives 28 and 33, with three of the Ferrar group. Since the word μογγός *hoarse* is attested (very rarely) from v/A.D.—see E. A. Sophocles *s.v.*—we must probably regard this as a real *v.l.*, rather than as a nasalising like some words mentioned below.

The insertion of μ in λήμψεσθαι, λημφθῆναι etc., is a Hellenistic analogy-product belonging to the flexion of that verb (see § 95). The (classical) loss of μ by dissimilation in compounds of πίμπλημι and πίμπρημι with ἐν and σύν is overcome by analogy in Ac 14^{17} DEP, 28^{6} cu^{3}: as Lobeck shows (*Phryn.* 95 f.), forms with μ appear frequently in classical MSS. In the latter place ℵ* reads ἐμπιπρᾶσθαι. The inserted ν in θηνσαυρούς Mt 2^{11} D is no doubt due to the Latin: we find the loan-word often in Plautus spelt thus (see Lindsay *Latin Language* 69). *Per contra*, in the Roman name *Clēmēns* the nom. (not in NT) was written Κλήμης, though *cēnsus* was transliterated κῆνσος. The *n* in Latin was faintly heard in these combinations. WH write Ἁδραμυντηνός as the adj. of *Hadrumetum* in Ac 27^{2}, following AB 33 and the Bohairic, with some minor cursives.

Sibilants.

Ζ in the Κοινή. § 43. It seems probable that in the Hellenistic period ζ had passed from its earlier double value as = *zd* or *dz* into the soft *z* as in English; that is, the MGr pronunciation was reached in the Ptolemaic age. A possible survival of *zd* in the Κοινή might be recognised in Ἄζωτος: in *IMAe* i. 406 we find Ἀσζωτ[ίς], with the note, "Semiticam formam *Ašdōd* optime reddit." The name presumably acquired this orthography before the sign had changed its value. That עֶזְרָא was transliterated Ἔσδρας in the same early period proves nothing, for the δ could be intrusive as in Ἰσδραήλ—see § 41. For the proof of this development of ζ see Mayser 209 and reff. there. It depends largely on the frequency with which ζ in our documents is substituted for σ before voiced sounds. In NT we find ζβέννυμι in Mt 12^{20} 25^{8} D, 1 Th 5^{19} B*D*$_2$FG, ἄζβεστος Mk 9^{43} N; ζμύρνα Mt 2^{11} DW, Jn 19^{39} ℵ (σζμ.) D^{supp}W; Ζμύρνα Rev 1^{11} 2^{8} ℵ and Latin. So in BGU iv. 1175 *ter* (B.C. 4) Ζμύρνα is the name of a woman of Persian birth; in P Oxy viii. 1088^{39} (early i/A.D.) ζμύρνα occurs in a medical prescription; and in P Ryl ii. 153^{18} (mid. ii/A.D.) we read ἐν Ζμύρνῃ τῆς Ἀσίας. We find *Zmyrna* in Catullus 95, and elsewhere in MSS of Latin authors. Lightfoot's note (ii. 331) on *Ep. Ign. ad Polyc.* (*ad init.*) gives abundant evidence that in the name of Smyrna the ζ and the σ were used impartially in ii/A.D. (*init.*). "In the earliest coins the ζ seems to be preferred, in the latest the σ." If so, ζ would rule in i/A.D. Crönert *Mem.* 95 gives a multitude of parallels from the Herculaneum papyri (before A.D. 79) and from inscriptions. It is in fact abundantly clear that if ζμ and ζβ are "Western" only (WH *App.*[2] 155), that is not so much a reason for banning the ζ as for approving the "δ Text" in its (characteristic!) use of spelling that was coeval with the autographs and true to the pronunciation. In MGr σβ and σμ are pronounced with voiceless ζ.

Σσ and ττ. The relations of σσ and ττ may be treated here: it must be remembered that in earlier Greek σσ(ττ) nearly always, and ζ very often, arise from a guttural followed by consonantal *y*. In MGr we find in Carpathos and Chios σσ (and σ*y*) becoming τσ, while "the transition from ζ to *d*ζ (*e.g.* παίdζω = παίζω) is more widely spread" (Thumb *Handb.* 22). One is tempted to regard both as survivals, and take *ts* as the old pronunciation of σσ (perhaps *tth* of ττ), just as we know *dz* was that of ζ in class. Greek. Without dwelling on this conjecture, we go on to note that the Κοινή has σσ almost exclusively where Attic had ττ, which was hardly used outside the contiguous districts of Attica and Boeotia. The following instances of ττ are accepted by WH in NT: κρεῖττον in Paul 1/4, 1 Pet 1/1, 2 Pet 1/1?, κρείττων etc. Heb 11/12 and one doubtful; ἐλάττων 2/4, ἐλαττόω 3/3, ἐλαττονέω 1/1; ἥττημα Paul 2/2, ἡττάω 2 Pet 2/2, but ἧσσον Paul 2/2 and ἡσσώθητε Paul 1/1; ἐκπλήττω 1/12 (in Ac 13[12]). These are mostly explained satisfactorily by Wackernagel's thesis referred to above (§ 42). The verb from ἥσσων was either ἑσσόω (Ionic) or ἡττάω (Attic): when the Κοινή took it over, it naturally did not fuse these alternatives into ἡσσάω. Ἥττημα accordingly was an Attic word, adopted as it stood. Wackernagel thinks that ἥττων followed ἡττᾶσθαι, and in its turn influenced its synonym ἐλάττων and its antithesis κρείττων, both of which appear in LXX—ἐλάττων with its derivative verbs greatly outnumbering the σσ form. Here the process was helped by the fact that the verb ἐλαττόω (and noun -ωσις) was specifically Attic and had no Ionic rival to endanger its ττ. No special explanation can be suggested for the isolated ἐκπληττόμενος, with which cf. καταπλήττεσθαι in P Petr ii. 45$^{\text{iii. 18}}$ (*c.* B.C. 246);[1] but similar isolated or occasional variations can be quoted from papyri and other Κοινή documents—see Wackernagel's samples. The influence of Attic was so commanding that we cannot be surprised if reminiscences of an Attic peculiarity slip in to disturb normal pronunciation.

ζ in transliteration. There remains the question of transliteration from Semitic, already raised on the name Ἄζωτος. Burkitt shows[2] that Ναζαρά (Ναζαρέτ) stands practically alone if we make its ζ represent a Semitic צ; for which reason among others he seeks to get the adjectives Ναζαρηνός and Ναζωραῖος from נָזִיר. Normally

[1] Wrongly given from P Grenf in Mayser 223.

[2] *Syriac Forms of NT Proper Names* (Brit. Acad. 1912), 16, 28 f.

צ was σ and ז was ζ, as we might expect, שׂ and שׁ being also σ, since Greek had no means of differentiating.

Gutturals.

Γμ, γν. § 44. The combinations γμ and γν were pronounced with γ as *ng* (as in *kingmaker* etc.). In Ionic during iv/B.C. -ιγν- became -ῑν- in γίνομαι and γινώσκω, perhaps through dissimilating influence of the initial γ (so Brugmann-Thumb *Gr.* 126): Thumb thinks that the same forms in Doric, Thessalian and Boeotian arose from later Attic (B.C. 300 and after) and Hellenistic influence. These forms are universal in the Κοινή, as innumerable papyrus records show—a few pedantic revivals of γιγν. serve as exceptions to prove the rule. It is curious that W, which has so many thoroughly vernacular spellings, uses γιγνώσκω often, and γίγνομαι, though less frequently (Sanders 23). Sporadic instances of the dropping of *ng* may be seen in λάρυξ Rom 3[18] AP 33 cu[7], and σάλπιξ 1 Co 14[8] ALP. The papyri show

Κ and γ. innumerable instances of ἐκ with κ softened before voiced sounds: thus the recurrent formula καθάπερ ἐγ δίκης. Mayser (225 f.) shows that it is normal, κ being quite exceptional. In NT it is curiously absent, but note ἔγγονα 1 Tim 5[4] D* cu[5] (see reff. in Mayser 228), ἀπεγδύσει Col 2[11] B*, ἀνέγλιπτος Lk 12[33] D, ἐγλύου Heb 12[5] 𝔭[13] (from Debrunner 14), also ἐπιδιγνύμεναι in Ac 9[39] A. So γναφεύς, which in old Attic was κν.: γν. is found in an Attic inscr. of iv/B.C., and exclusively in Ptolemaic papyri (Mayser 169 f.). It may be noted here

Contiguous κ and σ-. that ἐκ sometimes combined with initial σ to ξ: thus εξογ = ἐκ σοῦ Mt 2[6] ℵC *al.*, 21[19] D *al.* So in papyri ἐξυμφώνου etc. (*CR* xv. 31). The *v.l.* in Ac 27[39] ἐξῶσαι ℵAω, ἐκσῶσαι BC boh arm, is really perhaps a mere matter of orthography in its inception.

Κ and χ. On ὄρνιξ see § 55 (3) (*e*). Πανδοχεύς -εῖον has χ from the influence of its original δέχομαι: the κ (cf. Ionic δέκομαι) is still found in *Syll.* 901 (? i/B.C.) and even in P Gen 54[26] (iii/A.D.). For κ in Lk 10[34] stand ℵ*Ξ, *ib.*[35] ℵ*D*, against ABLWω: Ti takes the correction in ℵD as evidence that the κ form was obsolete. Forms like ἐκθρός—common in D[1]—and the converse ἐχθέσει (Wis 11[14], from ἔκθεσις: see Thackeray 103) show the development of θ into a spirant, which involved a strange articulation of the guttural before it. Metathesis of aspiration produces interchange of χ and κ in χιτών and other words: see § 40.

Semitic words with χ and κ. Semitic words show χ occasionally as a transliteration of the gutturals, including even א. So Ἀκελδαμάχ (ακ- BCD, αχ- ℵA) = Aram. חֲקֵל דְּמָא, and Σειράχ = סִירָא. See Kautzsch *Gramm. d. bibl. Aram.* (1884) 8. Dalman (*Gramm.* 161) compares Ἰωσήχ Lk 3[26] = יוסי, and says that

[1] See Rendel Harris, *Codex Bezae* 141. Also cf. Mayser 172.

the χ marks the word as an indeclinable. Elsewhere א always disappears : ἀββά=אַבָּא, σίκερα=שִׁכְרָא etc. But ἐφφαθά=אֶתְפְּתַח (Kautzsch 10), while ה and ח initial are often only a (presumed) rough breathing. ʽΡαχάβ in Mt 1[5] stands for רחב, which in Jas 2[25], Heb 11[31] is ʽΡαάβ, all without variant. In ʽΡοβοάμ for רְחַבְעָם both ע and ח disappear. The transliteration of ע by γ under certain conditions is rather a matter for Semitists than for us : it is enough to observe that in our period γ was generally a spirant, so that Γόμορρα represented עֲמֹרָה satisfactorily. The instances of χ standing for ק (cf. ἀχελδαμάχ above) may be due to the differentiation of ק and כ : χ when spirantised may have represented ק better as being articulated farther back. An instance of the opposite procedure is where Καναναῖος represents an initial ק, and Χαναναία a כ, on the evidence of the Syriac.[1] The representation of ח by κ in Κλωπᾶς cannot be accepted if it means direct transliteration, since חַלְפַי has ʼΑλφαῖος already to represent it ; but Dalman (*Gramm.* 142 n.[3]) suggests that it might be the Gentile name of a Jew חלפי—as a Saul took the similar-sounding "Paul," or a Silas "Silvanus." This presumes our identifying Κλωπᾶς with Κλεόπας, on which see above, § 38.

Labials.

Φ for π. § 45. Σφυρίς for σπυρίς is well attested in NT, and appears very often in papyri : *CR* xv. 33, xviii. 107, Mayser 173. So σφόγγος Mk 15[36] D, σφεκουλάτορα Mk 6[27] W. See Crönert *Mem.* 85 n.[3]. Meisterhans[3] 78 shows that σφόνδυλος was Attic in iv/B.C. He also cites Attic inscrr. of ii/A.D. and later for ʼΑφφιανός, where φφ is assumed to represent Latin *pp*, as in Phm[2] ʼΑφφίᾳ D*. So from mid. ii/B.C. the Latin *Sulpicius* becomes Σολπίκιος. (Contrast ʼΑππιανός *novies* in P Oxy i. 33 (ii/A.D.): so CP Herm 127 *vs* iii.[9] (? ii/A.D.), and BGU iii. 785[1] (i/A.D.).) But the inscriptional parallels from Asia Minor in Kretschmer's *Einleitung* 346 f. make it highly probable that this name in its various forms was affected by an Anatolian word (cf ἄπφα "papa" in Greek nursery speech) unconnected with *Appius*. This last appears in Ac 28[15], where 33 cu[2] read ʼΑπφίου. No doubt in Asia Minor this word influenced the spelling of really Latin names. Schweizer *Perg.* 110 remarks that when φ became a spirant it probably remained bilabial, and therefore not quite equivalent to the *f* of imperial Latin, which like ours was labiodental. The relations between π and φ are concerned in the *v.l.* at Ac 13[18] ἐτροποφόρησεν ℵBDω, ἐτροφ. AC*E 33 lat[vt] syr[vg hl] sah boh ; there is no probability that the former could arise from the latter phonetically. See § 28.

The addition of φ in ʼΑσάφ Mt 1[7f.] ℵBC 𝔭[1] (also D in Lk) 1 etc. lat[vt] sah boh is discussed by F. C. Burkitt in *Proc. Camb. Philolog. Soc.* for March 4, 1897. He shows from Latin evidence that the true LXX form of the

[1] F. C. Burkitt, *Syriac Forms of NT Proper Names* (Brit. Acad. 1912), 5.

name, however explained, was Ἀσάφ, so that Mt was following the Greek Bible: this disposes of Salmon's criticism on the NT uncials (*Some Thoughts on the Textual Criticism of NT* 29, 156).

B and ο(υ) for a *w* sound. An important point for Greek pronunciation is raised by the transliteration of דָּוִד and *Silvanus*. Uncials have only Δαυ(ε)ίδ (often abbreviated), and Δαβίδ comes in with the cursives. The earlier spelling is exactly parallel with the representation of Roman names like *Flavius*, for which in the papyri we find Φλαύιος as well as Φλαούιος: thus P Oxy ii. 237viii. 19 (A.D. 186), vi. p. 223 (and 356) (A.D. 154), 991 (A.D. 341)—the spelling with ου is much the commoner. The case of Silvanus is rather different, as *v* follows a consonant. Σιλουανός is the overwhelmingly attested form, but Σιλβανός has better warrant than Δαβίδ, appearing in B at 1 Pet 5[12] and in DEFG at 2 Co 1[19], 1 Th 1[1], 2 Th 1[1] (where also add 424**). Now in the papyri Σιλβανός stands alone from iii/A.D. onwards: the very few earlier instances of the name quotable from inscrr. and papyri seem to show that the β spelling did not arise (with one exception, which is not quite certain) till the end of ii/A.D.[1] That ℵ always and B 3/4 times should have preserved the long obsolete ου of the autographs is another of the striking trifles which go to prove their accuracy. It was only in later times that β became the normal representative of *F* (*i.e.* Eng. *w*): being a spirant like our *v* (but interlabial), it did not accurately express the Latin *u* or Hebrew ו. Earlier Egyptian contacts of β and υ may be seen in Mayser 115, where from ii/B.C words like ῥαύδους=ῥάβδους (P Par 40[33]), ἐμβλεύσαντες (P Lond 23[15]=i. p. 38)=-βλέφ-σαντες made up afresh with φ=f, etc., show the spirant value of both. Note that ο sometimes represents Latin consonant *u*, as Κοΐντος, Ὀαλέριος.

Dentals.

T and θ. § 46. Interchanges of θ and τ from metathesis of aspiration are treated in § 40. Μαστός varies: Lk 11[27] μασθοί DG 23[29] D*FG (μαζοί C), Rev 1[13] μασθοῖς ℵ (μαζοῖς A). Μαζός and μασθός are primitive doublets: cf. Skt. *mạ́du-* and *mạ́dha-* (Brugmann-Thumb *Gr.* 117, 125). Μαστός (the normal cl. form) may perhaps be independent: it might be a verbal from the root (cf. μαδάω) from which the other two are derived. See the material in Walde, *Lat. Etym. Wörterb.*[2] 453 f. Φόβηθρον Lk 21[11] BDW (Is 19[17] B) is presumably due to the analogy of words like κόρηθρον, κύκηθρον (W. F. Moulton in WM 119 n.[2]): add κάλλυνθρον BGU iv. 1120[17] (B.C. 5). See Brugmann-Thumb *Gr.* § 206, and Thackeray 104 (μασθός and φόβηθρον in LXX) Mayser 179 illustrates the frequent change of σθ to στ in papyri. Rendel Harris describes this as "very common in Codex Bezae": he instances Mk 4[1] καθῆσται, Ac 19[25] ἐπίστασται.

---

[1] See the facts concerning *Silvanus* in *Vocabulary*, *s.v.* It must be noted that in some names β represents Latin *u* much earlier: see Viereck *Sermo* 57, with instances from i/B.C. *Livia* is Λιβία in P Ryl ii. 127[26] (A.D. 29).

Οὐθείς, etc. The variation between οὐδείς μηδείς and οὐθείς μηθείς is one of peculiar importance as a test of our MSS: cf. what is said on ἐάν for ἄν in § 38. The history of this rather shortlived development is acutely traced by Thackeray (pp. 58–62 and 104 f.), whose account should be carefully followed. That οὐτεμία is never found proves that mixture of οὔτε and οὐδέ has nothing to do with it: there has been a re-formation οὐδ' εἶς, with $\delta + h$ producing θ—see Brugmann-Thumb 170 f "First found in an inscr. of 378 B.C.,[1] it is practically the only form in use throughout the Greek-speaking world during iii/B.C. and the first half of ii/B.C. In 132 B.C. the δ forms begin again to reassert themselves, and the period from that date to about 100 B.C. appears to have been one of transition, when the δ and θ forms are found side by side in the same documents. For i/B.C. we are in the dark, but in i/A.D. we find that οὐδείς has completely regained its ascendancy, and by the end of ii/A.D. οὐθείς, which still lingers on in i/ii A.D., mainly in a single phrase μηθὲν ἧσσον, is extinct, never apparently to reappear, at all events not within the period covered by the papyri."[2] It follows naturally that οὐθείς plays a very small part in NT. It is accepted by WH eight times: Lk 22³⁵ 23¹⁴, Ac 15⁹ 19²⁷ 26²⁶, 1 Co 13², 2 Co 11⁸ (οὐθ.), and Ac 27³³ (μηθ.). To these might be added Ac 20³³ ℵAE 27³⁴ A, 1 Co 13³ ℵA 33 cu²: since -θείς was obsolete long before our oldest MSS, we should incline towards accepting it as often as good uncials show it. But against these possible 11 instances we have some 220 of οὐδείς and 80 of μηδείς. We have to note the peculiar case of the verb ἐξουθενεῖν, a verb coined while οὐθείς was still in use: Thackeray shows (104 f.) that ἐξουδενοῦν was coined afresh when οὐδείς was reasserting itself, and mixed forms -δενεῖν and -θενοῦν appear in a few places in LXX. In Plutarch we have ἐξουδενίζω, perhaps a corrected form from ἐξουθενίζω which we have in a scholiast: ἐ[ξ]ουδενῆ[σαι is said by Schubart to be the most probable reading in BGU iv. 1117³¹ (B.C. 13), and it is printed by Mitteis in *Chrest.* ii. p. 129 without question. In NT ἐξουθενεῖν, as a long-established word which has detached itself from its origin, stands without doubt in 11 places. In Mk 9¹² there is doubt: ἐξουθενωθῇ ℵ 69 is confronted by ἐξουδενηθῇ in BD 565, while LNW have ἐξουθενηθῇ and ACXΔ *al.* ἐξουδενωθῇ—perhaps the most probable reading, since the general NT form -θενη- will explain the θ of the ℵ and the η of the BD reading. From other places the only variants are Lk 23¹¹ -ώσας X,

---

[1] But in *Amer. Journ. of Archaeol.* vii. 152, S. O. Dickerman gives an inscr. from Cleonae which has μηθέν, and he assigns it to early v/B.C. at latest. I cannot criticise this judgement.

[2] Thackeray *Gr.* 58. Since this was written, our "darkness" as to i/B.C. has been somewhat relieved by the publication (in BGU iv.) of about a hundred papyri from Alexandria, dated under Augustus. One of these documents, No. 1141, a private letter, and almost the only paper in the collection which is not formal, shows οὐθέν and μηθέν once each, and even this has μηδέν twice. Even the formal character of the remainder does not altogether discount the fact that οὐδείς appears 5 times and μηδείς 56 (largely in identic formulae).

-ίσας W (cf. Plutarch's verb, unless it is mere itacism—see § 34), Ac 4[11] -ωθείς cu[5] (-δενωθείς cu[1]), 1 Co 1[28] ἐξουδενωμένα 33 (-θενω- cu[1]), 16[11] ἐξουθενώσῃ 33 (-δενω- cu[2]), 2 Co 10[10] ἐξουδενημένος B (as in Mk 9[12]).

Miscellaneous variations. A few miscellaneous variant forms may be noted. A dental is dropped in ἄρκον Rev 13[2] (all unc.). It is explained in Brugmann-Thumb 151 as an effect of popular etymology, produced by ἀρκέω and τὸ ἄρκος "defence." The link hardly seems obvious: if we are seeking an etymon it is more plausible to try ἄρκυς, the bear being assimilated in name to the net that snared him. But Boisacq (*s.v.*) regards both forms as primitive Idg doublets. Add the old word ἄρκᾰλος "young panther." Ἄρκος is both literary (Aelian) and vernacular Κοινή (see *Vocab. s.v.*), and MGr. For the added dental in σφυδρά (Ac 3[7] ℵ*AB*C*) we have only Hesychius to quote. (Ἀνα)βαθμός came into the Κοινή from Ionic, according to Phrynichus; but G. Meyer (p. 365) gives inscr. evidence against this (cf Thumb *Hellen.* 73). Anyhow it is Hellenistic, while βασμός is Attic. See *Vocab.* on both words. On the other hand no trace survives of the old form ὀδμή, which figures in Herculaneum papyri and some later writers as *v.l.*: see Crönert *Mem.* 136, who notes dissidence among the old grammarians. Ἐθύθη 1 Co 5[7] is only a blunder in very late sources of TR. Δ and τ are concerned in the Hellenistic ποταπός, which comes from class. ποδαπός (see under Word-formation) by assimilation to πότε. There is no connexion with the frequent substitution of τ for δ in badly written papyri, which is due wholly to Egyptian native pronunciation.

A curious substitution of χ for θ occurs in D at Mk 6[21] γενεχλίοις. There is only a fortuitous resemblance to the χ in ὄρνιξ.

In foreign words. In foreign words there is some wavering between τ and θ, shown by doubling (as Μαθθαῖος) to be spirant, representing Aram. ת. So esp. Ναζαρέτ and Ναζαρέθ, the latter predominating in Mt and Lk, the former in Mk and Jn, according to Gregory 120. WH print only τ (Ναζαρά Mt 4[13]): the form with θ is attested by ℵ 4 times, B at least 4, D also 4. W oddly drops it in the best-attested place, Mt 21[11], and in Lk 4 times, but has it everywhere else, as the later MSS normally.

Movable Letters

Final ς movable. § 47. (1) Final -ς in οὕτως is practically fixed. Οὕτω is admitted by WH 10 times (W. F. Moulton in WM 44 n.) out of over 200, on the mechanical principle of accepting an omission found in ℵ or B supported by A or C—a principle they adopt also for movable -ν.[1] In Ptolemaic papyri οὕτω is found a few times, even before vowels, but οὕτως predominates (Mayser 242 f.). On the other hand, Crönert counts 75 instances of οὕτω to 25 of οὕτως before consonants, in the Herculaneum rolls included in his survey (*Mem.* 142). Since

---

[1] Their neglect of D in this matter is in accord with their general principle, but it is hard to defend it to-day.

these are literary, they need not disturb the impression that οὕτως is normal.

Ἄχρι and μέχρι were Attic, according to Thomas Mag. (p. 135) and Phrynichus (*al.*—see Rutherford *NP* 64): Moeris (p. 34) calls ἄχρις Hellenistic. But the record of the forms with -ς is not good enough to justify this claim. They appear first in the Roman period (Mayser 243): an early instance is BGU iii. 830^{13} (i/A.D.) ἄχρις ἄν. Instances before vowels appear in early Fathers (Reinhold 37). In NT "ἄχρι usually precedes vowels (14–16 times), Gal 3^{19} ἄχρις ἄν or οὗ being the only certain exception: μέχρι preceding a vowel is certain only Lk 16^{16}, μέχρις 2–3 times" (WH *App.*² 155). They give ἄχρις as alternative in Rom 11^{25}, and read ἄχρις in Heb 3^{13}, μέχρις in Heb 12^{4} with alternatives, in Mk 13^{30} Gal 4^{19} without alternative.

Ἄντικρυς Χίου is found in "all good MSS" at Ac 20^{15} (WH).

The omission of -ς in -κις adverbs (Crönert *Mem.* 142 f.), not uncommon in the Κοινή, has no place in NT.

Radermacher (*Gr.* 39) observes that final -ς and final -ν were alike feeble in the Hellenistic period. There are even instances of -ι written for -ς, as more often for -ν: thus τὰς ἅλωι P Tebt i. 61 *b* ^{373} (B.C. 118). See Mayser 136.

Final -ν. (2) Final -ν (ν ἐφελκυστικόν) is so universal in the forms which admit it at all, that it is only necessary to take note of omissions. Modern use, by which ν is inserted before vowels only, is known to be wrong even for classical writers, and in Hellenistic it is altogether to be set aside. Indeed a superfluous -ν appears largely in forms which had never known it. A conspicuous instance is ἦν, subj. of εἰμί, which has misled even Deissmann (*LAE* 155). See *Prol.* 49, where μείζων acc. sing. is quoted from Jn 5^{36} AB *al.* (add W). Cf. βορρᾶν gen. in ℵ in LXX (Thackeray 143). Cf. from papyri P Oxy iii. 505 (ii/A.D.) ἀπηλιώτουν, Preisigke *Samm.* 4317^{14} (*c.* A.D. 200) ἐν Ἀλεξανδρίᾳν, P Tebt i. 104 (i/B.C.) Ἀπολλωνίᾳν, P Oxy viii. 1088^{43} (i/A.D.) εἶταν, P Ryl ii. 90^{32} (iii/A.D.) τῷν ἡμῶν κινδύνῳν, *ib.* 160^{5} (A.D. 28–9) β]εβαιώσιν (dat.) etc. etc. Cf. Nachmanson *Beiträge* 66 f.

For the practice of ℵABC in the matter of movable -ν, see WH *App.*² 153–5, who explain there the admittedly mechanical rule by which they decide whether to print -ν or omit it: see under (1) above.

The irrational addition of -ν may be set beside its irrational omission, for which see many exx in Mayser 190 f. One recurrent instance may be named, πάλι for πάλιν, a vulgar by-form found in post-Ptolemaic nscrr. and papyri—cf. Mayser 241. It occurs in W at Jn 1^{35}.

Final -ν has the same uncertain tenure in MGr that it had in Hellenistic, and the range of its variation has been considerably extended. See Thumb's account, *Handbook* 24 f.

Final ι movable. (3) Final -ι after η or ω—the ι *subscript* of mediaeval and modern writing (see above, § 27)—was in i/B.C. and i/A.D. inserted and omitted so freely in papyri that it may be counted as a movable final indifferent for pronunciation, even beyond -ν. A finely concentrated instance is BGU iii. 883^{2} (ii/A.D.—by which time it was rare) ὀκτῶι, οὐλῆι δακτύλῳ πρώτωι: the ι is in these four words inserted once rightly, twice wrongly, and once wrongly omitted. It might be substituted for the other weak finals, as we have seen: add such exx. as BGU iv. 1188[14] (B.C. 15) εἰς τὴν κώμηι, and conversely Preisigke *Ostr.* 15[7] (B.C. 59) ἀριθμῷν dat. sg. Further instances are given in *CR* xviii. 108a. See in general on the long diphthongs in § 36. Since -ᾱι might be read -ᾰι and so pronounced -ε, the irrational -ι was naturally added to -ᾱ less often than to -η or -ω. The insertion of this irrational ι is best taken as a mere consequence of literary tradition: the proper limits of a now functionless letter were forgotten, and indiscriminate insertion paved the way for impartial omission from ii/A.D. According to Gregory *Prol.* 109 the ι is found very rarely in NT uncials: he quotes ἤιδισαν (=ᾔδεισαν) Mk 1[34] D, ὧι Mt 25[15] U, Lk 7[4] Λ, and ξύλωι Lk 23[31] K. He adds on Scrivener's authority that it is not found subscript in the minuscules before the time of cod. 71 (written A.D. 1160). (See §§ 27, 36.)

PART II.

ACCIDENCE.

The Noun and Verb paradigms that follow are printed in bold type (as **ἡμέρα**) whenever the forms themselves or forms on the same model actually occur in NT. Small type is used, as κύνα, when the word is isolated and only part of its flexion occurs, or when from actual instances in NT it is not possible to make up the flexion of a model word. When there is reason to doubt the continued existence of an inflexional type in Hellenistic, a blank is left.

PART II.

ACCIDENCE.

Definite Article.

§ 48. The forms of the Article should strictly be presented among the other Pronouns, to which it belongs by historical syntax. But in post-Homeric Greek, except for a few uses which will be treated under the Syntax, the Article had detached itself for special functions answering generally to those of our own *the*; and convenience demands that it should be given here. There are no irregularities. The base is *to-*, *tā-*, except in N. sing. m.f., where it is *so*, *sā* (as in Skt, Germanic etc.): this has in Attic and other dialects infected the plur., which was originally *τοί*.

Sing. *N.*	ὁ	ἡ	τό	*Plur.* οἱ	αἱ	τά
A.	τόν	τήν	τό	τούς	τάς	τά
G.	τοῦ	τῆς	τοῦ	τῶν	τῶν	τῶν
D.	τῷ	τῇ	τῷ	τοῖς	ταῖς	τοῖς

NOUNS.

First Declension.

§ 49. This declension includes nouns and adjectives with stems in *-ā*, masculine and feminine, together with those (distinct in their origin) which in Greek show a nom. sing. in *-ι̯ă*, feminine only. The feminine type is original in the *-ā-* nouns also: we shall present it first.

A. Feminine Nouns in *-ā*, *-η*, and *-ă*.

		ἡμέρā day.	*φωνή voice.*	*γλῶσσă tongue.*	*σπεῖρα cohort.*
Sing. *N.*	ἡ	ἡμέρα	φωνή	γλῶσσα	σπεῖρα
A.	τὴν	ἡμέραν	φωνήν	γλῶσσαν	σπεῖραν
G.	τῆς	ἡμέρας	φωνῆς	γλώσσης	σπείρης
D.	τῇ	ἡμέρᾳ	φωνῇ	γλώσσῃ	σπείρῃ
Plur. *N.*	αἱ	ἡμέραι	φωναί	and so	
A.	τὰς	ἡμέρας	φωνάς	all other First Declension words.	
G.	τῶν	ἡμερῶν	φωνῶν	Gen. plur. always perispomenon.	
D.	ταῖς	ἡμέραις	φωναῖς		

The Vocative is identical with the Nominative throughout.

It will be seen that Hellenistic agrees with Attic in its treatment of *ā pure* (see above, § 33). There are two divergences from Attic in this flexion, the first of which affects nouns in -ης as well.

(1) In spelling the dat. sing. in ῃ was unchanged, but in reality it was new. Attic ῃ was pronounced as ει (*ē* close as in *day*), while η was the open *ē* in *there*. Hence nom. and dat. sing. of barytone -η nouns were not mere graphic variants, as in Hellenistic, where η and ῃ were alike close *ē*, while ει was *ī* (as in *machine*). The new dative came from gen.—ἡμέρας : ἡμέρᾳ : : φωνῆς : φωνῇ, aided by the uniformity thus established throughout Decl. I. by nom. and acc. having the same relation to the dative in -ᾱ (-ᾱς) and -η (-ης) nouns alike.

(2) There is a partial levelling of -ᾰ stems: nouns in -ρᾰ and participles in -υῖα follow γλῶσσα in gen. and dat. sing.[1]

(*a*) The evidence of NT MSS is as follows. Μαχαίρης (-ῃ) ℵ $\frac{6}{9}$, B $\frac{4}{7}$, A $\frac{6}{8}$, C $\frac{4}{5}$, D $\frac{1}{2}$, D_2 $\frac{2}{2}$, L $\frac{2}{3}$, Δ $\frac{1}{3}$, W $\frac{0}{3}$, 𝔭[13] $\frac{1}{2}$: add single occurrences in T 33 81 124. Πλη(μ)μύρης $\frac{1}{1}$ in ℵB*LWΞ 33. Πρῴρης $\frac{1}{1}$ in ℵA 33. Σπείρης $\frac{3}{3}$ (Ac) with no serious variant except B in 10[1] and P twice. Σαπφείρῃ $\frac{1}{1}$ ℵAEP. Συνειδυίης $\frac{1}{1}$ ℵABE. In the papyri both -ρης and -υίης are normal A.D., exceptions being about as frequent relatively as in the older NT uncials. In its full development this flexion is characteristic of the second period of the Κοινή (i/A.D. and after), and is therefore only sporadic in LXX. Thackeray's evidence there may prove that the infection started in words with Ionic associations: this suggestion combines the alternatives discussed in *Prol. l.c.* It is difficult to say why the type ὀξεῖα did not conform to the new rule.[2]

(*b*) Στείρᾳ Lk 1[36] has no variant. It is the fem. of στεῖρος (usually of two terminations), and στεῖρα (*sic scrib.*) is a new fem.: see § 64. Note that the irreg. nom. ἑστηκυίη Wis 10[7] ℵ* has no parallel in NT, and very few elsewhere.

(*c*) On the form Νύμφᾰν in Col 4[15] B, as an instance of levelling in an opposite direction, see *Prol.* 48.

(*d*) Στοά (from στοιά) has ᾱ pure after the ι has disappeared.

(*e*) Πρύμνα is found in Ac 27[41] without variant: in cl. Grk πρύμνη alternates with it. In μάμμη and θέρμα, where there is similar fluctuation, the NT exx. are indeterminate (gen. or dat.), while ἄκανθα (Attic) only occurs in plur.: see Thackeray 143, G. Meyer *Gr.*[3] 94.

---

[1] *Prol.* 38, 48. Cf. Thumb *Hellen.* 69 ff., WS 81 n., Thackeray *Gr.* 140–2, Mayser 12 f., Schweizer *Perg.* 40 ff., Kretschmer *Entstehung* 30, Reinhold 48, Hatzidakis 84, *CR* xv. 34, 434 (papyrus evidence up to 1901), and xviii. 108.

[2] Blass and Thackeray would find a motive in Attic -ῦα for -υῖα (Meisterhans 59) which is assumed to make ᾰ impure. But Attic had gen. -ύας, and the power of ι and ρ to influence a following ę had ceased to act centuries earlier. That ἀλήθεια *et sim.* did not follow suit proves nothing, for nouns in -ία would supply a powerful analogy.

§ 50. *B.* Masculine Nouns in -ας and -ης.

	νεανίας *youth.*	κριτής *judge.*	βορρᾶς *north (wind).*	ᾅδης *Hades.*
Sing. N.	ὁ νεανίας	κριτής	βορρᾶς	ᾅδης
V.	νεανία	κριτά	βορρᾶ	ᾅδη
A.	τὸν νεανίαν	κριτήν	βορρᾶν	ᾅδην
G.	τοῦ νεανίου	κριτοῦ	βορρᾶ	ᾅδου
D.	τῷ νεανίᾳ	κριτῇ	βορρᾷ	ᾅδῃ

Non-Greek proper names will be dealt with separately. Greek names in -ᾶς and in -ας *impure* follow normally the third of these models, those in -ας *pure* the first.

(*a*) Βορρᾶς is the usual Κοινή form, though the older Attic βορέας is rarely found. It is not a "contracted noun"—βορέας → βορ̯ᾶς, as στερεός → στερ̯εός → στερρός. Meisterhans[3] 100 thinks the declension was adapted to the analogy of the "originally not Ionic-Attic abbreviated names in -ᾶς." Βορρᾶ gen. is the only NT form, but the whole of the above flexion is found in LXX (Thackeray 143).

(*b*) Ἅιδη only 1 Co 15^{55} ℵ^{c}A^{2} etc.: it is regular (K.Bl. i. 387). The only vocatives found in NT are δέσποτα, ἐπιστάτα, καρδιογνῶστα, ὑποκριτά, Αἰνέα, Ἀγρίππα, and four Hebrew names (see § 60 for foreign names).

(*c*) The gen. in -ου is specifically Attic (*e.g.* even βορροῦ), and naturally the alternative -ᾱ extends itself in the Κοινή, having a certain footing in Attic *Volkssprache*: in Lesbian (G. Meyer[3] 439) and in late Attic we even find exx. of gen. -η from nouns in -ης. (Cf. MGr κλέφτης, gen. -η.) It would probably have spread more if the Ionic had here agreed with the form characteristic of Greek outside Ion. Attic. Greek names in -ας *pure* take -ου, as Ἀνδρέου, Λυσανίου (K.Bl. i. 386 f.)—Josephus however shows many exceptions (Schmidt 489 f.); while those in -ᾶς and -ας *impure* have -ᾶ (-α)—thus Στεφανᾶ, Ἐπαφρᾶ, and (*e conj.*) Ἀντίπα (Rev 2^{13}—see *Prol.* 12). But usage differed for -ας *impure*: cf. Ἀγρίππα P Amh 75 *ter* (ii/A.D.), but Ἀγρίππου BGU ii. $511^{ii. 4}$ (ii/A.D., a copy of an official document of Claudius' reign), and Ἀκύλα in BGU i. 71 (i/A.D.). See Schmidt *Jos.* 487 f. for similar fluctuations in Josephus: -ου here slightly predominates, but -α is common, and greatly outnumbers -ου in other names. According to Herodian (K.Bl. i. 386) πατρολῴας and μητρολῴας (as we spell in NT—see p. 83) had "Doric" gen., but NT has only dat. pl. Cf. Thackeray 162 on the "vulgar and late" use of -α in Hebrew proper names in LXX: also below, § 60 (4).

(*d*) For cases of Metaplasmus see § 54.

§ 51. *C.* Contracted Nouns.

This category includes μνᾶ (like ἡμέρα) and γῆ, συκῆ, like φωνή. They differ only in that the accent is perispomenon throughout. The feminine of contracted adjectives (διπλοῦς, χρυσοῦς, ἀργυροῦς, σιδηροῦς) follows this model, with nom. διπλῆ, χρυσῆ, ἀργυρᾶ, σιδηρᾶ.

(*a*) Χρυσᾶν Rev 1[13] ℵ*AC follows the analogy of ἀργυρᾶν, its natural associate. The pair react on each other in both ways—thus P Lond 124[26] (iv/v A.D.) (=I. p. 122) χρυσᾶν ἢ ἀργυρᾶν, P Leid W [xxiii. 22] (ii/iii A.D.) χρυσῆν ἢ ἀργυρῆν. Blass (p. 25) gives a much less probable account of the genesis of this "gross blunder," as he calls it.

(*b*) Uncontracted forms are occasionally found from χρυσῆ in Rev: χρυσέας 5[8] ℵ, χρυσέων 2[1] AC. See below, § 64.

Second Declension.

(1) *Flexion.*

§ 52. *A.* Masculines and Feminines in -ος, and Neuters in -ον.

	φίλος *friend.*	ὁδός *way.*	τέκνον *child.*
Sing. N.	ὁ φίλος	ἡ ὁδός	τὸ τέκνον
V.	φίλε		τέκνον
A.	τὸν φίλον	τὴν ὁδόν	τὸ τέκνον
G.	τοῦ φίλου	τῆς ὁδοῦ	τοῦ τέκνου
D.	τῷ φίλῳ	τῇ ὁδῷ	τῷ τέκνῳ
Plur. N.	οἱ φίλοι	αἱ ὁδοί	τὰ τέκνα
V.	φίλοι		τέκνα
A.	τοὺς φίλους	τὰς ὁδούς	τὰ τέκνα
G.	τῶν φίλων	τῶν ὁδῶν	τῶν τέκνων
D.	τοῖς φίλοις	ταῖς ὁδοῖς	τοῖς τέκνοις

(*a*) Nearly thirty vocatives in -ε occur in NT: this formation survives in MGr. No feminine -ος nouns in the NT show the vocative. Θεός makes θεέ nearly always in LXX, as in Hellenistic generally (θεός Att.): cf. Thackeray 145, *CR* xv. 34, 434. Τιμόθεε (Lucian) answers to old Attic models. Note υἱός voc. once in Mt (1[20]—υἱέ appears four times): cf. Mayser 256

B. Contracted Nouns.

The norm may be seen in the masc. and neut. of adjectives: thus

Sing. N.	διπλοῦς	διπλοῦν	*Plur.* διπλοῖ	διπλᾶ
A.	διπλοῦν		διπλοῦς	διπλᾶ
G.	διπλοῦ		διπλῶν	
D.	διπλῷ		διπλοῖς	

(*a*) For νοῦς and πλοῦς, originally in this class, see § 59 (4).

(*b*) Open forms, presumably Ionic in origin (Thumb *Hellen.* 63), are found rather freely in the flexion of χρυσοῦς in Rev: thus 2[1] χρυσέων AC, 4[4] -έους א, 5[8] -έας א, 9[20] -αια א, 14[14] -εον (in 38 only); so χάλκεα 9[20] א. Thumb's statement that they were characteristic of the Eastern Κοινή is suggestive in connexion with the curious fact that they are peculiar to Rev. On the other hand the flexion of ὀστοῦν, the only substantive in this class in NT, shows open forms in the plural: ὀστέα Lk 24[39] (-ᾶ DN), ὀστέων Mt 23[27] Heb 11[22] (Eph 5[30] א^{c}D etc.). This differs from LXX, where the rule is that uncontracted forms come in gen. and dat. sing. and plur. (Thackeray 144: see also 172 f. on the adjectives). See *CR* xv. 35, 435; Schmidt *Jos.* 490 ff.; K.Bl. i. 402 (§ 113 n. 3).

(*c*) Χειμάρρου in Jn 18[1] may probably be accented thus (so Blass 25), as coming from a late shortened form χείμαρρος; but χειμάρρους occurs normally in LXX (Thackeray 144).

C. "Attic" Declension.

Strictly this declension affects a few words which by "metathesis of quantity" had substituted -ως for the final -ος. Thus νεώς, λεώς from νηός, ληός, for which Hellenistic replaced (except in the compound νεωκόρος) the general Greek νᾱός, λᾱός.

With a different history we have ἅλως (ὁ) *threshing-floor*, which still survives in LXX and papyri, though replaced in NT by ἅλων (ἡ): its flexion (sing.) is A. ἅλων, G. ἅλω, D. ἅλῳ. In Ptolemaic papyri (Mayser 259) A. plur. ἅλω(ς), G. ἅλων. See in general Meisterhans[3] 129–131.

(*a*) For the neuter ἀνώγεων Ti cites 15 cursives in Mk 14[15] and names two (with "*al*") in Lk 22[12]. See WS 47. It has no classical or Hellenistic warrant.

(*b*) Ἵλεως survives only in the nom. sing. It had been stereotyped largely by the phrase ἵλεώς σοι (etc.) "mercy on thee!": see *Prol.* 240. It was rather more alive in the LXX period—see Thackeray 173.

(*c*) Ἀπολλώς follows this model in N.A.G., with the same fluctuation as in Attic (Goodwin *Gram.* § 199) between -ών and -ώ in acc. Thus 1 Co 4[6] Ἀπολλών א*AB* but Ἀπολλώ Ac 19[1] exc. A[2]L 40. See Meisterhans[3] § 49*d*. There was hardly any difference in sound.

Κῶς in Ac 21[1] has acc. Κῶ exc. in HLP.

Both these nouns have been preserved by the influence of the mixed declension.

(2) *Gender.*

§ 53. (*a*) Neuter plurals attached to a masc. sing. in -ος are still found in NT. They were originally collectives,[1] and some traces of this sense survive.

Δεσμός has plur. δεσμά in Lk 8[29] Ac 16[26] 20[23], δεσμοί

[1] Giles[2] 266 ff.

Phil 1[13], the rest being ambiguous. Thackeray (p. 154) observes that in LXX as in NT *δεσμά* is literary.

Rutherford *Gram.* 9, asserts after Cobet that *δεσμά*=actual bonds, *δεσμοί*=bondage. The distinction cannot be pressed for the NT, though it would suit very well: Ac 20[23] gains vividness from it. The original differentia is in this case almost inverted.

Θεμέλιος (*sc.* λίθος) has masculine forms except in Ac 16[26]. *Τὰ θεμέλια* here shows the collective sense: contrast *οἱ θ.* in Rev 21[19].

It is common in LXX, where the masc. appears rarely. Thackeray (154) suggests that the earlier and later Κοινή levelled in different directions, "the former using the neuter throughout, the latter the masc." Thucydides however has *οἱ θ.* (i. 93) and so has Aristotle. Moeris and Thomas Magister declared the neuter alone Attic: it may be questioned whether they had adequate data. See Mayser 289, Crönert 175.

Σῖτος shows the old plur. *σῖτα* in Ac 7[12] HP, where Blass says *σιτία* does not suit; but see Wendt or Knowling. It survives in two literary LXX books (Thackeray 155).

Στάδιον retains the old double plural, but *στάδιοι* predominates: *στάδια* only Jn 6[19] ℵ*D 106 (against ℵ[a (?)] ABL etc.).

Thackeray assigns *στάδιοι* to the literary element, which NT use makes doubtful. Kälker (p. 239 f.) says that Polybius alternates the forms to avoid hiatus, which makes them mere equivalents.

Λύχνος and **χαλινός** have only masc. plur., as in LXX.

(*b*) Gender fluctuates in the following:—

Ἄβυσσος, an adj., becomes a fem. noun (*sc.* χώρα).

First in LXX (as Gn 1[2]), but a citation from Diogenes Laertius (ii/A.D.) shows it was a "profane" use: see Grimm-Thayer *s.v.*

Ἀλάβαστρος is fem. in Mk 14[3] ℵ[c]BCLΔ, masc. in ℵ*AD etc., and actually stands as neuter in GM 1 13–69 (Ferrar).

LS quote for the neuter Theocritus and the Anthology. The Attic *ὁ ἀλάβαστος* accounts for the second alternative, which occurs in LXX (4 K 21[13] B). Ti quotes a scholiast who writes *τὴν ἀ.*, observing that Herodotus made it masc. Blass (p. 26) says Attic should be *ἡ ἀ.*, though he quotes no authority and admits *ὁ ἀλάβαστος* for Aristophanes and *τὸ ἀλάβαστον* for Menander. The word probably comes from Arabic (see Boisacq *s.v.*), and naturally wavered when a gender had to be found, much as German wavers between der, die and das Awesta.

Ἄμφοδον neut. in Mk 11[4] as usual, but see Mayser 261 n.

Ἄψινθος in Rev 8[11] is ὁ ἄ., but ℵ* substitutes the more usual ἀψίνθιον.

Fem. in Aretaeus (medical—i/A.D.). From a pre-Greek place-name, according to Kretschmer: Boisacq gives Ἀψίνθιοι as a Thracian tribe. WS 83 accounts for masc. in Rev 8[11] by noting it is an angel's name.

Βάτος is fem. according to Moeris in Hellenistic. So in Luke's use: see Blass on Ac 7[35].

Thackeray (p. 145) appears to be wrong in making the LXX masc. the Κοινή norm, unless Moeris is the blunderer. Mk 12[26] has masc. (?). We might read here (with RV and Swete) ἐπὶ τοῦ Βάτου from τὸ "Βάτος," "the *Bush* passage." SH on Rom 11[2] show that ἐν without article is normal in this locution, but their evidence is hardly decisive. The order of the words in Mk favours the RV translation: Luke's change of order and gender may well mean that he took it locally—it was actually "at the Bush" that Moses made the pronouncement.

Δεῖπνον appears as masc. in Lk 14[16] B[3]DΛΠ[2], Rev 19[9] 046 cu[4], 19[17] cu[20]: so MGr.

Ζυγός is regular in the *Κοινή* since Polybius for ζυγόν: earlier masc. only in sense of *balance* (see LS).

Ληνός has (class.) fem. in Rev 14[20] *bis* 19[15]; but in 14[19] τὴν λ. . . . τὸν μέγαν (ℵ corrects)! It is only another instance of the breach of concord familiar in Rev. See Swete, also Charles *in loc.*

Ὁ ληνός is given by LS from Athenaeus xi. 49 (p. 474 fin.), and Is 63[2] (probably wrong—see Ottley *in loc.*). Thackeray quotes cursives of Gn 30[38, 41].

Λιβανωτός is written -ον, neut., in a few cursives at Rev 8[5].

Λίθος is no longer fem. when meaning *gem* (Rev 21[11] etc.): so LXX.

Meisterhans 129 says the fem. is frequent from 385 B.C. If it is specifically Attic, and late at that, it would naturally get no footing in the Κοινή. Cf. ὕαλος below, and see Mayser 262.

Λιμός wavers in gender: the fem. was a Doric element in the *Κοινή* (Thumb *Hellen.* 67) and as such unstable.

Phrynichus says τὴν λιμὸν Δωριεῖς: Lobeck (p. 188) supports it convincingly. Moeris calls the fem. Hellenistic: Mayser (p. 8) emphasises this with evidence. It is sporadic in LXX (Thackeray 146). NT instances are indeterminate except in Luke: fem. is certain in Lk 15[14] ℵABDL, Ac 11[28] ℵBD[2]; but in Lk 4[25] only 13–69 (Ferrar) evidences μεγάλη. See *Prol.* 60 for a case of wavering in papyri written by the same hand, which excuses our seeking an explanation in varying sources used by Luke.

Νῶτος in Rom 11^{10} (LXX) replaces classical νῶτον.

So in LXX, exc. Gen 9^{23} Jer 2^{27} (Thackeray 155).

Σάρδιον is masc. in a good many cursives in Rev 21^{20}.

Στάμνος keeps fem. gender in Heb 9^{4}: masc. in Ex 16^{33} (exc. one cursive).

Mayser (p. 262) cites three papyri (Ptolemaic) for ὁ σ., and notes that Sextus Empiricus gives the masc. as Peloponnesian, fem. as Attic.

Τρίβος (only in a LXX citation) keeps fem. without variant.

It wavers very much in LXX (Thackeray 146).

Ὕελος (or ὕαλος—see § 33. 1) fem. in Hdt. etc., masc. in Rev. 21^{18}.

LS cite Theophrastus for the masc.

Ὕσσωπος indeterminate in NT: see Thackeray 146.

Metaplasmus and Heteroclisis.

§ 54. Fluctuations of gender within the Second Declension have been already dealt with: we present here only Greek nouns which appear in various declensions. Proper names and foreign nouns are treated separately.

A. Declensions I. and II.

-άρχης and **-αρχος** compounds. The Decl. I. form has encroached very largely on the Attic -αρχος. In NT only one word keeps -αρχος without wavering, viz. χιλίαρχος (as LXX). Ἑκατόνταρχος is overwhelmingly predominant in LXX, but WH accept it only 4 times out of 17 places (apart from ambiguous gen. sing. and plur.). Στρατοπέδαρχος appears in HLP *al.* at Ac 28^{16}, but the clause (accepted by Blass for his β-text) has slender authority. No variants occur for ἐθνάρχης, πατριάρχης, πολιτάρχης and τετραάρχης. Ἀσιάρχης only occurs in gen. plur. (Ac 19^{31}), but we should probably accentuate -ῶν (cf. -χην in *IMAe* iii. 525, 526—Thera, ? ii/A.D.).

Ἑκατόνταρχος (excluding gen.) occurs in the great uncials in only five places viz. $\aleph\frac{2}{16}$, $B\frac{5}{12}$, $A\frac{4}{10}$, $D\frac{2}{7}$: WH give in Mt nom. *-ος* dat. *-ῃ*, in Luke *-ης* throughout, but acc. *-ον*. Such mixture is paralleled in papyri: see *CR* xv. 34, 434, xviii. 108, Mayser 256 f., where literature on the subject is given—add Thackeray 156. Mayser observes that *-άρχης* started in Ionic districts (so Herodotus), spread thence into Attic tragedy, and prevailed more and more in the Κοινή. New formations were almost exclusively of this form, while in compounds of numerals and old official titles the other kept its own until the Ptolemaic period was past. Thumb (*Hellen.* 59) calls attention to the significant fact that in Attica *-αρχος* persisted until A.D. (middle of i/A.D., to judge from exx. in Meisterhans³ 125): this will then be an element in the Κοινή decidedly traceable to non-Attic influences.

Δυσεντέριον in Ac 28⁸ ℵAB *al.* for *-ία*, was Hellenistic according to Moeris.

Ἔνεδρον (for *ἐνέδρα*) occurs in LXX (Thackeray 156), but not in NT (Ac 23[16] only HLP).

Ἦχος (masc.) replaces *ἠχή* from Aristotle down. So Heb 12[19], and other places where it might be Decl. III. (see below, B (*a*)).

Θεά seems to have been the *Κοινή* fem. of *θεός*: in Ac 19[37] we find *τὴν θεόν* used as the regular *term. techn.* for the city goddess—see *Prol.* 244.

Blass held that *ἡ θεός* was Hellenistic, except in the formula *ἡ μεγάλη* or *ἡ μεγίστη θεά*: inscriptional evidence from Magnesia strongly supports the other (Kuhring's) view. Ἡ *θεά* appeared in Attica itself in iii/B.C. (and earlier in direct antithesis to *ὁ θεός*): see Meisterhans³ 125.

B. Declensions I. or II. and III.

(*a*) Neuters in *-ος* have increased at the expense of the first and second declensions. This arises naturally from the coincidence of nom. sing. in the masc. and neut. *-ος* nouns, and their nearness in gen. sing., where an *-ς* was easily added or lost. Similarly even in classical times there was confusion between nouns in *-ης* gen. *-ου* (Decl. I.) and those in *-ης* gen. *-ους* (Decl. III.)—cf. G. Meyer *Gram.*³ 439 f. The confusion has developed in MGr: Thumb *Handb.* 64.

Δίψος and *δίψα* both occurred in Attic (Blass 28). NT only 2 Co 11[27], where B* has *δίψῃ*, and the rest *δίψει*.

P Flor ii. 176[12] (A.D. 256), an illiterate private letter, has gen. *δίψης*, while the medical fragment P Tebt ii. 272[17] (late ii/A.D.) has *τὸ δίψος*.

Ἔλεος as neuter always in NT, nearly always in LXX.

See Thackeray's interesting evidence (p. 158) as to the literary character of ὁ ἔ. (Attic) in its few LXX occurrences. (Add that it alternates with τὸ ἔ. in Pss. Sol). Adjectives like ἐλεεινός and σκοτεινός suggest that the neuter forms in these words were survivals. But to prove this we must postulate their coming into the Κοινή through some dialect that preserved the hypothetical old neuter: Brugmann (*Grd.*[2] II. i. 282) treats them as analogical extensions from φαεινός (=φαεσ-νός) and the like. The adj. νηλεής however goes the other way. Ἔλεος masc. only survives in later uncials, with one appearance in C (Mt 23^{23}).

Ἕλκος (τό) has acc. sing. ἕλκον in Rev 16^{2} ℵ*.

Ζῆλος is neuter in Ac 5^{17} B*, 2 Co 9^{2} ℵB 33, Phil 3^{6} ℵ*ABD*FG: ὁ ζ. occurs in seven places (eight, if we followed ℵCD^{c}ω in Gal 5^{20}).

Ὁ ζ rarely occurred in LXX. It is neuter in MGr, which makes for the view (WS 84) that the neuter was popular Greek in Hellenistic times.

Ἦχος is of Decl. II. in Heb 12^{19}, of III. in Lk 21^{25} (neut. or fem.).

In Lk *l.c.* WH (*App.*[2] 165) accentuate ἠχοῦς from ἠχώ f., Ln and Ti ἤχους from τὸ ἦχος. The existence of the latter is proved from LXX (Thackeray 159), and from several quotations collected by Schmiedel (WS 84 n.), who remarks that the meaning *sound* for ἠχώ is only poetical, except in Philo i. 588 and Job 4^{13} (see below). Whether ἠχώ survived in vernacular Greek can hardly be determined. Its influence may perhaps be traced in Job 4^{13}, where ἠχῷ is fem.: should we accent ἠχῷ with ῳ for οι[1] (see § 36)? In Lk perhaps ἤχους is slightly more probable: the OT original (Ps 65^{7}) to which WH assign it has ἤχους acc. pl.—gen. sing. is barely possible. (The ancient conjecture (?) ἠχούσης, found in D and Eusebius, would improve the construction.) Ἦχος is masc. in MGr.

Θάμβος is neuter in NT, but *θάμβου* gen. in Ac 3^{10} C: *θ. μέγας* Lk 4^{36} D.

It is masc. and neut. in classical Greek (Blass 28) and LXX (Thackeray 158).

Νῖκος (τό) has supplanted νίκη in true Hellenistic, though the latter survives in 1 Jn 5^{4}. *Τὸ ν.* in Mt 12^{20}, 1 Co $15^{54. 55. 57}$.

Neut. in BGU iv. 1002^{14} (55 B.C.). The old fem. is literary in LXX

---

[1] Cf. Λητῷ dat. in a Phrygian inscr. (*JHS* iv. 385) *ap.* Dieterich *Unters.* 163.

(Thackeray 157): cf. P Lond 1178[12] (=iii. p. 216), where it is used in a letter of Claudius. See Mayser 93 n.[8] for exx.

Πλοῦτος is neut. in nom. and acc. 8 times in Paul: masc. (nom. acc. gen.) 5 times, and 7 times in other NT writers.

Neut. only once in LXX, Is 29[2] (but ὁ π. BQ). It is MGr.

Σκότος, formerly masc. and neut., is always neut. in LXX and NT.

The gloss *σκότῳ* has intruded in late authorities at Heb 12[18].

Στρῆνος (*τό*) has gen. *στρήνου* in Rev 18[3] C cu[2].

(*b*) Contracted masc. nouns of Decl. II. (substantives only) have passed into Decl. III., with which they already coincided in nom. and acc. sing. (*βοῦς*, *βοῦν*). Thus **νοῦς** makes gen. *νοός*, dat. *νοΐ*, **πλοῦς** gen. *πλοός*.

So even the Atticising writer of 4 Macc (Thackeray 160). To the inscriptional exx. in WS 84 n.[7] add *ῥόας* from *ῥοῦς* P Oxy iv. 736[58] (c. A.D. 1). But *νόῳ* BGU ii. 385[5] (ii/iii A.D., an illit. letter), and Εὔπλοος *REGr* xvii. 205 f. (Rhodes, ii/A.D.). See further evidence in K.Bl. i. 516, G. Meyer 419, Crönert 166. The plural nom. *εὔνους* is found in Attica as early as 300 B.C.: the analogy given above could not have produced this, which is presumably an accus. influencing nom. **Χοῦς** (liquid measure) was declined like *βοῦς* even in Attic, and this may well have affected the other *χοῦς*, "earth" (*χοός*, *χοΐ* in LXX) so starting the type: cf. *χοΐ* in *IMAe* iii. 248 (ii/B.C.). See Mayser 257, whose papyrus evidence shows that the type had not developed far in the first (B.C.) period of the Κοινή.

(*c*) Miscellaneous instances under this heading are—

Ἅλων (*ἡ*, gen. *ἅλωνος*) has replaced *ἅλως* (see above, § 53).

Thayer cites it from Aristotle. In papyri it occurs, but far less often than *ἅλως*: see Mayser 258 f., 287, and add the early instance P Lille 13[3] (243 B.C.).

Γόης makes pl. after Decl. I. *γόηται* in 2 Ti 3[13] D*.

Δάκρυον has the dat. pl. *δάκρυσιν* Lk 7[38. 44], a survival from the old *δάκρυ*, which agrees with *δάκρυον* in nom. acc. gen. pl. See below, p. 141.

Κατήγωρ in Rev 12[10] A is said (WS 85) to be only the Aramaic term קטגור, a Greek loan sent back in damaged condition. But cf. Thumb *Hellen.* 126.

Blass calls in the analogy of *ῥήτωρ*: the two types coincide in gen. pl. Schmiedel compares the late forms *διάκων* for *διάκονος* and *πάτρων* for Latin *patronus* (a loan-word). But this is really an *alternative* to the explanation quoted from him above: these words, for which no foreign borrowing can be appealed to, must be explained by a mixture of declensions characteristic of the later periods of the Κοινή. This is Thumb's view.

Σάββατον was a Semitic word, and should properly come in below (p. 153). But its dat. pl. *σάββασιν* (once in LXX, always in NT) is on a good *Κοινή* model: cf. Lobeck *Par.* i. 175, where grammarians are cited showing that *πρόβατον* made *πρόβασιν* in dat. pl.—this case does not appear in NT.

WS 85 n.[8] cites *σάββασιν* from Jos. *Ant.* xvi. 6^4 and Meleager 83^4. W. F. Moulton (WM 73 n.[1]) gives *σαββάτοις* (the LXX form) from Mt $12^{1.12}$ B. See Schmidt *Jos.* 499 f.

(*d*) Heteroclisis in proper names (non-Semitic) may be noted in the following:—

Θυάτειρα is neuter pl. except in Rev 1^{11} AC 046 *Θυάτειραν* acc. (*-α* ℵ and so WH text), 2^{24} *-ρῃ* dat. $ℵ^c$ vg, and even *-ραις* dat. pl. in late MSS.

Λύστρα similarly has acc. *-αν*, dat. *-οις* in the same context: see *Prol.* 48, § 60 (10) below.

Μύρρα is neut. pl. in Ac 27^5, but 81 reads *Μύραν*, which Ramsay supports from the modern name: the gen. is *Μύρων* (or with *ρρ*).

Σαλαμίς (? nom. *Σαλαμίν* on analogy) has *Σαλαμίνῃ* as "a well attested substitute for" its regular dative (WH *App.*[2] 163): so in Ac 13^5 ℵAEL and some Latin texts—cf. Reinhold 56 for late vernacular evidence. Suidas (p. 413*a* Bekker) gives *Σαλαμίνη* (in gen.) as the older name of Constantia in Cyprus: WS 94 also cites *Salamina-ae* from Justinus for the more famous Salamis near Athens.

Third Declension.

§ 55. In this Declension are grouped together a great variety of stems, all ending in consonants or semivowels (*i̯* or *u̯*). As the semivowels and *σ* fall out between vowels, a good deal of contraction results. A marked feature of the declension is the (very limited) survival of "strong flexion," by which a stem varies through vowel-gradation (*Ablaut*) in different cases. The proper case-terminations will be seen in the types of nouns with consonant stems which do not contract, nor show strong flexion.

A. Stems ending in Mutes.

	σαρκ- (ἡ) *flesh.*	μαστῑγ- (ἡ) *scourge.*	πνευματ- (τό) *spirit.*	παιδ- (ὁ, ἡ) *boy, girl.*
Sing. N.	σάρξ	μάστῑξ	πνεῦμα	παῖς
A.	σάρκα	μάστῑγα	πνεῦμα	παῖδα
G.	σαρκός	μάστιγος	πνεύματος	παιδός
D.	σαρκί	μάστιγι	πνεύματι	παιδί
Plur. N.	σάρκες	μάστιγες	πνεύματα	παῖδες
A.	σάρκας	μάστιγας	πνεύματα	παῖδας
G.	σαρκῶν	μαστίγων	πνευμάτων	παίδων
D.	σαρξί(ν)	μάστῑξι(ν)	πνεύμασι(ν)	παισί(ν)

N.B.—(1) Vocatives will be specially mentioned in this declension whenever separate forms occur. There are none here except **γύναι**: the classical *παῖ* is obsolete.

(2) Monosyllables transfer the accent to the last syllable in gen. and dat.: *παίδων* is an exception.

(3) The acc. sing. in *-αν* is conspicuous in the vernacular throughout the 3rd decl., but the culture level of the documents that exhibit it is decidedly lower than anything we find in NT. It does not appear in Attic inscriptions till the later Roman period:[1] see Meisterhans^3 § 50. 7. For its currency generally cf. Schweizer *Perg.* 156 f., Schmid *Attic.* iv. 586, Crönert 169 (and reff. there), Jannaris pp. 542 f., *CR* xv. 34 f., 435. We will deal separately with the rather different case of *-ν* added to acc. *-η* or *-ῆ*: see below, § 58 (*d*). In LXX (Thackeray 22) the phenomenon is almost confined to ℵ and A; nor is the case very different in NT, for Scrivener (*Collation* p. liv) cites ten exx. from ℵ in NT and fourteen more from Barnabas and Hermas, while A has at least five. The following list is perhaps sufficiently complete. Mt 2^2 *ἀστέραν* ℵ* (for *ἀ. ἐν*), 2^{10} *ἀστέραν* ℵ*C, 5^{36} *τρίχαν* ℵ*EL etc., 9^{18} *χεῖραν* L, 12^{49} *χεῖραν* ℵ*—so far of course A *hiat.* Mt 27^{28} *χλαμύδαν* D, Mk 1^{41} *χεῖραν* Δ*, 6^{27} *σπεκολάτοραν* D*, 7^{30} *θυγατέραν* D, 7^{32} *χεῖραν* D, Jn 6^{54} *σάρκαν* D, 20^{25} *χεῖραν* ℵ*AB, Ac 6^5 *Ἀντιοχέαν* C, 14^{12} *Δίαν* DE *al.*, 16^8 *Τρωάδαν* 61, 17^6 *Ἰάσωναν* D*, 21^7 *Πτολεμαΐδαν* ℵ*, 22^{23} *ἀέραν* ℵ, 1 Pet 5^6 *χεῖραν* ℵA, Heb 8^5 *δειχθένταν* DE (10^{21} *ἱερέαν* L—but here there is *-ᾱ* final, which brings the case near to those in § 58 (*d*) below), Rev 6^9 and 9^4 *σφραγῖδαν* ℵ and a cursive or two, 12^{13} *ἄρσεναν* A, 13^{14} *εἰκόναν* A, 22^2 *μῆναν* A. On the case as it affects the NT, WH (*App.*^{2} 164) pronounce generally that the *ν* is

[1] *Δήμητραν* is printed in the Teubner text of Plato *Cratylus* 404*b*, but silently emended in the Oxford text: its MS attestation can hardly be regarded as evidence here.

due to transcribers, both where added to -ᾰ and in the contracted stems (p. 139). They are influenced by "the irregularity and apparent capriciousness of its occurrence," the generally scanty witness and especially "its extreme rarity in B." To this we may add the curious fact that it appears most often (except for Rev) in the writings where the Greek is good, while the papyri show it characteristically in documents of low culture. In later periods of the Κοινή the levelling process brought the final -ν everywhere into the acc. sing. in popular speech, to disappear again impartially except in certain dialects and under certain *sandhi* conditions. Thus in MGr we find τὴμ πίστι, τὴ μέρα, τὴν ἐρπίδα (πίστιν, ἡμέραν, ἐλπίδα): see Thumb *Hdb.* § 34.

(4) Acc. pl. m.f. in -ες, encouraged by the identity of nom. and acc. in such flexions as πόλις, γραμματεύς, πῆχυς, is fairly common in papyri of early and later periods. It was probably started by τέσσαρες, which in LXX and papyri is far the commonest instance (Thackeray 148): in some kinds of writing it outnumbers τέσσαρας; see *Prol.* 243 f., also 36, where it is noted that there is good uncial authority for -ες in every NT occurrence of the accus. That δύο, τρεῖς, πέντε κτλ. have no separate accus. form is enough to account for this form. Apart from this there are no NT exx.

(1) *Guttural Stems.*

Ἀλωπεκ- (ἡ) *fox*, pl. ἀλώπεκες, has nom. sing. ἀλώπηξ. For gender see under SYNTAX (Vol. III.).

Γυναικ- (ἡ) *woman* makes voc. γύναι (with final κ dropped), and takes for nom. sing. an old 1st decl. stem. γυνή (cf. Gothic *quinō*). Its accent follows the monosyllables—γυναῖκα, γυναικός, etc.

Θριχ- (ἡ) *hair* is affected by the law which forbids successive aspirates:[1] N. θρίξ, A. τρίχα(ν) (see above) D.Pl. θριξί(ν) etc.

Κηρῡκ- (ὁ) *herald*, like *Φοινῑκ-* (ὁ) *Phoenician* *Φηλικ-* (ὁ) *Felix* and χοινῑκ- (ἡ) *quart*, is variously accented in nom. sing. κῆρυξ (WH) and κήρυξ (Ti) according as we accept or reject express statements of ancient grammarians: see § 29, and especially K.Bl. i. 420.

Ὀρνῑχ- (ἡ) *hen*, nom. sing. ὄρνιξ Lk 13[34] אD. Ὄρνις (*q.v.*) is the reading of WH, but the rarer form has a strong claim.

Ὄρνιξι occurs six times in P Lond 131 (i/A.D.) (=i. 109–88). It was mentioned *Prol.* 45. An element drawn from Doric, it was probably

[[1] Aspirated tenues lost the aspirate in primitive Greek when the next syllable or next but one also began with an aspirate. Brugmann *Gr.*[4] 122.—ED.]

dialectic in the Κοινή, just as its descendant ὀρνίχ is local (Cappadocian) to-day. Photius (*ap.* Ti) says it was also used by the Ionians, with the oblique cases. This suits its modern survival very well. Crönert's instances of it (p. 174 n.) should be observed.

(2) *Labial Stems.*

Four nouns in π- and one in β- occur in NT. The nom. of course is in -ψ: there is nothing irregular or noteworthy.

(3) *Dental Stems.*

(*a*) Very many nouns make stem in -δ. Those in -άς gen. -άδος, -ίς gen. -ίδος, -ύς gen. -ύδος, keep the accent on this syllable throughout. In σφραγῑδ- (ἡ) *seal* the ῑ makes all oblique cases (exc. gen. pl.) and the nom. pl. properispomenon (σφραγῖδα etc.).

Συγγενιδ- (ἡ) *kinswoman*, nom. συγγενίς, serves as a Hellenistic fem. for συγγενής. By earlier rule only nouns in -της cf. (προφῆτις, πρεσβῦτις) and -εύς could form such fem. If the rule is to be maintained for later Greek, we might observe that συγγενής has sundry forms from the -ευς flexion (see § 59 (3)).

Ποδ- (ὁ) *foot* keeps its irregular nom. πούς: the rest is normal.

(*b*) Barytones in -ις (gen. -ιτος and -ιδος), being brought by their accent into asssociation with the -*ei̯* stems (§ 59 (1)) had in earlier Greek acc. sing. in -ιν. So in NT προφῆτιν from προφητιδ- (ἡ) *prophetess.* More or less stem-mixture appears in the following:—

Ἐριδ- (ἡ) *strife.* Acc. sing. ἔριν only, but also in pl. we find all the versions (exc. Eth.) supporting ἔρεις in Tit 3[9] (so ℵ[c] AC). WH reject it with ℵ*D*G, one singular being easily assimilated to the plurals around. Where ἔρεις nom. pl. occurs, there is always a variant ἔρις, and we cannot feel any confidence in it. WH place it in margin "with hesitation" at Gal 5[20]. But when ει and ι were identical in pronunciation it is unlikely that such a new form would oust the regular ἔριδες (1 Co 1[11]—no *v.l.*), and produce a needless ambiguity.

Κλειδ- (ἡ) *key* was not originally a δ- stem: cf. Lat. *clāvis*—the gen. κλῃ(ϝ)ῖδος is however as old as Homer. It kept in Attic its proper acc. κλεῖν, pl. κλείς (K.Bl. i. 461): so in NT Rev 3[7] 20[1] and 1[18] respectively, without serious variant, also Lk 11[52] D, Mt 16[19] ℵ[c]B[2]CD *al.* The LXX forms κλεῖδα κλεῖδας (Thackeray 150) stand in Mt 16[19] ℵ*B*L, Lk 11[52] (exc D), and are introduced in cursives (exc Mt *l.c.*): κλεῖδα is expressly said by Moeris to be Hellenistic, and it is also banned by Phrynichus, Thomas and the Antiatticista. But it is odd that Attic κλεῖν and κλεῖδα should appear as well as κλεῖδα -ας in the papyri,[1] and odder still to find the author of Rev. among the Atticists, with the other NT writers using correct Hellenistic!

Νηστιδ- (ὁ or ἡ) *fasting*, which strictly should be called an adj., shows in classical Greek the alternative stems νηστῐ- and νηστει-. Since the -ῐ- stems are obsolete in Hellenistic, we may safely reject νήστῖς as nom. sing. in Dn 6[18] or as acc. pl. in Mt 15[32] Mk 8[3]: it is only Itacism for νήστεις in the latter and νῆστις in the LXX of Dn *l.c.* The stem then may perhaps be set down best as νηστει-; but Phrynichus (Lobeck 326) seems to imply that the Hellenistic word was νήστης: cf. *Syll.* 805[9] (? i/A.D.), and the medical papyrus P Oxy viii. 1088[44] (early i/A.D.). Was the word heteroclite, with 1st decl. forms in the sing.? See WH *App.*[2] 164.

Χαριτ- (ἡ) *grace* keeps Attic acc. χάριν some forty times, but has χάριτα Ac 24[27] ℵ*ABC, 25[9] A, Jude[4] AB, which according to Moeris 213 was Hellenistic. It is well supported in the vernacular of the imperial age: see *CR* xv. 35; Thackeray 150; Mayser 271 f. and reff. there.

(*c*) Stems in -τ are mainly accounted for by the large class of neuters in -ματ-, and by the fem. abstracts in -τητ-. In the former the stem in *-mn̥-* has been extended by fusion with words in *-mn̥to-*. There is a small class of neuters in which hysterogenous -τ- forms have from an early period ousted more original ones from -ασ- base (see § 58 (3)): so κέρας *horn*, τὰ κέρᾱτα, πέρας *end*, τὰ πέρᾰτα, τέρας *marvel*, τὰ τέρᾰτα. The types coincide in D. plur. τέρασιν. Cf. Meisterhans[3] 143.

Ἅλας (τό) *salt*, gen. ἅλατος, has largely driven out the older ἅλς (ὁ). In Ptolemaic papyri and LXX ἅλς predominates (Mayser 286, Thackeray 152); but ἅλας is certain in 2 Esd 7[22] Sir 39[26].[2] In NT ἅλς disappears, except for ἁλί Mk 9[49] D (from LXX) and ἅλα Mk 9[50] acc. But this last may belong to the variant nom. ἅλα (Lk 14[34] *bis* ℵ*D, Mt 5[13] ℵ*bis* DW*bis*, Mk 9[50] LΔ*bis* ℵ**semel*), which appears also in Sir 39[26] ℵBC (ἅλας A). In Lev 2[13] we find ἅλα and ἅλας in the same verse translating the same Hebrew,[3] which starts a possible hint for the genesis of these forms. In 14 LXX occurrences of ἅλα and ἅλας accus. the article is absent, and there is nothing to show gender or number, if it were not for

---

[1] Mayser 272, *CR* xv. 35—add P Oxy iii. 502[34] (A.D. 164) θύρας καὶ κλεῖς.

[2] In a letter dated Jan. 10, 1911, Mr. Thackeray agrees with this statement, and adds that he would now regard "the other exx. of ἅλας (and perhaps ἅλα)" as "probably neuters. The only indubitable cases of the plural are in the local plural phrases ἡ θάλασσα (κοιλάς, φάραγξ) τῶν ἁλῶν. This looks as if the plur. was the regular form for salt-*areas* (salt-marshes etc.) in which the individual lumps or particles were widely distributed."

[3] There are variants both ways, but not in the major MSS: see the Cambridge LXX *in loc.*

17 places where ἁλός, ἁλί and ἁλῶν appear. Very possibly the new noun arose from these ambiguous forms: it may have been encouraged by the formal similarity of two other food-names naturally associated with it, **γάλα** and **μέλι**, which were both neuter. According to ancient grammarians (K.Bl. i. 456) γάλα as well as μέλι had a gen. formed by simply adding -τος, which may have helped the new flexion. The old ἁλός can be cited as late as iii/A.D., in P Lond 1170 *vs.* 124 (= iii. p. 196): cf. WS 90 n.

Γαλακτ- (τό) *milk* has acc. **γάλα**, gen. **γάλακτος**. This and νυκτ- (ἡ) *night*, nom. **νύξ**, are the only stems in which τ follows a mute.

Γελωτ- (ὁ) *laughter* only occurs in nom. **γέλως**, as does ἱδρωτ- (ὁ) *sweat*, nom. **ἱδρώς**. For earlier flexion see K.Bl. i. 516 and 509 f.

Ἐσθητ- (ἡ) *clothing* has acc **ἐσθῆτα** etc., but a heteroclite dat. pl. **ἐσθήσεσι** in Lk 24⁴ (all exc. ℵBD, which have ἐσθῆτι), Ac 1¹⁰ ℵABC: Deissmann supports this with BGU i. 16¹² (159 A.D., as amended, p. 395), and Crönert (p. 173) adds several citations from MSS of Κοινή writers.

Φωτ- (τό) *light* has nom. acc. **φῶς**, and χρωτ- (ὁ) *skin*, gen. **χρωτός**, nom. χρώς. Both have considerable variation of stem in the earlier Greek: see K.Bl. i. 436,511. **Φῶς** is accented like παῖς.

(*d*) The following neuter nouns with -τ- in oblique cases and plural have a divergent nom. acc. sing.:—

Γονατ- *knee* (*i.e.* γονϝ- ατ-) has nom. **γόνυ**, a -ŭ-stem, which was declined throughout in early Greek.

Ὠτ- *ear* has in papyri of iii/ and ii/B.C. a nom. acc. ὦς, levelled from **οὖς** by the influence of **ὦ-α**, ὠσίν etc. (Mayser 5). It is not found in NT.

Two remain of the very ancient declension which had -ρ in nom. acc. sing. and -ατος (= -ṇ-τος) in gen.:—

Ὑδατ- *water* has nom. acc. **ὕδωρ**: the whole flexion occurs in NT.

Φρεᾱτ- (for φρηᾱτ-) *well*, nom. acc. **φρέαρ**, gen. **φρέατος**. It is rarely contracted (φρῆτος) in the vernacular.

(*e*) One -θ- stem survives, ὀρνῑθ-, which has specialised its meaning just as our *fowl* has. **Ὄρνεον** or **πετεινόν** replace it in the wider sense *bird*. It only occurs once, Mt 23³⁷ **ὄρνις** nom.: the parallel passage in Lk 13³⁴ has probably (see (1) above) the dialectic variant **ὄρνιξ**.

In ABLR *al* the reading is assimilated to Mt. If WH are right in calling ὄρνιξ "Western," we have a small point which might go towards locating this type of text in Asia Minor, with Egypt (on the papyrus evidence) as an alternative. More probably ὄρνις is Mt's form and ὄρνιξ that of Luke, who has again refrained it would seem from altering an "incorrect" form of Q. But possibilities are many and evidence ambiguous, so that we must be cautious in inferences.

(4) *Stems in -ντ-.*

These form a special class, because of the phonetic results of the addition of -σ- suffixes: there is also the double type in nom. sing. from stems in -οντ-, which admits of more than one explanation—see Brugmann-Thumb *Gr.* 257.

	ἀρχοντ- (ὁ) *ruler.*	ὀδοντ- (ὁ) *tooth.*	ἱμαντ- (ὁ) *strap.*
Sing. N.	ἄρχων	ὀδούς	ἱμάς
A.	ἄρχοντα	ὀδόντα	ἱμάντα
G.	ἄρχοντος	ὀδόντος	ἱμάντος
D.	ἄρχοντι	ὀδόντι	ἱμάντι
Plur. N.	ἄρχοντες	ὀδόντες	ἱμάντες
A.	ἄρχοντας	ὀδόντας	ἱμάντας
G.	ἀρχόντων	ὀδόντων	ἱμάντων
D.	ἄρχουσι(ν)	ὀδοῦσι(ν)	ἱμᾶσι(ν)

There are no separate Vocatives. Under Adjectives and Participles will be found types of Neuters, and of stems in -εντ-, -ωντ- and -ουντ-. The flexion of the noun types ὀδούς and ἱμάς is incomplete in NT, but adjectives and participles justify their being printed as if complete.

Latin nouns in -εντ- made nom. in -ης (Lat -ēns): Κρήσκης = *Crescens* and Πούδης = *Pudens* (nom.), Κλήμεντος (gen.) = *Clemĕntis* (K.Bl. i. 421).

B. Nasal Stems.

§ 56. In Greek these all end in -ν, through the influence of a final μ becoming -ν in nom. sing. by phonetic rule: thus the very few μ- stems (as χιών, χθών, εἷς) were assimilated.

1. Stems with Strong Flexion.

	ποιμεν- (ὁ) *shepherd.*	ἡγεμον- (ὁ) *leader.*	κυον- (ὁ) *dog.*
Sing. N.	ποιμήν	ἡγεμών	κύων
A.	ποιμένα	ἡγεμόνα	κύνα
G.	ποιμένος	ἡγεμόνος	κυνός
D.	ποιμένι	ἡγεμόνι	κυνί
Plur. N.	ποιμένες	ἡγεμόνες	κύνες
A.	ποιμένας	ἡγεμόνας	κύνας
G.	ποιμένων	ἡγεμόνων	κυνῶν
D.	ποιμέσι(ν)	ἡγεμόσι(ν)	κυσί(ν)

There are no Vocatives surviving here (classical in barytone words, as δαῖμον, κύον). The voc. ἄφρων is presented in the old form ἄφρον in Lk 12[20] KMSUVΠ etc., 1 Co 15[36] KL etc.: there can be no doubt that the better MSS spell here according to Hellenistic use.

(*a*) **Κύων** lost from the earliest times in Greek its *middle stem* in the acc. sing. and nom. pl., where historically it was in place. It is the only ν- stem surviving in NT which preserves the *weak stem*, except the isolated **ἄρνας** (acc. pl.) Lk 10[3], which comes from the long obsolete nom. sing. *Ϝαρήν* (found only in two or three ancient inscriptions). In NT *lamb* is **ἀμνός** (= Lat. *agnus*—generally, as in classical Greek, in nom. sing.) or the derivative **ἀρνίον**: *ἄρνα, ἀρνός* etc. are common in LXX, but rare in papyri (Mayser 284). Dat. *ἄρνασι* occurs in literary Κοινή.

(*b*) The effects of strong flexion are seen, not only in the lengthened vowel of nom. sing., but in dat. pl., where the addition of -σι(ν) to the middle stem would have produced -ειcι(ν), -ουσι(ν). The *weak* stem leaves its traces here, -ἀσι(ν) (= -η -σι) being assimilated in its vowel to the rest of the flexion.

(*c*) About a dozen nouns in NT are declined on these models, and a good many adjectives (like ἡγεμών). One or two late uncials in Lk 14[12] 15[6] spell **γείτονας** with ω.

2. Stems without Strong Flexion.

	Ἑλλην- (ὁ) *Greek.*	αἰων- (ὁ) *age.*	ὠδῖν- (ἡ) *throe.*
Sing. N.	**Ἕλλην**	**αἰών**	**ὠδίν**
A.	**Ἕλληνα**	**αἰῶνα**	**ὠδῖνα**
G.	**Ἕλληνος**	**αἰῶνος**	**ὠδῖνος**
D.	**Ἕλληνι**	**αἰῶνι**	**ὠδῖνι**
Plur. N.	**Ἕλληνες**	**αἰῶνες**	**ὠδῖνες**
A.	**Ἕλληνας**	**αἰῶνας**	**ὠδῖνας**
G.	**Ἑλλήνων**	**αἰώνων**	**ὠδίνων**
D.	**Ἕλλησι(ν)**	**αἰῶσι(ν)**	**ὠδῖσι(ν)**

There are no separate Vocatives here, either in classical or in Hellenistic Greek.

(*a*) One divergence here must be noted, the levelling of the old nom. ὠδΐς *et sim.* to **ὠδῖν**, so as to agree with the rest of the flexion. It is normal in Hellenistic (cf. Mayser 285, Thackeray 151), and is even found in Lucian (δελφῖν, K.Bl. i. 415—as voc.), which strikingly shows how the old -ῖς had faded out of even literary memory. (W and WS wrongly compare κλειδίν from a late writer: it is of course only the vernacular form of κλειδίον.)

(*b*) Two nouns in -αν- are declined on the above model:—**Μεγιστᾶν-** (ὁ) *magnate* (only plural)—nom. -**ᾶνες**, dat. -**ᾶσι(ν)**. **Μελᾰν-** (τό) *ink* (only sing.)—gen. **μέλανος**, dat. **μέλανι**. It is the neuter of **μέλας, μέλαινα, μέλαν** *black* (see § 65 (3) *a*, p. 160).

(*c*) Μην- (ὁ) *month* has without variant the Attic nom. **μήν**, not the older *μείς*. Cases accented regularly, **μῆνα, μηνί, μῆνας**.

(*d*) Besides those already mentioned, there are fifteen nouns in NT declined like **αἰών**, together with the name Σαλαμῖν- (ἡ), like **ὠδίν** (**Σαλαμῖνι** dat.—for a heteroclite variant see above, § 54 *B* (*d*)). The inferior uncials and D would add **μυλῶνι** at Mt 24[41]. It is worth noting that foreign words (**ἀρ(ρ)αβών, λεγιών, κεντυρίων, χιτών**) and late formations make up the bulk of the list, in which **ἀγών, αἰών** (whose ancient locative *αἰέν ever* attests original strong flexion), **κλύδων** (**μυλών**), **χειμών, χιτών** are the only ones that claim classical antiquity. This is due of course to the fact that a simple flexion like this was naturally adopted for new words.

(*e*) Inferior uncials sometimes spell with *ο* for *ω* oblique cases of **ἀρτέμων, ἀφεδρών, κλύδων**.

C. Liquid Stems.

§ 57. **Ἅλς**, the only word with stem in λ, has been dealt with above (p. 132), so that we are exclusively concerned with stems in *ρ*, which are very numerous. In this class occur the most considerable survivals of vowel-gradation in the stem, especially in the old relationship-nouns.

(1) Nouns with Strong Flexion.

	πατερ- (ὁ) *father.*	μητερ- (ἡ) *mother.*	θυγατερ- (ἡ) *daughter.*	ἀνερ- (ὁ) *man.*
Sing. N.	πατήρ	μήτηρ	θυγάτηρ	ἀνήρ
V.	πάτερ		θύγατερ	ἄνερ
A.	πατέρα	μητέρα	θυγατέρα	ἄνδρα
G.	πατρός	μητρός	θυγατρός	ἀνδρός
D.	πατρί	μητρί	θυγατρί	ἀνδρί
Plur. N.V.	πατέρες	μητέρες	θυγατέρες	ἄνδρες
A.	πατέρας	μητέρας	θυγατέρας	ἄνδρας
G.	πατέρων	μητέρων	θυγατέρων	ἀνδρῶν
D.	πατράσι(ν)	μητράσι(ν)	θυγατράσι(ν)	ἀνδράσι(ν)

In the vocative *μῆτερ* is not given, as it is rather unsafe to assume a vocative that does not actually occur. Thus in BGU iii. 846[10] (ii/A.D.) (=Milligan no. 37) we have *μήτηρ* as voc. in an illiterate letter. **Πατήρ** and **θυγάτηρ** as vocatives appear three times each in the Synoptic Gospels in the best MSS (four times in Jn): there does not seem adequate reason (with WH) to accentuate this *πάτηρ* (*App.*[2] 165), as it is simply a nom. used as voc. (cf. **υἱός** above, § 52).

Strong flexion originally required the lengthened stem in nom. sing., the middle in acc. and locative (here = dat.) sing, and nom. plur., and the weak elsewhere. It will be seen that when we put the four nouns together these conditions appear in one or other of them throughout, except in dat. sing., where earlier Greek could use the middle stem (*μητέρι, ἀνέρι*). The weak stem *ἀνδρ-* has a transition sound *δ* between *n* and *r* (cf. our *thunder*). The *-ρᾰ-* in dat. pl. represents vocalic *r̥*.

Γαστερ- (*ἡ*) (*belly*), *womb*, is declined and accented like **πατήρ** but shows only dat. sg. **γαστρί** (and nom. pl. **γαστέρες**=*gluttons* in a quotation from Epimenides (vi/B.C.) at Tit 1[12]).

Ἀστερ- (*ὁ*) *star* might historically be placed here, though it has levelled away its gen. and dat. sing. into **ἀστέρος, ἀστέρι,** for its dat. pl. was *ἀστράσι(ν)*. But although this occurs in late writers, it cannot be shown to survive in the vernacular. In NT, where the whole flexion occurs except dat. sing. and pl., it is perhaps significant that **ἄστροις** appears in Lk 21[25], where *ἀστράσιν* would have served equally well. Crönert 173 quotes *ἀστῆρσι* and *ἀστέροις* as MS readings in Geminus, a writer of i/A.D.

(2) Stems with partial Strong Flexion or none.

	ῥητορ- (*ὁ*) *orator.*	*σωτηρ-* (*ὁ*) *saviour.*	*χειρ-* (*ἡ*) *hand.*	*μαρτυρ-* (*ὁ*) *witness.*
Sing. N.	**ῥήτωρ**	**σωτήρ**	**χείρ**	**μάρτυς**
A.	**ῥήτορα**	**σωτῆρα**	**χεῖρα**	**μάρτυρα**
G.	**ῥήτορος**	**σωτῆρος**	**χειρός**	**μάρτυρος**
D.	**ῥήτορι**	**σωτῆρι**	**χειρί**	*μάρτυρι*
Plur. N.	**ῥήτορες**	**σωτῆρες**	**χεῖρες**	**μάρτυρες**
A.	**ῥήτορας**	**σωτῆρας**	**χεῖρας**	**μάρτυρας**
G.	**ῥητόρων**	*σωτήρων*	**χειρῶν**	**μαρτύρων**
D.	*ῥήτορσι(ν)*	*σωτῆρσι(ν)*	**χερσί(ν)**	**μάρτυσι(ν)**

No Vocatives are found.

(*a*) The classical type *ῥῆτορ* is pointedly set aside in the recurrent LXX *κύριε παντοκράτωρ*; nor is the old *σῶτερ* (abnormal in a word with *-τήρ -τῆρος*) traceable in LXX or NT.

(*b*) Papyri and inscriptions guarantee datives like *Φιλομήτορσι, Σωτῆρσι,* and the gen. *σωτήρων*, which do not occur in NT.

(*c*) Two nouns in *-ήρ -έρος* may be declined after *ῥήτωρ mutatis mutandis*, but with no warrant for a dat. pl. (*φράτερσι* occurs in Attic). *Ἀερ-* (*ὁ*) *air* has nom. **ἀήρ**, acc. **ἀέρα**, gen. **ἀέρος**. For **ἀστήρ** see above, *C* (1).

(*d*) The real stem of χείρ is *χερσ-*, whence χειρός and χερσί came phonetically, the nom. being made up afresh from oblique cases (G. Meyer[3] 414).

(*e*) Like *μαρτυρ-* (sing. only) is *πῠρ-* (*τό*) *fire*, with nom. acc. πῦρ, gen. πυρός, dat. πυρί. The nom. μάρτυς occurs eight times in NT, with no sign of *μάρτυρ* : for the loss of *ρ* see Brugmann *Grundr.*[2] I. 435.

(*f*) There are five nouns in NT (one only in nom. sing.) with decl. after *σωτήρ*, and eight or nine after *ῥήτωρ*. The two in *-ηρ -ερος* may be added, and a compound each of *χείρ* and *μάρτυς*. On κατήγωρ see above, § 54 *B* (*c*).

D. Stems in *-σ-*.

§ 58. Since original *σ* disappeared in Greek between vowels, there are contractions of concurrent vowels in these stems everywhere except in nom. (acc. neut.) sing. and dat. pl. This class is in Hellenistic practically confined to one type, neuters in -ος, which in oblique cases show vowel-gradation (-εσ-).

(1) *Stems in -ος : -εσ-.*

	ἐθνεσ (*τό*) *nation.*	*συγγενεσ-* (*ὁ*) *kinsman.*
Sing. N.	ἔθνος	συγγενής
A.	ἔθνος	συγγενῆ (= - ε(σ)α)
G.	ἔθνους (= - ε(σ)ος)	συγγενοῦς
D.	ἔθνει (= -εσ-ι)	συγγενεῖ
Plur. N.	ἔθνη (= -εσ-ᾰ)	συγγενεῖς (= -εσ-ες)
A.	ἔθνη	συγγενεῖς
G.	ἐθνῶν (= -εσ -ων)	συγγενῶν
D.	ἔθνεσι(ν) (= -εσ-σι)	συγγενέσι(ν)

(*a*) Συγγενής was properly an adjective : its flexion as such is given as a model below, p. 162. Note another dat. pl. of this word, *συγγενεῦσιν* Mk 6[4] B*LΔ *al.*[6] 33 1 etc. (13) etc. *al.*[2] (*-έσιν* ℵACD*W *al.*), Lk 2[44] LWXΔΛ 1 etc. 13 etc. 33 *al.*[10] (*-έσιν* ℵABCD *al.*). Cf. 1 Mac 10[89]. The MSS which give this form in Lk (where all the great uncials have the normal form) have evidently been influenced by Mk, whose use of this vernacular heteroclisis is characteristic : since the passages are not parallel, Luke has not his common motive for using a popular form. The plurals of nouns in *-ής* and *-εύς* coincided in Hellenistic in nom. and acc., and the sing. in dat. ; while fluctuating usage in contraction would bring together acc. sing. and gen. pl. as well. In this case the plural of γονεύς would be the principal force. For other exx. of συγγενεῦσι, also *συγγενέων*, *συγγενέας* and acc. sing. *συγγενέα*, see Thackeray 153 n.[2], Crönert 173. WS 89 cites an Atticist's ban as evidence for *συγγενεῦσιν*.

(*b*) The acc. pl. masc. and fem. is borrowed from the nom.: otherwise -έας contracted to -ῆς would have been found.

(*c*) Gen. pl. without contraction appears in **ὀρέων** Rev 6^{15}, and **χειλέων** Heb 13^{15}, apparently with no variants: contracted forms occurring are **ἐθῶν, ἑλκῶν, κτηνῶν, μελῶν** (*bis*), **ἐθνῶν** (43 times), **ἐτῶν** (14 times), and in the adjective formation **ἀσεβῶν** (*ter*), **ἀσθενῶν** (*bis*), **συγγενῶν** (*bis*). The disparity is very great, but in the two words affected the open form seems firmly established: it is always found in LXX (**ὀρέων** some seventy times, **χειλέων** forty), while **ἔτος** and **σκεῦος** have -ῶν but **τεῖχος** usually -έων (gen. pl. not in NT): see Thackeray 151. For outside evidence see *CR* xv. 435, Mayser 17, 277, Crönert 172, Schweizer 153, Nachmanson 135. It seems clear that the uncontracted form was throughout kept mainly for certain words: *a priori* we should assume that these came into use in the Κοινή especially from districts (Ionic or other) in which the open forms were normal, but it would be hard to prove it. Schweizer himself expresses this as his opinion immediately after citing the evidence which shows that -ῶν was normal (even τειχῶν) in Pergamum—Ionic territory! Nachmanson's exx. prove the same for Magnesia: we may admit that neither touches ὄρος or χεῖλος. The infection did not reach Egypt, where P Tor 13^{14} βλαβέων (B.C. 137) is the only early example. See Thackeray 144, 151.

(*d*) The addition of -ν in acc. sing. masc. or fem. is distinguished from the case of -ᾰν (above, § 55) by the stronger influence of the 1st decl., combined with the strong tendency to add irrational final ν after *long* vowels. With *short* finals it was much less common. The -ης nouns in 1st and 3rd decl. agreed originally in nom. and dat. sing. (ει and ῃ being identical in Attic, though not in Κοινή); and the dropping of the gen. -ς was as easy as the adding of ν. Hence even in iv/B.C. proper names of 3rd decl. preferred -ην: Σωσθένην in Ac 18^{17} is Attic. See K.Bl. i. 512 f. But the later extension (ἀσφαλῆν etc.) is less obvious than it would seem, for the datives were no longer identical in sound—ῃ and η alike were ẹ̄, while ει was ī (see § 24). More serious is the difficulty of the accent. If the analogy of Decl. I. was still the operative force, we should naturally write συγγενήν, like κριτήν; but it is hardly likely that the addition of so fugitive an element—added so recklessly, as we saw (§ 47), to all manner of long vowel endings—should have altered the circumflex to an acute. We may regard it then as a special case of "irrational -ν," encouraged largely by the analogy of other accusatives in -ην: cf. the raising of the "freak" ἦν into something like a regular flexion form by the fact that it coincided with an existing form in the conjugation of **εἰμί**. It is presumably only a coincidence that in Lesbian Aeolic the -ης proper nouns took a flexion modelled on 1st decl. (Thumb *Dial.* 262). The occurrences of this -ῆν acc. in NT may be summarised thus: αἰσχροκερδῆν Tit 1^{7} FG, ἀσεβῆν Rom 4^{5} ℵD*FG, ἀσφαλῆν Heb 6^{19} ACD*P, αὐθαδῆν Tit 1^{7} FG, μονογενῆν Jn 3^{16} cu^{3} (including 13–346) Heb 11^{17} D*, ποδήρην Rev 1^{13} A cu^{1}, συγγενῆν Rom 16^{11} AB*D*, ὑγιῆν Jn 5^{11} ℵ*W, 7^{23} L, Tit 2^{8} G.

(*e*) The Attic acc. sg. **ὑγιᾶ** occurs in three cursives (incl. 1) at Tit 2^{8}.

(2) *Stems in -οσ-.*

One noun, once used, survives from this rare declension.

Αἰδοσ- (ἡ) *modesty*, makes nom. *αἰδώς*, gen. αἰδοῦς (= -οσ-ος). The type reappears among the adjectives and participles, where it accounts for the forms without ν in the -ίων comparative, and for some of the perf. partic. act. For these see § 65.

For the similarly declined ἠχώ see below, § 59 (6).

(3) *Stems in -ασ-.*

Two nouns show traces of this type, never common; and (as might be expected) levelling has worked even here. But see *Κοινή* instances in Schweizer *Perg.* 156.

Γηρασ- (τό) *old age* occurs in dat. Lk 1[36] γήρει—so all uncials and many cursives. Papyrus instances of γῆρ-ας -ως and -ᾳ are given in *Vocab. s.v.* *Kaibel* 426 (Christian) has γῆρος nom.

Γήρει is best taken as a simple assimilation to the -ος nouns. But it may be Ionic, for Herod. has κέρεος κέρει etc., and Homer οὔδεος οὔδει from οὖδας. Attic κνέφας has gen. κνέφους.

Κρεασ- (τό) *flesh* forms κρέα in Rom 14[21], 1 Co 8[13]: the plural is collective. Herodian says the *Κοινή* pronounced κρέᾰ, as from Homer down (K.Bl. i. 431). Other nouns of this class have passed into the -t- class: see § 55 (3) *c*.

§ 59. *E.* Stems in Semi-vowels.

(1) *Stems in* ει : ι *and* ευ : υ.

	πόλει- (ἡ) *city*.	σῑνᾱπει- (τό) *mustard*.	πηχευ- (ὁ) *ell*.
Sing. N.	πόλις	σίναπι	πῆχυς
A.	πόλιν	σίναπι	πῆχυν
G.	πόλεως	σινάπεως	πήχεως or πήχεος
D.	πόλει	σινάπει	πήχει
Plur. N.A.	πόλεις		πήχεις
G.	πόλεων		πηχῶν (πήχεων)
D.	πόλεσι(ν)		πήχεσι(ν)

Both in form and in accent the flexion of the πόλις type presents obvious irregularities, which are however all classical. Nouns in -teị (-σις, except πίστις) form the bulk of this class, which includes also one masculine noun, ὄφις *snake*, and a few more feminines. The neuter only occurs in one form, and was never more than sporadic among nouns. The papyri show the nouns ἄμι, σέσελι, στίμι, κόμμι, πέπερι —all foreign, like σίναπι itself. For corresponding forms in *-eụ-* we have mostly to refer to the adjectives. The common noun πῆχυς is the only one occurring in NT, and there are hardly any others in Hellenistic: its flexion is guaranteed from other Hellenistic sources. *Ἄστυ city*, the only native neuter, was obsolete.

The influence of the commoner *-u-* nouns is seen in the form πήχυος gen. P Oxy ii. 242[15] (A.D. 77). The LXX gen. sing. is πήχεος (Thackeray 151), but πήχεως (as Attic) appears in BGU iii. 910 [ii. 9] (A.D. 71). In the plural πηχῶν is always found in papyri, and has the additional recommendation of being δεινῶς ἀνάττικον for Phrynichus: see Mayser 267. I. is suggestive that in P Flor ii. 262[6] (ii/A.D.) πηχεων has the ε erased, The Attic form occurs often in LXX (Thackeray *l.c.*), and in Jn 21[8] AW, Rev 21[17] ℵ.

(2) *Stems in -υ-.*

	σταχυ- (ὁ) *ear of corn.*	ὀσφυ- (ἡ) *loins.*	δάκρυ- (τό) *tear.*
Sing. N.	στάχυς	ὀσφύς	(δάκρυ)
A.	στάχυν	ὀσφύν	(δάκρυ)
G.	στάχυος	ὀσφύος	(δάκρυος)
D.	στάχυϊ	ὀσφύι	(δάκρυϊ)
Plur. N.	στάχυες	ὀσφύες	δάκρυα
A.	στάχυας	ὀσφύας	δάκρυα
G.	σταχύων	ὀσφύων	δακρύων
D.	στάχυσι(ν)	ὀσφύσι(ν)	δάκρυσι(ν)

Δάκρυ is an isolated word, for which the heteroclite sing. N.A. δάκρυον appears in NT. The sing. certainly was obsolete in the *-υ* form, and in the plur. it is only the dat. (also Attic) that fixes it here.

K.Bl. i. 438 f., 488 follows Herodian in circumflexing sing. N.A. of the oxytone words ὁ ἰχθῦς *fish*, ἡ ὀφρῦς *brow* and ἡ ὀσφῦς. Brugmann *Grd.*[2] II. i. 137 does the same. Historically the *υ* is long in these oxytona—cf. Skt. *bhrūs brow*—the dat. pl. being shortened to match the barytones. See also Chandler § 620. Ὁ βότρυς *bunch of grapes*, ἡ ἀχλύς *mist*, ἡ ἰσχύς *strength* and ἡ ὗς *sow* are the only other words in this class. For small traces of the old acc. plur. in -ῦς for ύας see Thackeray 147; there are no signs of it in NT.

(3) *Stems in -ευ-.*

βασιλευ- (ὁ) *king*.

Sing. N.	βασιλεύς	*Plur. N.V.A.*	βασιλεῖς
V.	βασιλεῦ	*G.*	βασιλέων
A.	βασιλέᾱ	*D.*	βασιλεῦσι(ν)
G.	βασιλέως		
D.	βασιλεῖ		

So a dozen common nouns in NT. The flexion is like that of the later Attic, with no sign of the old acc. pl. in -έᾱς. Note that ὁ ἁλιεύς *fisherman* dissimilates ι to ε before the ῑ sound in plur. ἁλεεῖς, as in LXX (Thackeray 84). On heteroclite dat. pl. συγγενεῦσιν from συγγενής see above, § 58 (1). There are no traces of the not uncommon acc. sing. βασιλῆ.

The primitive noun Ζεύς (*I.E. dyēus*, gen. *diu̯ós*, with strong flexion) appears in the acc. Δία Ac 14[12] (Δίαν DEHLP[2]) gen. Διός.

(4) *Stems in -ου-.*

βου- (ὁ) *ox*.

Sing. N.	βοῦς	*Plur. N.*	βόες
A.	βοῦν	*A.*	βόας
G.	βοός	*G.*	βοῶν
D.	βοΐ	*D.*	βουσί(ν)

Ὁ νοῦς *mind*, ὁ πλοῦς *voyage*, ὁ χοῦς *dust*, have in Hellenistic transferred themselves to this class from Decl. II.: νοῦς is the only one in NT that has unambiguous forms of this flexion (G.D. sing.). See copious Hellenistic citations in WS 84 n., also Schmid *Attic.* iv. 24, 586.

(5) *Stem in -ᾱυ-.*

Ἡ *ναῦς ship* has acc. ναῦν in a passage which seems to be a literary reminiscence: cf. *Prol.* 25 f. The word with its medley of irregular forms naturally gave way to πλοῖον in the vernacular.

(6) *Stem in -οι̯.*

A few nouns, declined in sing. only, followed the norm of πειθοι- (ἡ) *persuasion*, which still is found in a papyrus of ii/A.D. (P Oxy iii. 474[37]).

N. πειθώ (or -ῴ)	*G.* πειθοῦς (= -όι̯ος)
A. πειθώ (= -όι̯α : accent irreg.)	*D.* πειθοῖ (= -όι̯ι)

See K.Bl. i. 453 f. The flexion concerns us if we regard ἤχους in Lk 21[25] as ἠχοῦς from ἠχώ *sound*: so WH. See above, §§ 54, 58 (2). In 1 Co 2[4] πειθοῖ is an extremely probable reading, involving only the dropping of c before another c, and the acceptance of the reading of FG omitting λόγοις. *Πειθοῖ* was read by the old Latin and the Sahidic and Peshitta: the adj. π(ε)ιθός cannot be proved to have existed at all. See § 35 (p. 78).

Declension of Semitic Names.

§ 60. The Greek Bible presents a very obvious contrast to writers like Josephus[1] in its treatment of Semitic names, which are very largely left indeclinable. Thackeray (*Gr.* 160) gives as the general rule for the LXX that

Names which in the Hebrew end in a consonant remain unaltered (Ἀδάμ, Ἀβραάμ, Δαυείδ, Ἰσραήλ, Ἰωσήφ etc.), while those which end in a vowel, especially in ָיה, are in most cases declined like nouns of the first declension, the feminines requiring no addition in the nominative, the masculines taking on the termination -ίας and being declined like Νικίας. Names ending in other vowels are either Hellenised by the addition of ς and form a new class of first declension names in -ᾶς, -ῆς, -οῦς etc. (Ἰωνᾶς, Μωυσῆς, Ἰησοῦς etc.), or remain indeclinable (Ἠλειού).

Since these rules may be transferred to the NT with little modification, it will be convenient to follow Thackeray's paragraphs and apply them successively.

A. Personal Names.

(1) *Indeclinables.*—The extent to which the use of indeclinable forms prevails is well seen in the genealogies of Mt 1 and Lk 3. In the former there are 46 names (42 men and 4 women), of which Ἰούδας, Σολομών,

[1] The contrast may be well seen in WS 91, where the Graecised proper names of Josephus and others are quoted in abundance. I have not thought it worth while to repeat them here.

Οὐρίας, Ὀζείας, Ἑζεκίας, Μανασσῆς, Ἰωσείας, Ἰεχονίας and **Ἰησοῦς** are declined: it is curious that **Ἀβιά** (N.A.G.) is not treated like other names in ־יָה, but the LXX (Ἀβιού in Kings, Ἀβιά in Chr) does the same. Of the 75 names in Lk 3[23ff.] none can be taken with perfect certainty out of the indeclinable category, though indecl. Ματταθιού (vv.[25. 26]) has no LXX authority, and Ἰησοῦ and Ἰούδα *bis* are presumably also from nom. in -ας. Λευεί *bis* probably is as elsewhere from Λευείς, but there is no strong reason for assigning to the Mixed Decl. (see (6) below) the other names with vowel endings. A summary may be added of Semitic names in NT (incl. Ἀκελδαμάχ, Βοανηργές, γέννεα, μαμωνᾶς, Σαβαώθ and χερουβείν) as in WH text:—

Ending in . .		α.	β.	γ.	δ.	ε.	η.	θ.	ι.	κ.	λ.	μ.	ν.	ρ.	ς.	τ.	υ.	φ.	χ.	ω.	
Persons, etc.	Decl. .	10	..	..	..	..	1	..	..	..	..	..	1	..	57	..	..	..	..	..	= 69
	Indecl.	12	4	2	6	4	..	5	9	6	20	20	19	14	7	5	2	2	6	1	=144
Places.	Decl. .	15	..	..	..	..	2	..	..	..	..	..	3	..	3	..	..	..	..	..	= 23
	Indecl.	8	..	..	..	..	1	..	1	..	..	9	8	2	1	2	..	..	..	1	= 33

To these should be added 28 gentilic names and the like derived from Semitic words: see (16).

(2) *Declension II.*—A few names have been Graecised in this way, viz. *(?)Ἄγαβος, Ἁλφαῖος, *Βαρθολομαῖος, Βαρτίμαιος, *Ἐλισαῖος, †Ζακχαῖος, *Ζεβεδαῖος, Θαδδαῖος, †Ἰάειρος, *Ἰάκωβός (not the patriarch, nor the person named in Mt 1[15f.]), Λάζαρος, Λεββαῖος (in δ-text, perhaps a duplicate of Λευείς), Μαθθαῖος, Μάλχος, *Σαῦλος (against Σαούλ as name of the king, and in a direct citation of Aramaic). Those marked * are names which are only indeclinable in LXX; in those with † the NT form is anticipated in LXX, with or without alternative. It should be added that Ἰάκουβος occurs once in LXX text (1 Es 9[48] A). We find Δανιήλου in Mt 24[15] D, Γαμαλιήλου Ac 22[3] B. (I have excluded Τιμαῖος above on the same principle as Σίμων in (7) below, *q.v.*: Βαρτίμαιος is counted.)

(3) *Feminines in Decl. I.*—Here we have Ἄννα (nom. only), Εὕα, Ἰωάνα (nom.), Μάρθα, Μαρία, Ῥεβέκκα (nom.), Σάρρα, Σουσάννα (nom.), also Σαλώμη. As in LXX the gen. and dat. are always -ας -ᾳ: so Μάρθας Jn 11[1], as well as Μαρίας and Σάρρας.[1] The variations in the name Μαρία are complex. In the gen. Μαρίας stands "virtually without variation" (WH) for all the women so named; and "Mary of Clopas is always Μαρία (nom.[8]), as is (acc.[1]) Paul's helper (Rom 16[6])," where, however, ℵD$_2$ read Μαριάμ. The mother of Jesus WH always give as Μαριάμ (nom., voc., acc., dat.), except in Mt 1[20] (BL 𝔭[1] 1), Lk 2[19] (ℵ*BDR); but even here ℵCDWω and ALWω could be quoted if we preferred to

[1] WS 92 quotes K.Bl. i. 381, where it is observed that names in Attic of foreign origin often keep -ᾱ throughout. Cf. Λύδδας in (10) below; also Τα]μύσθᾳς gen. in BGU iii. 883[5] (ii/A.D.).

make the rule absolute. The name appears thus, except in the genitive, "usually without important variation." They make the same rule for Mary of Bethany, though here they are content once with 33 as sole authority. The perpetual variation of the uncials, even in a continuous narrative like Jn 11, is inexplicable. Thus for Μαριάμ nom. in Jn 11[20] there is nothing but 33, in [32] we have BC*EL 33; for it is as acc. the range is less remarkable. Again in Lk 10[39] Μαριάμ nom. is in ℵCLPΞW 1 33, against AB*Dω: in [42] B and 1 alone support it. Only two or three MSS are consistent: B 33 have -μ 8/10 while ℵW have -α -αν 9/10. For Mary of Magdala the case is still more complex: see WH *App.*[2] 163, and add that W has -μ 3/13. Gregory (Ti iii. 116) notes that ℵD prefer the declined, and BLΔ the indeclinable form: it will be clear, however, that there are great inconsistencies, and a rule seems unattainable.

Σάπφειρα (dat. -η—see p. 118) belongs to this section if taken directly from Aram. שַׁפִּירָא "beautiful." If it is fem. of σάπφειρος it is Hebrew ultimately, for the name of the gem was naturalised in iv./B.C. Blass rightly prefers the former, but thinks the common noun influenced it (*Gr.* 7 n.: cf. WS 76).

(4) *Masculine names* in יָה־ (etc.), from the name יהוה. There are about a dozen of these in NT, declined like Νικίας, with voc. -α and gen. -ου. This is the Greek rule for -ας *pure* (K.Bl. i. § 105. 9). So Ἁνανία; Βαραχίου, Ζαχαρίου, Ἠσαίου, Ἰερεμίου, Ματταθίου, Οὐρίου. The only question arises with Ἠλείας, which in Lk 1[17] makes gen. Ἠλεία ℵBLW 565** (-ου ACD etc.), but in Lk 4[25] Ἠλεί -ου without variant. (In both places late uncials accent -οῦ or -ού, reading the indeclinable form found in the LXX (historical books): that the later LXX books (Mal, Sir, 1 Mac) show Ἠλείας confirms the reading of the better MSS in NT). Thackeray 162 argues the -α genitive "vulgar and late": this difference of Greek culture between the sources which Luke reproduces in these two places would be quite in keeping with their style.

Other masculines of Decl. I. are Μεσσίας, Ἰωάνης, Ἰσκαριώτης (Ἰσκαριώθ in Mk and in Lk 6[16]).[1] Note the dat. Ἰωάνει $\frac{4}{5}$ in WH: it will be explained like Μωυσεῖ below.

(5) The difficulty discussed under this section does not arise in NT. Ἀβιά Mt 1[7] is necessarily indeclinable, not being gen.: the possible accentuation Ἠλειοῦ or -ού was mentioned in (4).

(6) *Mixed Declension.*—This is a large type in NT, and need hardly be set down (with Thackeray) to Hebrew influence. For although it contrasts with the form prevailing in Egypt (Ἰησοῦς Ἰησοῦτος and the like), it tallies with a type used in Greek abbreviated names (Δημᾶς -ᾶ etc.) and in Roman masc. names like Ἀκύλας gen. Ἀκύλα.[2] It is moreover identical with the sing. flexion of a mass of MGr nouns—γέροντας A.G. γέροντα, κλέφτης A.G. κλέφτη, παπᾶς A.G. and Voc. παπᾶ, παπποῦς

[1] Note also Σκαριώθ Mk 3[19] and Lk 6[16] D. In Jn D has Ἰ. ἀπὸ Καρυώτου (exc. 6[71]), and in Lk 22[3] Ἰσκαριώδ.

[2] As early as Plato (*Phaedrus* 274*d*) we find the Egyptian name Θαμοῦς with acc. -οῦν, gen. -οῦ; but the crucial dat. does not occur there, so that Winer's citation is not decisive: it is only like νοῦς.

A.G. παππου̂. Many of these make plur. in -δες, as παπάδες, combining these alternative flexions. Βορρα̂ς is an Attic prototype. The general formula is that the bare stem, in a long vowel or diphthong, forms the gen., dat., and voc. if any, while -ς is added for nom. and -ν for acc. Only a few call for note :—

(*a*) In -ας or -α̂ς. Ἰούδας (with voc. Ἰούδα) is constant in NT, there being no sign of gen. Ἰούδου or of indecl. Ἰουδά. So Ἄννας, Ἁρέτας, Καιάφας, Κηφα̂ς, Βαρνάβας, Ἰωνα̂ς, Κλωπα̂ς, μαμωνα̂ς, Σατανα̂ς, Σκευα̂ς, Χουζα̂ς, to mention only those that have the gen. Σίλας (-αν -ᾳ) (=שְׁאִילָא) is not contracted from Σιλουανός, which is a case like Σίμων in (7) below (Dalman *Gramm.* 124).

(*b*) In -η̂ς. Μανασση̂ς may as well be counted here, though -ν is not attached in acc. : LXX has Μανασσή indecl. for the tribe, which is equally possible for Rev 7[6]. Μωυση̂ς has been transferred from the Mixed Decl. (normal in LXX) to a new flexion universal in and after i/A.D., with very marked Hellenisation. We may conjecture that the dat. -ει̂ began the type, as a natural dat. for a nom. in -η̂ς, and that the circumflexed -ει̂ led on to a gen. -έως and even an acc. -έα (Lk 16[29] all MSS), on the analogy of βασιλει̂ -έως -έα. The flexion thus agrees (as WS 94 notes) with that of Ἄρης in class. Gk. Μωυση̂ν the ordinary acc., and Μωυση̂ (Ac 7[44], under LXX influence) are the only survivals of the Mixed flexion. See WH *App.*[2] 165. Ἰωση̂ς makes gen. Ἰωση̂ Mt 27[56] ABC *al.*, Mk 6[3] ACW, 15[40] ℵ*ACW *al.*, [47] CW *al.* ; but Ἰωση̂τος Mk 6[3] BDLΔ 33 13 etc. (Ferrar) 565, 15[40. 47] same (exc. D at [47]). This last flexion has abundant analogues in papyri, but is solitary in NT, which makes for its genuineness.

(*c*) In -εύς. Λευείς in NT conforms throughout to this type.

(*d*) In -ου̂ς. Ἰησου̂ς has been assimilated to this class, the LXX dat. Ἰησοι̂ yielding to Ἰησου̂ (as in the Freer MS of Dt).

(7) *Names in* ων.—Σίμων -ωνος is declined fully, but it is rather a case of appropriating a Greek name of similar sound than adapting a Semitic one : Συμεών (indecl.) is the Semitic original. Similarly men named Jêshû could either adapt the name as Ἰησου̂ς or appropriate the Greek Ἰάσων. The only other name in -ων that is declined is that of Solomon. Thackeray shows that the Hellenising of שְׁלֹמֹה took the following order : (*a*) in orthography (1) Σαλωμών (2) Σαλομών (3) Σολομών, (*b*) in flexion (1) indeclinable (2) gen. ω̂ντος (3) gen. -ω̂νος. (See his note as to the phonological meaning of the successive spellings.) Of (*a*) (1) and (2) we have some traces in NT : thus nom. Σαλωμών Ac 7[47] ℵAC, and Σαλομ. in Mt 1[6] ℵ* 1, Ac 3[11] A 5[12] ℵ. For (*b*) (1) there is only Mt 1[6] Σαλομών acc. ℵ 1, Jn 10[23] W. For (2) the evidence is considerable. Σολομω̂ν (so accent) -ω̂ντος, like Ξενοφω̂ν -ω̂ντος and several Egyptian names, is supported by late uncials generally, with WΔ in Mt 1[6], C (*semel*) Δ Mt 12[42], CKLW *al.* Lk 11[31] *bis*, ℵ[c]AKLW etc. Jn 10[23] ; and it must be read in Ac throughout—3[11] ℵABCP 1. 33 *al.* (-ω̂νος DE 104), 5[12] ℵA 33 *al.* (-ω̂νος BDEP *al.*), 7[47] accent Σολομω̂ν (WH). The late uncials in accenting the nom. perispomenon agree with their preference for -ω̂ντος, which may

have been due to LXX influence : it is the only declined form that has even begun to appear there.

B. Place Names.

(8) *Places and peoples.*—Thackeray notes that "the Hellenised forms largely predominate" here. The table in (1) so far bears this out for the NT, in that indeclinable forms outnumber inflected by 43 per cent. in place-names, but by 110 per cent. in person-names.

(9) *Place-names in -a feminine.*—So Γάζα -αν (LXX gen. -ης), Σαμαρία -ας,[1] Λύδδα -ας (but see (10)), Ἰδουμαία -ας, Ἁριμαθαία -ας, Βηθανία -ας etc. Χαρρά -ᾶς is found twice in LXX, but χαρράν indecl. usually, and so in NT. As with the four feminine personal names in -α which only occur in the nominative (see (3) above), we are sometimes left without conclusive proof of their proper category : see (11) *b*. A place-name which almost becomes a common noun is γέεννα, gen. -ης (acc., gen., dat. sing.).

(10) *Towns in -a.*—Declined as neuter plural alone are Σόδομα (as LXX) and Σάρεπτα (acc. only, but LXX gen. -ων). Metaplasmus is conspicuous here. Λύδδα is twice acc. Ac $9^{32. 35}$ ℵAB 33 (hiat. v.^{32}), where CEω assimilate to the fem. form Λύδδας in v.^{38} (Λύδδης there in Eω): analogy of other forms proves this form Decl. II. and not indecl. (as Hort). Γόμορρα, in LXX and 2 Pet 2^{6} (Σοδόμων καὶ Γομόρρας), rather strangely fails to agree with its constant associate. In Mt 10^{15} however we have Γομόρρων. A non-Semitic NT name which behaves in the same way is Λύστρα, acc. -αν, dat. -οις. See Thackeray 167 f. and *Prol.* 48 for sundry parallels : add P Grenf ii. 74 (A.D. 302), where we have ἐν Τεντύρῃ *bis*, the village being elsewhere Τέντυρα neut. pl. Similarly the Zoroastrian capital Ragha appears in Tobit with Ῥάγας (acc) and Ῥάγῃ, against Ῥάγων -οις. WS 93 notes the varying flexion in 1 Mac of Ἁδιδά (indecl., dat. -οις), Βαιθσουρά (indecl., fem., neut. pl.), and Γαζάρα (fem. and neut. pl.).

Declined in 1st decl. only are Γάζα -αν, Βηθανία (but see (11) *b*), γέεννα, Σαμαρία (see also 14).

The examples of metaplasmus just given show that in foreign names it was rather the rule than the exception. This accounts for the flexion of the name *Jerusalem* when declined. Mt 2^{3} πᾶσα Ἱεροσόλυμα is of course fem., as in Tob 14^{4} B, and Mt 3^{5} may show the same. These are the only places where the word is nom., and the rule may be that Ἱεροσόλυμα in nom. follows the gender of ἡ Ἰερουσαλήμ, and passes into 2nd decl. for oblique cases.

(11) *a.* Ἱεροσόλυμα and Ἰερουσαλήμ.[2] The indeclinable continues the LXX tradition, for Ἱεροσόλυμα only appears in Tobit and Maccabees : even in these it is only invariable in 2–4 Mac (1 Mac $\frac{4}{60}$, Tob $\frac{8}{18}$, and not

[1] Σαμαρείας gen. in P Petr ii. p. 14, a papyrus of iii/B.C., relating to a settlement of Jews in the Fayyûm, mentioned by Josephus : see *Tebtunis Pap.* ii. p. 401.

[2] For the breathing see above, § 40.

without variants). Usage in NT varies largely, and without very obvious motive. It may be presented thus :

	Mt.	Mk.	Jn.	Lk.	Ac 1–12	Ac 13–28	Rom.	1 Co.	Gal.	Heb.	Rev.	
Ἰερουσαλήμ *N.*	...	...	...	1	...	1	...	...	1	...	...	= 3
,, *V.*	1	...	...	1	...	...	...	...	...	...	...	= 2
,, *A.*	...	...	...	12	11	10	2	1	...	...	2	=38
,, *G.*	...	...	...	9	4	1	1	...	...	...	1	=16
,, *D.*	...	...	...	3	7	2	1	...	1	1	...	=15
Total . .	1	...	...	26	22	14	4	1	2	1	3	=74
Ἱεροσόλυμα *N.*	2	...	...	...	...	...	...	...	...	...	...	= 2
,, *A.*	7	7	4	3	1	11	...	...	3	...	...	=36
,, *G.*	2	3	2	...	2	2	...	...	...	...	...	=11
,, *D.*	...	...	6	1	2	5	...	...	...	...	...	=14
Total . .	11	10	12	4	5	18	...	...	3	...	...	=63

The figures are for WH *text*. The only places where variants have any real support are :—Ἰερουσαλήμ Mk 11[1] A *al*, Ac 15[4] ℵCDE *al.* (against AB 81 vg), Ac 20[16] ℵAE 33 *al.* (against BCD etc.), and some places where only the case is concerned. It should be added that the "We" passages of Ac have Ἰερουσ. 3 times and Ἱεροσ. 4 ; while Q shows Ἰερουσαλήμ voc. (Mt 23[37] = Lk 13[34]), and according to Harnack also in Lk 4[9] (where however Mt has not the name). In writers who use both forms—which does not include Mt, since his one instance of the indecl. comes from Q – it has been largely assumed that (as Grimm puts it) "a certain sacred emphasis . . . resides in the very name" where the indecl. form is used. This may account for a good many passages, but other forces are likely to have co-operated. Since Luke uses Ἰερουσαλήμ 48 times in the Palestinian narrative (Ev, Ac 1–12) against Ἱεροσόλυμα 9 times, while in Ac 13–28 the proportion is markedly reversed (14 : 18), it is clear that he keeps the LXX form as congruent with the atmosphere of his story till he emerges into the Gentile world, where the Jews' capital was vaguely supposed to have some connexion with the Solymi (neighbours of the Lycians) and the name had been fixed by popular etymology.

(11) *b. Indeclinables in -α* are Δαλμανουθά (*si v.l.*), Κανά, Μαγδαλά (CM boh *al.*—the true reading is Μαγαδάν), Σινά. Βηθαβαρά [1] and Ῥαμά occur in the dative, and we could write -ᾷ if we liked; similarly ambiguous are Βηθζαθά with its variants (nom.), and Γαββαθά (probably nom.[2]). Γολγοθά is classed as indecl., though Γολγοθάν acc in Mk 15[22] might be assigned to the nom. Γολγοθά of Jn 19[17] and (probably[2])

[1] The true reading is Βηθανίᾳ. Burkitt assigns the variant to the influence of syr[vt].

[2] The syntax is like that of Ἐλαιών in Lk 19[29] : see *Proleg.* 69, 235, and Thackeray 23.

Mt 27[33]. If it is indecl., the -άν and -ά forms will have the same relation as in the certainly indecl. Βηθσαιδάν and -ά: this account is more probable. Βηθανία, normally declined, occurs as Βηθανιά indecl. in Mk 11[1] B*, Lk 19[29] ℵ*BD* 131, Mk 11[12] H. A special difficulty occurs with the name of Nazareth: it is written *e.g.* Ναζαρά (ἡ, indecl.) Mt 4[13] B*Z 33, Lk 4[16] ℵB*Ξ 33; Ναζαρέτ Mt 2[23] ℵDL, Lk 1[26] ℵBL, Ναζαρέθ Mt 21[11] ℵBCD etc., Ac 10[38] ℵBCDE, and in Δ and other MSS sometimes Ναζαράθ (-άτ). See WH *App.*[2] 167, Ti on Lk 1[26]. WH assert that the tangle "presents little ambiguity," and print -ά in Mt 4[13] Lk 4[16], -έθ later in the Gospel story (Mt 21[11]) and Ac *l.c.*, with -έτ elsewhere "certainly or probably." Sanders (p. 21) says that in W Ναζαρέτ occurs four times in Lk, who has Ναζαρέθ once (4[16]): this however stands alone in the other Evv, except for Mt 21[11] -έτ. Dalman (*Gr.*[2] 152) appears to trace the two types to נָצְרָה (Ναζαρά) and נְצָרַת respectively. The exact Greek name of this obscure little place, which was never heard of till the Gospel story was current, might easily fluctuate in oral and written sources.

In -η there is only Βηθφαγή indecl. Ἰόππη, a town in early contact with the outside world, naturally took a Greek flexion.

In -ω we find Φαραώ and the place-name Ἰεριχώ indecl.

(12) *Place-names in* -ων.—Thackeray makes the interesting point that these "are declined or indeclinable mainly according to their rank and situation on or away from the main routes." This obviously suits the NT names Βαβυλών -ῶνος, Σιδών -ῶνας; nor need Σαρῶνα from Σαρών rank as a serious exception, though indecl. in LXX. Uninflected are Μαγεδών (Rev 16[16] after Ἅρ—the compound phrase prob. nom.: see above, p. 148 n.[2]) and Αἰνών, Σιών. Κεδρων raises a difficulty in Jn 18[1]. In A(S)YΔ 123 latt syrr arm we find τοῦ Κεδρών, which would represent the indecl. found in LXX. But ℵ*DW a b sah aeth read τοῦ κέδρου, and all the other Greek MSS τῶν κέδρων, with boh Orig Chr. These would plausibly figure as independent attempts to regularise the reading of A, regarded as Greek; and so Lightfoot (*Bibl. Essays* 174) actually read. But it seems better with WH to accept τῶν κέδρων as a Greek popular etymology of Kidron: it is needless with them to labour a proof that this etymology was correct.[1] The Hellenised form starts in LXX, 2 K 15[23], 3 K 15[13]. An interesting parallel occurs in Ps 82[10], where "some inferior MSS" (Lightfoot) have τῶν κισσῶν, making Kishon into "ivy brook."

(14)[2] *Names of countries or districts.*—Thackeray shows that these were normally expressed by feminine adjectives in agreement with χώρα understood. The oldest suffixes were -ίς (-ίδος), -(ε)ία (-ας), and -ική (-ῆς) which are used for places away from Palestine. Ἀραβία, Σιδωνία and Συρία are NT representatives, with Σαμαρία as an old name of a district within Palestine. Φοινίκη is also Semitic in origin, but is of course not formed in this way: it is not included in the table above, being naturalised very early in Greek language history. About 200 B.C. the

[1] O. Schrader, *Reallexicon d. idg. Altertumskunde*, 926, gives a very different account of κέδρος, which originally meant "juniper."

[2] (13) does not concern Semitic words; nor have we NT instances for (15).

old indeclinables for names of Palestinian districts began to be replaced by adj. in *-αία* and *-(ε)ῖτις* (*-ιδος*): for the latter we may quote the appearance in Ptolemaic papyri of adjectives like *ξυλῖτις* (*γῆ*), *ἀμπελῖτις* (*γῆ*) "land under trees" or "vines," and Greek names like **Τραχωνεῖτις.** So *αἰγιαλῖτις γῆ* P Lond 924[7] (A.D. 187–8) (=III. p. 134)="land on the border of the lake." This last has no Semitic representative in NT: the *-αία* form appears in **Ἰτουραία, Γαλιλαία, Ἰουδαία, Ἰδουμαία. Ἀβειληνή** uses another adj. suffix.

(16) *Gentilic names*—of tribes, parties and inhabitants of towns or districts—are as in LXX formed largely with the adjective suffixes noted in (14), all of course native Greek. In *-αῖος* we have **Γαλιλαῖος, Ἑβραῖος** (fem. **Ἑβραΐς** as an adj.), **Ἰουδαῖος** (whence adj. **Ἰουδαϊκός**, and adv. **-κῶς**, and the verb **Ἰουδαΐζειν** and its derivative **Ἰουδαϊσμός**), **Καναναῖος, Ναζωραῖος, Σαδδουκαῖος, Φαρισαῖος, Χαλδαῖος, Χαναναῖος.** In *-είτης*, **Ἐλαμείτης, Ἱεροσολυμείτης, Ἰσραηλείτης, Λευείτης, Νινευείτης, Σαμαρείτης** (fem. **Σαμαρεῖτις**). In *-ηνός*, **Γαδαρηνός, Γερασηνός** (**Γεργεσηνός**), **Δαμασκηνός, Ναζαρηνός, Μαγδαληνός** (only fem.): this is hardly represented in the LXX. The less used suffixes are (1) *-ος* in **Σύρος**, (2) *-ιος*, **Σιδώνιος, Τύριος**, (3) *-ισσα* (fem.), **Συροφοινίκισσα**, (4) consonant noun, **Ἄραψ**, n. pl. **Ἄραβες** (D* *Ἄραβοι*).

The variation between Ναζωραῖος and Ναζαρηνός has been the basis of much theorising: it must be left to the Semitist to find out loose stones in these structures.[1] The former is used exclusively in Mt, Jn and Ac, the latter in Mk. Lk has both, in 18[37] and in 4[34] 24[19]. Luke presumably took *-ηνός* over from Mk in 4[34], and from the sources of his Resurrection story in 24[19]. Mark's form is obviously more closely related to Ναζαρά (*-έτ, -έθ*): Ναζωραῖος seems to be coloured by some popular etymology, or to represent some other word. Dalman (*Gr.*[2] 178) makes Ναζωραῖος "reproduce נָצוֹרַי, from the by-form נָצוֹרַת, synonymous with נָצְרַת," from which "נָצְרַי would be expected."

Declension of Non-Semitic Names.

§ 61. There is not much to remark in the flexion of Greek names, or even of Latin or other foreign names outside the Semitic. They may be briefly classified according to their declension.

(*a*) **Decl. I. and II.**—*Feminines in -ā and -η* are Εὐοδία (so certainly from the context in Ph 4[2. 3] (*αὐταῖς*)), Βερνίκη, Χλόη and such Latin names as Ἰουλία, Κλαυδία, with place-names Ἀπολλωνία, Ἀχαΐα etc., Ἰταλία, Σπανία, Λιβύη, Μιτυλήνη, Ῥώμη and various others, derived often from native names in sundry languages. In the *-ᾰ class* (gen. *-ης*) we should

[[1] See now *The Beginnings of Christianity*, I. i. 426 ff., Appendix B, Nazarene and Nazareth, by G. F. Moore.—Ed.]

put Νύμφα (see *Proleg.* 48), Σάπφειρα (§ 60 (3): ultimately, and perhaps immediately, Semitic), Τρύφαινα, Τρυφῶσα, and Latin names like Πρίσκα and Πρίσκιλλα (only nom. acc.), Δρούσιλλα (dat. -ῃ);[1] Ἀντιόχεια, Βέροια. In some of these the complete equivalence of ι and ει in Hellenistic makes the spelling, and therefore the accent in nom. and acc., indeterminate. There is no adequate reason to alter the classical spelling where we have evidence of it: see *Proleg.* 46f. and § 35. The plural names Ἀθῆναι, Κεγχρεαί, Κολοσσαί, Συράκουσαι are classed here. Neuter plurals in -α are Θυάτειρα, Λύστρα, Μύρρα, Πάταρα. But metaplasmus is here strongly felt: see above, § 54.

Masculine person- or place-names in Decl. I. include (*a*) Greek names, normally declined, such as Αἰνέας, Ἀνδρέας, Ἁδρίας, Ἅιδης, Λυσανίας, Ἡρῴδης, Σωσθένης, Εὐφράτης (old Persian *Ufrâtu*, in Greek since Herodotus), Ἀσιάρχης (see § 54) and two in -ίτης; (*b*) Greek and Latin names with gen. -α or -ᾶ, which might be classed with the Mixed Declension. See § 60 (6) above.

Second Declension names are naturally numerous. Masculine personal names in -ος call for no comment. Many of them of course are Latin, coming from Decl. II. names. Place-names of towns or islands in -ος are feminine, as Ἄσσος, Ἔφεσος, but plurals masculine, Φίλιπποι and Ποτίολοι (both indeterminate in NT). Among names of countries we have ὁ Πόντος (gender indeterminate in NT), but ἡ Αἴγυπτος (Ac 7[11] and probably [36]—Blass's "wrong reading" in the former only disagrees with his own conjectural emendation). Adjectives are numerous, as Ἁδραμυντηνός, Ἀσιανός, Βεροιαῖος, Ἑλληνικός. The Mixed Declension rather than the obsolete "Attic" is responsible for Ἀπολλώς acc. -ώ or -ών gen. -ώ (Blass -ῶς -ῶν -ῶ), and for ἡ Κῶς acc. Κῶ: see § 52 *C* (*c*). Neuter place-names are Ἰκόνιον, Ἰλλυρικόν etc. Πέργαμον acc. may be from either -ος fem. or -ον neut.: "ἡ Π. in Xenophon, Pausanias and Dion Cassius, but τὸ Π. in Strabo and Polybius and most other writers and in the inscriptions" (Swete on Rev 2[12]).

(*b*) **Decl. III.**—Normal consonant nouns, Greek or Latin, such as Φῆλιξ -ῖκος, Φοῖνιξ -ῖκα, Αἰθίοψ -οπος, Κρής -τός, Ἑλληνίς -ίδος, Καῖσαρ -αρος, Μνάσων -ωνος, Γαλλίων -ωνος, Ἕλλην -ος, need only be named. On Σαλαμίς (metaplasmus) see above, § 54. With strong flexion we have Μακεδών, Ἰάσων and Φιλήμων -ονος, Φλέγων -οντος, Νικάνωρ -ορος. Stems in semi-vowels are Νηρεύς, Ἀντιοχεύς and other gentilic adjectives; compounds of πόλις, declined like the noun;[2] Σύρτις and Σάρδεις (pl.); Στάχυς (acc. -υν) and Ζεύς acc. Δία gen. Διός. It should be noted that in Ac 16[11] Νέαν Πόλιν ℵABD[2] (against CD*ω) and Col 4[13] Ἱερᾷ Πόλει (where MSS are indeterminate) the writing *divisim* agrees with earlier Greek rules: cf. Ἄρειος Πάγος Ac 17[19. 22] (whence regularly Ἀρεοπαγείτης *ib.*[34]). See on this rule further § 106 below.

A special case under this heading is the name of the Mount of Olives,

---

[1] But note gen. Σεκόνδας P Oxy ii. 294[9] (A.D. 22).

[2] Ἱερὰ πόλις and Νέα πόλις are best written *divisim*: see § 106. For Πρόπολις see *Proleg.* 228.

on which it will be enough to refer to the discussion in *Proleg.* 69, 233 (*Einl.* 104 f.). There I have tried to show that Ἐλαιών, a common noun =*oliveyard*,[1] occurring very frequently in the papyri, is beginning to be used as a proper name to be a short substitute for τὸ ὄρος τῶν ἐλαιῶν : we are to print πρὸς τὸ ὄρος τὸ καλούμενον Ἐλαιών (nom.) or Ἐλαιῶνα with W in Lk 19^{29} and (εἰς τὸ κτλ.) 21^{37}, and retain Ἐλαιῶνος with all MSS in Ac 1^{12}, the καλούμενον being an indication, common to Luke and Josephus, that the adaptation had not yet thoroughly established itself.

The **Gender** of Proper Names shows few irregularities. *Towns* are fem., except when the suffix determines otherwise ; *streams* follow ποταμός[2] and *hills* ὄρος in gender, but instances are few. Among *personal names* naturally the gender determines itself ; but there is the curious *Q'rî perpetuum* of ἡ Βάαλ Rom 11^{4}, and always in LXX in the later books (Chron, Prophets and Tob) : in Gen—4 K only thrice (4 K $1^{6.\,16}$, 21^{3}) except as a variant in A only. (In *Proleg* 59 (=*Einl.* 88) I have unaccountably given it as occurring only three times in LXX.) The *Q'rî* is actually written in 3 K $18^{19.\,25}$ οἱ προφῆται τῆς αἰσχύνης, and in the marginal gloss in Q at Jer 11^{13} τη αισχυνη θυσιαστηρια. The explanation, due to Dillmann, "has superseded all others" (SH on Rom 11^{4}). Χερουβείν is neut. pl. in Heb 9^{5}, as in Philo and generally in LXX, presumably following the association with ζῷα. LXX has χερούβ sing. masc. four times, once neut. ; χερουβίμ (when treated as pl.) masc. four times, neuter twenty. Josephus *Ant.* viii. $3^{72f.}$ has τὰς χερουβεῖς. (In *Ant.* iii. 5^{137} WS wrongly infers οἱ χ. : αὐτούς there refers to πρόστυποι.)

Miscellaneous Foreign Words and Irregular Flexions.

§ 62. In addition to the proper names already catalogued, there are a few Semitic words in NT, written in Greek characters, which may be collected here, though some of them are not nouns.

(*a*) *Indeclinable nouns, or vocatives.*—Ἀββά (אַבָּא Aramaic of אב in *stat. emphat.*) is exactly translated by ὁ πατήρ, used in address : see *Proleg.* 233 ; Ῥαββεί (רַבִּי Aram.) διδάσκαλε Jn 1^{38} and Ῥαββουνεί (רַבּוֹנִי Aram. "mein Gebieter," Dalman *Gramm.*[2] 176) ; Ῥακά, an Aramaic term of contempt (רֵיקָא, *ib.* 173)[3]—all these appear only in address, and do not develop into regular nouns. The question has been raised whether Μωρέ in Mt 5^{22} is to be read as Greek—so="Fool !" in the ethical sense (RV text)—or as the Hebrew מֹרֶה : cf. Num 20^{10}, where LXX οἱ ἀπειθεῖς. Field (*Notes in loc.*) observes that no other pure Hebrew word appears in

---

[1] How fertile this formation was in the vernacular may be seen in the list collected *s.v.* Ἐλαιών in *Vocabulary.*

[2] Thus τὸν Σιλωάμ *ter* : contr. Josephus *Wars* v. 4^{2}, 12^{2}, ἡ Σ., *sc.* πηγή.

[3] Dalman suggests that the word took the form ῥακά instead of ῥηκά because of similarity of sound to ῥάκος "rascal." It must be admitted that this is a sufficiently rare meaning of ῥάκος (*ib.* 173 n.[2]).

NT except through the medium of the LXX; while Zahn (*Matthäus* p. 225 n.) shows that Jewish Midrash writers took מוֹרֶה in voc. as a Greek word. This seems decisive, added to the obvious consideration that Mt's Greek readers would naturally have been warned if the author had meant them to take the familiar word as Hebrew. Πάσχα (Aram. פִּסְחָא), μάννα (מַנָּא), and σίκερα (Aram. שִׁכְרָא, according to Dalman[1] *Gr.*[1] 126 n.[2]) are indeclinables. So also the plural Χερουβείν (Heb. כְּרוּבִים, with Aram. pl. ין״): see above, § 61. This last has been included among the proper names. So has Ἀκελδαμάχ, in Ac 1[19] tr. χωρίον αἵματος (חֲקַל דְּמָא), where Dalman 202 says the final -χ is sign of the indeclinable.[2] The NT has no trace of declined forms πάσχων, μάννας or -ης, σίκερος or -ατος, οἱ or αἱ Χερουβεῖς, which are found in sundry writers (WS 91 f.); nor again of the Hebrew form φασεκ for πάσχα (LXX.)

(*b*) *Nouns with Greek suffixes and flexion.*—Ἀρ(ρ)αβών, -ῶνος (see § 41) was borrowed in iv/B.C. from Phœnician (Heb. עֲרָבוֹן). Γέεννα (originally γαί., as in Jos 18[16] B) = Heb. גֵּי־הִנּוֹם, Aram. גֵּיהִנָּם, with final ם dropped (Dalman[2] 183): it has been included among place-names above, as also Σατανᾶς among the person-names (Heb. שָׂטָן, Aram. סָטָנָא). So too μαμωνᾶς (= מַאָמוֹן "deposit," according to Dalman[2] 170 n.), and σαβαώθ (pl. of צָבָא "army"). Κορβανᾶς "treasury" (Mt 27[6]) is inflected (Aram. קָרְבָּנָא), while κορβάν, in Mk 7[11] tr. δῶρον, is in Dalman's view (*Gr.*[2] 174) a Hebrew word (קָרְבָּן). In Decl. II. we have βάτος (בַּת), κόρος (כֹּר) and σάτον (סְאָה), all Hebrew measures, but the form of the last clearly depends on Aram. סָאתָא. So with the thoroughly Hellenised σάββατα —for decl. see § 54 *c*—which Dalman ([2] 160) thinks was spelt with τ for θ in virtue of its Greek ending. Συκάμινος is supposed to have been borrowed from Heb. שִׁקְמָה, at least as early as Theophrastus (iv/B.C.): popular etymology doubtless affected it. That in OT it is exclusively plural suggests that an Aram. שִׁיקְמִין started the form: the sing. שִׁיקְמָא is cited in BDB.

(*c*) *Semitic quotations.*—Some fragments of original Semitic language appear in NT, simply transferred as spoken. From the *ipsissima verba* of Jesus we have Ἀββά (glossed ὁ Πατήρ), ῥακά (see (*a*) above), ἐφφαθά *be opened* (אֶפְּתַחָא—Dalman[2] 278 n.), Ταλιθὰ κούμ (טַלְיְתָא קוּמִי, in which the ־ִי had become silent—see Dalman[2] 150, 321), and Ἐλωΐ Ἐλωΐ λαμὰ σαβαχθανεί. In this last (Mk 15[34] WH) there has been slight Hebraisation, which D carries further by substituting ζαφθανεί for the verb. See Dalman[2] 156, 221, 365: he makes the Aramaic original to have been אֱלָהִי אֱלָהִי לְמָא שְׁבַקְתַּנִי. The bearing of Mark's authentic record on the question of our Lord's ordinary language is obvious: had it been words

---

[1] Apparently dropped in ed.[2]—by oversight?

[2] See however WS 63 n., quoting Kautzsch.

of a sacred text that rose to His lips, we should have had Hebrew—the Aramaic attests the speech in which He most naturally expressed Himself when there was no question as to making others understand. In this category of *Dominica verba* we should include ἀμήν *truth!* It established itself in the Christian vocabulary because of its characteristic use by Jesus: Jn shows (cf. also Mt 5^{37}) that He was wont to double it for emphasis. Dalman[2] 183 gives אָמֵן as Aramaic, but notes (243) that Rabbinic literature has no parallel to such a phrase as ἀμὴν λέγω ὑμῖν. Ὡσαννά *save!* (הוֹשַׁע נָא, Dalman[2] 249) comes from the Gospel story, but was well established among the Jews. Another Jewish liturgical term taken over was ἀλληλουιά *praise ye Jah!* (= הַלְלוּיָהּ—Dalman[2] 191 n.[2]). Μαρανα θά is of special interest, as found only in a letter addressed to Greeks (1 Co 16^{22}: cf. *Didache* 10^{6}). Dalman (*Gr.*[2] 152 n.[3]) makes it מָרַנָא תָא *our Lord, come!* (ἔρχου Κύριε in Rev 22^{20}). See Findlay *in loc.* A password in a foreign language, which embodied the Christian hope so as to be unintelligible to the uninitiated, is a very natural and suggestive touch in the picture of the primitive Church. Dalman's note seems to dispose of an alleged grammatical difficulty.

Variants in MSS where these Semitic words are reported belong to a Semitic grammar: I have merely reproduced Dalman, with the ordinary pointing in place of the supralinear vowels.

(*d*) In a category by itself comes Rev 1^{4} ἀπὸ ὁ ὢν καὶ ὁ ἦν καὶ ὁ ἐρχόμενος. It is deliberately left in nom. after ἀπό "in order to preserve the immutability and absoluteness of the divine name from declension" (Moffatt). The writer aimed at focusing in a phrase the LXX and Targums view of Ex 3^{14}: cf. also Heb 13^{8}. A further *tour de force* makes "the He was" serve as correlative to the present ὁ ὤν, there being no participle to express the continuous past. A Greek might have said ἀπ' ἐκείνου ὃς ἔστι καὶ ἦν καὶ ἔσται: cf. the well-known line—

Ζεὺς ἦν, Ζεὺς ἔστιν, Ζεὺς ἔσσεται· ὦ μεγάλε Ζεῦ.[1]

Winer's parallels from Greek philosophical writing—μετὰ τοῦ ἕν, χωρὶς τοῦ ἕν, τοῦ μηθέν (Aristotle *Politics* viii. 3^{10}—Congreve[2] p. 347) etc. (WM 79)—illustrate the idea underlying the indeclinable, but the presence of the article regularises the grammar. Erasmus (supported subsequently by two cursives) performed the same service to the text by conjecturing ἀπὸ τοῦ ὁ ὤν. For the solecism deliberately conveying dogma we may compare Charles Wesley's couplet—

The Father, Son and Holy Ghost
Is ready, with the shining host.

---

[1] Cf. Preisigke *Sammelbuch* 1540, a tombstone of A.D. 408, beginning θεὸς ὁ παντοκράτωρ, ὁ ὢν προὼν καὶ μέλλων, which is a Christian translation of Rev 1^{4} into idiomatic Greek. Cf. also *Syll.* 757 (reign of Augustus), where Αἰών as a divinity is described, ὁποῖος ἔστι καὶ ἦν καὶ ἔσται, and again ἀρχὴν μεσότητα τέλος οὐκ ἔχων.

Latin Nouns.

§ 63. Proper names are very numerous. We have *praenomina*, such as *Gaius*,[1] *Marcus, Lucius, Titus, Tiberius, Publius; nomina*, as *Quirinius, Sergius, Titius, Iulius, Porcius, Cornelius; cognomina*, as *Paulus, Caesar* etc.; *agnomina*, as *Augustus*; women's names, as *Prisca, Iunia, Drusilla, Iulia.* Words of the 1st and 2nd declensions in Latin fall naturally into the same class in Greek: masculines in -*a* make nom. -*ας*, and gen. -*α*, as Ἀγρίππας -α (ultimately Greek), Ἀκύλας -α (in papyri—gen. does not occur in NT), Ἁδρίας (dat. -ᾳ). Names of the 3rd decl., as *Caesar, Felix, Gallio*, are generally simple: we need only note that -*ēns* is transliterated -ης, in agreement with the pronunciation (*n* before *s* being evanescent), so that Κρήσκης and Πούδης nom., Κλήμεντος gen. belong to the same flexion. Place-names are also simple, but the Latin -*ă* is not maintained as it is in person-names. Hence *Roma* Ῥώμη: of course it is -α when pure, as Καισαρία (so write, preserving the accent of *Caesarēa*), Ἰταλία. Two Latin place-names form a link with the common nouns—Ἀππίου Φόρον = *Appi Forum* and Τρεῖς Ταβέρναι = *Tres Tabernae*, which are of the same kind as Καλοὶ Λιμένες, *Market Drayton, Sevenoaks, Moses Gate.*

Common nouns borrowed from Latin include:—Decl. I. κολωνία, μεμβράνη,[2] κουστωδία (κ̣οσ[τ]ωδε[ία̣] dat., P Oxy ii. 294[20]), and the masculines κοδράντης (possibly starting from acc. κοδράντην = *quadrantem?*), ξέστης (if this really is a Latin word);[3] also the curiously transformed φελόνης, which NT and MGr (φελόνι) show for φαινόλης = *paenula*, which is found with the other in papyri. For the metathesis see Brugmann *KVG* 249. The Keltic (Gaulish) *rēda* passed into Greek (ῥεδῶν gen. pl. in Rev 18[13]) from Latin. Decl. II. includes κῆνσος, τίτλος, μίλιον (a new formation from the plural *milia* (passuum)), πραιτώριον and others. In Decl. III. are words in -ων, of which only λεγιών -ῶνος need be named: in papyri λεγεών is also found, but λεγιών predominates.[4] Σπεκουλάτωρ makes its acc. σπεκουλάτορα, according to the normal flexion of nouns in -ωρ.

ADJECTIVES.

§ 64. Adjective flexions need not generally be presented in full, as they simply combine types which have already appeared among the nouns. We have only to classify the types and note some irregularities.

[1] Not *Caius*, which is a pure blunder, due to the misunderstanding of the archaic abbreviation C.

[2] No early ex. of the sing. is quoted.

[3] A vulgar Latin *xexta* = *sexta* might support a kind of metathesis: see Brugmann *Grd.*[2] I. 871. But the difficulties are great—see also Brugmann-Thumb *Gr.* 159, where the connexion with ἕξ is queried.

[4] See *CR* xv. 33, 434: many more could be added—see *Vocab. s.v.*

I. Second and First Declensions. (Three Terminations.)

Thus *καλός noble*, *ἅγιος holy*, forming the commonest type:

N. καλός	καλή	καλόν	ἅγιος	ἁγία	ἅγιον
V. καλέ etc.			ἅγιε etc.		
like φίλος ...	φωνή ...	τέκνον	like φίλος ...	ἡμέρα ...	τέκνον

Contracted adjectives, from stems in which ε or ο precedes the termination, may be declined by combining the flexion of διπλοῦς (§ 52 *B*) with that of γῆ or μνᾶ (§ 51), according as the last syllable of the contracted word is impure or pure: thus χαλκοῦς -ῆ -οῦν *brazen*, χρυσοῦς -ῆ -οῦν *golden*, ἁπλοῦς -ῆ -οῦν *single*, διπλοῦς -ῆ -οῦν *double*, τετραπλοῦς -ῆ -οῦν *fourfold*, but ἀργυροῦς -ᾶ -οῦν *silvern*, σιδηροῦς -ᾶ -οῦν *iron*: πορφυροῦς (only in neut.) would follow the same flexion. For irregularities in this respect, and for the appearance of uncontracted forms, see §§ 51, 52 *B* (*b*). The contracted forms are perispomenon throughout. Νέος and στερεός, ὑπήκοος and ὄγδοος do not contract (the last-named sometimes -ους in papyri). On ἵλεως (only nom. sing. masc.), the solitary survival of the "Attic Declension," see above, § 52 *C* (*b*). Ἀνίλεως *merciless* appears in nom. sg. fem. in Jas 2[13] ω, but ἀνέλεος (ℵABC etc.) is the true Hellenistic form. For a discussion of στείρᾳ (Lk 1[36]) see below, II. (*a*).

II. Second Declension. (Two Terminations.)

An adjective flexion in -ος -ον, like those given above with the separate feminine dropped, belongs regularly to compound adjectives, *e.g.* ἡ γυνὴ ἡ ἄγαμος (1 Co 7[33]) *the unmarried woman.* Exceptions were allowed especially where the fem. would be -α (pure), not -η. But there are also a few simplicia, which Brugmann (*Grundriss*[2] II. ii. 105) explains as being originally nouns. We should not press this in the case of adjectives falling into this class in the later language. It should be noticed that the tendency of the language set ultimately towards eliminating the class: in MGr "all adjectives have a separate form for masc. fem. and neut." (Thumb *Handb.* 67). We must pause for comment on some compounds which have taken separate fem. form, and on simplicia falling into this class II., noting also variations from earlier Greek.

(*a*) *Simplicia with two terminations.*

Adjectives in -ιος admit of both flexions, even when compound (Blass). Kälker p. 239 remarks that Polybius uses παραπλήσιος fem. simply to avoid hiatus: this will show that the choice was often very free. In this class are—

Αἰώνιος -ον very often (52 times, of which 43 with ζωή), as usually in Attic. But αἰωνίαν occurs twice, 2 Th 2[16] (exc. FG), He 9[12]; also Mk 10[30] B, Ac 13[48] B, 1 Jn 2[25] B, 2 P 1[11] C*, 42.

Κόσμιος has dat. fem. κοσμίῳ 1 Ti 2[9] ℵ*A (*al.* κοσμίως): Att. -ᾳ.

Μάταιος has fem. -ος in Tit 3[9] and Jas 1[26], but -α in 1 Co 15[17] and 1 P 1[18]: our classical texts show similar fluctuation even within the same book

Νηφάλιος has -ους acc. fem. pl. 1 Ti 3[11]. So in Plutarch: normally -ος -α -ον.

Ὅσιος apparently has acc. fem. pl. -ους in 1 Ti 2[8], except in some cursives (incl. 33 and 1). Here Winer admitted the possibility of Fritzsche's construction (ὁσίους with ἐπαίροντας): against this W. F. Moulton referred to Ellicott *in loc.* The fem. has no parallel here, not even in LXX, but an isolated slip, affected by the analogy of other adj. in -ιος fem., is not strange.

Οὐράνιος (Att. fem. -ία) makes gen. fem. -ου in Lk 2[13] (but οὐρανοῦ in B*D*), dat. -ῳ Ac 26[19].

Σωτήριος, as in earlier Greek, has nom. fem. -ος (Tit 2[11]).

On the other hand—

Βέβαιος has fem. -α alone, Attic showing -ος also. But

Ἐπάρχειος dat. -ᾳ Ac 25[1] B*C is of course the noun ἐπαρχία, ἐπαρχείῳ ℵ*A being the adj. in its regular form (ἡ ἐ. *sc.* ἐξουσία).

Ὅμοιος has fem. -α except in Rev 4[3], where however the agreement of ὅμοιος with ἶρις is only an instance of the writer's normal defiance of concord: he has θάλασσα ὑαλίνη ὁμοία κρυστάλλῳ in v.[6]. Similarly in 9[19] ὅμοιοι in two cursives needs no explanation.

Other two term. adj. in -ιος are ἀΐδιος, αἰφνίδιος, ἐπίγειος, ἐπουράνιος, παράλιος, all in accord with earlier Greek.

Of adjectives not in -ιος we find—

Ἔρημος fem. always -ος (Attic also -η), but as a noun (*sc.* γῆ) except in Ac 1[20] 8[26] Gal 4[27]

Ἕτοιμος fluctuates as in Attic—fem. pl. -οι in Mt 25[10] (exc. A), elsewhere -ος -η -ον.

Σεμνός has acc. fem. in -ούς 1 Ti 3[11] A—a mere casual slip.

Στεῖρος -ον (so in classical Greek) is a peculiar case. It seems best to regard the fem. as στεῖρα in NT, since στεῖρα would have made dat. στείρῃ (see p. 118). The assumption that the NT form is simply a new fem. attached to the old adj. of two terminations, and not the independent fem. noun στεῖρα (Hom., cf. Skt. *starī*), cuts out the only exception to the rule that -ρᾰ makes -ης -η. Cf. Gothic *stairō* fem., which would answer to *στέρᾱ in Greek.

Other simplicia with fem. in -ος are ἁμαρτωλός, βέβηλος, φλύαρος, and those in -ιμος (φρόνιμος, ὠφέλιμος), all in accord with the sole or predominant usage in earlier Greek.

(*b*) *Compounds with three terminations* are—

Ἀργός (=ἀ-ϝ-εργός), nom. fem. ἀργή Ja 2^{20}, ἀργαί in 1 Ti 5^{13}, as well as in the line of Epimenides Tit 1^{12}, which establishes it as older Greek if the reading has not been assimilated. The ban of Phrynichus rests on fem. ἀργή, which Rutherford (*NP* 185) thinks may be genuine in Xenophon : Lobeck, *Phr.* 104 f. gives plentiful exx. of ἀργή in later literature.

Αὐτόματος fem. -η in Mk 4^{28}, Ac 12^{10} ("not unclassical," says Blass).

Καθημερινός, like its classical predecessor καθημέριος, has three terminations (Ac 6^{1}).

Παραθαλάσσιος Mt 4^{13} -ίαν (-ιον D, παρὰ θάλασσαν ℵ*), but ἡ παράλιος Lk 6^{17}.

III. Third and First Declensions. (Three Terminations.)

§ 65. Third decl. stems form their fem. with the suffix -(*i*)*i̯ā* : -*ī*-, which in Greek becomes -ι̯ᾰ gen. -ι̯ης. It will be convenient to include participles here.

(1) *Stems in* -ντ- (cf. § 55 (4) above for the nouns).

(*a*) *Stems in* -αντ-.

	πάντ- *all.* *Sing.*			*Plur.*		
Sing. N.	πᾶς	πᾶσα	πᾶν	πάντες	πᾶσαι	πάντα
A.	πάντα	πᾶσαν	πᾶν	πάντας	πάσας	πάντα
G.	παντός	πάσης	παντός	πάντων	πασῶν	πάντων
D.	παντί	πάσῃ	παντί	πᾶσι(ν)	πάσαις	πᾶσι(ν)

So ἅπας, and all participles in -ας.

(*b*) *Stems in* -εντ-

So participles like τιθέντ- (pres.), πεισθέντ- (wk. aor.).

Nom. sing. -είς -εῖσα -έν ; *gen.* -έντος -είσης ; *dat. pl.* -εῖσι(ν), -είσαις.

Adjectives in -εις -εσσα -εν are not found in NT and seem to be obsolete.

(*c*) *Stems in* -οντ-.

So ἑκοντ- *willing*, ἀκοντ- *unwilling* (orig. participles) and participles in -οντ-, as ἄρχοντ- *ruling* (pres.), ἰδόντ- (strong aor.) *having seen.*

Nom. sing. -ων -ουσα -ον ; *gen.* -οντος -ούσης.
-ών -οῦσα -όν ; -όντος.
Dat. pl. -ουσι(ν) -ούσαις.
-οῦσι(ν).

One or two formations (from non-thematic verbs—see § 86) make nom. sing. masc. in -ούς, as διδούς pres., δούς aor., from δίδωμι *give* (stems διδόντ-, δόντ-).

(*d*) *Stems in* -ουντ- (= -εοντ- or -οοντ-).

From Contract Verbs in -έω- and -όω : thus φιλουντ- (φιλέω *love*), δηλουντ- (δηλόω *make clear*).

Nom. sing. -οῦσα -οῦν ; *gen.* -οῦντος -ούσης ; *dat. pl.* -οῦσι(ν) -ούσαις.

(*e*) *Stems in* -ωντ- (= -αοντ- or -ηοντ-).

From Contract Verbs in -άω and -ήω : thus τιμωντ- (τιμάω *honour*), ζωντ- (ζήω *live*—entered as ζάω in lexica).

Nom. sing. -ῶν -ῶσα -ῶν ; *gen.* -ῶντος -ώσης ; *dat. pl.* -ῶσι(ν) -ώσαις.

(*f*) *Stems in* -υντ-. Only two forms survive in NT, from participles like δεικνύς, *showing.*

Nom. sing. -ύς -ῦσα -ύν ; *gen.* -ύντος -ύσης ; *dat. pl.* -ῦσι(ν) -ύσαις.

(2) *Participle stems in* -*u̯os*- : -*us*- (-*u̯ot*-). On the primitive stem-mixture here see Brugmann *Grd.*[2] II. i. 563 ff. In addition to the normal form used in the perfect partic. act., there is a type of which ἑστώς *standing* (from ἵστημι) is the only NT survival in which contraction has taken place, and a new fem. introduced from the present participle. So decline εἰδώς *knowing* and ἑστώς.

Sing.	*N.*	εἰδώς	εἰδυῖα	εἰδός	ἑστώς	ἑστῶσα	ἑστός
	G.	εἰδότος	εἰδυίης	εἰδότος	ἑστῶτος	ἑστώσης	ἑστῶτος
Pl.	*D.*	εἰδόσι(ν)	εἰδυίαις	εἰδόσι(ν)	ἑστῶσι(ν)	ἑστώσαις	ἑστῶσι(ν)

On εἰδυίης see above, § 49 (2) *a*. Ἑστός shortens its proper ω (from -αϝο-) by analogy. In Rev 5[6] ℵ and some cursives have a neuter ἑστηκώς, which if genuine will be due to the writer's peculiar concord : ω and ο were hardly distinguished even in his day (§ 34 (4)). So also ἑστώς neut. Mt 24[15] D*ω ; Rev 14[1] in 046 and a dozen cursives.

(3) *Stems in -n-.*

(*a*) Μελαν- *black* is thus declined:

Sing. N. μέλας μέλαινα μέλαν; *G.* μέλανος μελαίνης; *Plur. D.* μέλασι(ν) μελαίναις.

(*b*) An old noun (μέγῃ) μέγα = *greatness* appears to have produced the adjective flexion nom. masc. μέγας neut. μέγα *great*, acc. masc. μέγαν (Brugmann *Grd.*² II. ii. 656). The rest of the flexion of this adjective is still in NT supplied by the stem μεγαλο-, declined like καλός, which in MGr supplies the whole of the flexion, regularly formed (Thumb *Handb.* 69).

(4) *Stems in -eu- : -u-.*

(*a*) One very common adjective may be named first, in which Brugmann (*l.c.*) holds that an old neuter noun πολύ *plenty* has produced a nom. masc. πολύς neut. πολύ *much* (pl. *many*), acc. masc. πολύν. The rest of the flexion is from the ordinary stem πολλο- -η- like καλός: the adj. is thus parallel altogether to μέγας above, *q.v.*, except that here the old irregular flexion survives in MGr (Thumb *Handb.* 71).

(*b*) Adjectives in -ύς form a class which has maintained and even extended its ground in MGr: see Thumb *Handb.* 70 f. Thus decline ὀξύς *sharp.*

Sing. N.	ὀξύς	ὀξεῖα	ὀξύ	*Pl.*	ὀξεῖς	ὀξεῖαι	ὀξέα
A.	ὀξύν	ὀξεῖαν	ὀξύ		ὀξεῖς	ὀξείας	ὀξέα
G.	ὀξέως	ὀξείας	ὀξέως		ὀξέων	ὀξειῶν	ὀξέων
D.	ὀξεῖ	ὀξείᾳ	ὀξεῖ		ὀξέσι(ν)	ὀξείαις	ὀξέσι(ν)

In this class the NT shows a few forms each of βαθύς *deep*, βαρύς *heavy*, βραδύς *slow*, βραχύς *short*, γλυκύς *sweet*, εὐθύς *direct*, θῆλυς *female*, πλατύς *broad* (only fem., esp. as a noun = *broad way, street*), πραΰς *unassuming* (the Attic masc. πρᾶος is obsolete), ταχύς *swift*, τρᾱχύς *rough*.

The Attic gen. sing. in -έος occurs in inferior MSS: βαθέος Lk 24[1] later uncials (-έως ℵABCDL etc.), πραέος 1 Pet 3[4] ACP (-έως ℵBKL). For variations in LXX see Thackeray 179.

The neut. pl. βαθέα in Rev 2[24] AC 046 is replaced by βάθη ℵP, which is however not a contraction but the pl. of βάθος.

Nom. sing. neut. θῆλυν occurs in D* at Mt 19[4] Mk 10[6], and πολύν Ac

18[27]. For ἥμισυς (derived from the neuter noun ἥμισυ, which may even have survived in popular speech, being very common in the papyri) see § 73.

IV. Third Declension. (Two Terminations.)

(1) *Stems in* n.

(*a*) *Stems in -ον- and -εν-.*

These are declined like ἡγεμών and ποιμήν above (§ 56. 1), except for the addition of a neuter. Thus σώφρων *sober*, ἄρσην *male* (ἄρρην—see § 42).

Sing. N.	σώφρων	σῶφρον	ἄρσην	ἄρσεν
A.	σώφρονα		ἄρσενα	
Plur. N.	σώφρονες	σώφρονα	ἄρσενες	ἄρσενα
A.	σώφρονας		ἄρσενας	

In Rev 12[5] by the usual neglect of concord we have the neut. ἄρσεν in apposition to υἱόν : contrast τὸν ἄρσενα v.[13].

(*b*) Comparatives in -ων (like participles in -ώς above) combine two stems in their flexion, viz. (-ī)-i̯es- : (-ī)-i̯os- and the same in weak gradation with a nasal stem added, -*is-on-*. See Brugmann *Grd.*[2] II. i. 547 ff. for the details.[1] Forms in Hellenistic are restricted to those in -ι̯οσ- and those in -ι̯ον-. Thus :

	Sing.		*Plur.*	
N.	μείζων	μεῖζον	μείζονες and μείζους (=-ο(σ)ες)	μείζονα and μείζω (=ο(σ)α)
A.	μείζονα and μείζω (=-ο(σ)α)	μεῖζον	μείζονας and μείζους (=nom.)	μείζονα and μείζω
G.	μείζονος		μειζόνων	
D.	μείζονι		μείζοσι(ν)	

(1) The shorter forms occur in Mt 26[53], Lk 21[3] DW, Jn 1[51] (exc. ℵ), 2[10], 4[41], 5[36] (exc. D), Ac 13[31] (not D), 19[32], 21[10], 23[13], [21], 24[11], 25[6] (not B), [14].

(2) The form in -ω has in Hellenistic an indeclinable use, of which there are one or two traces in NT. See for this *Proleg.* 50 and Thackeray 186. So Mt 26[53] ℵBD παραστήσει μοι πλείω δώδεκα λεγιῶνας ἀγγέλων, Mt 23[19] D τί γὰρ μείζω ; P Leid C *verso* [ll. 17] (p. 118—B.C. 100), πλήω μου ἔχει χαλκοῦς, P Oxy vii. 1029[24] πλείω τούτων (men) μὴ εἶναι etc. In Jn 1[50] MXΔ, 5[36] ABω etc. μείζων, and 2[10] G ἐλάσσων, we find irrational ν added to the acc. sing or neut. pl.

---

[1] As the old mistake by which -ους was supposed to be contracted from -ονες is still found in WS 88, the warning against this impossibility is not needless.

(2) *Stems in* es.

These answer to the noun flexion συγγενής in § 58: we only have to add neut. sing. συγγενές and pl. συγγενῆ (= -ε(σ)α). There are some sixty adjectives in NT belonging to this class, which has however rather strangely vanished in the modern vernacular, though that in -ύς, which it outnumbers five times or more in NT, has survived. See Thumb *Handb.* 72 f.

Πλήρης has considerable traces of an indeclinable use, which is often found in LXX uncials, and must probably be read in Mk 4[28] (C* cu[2]—it alone explains the variants), Jn 1[14] (all but D), and—if we must follow the MSS—Ac 6[5] (all but B). Add Mk 8[19] AFGM *al.*, Ac 6[3] AEHP *al.*, 19[28] AEL 33 cu[1], 2 Jn[8] L. The vernacular evidence will be given in full in *Vocab. s.v.*: meanwhile see Thackeray 176 f. and references in *Prol.* 50 n. Despite the rather abundant instances in MSS, Thackeray is not inclined to accept the indecl. for the LXX, unless in Sir 19[26] and Job 21[24] (where a σ follows, and the mere transcriptional account mentioned above, § 31, may be applied). Deissmann *LAE* 125–7 thinks the evidence from papyri early enough to justify acceptance in Jn: his view that "in the Gospels and in St. Paul popular forms have always a fair claim to preference" leaves us free to exclude it from Ac. Then why follow the MSS in one place and not in the other? Can Luke have been faithfully copying the popular Greek of his source? But it must be admitted that early evidence is local and scanty. P Leid C *verso* ii. 14 (p. 118—B.C. 160) is much the oldest. Next comes a mummy label in Preisigke *Sammelb.* 2632, which Deissmann dates from Augustus. P Lond *recto* 131[133] (=i. p. 174—A.D. 78–9) has πληρ[η] acc. pl. This is all I know from i/A.D. and earlier.

V. Miscellaneous. (Mainly One Termination.)

The remaining adjectives found in NT only occur in one or two forms.

Ἀμήτωρ and ἀπάτωρ (only N. sing.) make gen. -ορος: so ἀπάτορος gen. "with father unknown"—see *Vocab. s.v.* The neut. would be -ορ (with τέκνον or the like), but I have not seen it.

Ἅρπαξ, nom. pl. ἅρπαγες, *ravening.*

Αὐτόχειρ, nom. pl. αὐτόχειρες, *with one's own hand.*

Νῆστις *fasting*, acc. pl. νήστεις: see above, p. 132.

Πένης *poor*, dat. pl. πένησι(ν), might as well be called a noun (stem in -τ-). Similarly declined is

Πλάνης *wandering, planet* (with ἀστέρες), nom. pl. πλάνητες Jud [13] B: other MSS have πλανῆται (1st decl.), an alternative form found like πλάνης in earlier Greek in this connexion.

Τετράπους *quadruped* is only used as a neuter noun, in plural, τετράποδα -ων.

ADVERBS.

§ 66. As might be expected, the normal termination -ως extends its borders considerably in Hellenistic. (It has receded since almost entirely: see Thumb *Handb.* 77.) In NT there are about a hundred of these, fully a third of the total number of adverbs (not counting adverbial phrases) occurring there. The empiric rule that the adverb may be formed by changing the final -ων (-ῶν) of the gen. pl. masc. of an adjective into -ως (-ῶς) holds as in earlier Greek. They are attached to adjectives of all kinds, including participles used adjectivally (as **ὄντως, ὑπερβαλλόντως, ὁμολογουμένως, φειδομένως**). **Νουνεχῶς** (from -ής adj.) may be noticed as replacing the classical νουνεχόντως (in Plato even ἐχόντως νοῦν!) from Aristotle down. **Πρώτως** (Aristotle) occurs in Ac 11[26] (ℵBD[2] and some cursives) for the still far commoner classical **πρῶτον**: cf. P Tebt ii. 295[7] and 472 (ii/A.D.), and Rutherford *NP* 366. There is also some tendency to bring -ως into cpve. and superl.: thus in NT **ἐσχάτως** (not obviously superl. in form: it is moreover as old as Hippocrates), **σπουδαιοτέρως, περισσοτέρως**. Radermacher (p. 54) asserts that the extension of -ως belongs essentially to the written language: we might note the appearance of the new adverb **ὀλίγως** (2 Pet 2[18]) as characteristic of the writer's bookish style—Aquila and the Anthology appear to be its only supporters.

In the vernacular, where as Völker notes[1] -ως differed less and less from -ος, the tendency was (as in MGr) to extend the adverbial use of the accus. neut. Thus **πολλά, πάντα, οὐδέν** (whence MGr δέν), **ἐξάπινα, μέσον, ἐνώπιον**. In cpve. and superl. this was traditional: **ἐκτενέστερον, κάλλιον**, etc. (see below, § 67), follow classical rule, so do **μάλιστα, ἥδιστα, τάχιστα,** πλεῖστα (papp. *passim*).

Other case-endings appear in adverbial use: only a few instances need be named, since case-consciousness disappeared centuries before our period in nearly all of our exx. The fem. accus. appears in **μακράν** (*sc.* ὁδόν), **ἀκμήν, δωρεάν**. Old instrumentals have been recognised in **λάθρᾱ, πάντη** (formed on the analogy of ταύτῃ, Brugmann *Grd.*[2] II. ii. 713), **εἰκῆ, πεζῆ, κρυφῆ, πόρρω** etc. Since there are adverbial datives, like **ἰδίᾳ, δημοσίᾳ**, and the ancient inscriptional witness shows some confusion, we cannot be perfectly certain whether to write εἰκῆ or εἰκῇ. See Brugmann's discussion *Grd.*[2] II. ii. 705: it is of course a mere matter of orthography for Hellenistic. Forms in -ω have no claim to the ι, and in the rest we may leave the matter open. Locatives are recognisable in **ἀεί** (from the stem *ai̯u̯o-*, cf. Lat. *aevom*), **πανοικεί**, and with short -ῐ (cf. Brugmann *l.c.* 710) in the special class in -ιστί, answering the question *in what language?*, viz. **Ἑλληνιστί, Ῥωμαϊστί, Ἐβραιστί, Λυκαονιστί,** Συριστί (*in Aramaic*) etc. Add the old word **πέρυσι** (see § 106).

---

[1] *Papyrorum gr. Syntaxis Specimen*, p. 9—quoted with approval by Radermacher, *l.c.*

Accretions of -ς are found in **ἐγγύ-ς, εὐθύ-ς** (orig. neut. acc. sing.), **μέχρι-ς, ἄχρι-ς** (see the chapter on Prepositions), **πολλάκι-ς** and the numeral adverbs. An originally quasi-ablative -*θεν* has been attached in **ἐκεῖθεν, πόρρωθεν, πάντοθεν** etc., and in a noun (**παιδιόθεν**), where the strengthening with *ἐκ* (Mk 9[21]) reminds us that the original force of the suffix is wearing thin. The suffix -*δον* should be noted in **ῥοιζηδόν, ὁμοθυμαδόν, σχεδόν**.

For *Compound* adverbs and *Prepositions*, see under WORD-FORMATION; and for *adverbial phrases* the sections on the several cases in the SYNTAX (Vol. III.).

COMPARISON OF ADJECTIVES AND ADVERBS.

§ 67. The syntactical developments which have affected so seriously the comparison of adjectives and adverbs have been described in *Proleg.* 77 ff. (= *Einl.* 120 ff.). They affect us at this point by driving out of use many forms that were largely employed in the classical period: the mixture of compar. and superl. has also produced some strengthened forms. There are two forms of comparison, surviving from the classical period, one of them of Indo-European antiquity, and the other partially so. Adjectives will be given in the nom. sing. masc., so that adverbs can be distinguished by their ending.

(1) *With suffix -ίων or γων, -ιστος.*

One new formation appears frequently in papyri and Hellenistic writers,[1] and four or five times in NT, viz. **τάχειον** (better **τάχῖον**), which takes the place of *θᾶσσον* or *θᾶττον* (=*θαχ-ιον*—Brugmann, *Grd.*[2] I. 363). This fell by its form out of association with the positive and superlative, and a new form was made on the model *βέλτιον* : *βέλτιστα, κάλλιον* : *κάλλιστα* etc. There is no reason whatever for assuming (with WS) that a "more original" form emerged for the first time in later Greek, though *ταχίων* and *θάσσων* might have coexisted (-*ῑγον*- as *lento*-form, -*γον*- as *allegro*): where analogy formation explains so easily, we cannot assume antiquity without any evidence. The remaining forms are all classical. Their obvious shrinking foreshadows their disappearance in later times: only *κάλλιον* survives in MGr (Thumb *Handb.* 74).

Ἆσσον *nearer*, from *ἄγχι* (cf. Ger. *enger*).

Βέλτιον *better*, used as cpve. of **εὖ** (elative in 2 Ti 1[18], Ac 10[28] D).

Ἔγγιστα *nearest* (Mk 6[36] D), sup. of **ἐγγύς**, which has cpve. **ἐγγύτερος** in class (2).

{ **Ἐλάσσων** *lesser*, **ἐλάχιστος**. See below, (3). On the -*ττ*- form see § 43. Cf. *Proleg.* 236.
{ **Ἔλαττον** *less*.

[1] Rutherford *NP* 150; *CR* xv. 35.

Ἥδιστα *most gladly*, sup. of ἡδέως (elative), Ac 13⁸ D, 2 Co 12⁹· ¹⁵.

Ἥσσων *worse*. The -σσ- is in all the good uncials.
Ἧσσον *worse, less*.

Κάλλιον *very well*. From **καλῶς**. See above.

Κρείσσων, κρείττων *better*, **κράτιστος**. Sup. only as title. For -ττ- see § 43. The most frequent cpve. of ἀγαθός in LXX.
Κρεῖσσον, κρεῖττον *better*.

Μᾶλλον *more, rather*, **μάλιστα**. Positive μάλα not in NT. Sup. generally not elative.[1]

Μείζων *greater, greatest*, **μέγιστος**. Sup. only once (2 Pet 1⁴, elative, as always in Κοινή).
Μεῖζον *more* (only Mt 20³¹).

Πλείων, πλέων *more*, **πλεῖστος**. Sup. only four times, of which two at least are elative: so sometimes πλείων. The forms without ι occur in Lk 3¹³, Jn 21¹⁵ ℵBCD (adv.), Ac 15²⁸ (exc. D cu⁴), and in one or two primary uncials at Mt 5²⁰, Mk 12⁴³, Lk 7⁴²⁻⁴³ 11³¹ 12²³ 21³, Jn 7³¹, 2 Co 2⁶. MGr πιό or πλιό (from πλεῖον rather than πλέον) takes the place μᾶλλον had in forming comparatives.
Πλεῖον, πλέον *more*.

Τάχιον *faster* (see above), **τάχιστα**. Sup. only in Ac 17¹⁵. Positive **τάχα** or **ταχέως**.

Ὕψιστος *highest*. Exc. in the phrase ἐν τ. ὑψίστοις, only used as title of God.

Χείρων *worse*, used as cpve. of **κακός**.

(2) *With suffix* -τερος -τατος.

§ 68. The following forms are found in NT:

(1) Compar.: ἀκριβέστερον, ἀλυπότερος, ἀναγκαιότερος, ἀνεκτότερος, ἀσθενέστερος, ἀτιμότερος, βαρύτερος, βεβαιότερος, δεισιδαιμονέστερος, διαφορώτερος, διπλότερος, ἐγγύτερον, ἐκτενέστερον, ἐλαχιστότερος, ἐλεεινότερος, ἐντιμότερος, εὐγενέστερος (εὐθυμότερος T.R.), εὐκοπώτερος, ἰσχυρότερος, καινότερος, κομψότερον, μακαριώτερος, μειζότερος, μικρότερος, νεώτερος, περισσότερος -ον -ως, πολυτιμότερος, πονηρότερος, πρεσβύτερος, πυκνότερον, σοφώτερος, σπουδαιότερος -ως, τελειότερος, τολμηροτέρως or -ον, τομώτερος, ὑψηλότερος, φρονιμώτερος (χρηστότερος T.R.)—see also (3) below.
(2) Superl.: ἁγιώτατος, ἀκριβέστατος, τιμιώτατος.[2]

The formations here are altogether upon the old models. As may be expected, there are occasional substitutions of -ώτερος for -ότερος, and *vice versa*: the two were equivalent long before the later uncials were written, and the traditional

[1] There are places where μᾶλλον appears to be elative, as Mt 6²⁶. In 1 Co 7²¹ we may translate "by all means seize (the opportunity)": cf. *Prol.* 247.
[2] Overlooked by Blass, p. 33 (also by Debrunner, p. 36).

distinction meant no more than it does in MGr (cf. Thumb *Handb.* 73). The three superl. in -τατος, of which only ἀκριβέστατος is true superl., tell of the vanishing of this form, which is however still common in the papyri:[1] Thumb *l.c.* shows how it has a limited elative use to-day. Among the details note—

(*a*) Διπλότερος Mt 23[15] is irregular (cf. class. ἁπλούστερος): it occurs in Appian (ii/A.D.) *Praef. Hist. Rom.* 10 διπλότερα τούτων. The form ἁπλότερος occurs in *Anth. Pal.* vi. 185, and διπλός *ib.* x. 101. Cf. Lat. *duplus*, and see Lobeck *Phryn.* 234.

(*b*) On comparative adverbs in -ως instead of -ον see K.Bl. i. 577 n.[1]. Both are classical.

(*c*) *Double comparison.*—μειζότερος 3 Jn [4] and its parallels[2] are best explained (like Eng. *more, lesser, worser*, Ger. *mehrere*) as efforts to add fresh strength to a form the comparative force of which was somewhat blunted through its not having the normal termination. MGr π(λ)ειότερος and χερότερος, from πλείων and χείρων, πρωτύτερος from πρῶτος, continue the tendency. Ἐλαχιστότερος in Eph 3[8] is on the other hand, when compared with 1 Co 15[9], a kind of *tour de force* in expression, like Aristotle's τοῦ ἐσχάτου ἐσχατώτερος (*Metaph.* ix. 4).[3] To this heading practically belongs also the frequent use of pleonastic μᾶλλον with cpve.

(3) *Miscellaneous.*

§ 69. (*a*) A number of comparative formations in -τερος from adverb bases may be put in a class together:

Ἀνώτερον *higher*, from ἄνω.

Ἐξώτερος *outer*, from ἔξω.

Ἐσώτερος *inner*, from ἔσω.

Κατώτερος *lower*, from κάτω, Eph 4[9]. There is a significant alteration of this to κατώτατα (μέρη) when quoted by sundry Greek fathers.

Κατώτερω *lower*.

Περαιτέρω *further*, from πέραν.

Πορρώτερον *further*, from πόρρω. So BA, -ρω ℵD etc.

---

[1] As in Hermas (Blass 33, Bl.-Debr. 36): Blass's suggestion that the Κοινή at Rome differed in this respect from that found elsewhere (as in Egypt) is thus seen to be unproved.

[2] WS wrongly cft. θεομακαριστότατος Ignat. *Polyc.* 7[2]: θεομακάριστος is not a superl. (see Lightfoot *Ignat.* ii. 292). Does this suggest the origin of the MGr superl. formations beginning with θεο- (Thumb *Handb.* 74)? One compares ἀστεῖος τῷ θεῷ, which is assumed to be Hebraic. An early ex. in Mimnermus (fr. 11[9]—vii/cent.) ἀμεινότερος. Exx. from papyri in *CR* xv. 35. See Hatzidakis 177, K.Bl. i. 573.

[3] We have however ἐλαχιστότατος in Sextus Empiricus (iii/A.D.).

Πρότερος *former*, from **πρό** : see below.
Ὕστερος *later, last.* From the adverb which appears in Skt. as *ud* and in English as *out.*
Ὕστερον *afterwards, last.*

(*b*) Two superlatives are formed with suffix -ατος, viz. **πρῶτος** (from *πρωϝός, Skt. *pūrva* "former") and **ἔσχατος** (from *ἔσχος, akin to ἐξ—Brugmann *Gr.*[4] 241). Cf. ὕπατος (**ἀνθύπατος** *proconsul*) from ὑπό. On the relations of πρότερος and πρῶτος see *Proleg.* 79.

(*c*) Many of the substitutes for comparison must be left to the Syntax; but one word deserves quoting from MGr, περισσότερος as cpve. of πολύς. That περισσός and its cpve. are practically *suppletiva* for πολύς is clear in NT.

NUMERALS.

§ 70. The following occur in NT: see § 71 (*b*) for their combinations.

Value.	Sign.	Cardinals.	Ordinals.	Adverbials.
1	ᾱ	εἷς *one*	πρῶτος *first*	ἅπαξ *once*
2	β̄	δύο	δεύτερος	δίς
3	γ̄	τρεῖς	τρίτος	τρίς
4	δ̄	τέσσαρες	τέταρτος	τετράκις
5	ε̄	πέντε	πέμπτος	πεντάκις
6	ϛ̄	ἕξ	ἕκτος	
7	ζ̄	ἑπτά	ἕβδομος	ἑπτάκις
8	η̄	ὀκτώ	ὄγδοος	
9	θ	ἐννέα	ἔνατος	
10	ῑ	δέκα	δέκατος	
11	ιᾱ	ἕνδεκα	ἑνδέκατος	
12	ιβ̄	δώδεκα δεκαδύο	δωδέκατος	
14	ιδ̄	δεκατέσσαρες	τεσσαρεσκαιδέκατος	
15	ιε̄	δεκαπέντε	πεντεκαιδέκατος	
16	ιϛ̄	δέκα ἕξ		
18	ιη̄	δέκα ὀκτώ or δέκα καὶ ὀκτώ		
20	κ̄	εἴκοσι(ν)		
30	λ̄	τριάκοντα		
40	μ̄	τεσσαράκοντα τεσσεράκοντα		
50	ν̄	πεντήκοντα	πεντηκοστός	
60	ξ̄	ἑξήκοντα		

70	ō	ἑβδομήκοντα	ἑβδομηκοντάκις
80	π̄	ὀγδοήκοντα	
90	ϙ̄	ἐνενήκοντα	
100	ρ̄	ἑκατόν	
200	σ̄	διακόσιοι	
300	τ̄	τριακόσιοι	
400	ῡ	τετρακόσιοι	
500	φ̄	πεντακόσιοι	
600	χ̄	ἑξακόσιοι	
1,000	͵α	χίλιοι	
2,000	͵β	δισχίλιοι	
3,000	͵γ	τρισχίλιοι	
4,000	͵δ	τετρακισχίλιοι	
5,000	͵ε	πεντακισχίλιοι or χιλιάδες πέντε	
7,000	͵ζ	χιλιάδες ἑπτά or ἑπτακισχίλιοι	
10,000	$\overset{\alpha}{\mathrm{M}}$	μύριοι or δέκα χιλιάδες	
12,000	$\overset{\alpha}{\mathrm{M}}$͵β	δώδεκα χιλιάδες	
20,000	$\overset{\beta}{\mathrm{M}}$	εἴκοσι χιλιάδες or (δισμύριοι—see below, § 71 *b* (4))	
50,000	$\overset{\epsilon}{\mathrm{M}}$	μυριάδες πέντε	
100,000,000		μυριάδες μυριάδων. [For the sign see below.]	

Those which do not happen to occur in the NT may be supplied.

Cardinals: 700 ψ̄ ἑπτακόσιοι—800 ω̄ ὀκτακόσιοι—900 ϡ̄ ἐνακόσιοι.

Ordinals: 20th εἰκοστός, 100th ἑκατοστός, 400th τετρακοσιοστός (*et sim.* for the rest), 1000th χιλιοστός.

Adverbial: 6 times ἑξάκις, 8 ὀκτάκις, 9 ἐνάκις, 10 δεκάκις (*et sim.*), 20 εἰκοσάκις, 100 ἑκατοντάκις, 1000 χιλιάκις, 10,000 μυριάκις.

Since many of these are on the way to become obsolete (see below), we cannot expect always to find actual instances in Hellenistic texts. All the supplements just mentioned occur in the LXX, except the ordinals 1,000th and 10,000th and the adverbials 9 times, 100 times, 1000 times, and 10,000 times. In the case of the higher numbers this is probably not accidental: it is suggestive that we find μυριάκις μύριοι otherwise expressed in Rev 5[11] 9[16].

A. Signs.

Three supplementary signs, drawn from older forms of the alphabet, made the available ciphers 27: these were στίγμα for 6 (ϛ, in papyri C), κόππα for 90 (ϙ or ϟ), σάν or σαμπῖ for 900 (ϡ or ͳ). The signs thus fell into three sets of nine each; ᾱ–θ̄ units, ῑ–ϙ̄ tens, ρ̄–ͳ hundreds. These horizontal straight strokes (in MSS sometimes curled thus ~, as in D) preserve the ciphers from confusion with the letters in their ordinary use; but their employment was not essential. From 1000 to 9000 the unit ciphers are used over again, differentiated in papyri by a large curved flourish at the top (͵A), in MSS by a sloping line below (together with the other line sometimes), as ͵ε̃, 5000 (D). The ciphers were usually, but not necessarily, placed in order of magnitude with the highest at the left, as ͵αϙιϛ = 1916. From 10,000 upwards the system started afresh, the signs being written over a large M, the initial of *μυριάδες*: thus $\overset{\epsilon}{\mathrm{M}}$ = 50,000.

In printed books ordinary accents are usually employed for the horizontal line.

(*a*) "In this way the Greeks could express by symbols any number less than a hundred millions . . . ; and hence perhaps we may understand why it was that in nations which used this system of notation, the next highest number, ten thousand times ten thousand, was used to represent a multitude which no man could number, as in Dn 7[10], Rev 5[11]."[1]

(*b*) The dropping of the horizontal line, which in ordinary arithmetic was not needed, made these series of ciphers exactly like words, the more so as their order did not matter, and they could be arranged very often so as to be pronounceable. Hence no doubt arose the link between numbers and names, which on the one side produced mystic words like *αβρασαξ*, the number of the year (since 1+2+100+1+200+1+60=365), and on the other made a name numerically significant, as Ἰησοῦς=888. For the Greek custom as applied to Rev 13[18], see Deissmann *LAE* 275–7: see also Moffatt *EGT*, or Charles *ICC*, *in loc.*, for the view which finds a Hebrew "gematria" here.

(*c*) Fractions could be expressed in words or in the alphabetic notation. Sometimes both are found together, as in P Ryl ii. 202 (*a*)[9. 10] (A.D. 108) (πυροῦ) ὀκτὼ τρίτο(ν) ιβ′, (γίνεται) (πυροῦ) ηγ′ιβ′ "eight and a third and $\frac{1}{12}$ artabae of wheat, total $8\frac{5}{12}$ of wheat." $\frac{1}{2}$ was abbreviated ∠: neither this nor γ′ nor δ′ is found in NT. See Mayser 52 for further information.

B. Cardinals.

§ 71. (*a*) *Declension and Orthography.*—Cardinals are indeclinable, except the first four, and those in the table above from *διακόσιοι* onward: these are ordinary plural adjectives, while *χιλιάς* and *μυριάς* are singular collective nouns (gen. -*άδος*). The first four are thus declined:

N.	εἷς	μία	ἕν	δύο	τρεῖς τρία	τέσσαρες τέσσαρα
A.	ἕνα	μίαν	ἕν	δύο	τρεῖς τρία	τέσσαρας τέσσαρα
G.	ἑνός	μιᾶς	ἑνός	δύο	τριῶν	τεσσάρων
D.	ἑνί	μιᾷ	ἑνί	δυσί(ν)	τρισί(ν)	τέσσαρσι(ν)

[1] "The Employment of the Alphabet in Greek Logistic," by J. G. Smyly *Mélanges Nicole* 519.

These flexions are followed also when standing at the end of a combination, as *δεκατεσσάρων*.

(*a*) Like *εἷς* are *οὐδείς οὐδεμία οὐδέν* and *μηδείς*: for the alternative forms (masc. and neut.) *οὐθείς μηθείς* see § 46.

(*β*) The disappearance of the dual flexion of *δύο* is in line with the general development of Κοινή Greek: see *Prol.* 77 ff. Δύω (pre-classical) is found in Ptolemaic papyri by Mayser (p. 313), probably a sheer mistake. NT shows neither the gen. *δυῶν* (Mayser 314) nor the literary Hellenistic *δυεῖν* (late Attic), which appears in some parts of LXX (Thackeray 187), as in Josephus, and not seldom in papyri. Δύο indecl., a primitive form, was ousted from the dative in Hellenistic by the pluralised form *δυσί(ν)*. This appears first in Hippocrates, and is traced by Brugmann (*Grd.*² II. ii. 9) to Ionic. It is regular in literary Κοινή from Aristotle's time, and in papyri from the end of ii/B.C.: see reff. in Mayser 314. Δυσίν is of course lost in MGr., which has sometimes *δυῶ(νε)* (Thumb *Handb.* 81). See *Vocabulary s.v.* for the papyrus record.

(*γ*) (1) Τέσσαρες is found as accus. extremely often in papyri, and is actually normal in LXX (Thackeray 148). We should have expected it in NT uncials, where however it is not adequately attested: see citations in *Prol.* 36 n. WH (*App.*² 157) make Rev 4⁴ (2nd) the one occurrence out of eight where there is not some good authority for *τέσσαρες* acc.: cf. also *ib.* 138, and *Prol.* 243, where its predominance in Egyptian business documents is noted. It is rather tempting to connect it specially with Egyptian Κοινή, in view of its record (*a*) in LXX, (*b*) in papyri and ostraca, (*c*) in ℵ,[1] the Alexandrian origin of which is becoming more and more probable. To associate it with the acc. in -*ες* as an element drawn from Achaean-Dorian Κοινή (as *Prol.* 36) is on the whole a less probable account of its origin than we get by calling in the influence of *δύο* and *τρεῖς*, neither of which has a separate acc. form. But both causes may have operated.

(2) Τέσσερα appears in Jn 19²³ ℵALM (not BW), Rev 4⁶ A (not ℵP 046), 4⁸ ℵA (not P 046), 5⁸ ℵA, 5¹⁴ A, 19⁴ ℵAC: the word itself does not occur elsewhere. WH are clearly justified in editing it for Rev., on the principle that the MSS are to be followed: it is not so easy to admit it in Jn. Τέσσερες and *τέσσερας* (Rev 4⁴ A) have in any case no place in NT, nor in LXX, where *τέσσερα* is normal (Thackeray 187). We cannot therefore regard *τέσσερα* as Ionic, as the other Ionic forms would have accompanied it, recommended further by uniformity. But even *τέσσερα* does not appear in papyri till ii/A.D., and then but rarely.[2] The Ionic sphere of influence, Asia Minor, behaved in this matter quite

---

[1] Curiously enough, it is B which shows it in LXX (Octateuch), ℵ only having it twice (Thackeray, 73).

[2] In *CR* xv. 33 I quoted *τέσσερας* from CPR 242 (A.D 40), but it must be corrected to *τέσσαρες* acc. Mr. Thackeray also fell into a slip on this matter, in his statement (*Gr.* 74) that the form starts in i/A.D.: he admits it in a letter to me (Dec. 1910). An Egyptian inscr. of i/B.C., in *Archiv* i. 209, no. 22, has *δεκατέσ*]*σερα*, and the same word occurs in BGU i. 133⁹ (A.D. 144–5).

differently: see Schweizer *Perg.* 163. If we could assume that a strictly localised phonetic change produced ερα out of αρα, in the period just preceding that of ℵ, we might explain the absence of τέσσερας by the prevalence of the nominative form (above (1)). The normal acc. thus was τέσσαρες, τέσσερα, which constrained scribes within its area to forsake the αρα of the LXX and NT autographs.

(3) Τεσσάρων is invariable in LXX and NT, and τέσσαρσι(ν) is normal in both (5 times in NT). But the Homeric and poetical τέτρασι(ν) appears in Ac 10[11] E Orig, 11[5] D Epiph, Rev. 20[8] ℵ (Jud 9[34] B): Crönert shows (p. 199) it was common in literary Hellenistic. In Rev 7[2] ℵ has the indeclinable form τοῖς τέσσαρες. MGr preserves the distinction in vocalism between nom.-acc. and gen., the former usually being τέσσερις, the gen. always τεσσάρω(ν) (Thumb *Handb.* 81).

(δ) (1) Between 13 and 19 the forms in the table are firmly established from iii/B.C. down. These were in use as far back as v/B.C. in Attic, in places where the substantive preceded the numeral (Thumb *Hell.* 82). In LXX it alternates with the other form (τρεισκαιδέκα etc.), but it is almost universal in NT, and MGr has no alternative. Lk 13[16] has δέκα καὶ ὀκτὼ ἔτη (D ἔτη ῑη̄), while ἔτη δέκα ὀκτώ in v.[11] happens to preserve the classical rule mentioned above: the agreement is mere coincidence, as the frequency of such numerals preceding the noun in NT shows. Δέκα καὶ ὀκτώ—which is also found in Lk 13[4] AW, [11] AL—is a compromise form found sometimes in LXX (Thackeray 188): the old ὀκτωκαίδεκα is reversed by the influence of the cipher ῑη̄, the commonest way of writing.[1] Whether we should write δεκαοκτώ as well as δεκα·τέσσαρες and δεκαπέντε as one word is hard to determine. Ti.-Gregory (p. 109) give δεκαοκτώ on the witness of the cursives: WH make an exception and print δέκα ὀκτώ, which is perhaps supported by the fact that the numeral may be δέκα ὀχτώ as well as δεκοχτώ in MGr, like δεκαννιά or δέκα ἐννιά for 19 (Thumb *Handb.* 80).

(2) Analogy attempted to extend the rule to 11 and 12. For the former δεκαμίαν in an ostracon of ii/B.C. and δεκαμιᾶς in P Oxy ii. 248 (i/A.D.) are isolated instances. But δεκαδύο flourished during the Ptolemaic age, from which Mayser (p. 316) can only cite one instance of δώδεκα. Δεκαδύο appeared in Attica about B.C. 100, and in Asia Minor a little earlier. Polybius has it, and sometimes MSS of Josephus.[2] But it died out rapidly, for δώδεκα predominates already in Wilcken's ostraca (*Proleg.* 246), and MGr has only ἕντεκα and δώδεκα. Wellhausen[3] states about D that "*twelve*, in the two places where the number is written out, is δεκαδύο, not δώδεκα." There are in fact *eight* instances of δώδεκα in D,[4] with δεκαδύο in Mt 19[28], Lk 9[17], and ῑβ̄ in 38 places (Lk 8[43] β̄ι). Δεκαδύο

[1] The great frequency of this writing in such a MS as D suggests the probability that the autographs used symbols rather than words for numbers. So in our oldest papyrus scrap (𝔭[1] in Souter) we find ῑδ̄ ter in Mt 1[17].

[2] Meisterhans[3] 159; Schweizer *Perg.* 164; Schmidt *Jos.* 508.

[3] *Einleitung*[1] 11: cf. *Proleg.* 96 and Thackeray *Gr.* 188. It does not always do to trust in German accuracy without verifying references!

[4] See the facsimile in Mt 9[20] 11[1], Lk 9[12], Jn 6[13. 67. 71] 11[9], Ac 19[7].

appears also in Ac 19⁷ 24¹¹ HLPω : Ti on the former passage cites very scanty cursive witness in six places. As we might expect, δεκαδύο makes a rather better show, though still a poor one, in LXX (Thackeray 188).

(ε) Τεσσεράκοντα is much better supported in papyri than the corresponding forms of *four*, and in NT the uncials give decisive testimony. No single quotation of -αρ- can be made from אABC, except Rev 7⁴ A. D wavers, having -ερ- once and -αρ- twice (often μ̄, after its manner). W has -αρ- twice in Mt 4², and μ̄ elsewhere (*ter*). The papyri however tell a very different tale;[1] and MGr σαράντα, the only form given in Thumb *Handb.* 80, shows that the ε infection was not lasting. It is not probable that it appeared in the NT autographs. If they had μ̄, as suggested above, we can assign the uncial tradition to an age when the -ερ- form was temporarily established. The fact that *forty* had the syllable before the accent, and *four* after it, was noted in § 33 as the probable cause of the difference between them.

Note σεράκοντα in Ac 7³⁰ C—a first step in the vernacular towards the apocopated form of MGr. An ostracon of vi/vii A.D., now in the Rylands Library, Manchester, shows the numerals from 44 to 49 written out as "μζ σερακονταεπτα" etc. A yet more remarkable anticipation was developing in the first centuries A.D. Dieterich *Unters.* 186 cites τριάντα from an early inscr., and by ix/A.D. σαράντα and the rest of the series were established as they are now.

(ζ) Ἐνενήκοντα in several cursives at Mt 18¹²ᶠ· and Lk 15⁴·⁷ is written ἐννεν.: it was natural that ἐννέα should sometimes assimilate the other 9 forms in which the single ν was correct.

(*b*) Arrangement.

(1) The order which Hellenistic has adopted for the 'teens is kept up usually in higher combinations, as 99 ἐνενήκοντα ἐννέα, 153 (gen.) ἑκατὸν πεντήκοντα τριῶν, 616 ἑξακόσιοι δέκα ἕξ. In four places καί is added, as in Lk 13¹⁶ above, viz. Jn 2²⁰ 5⁵ (where B and minor uncials omit), Ac 13²⁰, Gal 3¹⁷. It is probably not accidental that all five are in time-reckonings with ἔτη: there are however exceptions enough to make any rule doubtful—thus Lk 2³⁷ 13¹¹, Gal 2¹, 2 Co 12². In Rev 11² and 13⁵ we have μῆνας τεσσεράκοντα [καὶ] δύο: the καί is dropped by אP, with C in 13⁵. Ptolemaic papyri agree with NT usage, with καί proportionately rare. The rule was for the numeral to follow the noun (Mayser 316 f.). This however does not hold in NT Greek,

[1] Τεσσερ. seems to appear first in BGU iv. 1105¹², 1170⁶, both Alexandrian, from about B.C. 10. P Lond 262¹ (A.D. 11) (=ii. p. 177) has τεσσερακοστοῦ, but also τεσσαρ. *bis*. Lists kindly lent me by Mr. Thackeray (completed in 1906) show -αρ- in i/ A.D. 21 : 2, in ii/ 18 : 13, in iii/ 8 : 7. See § 33 for fuller notes.

where for the earlier numbers the other order predominates: from 14 on the numeral more often follows.

(2) The old method of representing by subtraction numbers ending in 8 and 9 has not survived, except in 2 Co 11[24] *τεσσεράκοντα παρὰ μίαν forty less one.* It is not found in MGr.

(3) Arithmetical processes are not represented in NT. We may just note that an addition sum ends with *γίνεται* (usually abbreviated) = *comes to*: cf. Ac 4[4] *ἐγενήθη ἀριθμὸς τῶν ἀνδρῶν ὡς χιλιάδες ε̄* (D). Ἐπὶ *τὸ αὐτό* also has an arithmetical connotation,[1] which suggests itself in Ac 2[47]. Προσθεῖναι *ἐπὶ* c. acc. may be noted in Mt 6[27] = Lk 12[25] (cf. Rev 22[18]). Ἐπί is often multiplicative, as *χιλιάδες ἐπὶ δεκάδας γίνονται μυριάδες* (͵α ἐπὶ ῑ / Μ̊) 1000 × 10 = 10,000. This use of *ἐπί* is not unlike Phil 2[27] *ἵνα μὴ λύπην ἐπὶ λύπην σχῶ.*

(4) It is noteworthy that *χίλιοι* with numeral adverbs is supplanted after 5000 by *χιδιάδες* with cardinal: in Ac 4[4] we have this for 5000 as well. It is curious therefore that in Ro 11[4] the *ἑπτὰ χιλιάδας* of LXX should be deliberately replaced by *ἑπτακισχιλίους*. In MGr *χιλιάδες* has driven *χίλιοι* out, except for *χίλιοι* 1000. Just so in NT we note that *χιλιάς* does not come in for the single thousand: it begins where it has to be plural. In Rev 14[3] it is still an nflected fem. noun, and in 5[11] it keeps its substantive constr.; but in 7[4ff.] and elsewhere it is already, as in MGr, an adjective agreeing with its noun, expressed or understood.[2] Similarly *μύριοι* gives place to *μυριάδες* after the unit, but the latter retains its substantive character. (So even in late papyri, as P Oxy vi. 896[17] (A.D. 316) [*ἀργυρίου δηναρίων μυ*]*ριάδαν μίαν.*[3]) In Rev 9[16] we have it qualified by an adverb, as if *δισμύριοι*; but as it has a dependent genitive following it is better to write *δὶς μυριάδες*, a noun, or to follow ℵ and two or three cursives with *δύο*. The autograph may well have had *β̄*. *Μύριοι* and -*άς* are obsolete in MGr.

C. Ordinals.

§ 72. It is significant that no ordinals beyond *fifteenth* occur in the NT. *Πεντηκοστή* was specialised as a feast-

[1] [For another explanation of this phrase see *Harvard Theol. St.* i. 10 ff. (C. C. Torrey); also discussions in *JBL* xxxvii. 105 ff. For further treatment see the Appendix on Semitisms.—ED.]

[2] Rev 21[16] is ambiguous, but 14[20] makes the adj. more probable.

[3] Cf. for this common combination P Oxy vii. index, p. 256.

name: in papyri it and ἑκατοστή similarly survive, as names of taxes. MGr on the same lines uses πέφτη *fifth* as the name of Thursday; but neither this nor the higher ordinals are now found, the cardinals supplanting them after τέταρτος. This use apparently goes back to Byzantine times, but it does not occur in NT, except in the case of εἷς. That this use of εἷς is not due to Hebraism, apart from a modicum of influence due to "translation Greek," may be inferred from considerations set forth in *Prol.* 96. We may add to them the fact that the locution εἷς καὶ εἰκοστός or εἰκάς does not go beyond the first unit: ἡ μία καὶ εἰκάς is *the 21st* (day of the month), but ἡ ἕκτη καὶ εἰκάς *the 26th.*

The ordinals in the 'teens are formed from the old cardinals in which δέκα stands last, after καί. Thackeray gives them as "possibly of Ionic origin." They were at any rate found in Boeotian: thus ἐνακηδεκάτη (Larfeld 16[172]—iii/ii B.C.), ἑσκηδεκάτη (Thumb *Dial.* 231) etc. We may note that compounds also prefer this older form of the cardinal as base: so the series with ἔτος, as ἑπτακαιδεκαετής. What NT writers would have used for ordinals between 21st and 99th we might infer from such forms as δυοτριακοστόν 32nd (P Ryl ii. 157[8]—A.D. 135), τετρακαιεξηκοστόν 64th, τεσσερακοσθόγδον 48th. We have also ἑκατοπεντηκοστόν 150th.

The type εἰκοστὸς πρῶτος still retains signs of life in LXX (Thackeray 189), but neither this nor εἷς δεύτερος καὶ εἰκοστός—found in Ptolemaic papyri (Mayser 318)—appears in NT. In the later LXX books there was a tendency to reverse the order, conforming to the normal order of the alphabetic signs, which had already affected the cardinals. Thus in a petition of iv/A.D. (P Oxy vi. 889[17]) we find ἑβδο]μηκοστὸν καὶ τρίτον. Sundry eccentric forms survived: $\frac{1}{24}$ is τετρακαιεικοστόν in early Ptolemaic papyri, and is seen still in ii/A.D. (as P Fay 82 and 83) and even in iv/A.D. (P Lips 87[5] τετρακαικοστόν). Ordinals in fractions and days of the month were so often written with symbols—as ιη̄ = *the 18th*, κ'ς' = $\frac{1}{26}$ etc.—that the papyri present us with relatively few written out in full

The absence in NT of τετράς, εἰκάς, τριακάς (words of the same class as χιλιάς) to denote the 4th, 20th, and 30th of the month is only due to lack of opportunity. They were used in LXX as in classical Greek, and in papyri well after the NT period. Τετράς was transferred to name a day of the week (Ps 94 (93) title), and τετράδη to-day means *Wednesday.* The only sign of obsolescence is that they were unused by Theodotion and his school (Thackeray 189); but the frequency even of τριακάς in papyri—

note for example P Oxy vi. 967, a private letter of ii/A D.—disposes of any inference.

The forms of ordinals that do occur in NT are in other respects normal. Ὄγδοος is nowhere contracted, as (rarely) in papyri. Τεσσαρεσκαιδέκατος in Ac 27[27. 33] is written τεσσαρασκ. in 81, perhaps under the influence of τεσσαρακ., which occasionally appears in papyri. B[3] writes τεσσαρισκ., as does H the second time: this is found frequently in LXX in correctors of B, and once in B*A (Thackeray). It is assimilated to τρισκαιδέκατος, an orthographic variant of τρεισκ.; but we may remember that τέσσαρις is the normal MGr for the cardinal *four*. In πεντεκαιδεκάτῳ Lk 3[1] L drops the -και-.

The ghost-word δευτεροπρώτῳ Lk 6[1] (all but 𝔭[4] ℵBLW, some important cursives, and the best versions) will be dealt with under Word-composition (§ 104).

D. Adverbials.

That in MGr these multiplicatives have disappeared from ordinary use—there are survivals like τρίσβαθος "thrice deep," *i.e.* "very deep"—makes their fewness in NT easily intelligible. There is no sign among NT MSS (so fâr as Ti records) of the forms in -κι, found rarely in LXX and papyri (Thackeray 136, Mayser 244): Crönert p. 143 f. gives a considerable list of instances from MSS, especially in Josephus.

In Mt 18[22] ἑβδομηκοντάκις ἑπτά is in any case abbreviated for ἑπτάκις (which is read by D). But the question arises whether the -κις has not been added to the wrong element: see *Prol.* 98. W. C. Allen (Comm. *in loc.*) accepts the allusion to Gn 4[24] (first noticed by Tertullian), but suggests that in the LXX there and in Mt *l.c.* we should alike translate *seventy times seven.* In that case the LXX mistranslated the Hebrew. Origen took it as 77 times, as McNeile notes *in loc.* Mr. H. Scott notes the reference in the Testaments, *Benj.* 7[4], where the phrase is quoted with 70 × 7 as the meaning.

E. Distributives.

Two each, etc., are expressed by δύο δύο, or by ἀνὰ δύο or κατὰ δύο—sometimes the two forms are combined. On these see *Prol.* 97; also Thumb *Handb.* 83 for the corresponding usage in MGr. Further discussion is reserved for the Syntax: see also the Semitism examined in the Appendix.

F. Other Numeral Series.

§ 73. Definite compounds with extant words (such as τετράμηνος *κτλ.*, διετής *κτλ.*) will be reserved for the section on Word-composition (§ 107); but we may bring in here those series in which the numerals are specialised for certain uses by agglutinative suffixes—for their history see the section on Word-formation by suffixes.

Abstract numerals, like *τριάς triad,* do not occur in the NT, except for those like χιλιάς, μυριάς, which have been appropriated for a different purpose: on these see above, *B.* They survive in MGr only in specialised senses, as *ἡ Τριάδα the Trinity* (Thumb *Handb.* 84). A derivative τετράδιον occurs (Ac 12[4]), meaning *a company of four*: it is an instance of the specialising force of the suffix *-ιον* (Petersen *Greek Diminutives in -ιον*, p. 84 ff., where *τετράδιον* is not mentioned).

Multiplicative numeral adjectives are found with the suffixes *-πλοῦς* (ἁπλοῦς, διπλοῦς, τετραπλοῦς) and *-πλασίων* (akin to our *-fold* (ἑκατονταπλασίων). It is significant that *30-fold* and *60-fold* are otherwise expressed in Mk 4[8], though *τριακονταπλάσιος* (and *-ων*) had existed: analogy had clearly ceased to be productive. *Ἁπλός*, *διπλός* still survive, and *διπλός* makes a new series *τρίδιπλος* etc. (Thumb *Handb.* 83).

Of the n-*th day* is expressed by a series in *-αῖος*: so in NT δευτεραῖος, τεταρταῖος, and cf. ὀκταήμερος, which shows that the series did not develop in popular Greek. Polybius has the regular *ὀγδοαῖος*, and literary Greek shows a large number of these forms.

Fractions scarcely appear in NT. Τὸ τρίτον $\frac{1}{3}$ (sign *γ'*) occurs in Rev 8 *sexies*, and τὸ τέταρτον $\frac{1}{4}$ (*δ'*) in Rev 6[8]. We have also the word for *half* (sign ∠), ἥμισυς, in classical Greek declined *-εια -υ* regularly. It is derived from the proethnic *sēmi-* (*ἡμι-*, Lat. *sēmi-*, O.E. *sām* (in Shakespeare's *sand*blind) with the suffix *-tu.* *Ἡμι-* occurs in many compounds, as ἡμίωρον *half an hour*, *ἡμιόλιος one and a half* (adj.). Some curious features arise in the spelling and declension of *ἥμισυς* in NT times. The fem. ἡμίσεια has been cut loose from the declension, and is only used as a noun (*sc.* μοῖρα); while ἥμισυς, as an adj. of two terminations, or even as an indeclinable quasi-numeral ἥμισυ, is almost entirely confined to the forms ἥμισυ (ἥμισου) and (much less frequently) ἡμίσους and ἡμίσει.

(*a*) The spelling ἥμυσυς -υ is common between iv/ and i/B.C., the second syllable being assimilated to the third: very rarely it is carried into forms where -υ does not form part of the suffix "In the Ptolemaic papyri this form predominates in iii/B.C., in ii/i B.C. ἥμυσυς and ἥμισυς are represented by nearly equal numbers" (Thackeray 95): he adds that the absence of ἥμυσυ from the LXX is unfavourable to the trustworthiness of the uncials.[1] Its absence from the NT will, on the same showing, be a good sign, for with the rapid movement of υ towards the simple *i*-sound ἥμυσυ became obsolete: only six instances can be cited from the imperial age by Crönert, and in NT it is represented only by τὰ ἥμυσοι (-οι = -υ) in Lk 19^{8} D*—indecl., with ἡμίση in correction: see § 35.

(*b*) Another peculiarity is thus noted by WH (*App.*[2] 165): "In Ap[3] ἥμισυ each time has the *v.l.* ἡμίσου (A^{a}, ℵA, ℵ*: cf. Is 44^{16} B), which likewise is one of the variants for ἡμίσους Mc[1]." In Mk 6^{23} LΔW read ἕως ἥμισυ, and it seems better to regard ἡμίσου (? ἥμισου) there as the same reading: for this curious form see (*e*) below. The indecl. ἥμισυ appears also in Lk 19^{8} τὰ ἥμισυ AD* (ημυσοι) RΔ 69: cf. Tob 19^{10} B.

(*c*) Τὰ ἡμίσια Lk 19^{8} ℵB*Q 382 and L (-εια) may be supported by a Pisidian inscr. of the imperial age (*Papers of Amer. School* iii. 204), whence Crönert cites ἡμυσίοις. It is obviously useless to cite *fem.* forms in -σια (with WH). W. F. Moulton (WM 75 n.[1]) compares ὀξεῖα χρέμισαν in Hesiod *Sc.* 348, and θήλεια neut. in Aratus 1068: WS 87 adds from Meisterhans a neuter πλατεῖα dated B.C. 358. Thackeray 179 gives LXX parallels. MGr, which has developed the adj. in -ύς, makes plur. βαθειοί -ές -ά, which is the descendant of these forms.

(*d*) The older forms of the gen do not appear in NT uncials, except for ἡμίσεως Mk 6^{23} S and ἡμίσεος *ib.* Π.

(*e*) Some account of general papyrus usage may be added, drawn mainly from Mayser (294 f.), supplemented from an analysis of a large number of documents dated A.D., containing about 90 occurrences. In these last no plural occurs—the Hellenistic ἡμίσεις and ἡμίση are barely quotable A.D.—and ἡμίσια (so spelt, 8 times) is only used as a noun. (It is absent altogether in LXX.) Τὸ ἥμισυ, with or without μέρος, increases in frequency. Ἡμίσους gen. and (less frequently) ἡμίσει dat. occur freely, and may agree with fem. nouns, as ἀρούρη[ς ἡ]μίσους BGU ii. 422^{19} (ii/A.D.). Ἥμισυ (-ου) indecl. is in these documents restricted to the position following an integer, as ἀρταβῶν ἑβδομήκοντα δύο ἥμυσυ BGU ii. 538^{33} (100 A.D.), another hand having already written the same phrase with

[1] To his one ex. (Dn Θ 7^{25} B) Crönert adds Nu 28^{13} in a palimpsest edited by Tischendorf; also one from Cod. G of the Octateuch (iv/v A.D.).

ἡμίσους. Evidence for its wider use may be seen in Thackeray p. 180. For ἥμισου (Thackeray 180 n.[1]) five documents may be cited from ii/iii A.D.: add a papyrus cited by Crönert (*Mem.* 23) with οἵμυσου (A.D. 261), and NT uncials as above.

(*f*) The MGr μισός is prepared for in the Doric ἥμισσος (*Syll.* 594 *bis*, 598[58], both ii/B.C.), and ἡμίσωι *IMAe* iii. 168 (i/B.C.), *Syll.* 493[11], τὸ ἥμισον *Syll.* 596[7] (ii/B.C.): we might even accent this derivative oxytone, as in MGr.

(*g*) No instance can be quoted in which καί links ἥμισυ with an integer preceding. It is natural therefore that 046 and a good many cursives should omit the irregular conjunction in Rev 11[9] ἡμέρας τρεῖς καὶ ἥμισυ: it is significant that in v.[11], where the order is changed to τρεῖς ἡμέρας καὶ ἥμισυ, only two cursives omit. This is of course only one more irregularity added to the special grammar of this Book: we need not suspect the reading. Note that the idiomatic use of ἥμισυ indecl. following an integer survives in MGr, as δυό 'μισυ 2½, τρεῖς ἥμισυ 3½ (Thumb *Handb.* 82).

PRONOUNS.

§ 74. The Pronoun system retains one or two special flexions which from prehistoric times differentiated it from the Noun. Chief among them is the nom. acc. neut. sing in -ο(δ), with which we compare the form surviving in Skt. *tad*, Lat. *istud*, Eng. *that*, etc.

Demonstrative Pronouns include ὁ (the Definite Article), οὗτος *this*, ὅδε *this*, ἐκεῖνος *that*, τοιοῦτος *such*, τοσοῦτος *so much*, τηλικοῦτος *so great*, τοιόσδε *such*.

Thus decline

Sing.	*N.* ὁ ἡ τό	οὗτος	αὕτη	τοῦτο	ἐκεῖνος ἐκείνη ἐκεῖνο
	A. (see § 48)	τοῦτον	ταύτην	τοῦτο	and the rest like καλός
	G.	τούτου	ταύτης	τούτου	
	D.	τούτῳ	ταύτῃ	τούτῳ	
Plur.	*N.*	οὗτοι	αὗται	ταῦτα	
	A.	τούτους	ταύτας	ταῦτα	
	G.	τούτων			
	D.	τούτοις	ταύταις	τούτοις	

Ὅδε (rare) is declined as ὁ with enclitic δε added: similarly τοιόσδε is τοιός like ἅγιος with δε (only once found 2 Pet 1[17]). The others are like οὗτος: eject the initial τ and prefix τοι-, τοσ-, τηλικ- respectively.

They may however take -ον in nom acc. sing. neut.: thus τοσοῦτον Heb 12[1], τηλικοῦτον *ib.* ℵ*, but τοσοῦτο Heb 7[22] ℵ*ABCD*P 33 cu[3]; in

Mt 18[5] τοιοῦτο ℵBLW *al.*, τοιοῦτον D etc. In Heb. Blass might have regarded it as significant that τοσοῦτον precedes a vowel, and τοσοῦτο a consonant. Both are inherited from earlier Greek.

Ἄλλος -η -ο (otherwise like καλός) *other*, and ἕτερος (like ἅγιος) *different* (sometimes still *other of two*).

Ὁ δεῖνα so-and-so (A τὸν δεῖνα, G τοῦ δεῖνος, D τῷ δεῖνι) occurs once (in acc. Mt 26[18]).

Ἕκαστος each (like καλός).

§ 75. **Relative** Pronouns are ὅς and ὅστις *who* (see SYNTAX), ὅσ-γε and ὅσ-περ (*i.e.* ὅς with enclitics—see SYNTAX), οἷος *of which kind, such as*, ὅσος *as many as, as much as*, ὁποῖος *such as*: the last three are declined like καλός or ἅγιος regularly.

Interrogative Pronouns are τίς *who?*, ποῖος *of what sort?*, πηλίκος *how great?*, πόσος *how many?* (like ἅγιος and καλός).

The **Indefinite** Pronoun is τις *some, any* (enclitic).

Thus decline:

Sing.	*N.*	ὅς ἥ ὅ	ὅστις	ἥτις	ὅτι	τίς	τί	τις	τι
	A.	ὅν ἥν ὅ	(ὅς with enclitic			τίνα	τί	τινά	τι
	G.	etc., like	ὅτου		τις)	τίνος		τινός	
	D.	Article,				τίνι		τινί	
Plur.	*N.*	but accented	οἵτινες	αἵτινες	ἅτινα	τίνες	τίνα	τινές	τινά
	A.	and without τ.				τίνας	τίνα	τινάς	τινά
	G.					τίνων		τινῶν	
	D.					τίσι(ν)		τισί(ν)	

Ὅστις is only used in nom. (and acc. neut.), apart from the old additional gen. neut. ὅτου, surviving in the stereotyped phrase ἕως ὅτου (*as far as what*) *until*, and in Lk 13[25] ἀφ' ὅτου D. Its oblique cases are rare in vernacular *Κοινή*: sometimes we have them with additions equivalent to our *-soever*, as ὁντιναδηποτοῦν *whomsoever*. The neuter ὅτι is often (very needlessly) printed ὅ τι or even ὅ,τι to distinguish it from ὅτι *that*.

§ 76. **Personal** Pronouns are ἐγώ *I*, σύ *thou*, αὐτός -ή -ό *he, she, it*.

Thus decline:

Sing.	*N.* ἐγώ	*N.V.*	σύ	*N.*	αὐτός	-ή	-ό
	A. ἐμέ με		σέ σε		αὐτόν	-ήν	-ό
	G. ἐμοῦ μου		σοῦ σου		αὐτοῦ	-ῆς	-οῦ
	D. ἐμοί μοι		σοί σοι		αὐτῷ	-ῇ	-ῷ
Plur.	*N.* ἡμεῖς	*N.V.*	ὑμεῖς	*N.*	αὐτοί	-αί	-ά
	A. ἡμᾶς		ὑμᾶς		αὐτούς	-άς	-ά
	G. ἡμῶν		ὑμῶν		αὐτῶν		
	D. ἡμῖν		ὑμῖν		αὐτοῖς	-αῖς	-οῖς

For the use of the enclitic forms see the SYNTAX. After prepositions the enclitic forms are not used, except with πρός (generally).

Αὐτός is properly demonstrative, and has an adjective use = *self*, *same*, for which see SYNTAX.

§ 77. The **Reflexive** Pronouns are *ἐμαυτόν -ήν myself*, *σεαυτόν -ήν thyself*, *ἑαυτόν -ήν -ό* (rarely *αὑτόν -ήν -ό*) *himself*, *herself*, *itself*. Thus decline:

Sing.	*A.* ἐμαυτόν -ήν	σεαυτόν -ήν	ἑαυτόν -ήν -ό
	G. ἐμαυτοῦ -ῆς	σεαυτοῦ -ῆς	ἑαυτοῦ -ῆς -οῦ
	D. ἐμαυτῷ -ῇ	σεαυτῷ -ῇ	ἑαυτῷ -ῇ -ῷ
Plur.	*A.* ἑαυτούς -άς -ά	all persons	
	G. ἑαυτῶν		
	D. ἑαυτοῖς -αῖς -οῖς		

For the vernacular spelling *ἐμᾱτόν* see § 37.

The shortened forms *σαυτόν* and *αὑτόν* occupy a somewhat ambiguous position. The former is non-existent in NT, except for one appearance in B (Jas 2^{8}) and one in a few cursives (Rom 14^{22}). But the latter is read by WH in some twenty places, and the strength of their case seems irresistible: in Jn 2^{24} *αὐτὸς δὲ Ἰησοῦς οὐκ ἐπίστευεν αὑτὸν αὐτοῖς*, and Lk 23^{12} *προϋπῆρχον γὰρ ἐν ἔχθρᾳ ὄντες πρὸς αὑτούς*, it is simply impossible to read the ordinary demonstrative. The *h* was faint at this time, but still heard; and in spite of serious difficulties it seems imperative to believe it could sometimes differentiate the pronouns as in much earlier Greek. See *Vocabulary s.v. αὑτοῦ.*

The difficulty lies mostly in the fact that our outside evidence proves overwhelmingly the disappearance of the dissyllabic forms of 2nd and 3rd person reflexives before the age of the NT. In Attic inscrr. ἑαυτ. has to *αὑτ.* the ratio 31 : 23 from B.C. 403 to 300, while from 300 to 30 it rises to 100 : 7 (Meisterhans[3] 153). In Egypt, in the Ptolemaic inscrr. and papyri included in Mayser's survey (p. 305 f.), *αὑτ.* outnumbers *ἑαυτ.* by 3 : 1 in iii/B.C., the proportion is reversed in ii/B.C., and in i/B.C. *ἑαυτ.* stands alone. In Pergamon during the pre-Roman period *ἑαυτ.* stands at 24 : 5 above *αὑτ.*, while under Roman rule it rises to 18 : 2 (Schweizer *Perg.* 162). In Magnesia no certain instance of *αὑτ.* is forthcoming (Nachmanson *Magn.* 144). These statistics suffice to show that *αὑτ.* was very near extinction before A.D. But as we look at Mayser's analysis for the second half of the Ptolemaic period, we find that the large majority against *αὑτ.* is secured by official papyri and inscrr.: in private documents there is absolute equality. *A priori* we should expect to find *αὑτ.* vanish first in a country where psilosis was complete, since it would no longer be distinguishable from *αὐτ.* This is true of Asia Minor, as Pergamon and Magnesia attest. But the *h* may have survived elsewhere, and the actual citations that are given from Egyptian documents show that *αὑτ.* had not yet ceased to make sporadic appearances. Thackeray (*Gr.* 190) shows that *αὑτοῦ* still exists in LXX, though scantily). Against Blass's denial, we must leave room for the possibility of very occasional retention of the dissyllabic form. See *Vocab. s.v.* *ἑαυτοῦ* for post-Ptolemaic instances of *αὑτοῦ*.

For the plural of the reflexive, *ἑαυτούς* stands alone in the Hellenistic age. A survival of *ὑμῶν αὐτῶν* may be noted in 1 Co 5[13], which is quoted from the Pentateuch: in this part of the LXX (Thackeray 191) these forms were still current. On *ἑαυτούς* as the common plural for all persons, coupled with the exclusion of *ἑαυτόν* from 1st and 2nd person, see *Proleg.* 87. 1 Co 10[29] has *τὴν ἑαυτοῦ* where *τὴν σεαυτοῦ* might have stood (so D_2*); but we may render impersonally "one's own."

Only negligible MSS violate this rule, except in Jn 18[34], where A and W join the crowd with *ἀφ' ἑαυτοῦ* "of thyself," and Jn 14[22] *ἐμφανίζειν ἑαυτόν*, read by three Ferrar cursives and therefore presumably their archetype. In Mk 1[44] W has *δεῖξον ἑαυτόν*, and in Lk 23[39] actually *σῶσον καὶ αὐτὸν καὶ ἡμᾶς*. The LXX citation in Lk 10[27] has *ὡς ἑαυτόν* in A, as elsewhere in inferior uncials. See Thackeray 190 f.

§ 78. The **Reciprocal** Pronoun is *ἀλλήλους -ων -οις*: no fem. or neut. forms occur in NT. *Ἑαυτούς* is also used, and sometimes phrases with *ἄλλος* or *εἷς*—see the SYNTAX.

Possessive Pronouns, attached to the Personal, are *ἐμός* *my*, *σός* *thy*, *ἡμέτερος* *our*, *ὑμέτερος* *your*, all declined as regular adj. *Ἴδιος* *own* belongs to the same category.

§ 79. Pronouns indicating duality, as *πότερος* *which of*

two?, ἑκάτερος *each of two*, against τίς *which* and ἕκαστος *each*, are obsolete in the vernacular: see the SYNTAX. The NT has only ἀμφότεροι *both*, and ἕτερος *other*; but the former has begun to lose its duality, and the latter has almost entirely lost it—see *Prol.* 79 f. and further in SYNTAX. For this place also will be reserved tables of Correlative Pronouns and Pronominal Adverbs.

VERBS.

§ 80. The verb in Hellenistic Greek has been simplified in many directions, as compared with earlier profusion of forms; but except for the complete elimination of the Dual no category has been definitely removed. MGr has entirely lost two Moods, the Optative and (except dialectically) the Infinitive. It has also treated the Middle Voice and the verbs in -μι just as Latin treated them in prehistoric times. A few survivals serve as exceptions to prove the rule. These and other tendencies, the issue of which is seen in MGr, were all at work early in Hellenistic; but they had not travelled far enough to relieve the accidence of much grammatical lumber, once significant but now outworn. A brief summary may be given before we present the paradigms.

Conjugations.—For practical purposes the verb may still be divided into the familiar categories of Simple -ω Verbs, Contract Verbs, and verbs in -μι. The last-named are being largely replaced by forms of the other two classes; and among the Contract Verbs there is a tendency towards the fusion of -άω and -έω forms, which however has not yet gone far.

Voice.—The Middle and the Passive have drawn closer together in form, while Active endings have replaced a good many Middle where there was no clear distinction of function.

Mood.—The Optative has very largely disappeared, being restricted to a few uses; but for a semi-literary predilection in the Lucan writings, we might leave it out of the paradigms and merely set down isolated forms.

Tense.—The Strong Aorist survives (in one or more Voices) in less than seventy verbs, and most of its occurrences are accounted for by the commonness of a verb's use preserving ancient forms. The Weak Aorist is constantly encroaching; and its endings are steadily driving out those special to the Strong Aorist, even in the verbs which keep the old root form. Weak Aorist endings moreover tend to oust the proper suffix of the 3rd plural Perfect Active, and so complete the identity of person-endings between these tenses. In past tenses of the Indicative a weakening of the Augment's hold has begun in compound verbs.

Conjugation and Tense Stems.

§ 81. The complexities of the Greek verb are due mainly to the survival of conjugation stems, which give great variety to the present tense and its attendant imperfect. In prehistoric Indo-Germanic these stems may have carried some functional distinctions; but it is difficult to prove these distinctions in all cases, and most of them were obsolete before Hellenistic Greek arose, even if they could be claimed for earlier stages. A brief sketch of the historical classification of present stems may be given, so far as concerns words occurring in NT: for a full account reference may be made to Brugmann-Thumb *Gr.* 316 ff., or to Giles 425 ff. from which the numeration of the classes is taken.

The primary division is that between Thematic and Unthematic formations, which accounts for the obvious classes of -ω verbs and -μι verbs, and for other peculiarities of I.E. verb-systems. Thematic formations show the vowel *o* in the 1 sing. and plur. and 3 plur. (exc. imper.) and ϵ in 2 sing. and plur. and 3 sing. In unthematic formations the person-ending is added directly to the root or the tense-stem. We need not here discuss whether the *o* : *e* is historically a part of the root, ejected in unthematic formations by the prehistoric action of accent, or a functional suffix: all these questions belong to a period which was over for Greek ages before Homer. The study of the Hellenistic verb soon shows that unthematic formations were receding fast before thematic, which in MGr cover the whole field except for the substantive verb. This moreover is of Middle form; and Hellenistic largely retains unthematic Middles where the Active has become thematic.

A. Conjugation Classes, Present Stem.

The following are the conjugation classes: in each case (*a*) is thematic, and (*b*) unthematic. Where no unthematic forms survive in Hellenistic, no distinction is attached.

I. Person suffixes are added to the root—
(*a*) with thematic vowel.
Thus ἔλυο-ν, ἔλυε-ς, λυό-μεθα, λύε-σθε.
(*b*) without thematic vowel.
Thus ἔσ-τι, pl. εἰσί (for ἐντί, i.e. *senti*);
ἔφη-ν, pl. ἔφἄ-μεν, mid. ἐφἄ-μην.
The singular active had strong root-form, the plural and the whole middle had it weakened: thus φη : φἄ, εσ : σ. Here levelling has obliterated much of a distinction which served no special purpose.

I*a*. Reduplicated forms (with ι in redupl. syllable).
(*a*) thematic.
Thus πί-πτ-ο-μεν (√ *pet*), ἵ-ζ-ε-τε (= *si-zd-*, √ *sed*).
(*b*) unthematic.
Thus ἵ-στη-μι, pl. ἵ-στἄ-μεν, mid. ἵ-στἄ-μαι
τί-θη-σι, pl. τι-θέ-ασι, mid. ἐ-τι-θέ-ντο.

II. With formative suffix in *-n-*.
(*α*)
(*a*) suffix νο : νε or ανο : ανε.
(i.) added to root.
Thus αὐξ-άνο-μεν, τέμ-νε-ται.
(ii.) added to root with a nasal inserted (only -άνω).
Thus λαμ-βάνο-μεν (λαβ-εῖν), ἐλάνθ-ανε (λαθ-εῖν), λαγχ-άνε-τε (λαχ-εῖν).
(*b*) suffix νη : νἄ added to root.
Thus δύ-νἄ-ται.
(*β*)
(*a*) (i.) suffix νυο : νυε.
Thus δεικ-νύε-τε etc.: verbs in -νυμι from classical times thus tended to become thematic.

(ii.) suffix *νϝο : νϝε*.

Thus *φθά-νο-μεν, τί-νε-τε*.

(iii.) suffix *νεϝο : νεϝε*.

Thus *κινούμεθα* (= *-νεϝό-μεθα*), *ἀφικνεῖτο* (= *-νέϝε-το*).

(*b*) suffix *νῡ : νῠ* (from *neu* : *nu*) added to root.

Thus *δείκ-νῡ-μι, ἐδείκ-νῠ-τε, δεικ-νῠ́-μεθα*.

III. With formative suffix in *so* : *se*.

Thus *κλά-(σ)-ω, σπά-(σ)-ω αὔξ-ω* (= *aug-so-*).

IV. *Stems in* sko : ske.

The suffix is added to simple or reduplicated stems, sometimes with *ι* before it.

Thus *βό-σκω, εὑρ-ίσκω, δι-δά(κ)-σκω, γι-(γ)νώ-σκω*.

V. *Stems in* to : te.

This class may be ignored for our purpose. Verbs in *-πτω* do not belong to it: see VII.

VI. *Stems in θο : θε*.

Thus *πρή-θω, ἔσ-θω*: it is very small.

VII. *Stems in yo : yε*.

This is a very large class, varying greatly in form according to the consonant or vowel preceding. A large proportion of these verbs are formed from nouns. Among the principal types are:

(i.) with *yo*: *yε* added to root.

Thus *βαίνω* (= I.E. *g*^{u}*m̥-i̯o-*), *χαίρω* (*-r̥-i̯o-*).

(ii.) added to another suffix.

Thus *κρῖνω* (*κρῐν-yω*: *κριν* = *κρῐ-ν*).

(iii.) added to the stem of a noun.

Thus *φυλάσσω* (*κy*), *ἀστράπτω* (*πy*), *ποιμαίνω* (*n̥y*), *ἐλπίζω* (*δy*), *μαρτῦρομαι* (*ῠρy*), *τιμάω* (*āy*) *ζήω*, *φιλέω* (*εy*), *μεθύω*, etc.

Tense Stems.

§ 82. These are essentially of the same nature as the conjugation stems; but having developed definite functions, they came to be formed from roots belonging to any one, or more than one, of the stems given above.

B. Strong Aorist.

This is a special use of formations already described under *A.* I. In the indicative it has of course only the augmented form.

(*a*) = I. (*a*) with weak gradation in the root.

Thus *ἔλιπο-ν* (√λειπ), *ἐσπάρ-ην* (√σπερ, with *r̥r* in weak gradation, and passive suffix), *ἔπαθο-ν* (√πενθ, with *α* = *n̥*), *ἔσχο-ν* (√σεχ).

Sometimes the rule of weak gradation is broken, when the present stem is differentiated by the formative of another class. Thus *αἰσθέ-σθαι* from *αἰσθ-άνο-μαι*, *ἔτεμο-ν* from *τέμ-νω*, *ἔπεσο-ν* (for *ἔπετον*) from *πί-πτ-ω*, *εὗρο-ν* from *εὑρ-ίσκω*, *ἐγενό-μην* from *γίνομαι* (= *γι-γν-*).

(*b*) = I. (*b*).

Thus *ἔστη-ν*, *ἔθε-μεν*, *δό-σθε*, *γνῶ-θι*.

The Strong Aorist in the passive is not thematic, being formed with an *η* which has no connexion with the thematic vowel.

C. Weak Aorist.

The stem is formed by adding *σ* to the root, with the suffixes attached directly. Forms answering to this description have disappeared from Greek, except for the 1st sg. (*ἔδειξα* = *édeiks-m̥*), and in active and middle, apart from the subj. and two or three other forms, the characteristic of the tense is *σα*. After liquids this *σ* is obscured.

Thus *ἔλεξα* (√λεγ), *ἐλυσά-μεθα* (√λυ), *ἔκρῖνα* (*κρῐν*), *ἔσπειρα* (√σπερ), *ἔνειμα* (√νεμ), *ἔκτεινα* (√κτεν), *ἔστειλα* (√στελ).

The Weak Aorist in the passive is formed in a wholly different way. A new formative *θη*, drawn originally from a middle person-ending (2nd sing.) *-θης*, has extended through the whole tense system, with endings following those of the Strong Aorist.

Thus *ἐδό-θης*, *κρι-θῆ-ναι*.

D. Future Stems.

The Future is partly extended from the Weak Aorist subj., which before the analogy of the pres. subj. of thematic verbs affected it had the flexion λύσω -εις -ει -ομεν -ετε -ουσι, and similarly in the middle. Probably there was also some influence from a special future stem in *syo* : *sye*, found in Aryan and Lithuanian, which coincided in form. In most verbs accordingly the Future act. and mid. coincide in stem with the Weak Aorist, but keep -σω when the aorist has a special form, as δώσω (aor. ἔδωκα).

In verbs with Liquid stems, and in a few others which may be sought in the Table, the Future stem is formed with -έ(σ)ω instead of -σω, and a flexion results identical with that of the Contracta in -έω. Thus from κρῐν (κρῐνέ(σ)ω) κρινῶ, from σπερ σπερῶ, from ἐλπίζω ἐλπιοῦμαι.

In LXX and occasionally in papyri and inscriptions we find a similar future from stems in -άζω : thus ἐργᾶται from ἐργάζομαι. The absence of this in NT is marked, and shows a dialectic distinction : thus in 1 Co 2[16] the LXX συμβιβᾶ is altered to συμβιβάσει. The formation is found in Ionic : see Thumb *Dial.* 358.

In the Passive the Future is formed from the (Strong and Weak) Aorist stems by adding -σομαι to the characteristic (θ)η. Thus κριθήσομαι, ἀνοιγήσομαι. The "Third" Future, or Future Perfect, is obsolete ; but the form κεκράξομαι (from κέκραγα) is on the same model.

E. Perfect Stem.

This stem is unthematic, and in the earliest period (as in classical Sanskrit, and in our own speech-family up to the Middle English period) had vowel gradation, with strong root in singular active and weak elsewhere. So in classical Greek οἶδα, 2 pl. ἴστε, just as in Chaucer's English *I wot, we witen.* In Hellenistic this verb is assimilated to other perfects ; and the only trace of gradation is that the middle stem sometimes differs from the active.

The Perfect stem (except in the verb οἶδα) is reduplicated, with ε in the reduplicating syllable. It has in the Active two formations, Strong, with internal change as in our own Strong Perfect, and Weak, with a formative suffix κ. Thus λέλοιπα from λείπω is historically parallel with our *rode* from *ride.* Roots with radical *ε* show *ο* in its place in the Strong Perfect active, except when combined with *υ* (*πέφευγα* from *φεύγω*). The suffix *κ* only appears when the verb stem ends in a vowel or a dental mute: thus **λέλυ-κα** from **λύ-ω**, **πέπει-κα** from **πείθω**.

The past tense of this stem, called Pluperfect, has (usually) the augment, and a special set of person-endings with the connecting vowel *ει*, which in Hellenistic goes right through.

The Middle and Passive have one set of forms, Perfect and Pluperfect, which are normal unthematic forms from the Perfect stem.

F. Verbals.

Two adjectives are formed from verbal roots, unconnected with the tense system. One in -*τός*, historically identical with the Latin perf. partic. passive in -*tus* (-*sus*) and our English -*d* participle, is extended to derived verbs and attached to their stem: the form can usually be deduced empirically by putting -*τος* for the -*σω* of the Future. For the function of this verbal adjective, see *Proleg.* p. 221 f.

The gerundive in -*τέος*, formed in the same way, is very rare in Hellenistic (only once in NT—Lk 5[38]).

VERBS.

Augment and Reduplication.

1. Augment with ἠ.

§ 83. The augment with *ἠ* is found in later Attic (since 300 B.C.) in the verbs *μέλλω*, *δύναμαι*, *βούλομαι*, probably by analogy of *ἤ-θελον*, where *ἠ*- was a preposition (Lat. *ē*, Skt. *ā*).[1] Of these forms *ἠβουλ.* never occurs in NT (exc. ℵ in Philem [13], HLP in Ac 28[18] and cursives in 2 Jn [12]), though sometimes in LXX, and once in a i/A.D. papyrus (P Oxy ii. 281[16]). So also in patr. often, esp. in aor. *Ἤμελλον* and *ἔμελλον* alternate: WH print *ἤμ.* always in Lk and Ac, exc. Ac 21[27], but in Jn both forms about equally. *Δύναμαι* has aor. *ἠδ.* (often with variant *ἐδ.*), but great fluctuation in the impf.: *ἠδ.* is read by WH 7 times and *ἐδ.* 12 times. See on both MG *s.v.* and WH *App.*[2] 169. *Θέλω* (never *ἐθέλω*) makes *ἠθ.* always, as in class. Gr. To the same class are generally assigned *ἑώρων*, *ἀνέῳξα* (and other forms from *ἀνοίγω*), *ἐάγην*, in which by "quantity metathesis" *ηο* etc. would become *εω*, *εῳ*

---

[1] See for its extent Meisterhans[3] 169; for its origin, Brugmann *Grd.*[2] II. ii. § 634, Giles[2] 408. It appears occasionally in earlier poetry: see Veitch *s.vv.*

εα̅.[1] Ἑώρων only Jn 6² ℵΓ etc. where ἐθεώρουν BDL(W) is the better reading. Ἀνοίγω (διανοίγω), as the simple verb became obsolete, took an augment in the preposition, either with or without that in the root syllable: hence the triple types ἠνεῳ. (with inf. ἀνεῳχθῆναι), ἠνοι., ἀνεῳ. For the distribution of forms between the types see WH *App.*² 168. Κατάγνυμι has aor. κατέαξα, pass. -εαγην, but in the latter the augm. is continued in subj. κατεαγῶσι Jn 19³¹ (as in ἀνεῳχθῆναι above). Veitch quotes κατεάξαντες from Lysias and κατ-εαγῇ -εαγείη -εαγείς from the Ionic Hippocrates. A more difficult peculiarity is the fut. κατεάξω Mt 12²⁰ (=Is 42³, but not LXX), which must go with the nouns κατέαγμα (BGU ii. 647 *bis*, P Amh ii. 93¹⁹, both ii/A.D.), ἔαγμα (*ap.* G. Meyer³ 165). Possibly -εάξας -εάξω -έαγμα may be explained side by side with ἐθελήσας ἐθελήσω ἐθελημός, on which see reff. above.[2] In LXX (Hab 3¹² *al.*) the fut. is κατάξω, but κατεάξω in Symm. Ps 47⁸.

2. Double Augment.

Ἀποκαθίστημι (as in LXX)[3] in Mk 8²⁵ ἀπεκατέστη, Mk 3⁵=Mt 12¹³, Lk 6¹⁰ ἀπεκατεστάθη, inserts an augment after both prepositions, which seems a well-established vernacular usage. So ἀντεκατέστητε Heb 12⁴ L* (WH alt.), (παρεσυνεβλήθη Ps 48 (49)¹³· ²¹ AT). The forms of ἀνοίγω described in (1) above are the only surviving exx. of augment attached both to verb and preposition. See the list for Attic in Rutherford *NP* 83: of these only ἀνέχεσθαι shows double augment even as a variant in NT. Cf. Ac 18¹⁴, where ℵ*B support ἀνεσχόμην, the form attested by Moeris as Hellenistic (Ti *in loc.*).[4] From ἀφίημι the impf. is read by WH with ἠφ. in Mk 1³⁴ 11¹⁶: this form is perhaps not Attic (Meisterh.³ 173, but only one ex., which is not decisive). Note ἐπροεφήτευσεν Mk 7⁶ W.

3. Syllabic Augment for Temporal.

In verbs which originally began with *s* or *w* the primitive syllabic augment often leaves its traces behind, contraction following the loss of the consonant: thus εἶχον (not ἦχον) for ἔ-εχον (=ἔσεχον), εἵλκυσα for ἐ-έλκυσα. In Attic ὠθέω and ὠνέομαι normally augmented ἐω. (from ἐ-Fω.); but ἐξέωσεν Ac 7⁴⁵ ℵ*E (Ti) is the only trace in NT of such forms.[5] Ἐργάζομαι and cpds. have ἠργ. in Attic,[6] which prevails in NT;

---

[1] See Brugmann-Thumb *Gr.* 310.

[2] Various unsatisfactory explanations of the word have been given; by Thom. Mag. (who would accent κατεάγωσι as perf. subj. act.), by W. (who thinks differentiation from fut. of κατάγω adequate—see WM 82), and by G. Meyer *l.c.* (see *CR* xv. 36). See Cobet on the word (*NT Vatic.* lxxix).

[3] Add Letr. 525 (ii/A.D.) and other parallels in WS § 12. 7 n. But ἀποκατεστάθη P Oxy i. 38¹² (i/A.D.). See Dieterich 213.

[4] Ἐνοχλέω retains double augment in perf. as late as ii/B.C. (P Amh ii. 37⁹, ἠνώχλησαι). Cf. Reinhold 68.

[5] The perf. ἐώνημαι is found twice in papyri of ii/A.D. (P Oxy ii. 252⁶, P Amh ii. 68⁸).

[6] Perhaps from ἠ-Fεργ., which would account for the different form in the perfect. See Meisterhans³ 171; *CR* xv. 35.

but the aor. κατειργ. (mid. and pass.) is read by WH with ℵ* four times in Paul, B* however thrice opposing.

4. Dropped Augment.

In the *pluperfect* the augment is usually dropped: so Mt 7^{25}, Mk 14^{44} $15^{7.10}$ [Mk] 16^{9}, Lk 19^{15}, Jn 11^{57}, Ac 4^{22} 14^{23}, 1 Jn 2^{19}, and temporal augment dropped Jn 11^{30} 14^{7}. Among these passages only Ac 4^{22} (ἐγεγόνει ℵAEP *al.*) shows respectable attestation for the augmented form. It appears however unquestionably in Lk 11^{22} 16^{20}, Jn 9^{22} 11^{44} (D*om.), Ac 26^{32} (AL om.). In Attic writers the temporal augment is omitted, but not the syllabic, MSS and edd. notwithstanding (see *e.g.* Ti on Ac 4^{22}, Shilleto on Dem. *FL* p. 38). Attic inscr. down to iii/B.C. show 6 augmented forms and no omissions (Meisterh.[3] 170); and Ptolemaic papyri in P Tebt, P Amh and P Fay show 5 augmented against 2 unaugmented.[1] The evidence in Schweizer also goes strongly against omission. In such a point the evidence of MSS cannot be trusted far, but it may be noted that Jos. (according to Schmidt) prefers omission in act., retention in pass. of compound verbs, while in simplicia omission is fairly common though not preponderant, even where hiatus is not concerned. In Polybius the augment greatly preponderates in simplicia, though often dropped in compounds, esp. in act. forms.[2] The pluperf. of ἵστημι is a case by itself. The augmentless ἑστήκειν occurs Rev 7^{11} C, and is not uncommon outside NT. WH accept throughout the spelling ἱστήκειν, in which they think the analogy of the present is to be recognised, and not mere itacism. WS brings strong arguments against this view, which must be regarded as decidedly questionable. As in the case of ἴδον below, the complete identity of ει and ι in popular speech makes it only a question of the extent to which the literary tradition was remembered.

Omission of *syllabic* augment in other tenses occurs only in προορώμην Ac 2^{25}=Ps 15 $(16)^{8}$ LXX. Here also, since εἶδον arises from ἔ-Ϝιδον, would be placed the more than dubious ἴδον in Rev (Ti, WH alt.) and LXX: it seems as though editors and commentators will persist in this writing, whatever grammarians say.[3] Those who will may consult Gregory's tabular statement in his *Prol.* 89. In Jn 5^{9} 10^{23} AL read περιπάτει, and in Rom 5^{13} A has ἐλλογᾶτο: such omissions became frequent in later times.

Temporal augment is more often dropped, but only in compounds, for we should not accept ὁμοιώθημεν Rom 9^{29} AFGLP=Is 1^{9} (LXX) AQ*Γ. So διερμήνευσεν Lk 24^{27}, διεγείρετο Jn 6^{18} BGL *al.*, ἀνέθη Ac 16^{26}, ἀφέθησαν Rom 4^{7}=Ps 31 $(32)^{1}$ B, ἀφέθη Mk 13^{2} W, ἀνορθώθη Lk 13^{13} ABD *al.* The first two out of this short list are directly paralleled in

[1] Cf. Mayser p. 333 f.

[2] Wackernagel (reviewing Hultsch) *Idg. Fors.* v. *Anz.* 59.

[3] Schweizer 170 and Reinhold 11 may be referred to. If the MSS were any evidence on the question of this itacism, we might not unreasonably call in the principle of levelling as a *vera causa* of indic. assimilated to infin. But who that has read the papyri would care to build anything on such evidence?

papyri (*CR l.c.*) and in Reinhold's exx. (p. 66), which casts doubt on Blass's "clerical error." Historically ὄφελον is a case of dropped augment.

5. Temporal Augment for Reduplication.

What has been said of the temporal augment applies to the nearly always identical form taken for reduplication by verbs with initial vowel. An original distinction is still preserved faintly in the difference between the perf. εἴργασμαι and the impf. and aor. ἠργ—see 2 above. In ἀφομοιωμένος Heb 7³ CDELP, ἀπαλλάχθαι Lk 12⁵⁸ AΔ (neither in Ti nor WH), the redupl. is dropped.[1] WH (*App.*² 179) would add εὐοδῶται 1 Co 16² ℵ*B *al.*, which they suggest is a perf. subj. mid., comparing those noticed in KBl. § 224. 2 (ii. p. 100): the verb is regularly unaugmented in LXX. But the present subj. is exegetically sound (see Findlay EGT *in loc.*), and this perf. subj. type, except for one word from Hippocrates,[2] is entirely confined to verbs where the long vowel is radical (κεκτῶμαι = κεκτή-ομαι, etc.). Nor is that vowel in Attic ever ω, so that the link for an analogy-process is wanting, and without such a process a late denominative verb could never have made such a form. Hort favoured this account of εὐοδῶται as fitting in with his view of the pres. subj. of -όω verbs (*App.*² 174), on which see below, p. 200.

6. Initial Diphthongs.

The short diphthongs are found as follows in the matter of augment (reduplication):—Αἰ. normally augmented, except ἐπαισχύνθη 2 Ti 1¹⁶ ℵᶜACDLP *al.* (WH). The spelling ει for η, common in papyri,[3] is found in some MSS of 2 Co 9⁷.—Εἰ. unchanged Gal 2⁵ εἴξαμεν, Mk 15⁴⁶ ἐνείλησεν, as in Attic.[4]—Οἰ. was augmented ῳ, except κατοίκησεν Mt 4¹³ D, ἐνοίκησεν 2 Ti 1⁵ D₂* 17, οἰκοδομήθη Jn 2²⁰ ℵB*TW 33, ἐποικοδόμησεν 1 Co 3¹⁴ ℵAB* *al.* (ῳ B³C). The omission was Attic only when οι preceded a vowel. It is common in patr. In οἰκοδομέω WH accept οἰ. in Ac 7⁴⁷, and gave it as alt. form everywhere exc. Mt 21³³, Lk 4²⁹. Cf. *Logion* 7 (P Oxy i. 1).[5]—Αὐ. augmented regularly ηὐ. in parts of αὐλέομαι, αὐλίζομαι, αὐξάνω, occurring 12 times. Once (Ac 12²⁴) εὔξανε in D*, with the identically pronounced ευ for ηυ: cf. Blass *Pron.* 44, who thinks the grammarians chiefly responsible for the maintenance of ηυ.[6]—Εὐ. without augment usually, as in Attic inscrr. since 300 B.C.: so εὐπορέομαι, εὐφορέω, εὐθυδρομέω, εὐνουχίζω, εὐλογέω (with var.). Εὐφραίνομαι, εὐκαιρέω, εὐχαριστέω show ηὐ. in Ac 2²⁶ 17²¹, Ro 1²¹, εὐ. elsewhere (one

---

[1] Parallels in papyri in *CR l.c.* (4 above).

[2] ἧλκωται (so in K.Bl., but perhaps ἡλκῶται is better for Ionic), which in H has βεβρῶται to set the type.

[3] Cf. Meisterh.³ 38 f., Blass *Pron.* 47.

[4] But see Meisterh.³ 171, Rutherford *NP* 244.

[5] Blass notes that ῳ (pron. ō) "no longer bore much resemblance to οι" (Ger. ö, pron. nearly like ü).

[6] In *Gr.*² § 15. 4 n. 1 he further notes that ηυ was in later times dissyllabic, as seen in the writing ηϋ in ℵA.

each). In εὔχομαι and προσεύχομαι ηὐ. is general, with var. occasionally (εὐ. twice in Ti, Ac 26^{29} ℵ 27^{29} B*). In the impf. of εὑρίσκω WH read ηὑ. Mk 14^{55}, Lk 19^{48}, Ac 7^{11}, Heb 11^{5} with alt. each time, but εὑ. in the other tenses.[1] In εὐδοκέω they read εὐ. in the Gospels, noting that ηὐ. is sometimes well supported : in the Epp. ηὐ. 5 times, εὐ. 6. For words with εὐ- followed by a vowel see 7 below.

7. Augment and Reduplication in Compounds.

The primitive rule that in a verb compounded with one or more prepositions the augment or reduplication falls between the last preposition and the verb has produced a tendency to place them thus where there is no real composition,[2] and even where the presence of the preposition is imaginary. So διηκόνουν (denom. from διᾱκονος), ἀπεδήμησα (ἀπόδημος), ἀπελογούμην (ἀπόλογος) ἐπεθύμησα (*ἐπίθυμος), ἐπεχείρησα (ἐπὶ χεῖρα sc. βάλλω), κατηγόρουν (κατήγορος), συνήργουν (σύνεργος). Sometimes the association with the original noun was so vividly present that the rule was resisted. Hence ἐπροφήτευσα (προφήτης: Attic προεφ., often in LXX, normal in Jos., and as var. in NT, as Jude [14] AC *al.*), ἐπερίσσευσα (περισσός, a deriv. from περί: Phr. mentions ἐπεριέσσευσε (cf. περιέσσευον Ac 16^{5} E) as a solecism).[3] In some words the presence of the preposition was forgotten (the simple verb being obsolete), and augment (redupl.) put at the beginning: ἐκάθευδον, ἐκάθισα, ἐκαθεζόμην, ἐκαθήμην, ἠμφιεσμένος (class.), also ἤφιον (above), ἐκάμμυσα (κατ(α)μύω). This process became commoner in Byzantine Greek,[4] and survives in MGr. The combination of the two tendencies produces the Attic verbs with double augment (2 above). The treatment of εὖ as a preposition for this purpose—seen in εὐηγγελιζόμην and aor., εὐηρεστηκέναι Heb 11^{5} ℵDEP *al.* (Ti)[5]—is due to the frequency with which it is used separately with verbs, as εὖ ποιεῖν etc.

8. Reduplication.

On analogy of ἕλκω, the denominative ἑλκόω (originally with init. ϝ: cf. Lat. *ulcus* reduplicates εἱλκ. Lk 16^{20} in all older uncials. In ῥεραντισμένοι Heb 10^{22} ℵ*ACD* *al.* and Rev 19^{13} (where WH suspect ῥεραμμένον and Ti reads περιρεραμμένον with ℵ*) verbs with init. ρ have analogical redupl.:[6] so D in Mt 9^{36} ῥεριμμένοι. WH print ῥ (*App.*² 170):[7] ancient

---

[1] Reinhold 65 notes that two MSS which most faithfully represent common speech entirely avoid ηὗρον. Hὕρισκον once in Hermas (ℵ) not elsewhere.

[2] See list in K.Bl. § 204 n. 1 (ii. p. 34); also Rutherford *NP* 79 ff.

[3] K.Bl., followed by WS, gives ἐπαρρησιασάμην here, but the old etym. from πᾶν is unexceptionable. Blass corrects this in *Gr.* 39 n.².

[4] See Hatzidakis 67 f.

[5] It is only found when εὐ- precedes a short vowel: cf. the usage in Att. described by Rutherford *NP* 245.

[6] Moeris 459 app. (ed. Koch 417) expressly mentions ῥέρανται as a solecism. Ῥεριμμένον Jer 43 $(37)^{30}$ A (ἐριμ. B) Jdth $6^{13\,(9)}$ A. As early as Homer (*Od.* 6^{59}) we find ῥερυπωμένα, and in Pindar ῥερῖφθαι (*Frag.* 314 Bergk).

[7] So Lachm. Lobeck (*Par.* 14 n.) favours ῥεῤ.

authorities vary—see K.Bl. § 67. 3 n. 5, § 200. 1 n. 2. In the latter place K.Bl. gives classical parallels for this kind of redupl. Verbs in ῥ. usually redupl. ἐρρ. (orig. σε-σρ. or ϝε-ϝρ.): so Lk 17^{2}, Ac 15^{29}, Eph 3^{17}, Col 2^{7}. See G Meyer^{3} 237, also 624. The ρρ was ultimately made single, to resemble other augments: so ἐριμμένοι Mt *l.c.* ℵBCL (Ti WH), ἔριπται Lk 17^{2} Π* *al.* (WH alt.). The substitution of syllabic augment for redupl. appears as in Attic in various verbs with init. consonant group. So (with var.) ἐμνήστευμαι Lk 1^{27} ℵ*AB*LW, 2^{5} ℵ*AB*C*DW (Ti WH): μεμν. Diodorus *al. ap.* Veitch, and in LXX, on anal. of μέμνημαι. For later encroachments of augment on redupl. see Dieterich 214 f., *CR* xv. 36. The classical perfect is maintained in two words with init. cons. The distinctive ει in the perf. εἴργασμαι (=ϝεϝεργ.) Jn 3^{21}, 1 Pet 4^{3} is practically without variant. Cf. Schweizer 170 f. WH read ἑόρακα (ϝεϝορ.) in Paul (1 Co 9^{1} ℵ*B *al.*,[1] Col 2^{1} ℵ*C, 2^{18} ℵB* *al.*), and as alt. (with B*), 7 times in 1 and 3 Jn; but ἑώρακα (-ειν) 24 times in Gospels and Ac. Ἑόρακα is Attic and original: ἑωρ. (from pluperf. ἑωρ.=*ἠορ.?) is well attested in MSS of Attic prose writers. The double reduplication curiously known as "Attic" is maintained intact: so ἀκήκοα, ἀπόλωλα, ἐγήγερμαι, ἐλήλακα, ἐλήλυθα, προσενήνοχα. Neither this nor the ordinary redupl. is ever dropped, as so often in later times. From λαμβάνω we have only the original εἴληφα, εἴλημμαι (=σε-σλ.). (The similar aor. κατειλήφθη in [Jn] 8^{4} seems only a mistake of ϛ: WS wrongly accuses Ti of endorsing it.)

9. Augmented Tenses of Verbs in ῥ.

As noted in § 41, and for the reduplicated tenses in 8 above, the single ρ prevails over the double. So from ῥαβδίζω 2 Co 11^{25}, ῥαντίζω Heb 9$^{19. 21}$, ῥαπίζω Mt 26^{67}, ῥήσσω and cpds. Lk 5^{6} 6$^{48f.}$ (but ερρ. Mt 26^{65}, Lk 9^{42}), ῥίπτω Mt 15^{30}, Ac 27^{19}, ῥύομαι 2 Co 1^{10}, Col 1^{13}, 2 Ti 3^{11} 4^{17}, 2 Pet 2^{7} (Ti twice ἐρρ.). Ἐρρέθην always.

A. PRESENT STEM.

(*a*) Thematic.

ACTIVE VOICE.

Stem:

λυ°/ε	τιμα°/ε	ζη°/ε	φιλε°/ε	πλεϝ°/ε	δηλο°/ε
loose	*honour*	*live*	*love*	*sail*	*make clear*

§ 84. **Present Indicative**—

Sg. 1	λύω	τιμῶ	ζῶ	φιλῶ	πλέω	δηλῶ
2	λύεις	τιμᾷς	ζῇς	φιλεῖς	πλεῖς	δηλοῖς
3	λύει	τιμᾷ	ζῇ	φιλεῖ	πλεῖ	δηλοῖ
Pl. 1	λύομεν	τιμῶμεν	ζῶμεν	φιλοῦμεν	πλέομεν	δηλοῦμεν
2	λύετε	τιμᾶτε	ζῆτε	φιλεῖτε	πλεῖτε	δηλοῦτε
3	λύουσι(ν)	τιμῶσι(ν)	ζῶσι(ν)	φιλοῦσι(ν)	πλέουσι(ν)	δηλοῦσι(ν)

[1] In *App.*^{2} 170 ἑόρακα as *alternative* reading here is presumably a misprint for ἑώ.

Imperfect Indicative—

Sg. 1	ἔλυον	ἐτίμων	ἔζων	ἐφίλουν	ἔπλεον	ἐδήλουν
2	ἔλυες	ἐτίμας	ἔζης	ἐφίλεις	ἔπλεις	ἐδήλους
3	ἔλυε(ν)	ἐτίμα	ἔζη	ἐφίλει	ἔπλει	ἐδήλου
Pl. 1	ἐλύομεν	ἐτιμῶμεν	ἐζῶμεν	ἐφιλοῦμεν	ἐπλέομεν	ἐδηλοῦμεν
2	ἐλύετε	ἐτιμᾶτε	ἐζῆτε	ἐφιλεῖτε	ἐπλεῖτε	ἐδηλοῦτε
3	ἔλυον	ἐτίμων	ἔζων	ἐφίλουν	ἔπλεον	ἐδήλουν

NOTE.—1. In 1 sg. impf. the form ἔζην is found in Rom 7[9] B (where 33 has ἔζουν, with the mixture noted under 5 below): it occurs in LXX, and in all MSS but one of Demosth. *Timocr.* 7. See Mayser 347. The analogy of flexions like ἔβη-ν, ἔβης, ἔστην ἔστης accounts for it.

2. Sporadic instances of the ἔλυα type (weak aor. ending) begin to appear in the plural: WS p. 112 cites εἶχαν Mk 8[7] (אBDΔ), Ac 28[2] (אAB), Rev 9[8] (אA), Lk 4[40] (D), Ac 8[10] (א), Jn 15[22. 24] (D*); εἴχαμεν 2 Jn [5] (אA), εἴχατε Jn 9[41] ("als Var."—but it does not appear in Ti), ἔλεγαν Jn 11[56] (D) 9[10] 11[36] (א*), to which Blass adds Ac 28[6] B. Scrivener's list (*Codex Bezae* p. xlvi) shows that the search has been imperfect: he adds from D ἔκραζαν Mt 21[9], ἔλεγαν Jn 7[31. 41] 8[22] 9[16] 10[24], Lk 23[35] 24[10], ὑπέστρεφαν Lk 23[48], εἶχαν Mk 8[16], Ac 19[14], ἔσυραν [which however might be aorist] Ac 14[19] 17[6], ἤθελαν Ac 16[7]. Outside D, accordingly, this imperfect is limited to two common verbs, and that mainly in א. It appears very sparingly before ii/A.D. (see Crönert 210, Thackeray 212, Mayser 369, Reinhold 81), but ultimately established itself, as in MGr. Mk 8[7] is the only instance that is at all likely to be original. (For -α- forms in flexion of ἥκω, due to its perfect meaning, see *Prol.* 53 and below, § 92.)

3. Older than this infection is the 3rd pl. impf. in -σαν, which is well attested for a non-contract verb in εἴχοσαν Jn 15[22. 24] אBL*N* 1. 33 (D* εἶχαν): WH *App.*[2] 172 note that "in a few other places forms in -οσαν [impf. or aor.] have some Western attestation"—thus Mk 1[32] ἐφέροσαν, 6[14] ἐλέγοσαν (Scrivener).[1] Instances for the strong aorist are discussed below, § 88 (p. 209). Thackeray 213 f. observes that "these forms in -οσαν are exceedingly frequent in LXX, being distributed over all the translations (except [1–4 K.]) from the Hexateuch to 2 Esdras." The question therefore is how to explain their almost complete absence from NT. The extension of the suffix -σαν began in the -μι verbs in the earliest Greek, and passed into -ω verbs in the dialects of Phocis and Delphi (in the NW Greek group): see Thumb *Dial.* 191, Valaori *Delphische Dialekt* 60. We may probably regard it as a dialectic form in the Κοινή, which ultimately failed to establish itself.

4. In Contract Verbs the -σαν form becomes rather more prominent, though it leaves even less trace in NT. There are about 30 places in NT where the 3rd pl. impf. act. of an -άω verb is read by one or more of the authorities given in MG; but nowhere does Ti cite a form in -ῶσαν. From -έω verbs Blass cites ἐθορυβοῦσαν Ac 17[5] D, and doubtfully κατοι-

---

[1] We may add ἐτίθοσαν Ac 8[17] B, as a clear step towards thematising.

κοῦσαν Ac 2^{46} D,[1] with two instances from Hermas. We may add διηκονοῦσαν Mk 15^{41} W. In one place only is there an imperfect from the -όω verbs, and that is ἐδολιοῦσαν (Rom 3^{13}).[2] But this is a quotation from the LXX, where these forms are common (Thackeray 214).[3] See *Proleg.* 52. In NT Greek the -σαν form was even ousted from the -μι verbs, ἐτίθουν and ἐδίδουν largely replacing ἐτίθεσαν and ἐδίδοσαν. Clearly therefore this type was still dialectic, though destined to survive into MGr.

5. Incipient passage of -άω into -έω forms shows itself here in the MSS, as in some other parts of the verb: we may deal with it here in advance. Radermacher (p. 73) remarks that it did not extend far till iii/A.D., though some traces of the opposite tendency may be found earlier. In 3rd plur. impf. we find ἠρώτουν Mt 15^{23} ℵBCDX, Mk 4^{10} ℵC, Ac 16^{39} A, κατεγέλουν Lk 8^{53} D*KX, ἐπετίμουν Lk 18^{39} AΓ; but among the older uncials only C shows the form frequently (ἐπηρώτουν Mk 9^{28} $10^{2.10}$ 12^{18}, ἠρώτουν Jn 4^{31}, Ac 1^{6}, ἐσιώπουν Mk 9^{34} with N). It is noteworthy that C does not show the form in Lk (once in Ac). A few later uncials and cursives give -ουν forms in a dozen places. Note the reverse change in θεωρῶσιν Mk 5^{15} L, ἐθεώρων Jn 6^{2} A 13, ἐλεᾷ Rom 9^{18} DFG: see further p. 196 ff. below. Sometimes the variant -ον has support in inferior authorities. Hort and Radermacher are probably right in refusing to consider the claim of any of these except in Mt 15^{23}. Κοπιοῦσιν Mt 6^{28} B 33 is not accepted even by WH: see *App.*[2] 173. For other instances see p. 197. MGr has taken -έω forms into 1st and 3rd plur. (and 1st sing. mid.) of all -άω verbs, and the whole of the impf.: see Thumb *Handb.* § 237 ff.

6. Verbs in which original ϝ prevented contraction of εω, εου, εοι, εο, εη, are πλέω, δεῖ (impers.), δέομαι, ζέω, πνέω, (ῥέω), (-χέω).[4] The NT forms are not numerous, but except for πνέει Jn 3^{8} L Chrys and ἐδέετο Lk 8^{38} ℵ*C*ω (see below) there is nothing to suggest deviation from Attic norm: early papyri likewise preserve this (Mayser 346). Lobeck *Phryn.* 220 ff. collects a good many instances of uncontracted forms from later literature, which are more likely to be assimilations of πλέω type to λύω than a survival of Ionic, as Phrynichus suggested.

7. Διψάω and πεινάω have left the -ήω class, which in Hellenistic only retains ζήω and χρήομαι. Πεινᾷ 1 Co $11^{21.34}$ stands without variant.

Imperative—

Sing.	2 λῦε	τίμα	φίλει	δήλου
	3 λυέτω	τιμάτω	φιλείτω	δηλούτω
Plur.	2 λύετε	τιμᾶτε	φιλεῖτε	δηλοῦτε
	3 λυέτωσαν	τιμάτωσαν	φιλείτωσαν	δηλούτωσαν

[1] Cf. κατωικοῦσαν (ii/B.C.) *Magn.* 17^{8}, ἀξιοῦσαν 47^{4} (Nachmanson 148). The accent is proved by Wackernagel *ThLZ*, 1908, p. 638.

[2] Perhaps we should add παρεδιδοῦσαν Ac 16^{4} C.

[3] Note that ἐῶσαν is not the only -άω form: there is ἐγεννῶσαν from γεννᾶν in Gn 6^{4}.

[4] The new present -χύννω probably stands alone in the active, where it avails to prevent confusion with fut. χεῶ. Συνέχεον Ac 21^{27} may be imperf.: see § 95.

NOTE.—1. The imperative of ζήω does not happen to occur. In LXX we find ζῆθι (Thackeray 242), ζήτω.

2. The old Attic 3rd pl. in -όντων, -ώντων, -ούντων, disappeared even from Attic in iii/B.C., with an isolated exception: see Meisterhans[3] 167 f.

3. Ἐλλόγα Phm [18] ℵ*ACD*FG 33 (cf. Rom 5[13] and p. 198 below) is an instance of -έω form yielding to -άω. So is ἐλεᾶτε Jude [22f.] ℵB (see p. 197 below).

4. Ἐκχέετε Rev 16[1] ℵACP is discussed under χέω in § 95.

Subjunctive—

Sing.	1 λύω	φιλῶ	πλέω	and the rest
	2 λύῃς	φιλῇς	πλέῃς	as pres. indic.
	3 λύῃ	φιλῇ	πλέῃ	
Plur.	1 λύωμεν	φιλῶμεν	πλέωμεν	
	2 λύητε	φιλῆτε	πλέητε	
	3 λύωσι(ν)	φιλῶσι(ν)	πλέωσι(ν)	

NOTE.—1. The above statement is somewhat doubtfully true about the subjunctive of δηλόω: see *Proleg.* 54. That in 1 Co 10[22] παραζηλοῦμεν and Gal 4[17] ζηλοῦτε are subjunctive seems the most probable view: it has been accepted by Radermacher 67 n., who remarks on the assistance given to this fusion at a later period by the convergence of ου and ω in pronunciation, which he dates in iii/A.D. See below, § 85 (p. 200).

2. Πεινᾷ Rom 12[20] and διψᾷ *ib.* and Jn 7[37] (Orig.[1] διψῇ) continue the evidence that these verbs have left the -ήω class: the LXX of Prov 25[21] supplies the forms in Rom *l.c.*

Optative—

Sing.	1 λύοιμι	*Plur.*	1 λύοιμεν
	2 λύοις		2 λύοιτε
	3 λύοι		3 λύοιεν

NOTE.—1. Optatives of Contract Verbs are not quotable in the NT. The forms in Hellenistic included according to Moeris (p. 208) ποιῴη, after the model of τιμῴη. See further Schmid *Atticismus* iv. 587 f., Schweizer *Perg.* 191.

2. The paradigm even of the uncontracted verb cannot be completed from NT, but its forms are not doubtful. In 3rd pl. we find εὕροισαν (strong aor.) in Ac 17[27] D*, according to a type common in LXX (Thackeray 215). Blass *Gr.* 46 f. thinks this "may be correct, . . . since the scribes of D and of its ancestors certainly did not find the optative in the living language." This statement is very questionable, for before the date of D there was a curious recrudescence of the optative even in illiterate papyri. On the whole it seems better to link D with the evidence of the LXX, and regard the -σαν as a dialectic element (here as in p. 194, n. 3) which has not touched the NT. Were the phenomenon less isolated, it would be tempting to seek light on the history of D. See *Prol.*[3] 56 n.

Infinitive—

λύειν τιμᾶν ζῆν φιλεῖν πλεῖν δηλοῦν

NOTE.—1. Since -ειν is historically from -ε(σ)εν, and therefore does not contain iota, the contraction from the first shows no ι. Δηλοῦν is unchallenged for the period before iv/A.D., with two or three isolated exceptions: see the discussion in *Prol.* 53, and add Thackeray 244. Crönert 220 n. gives a number of instances of -οῖν from late MSS. Though in five NT occurrences of the infin. B has -οῖν thrice, we cannot regard this as evidence for the autographs. How the late form arose is explained in *Prol. l.c.*

2. The printing of ι *subscr.* in τιμᾶν and ζῆν is wholly wrong for classical texts:[1] it never appears in Attic inscriptions—see Meisterhans[3] 175—nor in papyri during the age when the presence or absence of ι *subscr.* counted for anything (Mayser 347). In NT times of course it is a mere orthographical question, but there is no reason whatever for retaining the ι.

3. Inf. πεινᾶν Phil 4^{12}.

Participle. (For declension see § 65.)

λύ-ων	-ουσα	-ον	τιμ-ῶν	-ῶσα	-ῶν	φιλ-ῶν	-οῦσα	-οῦν
πλέ-ων	,,	,,	ζῶν	,,	,,	δηλῶν	,,	,,

NOTE.—Passage of -άω into -έω occurs in νικοῦντι Rev 2^{17} AC 2^{7} A, νικοῦντας 15^{2} C, προσδοκούντων Ac 28^{6} A 25, πλανούντων 1 Jn 2^{26} A; ἐλεῶντος Rom 9^{16} ℵAB*DFGP *al.* (cf. above, p. 195), and θεωρώντων Ac 28^{6} ℵ* afford instances of the converse.

MIDDLE AND PASSIVE VOICE.

§ 85. **Present Indicative**—

			χρη$^{o}/_{\epsilon}$ *use*		δεϝ$^{o}/_{\epsilon}$ *entreat*	
Sg. 1	λύομαι	τιμῶμαι	χρῶμαι	φιλοῦμαι	δέομαι	δηλοῦμαι
2	λύῃ	τιμᾶσαι	χρᾶσαι	φιλῇ	δέῃ	δηλοῖ
3	λύεται	τιμᾶται	χρᾶται	φιλεῖται	δεῖται	δηλοῦται
Pl. 1	λυόμεθα	τιμώμεθα	χρώμεθα	φιλούμεθα	δεόμεθα	δηλούμεθα
2	λύεσθε	τιμᾶσθε	χρᾶσθε	φιλεῖσθε	δεῖσθε	δηλοῦσθε
3	λύονται	τιμῶνται	χρῶνται	φιλοῦνται	δέονται	δηλοῦνται

NOTE.—1. In 2nd sing. the suffix -ει of later Attic takes the place of -ῃ in the word βούλει (Lk 22^{42}): the two were no longer equivalent in sound as in Attic, for ῃ was identical with η (see p. 97). Since βούλομαι was not a "literary" word, as Blass supposed,[2] we cannot interpret the variation by the help of this assumption; but βούλει may have been

[1] The "high authorities" to whom Hort appeals (*Introd.*[2] 314) lived unfortunately before the days of scientific philology.

[2] See *Gr.* 47.

stereotyped in general use from use in phrases derived from literature. Ὄψῃ (future) has been levelled (p. 97): its Attic orthography was ὄψει.

2. In the -άω verbs—and probably in the one -ήομαι verb—the 2nd sing. has established a new analogy form in -σαι, drawn from the model of the Perfect and from the present of verbs in -αμαι. So in NT καυχᾶσαι, ὀδυνᾶσαι, in five places, with no exx. of -ᾷ: Blass quotes πλανᾶσαι and ἐπισπᾶσαι from Hermas. The other contracta did not follow suit in NT. Blass notes αἰτεῖσαι from Hermas 10[7] ℵ: the -ῇ form is however found in that book, as in Lk 23[40] φοβῇ (where he suggests that φοβεῖσαι for φοβῇ σύ would be an easy correction). The LXX has very small traces of this formation. Thackeray 218 gives κτᾶσαι Sir 6[7] and ἀποξενοῦσαι 3 K 14[6] Aquila (ἀπεξ. in the MS) as the only certain exx. from Contract Verbs. Moeris contrasts the Attic ἀκροᾷ with Hellenistic ἀκροᾶσαι; but this is witness no older than the NT, and the same is true of Phrynichus. Apart from the solitary form χαριεῖσαι (P Grenf ii. 14 (c)[7] —iii/B.C.), which may be a mere blunder,[1] there is accordingly no real evidence of this form, outside the LXX, before the second period of the Κοινή, which dates roughly from A.D. Wackernagel *ThLZ*, 1908, p. 639 thinks it started from the future form πίεσαι, which alone is steadfast in LXX: this he derives from the analogy ἴεται : ἴεσαι : : πίεται : *x*. Thence naturally φάγεσαι followed, but not in the earliest stratum of LXX:[2] both are firmly established in NT. The future χαρίεσαι may perhaps be accepted in P Oxy ii. 292[9] (25 A.D.). The extension of the form from the -άω verbs to the other contracta may have taken place in i/A.D. Later writers show it in abundance (see Hatzidakis p. 188), and it stands in MGr now.

3. Χρήομαι is entered tentatively as assimilated to τιμάω. Only one material form occurs in NT, and that is in subj., where the η of the non-contracta may have exercised influence. Hermas *Vis.* iii. 6[7] has χρᾶσαι for 2 sg., and Moeris expressly says χρῆται Ἀττικοί, χρᾶται Ἕλληνες.[3] Traces of the old flexion appear in some of its moods sporadically.

4. Mixture of classes occurs in ἐλλογᾶται Rom 5[13] ℵ[a] (accepted by WH—rest -εῖται): the impf. appears in A ἐλλογᾶτο and ℵ* ἐνελογεῖτο. Cf. above, p. 196, and see p. 198, n. 3, below. Of a rather different kind is ἐμβριμόομαι (simplex once in Xen.), as evidenced by ἐνεβριμοῦντο Mk 14[5] ℵC*W (rest the normal -ῶντο) and ptc. (*q.v.*). See below, p. 201.

Imperfect—

Sg. 1	**ἐλυόμην**	**ἐτιμώμην**	ἐχρώμην	**ἐφιλούμην**	ἐδεόμην	**ἐδηλούμην**
2	**ἐλύου**	**ἐτιμῶ**	ἐχρῶ	**ἐφιλοῦ**	ἐδέου	**ἐδηλοῦ**
3	**ἐλύετο**	**ἐτιμᾶτο**	ἐχρᾶτο	**ἐφιλεῖτο**	**ἐδεῖτο**	**ἐδηλοῦτο**

[1] Grenfell and Hunt thought it "due to a confusion of χάρισαι with χαριεῖ": they may be right.

[2] Wackernagel says its appearance in A (*ter*) is to be reckoned among the vulgarisms of that MS.

[3] Brugmann *Gram.*[4] 348 says, "The Ionic flexion with α for η . . ., which from Aristotle's time passed over into Attic, . . . is explained by assimilation to verbs in -αω."

Pl.	1 **ἐλυόμεθα**	**ἐτιμώμεθα**	*ἐχρώμεθα*	**ἐφιλούμεθα**	*ἐδεόμεθα*	**ἐδηλούμεθα**
	2 **ἐλύεσθε**	**ἐτιμᾶσθε**	*ἐχρᾶσθε*	**ἐφιλεῖσθε**	*ἐδεῖσθε*	**ἐδηλοῦσθε**
	3 **ἐλύοντο**	**ἐτιμῶντο**	**ἐχρῶντο**	**ἐφιλοῦντο**	*ἐδέοντο*	**ἐδηλοῦντο**

NOTE.—1. There is no decisive reason in NT why we should not make ἐδεόμην follow ἐλυόμην throughout, and ἐχρώμην take ῆ in 3 sg. and 2 pl. Ἐδεῖσθε is absent, and for ἐδεῖτο in Lk 8[38] BLX 33 ἐδέετο is read by ℵ*C*ω : AP have the conflate ἐδεεῖτο. Phrynichus gives the uncontracted forms as Ionic in two articles out of three : see Rutherford *NP* 296 f. There is good LXX evidence (Thackeray 243) for all three types. See *Prol.* 54 and 234. Late forms like καλέω, there quoted, do not invalidate Schweizer's argument (*Perg.* 174 n.) that in ἐδέετο *et sim.* we have new analogy forms rather than survivals of Ionic. WH *App.*[2] 173 quote also Jn (3[8]) πνέει L Chrys[1], and inf. πλέειν Ac 27[2] 112 and 137. Their assertion that ἐδεῖτο in Lk *l.c.* is "better attested" than ἐδέετο may only mean that it is in B, or that it is more "correct." Of the impf. of χρήομαι only 3 pl. occurs. A noteworthy form ἐχρήμεθα occurs in Gn 26[29] A (not noted by Thackeray): it is tempting to accept it as parallel to ἔζην (above, p. 194), but Brooke and McLean make A the solitary witness, and ἐχρησάμεθα matches the surrounding aorists.

2. No sign appears of the impf. 2 sg. -ᾶσο, corresponding with -ᾶσαι above. Tenses with -μην -σο -το were in much more limited use than those in -μαι -σαι -ται, and the force of analogy was therefore much less powerful. Grammarians give ἠκροᾶσο (see Hatzidakis 188), but we have no reason to believe that it was at all widely used.

3. For mixture of classes see p. 198, n. 4.

Imperative—

Sg.	2 **λύου**	**τιμῶ**	**χρῶ**	**φιλοῦ**	*δέου*	**δηλοῦ**
	3 **λυέσθω**	**τιμάσθω**	*χράσθω*	**φιλείσθω**	*δείσθω*	**δηλούσθω**
Pl.	2 **λύεσθε**	**τιμᾶσθε**	*χρᾶσθε*	**φιλεῖσθε**	*δεῖσθε*	**δηλοῦσθε**
	3 **λυέσθωσαν**	**τιμάσθωσαν**	*χράσθωσαν*	**φιλείσθωσαν**	*δείσθωσαν*	**δηλούσθωσαν**

NOTE.—1. The Attic 3 pl. in -σθων has gone the way of the active in -όντων.

2. From χρήομαι we have only 2 sg. χρῶ in NT. Χράσθω can be cited from P Oxy vi. 912[16] (235 A.D.), vii. 1036[25] (273 A.D.), and χράσθωσαν from P Giss i. 49[26] (mid. iii/A.D.) and Viereck *Sermo Graecus* 16[89] (81 B.C.).

3. Νικοῦ Rom 12[21] A is a case of mixture. Ξυράσθω 1 Co 11[6] B must be aorist like κειράσθω : see below, p. 200, n. 3.

Subjunctive—

Sing.	1 **λύωμαι**	**τιμῶμαι**	*χρῶμαι*	**φιλῶμαι**	**δηλῶμαι**
	2 **λύῃ**	*τιμᾷ*	*χρῇ*	*φιλῇ*	*δηλοῖ*
	3 **λύηται**	**τιμᾶται**	**χρῆται**	**φιλῆται**	**δηλῶται**
Plur.	1 **λυώμεθα**	**τιμώμεθα**	*χρώμεθα*	**φιλώμεθα**	*δηλώμεθα*
	2 **λύησθε**	**τιμᾶσθε**	*χρῆσθε*	**φιλῆσθε**	*δηλῶσθε*
	3 **λύωνται**	**τιμῶνται**	*χρῶνται*	**φιλῶνται**	*δηλῶνται*

NOTE.—1. The contracta have 2 sg. set down in the old form: evidence fails for forms in -σαι. The solitary form χρῆται in 1 Ti 1[8] accounts for the flexion given: see p. 198, n. 3 above.

2. As in the active, there is strong reason to believe that the -οω verbs made subj. identical with indic. pres., at any rate in the plur.: see *Prol.* 54. Hort (WH *App.*[2] 174) takes thus φυσιοῦσθε 1 Co 4[6] and διαβεβαιοῦνται 1 Ti 1[7], as well as the active forms cited above. This is certainly true of the former, though it can hardly be admitted that Rom 8[26], an unambiguous *conj. deliberat.*, enforces the same construction in Ti *l.c.*: the indic. gives as good sense. On the other hand Hort's view (*ib.* 179), that εὐοδῶται in 1 Co 16[2] is anything but pres. subj., can safely be rejected: see *Prol.* 54 (also above, p. 191).

Optative—

Sing. 1	λυοίμην	*Plur.* 1	λυοίμεθα
2	λύοιο	2	λύοισθε
3	λύοιτο	3	λύοιντο

NOTE.—Literature and late papyri,[1] during the period when the optative enjoyed a brief resuscitation, warrant the setting down of the old forms.

Infinitive—

λύεσθαι τιμᾶσθαι χρᾶσθαι φιλεῖσθαι δεῖσθαι δηλοῦσθαι

NOTE.—1. Itacism produces in MSS many spellings with -ε, some of which raise the question whether the imperative may be read: *e.g.* Lk 14[17] ἔρχεσθαι all Greek MSS, 19[13] πραγματεύσασθαι, Gal 4[18] ζηλοῦσθε ℵB 33 (where the infin. seems decidedly more probable)—see WH *Introd.*[2] 309 f.

2. The well-attested Hellenistic infin. χρᾶσθαι appears (καταχ.) in 1 Co 9[18] A 33 Orig.: correct *Prol.* 54 n.[3]. Early exx. are *Syll* 177[50. 59] (303 B.C., a rescript of Antigonus), *OGIS* 214[19] (iii/B.C., a dedication by Seleucus I. (?)). But χρῆσθ[αι can be quoted from BGU iv. 1130[15] (4 B.C., Alexandria). In Attica itself χρᾶσθαι prevailed from ii/B.C., though instances of χρῆσθαι can be quoted: see Meisterhans[3] 175. From Pergamon Schweizer quotes an ex. of χρῆσθαι from 135 B.C (p. 175).

3. The accentuation of ξυρασθαι in 1 Co 11[6] is questioned. It is most generally read ξυρᾶσθαι ("to go shaven"), with the mixed form found in the same verse in B—see above, p. 199, n. 3: it is quoted from Diodorus. Ξυρέω accounts for all the other tenses. In view of the association with the aor. κείρασθαι, Heinrici[2] proposed to read ξύρασθαι, aor. of ξύρω, which seems (Lobeck *Phryn.* 205 n.) to have quite as good Hellenistic warrant as ξυράω: cf. Veitch *s.v.* Since ξυράω has no probable place in NT, and the change to the present seems without

[1] See Harsing, *De Optativi in Chartis Aegyptiis Usu.*

[2] Not however in ed.[8]

adequate motive, we may follow WH (*App.*[2] 173) in preferring *ξύρασθαι*, which occurs in Plutarch *Mor.* 336 E and [Lucian] *Dea Syra* 55 (active in Diodorus and Hippocrates).

Participle—

λυόμενος -η -ον τιμώμενος χρώμενος φιλούμενος δεόμενος δηλούμενος

NOTE.—Ἐμβριμούμενος Jn 11[38] ℵAU, -ώμενος BDL *al.*: see p. 198, n. 4.

(*b*) UNTHEMATIC.

ACTIVE VOICE.

§ 86. [*N.B.*—In these obsolescent forms bold type implies that the type so printed actually occurs in NT. Forms printed otherwise are quotable or inferable from other Hellenistic sources.]

Active forms on these models occur to some extent in NT from *φημί* (1); *ἀνίημι, ἀφίημι, παρίημι, συνίημι* (2); *ἀμφιέννυμι, ἀποκτέννυμι, ζώννυμι, ὄμνυμι, σβέννυμι* (4).

(1) *ἱστη/ᾰ* **φη/ᾰ** (2) *τιθη/ε ἱη/ε* (3) *διδω/ο* (4) *δεικ-νῡ/νῠ* (5) *ἐσ*

Present Indicative—

Sg.	1	**ἵστημι**	**φημί**	**τίθημι**	**δίδωμι**	**δείκνυμι**	**εἰμί**
	2	*ἵστης*		*τιθης*	**δίδως**	*δείκνῡς*	**εἶ**
	3	**ἵστησι(ν)**	**φησί**	**τίθησι(ν)**	**δίδωσι(ν)**	**δείκνῡσι(ν)**	**ἔστι(ν)**
Pl.	1	*ἵσταμεν*		**τίθεμεν**	*δίδομεν*	*δείκνῠμεν*	**ἐσμέν**
	2	*ἵστατε*		**τίθετε**	*δίδοτε*	*δείκνῠτε*	**ἐστέ**
	3	*ἱστᾶσι(ν)*	**φασί**	**τιθέᾱσι(ν)** **-ιᾶσι(ν)**	**διδόᾱσι(ν)**	*δεικνύᾱσι(ν)*	**εἰσί(ν)**

Imperfect—

Sg.	1	*ἵστην*		*ἐτίθην*	*ἐδίδουν*	*ἐδείκνῡν*	**ἤμην**
	2	*ἵστης*		**ἐτίθεις**	*ἐδίδους*	*ἐδείκνῡς*	**ἦς, ἦσθα**
	3	*ἵστη*	**ἔφη**	**ἐτίθει**	**ἐδίδου**	*ἐδείκνῡ*	**ἦν**
Pl.	1	*ἵσταμεν*		*ἐτίθεμεν*	*ἐδίδομεν*	*ἐδείκνῠμεν*	**ἦμεν** **ἤμεθα**
	2	*ἵστατε*		**ἐτίθετε**	*ἐδίδοτε*	*ἐδείκνῠτε*	**ἦτε**
	3	*ἵστασαν*		**ἐτίθεσαν**	*ἐδίδοσαν*	*ἐδείκνῠσαν*	**ἦσαν**

To these should be added the few surviving forms of the mainly literary verb *ει/ι go*, viz. 3 pl. pres. **-ίᾱσι(ν)**, 3 sg. impf. **-ῄει**, 3 pl. **-ῄεσαν**.

NOTE.—1. Forms from the Thematic conjugations invaded these Unthematic survivals even in the classical period, as ἐτίθεις -ει, ἐδίδουν -ους -ου, and many forms from δεικνύω. In NT none of the models given here can be completely evidenced.

(a) From ἵστημι occur 1 sg. (only Rom 16[1] in good MSS) and 3 sg. pres., but no impf. act. Forms occur from -ἱστάνω and -στάνω: the latter is not in LXX, but ultimately secured a permanent place—it is MGr. (see *Prol.*[3] 55 n.). The impf. καθίστη appears in a fragmentary (and rather literary) papyrus of the Roman age, CP Herm 6[9]. From φημί we have in NT only the four forms noted above. In the imperf. the analogy of ἔστην and ἔβην naturally produced levelling of vowel: hence such forms as ἔφημεν in Justin Martyr. In papyri we have some middle forms, like φάμενος: their prominence in Herodotus suggests that they may have been an Ionic element in the Κοινή. How far the old forms ἔφαμεν, ἔφατε, ἔφασαν survived in the spoken language is questionable: these and other forms not found in NT are omitted above.

(β) From τίθημι occur 1 sg. and 1 and 3 pl. pres., and from impf. 3 pl., as well as 3 sg., which is already of the contract type. This was extended into 3 pl. ἐτίθουν (Ac 3[2] 4[35] 8[17] D*EHLP *al.*, Mk 6[56] ADNX *al.*). Apparently τιθι in Lk 8[16] D is τιθεῖ, for τίθησι. Mixed forms appear in -ετίθοσαν B -ετίθεισαν C (Ac 8[17]). The five compounds of ἵημι show between them 1 and 3 sg. and 2 and 3 plur. pres., but no impf. Non-contract forms from -ίω are common, as ἀφίομεν, impf. ἤφιον. Late uncials restore the classical ἀφίεμεν in Mt 6[12]. Neither in LXX (Thackeray 250 f.) nor NT are there contract forms, unless we are to recognise with WH (so WS §§ 14, 16) a type -έω, formed from the future -ήσω in ἀφεῖς Rev 2[20] and συνεῖτε Mk 8[17] B*: cf. ἀφῶ in *OGIS* 201[18] (vi/A.D., rescript of the Nubian king Silko), and ἐπαφῶ in a Lycian inscr. But I agree with Thackeray in treating ἀφεῖς as a regular contraction for ἀφίεις: see *Prol.*[3] 45, where add ἀνασεῖς from ἀνασείω, *Zauberpap.* p. 116. In that case συνεῖτε would be aor., which is quite idiomatic, and even a plausible reading as differing from συνίετε in v.[21]; but accidental transposition of letters is more probable. Evidence for -έω is wholly inadequate, and for -ιέω *nil*, though the latter is sometimes brought in by faulty accentuation (as by Ti in Mt 13[13], Rom 3[11]).

(γ) From δίδωμι we find 1, 2 and 3 sg. and 3 pl. pres. and 3 sg. and pl. impf. But while ἐδίδοσαν survives in Mk 4[8] C, Jn 19[3] ℵB, Ac 16[4] ℵABDE 33 40 61 68 (παρεδιδοῦσαν C—see above, p. 195, n. 4), even the risk of confusion with 1 sg. has not kept out the form ἐδίδουν (Mt 13[8] D, Mk 3[6] BL, 15[23], Jn 19[3] AD *al.*, Ac 4[33] (*omn.*) 16[4] HLP 27[1] (A has sg.). Contract forms like ἐκδιδοῖ (Arrian *Anab.* i. 3. 2) do not happen to occur in NT, except for διδῶ Rev 3[9] AC. This might be written δίδω (as MGr.). Mk 4[8] ἐδίδει W follows ἐτίθει: cf. ἐδείδι in BGU ii. 602[6] (ii/A.D.), and see *CR* xv. 37.

(δ) From classical times forms with -νύω supplanted those in -νυμι very largely, especially in active. From NT we can quote only 1 sg. δείκνυμι 1 Co 12[31] (-ύω 33); 3 sg. δείκνυσι Mt 4[8] (-ύει ℵ), Jn 5[20] (-ύει D* *semel*, -υσι *semel*); ἀμφιέννυσι Mt 6[30] (Lk 12[28] has the vernacular ἀμφιάζει

B or -έζει DLT, no doubt from Q[1]). There is no impf. (ἐζώννυες Jn 21^{18}, ἐστρώννυον Mt 21^{8}, Lk 19^{36}). In LXX ἀπόλλυμι has still some active forms (Thackeray 246).

2. (a) Ἔστι retains its accent at the beginning of a sentence, and when it=*exists* or *is possible*; also after οὐκ, μή, εἰ, ὡς, καί, ἀλλά, τοῦτο. Only εἶ, among the present forms, is never enclitic.

(β) Middle forms in the flexion of εἰμί began to come in very early in the dialects: cf. *Prol.* 55 f. In MGr εἶμαι εἶσαι etc., they have invaded the pres. Class. ἦν 1 sg. has been entirely thrust out by ἤμην (except in Ac 20^{18} D), and ἤμεθα stands side by side with ἦμεν: in Gal 4^{3} both appear. The active is some three times as frequent: and ἦσο, ἦτο, have not yet begun to show themselves.

(γ) For ἔστι in practically identical sense occurs in Hellenistic[2] (Paul[3], Jas[1]) ἔνι (=ἐν, used in the sense of ἔνεστι or ἔνεισι). In MGr this has thrust out ἔστι and εἰσί: the change of each vowel in its new form εἶναι (*ine* for *eni*) is caused by assimiliation to εἶμαι εἶσαι.

(δ) Ἦσθα, an old perfect form, was used in Attic (Rutherford *NP* 226) for the genuine impf. ἦς of some other dialects. Both survive in the Κοινή, but the latter is commoner in NT, where ἦσθα occurs only in Mk 14^{67} (ἦς 1 etc. 13 etc. Eus.) and its parallel in Mt 26^{69}, against seven instances of ἦς. The reverse was the case in LXX (Thackeray 256). Is it possible that this ἦσθα started in Mt under LXX influence, and that the text of Mk was harmonised?

Imperative—

Sg. 2	ἵστη	τίθει	δίδου	δείκνῡ	ἴσθι (ἔσο)
3	ἱστάτω	τιθέτω	διδότω	δεικνῡ́τω	ἔστω or ἤτω
Pl. 2	ἵστατε	τίθετε	δίδοτε	δείκνῡτε	(ἔστε)
3	ἱστάτωσαν	τιθέτωσαν	διδότωσαν	δεικνῡ́τωσαν	ἔστωσαν (ἤτωσαν)

Add -ἴθι from -εἶμι.

NOTE.—1. No form from ἵστημι occurs. Ἐπιτίθει (1 Ti 5^{22}) and τιθέτω (1 Co 16^{2}), ἀφιέτω (1 Co $7^{12f.}$) and ἀφίετε συνίετε coincide with contract and non-contract -ω verbs respectively, and were thus naturally preserved. Δίδου, διδότω and δίδοτε remain, though in 1 Co 7^{3} A has ἀποδιδέτω. Among the -νυμι verbs σβέννυτε 1 Th 5^{19} stands alone—contr. ἀπόλλυε, ὀμνύετε: cf. ὑποδίκνυ P Oxy vii. 1066^{21} (iii/A.D.).

2. Ἔστε appears to have become obsolete, or very nearly so. It does not occur, in LXX or NT, where γίνεσθε or ἔσεσθε replaces it: see also *Prol.* 180. It can be quoted from *Test. Reuben* 6^{1}, in one recension, and from Eph 5^{5} D^cKL *al.* τοῦτο γὰρ ἔστε γινώσκοντες, as Blass would read (p. 320). But ἴστε is overwhelmingly supported, and can be well explained as imper.: see *Prol.*[3] 245. Blass (p. 308) would make ἦτε in 1 Co 7^{5} imperative, which would suit very well if any instance of this

[1] Harnack *Sayings of Jesus* 140, overlooks this certain ex. of the stylistic emendation of Mt. See my note in *Cambridge Biblical Essays*, 486.

[2] Late, says Wackernagel *Hellen.* 6 n.

form were quotable. For ἤτω, ἤτωσαν and ἔσο (the last two not in NT, ἤτω in Jas 5[12], 1 Co 16[22]) see Radermacher *Gram.* 82, WS 117 n. and *CR* xv. 38, 436: their existence in i/A.D. Hellenistic is not very certain. But see Thackeray 256 f.

Subjunctive—

Sing. 1	ἱστῶ	τιθῶ	διδῶ	δεικνύω	ὦ
2	ἱστῇς	τιθῇς	διδῷς or διδοῖς	δεικνύῃς	ᾖς
			διδῷ or διδοῖ		

and so on like λύω, except for accent: in διδῶ the η is replaced by ω.

NOTE.—1. Since ᾖς and ἦς are only orthographic variants, and ν was easily added after a long vowel, the subj. only differed from impf. in 1 sg. and 1 and 3 pl. Hence in the papyri ἦν, *i.e.* ᾖ(ν), is very often subjunctive: see *CR* xv. 38, 436, xviii. 108, *Prol.*[3] 168, to which a good many more instances may be added now. From this start we get ἐὰν ἦσθα (*Prol.*[3] *l.c.*) in LXX and a papyrus of iii/B.C., and ἐὰν ἦσαν P Oxy viii. 1157[15] (iii/A.D.), P Tebt ii. 333[13] (iii/A.D.), where a past tense is excluded by the context. In NT we find ᾖν subj. in Mt 10[13] C*, Mk 5[18] B*Δ, Lk 5[14] D*, 20[28] ℵ[c], 1 Co 16[4] A, 2 Jn [12] ℵ*.

2. Forms from ἵστημι do not occur in NT. From ἀφίημι we have ἀφιῇ Mk 11[25] X, ἀφιῆτε Jn 16[32] L, συνιῶσι Lk 8[10], Mk 4[12] (where D*LW 1 etc. read συνῶσι), which of course might equally well come from (ἀφ)ίω, were there any particular reason for so accentuating. Τίθημι only gives us τιθῶ Lk 20[43] D and παρατιθῶσι Mk 6[41] (-θῶσιν AD) 8[6] (-θῶσιν ADNWΔ—probably right, the other being assimilated to 6[41]). From δίδωμι comes 3 pl. παραδιδῶσι Mt 10[19] Cω (*leg.* aor. or fut.), and 3 sg. διδῷ or διδοῖ. These forms remind us of the Hellenistic variations between οι and ῳ described in § 36*c*; but διδοῖ of course comes easily enough from the contract type found in indic. as early as Herodotus. The evidence is in no case unanimous: for -ῷ we have 1 Co 14[7] D[c]ELPω and 15[24] ℵADEP 67**, for -οῖ 1 Co 15[24] BFG (ω read aor.). BGU iv. 1127[40] (18 B.C.) has προσαποδιδῷ.

Optative—

There are no forms in NT, except 3 sg. εἴη *undecies* in Lk and Ac, and in Jn 13[24] ℵADW*ΓΔΛΠ al.* 13 etc. The Hellenistic forms of the plural have discarded the primitive εἶμεν, εἶτε, εἶεν, in favour of εἴημεν, εἴητε, εἴησαν (as in Ionic), due to levelling from the singular: εἶεν has however a better record than the 1st and 2nd pl. of the longer form.

Infinitive—

ἱστάναι	τιθέναι	διδόναι	δεικνύναι	εἶναι

NOTE.—1. *-ἱστάναι* occurs in 1 Co 13^{2} ℵBDEFG 33 (*-ἱστάνειν* ACKL) and in 2 Co 3^{1} FG (*-ιστάνειν* ℵAC *al.*). In 2 Co *l.c.* a contract form *συνιστᾶν* is read by BD* 33, and has a good claim.

2. *Ἀφιέναι* and *τιθέναι* have no rivals, nor has *διδόναι*,[1] nor *εἶναι*. For the *-νύναι* type may be cited *δεικνύναι* Mt 16^{21} B (rest *-ύειν*), *ὀμνύναι* Mk 14^{71} BL unc^{7} (*-ύειν* ℵACWΔ *al.*), while *-ύειν* also occurs in Mt 26^{74} (*sine var.*) : *ἀπολλύειν* occurs in Rom 14^{15} FG.

Participle—

ἱστάς	τιθείς	διδούς	δεικνύς	ὤν
(like *πᾶς*)	-εῖσα -έν	-οῦσα -όν	-ῦσα -ύν	οὖσα ὄν
	(§ 65. 1*b*)	(§ 65. 1*c*)	(§ 65. 1*f*)	like λύων

NOTE.—1. *Ἐμπίπλημι* makes *ἐμπιπλῶν*, from *-άω* type. *-Ἱστάς* is found in 2 Co 4^{2} ℵCD*FG 33 *al.* (*-άνοντες* A probably, BP 424**— *-ῶντες* rest), 6^{4} ℵ*CD*FG 33 (*-άνοντες* BP cu^{2}— *-ῶντες* rest) : WH reasonably choose the form *-άνοντες*, which was certainly the prevailing conjugation, though *-άω* forms had a temporary vogue (cf. Thackeray 245), starting in old Ionic.

2. *Ἀνιέντες* Eph 6^{9} and *συνιέντος* Mt 13^{19} (DF(L) *συνίοντος*) *συνιείς* 13^{23} ℵBD (*συνίων* CLWω) stand against *συνίων* (etc.) in Mk 4^{9} D vt lat Rom 3^{11}. Neither here nor in indic. do accents in late MSS justify our bringing in a type *-ιέω*, which never shows itself in distinct contracted forms. *Τιθείς* stands in Mk 10^{6} (*τιθῶν* 1 28 13–346), Lk 4^{40} BD vg, Jude^{4} : cf. *ὑποτιθοῦσα* BGU i. 350 (ii/A.D.), *ἐπιτιθο(ῦντι)* P Oxy vi. 986 (i/A.D.), and LXX once (1 Es 4^{30} BA) *ἐπιτιθοῦσαν*.

3. *Διδούς* naturally prevails, since except for nom. sg. m. its flexion is identical with that of *λύων*. But *ἀποδιδοῦν* Rev 22^{2} A *al.* (a correction to secure concord), *παραδιδῶν* Mt 26^{46} ℵ*, Mk 14^{42} D : *διδώς* in Jn 6^{33} D is a case of virtual itacism, like *ἐδίδων* 3 pl. impf. in Mk 15^{23} M*. Thackeray 250 gives *διδοῦντι* from Pr 26^{8} ℵ (*-όντι* BA). Cf. *διδοῦντος* BGU i. 86^{22}, *ἀνδιδοῦντα* *ib.* 44, P Oxy iii. 532^{11}—all ii/A.D.

4. *Ἀπόλλυμι*, as in its whole active flexion, makes a thematic ptc. (Rev 9^{11}), but *-ύς* is found in other verbs. Thus *ὑποζωννύντες* Ac 27^{17}, *δεικνύντος* Rev 22^{8} ℵ cu^{11} (*-ύοντος* A 046 *al.*), *ἐπιδεικνύς* Ac 18^{28}, *ἀποδεικνύντα* 2 Th 2^{4} (*-ύοντα* AFG). In Rev the *-ύων* type is *a priori* more probable.

MIDDLE AND PASSIVE VOICES.

§ 87. Present Indicative—

					ἡσ *sit*	κει *lie*
Sing. 1	ἵσταμαι	τίθεμαι	*δίδομαι*	δείκνῦμαι	κάθημαι	κεῖμαι
2	ἵστασαι	*τίθεσαι*	*δίδοσαι*	*δείκνυσαι*	κάθῃ	*κεῖσαι*
3	ἵσταται	τίθεται	δίδοται	δείκνυται	κάθηται	κεῖται
Plur. 1	ἱστάμεθα	*τιθέμεθα*	διδόμεθα	δεικνύμεθα	*καθήμεθα*	κείμεθα
2	ἵστασθε	τίθεσθε	*δίδοσθε*	*δείκνυσθε*	*κάθησθε*	*κεῖσθε*
3	ἵστανται	τίθενται	*δίδονται*	δείκνυνται	κάθηνται	κεῖνται

[1] *Προσδιδέναι* BGU iv. 1115^{43} (13 B.C.).

Imperfect Indicative—

Sing. 1	**ἱστάμην**	*ἐτιθέμην*	*ἐδιδόμην*	*ἐδεικνύμην*	*ἐκαθήμην*	*ἐκείμην*
2	*ἵστασο*	*ἐτίθεσο*	*ἐδίδοσο*	*ἐδείκνυσο*	*ἐκάθησο*	*ἔκεισο*
3	**ἵστατο**	**ἐτίθετο**	**ἐδίδοτο**	**ἐδείκνυτο**	**ἐκάθητο**	**ἔκειτο**
Plur. 1	**ἱστάμεθα**	*ἐτιθέμεθα*	*ἐδιδόμεθα*	*ἐδεικνύμεθα*	*ἐκαθήμεθα*	*ἐκείμεθα*
2	**ἵστασθε**	*ἐτίθεσθε*	*ἐδίδοσθε*	*ἐδείκνυσθε*	*ἐκάθησθε*	*ἔκεισθε*
3	**ἵσταντο**	**ἐτίθεντο**	*ἐδίδοντο*	**ἐδείκνυντο**	**ἐκάθηντο**	**ἔκειντο**

NOTE.—1. As in LXX and Ptolemaic papyri (Thackeray 245, Mayser 351 f.) the unthematic forms are much better preserved in the Middle than in the Active. Additional verbs of these classes, besides some of those named under the Active, are (1) *δύναμαι, ὀνίναμαι, κρέμαμαι, ἐπίσταμαι, πίμπραμαι*, (4) *μίγνυμαι, ῥήγνυμαι, ἀπόλλυμαι*.

2. Two roots, peculiar in that they appear in the Middle (in Sanskrit as well as Greek) without vowel-reduction, have a partial flexion in this class, preserved mainly by virtue of their similarity to the Perfect. Κεῖμαι is common and presents no irregularities : 2 sg. and pl. pres. and 1 and 2 sg. and pl. impf. do not happen to occur in NT. From the root *ἡσ* only *κάθημαι* has survived, and augment and accent alike show that it was not felt to be a compound. The impf. only occurs in 3 sg. (*undecies*) and 3 pl. (Mk 3^{32} Δ *al.*). In LXX the regular 2 sg. *κάθησαι* still occurs, but *κάθῃ* (from *κάθομαι*—cf. imper.) appears without variant in Ac 23^{3}, the only NT occurrence : cf. P Oxy i. $33^{\text{iii. }13}$ (ii/A.D.).

3. The two tenses can be made up for the *ἵσταμαι* type out of the four verbs that contribute forms, except for the 2 sg. impf., the form of which is not quite certain : Dt 28^{64}, Is 48^{8} have *ἠπίστω* preserving an old classical alternative (Kühner^{3} I. ii. § 213, n. 1), which Moeris even calls Attic against Hellenistic *-ασο* (Schweizer *Perg.* 168, who quotes *δύστω* from Pergamum). *Δύνασαι* is normal, appearing six times without variant : *δύνῃ*, from *δύνομαι*,[1] occurs in Mk 9^{22} ℵBDLWΔ (*-ασαι* ACNX), ^{23} ℵ*BDNWΔ (*-ασαι* ℵ^{c}ACLX), Lk 16^{2} ℵBDPW (*al.* future), Mk 1^{40} B (*-ασαι* ℵACDL *al.*), Rev 2^{2}. Similarly for (*ἐξ*) *-εκρέματο* Lk 19^{48} ADLQRW we have *ἐξεκρέμετο* ℵB.

4. From *ἀφίεμαι* we have 3 sg. and 3 pl. pres. Ἀφίενται is in Mt $9^{2.\,5}$ ℵB, Mk 2^{5} B 28 33, 2^{9} ℵB 28 565, Jn 20^{23} W and later uncials, Lk 7^{47} W ; while we find *ἀφίονται* Jn 20^{23} B*, Mk 2^{5} Δ, Lk 7^{47} F. *Τίθεμαι* shows 1 sg. and 2 pl. pres., 3 sg. and pl. impf. Προσετίθοντο is read by cu.^{4} (incl. 1) in Ac 5^{14}. Cf. *παρακατατίθομαι* BGU i. 326 (ii/A.D.).

5. *Δίδομαι* has 3 sg. and 1 pl. pres., but in impf. *διεδίδετο* Ac 4^{35} ℵB*ADE, *παρεδίδετο* 1 Co 11^{23} ℵB*ACDEFGK 33, with P and late authorities for *-οτο*. See under the Aorist, and cf. LXX in Thackeray 250.

6. For *-νυμαι* forms may be quoted *ἐνδείκνυνται* Ro 2^{15}, *ῥήγνυνται* Mt 9^{17}, *διερήγνυτο* Lk 5^{6} A unc^{13}, *ἀπόλλυμαι* Lk 15^{17}, *-υται* 1 Co 8^{11} ℵABDP 33, Mk 2^{22} BL, *-ύμεθα* Mt 8^{25}, Mk 4^{38}, Lk 8^{24}, *-υνται* Mt 9^{17} ℵB 1 13, *ἀπώλλυντο* 1 Co 10^{9} ℵBA, 10^{10} A, *σβέννυνται* Mk 9^{48}, *-υνται* Mt 25^{8}. The are no *-ύω* forms at all.

---

[1] WS 118 wrongly calls it contracted. The type *δύνομαι* occurs fairly often in papyri : see Thackeray 249, Mayser 355, *CR* xviii. 112.

Imperative—

Sing. 2	ἵστασο	τίθεσο	δίδοσο	δείκνυσο
3	ἱστάσθω	τιθέσθω	διδόσθω	δεικνύσθω
Plur. 2	ἵστασθε	τίθεσθε	δίδοσθε	δείκνυσθε
3	ἱστάσθωσαν	τιθέσθωσαν	διδόσθωσαν	δεικνύσθωσαν

NOTE.—1. The imper. κάθησο, still found in LXX, is supplanted in NT by κάθου (as from κάθομαι), which occurs six times with no trace of the older form. No other imper. appears; nor any imper. of κεῖμαι. Καθήσθω etc., and κεῖσο etc., may be postulated as the only conceivable forms if the tense was ever wanted.

2. -ἵστασο (περι- *bis*, ἀφ- *semel* in late MSS) has no variant form. (See p 206, n. 3.) Παρατιθέσθωσαν 1 P 4[19] is the only quotable part of τίθεσο; while συναναμίγνυσθε 2 Th 3[14] Εω (an itacism) alone represents the other types. Ἐπιτιθοῦ (as from a contract verb) occurs in 1 Ti 5[22] D: we might equally well write ἐπιτίθου, as from -τίθομαι.

Subjunctive—

Sing. 1	δύνωμαι	τιθῶμαι	διδῶμαι	δεικνύωμαι	καθῶμαι
2	δύνῃ	τιθῇ	διδῷ	δεικνύῃ	καθῇ

and so on like λύωμαι, except for accent: in διδῶμαι the η is replaced by ω.

NOTE.—Καθῆσθε Lk 22[30] B*TΔ represents the subj. of κάθημαι. From the rest no forms occur except δύνηται δύνωνται.

Optative—

Sing. 1	δυναίμην	*Plur.* 1	δυναίμεθα
2	δύναιο	2	δύναισθε
3	δύναιτο	3	δύναιντο

NOTE.—The only optative from which forms occur (1 sg. and 3 pl.) is cited by itself, as there is no evidence that NT writers would have used any of the rest.

Infinitive—

ἵστασθαι τίθεσθαι δίδοσθαι δείκνυσθαι καθῆσθαι κεῖσθαι

NOTE.—All these types occur without alternatives. This fact makes it very improbable that we should accent πιμπρᾶσθαι or ἐμπιπρᾶσθαι in Ac 28[6] as if from a contract verb, which we should naturally accept in the active.

Participle—

ἱστάμενος τιθέμενος διδόμενος δεικνύμενος καθήμενος κείμενος

NOTE.—All these are well represented in NT, and there are no alternative forms.

B. STRONG AORIST STEM.

§ 88. On the formation of this stem see above, § 82. It only concerns non-contract -*ω* verbs and the verbs in -*μι*. There is no present tense for this stem.

(*a*) Thematic, (*b*) Unthematic.

(*a*) *βαλ*$^{ό}/_{έ}$ *cast*; (*b*) (1) *στ*$^{η}/_{(α)}$ *stand*, (2) *θ*$^{η}/_{ε}$ *place*, (3) *δ*$^{ω}/_{ο}$ *give*, (4) *δῡ* *sink*.

(*b*) Like (1) are *ἔβην* from *βαίνω* and (opt. only) *ὠνάμην* from *ὀνίνημι*.

Like (2) are compounds of *ἵημι*.

Like (3) is *ἔγνων* from *γινώσκω*, but varying strongly in parts.

In (4) *ἔδυν* is nearly obsolete, and *ἔφυν* (from *φύω*) seems wholly so.

ACTIVE VOICE.

Indicative—

Sing.	1	ἔβαλον	ἔστην	sing. supplied by		ἔγνων	ἔδυν
	2	ἔβαλες	ἔστης	1st aor., ἔθηκα,		ἔγνως	ἔδυς
	3	ἔβαλε(ν)	ἔστη	ἔδωκα		ἔγνω	ἔδυ
Plur.	1	ἐβάλομεν	ἔστημεν	ἔθεμεν	ἔδομεν	ἔγνωμεν	ἔδυμεν
	2	ἐβάλετε	ἔστητε	ἔθετε	ἔδοτε	ἔγνωτε	ἔδυτε
	3	ἔβαλον	ἔστησαν	ἔθεσαν	ἔδοσαν	ἔγνωσαν	ἔδυσαν

NOTE.—1. In Thematic Verbs there is a large infusion of Weak Aorist terminations, as in other parts of the system. It began in Attic, where *εἶπον* is inflected -*ον* -*ας* -*ε*(*ν*), -*ατον* -*άτην*, -*ομεν* -*ατε* -*ον*: similarly *ἤνεγκον* (from *φέρω*), but with 1 pl. -*αμεν* (Rutherford *NP* 219 f.). In these verbs the double tenseformation was primitive: see Brugmann *Gr.*[4] 322. Cf. *Prol.* 51,[1] and Thackeray 210 f., who shows that except in these two verbs the -*α* forms did not become common till i/A.D., when the papyri begin to show them freely: cf. *CR* xv. 36, xviii. 110. In NT these two verbs are almost exclusively found with -*α*- in indic.: *εἶπες* Mk 12[32] ℵDL *al.*, Jn 4[17] ℵB*, with *εἶπον* 1 sg. usually, are about the only exceptions, with *εἶπον* 3 pl. rarely. Ἔπεσα -*ατε* -*αν* were helped towards predominance by the *σ*; *ἤλθαμεν* -*αν* and once -*α* (Rev 10[9]) are found; *εἴδαμεν* -*αν* and less certainly -*ατε*, with *εἶδα* in Rev; *εὕραμεν* and -*αν*, but only -*ον* in 1 sg.; -*εῖλατε* -*αν*: in other verbs the instances are more isolated—*ἔβαλαν* (*ἐπ*-) is thrice provisionally accepted by WH, with *ἐξεβάλαμεν* rejected in Mt 7[22], *ἐλάβαμεν* -*ατε* -*αν* in Lk 5[5], 1 Jn 2[27], Jn 1[12], *ἔπιαν* in 1 Co 10[4], *ἀπέθαναν* in Mt 8[32], Lk 20[31], Jn 8[53]. See WH *App.*[2] 171 f., WS 111 f., and for exx. in D see

---

[1] Correct the total given there for verbs forming strong aor. act. or mid.: there are over forty.

Scrivener *Codex Bezae* xlvi. The increasing prominence of these forms, especially in the plural, is thus well seen. The MGr aorist flexion -α -ες (§ 89) -ε -αμε -ετε (and -ατε) -αν, shows how these forms lived on. Cf. on impf. above, p. 194, n. 2.

2. In 3 pl. the suffix -οσαν—as in the impf. (p. 194, n. 3, 4)—obtained a footing for a time, but it makes no claim in the NT for the aorist except in παρελάβοσαν 2 Th 3[6] ℵ*AD* 33. BGg read παρελάβετε, which WH put in their text, remarking that the uniqueness of this termination in Paul renders it "somewhat suspicious": the mistake may have arisen from an ocular confusion if ΠΑΡΑΔΟϹΙΝ stood in the line above just over ΠΑΡΕΛΑΒΕΤΕ. Blass 46 argues that this and the impf. are probably authentic, since they could not have been very familiar to the scribes except in contract verbs. Scrivener cites from D ἤλθοσαν Mk 8[11] 9[33], εἴδοσαν 9[9]. As observed above, the form had only a temporary vogue, except in the Contracta (impf.), where it remains in MGr.

3. The aor. indic. of -ἵημι is supplied wholly by ἀφῆκα, as is that of τίθημι by ἔθηκα, and of δίδωμι by ἔδωκα, with the significant exception of παρέδοσαν in Luke's literary Preface (1[2]): contrast the Middle below. In Mk 7[13] W reads παρέδοτε, whence ἔδοτε is marked as NT above. Ἔστην and -έβην between them form a complete flexion (exc. 2 sg.), and ἔγνων is complete. Ἔδυν occurs in 3 sg. Mk 1[32] ℵACLWΓΔΠ *al.* (ἔδυσεν BD 28), and in 3 pl. παρεισέδυσαν Jude [4] ℵACP etc. (-εδύησαν B alone). If we read ἔδυσεν in Mk *l.c.*, both passages show the weak aorist dropping the transitive sense, which is likely enough. The aor. pass in Jude [4] is parallel to ἐφύην which has supplanted ἔφυν, and it is quoted by Veitch from Hippocrates and Hesiod (?). Whichever reading be adopted, the solitary survival of ἔδυ in Mk *l.c.* seems highly improbable.

Imperative—

Sg. 2	**βάλε**	**στῆθι** / **-στα**	**-βηθι** / **-βα**	**θές**	**ἄφες**	**δός**	**γνῶθι**
3	**βαλέτω**	**στήτω**	**-βάτω**	θέτω	ἀφέτω	**δότω**	**γνώτω**
Pl. 2	**βάλετε**	**στῆτε**	**-βατε**	**θέτε**	**ἄφετε**	**δότε**	**γνῶτε**
3	**βαλέτωσαν**	στήτωσαν	-βάτωσαν	θέτωσαν	ἀφέτωσαν	δότωσαν	γνώτωσαν

NOTE.—1. From εἶπον the imper. has exclusively weak aor. endings, except that εἰπέ also occurs: εἰπόν [1] is said by WH (*App.*[2] 171) to stand chiefly before consonants. They accept -ένεγκε four times, -ένεγκον once (Mt 8[4]), and ἐνέγκατε without variant From ἔπεσον however -πέσε and πέσετε are best attested; from ἦλθον ἔλθατε ἐλθάτω, though B has -ε- five times.

2. In compounds -στηθι and -στᾱ, -βηθι and -βᾱ alternate without very clear rationale. The short forms are found in Attic poets (Blass [2] 50 n.)

---

[1] The imper. εἰπέ, ἐλθέ, εὑρέ were oxytone in Attic and the Κοινή, as were ἰδέ and λαβέ in Attic: see Kühner[3] § 217. 3. *a* (I. ii. 84). It is a survival of the original accent: cf. Brugmann *Gr.*[4] 183, who accepts πιέ, φαγέ as well. Blass 45 follows Lobeck *Phryn.* 348 in accenting the imper. εἶπον.

but *v. inf.*—and in MGr: so Hatzidakis 101, where ἀνέβα ἀνεβᾶτε, ἔμβα ἐμβᾶτε and the like are cited. But in some MGr dialects ἀνεβῆτε etc. appear (*ib.*). This suits the fact that the η forms sg. and pl. still survived in ancient Κοινή: in LXX exclusively in -βαίνω, though -στα occurs as well as -στηθι.[1] In NT στῆθι occurs thrice simple and eight times compound; -στᾰ occurs Ac 12^{7}, Eph 5^{14}, Ac 9^{11} B, 10^{20} D*, 11^{19} D* (against ἀναστάς). For -βα we have Rev 4^{1} (exc. A), Mk 15^{32} L, Mt 17^{20} ℵB 1 etc. 13 etc. (against -βηθι CDω); for -βηθι also Mt 27^{40}, Lk 14^{10} 19^{5}, Jn 4^{49} 7^{3}, Ac 10^{20}. The other persons are always in η with στήτω etc.; but the analogy of τίμα τιμᾶτε has made καταβάτω five times (only Mk 13^{15} XΔ -βήτω) and ἀνάβατε Rev 11^{12} ℵACP (only 046 -βητε).[2] The accent of τίμα τιμᾶτε combines with MGr ἀνέβα ἀνεβᾶτε (see above) to make it probable that we should write ἀναβᾶτε in Rev 11^{12}, instead of following the older ἀνάβητε. It may be noted that ἀνάβα appears on an Attic vase-painting: see Kretschmer *Vaseninschriften* p. 197. Its occurrence in Attic comedy (as Arist. *Ran.* 35, ἔμβα *ib.* 377) suggests that it was Attic vernacular already, and not really poetical, though used by Euripides.

3. Ἄφες ἄφετε became a quasi-auxiliary: see *Prol.* 175. Θές θέτε, δός δότω δότε, γνῶθι γνώτω γνῶτε, show no signs of obsolescence. The 3rd pl. does not happen to occur. MGr θές, δός and ἄς (=ἄφες) show that the 2 sg. was the most firmly rooted.

Subjunctive—

Sg.	1	βάλω	στῶ	θῶ	ἀφῶ	δῶ	γνῶ
	2	βάλῃς	στῇς	θῇς	ἀφῇς	δῷς, δοῖς	γνῷς
	3	βάλῃ	στῇ	θῇ	ἀφῇ	δῷ, δοῖ, δώῃ	γνῷ, γνοῖ
Pl.	1	βάλωμεν	στῶμεν	θῶμεν	ἀφῶμεν	δῶμεν	γνῶμεν
	2	βάλητε	στῆτε	θῆτε	ἀφῆτε	δῶτε	γνῶτε
	3	βάλωσι	στῶσι(ν)	θῶσι(ν)	ἀφῶσι(ν)	δῶσι(ν)	γνῶσι(ν)

NOTE.—1. Στῶ suffers somewhat, like the rest of the paradigm of ἔστην, from the competition of the weak aor. pass., but it occurs (3 sg. and pl., and 2 pl.) six or seven times. -Βῶ is found in 3 sg. From τίθημι and -ἵημι forms are common, and abundant from the two -ω- verbs.

2. Where ῷ occurs in the flexion of δῶ and γνῶ there was a strong Hellenistic bias towards οῖ: in papyri it affects 2 sg. as well as 3 sg.,[3] and D shows this in Lk 12^{59}. The analogy of contract verbs might work directly on an aor. form—cf. ἀναβᾶτε just discussed—and there would be a natural tendency to eject unique subj. forms like -ῷς and -ῷ. But it may be also observed that there are several instances of Hellenistic οι replacing earlier ῳ: see *CR* xv. 37, 435 The figures for NT MSS are interesting. ℵ has δοῖ $\frac{3}{9}$ times, B $\frac{4}{10}$, A $\frac{0}{6}$, C $\frac{0}{3}$, D $\frac{5}{8}$, L $\frac{0}{11}$, W $\frac{1}{9}$ in the

---

[1] Thackeray 254: he says -στα is poetical in LXX.

[2] [Against this we have ἀνάβητε without variant in Jn 7^{8}.—ED.]

[3] See *Prol.*[3] 55 n.[3] and add—e.g. *Mél. Nic.* 185 (Ptol.), P Tebt ii. 409^{5} (A.D. 5).

Gospels: in Paul ℵ $\frac{1}{6}$, B $\frac{1}{7}$, A $\frac{0}{6}$, C $\frac{0}{1}$, D_2 $\frac{1}{3}$, G $\frac{2}{5}$ KLP $\frac{0}{6}$. (These last only stand for $\frac{\delta o\hat{\iota}}{\delta\hat{\varphi}}$: in Paul we have to add the places where *δώῃ* appears, viz. ℵ 2, B 0, A 2, C 1, D_2 5, G 3 and KLP 2.) Thus the δ-text shows *δοῖ* most, importing it even into Lk (22^{4} D): otherwise Luke and Paul show no trace of it (exc. in 1 Th 5^{15}, where ℵ joins DG). An obviously vernacular form—as its papyrus record shows—it may safely be assumed right in Mk 4^{29} ℵBD, $14^{10f.}$ BDW, 8^{37} ℵB, Jn 13^{2} ℵBD and perhaps Jn 13^{29} D. Though a late form of the opt. coincides with it, there is not the slightest syntactical reason for doubt that in NT it is always subj., as W. F. Moulton proved long ago (WM 360 n.). With *δοῖ* goes *γνοῖ*, read by WH in Mk and Lk (Mk 5^{43} ABDLW, 9^{30} ℵBCDL, Lk 19^{15} ℵBDL 33) against *γνῷ* in Jn 7^{51} 11^{57} (*γνοῖ* D*) 14^{31}, and as *v.l.* in Mk and Lk *l.c.* (A *bis*, ℵ and C *semel*, W *bis*).

3. A third form, *δώῃ*, occurs in Paul: ℵ $\frac{2}{8}$, B $\frac{0}{7}$, A $\frac{2}{8}$, C $\frac{1}{2}$, D_2 $\frac{5}{8}$, G $\frac{3}{8}$, and even KLP $\frac{2}{8}$—cf. Jn 15^{16} in 33 and late uncials. For proof that the form *δωη* is subj. as well as opt.—the different placing of *ι subscr.* is only orthographical—see *Prol.*³ 55 and 193 f.: a clear instance of *γνώῃ* subj. is there cited from Clement, with a ref. to Reinhold 90 f. for *δώῃ* in apocrypha, and to a new reading (*ἀποδούηι*) in a pre-Christian papyrus.[1]

Optative—

The 3 sg. δῴη occurs in Paul 4 (Rom 15^{5}, 2 Th 3^{16}, 2 Ti $1^{16.18}$), and in late texts of 2 Ti 2^{7} 4^{14}. *Δοῖ* was also a Hellenistic form. From thematic verbs the flexion was *βάλοιμι -οις -οι, -οιμεν -οιτε -οιεν* with no possible alternatives except in 3 pl. Here the form in *-σαν* appears in *εὕροισαν* Ac 17^{27} D*, as in LXX: see above, § 84, p. 196.

Infinitive—

Βαλεῖν στῆναι -βῆναι θεῖναι ἀφεῖναι δοῦναι γνῶναι

NOTE.—1. All these are well represented, and there are no signs of variants (such as *στάναι, -βάναι, δῶναι, γνοῦναι,* due to mixture with present forms, and confusion between the two -ω- roots), which appear in papyri: see *CR* xv. 37, 435.

2. *Ἀνενέγκαι* 1 Pet 2^{5} is the only weak aorist form.

Participle—

βαλών	στάς	βάς	θείς	ἀφείς	δούς	γνούς
-οῦσα -όν	-ᾶσα -άν		-εῖσα -έν		-οῦσα -όν	

NOTE.—*Εἴπας* appears, though rarer than *εἰπών*: the two occur together in Jn 11^{28} BC*. WH reject the oblique cases.

[1] [Mr. H. Scott cites *Test. Simeon* 4^{5} *ἵνα δῷ ὁ θεὸς χάριν*, *v.ll.* *δῴη, δώει*. *Test. Reuben* 4^{1} *ἕως οὗ ὁ κύριος δώῃ ὑμῖν σύζυγον*.—ED.]

MIDDLE VOICE.

Indicative—

ἐβαλόμην	ἐθέμην	ἐδόμην
ἐβάλου	ἔθου	ἔδου
ἐβάλετο	ἔθετο	ἔδοτο
ἐβαλόμεθα	ἐθέμεθα	ἐδόμεθα
ἐβάλεσθε	ἔθεσθε	ἔδοσθε
ἐβάλοντο	ἔθεντο	ἔδοντο

NOTE.—1. Forms of the thematic verb with *a* include ἀπειπάμεθα 2 Co 4², and (as in act.) the quotable forms of the aor. of αἱρέομαι: ἐξειλάμην, εἵλατο and ἀν- and ἐξ- είλατο. In this word the resemblance to the weak aorist of a liquid verb no doubt helped the mixture: see under the Participle.

2. Mk 8¹⁴ B has ἐπελάθεντο, which occurs 8 times in LXX, according to Thackeray, who calls in the analogy of ἐτίθεντο, and the occasional 3 pl. -εσαν for -οσαν. That the variation affects this verb only, and in LXX as well as NT, makes some special cause probable.

3. Ἐξέθοντο Ac 18²⁶ D shows thematising, also συνεπείθοντο Ac 24⁹ 33 and 23²⁰ συνέθοντο H*.

4. For thematic ἔδετο there is quotable ἀπέδετο Heb 12¹⁶ AC, ἐξέδετο Mt 21³³ א*B*CL, with A added in the ‖ Lk 20⁹, and AK in Mk 12¹. In Heb *l.c.* the "correct" form is read by אDKLP 33, and is what we expect: in Mk 12¹ the vernacular flexion is equally to be expected, and we find Mt and Lk faithfully copying it. W has ἐξέδοτο only. None of the other moods of ἐδόμην occur in NT.

Imperative—

βαλοῦ	θοῦ
βαλέσθω	θέσθω
βάλεσθε	θέσθε
βαλέσθωσαν	θέσθωσαν

NOTE.—The three occurrences of -θοῦ and θέσθε are in Luke and Paul.

Subjunctive—

βάλωμαι	θῶμαι
βάλῃ	θῇ
βάληται	θῆται
βαλώμεθα	θώμεθα
βάλησθε	θῆσθε
βάλωνται	θῶνται

NOTE.—Ἀποθώμεθα in Rom 13¹² is the only occurrence.

Optative—

In the NT no forms occur from unthematic verbs except **ὀναίμην** (Phm [20]) from *ὀνίναμαι*: cf. *ὄναιντο* in *Audollent* 92[3] (iii/B.C.). **Γένοιτο** from *γίνομαι* is also a living form in the vernacular, esp. in the expression *μὴ γένοιτο*. *Λάβοιντο* can be quoted from a very illiterate Christian letter of iv/v A.D., P Giss 54[12]. The forms are the old ones throughout, so far as they survive at all.

Infinitive—

βαλέσθαι	**θέσθαι**

NOTE.—*Εὕρασθαι* can be cited from P Oxy ix 1204[13] (299 A.D.). There are no NT parallels: see below.

Participle—

βαλόμενος	**θέμενος**

NOTE.—**Εὑράμενος** (Heb 9[12]) is a well-attested form, whose passage into the weak flexion is explained, like *εἵλατο* etc. above, by the closeness of the weak aor. in liquid verbs. So *γενάμενος*, which is plentiful in papyri, but very rare in good NT texts (*e.g.* Lk 22[44] ℵ, 24[22] B): see *Proleg.* 51 n.[1]

PASSIVE VOICE.

Indicative—

ἠλλάγην	**ἠλλάγημεν**
ἠλλάγης	**ἠλλάγητε**
ἠλλάγη	**ἠλλάγησαν**

Imperative—

ἀλλάγηθι	**ἀλλάγητε**
ἀλλαγήτω	**ἀλλαγήτωσαν**

Subjunctive—

ἀλλαγῶ	**ἀλλαγῶμεν**
ἀλλαγῇς	**ἀλλαγῆτε**
ἀλλαγῇ	**ἀλλαγῶσι(ν)**

Optative—

Not found in NT: it runs *ἀλλαγ-είην -είης -είη -είημεν -είητε -είησαν.*

Infinitive—

ἀλλαγῆναι

Participle—

ἀλλαγείς -εῖσα -έν

Note.—Twenty-five roots are found in NT with this strong aorist, and some of them belong to the post-classical age, so that the formation was still alive. Sometimes it even ejected an older weak aorist: *e.g.* ἠγγέλην for ἠγγέλθην—a denominative like ἀγγέλλω could not make strong tense-stems in earlier Greek.

C. WEAK AORIST STEM.

§ 89. For the general formation of this stem see above, § 82. It proved in later Greek a pivot of the verb, very frequently producing new present stems. See Thumb *Handb.* 143 f.

Note.—1. The development in the MGr verb throws much light on tendencies already visible in NT Greek. Strong and weak aorists are now fused, and the characteristic α of the weak aorist endings dominates the active, banishing completely the endings with -ο-. The impf. has taken the same set of endings— -α -ες -ε, -αμε -ετε (and -ατε) -αν(ε). Accordingly the Hellenistic tendency to assimilate the two aorists, and at the same time to keep the imperfect in touch with the aorist, has worked itself out to a symmetrical result. The same historical connexion is seen in the stems. Thumb (*l.c.*) remarks that the MGr aor. act. "corresponds exactly" to its old Greek predecessor. "Only in a few cases the sigmatic aorist has encroached upon the territory of the non-sigmatic; thus ἐκέρδεσα fr. κερδαίνω, ἐσύναξα fr. συνάγω (συνάζω), ἐπρόσεξα fr. προσέχω, ἁμάρτησα fr. ἁμαρτάνω." All these have parallels in the Κοινή. NT Greek shows κερδῆσαι as well as κερδᾶναι, συνάξαι as well as συναγαγεῖν, and ἡμάρτησα beside ἥμαρτον (cf. MGr ἥμαρτο="beg pardon!"); while προσέξαι can be illustrated from papyri.[1] Thumb goes on to say, "While in general the ancient aorist has maintained its place, the present [MGr] stem has been quite frequently remodelled, and that on the basis of the aorist." This process can be easily recognised in NT. The present suffix -νω, extremely productive in MGr, has made new present stems in δύνω (ἔδυσα), -κτέν(ν)ω (-ἔκτεινα, like MGr σπέρνω: ἔσπειρα etc.), λιμπάνω (ἔλιπον), -χύν(ν)ω (-εχύθην), -στάνω (ἐστάθην—see § 95): some of these began to appear in classical times. The simplification of present stems under an impulse from the aorist may be seen also in classical or Hellenistic exx. such as κυλίω (ἐκύλισα), νίπτω (ἔνιψα), ῥήσσω (ἔρηξα), στείλω (Ac 7[34]—ἔστειλα), σκέπτομαι (ἐσκεψάμην, which secured the victory of its present over the Attic rival σκοπέω), ἀμφιάζω or -έζω (ἠμφίεσα—see § 33. 2), κρύβω (Lk 1[24] ?—see § 95—ἐκρύβην), βλαστάω (ἐβλάστησα), ὀπτάνομαι (ὤφθην).

2. Verbs in -αίνω and -αίρω make weak aorist in -ᾱνα, -ᾱρα, without regard to the sound preceding this suffix: this is explained by Brugmann-

[1] Cf. παρέξασθαι CPR 175[18] (ii/A.D.) *al.*

Thumb *Gr.* 39 as due to the analogy of verbs in which the ᾱ was "pure." Perhaps the working of this analogy, in the opposite direction to the general tendency of the Κοινή, may have been helped by the quality of the α vowel which kept its place in the rest of the verb.

3. Χύν(ν)ω (the older χέω) forms an abnormal aorist ἔχεα, best taken as a primitive strong aorist (ἔχε- ϝm̥, with weakened root in mid. ἐχύμην, ἐχύθης, ἔχυτο): see Thumb in Brugmann *Gram.*[4] 676. This is the regular form in NT: on some ambiguities see the List, § 95.

ACTIVE VOICE.

Indicative—

ἔλυσα	ἐλύσαμεν	ἔκρῑνα	ἐκρίναμεν
ἔλυσας	ἐλύσατε	ἔκρινας	ἐκρίνατε
ἔλυσε(ν)	ἔλυσαν	ἔκρινε(ν)	ἔκριναν

Note. — The infection of strong aor. endings is found in 2 sg. (from the influence of the common 3 sg. -ε) in illiterate papyri of the Roman age, as P Oxy vii. 1067[5] (iii/A.D.) ἀφῆκες, i. 119[2] (ii/iii A.D.) ἐποίησες [11] ἔπεμψες [13] ἔπλευσες, etc.: it is fixed in MGr. It appears in Rev 2[4] ℵ*C ἀφῆκες, Mt 11[25] D ἀπεκάλυψες, ἔδωκες Jn 17[7] ℵB ἔδωκες, [8] B, and even ἀφήκετε in Mt 23[23] B. Apparently it began in the Perfect, which accounts for its appearance at first mainly in -κα aorists: see § 92.

Imperative—

λῦσον	λύσατε
λυσάτω	λυσάτωσαν

Note.—1. The MGr type δέσε, δέσετε is foreshadowed by some late forms in vernacular Κοινή: cf. Dieterich *Unters.* 248. Radermacher suggests that the middle λῦσαι, pronounced as λῦσε, may have started the assimilation to the present.

2. There is no trace in Hellenistic of the 3rd pl. λυσάντων, which is regular in Attic until 300 B.C. (Meisterhans[3] 167).

Subjunctive—

λύσω	λύσωμεν
λύσῃς	λύσητε
λύσῃ	λύσωσι

Optative—

λύσαιμι	λύσαιμεν
λύσαις	λύσαιτε
λύσαι	λύσειαν or -αιεν

Note.—1. In papyri (Harsing 14) the 3 sg. is λύσειε(ν) more often than λύσαι, but the exx. of -ειε(ν) are all from iii/A.D. or later (except one of ii/B.C.), and belong accordingly to the period in which the language of the schools gave the optative a short spell of renewed life. It seems that -αι was the suffix in the natural vernacular before this revival, and this is the only form evidenced in NT, unless we count Lk 6^{11} ποιήσειεν in ℵAW cu[5], Ac 17^{27} ψηλαφήσειεν in ℵE cu[9], which are ruled out by the demand for a 3 pl. Cf. Crönert *Mem.* 213, Meisterhans[3] 166 ("the so-called Aeolic forms in the aorist do not occur" in Attic inscrr.), Thackeray 215.

2. In the pl. the evidence is somewhat conflicting. Lk 6^{11} BLΔ 1 etc. 13 etc. 33 *al.* has ποιήσαιεν (ω -ειαν, ℵAW -ειεν), but Ac 17^{27} ABω ψηλαφήσ(ε)ιαν (see note 1), where only cu[5] have -αιεν. Here D reads -αισαν, which Blass wanted to accept, mainly because it is regular in LXX (Thackeray 215). It must be remembered however that the LXX has other extensions of the 3 pl. -σαν which are not shared by NT, and may be dialectic variations: the MS attestation is not strong enough to force this form on a writer of Luke's Greek culture.

Infinitive—

λῦσαι

Note.—There is a strong tendency in vernacular Κοινή to substitute the ending of the pres. inf. in act. and mid., so that the aor. infin. may be confused with the practically obsolete fut. infin. See *Prol.* 204 n.[2], where it is noted that ἔσεσθαι is the only fut. inf. in NT except καταντήσειν Ac 26^{7} B, εἰσελεύσεσθαι Heb 3^{18}, and χωρήσειν Jn 21^{25} ℵBC. Heb *l.c.* is the only clear fut. here: the other two are probably mere aorists. The aor. inf. would carry the same meaning, and the -ῆσαι of the other MSS is best taken as a correction.

Participle—

λύσας -ασα -αν

§ 90. MIDDLE VOICE.

Indicative—

ἐλυσάμην	ἐλυσάμεθα
ἐλύσω	ἐλύσασθε
ἐλύσατο	ἐλύσαντο

Imperative—

λῦσαι	λύσασθε
λυσάσθω	λυσάσθωσαν

Subjunctive—

λύσωμαι	λυσώμεθα
λύσῃ	λύσησθε
λύσηται	λύσωνται

Optative—

λυσαίμην	λυσαίμεθα
λύσαιο	λύσαισθε
λύσαιτο	λύσαιντο

NOTE.—*Εὐξαίμην* is the only quotable instance, but the rest of the tense could have no other form.

Infinitive—

λύσασθαι

NOTE.—The substitution of *-εσθαι*, making the form identical with that of the obsolete future, is parallel with that noted under the active; but there is no instance in NT.

Participle—

λυσάμενος

PASSIVE VOICE.

Indicative—

ἐλύθην	ἐλύθημεν
ἐλύθης	ἐλύθητε
ἐλύθη	ἐλύθησαν

Imperative—

λύθητι	λύθητε
λυθήτω	λυθήτωσαν

NOTE.—The 2 sing. *-τι* is for *-θι* by aspirate dissimilation.

Subjunctive—

λυθῶ	λυθῶμεν
λυθῇς	λυθῆτε
λυθῇ	λυθῶσι(ν)

Optative—

λυθείην	λυθείημεν
λυθείης	λυθείητε
λυθείη	λυθείησαν

NOTE.—A few instances occur in NT *πληθυνθείη* (1 Pet 1[2], 2 Pet 1[2], Jude[2]), *λογισθείη* (2 Ti 4[16]), *τηρηθείη* (1 Th 5[23]) — but the forms in Hellenistic are certain. Even the Atticisers hardly show the primitive (and Attic) short forms *λυθεῖμεν -εῖτε*, though Moeris commended them. Cf. Scham *Opt. bei Clem. Alex.* 34; Harsing 22; whence it appears that the 3rd pl. *-εῖεν* survived where *-εῖμεν -εῖτε* did not.

Infinitive—

λυθῆναι

Participle—

λυθείς -εῖσα -έν

D. FUTURE STEM.

§ 91. For the formation of Future Stems see above, § 82.

ACTIVE AND MIDDLE VOICES.

From the earliest times in Greek the Future has a large proportion of Middle forms, there being whole categories of verbs in which a present active took a future middle without any ascertainable reason. On this subject, and on the assimilations which took place in Hellenistic, see *Proleg.* 154 f. Notes on the individual verbs will be found in the List.

Verbs in *-ίζω* show some wavering between the *-σ-* and the *-ε(σ)-* formation. Moeris (see Schweizer *Perg.* 178) makes *-εῖται* Attic and *-σεται* Hellenistic. The more normal form naturally secured a lead over its rival, which held its own perforce in the liquid verbs. All cases where the Contracted Future is found in NT will be noted in the List. WH (*App.*[2] 170 f.) make *-ῶ* $\frac{1}{3}$, *-σει* habitually (exc. twice *(δια)καθαριεῖ*), *-σομεν* $\frac{2}{2}$, *-οῦσι* except *γνωρίσουσι*, *-σεται* $\frac{2 \text{ or } 3}{3}$, *-εῖσθε* $\frac{1}{1}$. See the note above on the difference between LXX and NT in the future of verbs in *-άζω* (§ 82).

Indicative—

Active.		*Middle.*		
λύσω	κρινῶ	λύσομαι	ἔσομαι	κρινοῦμαι
λύσεις	κρινεῖς	λύσῃ	ἔσῃ	κρινῇ
λύσει	κρινεῖ	λύσεται	ἔσται	κρινεῖται
λύσομεν	κρινοῦμεν	λυσόμεθα	ἐσόμεθα	κρινούμεθα
λύσετε	κρινεῖτε	λύσεσθε	ἔσεσθε	κρινεῖσθε
λύσουσι(ν)	κρινοῦσι(ν)	λύσονται	ἔσονται	κρινοῦνται

Subjunctive—

Alleged exx. of this imaginary mood are *δώσῃ* Jn 17[2], Rev 8[3], *ὄψησθε* Lk 13[28], which are only new aorists made from the future stem by the usual analogy.

Optative—

This mood, which in classical Greek only existed for one syntactical category, the representation of a fut. indic. in *orat. obl.* in past sequence, is entirely obsolete in Hellenistic, except for one or two artificialities of a late period.

Infinitive—

Active.	*Middle.*
λύσειν κρινεῖν	λύσεσθαι ἔσεσθαι κρινεῖσθαι

NOTE.—This form can hardly be said to have any real vernacular existence: see § 89. In Jn 21[25] χωρήσειν was probably an aor., as far as the writer's consciousness went;[1] and the substitution of -ασθαι in many places where so clear a future as ἐπελεύσεσθαι appeared in a formula shows that even this was felt as an aorist. Ἔσεσθαι is the one real exception, and even this only occurs in Ac: μέλλειν ἔσεσθαι (*ter*) is a set phrase, and 23[30] μηνυθείσης δέ μοι ἐπιβουλῆς εἰς τὸν ἄνδρα ἔσεσθαι is in an official letter in stilted style. Outside Ac and Heb (and Jn 21[25]—see above) the infin. is not found: cf. Heb 3[18], Ac 26[7] B.

Participle—

Active.

λύσων -ουσα -ον κρινῶν -οῦσα -οῦν λυσόμενος ἐσόμενος κρινούμενος

NOTE.—This also is very rare, but shows more signs of life than the infin. The only warrant for the contracted form is κατακρινῶν (Rom 8[34]), which might as well be present, and κομιούμενοι 2 Pet 2[13] ACω vg syr[hl] sah boh, which is certainly corrupt; but of course these forms would be used if the future ptc. of a liquid verb were wanted. As before, the Lucan writings and Heb show the survival most.

PASSIVE VOICE.

The Strong Future (ἀλλαγήσομαι etc.) agrees exactly with the model of the Weak, which alone need be given.

Indicative—

λυθήσομαι	λυθησόμεθα
λυθήσῃ	λυθήσεσθε
λυθήσεται	λυθήσονται

NOTE.—Καυθήσωμαι in 1 Co 13[3] CK *al.* seems to be a mere fusion of the *vv.ll.* καυθήσομαι and καυχήσωμαι—if indeed we should take it as seriously as even this; it does not in any case provide us with a future subj.!

---

[1] Blass's remark about "the spurious concluding verse" of Jn (*Gr.*[2] 202 n.) rests on no evidence at all: see Lake's introduction (*Cod. Sin.* p. xx) for the supposed hostile witness of ℵ*.

Infinitive—

λυθήσεσθαι

NOTE.—Not in NT, but quotable *e.g.* from P Tebt i. 61 (a)[186] (land survey, B.C. 118).

Participle—

λυθησόμενος

NOTE.—Found once (Heb 3[5]), and quotable from papyri.

E. PERFECT STEM.

ACTIVE VOICE.

§ 92. The formation of the Strong Perfect Active is described above, § 82 *E*; its frequent intransitive use, which caused it in old grammars to be counted as a middle, is noted in *Prol.* 154, with the theory that its unique person-endings betray a formation which in its prehistoric stages was neither active nor middle.

Perfect stems with the *o*-gradation (historically identical with the proethnic Germanic vowel in *sat*, *rang*, *wrote* etc.) are still numerous in Hellenistic. Thus οἶδα, λέλοιπα, πέποιθα, γέγονα, ἐνήνοχα, πέπονθα. In the other vowel-series there are no traces left of the corresponding gradation, except εἴωθα compared with ἦθος. Thus εἴληφα has the same vowel as λήμψομαι, κέκρᾱγα as κράζω, σέσηπα as σήπω. The roots with ευ do not seem to preserve any ο forms in the perfect: φεύγω makes πέφευγα, while τέτυχα keeps the weak gradation, originally characteristic of the plur.: cf. Eng. *wrung*, and the perfects *begun* etc., which were normal a few generations back. So γέγραφα, τέταχα, ἐλήλυθα.

In two cases an old Perfect has produced in Hellenistic a new Present Stem: στήκω from ἕστηκα *stand*, and γρηγορέω from ἐγρήγορα *am awake*.

The Person-endings in Hellenistic are levelled so as to be identical with those of the Weak Aorist in the indicative, except for the 3rd pl.: on this see below. The difference of gradation in the root of sing. and plur. no longer survives even in οἶδα.

Strong and Weak Perfects may be taken together, their terminations being identical.

Indicative—

Perfect.

οἶδα	οἴδαμεν	λέλυκα	λελύκαμεν
οἶδας	οἴδατε	λέλυκας	λελύκατε
οἶδε(ν)	οἴδασι(ν)	λέλυκε(ν)	λελύκασι(ν)

NOTE.—1. The old forms of οἶδα, 2 sg. οἶσθα and pl. ἴσμεν, ἴστε, ἴσασι(ν), were obsolete in vernacular Hellenistic. Moeris (ed. Pierson) p. 205 writes: "ἴσασι· Ἀττικῶς: οἴδασι· κοινῶς, and cf. Phryn. (ed. Lobeck) p. 236 f., where instances of οἶδας from older Greek are cited." It appears as early as B.C. 255 in P Petr ii. 4 (7)[2] (9)[8], but οἶσθα in P Lille 11[4] (mid iii/B.C.), an official letter, and even P Oxy viii. 1119[15] (A.D. 254) —cf. also Thackeray 278. Οἶδας appear 11 times in NT without variant, and the "regular" pl. very frequently in all persons, again agreeing with papyri: see *Prol.* 55, where Ionic is noted as the source of the levelled flexion. There is one certain ex. of the old forms, Ac 26[4] ἴσασι (no *v.l.*): Heb 12[17] ἴστε may also be a mark of this literary survival, appropriate in Heb, and in the speech of an educated man before a court. Cf. BGU i. 163[14] (A.D. 108) also official. See further under Imper.

2. Assimilation to the 3rd sg., on the lines of Impf. and Strong Aor., produced in the lower vernacular a 2nd sg. in -ες, which passed on into the Weak Aor.: § 89. It is rare in earlier papyri: see Thackeray 216, and some later exx. in *CR* xv. 36, xviii. 110, also Mayser's note p. 321. In NT we find it plausibly read in Rev 2[3] AC κεκοπίακες, [5] ℵ πέπτωκες, 11[17] C εἴληφες—also in Jn 8[57] B* ἑώρακες, Ac 21[22] B ἐλήλυθες, which last at any rate is highly improbable.

3. In 3rd pl. the Weak Aor. -αν secured a firm hold in the vernacular, being the last remaining difference between the aor. and perf. endings. (In some illiterate papyri the perf. -ασι invaded the aor.) It seems to begin in ii/B.C., and is found widely spread through the Κοινή: see *Prol.* 52, Thumb *Hellen.* 170, Mayser 323 f., Thackeray 212, *CR* xv. 36, 435, xviii. 110. In NT we find it in Ac 16[36], Rom 16[7], Lk 9[36], Col 2[1] (see *Prol. l.c.*), with Rev 21[6] A, 19[3] ℵAP, 18[3] AC, Jn 17[7] ABCDL *al.*, 17[6] BDLW, Jas 5[4] BP—too good a record perhaps to justify the suspicion I expressed: I must admit moreover that I aspersed unfairly the culture of some early papyri showing -αν.

4. The verb ἥκω "I have come," which is a perfect in meaning, and by its κ suggests a formal connexion also with the perfect tense, developed a corresponding flexion in the pl. Thus ἥκαμεν P Par 48[9] (B.C. 153), ἥκατε P Grenf ii. 36[18] (B.C. 95), ἥκασι Mk 8[3] ℵADW syr[s] latt *al.* (BLΔ boh substitute εἰσίν). Thackeray 269 and Mayser 372 show how well established this flexion is throughout, except in sing. indic. It is probably to be accepted in Mk *l.c.*: see *Prol.* 53.

Pluperfect.

ᾔδειν	ᾔδειμεν	(ἐ)λελύκειν	(ἐ)λελύκειμεν
ᾔδεις	ᾔδειτε	(ἐ)λελύκεις	(ἐ)λελύκειτε
ᾔδει	ᾔδεισαν	(ἐ)λελύκει	(ἐ)λελύκεισαν

NOTE.—1. The past tense of οἶδα has been assimilated to the other pluperfects. The sound of its initial vowel was in our period decidedly less removed from that of οἶδα than in Attic had been the case.

2. The characteristic ει runs through the tense in NT forms. There are a few isolated irregularities in papyri: thus εἰώθησαν BGU i. 250[7]

(ii/A.D.) (=*Chrest.* i. p. 114), εἰρήκης (pap. εἰρήκαις) P Par 32[16] (B.C. 162), ὀμωμόκεμεν P Par 46[12] (B.C. 153). See Mayser 324.

3. On the dropping of the augment in pluperf. see § 83.

Imperative—

ἴσθι	ἴστε
ἴστω	ἴστωσαν

NOTE.—1. No perf. act. imper. forms occur in NT. In LXX we find such forms as κεκραγέτωσαν, πεποίθατε, πεποιθέτω (Job 12[5]).

2. It is best, except perhaps in Heb 12[17] (see above, p. 221), to treat ἴστε as imper. wherever it occurs. In Jas 1[19] Mayor expresses a preference for indic., as also in Eph 5[5] and Heb *l.c.* But the only justification of this literary survival would be a clearly proved tendency in the author's general style; and οἴδατε in Jas 4[4] matches the Greek of the writer. "Be sure of this," Mayor's alternative, is decidedly preferable; and so in Eph *l.c.* (on which see *Prol.*[3] 245 also p. 22 f. above).

Subjunctive—

εἰδῶ	εἰδῶμεν
εἰδῇς	εἰδῆτε
εἰδῇ	εἰδῶσι(ν)

NOTE. — The ordinary verb makes its subjunctive by combining participle and the verb εἶναι, as πεποιθὼς ὦ.

Infinitive—

εἰδέναι	λελυκέναι	ἑστάναι

NOTE. — The old strong perf. ἑστάναι occurs three times in NT, ἑστηκέναι never.

Participle—

εἰδώς -υῖα -ός   λελυκώς   ἑστώς -ῶσα -ός (gen. ἑστῶτος)

NOTE.—1. On the gen. sing. fem. συνειδυίης see above, §§ 37, 51.

2. The strong ptc. ἑστώς, in simplex and compounds, maintains itself without serious challenge: it occurs in NT 57 times to 18 instances of ἑστηκώς, apart from places where the MSS are divided. Mk has 3 : 5, but all other writers use ἑστώς more frequently—except that Heb has ἑστηκώς in the one occurrence. The Lucan books show ἑστώς 22 times, and ἑστηκώς only twice; Rev has 9 ἑστώς against only 2. It is therefore no consequence of literary style one way or the other.

3. Both ἑστηκώς (Rev 5[6] ℵ) and ἑστώς (Mk 13[14] late uncials, Rev 14[1] 046 and cu[11]+) appear sporadically in neut. Since in both cases *ad sensum* construction would produce ἑστηκότα -ῶτα, this probably belongs to the general levelling of participial flexion: cf. § 65 (2).

MIDDLE AND PASSIVE VOICE.

§ 93. The flexion of this tense system depends on the character of the sound which ends the stem. Stems ending in a consonant have to use periphrastic 3 pl. in perf. and pluperf. indic.: the old forms with *-αται -ατο* (= *-n̥tai -n̥to*), like *τετάχαται*, were liable to be mistaken for 3 sg., and did not survive in the *Κοινή*. Hence types like *πεπεισμένοι -αι -α εἰσίν, ἦσαν*, had to supply the place.

Vowel Stems.	Guttural Stems.	Labial Stems.	Dental Stems.	Liquid Stems.	Nasal Stems.
λελυ-	τεταγ-	γεγραφ-	πεπειθ-	ἐσταλ-	μεμιαν-

Indicative—

Perfect.

λέλυμαι	τέταγμαι	γέγραμμαι	πέπεισμαι	ἔσταλμαι	μεμίαμμαι
λέλυσαι	τέταξαι	γέγραψαι	πέπεισαι	ἔσταλσαι	μεμίανσαι
λέλυται	τέτακται	γέγραπται	πέπεισται	ἔσταλται	μεμίανται
λελύμεθα	τετάγμεθα	γεγράμμεθα	πεπείσμεθα	ἐστάλμεθα	μεμιάμμεθα
λέλυσθε	τέταχθε	γέγραφθε	πέπεισθε	ἔσταλθε	μεμίανθε
λέλυνται		Periphrastic			

Note.—1. The last column is not quite certain, and some persons do not occur. Tit 1^{15} μεμιαμμένοις, Mk 3^{1} 11^{20} ἐξηραμμένην, together with μεμαραμμένος and κατησχυμμένος in Hermas and κατασεσημημμένα in P Oxy i. 117^{14} (cited by Blass) justify the μμ against earlier σμ; but note συνκαθυφασμένα Is 3^{23} *al.* (Thackeray 224). The rest of the flexion may be assumed to be as in Attic.

2. Stems in σ, as τετελεσ-, are like the dental stems.

Pluperfect.

(ἐ)λελύμην	(ἐ)τετάγμην	(ἐ)γεγράμμην	(ἐ)πεπείσμην	ἐστάλμην
(ἐ)λέλυσο	(ἐ)τέταξο	(ἐ)γέγραψο	(ἐ)πέπεισο	ἔσταλσο
(ἐ)λέλυτο	(ἐ)τέτακτο	(ἐ)γέγραπτο	(ἐ)πέπειστο	ἔσταλτο
(ἐ)λελύμεθα	(ἐ)τετάγμεθα	(ἐ)γεγράμμεθα	(ἐ)πεπείσμεθα	ἐστάλμεθα
(ἐ)λέλυσθε	(ἐ)τέταχθε	(ἐ)γέγραφθε	(ἐ)πέπεισθε	ἔσταλθε
(ἐ)λέλυντο		Periphrastic		

Note. — Some of these forms are inferred. No form of the (ἐ)μεμιάμμην type occurs.

Imperative—

λέλυσο	λελύσθω	λέλυσθε	λελύσθωσαν

Note.—The form πεφίμωσο, from φιμόω *muzzle*, can be quoted. The tense is very rare: if speakers of the Κοινή had occasion to use it they presumably used the old forms, which can be inferred from the flexions given.

Subjunctive—

Like the Optative, this was periphrastic (*λελυμένος ὦ* etc.) in earlier and later Greek.

Infinitive—

λελύσθαι *τετάχθαι* *γεγράφθαι* *πεπεῖσθαι* *ἐστάλθαι*

Participle—

λελυμένος τεταγμένος γεγραμμένος πεπεισμένος ἐσταλμένος μεμιαμμένος

F. VERBALS.

§ 94. One form of the gerundive in -*τέος* can be quoted from NT, viz. **βλητέον** from *βάλλω* (Lk 5[38]): see *Prol.* 222. In form it agrees with the verbal in -*τός*, the meaning of which is discussed in *Prol.* 221 f.

Papyrus instances of the gerundive are P Giss i. 40 [ii. 22] (A.D. 215) *διὰ τοῦτο οὔκ εἰσιν κωλυτέοι*, P Tebt i. 61 (*b*) [220 f.] (B.C. 118—a land survey) *εἰ [α]ὐτὴ [ἀνταναι]ρετέα [ἄλλη δὲ] ἀπὸ ὑπολόγου ἀνταναιρεθεῖσα ἀποκαταστατέα* (the whole formula elsewhere), P Par 63 (ii/B.C.) [53] *χρηστέον*, [119] *ἐνγραπτέον*, [120] *μεριστέον*. These are all official, and in themselves inadequate warrant for really vernacular use.

Verbal adjectives in -*τός* have recessive accent when compounded. There are about 150 of them in NT, and the formation seems to be still living, so that it can be made from new verbs. The -*τός* suffix in non-derivative verbs was originally added to the weakened root, as we may see in *θετός*, *πιστός*, *φθαρτός*, -*ιτός* (*ἀπρόσιτος*): contract verbs add it to the long vowel seen in future, as *ἀγαπη-τός*, *ἀλάλη-τος*, *μισθω-τός*, and other derivative verbs to the bare stem, as *βδελυκ-τός*, *σιτισ-τός*, etc.

LIST OF VERBS.

§ 95. This list includes all verbs occurring in NT (or in good MSS thereof), except—

(1) regular Contracta.

(2) regular verbs in -*ύω* and -*άζω*, and those in -*ίζω* which show no future act. or mid.

(3) verbs with no forms outside the present stem, and with nothing noteworthy to record.

"Regular" reduplication of verbs with initial σ implies σεσ- where a vowel follows, ἐσ- where a consonant.

Verbs are set down in the simplex, preceded by a hyphen when the form only occurs in a compound. The list of quotable compounds is appended in each case. A few Compound Verbs are given in their alphabetic place for points affecting the preposition. The prepositions are given in the assimilated form for the present indicative, according to classical orthography.

Roman numerals attached to the present stem denote conjugation classes.

An obelus denotes a form apparently not older than the Hellenistic age. When placed on the extreme left it means that the whole verb is late. Suppletives are enclosed in square brackets.

The indicative form stands for anything occurring in the tense paradigm. Occasionally the mood form is quoted for special reasons.

The regular tense-formations of verbs not included in this List (see above) are as follows:—

	PRESENT.	WEAK AORIST.	FUTURE.	PERFECT.
(1)	-άω (α *pure*)	-ᾱσα	-ᾱ́σω	-ᾱκα
		-ᾱσάμην	-ᾱ́σομαι	-ᾱμαι
		-ᾱ́θην	-ᾱθήσομαι	
	-άω (α *impure*), -έω	-ησα etc.	-ήσω etc.	-ηκα etc.
	-όω	-ωσα etc.	-ώσω etc.	-ωκα etc.
	-ίζω	-ισα etc.	[in List]	-ικα
		-ίσθην		-ισμαι
(2)	-ύω (αύω etc.)	-υσα etc.	-ύσω etc.	-υκα etc.
	-άζω	-ᾰσα	-ᾰ́σω	-ακα
		-ᾰσάμην	-ᾰ́σομαι	-ασμαι
		-άσθην	-ασθήσομαι	

A. PRESENT.	*B*. STRONG AORIST.	*C*. WEAK AORIST.	*D*. FUTURE.	*E*. PERFECT.
† ἀγαλλιάω (VII.) *exult*		ἠγαλλίασα		
		ἠγαλλιασάμην		
ἀγαλλιῶμαι		ἠγαλλιάθην		
		ἠγαλλιάσθην (Jn 5[35] BL)		

"A Hellenistic variation on ἀγάλλεσθαι after ναυτιᾶν, κοπιᾶν ἀγωνιᾶν," etc. (Blass-Debrunner).

ἀγγέλλω (VII.)	-ἠγγέλην †	ἤγγειλα	-ἀγγελῶ	-ἤγγελμαι
announce		ἠγγειλάμην		
-ἤγγελλον				

COMP. ἀν-, ἀπ-, δι-. ἐξ-, ἐπ-, κατ-, παρ-, προ-επ-, προ-κατ-

-ἄγνυμι (II. β.b)	-ἐάγην	-ἔαξα	-ἐάξω †
break	Subj. κατεαγῶσιν † Jn 19^{31}: see § 83 (1).		See § 83 (1).

COMP. κατ-

-ἄγχω (I. *a*)		ἠγξάμην
choke		

COMP. ἀπ-

ἄγω (I. *b*)	ἤγαγον	-ἧξα	ἄξω	ἦγμαι
lead		Not Attic, but old. Found in illiterate papyri.	ἀχθήσομαι	
ἦγον				
ἄγομαι				
ἠγόμην				
VERBAL -ἀκτός		ἤχθην		

COMP. ἀν-, ἐπ-αν-, ἀπ-, συν-απ-, δι-, εἰσ-, παρ-εισ-, ἐξ-, ἐπ-, κατ-, μετ-, παρ-, περι-, προ-, προσ-, συν-, ἐπι-συν-, ὑπ-

αἰνέω (VII.)		-ῄνεσα	-αἰνέσω
praise			
-ῄνουν			Ἐπαινέσω in 1 Co 11^{22} is prob. aor. subj.
VERBAL -αἰνετός			

COMP. ἐπ-, παρ-

αἱρέω (VII.)	-εἷλον (ἑλεῖν)	῾ρέθην	ἑλῶ †	-ῄρημαι
take	εἱλόμην		(LXX and papp.—from aor.).	On the general Κοινή spelling -εἵρημαι, see above, § 83 (6).
-αἱροῦμαι				
-ῃρούμην	(-α forms: § 88c).		αἱρήσομαι	
			-αἱρεθήσομαι	

VERBAL -αἱρετός

COMP. ἀν-, ἀφ-, δι-, ἐξ, καθ-, περι-, προ-

αἴρω (VII.)	ἦρα (ἆραι)	ἀρῶ	ἦρκα
raise	ἤρθην	ἀρθήσομαι	ἦρμαι
αἴρομαι			

COMP. ἀπ-, ἐξ-, ἐπ-, μετ-, συν-, ὑπερ-

From ϝαριω: not contracted from cognate ἀείρω. The aor. must not be written with ι subscript.

αἰσθάνομαι (II. *a*) *perceive* — ἠσθόμην

-αἰσχύνω (VII.) *shame*
αἰσχύνομαι
ᾐσχυνόμην
VERBAL -αἰσχυντός
COMP. ἐπ-, κατ-
— ᾐσχύνθην (-αισχ.: see § 83 (6)) — αἰσχυνθήσομαι

ἀκούω (VII.) *hear*
ἤκουον
ἀκούομαι
COMP. δι-, εἰσ-, ἐπ-, παρ-, προ-, ὑπ-
— ἤκουσα, ἠκούσθην — ἀκούσω †, ἀκούσομαι, ἀκουσθήσομαι — ἀκήκοα

ἀλείφω (I. *a*) *anoint*
ἤλειφον
COMP. ἐξ-
— ἤλειψα, ἠλειψάμην, -ἠλείφθην (Ac 3[19] ἐξαλιφθῆναι WH: see § 35). — -ἀλείψω

ἁλίσκομαι: see ἀναλίσκω
VERBAL -ἁλωτός

-ἀλλάσσω (VII.) *change* — -ἠλλάγην
-ἤλλασσον
-ἀλλάσσομαι
COMP. ἀπ-, δι-, κατ-, ἀπο-κατ-, μετ-, συν-
— ἤλλαξα — ἀλλάξω, ἀλλαγήσομαι — -ἤλλαγμαι

ἅλλομαι *leap* — -ἡλόμην (-α forms: see § 88).
COMP. ἀν-, ἐξ-, ἐφ-

ἁμαρτάνω (II. *a*) ἥμαρτον *sin*
VERBAL -ἁμαρτητός
COMP. προ-
— ἡμάρτησα † (see § 89). — ἁμαρτήσω † — ἡμάρτηκα

ἀμύνομαι (VII.) *take revenge* — ἠμυνάμην

ἀμφιέννυμι (II. *β. b*)				**ἠμφίεσμαι**
ἀμφιάζω † (VII.)				(See § 83 (7))
clothe				

The simplex ἕννυμι had long been obsolete: so was the II. β present-stem except in semi-literary language. On the variant Κοινή presents -άζω and -έζω, both found in good uncials of Lk 12[28], see *Vocabulary*, *s.v.*, and *supra*, p. 68.

ἀναλίσκω (IV.)		**ἀνήλωσα**	**ἀνᾱλώσω**
ἀνᾱλόω † (VII.)		(**ἀνᾱλῶσαι**)	
spend, *destroy*		**ἀνηλώθην**	

Comp. **κατ-**, **προσ-**

A very early compound (ἀνα-ϝαλίσκω), with αϝα contracted to ᾱ: cf. ἁλίσκομαι. The late "regular" present (2 Th 2[8] ℵ*) is a back-formation from the future and aorist.

ἀνοίγω (I. *a*)	**ἠνοίγην** †	**ἀνέῳξα**	**ἀνοίξω**	**ἀνέῳγα**
open		**ἤνοιξα**	**ἀνοιχθήσομαι** †	**ἀνέῳγμαι**
ἀνοίγομαι		**ἠνέῳξα** †	**ἀνοιγήσομαι** †	**ἠνέῳγμαι** †
-ἤνοιγον		(**ἀνοῖξαι**)		**ἤνοιγμαι** †
Comp. **δι-**		**ἀνεώχθην**		
See *Vocabulary*, *s.v.*		**ἠνοίχθην** †		
For the strange irregularities of augment and reduplication, see § 83 (1). The simplex οἴγω or οἴγνυμι (on which see Brugmann[4] 310 n.) was extinct in Hellenistic.		**ἠνεῴχθην** † (**ἀνεῳχθῆναι**)		

-ἀντάω (VII.)		**-ἤντησα**	**-ἀντήσω** †	**-ἤντηκα**
meet			(cl. **-ομαι**)	

Comp. **ἀπ-**, **κατ-**, **συν-**, **ὑπ-**

The simplex became obsolete early.

ἅπτω (VII.)		**ἧψα**
grasp, *kindle*		**ἡψάμην**
ἅπτομαι		**ἥφθην**
ἡπτόμην		

Comp. **ἀν-**, **καθ-**, **περι-**

ἀρέσκω (IV.)			
please	**ἤρεσα**	**ἀρέσω**	
ἤρεσκον			
VERBAL **ἀρεστός**			
ἀρκέω (VII.)	**ἤρκεσα**	**ἀρκέσω**	
suffice		**ἀρκεσθήσομαι** †	
VERBAL **ἀρκετός**			
COMP. **ἐπ-**			
ἁρμόζω † (VII.)	**ἡρμοσάμην**		
fit			
The Attic pres. was ἁρμόττω.			
ἁρπάζω (VII.) **ἡρπάγην** †	**ἥρπασα**	**ἁρπάσω** †	**-ἡρπάκειν**
seize	**ἡρπάσθην**	**ἁρπαγήσομαι** †	
		see Rutherford *NP* 407.	
COMP. **δι-**, **συν-**			
On the mixture of guttural and dental stem see *Proleg.* 56; also Brugmann *Gr.*[4] 359.			
ἄρχω (I. *a*)	**ἠρξάμην**	**ἄρξομαι**	
be first			
ἄρχομαι			
-ἦρχον			
COMP. **ἐν-**, **προ-εν-**, **ὑπ-**, **προ-υπ-**			
ἀστράπτω (VII.)	**-ἤστραψα**		
lighten			
COMP. **ἐξ-**, **περι-**			
αὐξάνω (II. *a*)	**ηὔξησα**	**αὐξήσω**	
αὔξω (III.)	**ηὐξήθην**		
wax			
ηὔξανον			
αὐξάνομαι			
COMP. **συν-**, **ὑπερ-(αυξάνω)**			

ἀφίημι, imperf. **ἤφιον**: for other forms see under **-ἵημι**.

-βαίνω (VII.) **-ἔβην** (§ 88)		**-βήσομαι**	**-βέβηκα**
go			
-ἔβαινον			
CAUSAL **-βιβάζω** (**ἀνα-**, **ἐμ-**, **ἐπι-**, **κατα-**, **προ-**, **συν-**), conjugated regularly.			
VERBAL **-βατός**			

COMP. ἀνα-, ἀπο-, δια-, ἐκ-, ἐμ-, ἐπι-, κατα-, μετα-, παρα-, προ-, προσ-ανα-, συμ-, συγ-κατα-, συν-ανα-, ὑπερ-

The simplex was very nearly extinct in common speech when the Κοινή arose. See *Vocabulary*, *s.v.*

βάλλω (VII.)	ἔβαλον	ἐβλήθην	βαλῶ	βέβληκα
cast	-ἐβαλόμην		-βαλοῦμαι	-βεβλήκειν
βάλλομαι	(For -α forms		βληθήσομαι	βέβλημαι
-ἔβαλλον	see § 88.)			ἐβεβλήμην

VERBALS -βλητός, βλητέος

COMP. ἀμφι- ἀνα-, ἀντι-, ἀπο-, δια-, ἐκ-, ἐμ-, ἐπι-, κατα-, μετα-, παρα-, παρ-εμ-, περι-, προ-, συν-, ὑπερ-, ὑπο-

βαπτίζω (VII.)	ἐβάπτισα	βαπτίσω †	βεβάπτισμαι
baptize	ἐβαπτισάμην	βαπτισθήσο-	
βαπτίζομαι	ἐβαπτίσθην	μαι	
ἐβάπτιζον			
ἐβαπτιζόμην			

βάπτω (VII.)	ἔβαψα	βάψω	βέβαμμαι
dip			(Rev 19[13] A)

COMP. ἐμ-

βαρέω † (VII.)	-ἐβάρησα †		βεβάρημαι
burden	ἐβαρήθην †		
βαροῦμαι			

COMP. ἐπι-, κατα-

The verb was apparently a back-formation from the perf. pass. The alternative βαρύνω is found in Lk 21[34] βαρυνθῶσι DH and Mk 14[40] καταβαρυνόμενοι.

βασκαίνω (VII.)	ἐβάσκᾱνα		
bewitch			

βαστάζω (VII.)	ἐβάστασα	βαστάσω	
carry			
ἐβάσταζον			

VERBAL -βαστακτός

The guttural forms are not found in NT exc. in verbal and in Rev 2[2] βαστάξαι P 1, 38 : they are frequent in papyri.

βδελύσσομαι (VII.)			ἐβδέλυγμαι
loathe			

VERBAL βδελυκτός

βιβρώσκω (IV.)			βέβρωκα
eat			

VERBAL -βρωτός

βιόω (VII.) — **ἐβίωσα**
live — supplanted strong aor. *ἐβίων*.
Supplied in earlier Greek an aorist to *ζήω*.

βλάπτω (VII.) — **ἔβλαψα**
hurt

βλαστάνω (II. *a*) — **ἐβλάστησα**
βλαστάω †(VII.) — Perhaps Ionic (Hippocrates): replaces strong aor. *ἔβλαστον*.
grow

Βλαστᾷ (Mk 4[27]) is an instance of confusion between the two classes of Contracta which make fut. in -*ήσω* (see § 84): the back-formation *βλαστέω* is perhaps quotable even in Aeschylus.

βλέπω (I. *a*) — **ἔβλεψα** — **βλέψω** †
ἔβλεπον, *look* — **-ἐβλεψάμην** † — Herodotus has *ἀναβλέψω*.
βλέπομαι

COMP. **ἀνα-, ἀπο-, δια-, ἐμ-, ἐπι-, περι-, προ-**

The simplex appears once in aor. and once in fut., over hundred times in present stem, as the suppletive of **εἶδον** (so *βλέπω*, **εἶδα** in MGr).

βούλομαι (II. *a*) — **ἐβουλήθην**
wish
ἐβουλόμην

Blass's statement (cf. *Gramm.*[4] § 66[3], also p. 58) that this verb is "taken from the literary language," fits badly with its abundance in the papyri: see *Vocabulary*, *s.v.* On its augment see § 83 (1), on *βούλει*, § 85.

βρέχω (I. *a*) — **ἔβρεξα**
wet, rain

γαμέω (VII.) — **ἔγημα** — **γεγάμηκα**
marry — **ἐγάμησα** †
ἐγάμουν — **ἐγαμήθην**

The use of *γαμοῦμαι* = *nubo* is obsolete, except occasionally in legal documents: see *Prol.* 159. Cf. the derivative present stems **γαμίζω** † and **γαμίσκομαι**.

γελάω (VII.) — **γελάσω** †
laugh
-ἐγέλων

COMP. **κατα-**

γηράσκω (IV.) — **ἐγήρασα**
grow old — Trans. in older Greek, as against strong aor.

γίνομαι (I.α.*a*) *become* **ἐγινόμην**	**ἐγενόμην** For -α forms see § 88.	**ἐγενήθην**	**γενήσομαι**	**γέγονα** **(ἐ)γεγόνειν** **γεγένημαι**

COMP. **ἀπο-, δια-, ἐπι-, παρα-, συμ-παρα-, προ-**

The older form *γί-γν-ομαι* passed phonetically into *γīν.* in Ionic—see Thumb, *Gr. Dial*, p. 352—and thence spread in the Κοινή. It is most frequently *γείνομαι* in MSS: see WH *App.*[2] 160. W still shows *γιγν.* sometimes.

γινώσκω (IV.) *perceive* **γινώσκομαι** **ἐγίνωσκον**	**ἔγνων** (see § 88)	**ἐγνώσθην**	**γνώσομαι** **γνωσθήσομαι**	**ἔγνωκα** **ἐγνώκειν** **ἔγνωσμαι**

VERBAL **γνωστός**

COMP. **ἀνα-, δια-, ἐπι-, κατα-, προ-**

For *γι-γνώ-σκω* (Attic), as with *γίνομαι* above, and like it spelt *γειν.* (*Γιγν.* in W sometimes).

γνωρίζω (VII.) *make known* **γνωρίζομαι**		**ἐγνώρισα** **ἐγνωρίσθην**	**γνωριῶ** (Col 4⁹ ℵ*) **γνωρίσω** †	

COMP. **ἀνα-, δι-** (only Lk 2¹⁷ APω)

†**γογγύζω** (VII.) *grumble* **-ἐγόγγυζον**		**ἐγόγγυσα**		

COMP. **δια-**

γράφω *write* **γράφομαι**	**ἐγράφην**	**ἔγραψα** **-ἐγραψάμην**	**γράψω**	**γέγραφα** **γέγραμμαι** **-ἐγεγράμμην**

VERBAL **γραπτός**

COMP. **ἀπο-, ἐγ-, ἐπι-, κατα-, προ-**

δεῖ (I. *a*)
impers. *must*
ἔδει
The only other forms occurring are **δέῃ** subj., and **δέον δέοντα** ptc. See *δέομαι.*

δείκνυμι (II.β.*b*) *show* **δείκνυμαι**		**ἔδειξα** **-ἐδειξάμην** **ἐδείχθην**	**δείξω**	**δέδειγμαι**

COMP. **ἀνα-, ἀπο-, ἐν-, ἐπι-, ὑπο-**

For forms as from **δεικνύω**, see § 86.

δέομαι *need* **ἐδεόμην**		**ἐδεήθην**		

Comp. προσ-

For flexion see § 85. The active forms the impersonal δεῖ.

δέρω (I. *a*) ἔδειρα δαρήσομαι
beat

δέχομαι (I. *a*) ἐδεξάμην δέξομαι δέδεγμαι
receive -ἐδέχθην
-ἐδεχόμην

Verbal δεκτός

Comp. ἀνα-, ἀπο-, ἀπ-εκ-, δια-, εἰσ-, ἐκ-, ἐν-, ἐπι-, παρα-, προσ-, ὑπο-

δέω (VII.) ἔδησα δήσω δέδεκα
bind -ἐδησάμην δέδεμαι
ἐδέθην -ἐδεδέμην

Comp. κατα-, περι-, συν-, ὑπο-

The present stem (inflected like φιλέω) is not found in NT.

διᾱκονέω (VII.) διηκόνησα † διακονήσω
minister (inf.) διακονη-
διακονοῦμαι θῆναι
διηκόνουν

Attic used doubly augmented forms, ἐδιηκόνουν, etc.

διδάσκω (IV.) ἐδίδαξα διδάξω
teach ἐδιδάχθην
ἐδίδασκον

Verbal διδακτός

δίδωμι (I. *a. b*) (pl.) ἔδομεν ἔδωκα δώσω δέδωκα
give -ἐδόμην (subj.) δώσω ? -δώσομαι δέδομαι
δίδομαι (§ 91) δοθήσομαι (ἐ)δεδώκειν
ἐδίδουν ἐδόθην
-ἐδιδόμην

Verbal -δοτός

Comp. ἀνα-, ἀντ-ἀπο-, ἀπο-, δια-, ἐκ-, ἐπι-, μετα-, παρα-, προ-

See for flexion, and for later thematic forms in present stem, §§ 86–88.

διψάω (VII.) ἐδίψησα διψήσω
thirst

Inserted here because no longer from stem διψη- (inf. διψῆν) as in cl. Gr. It is now like τιμάω.

διώκω (I. *a*) ἐδίωξα διώξω δεδίωγμαι
pursue διωχθήσομαι
διώκομαι
ἐδίωκον

COMP. ἐκ-, κατα-

√δρεμ *run*—see under τρέχω, to which it acts as suppletive.

δοκέω (VII.)		ἔδοξα		
suppose				
ἐδόκουν				

δύναμαι (II. *a. b*)		ἠδυνήθην	δυνήσομαι	
can		ἠδυνάσθην		
ἐδυνάμην		The latter was Ionic: the two forms represent varying dialects contributing to the Κοινή.		
ἠδυνάμην				
On the augm. see § 83 (1).				
VERBAL δυνατός				

δύνω (II.)	ἔδυν (§ 88)	ἔδυσα		-δέδυμαι
-δύω		-ἐδυσάμην		
plunge				
-δύομαι				

COMP. ἀπ-εκ-, ἐκ-, ἐν-, ἐπι-, ἐπ-εν-, παρ-εισ-

From the same root the new present stem ἐνδιδύσκω (IV.).†

ἐάω (VII.)		εἴᾱσα	ἐάσω	
allow				
εἴων				

COMP. προσ-

† ἐγγίζω (VII.)		ἤγγισα	ἐγγιῶ	ἤγγικα
approach			(ἐγγίσω Jas 4[8] A)	
ἤγγιζον				

COMP. προσ-

A Κοινή verb, starting in Polybius.

ἐγείρω (VII.)		ἤγειρα	ἐγερῶ	ἐγήγερμαι
rouse		ἠγέρθην	ἐγερθήσομαι	
ἐγείρομαι				
-ἐγειρόμην (§ 83 (4))				

COMP. δι-, ἐξ-, ἐπ-, συν-

† ἐδαφίζω (VII.)			ἐδαφιῶ	
raze				

ἐθίζω (VII.)				εἴθισμαι
accustom				

ἔθω				εἴωθα
be wont				εἰώθειν

The present stem only occurs in ptc. (twice in Homer).

* Ϝειδ	εἶδον (-α, see § 88)		εἰδήσω	οἶδα (§ 92)
perceive				ᾔδειν

COMP. ἀπ-, ἐπ-, προ-, συν-, ὑπερ-

This root forms no present stem: εἶδον is used as aor. to βλέπω, and οἶδα makes a separate verb.

* ϝεικ — ἔοικα

resemble

Like √ϝειδ, this root forms no present stem. The present only occurs in one NT writer (Jas 1^{6. 23}).

-εἴκω (I. *a*) — εἶξα

yield

Comp. ὑπ-

-εἶμι (I. *b*)

go

-ᾔειν

Verbal -ιτός

Comp. ἄπ-, εἴσ-, ἔξ-, ἔπ-, σύν-

For the flexion of the few surviving forms, see § 86.

εἰμί (I. *b*) — ἔσομαι

be — 3 sg. ἔσται, otherwise regular.

ἤμην †

Comp. ἄπ-, ἔν-, ἔξ(εστι), πάρ-, συμ-πάρ, σύν-

For the flexion see § 86.

εἴρω (VII.) — ἐρρέθην (inf. ῥηθῆναι, ptc. ῥηθείς). — ἐρῶ — εἴρηκα, εἰρήκειν, εἴρημαι

say

Verbal ῥητός

Comp. προ- — The ε (Ionic) is only found in indic.

The present stem in use is λέγω, *q.v.*; the aor. act. εἶπον—see *ϝεπ-. The present εἴρω is obsolete early.

ἐλαύνω (VII.) — -ἤλασα — ἐλήλακα

drive

ἐλαύνομαι

ἠλαυνόμην

Comp. ἀπ-

The root is ἐλα-: the difficult present stem is held by Brugmann (*Gramm.*[4] 221) to be a denominative from a noun *ἐλαυνός.

ἐλέγχω (I. *a*) — ἤλεγξα, ἠλέγχθην — ἐλέγξω

convict

ἐλέγχομαι

Comp. δια-κατ-, ἐξ- (Jude[15], a few cursives only).

ἐλεέω, ἐλεάω † (VII.) — ἠλέησα, ἠλεήθην — ἐλεήσω, ἐλεηθήσομαι — ἠλέημαι

pity

On the variation in present stem see § 84.

ἑλίσσω (VII.) ἑλίξω
roll up
ἑλίσσομαι
The ("poetic, Ionic and late prose") pres. εἱλίσσω (≡ ἐϝελίσσω) is found in Rev 6[14] P cu[mu.] Blass (Kühner ii. 417) shows that spir. lenis is older, but the analogy of ἕλιξ, etc., produced ἑ. in later times.

ἑλκόω (VII.) εἵλκωμαι
make sore

ἕλκω (I. *a*) εἵλκυσα ἑλκύσω †
drag
εἷλκον
Comp. ἐξ-
The addition -υσα is due to the analogy of the synonym εἴρυσα: in its turn it produced a new future.

† ἐλλογάω (VII.)
impute
ἐλλογοῦμαι and -ῶμαι
On the variation in present stem see § 85.

ἐλπίζω (VII.) ἤλπισα ἐλπιῶ † ἤλπικα
hope
ἤλπιζον
ἐλπίζομαι
Comp. ἀπ- (ἀφ-, see p. 98), προ-
Veitch notes that "the early Greeks . . . were chary in expressing confidence in the future." Ἐλπιῶ is a late form built on Attic models.

ἐμβριμάομαι ἐνεβριμησάμην
and -έομαι (VII.) ἐνεβριμήθην †
groan
Cited for varying present stem: see § 85, pp. 198, 201.

ἐμέω (I. *a*) ἤμεσα
vomit
Probably a very early thematising of *ϝέμεμι (Skt. *vámimi*).

ἐμφανίζω (VII.) ἐνεφάνισα ἐμφανίσω
manifest ἐνεφανίσθην
A denominative from ἐμφανής: on the place of the augment see § 83 (7).

ἐπιορκέω (VII.) ἐπιορκήσω
perjure ἐφι. Mt 5[33] ℵ: see p. 99.

ἐπίσταμαι (I. *b*)
understand

For flexion see § 87. In NT only in present stem. It is an aorist-present from the middle of στῆναι.

*ϝεπ *speak* εἶπον (-α: § 88).
COMP. ἀντ-, ἀπ-, προ-
The aor. (a reduplication, the ει constant accordingly in the moods) is used for λέγω and the family of (εἴρω), *q.v.*

-ἕπομαι (I. *a*)
follow
-εἱπόμην
COMP. συν-

† ἐραυνάω (VII.) ἠραύνησα
search
VERBAL -ἐραυνητός
COMP. ἐξ-
The older form ἐρευνάω occurs in the mass of MSS: see § 37 and *Prol.* 46 n.[2].

ἐργάζομαι (VII.) ἠργασάμην (εἰργ.) εἴργασμαι
work -εἰργάσθην
ἠργαζόμην
COMP. κατ-, περι-, προσ-
On the augment see § 83 (3).

ἐρείδω (I. *a*) ἤρεισα
stick fast

ἐρεύγομαι (I. *a*) ἐρεύξομαι
utter

ἐρίζω (VII.) ἐρίσω †
strive

ἑρμηνεύω (VII.) -ἑρμήνευσα
interpret On dropped augment see § 83 (4).
ἑρμηνεύομαι
VERBAL -ἑρμηνευτός
COMP. δι-, μεθ-

ἔρχομαι (I. *a*) ἦλθον (-α, § 88) ἐλεύσομαι ἐλήλυθα
come ἐληλύθειν
ἠρχόμην † (διέρχοντο Jn 20[3] DΔ*—see § 83 (4)) (§ 83 (4))
VERBAL -ἡλυτός
COMP. ἀν-, ἀντι-παρ-, ἀπ-, δι-, δι-εξ-, εἰσ-, ἐξ-, ἐπ-, ἐπ-αν-, ἐπ-εισ-, κατ-, παρ-, παρ-εισ-, περι-, προ-, προσ-, συν-, συν-εισ-
The conjugation is made up from three roots, ἐρθ, ἐλυ and ἐνθ

(Doric ἦνθον), which have influenced one another's forms. On Attic usage of present and future stems, see Rutherford *NP* 103 ff.

ἐρωτάω (-έω †) (VII.) *ask* **ἠρώτων** (-ουν †) Comp. **δι-, ἐπ-**	**ἠρώτησα** **ἠρωτήθην** On the present stem see § 84.	**ἐρωτήθω**
ἐσθίω (VII.) **ἔσθω** (VI.) *eat* **ἤσθιον** Comp. **κατ-, συν-**	[**ἔφαγον**]	[**φάγομαι** †] Κοινή form, made (like φύγομαι and λάβομαι) on the analogy ἔπιον : πίομαι :: ἔφαγον : φάγομαι — see Brugmann *Gr.*[4] 383. Cf. § 85 above.

Ἔσθω (whence ἐσθίω by addition of a further suffix) is as old as Homer: it appears five times in ptc. and once (Lk 22^{30}) in subj. The suppletive **τρώγω** is used in present stem.

εὐ- For augment of verbs in **εὐ-** see § 83 (6)—the variants will not be noted here, forms being given as in WH.

εὐαγγελίζω † (VII.) *evangelise* **εὐαγγελίζομαι** **εὐηγγελιζόμην** Comp. **προ-**	**εὐηγγέλισα** † **εὐηγγελισάμην** **εὐηγγελίσθην**	**εὐηγγέλισμαι**
† **εὐαρεστέω** (VII.) *please* **εὐαρεστοῦμαι**	**εὐαρεστῆσαι**	**εὐαρέστηκα** (εὐηρ. — see § 83 (7)).
εὐθύνω (VII.) *straighten* Comp. **κατ-**	**εὔθυνα** (in moods)	
εὐοδόω (VII.) *give a fair way* **εὐοδοῦμαι**	**εὐοδωθῶ** (1 Co 16^{2} AC *al.*)	**εὐοδωθήσομαι**

On Hort's proposal to read the pres. subj. **εὐοδῶται** as perf. see § 83 (5).

εὑρίσκω (IV.) *find*	**εὗρον** (-α forms see § 88).	**εὑρέθην**	**εὑρήσω** **εὑρεθήσομαι**	**εὕρηκα**
εὑρίσκομαι	**εὑρόμην**			
ηὕρισκον (εὑρ.) **ηὑρισκόμην** Comp. **ἀν-**				

εὐφραίνω (VII.) ηὐφράνθην εὐφρανθήσομαι
gladden
εὐφραίνομαι
εὐφραινόμην

εὔχομαι (I. *a*) εὐξάμην -εὔξομαι
pray
ηὐχόμην (εὐ.)
Comp. προσ-

ἔχω (I. *a*) ἔσχον ἕξω ἔσχηκα
have ἐσχόμην ἕξομαι
ἔχομαι
εἶχον
εἰχόμην
Verbal -ἑκτός and -σχετός
Comp. ἀν-, ἀντ-, ἀπ-, ἐν-, ἐπ-, κατ-, μετ-, παρ-, περι-, προ-, προσ-, προσ-αν-, συν-. ὑπερ-, ὑπ-
On -α forms in imperf. and aor. see §§ 84, 88; on εἴχοσαν § 84, p. 194.

ζεύγνυμι (II. β. *b*) -ἔζευξα
yoke
Comp. συν-

ζέω (I. *a*)
boil
Verbal ζεστός
For ζέσω, but inflected like πλέω (only ptc.).

ζήω (VII.) ἔζησα † ζήσω
live (The strong ζήσομαι
aor. ἐβίων, from a cognate stem, was used in Attic.)
Comp. ἀνα-, συν-. For flexion see § 84.

ζωγρέω Periphr. ἐζώγρημαι
take alive (ἔσῃ ζωγρῶν)

ζώννυμι (II. β. *b*) -ἔζωσα ζώσω -ἔζωσμαι
gird ἐζωσάμην -ζώσομαι
ἐζώννυον
Comp. ἀνα-, δια-, περι-, ὑπο-
For flexion of present stem, and thematic forms in it, see § 86.

ἥκω (I. *a*) ἧξα ἥξω
have come
ἧκον
Comp. ἀν-, καθ-
For perfect endings in the present indic. see § 92.

ἡσσόω (VII.)		ἡσσώθην		ἥττημαι
ἡττάω ,,				
defeat				
ἡττῶμαι				
For variation of σσ and ττ see § 43; for confusion of classes of Contracta § 84.				
θάλλω (VII.)	-ἔθαλον †			
bloom				
Comp. ἀνα-				
θάπτω (VII.)	ἐτάφην	ἔθαψα		
bury				
Comp. συν-				
θέλω (I. *a*)		ἠθέλησα	θελήσω	
will				
ἤθελον (§ 83 (1))				
never ἐθέλω				
θεμελιοώ (VII.)		ἐθεμελίωσα	θεμελιώσω	τεθεμελίωμαι
found				τεθεμελιώμην (on augm. see § 83 (4)).
θερίζω (VII.)		ἐθέρισα	θερίσω †	
reap		ἐθερίσθην		
θιγγάνω (II. *a*)	ἔθιγον			
touch				
θλάω (I. *a*)			-θλασθήσομαι	
crush				
Comp. συν-				
θλίβω (I. *a*)				τέθλιμμαι
press				
θλίβομαι				
-ἔθλιβον				
Comp. ἀπο-, συν-				
-θνήσκω (IV.)	-ἔθανον		-θανοῦμαι	τέθνηκα
die				ἐτεθνήκειν
-ἔθνησκον				Never compounded: see *Prol.* 114. Inf. τεθνάναι Ac 14[19] D.
Verbal θνητός				
Comp. ἀπο-, συν-απο-				

θραύω (I. *a*) *bruise*				**τέθραυσμαι**
θύω (VII.) *sacrifice* **ἔθυον** **θύομαι**		**ἔθυσα** **ἐτύθην**		**τέθυμαι**

VERBAL **θυτός**

-ἵημι (I. *β*. *b*) *send*	**-εἶναι** (not indic.—see § 88, p. 209).	**-ἧκα** **-ἕθην** (see § 83 (4))	**-ἥσω** **-ἐθήσομαι**	**-εἶκα** (Lk 10^{30} C*) **-ἕωμαι** (indic.) **-εἷμαι** (ptc.)

Imperf. see **ἀφίημι**
VERBAL **-ἑτός**
COMP. **ἀν-, ἀφ-, καθ-, παρ-, συν-**
For flexion of present and strong aor. stems see § 86 ff.

-ἱκνέομαι (II. *β*. *a*. iii.) *arrive*	**-ἱκόμην**			

COMP. **ἀφ-, δι-, ἐφ-**

ἱλάσκομαι (IV.) *propitiate*		**ἱλάσθην**		
-ἵστημι (I. *β*. *b*) *stand* **-ἱστάμην**	**ἔστην**	**ἔστησα** **ἐστάθην**	**στήσω** **στήσομαι** **σταθήσομαι**	**ἕστηκα** **(ε)ἱστήκειν** **-ἑστώς** (ptc.) (§§ 65, 92) **-ἕστᾰκα** †

VERBAL **-στατός**

COMP. **ἀν-, ἀνθ-, ἀντι-καθ-** (augm., § 83 (2)), **ἀφ-, ἀπο-καθ-** (**-κατ-** § 83 (2)), **δι-, ἐν-, ἐξ-, ἐξ-αν-, ἐφ-, ἐπ-αν-, καθ-, κατ-εφ-, μεθ-, παρ-, περι-, προ-, συν-, συν-εφ-**

For the flexion of present and strong aorist stems, and thematic substitutes occurring there, see § 86. Present, weak aor. and future act. are transitive, as is the new perf. -ἕστακα. From the intrans. perf. ἕστηκα comes a new verb στήκω *stand* (intr.), and from the present two new verbs ἱστάνω and στάνω *stand* (tr.): cf. the early formation ὀλέκω from ὀλώλεκα, etc.

καθαίρω (VII.) *cleanse*		**ἐκάθᾰρα** † see § 89, p. 214, n. 2.		**κεκάθαρμαι**

VERBAL **καθαρτός**
COMP. **δια-, ἐκ-**
A denominative from καθαρός

καθαρίζω (VII.)	ἐκαθέρισα †	καθαριῶ	κεκαθέρισμαι
cleanse	ἐκαθερίσθην †	(-ίσω 1 Jn 1[9] A 33)	

Comp. δια-

Forms where augment or reduplication appear show in good MSS an ϵ after θ (ℵ $\frac{0}{8}$, B $\frac{2}{7}$, A $\frac{7}{7}$, C $\frac{4}{5}$, D $\frac{0}{6}$, L $\frac{4}{5}$), which is certainly felt to be a second augment following what popular etymology took to be κατά. It seems better not to allow any phonetic cause here, despite Thackeray 74. Such a combination as Mk 1[42] καθαρίσθητι . . . ἐκαθερίσθη seems decisive (see § 33).

καθέζομαι (VII.)	-καθεσθείς
sit	
ἐκαθεζόμην	

Comp. παρα-

The simplex ἕζομαι was extinct, and the compound was not felt to be such: cf. κάθημαι.

καθεύδω (I. *a*)
sleep
ἐκάθευδον

Another verb with simplex extinct.

καθίζω	ἐκάθισα	καθίσω	κεκάθικα †
sit (*seat*)		καθίσομαι	

Comp. ἀνα-, ἐπι-, παρα-, περι-, συγ-. See on καθέζομαι.

καίω (VII.)	-ἐκάην	ἔκαυσα	καύσω	κέκαυμαι
burn		ἐκαύθην	καυθήσομαι	
καίομαι			-καήσομαι	
-ἔκαιον				

Comp. ἐκ-, κατα-

There is no reason for following Veitch in parsing καυσούμενα (2 Pet 3[10]) as a future. Καυσόω is extant in medd. and elsewhere.

The present stem κᾱ́ω (not κᾴω), found often in Attic, is obsolete.

καλέω (VII.)	ἐκάλεσα	καλέσω †	κέκληκα
call	ἐκαλεσάμην	καλέσομαι †	κέκλημαι
καλοῦμαι	ἐκλήθην	κληθήσομαι	(ἐ)κεκλήμην
ἐκάλουν			

Verbal κλητός

Comp. ἀντι-, εἰσ-, ἐγ-, ἐπι-, μετα-, παρα-, προ-, προσ-, συν-, συμ-παρα-

Fut. a. m. is developed from the aor. (Att. καλῶ, -οῦμαι), perhaps in class. times.

καλύπτω (VII.)	Papyri have ἐκάλυψα	καλύψω	κεκάλυμμαι
cover	instances of ἐκαλύφθην	καλυφθήσομαι	

καλύπτομαι ἐκαλύφην.

VERBAL **καλυπτός**

COMP. **ἀνα-, ἀπο-, ἐπι-, κατα-, παρα-, περι-, συγ-**

† *καμμύω* (VII.) **ἐκάμμυσα**

shut (*eyes*)

For *κατα-μύω*, from the dialectic form *κατ-*: it was dissociated from *κατά* by its abnormal form, and its compound character forgotten.

κάμνω (II. *a*) **ἔκαμον**

grow weary

κάμπτω (VII.) **ἔκαμψα** **κάμψω**

bend

COMP. **ἀνα-, συγ-**

καυχάομαι (VII.) **ἐκαυχησάμην** **καυχήσομαι** **κεκαύχημαι**

boast

COMP. **ἐγ-, κατα-**

For 2 sg. pres. *καυχᾶσαι* see § 85.

κεῖμαι (I. *b*)

lie

ἐκείμην

COMP. **ἀνα-, ἀντι-, ἀπο-, ἐπι-, κατα-, παρα-, περι-, προ-, συν-ανα**

For flexion see § 87.

κείρω (VII.) **ἔκειρα**

shear **ἐκειράμην**

-κέλλω (VII.) **-ἔκειλα**

run ashore

COMP. **ἐπι-**

In Ac. 27[41] *ἐπώκειλαν* appears in ω (against ℵAB*C 33): this is from *ὀκέλλω*, probably in origin a compound (*ὠ = Skt. *ā-*, seen in *ὠκεανός*, *ὀδύρομαι* etc.).

κεράννυμι (I. *β*) **ἐκέρᾰσα** **κεκέρασμαι** †

mix **κέκρᾱμαι**

VERBAL **-κρᾱτός**

COMP. **συγ-**

κερδαίνω (VII.) **ἐκέρδᾱνα** **κερδᾰνῶ**

gain **ἐκέρδησα** **κερδήσω**

κερδηθήσομαι

These alternatives occur together even in one context (1 Co 9[21f.], where read *κερδάνω*).

κινέω (II. β)		**ἐκίνησα**	**κινήσω**	
move		**ἐκινήθην**		
κινοῦμαι				
VERBAL **-κινητός**				
COMP. **μετα-, συγ-**				

The root is *κῑ-*: the older non-thematic present *κίνυμαι* may have stood in the quotation adapted in Ac 17[28] (see *Camb. Bibl. Essays* 481).

κίχρημι (I. *a. b*)		**ἔχρησα**		
lend				
κλαίω (VII.)		**ἔκλαυσα**	**κλαύσω†**	
weep			**κλαύσομαι**	
ἔκλαιον				

The Attic *κλᾴω* (cf. on *καίω* above) is obsolete.

κλάω (III.)		**ἔκλασα**		
break		**ἐκλάσθην**		
κλῶμαι				
COMP. **ἐκ-, κατα-**				
κλείω (VII.)		**-ἔκλεισα**		
lock		**-ἐκλείσθην**	**κλείσω**	**κέκλεισμαι**
COMP. **ἀπο-, ἐκ-, κατα-, συγ-**				
κλίνω (VII.)		**ἔκλῑνα**	**κλῐνῶ**	**κέκλῐκα**
lean		**ἐκλίθην**	**κλιθήσομαι**	
COMP. **ἀνα-, ἐκ-, κατα-, προσ-**				
κομίζω (VII.)		**ἐκόμισα**	**κομίσομαι†**	
carry		**ἐκομισάμην**	**κομιοῦμαι**	
-ἐκομιζόμην				
COMP. **ἐκ-, συγ-**				
κόπτω (VII.)	**-ἐκόπην**	**ἔκοψα**	**κόψω**	
beat		**ἐκοψάμην**	**κόψομαι**	
κόπτομαι			**κοπήσομαι**	
ἔκοπτον				
ἐκοπτόμην				
COMP. **ἀνα-, ἀπο-, ἐκ-, ἐγ-, κατα-, προ-, προσ-**				
κορέννυμι (II. β)		**ἐκορέσθην**		**κεκόρεσμαι**
satiate				
κράζω (VII.)	**ἔκρᾰγον**	**ἔκραξα**	**κράξω**	**κέκρᾱγα**
cry		**ἐκέκραξα**	**κεκράξομαι**	
ἔκραζον				
COMP. **ἀνα-**				

See *Prol.* 147.

κρέμαμαι (I. υ)	ἐκρέμασα		
hang	ἐκρεμάσθην		
-ἐκρέμετο			

COMP. ἐκ-
For the flexion see § 87: the imperfect is thematised.

κρΐνω (VII.)	ἔκρῖνα	κρῐνῶ	κέκρῐκα
judge	ἐκρῑνάμην	κριθήσομαι	κεκρίκειν
κρίνομαι	ἐκρῐθην		κέκριμαι
ἔκρινον			
ἐκρινόμην			

VERBAL -κρῐτός
COMP. ἀνα-, ἀντ-απο-, ἀπο-, δια-, ἐγ-, ἐπι-, κατα-, συγ-, συν-υπο-, ὑπο-

κρύπτω (VII.) ἐκρύβην †	ἔκρυψα		κέκρυμμαι
-κρύβω † (I. α)			
hide			
-ἔκρυβον			

VERBAL κρυπτός
COMP. ἀπο-, ἐγ-, περι-
Present stem only in περιέκρυβεν (Lk 1[24]), which is probably impf., and not a newly-formed aorist.

-κτείνω (VII.)	-ἔκτεινα	-κτενῶ	
-κτέννω (II.)	-ἐκτάνθην		
-κτέννυμι (II.)			
kill			

COMP. ἀπο-. The simplex is obsolete. See *Vocabulary*, *s.v.* ἀποκτείνω, for the strange absence of this verb from vernacular sources till late. The pres. stem in -*νυμι*, a modification of the classical ἀποκτίννυμι (Kühner-Blass 469) under the influence of the ε found in the future, is quotable from Mk 12[5] B, where ℵ*ACD have ἀποκτέννοντες and ℵ[c] the older ἀποκτιννύντες: B is presumably right here, but the -εννο- may be recognised in Lk 12[4] ℵA, unless D be followed with -ενο- —here B adopts the normal form and is probably wrong. We may explain -κτένω as developed from ἔκτεινα by the proportion ἔμεινα : μένω. -Κτέννω is possibly a thematising of κτέννυμι. The welter of variants in present stem may perhaps be linked with the word's record, which is not at all clear. See for these forms the *app. crit.* at Mt 10[28] 23[7], Mk 12[5], Lk 12[4] 13[34], 2 Co 3[6] and Rev 6[11].

κτίζω (VII.)	ἔκτισα		ἔκτισμαι
found	ἐκτίσθην		

-κυέω (VII.) **-ἐκύησα**

-κύω (VII.)
bring forth

COMP. **ἀπο-**. The simplex was not obsolete: see *Vocabulary*, *s.v.* ἀποκυέω. The NT occurrence of the present is not decisive between κύω and κυέω: ἐκύομεν in Is 59[13] encourages us to accent ἀποκύει (with Ti) in Jas 1[15].

-κυλίω (VII.) **-ἐκύλῖσα** **-κυλίσω** **-κεκύλισμαι**
roll
ἐκυλιόμην

COMP. **ἀνα-, ἀπο-, προσ-**. The pres. stem, reformed from the aorist (*ἐκυλινδ-σα) as early as Aristophanes, has naturally ousted such forms as κυλίνδω (etc.): cf. Brugmann-Thumb *Gr.* 360.

-κυνέω (II. *β. a*) **-ἐκύνησα** **-κυνήσω**
kiss
-ἐκύνουν

COMP. **προσ-**. The simplex is obsolete, and the stem-forming suffix -νε- has been taken over in other tense-stems, so that προσκυνέω has the normal flexion of a contract verb. (Aor. ἔκυσα as late as Aristotle.)

-κύπτω (VII.) **ἔκυψα**
stoop

COMP. **ἀνα-, κατα-, παρα-, συγ-**

λαγχάνω **ἔλαχον**
(II. *a. a*)
draw by lot

λᾱκέω (VII.) **ἐλάκησα**
burst

Blass (on Ac 1[18]) compares διαλᾱκήσασα in Aristoph. *Nub.* 410, as giving a better meaning than λάσκω (aor. ἔλακον, weak aor. ἐλᾰ́κησα), to which the NT word is usually referred.

λαμβάνω	**ἔλαβον**	**ἐλήμφθην** †	**λήμψομαι** †	**εἴληφα**
(II. *a. a*)	(-α, p. 208)		**-λημφθή-**	**εἴλημμαι**
take	**ἐλαβόμην**		**σομαι** †	(3 sg. **-εἴληπ-**
λαμβάνομαι				**ται.**)
ἐλάμβανον				

VERBAL **-λημπτός** †

COMP. **ἀνα, ἀντι-, ἀπο-, ἐπι-, κατα-, μετα-, παρα-, προ-, προσ-, προσ-ανα-, συλ-, συν-αντι-, συμ-παρα-, συμ-περι-, ὑπο-**

The intruded μ (from present stem) is firmly established in fut. and weak aor., and in the verbal: see *Prol.* 56. Literary influence produced numerous relapses in late MSS: cf. also Mt 21[22] C, Jn 14[3] CL 16[24] C, 1 Co 3[8] C, Jas 1[12] C.

λάμπω (I. *a*) ἔλαμψα λάμψω
shine
COMP. ἐκ-, περι-

λανθάνω ἔλαθον -λέλησμαι
(II. *a. a*) -ἐλαθόμην
escape notice
COMP. ἐκ-, ἐπι-

λέγω (I. *a*) -ἐλεξάμην
say -ἐλέχθην
λέγομαι
ἔλεγον
ἐλεγόμην
VERBAL -λεκτός
COMP. ἀντι-, δια-, ἐπι-, προ-
For its suppletives see under εἴρω and √Fεπ.

λέγω (I. *a*) -ἔλεξα -λέξω λέλεγμαι
gather -ἐλεξάμην
-λέγομαι
-ἐλεγόμην
VERBAL -λεκτός
COMP. ἐκ-, ἐπι-, κατα-, παρα-, συλ-

λείπω (I. *a*) -ἔλιπον ἔλειψα † λείψω λέλειμμαι
λιμπάνω (II. *a. a*) ἐλείφην
leave
ἔλειπον
ἐλειπόμην
ἐλίμπανον
VERBAL -λειπτός
COMP. ἀπο-, *δια-, ἐγ-κατα-, ἐκ-, ἐπι-, κατα-, περι-, *ὑπο- (*λείπω and λιμπάνω).

There is a good deal of variation in MSS between ἔλειπον and ἔλιπον. Since itacism does not produce λίψω or ἐλίφθην, we may probably assume that the scribes of our uncials meant aorist-stem forms when they wrote λιπ-: they may often be repeating variants taken from unprofessional copies where itacism was really responsible. See WH *App.*[2] 162.

λούω (I. *a*) *wash* **λούομαι** Comp. **ἀπο-**		**ἔλουσα** **ἐλουσάμην**		**λέλουμαι** Heb 10[22] λελουσμένοι ℵD*P: so Jn 13[10] E, and LXX.
μακαρίζω (VII.) *congratulate*			**μακαριῶ**	
μανθάνω (II. *a*. *a*) *learn* Comp. **κατα-**	**ἔμαθον**			**μεμάθηκα**
μαρτῦρομαι (VII.) *protest* **ἐμαρτυρόμην** Comp. **δια-**, **προ-**		**ἐμαρτῦράμην**		
-μάσσω (VII.) *wipe* **-ἔμασσον** **-μάσσομαι** Comp. **ἀπο-**, **ἐκ-**		**-ἔμαξα**		
μεγαλύνω (VII.) *magnify* **ἐμεγάλυνον** **ἐμεγαλυνόμην**		**ἐμεγάλυνα** **ἐμεγαλύνθην**	**μεγαλυνθήσομαι**	
μεθύω (VII.) *be drunken*		**ἐμεθύσθην**		
μεθύσκομαι (IV.) *get drunk*				
μέλλω (? II. *a*. *a*) *intend* **ἤμελλον** **ἔμελλον**. On augment see § 83 (1).			**μελλήσω**	
μέλει (I. *a*) impers. *it matters* **ἔμελε**		**-ἐμελήθην**	**-μελήσομαι** **-μεληθήσομαι**	
-μέλομαι (I. *a*) *care* **-ἐμελόμην**				

VERBAL -μελητός
COMP. ἐπι-, μετα-

μέμφομαι (I. *a*)	ἐμεμψάμην		
blame	(later uncials at Mk 7[2]).		
VERBAL -μεμπτός			
μένω (I. *a*)	ἔμεινα	μενῶ	μεμένηκα
remain			μεμενήκειν
ἔμενον			

COMP. ἀνα-, δια-, ἐμ-, ἐπι-, κατα-, παρα-, περι-, προσ-, συμ-παρα-, ὑπο-

μιαίνω (VII.)	ἐμιάνθην		μεμίαμμαι †
defile			cl. μεμίασμαι
VERBAL -μιαντός			
-μίγνυμι (II. *β*. *b*)	ἔμιξα		μέμιγμαι
mix			
-μίγνυμαι			

COMP. συν-ανα-

Present stem only middle. The correct spelling in pres., weak aor. and perf. pass. is μει-, but in Hellenistic this is a mere matter of orthography.

μιμνήσκω (IV.)	-ἔμνησα	-μνήσω	μέμνημαι
remind	ἐμνήσθην	μνησθήσομαι	
μιμνήσκομαι			
COMP. ἀνα-, ἐπ-ανα-, ὑπο-			
μνηστεύω (VII.)	ἐμνηστεύθην		ἐμνήστευμαι
betroth			Lk 1[27] μεμν. CD.
μολῦνω (VII.)	ἐμόλῦνα		
defile	ἐμολύνθην		
μολύνομαι			
μωραίνω (VII.)	ἐμώρᾱνα		
make foolish	ἐμωράνθην		
-νέμω (I. *a*)	-ἐνεμήθην		
distribute			
COMP. ἀπο-, δια-			
νήφω (I. *a*)	ἔνηψα †		
be sober			
COMP. ἀνα-, ἐκ-			
νῑκάω (VII.)	ἐνίκησα	νικήσω	νενίκηκα
conquer			
νικῶμαι			

Comp. ὑπερ-

In Rev 2[17] νικοῦντι appears in AC, but in 2[7] only A, in 15[2] C: for these confusions of -άω and -έω stems see § 84.

νίπτω † (VII.)	ἔνιψα		
νίπτομαι †	ἐνιψάμην		
wash			

Comp. ἀπο-

The pres. stem is a back-formation, replacing cl. νίζω, where ζ is the regular resultant of *y* following velar g^u.

νύσσω (VII.) -ενύγην	ἔνυξα		
pierce			

Comp. κατα-

νυστάζω (VII.)	ἐνύσταξα		
nod			

ξηραίνω (VII.)	ἐξήρᾱνα		ἐξήραμμαι
dry up	ἐξηράνθην		Also -σμαι
ξηραίνομαι			in earlier Greek.

ξυρέω (VII.)	ἐξῡράμην	ξυρήσομαι	ἐξύρημαι
ξύρω (VII.)			
shave			

Ξυρασθαι, 1 Co 11[6], following κείρασθαι, is not easily construed as present (ξυρᾶσθαι, by confusion of -έω and -άω classes), and is better taken (ξύρασθαι) as aor. from ξύρω, quotable from Hippocrates and Plutarch: see WH *App.*[2] 173 (also above, p. 200).

-οἴγω, see ἀνοίγω

οἶδα, see √ϝειδ

οἰκοδομέω (VII.)	ᾠκοδόμησα	οἰκοδομήσω	οἰκοδόμημαι
build	οἰκοδομήθην	οἰκοδομη-	(Lk 6[48] ℵBL
ᾠκοδόμουν	For the augment see	θήσομαι	33 οἰ. *ib.*
οἰκοδομοῦμαι	§ 83 (6).		4[29] D.)
Comp. ἀν-, ἐπ-, συν-			ᾠκοδομήμην

οἰκτίρω (VII.)		οἰκτιρήσω †	
pity			

In later authorities generally spelt οἰκτείρω.

οἴομαι (VII.)
think

The 1st sing. pres. οἶμαι survives—perhaps originally an "*allegro*-form" of οἴομαι, used in parenthesis (Thumb in Brugmann *Gr.*[4] 80).

-οἴχομαι (I. *a*) — **-ᾤχημαι**
have gone
Comp. **παρ-**

-ὀκέλλω, see **-κέλλω**

-ὄλλυμι (II. *β. b*) — **-ὠλόμην** — **-ὤλεσα** — **-ὀλέσω**, **-ὀλῶ**, **-ὀλοῦμαι** — **-ὄλωλα**
destroy
-ὄλλυμαι
-ὤλλύμην
Comp. **ἀπ-**, **συν-απ-**
For flexion see §§ 86–87, also for thematic forms included.

ὀμείρομαι (VII.)
desire
Ἀπ. λεγ. in 1 Th 2[8] (cf. Job 3[21], Ps 62[2] Symm., *ὑπερομ.* in Irenaeus 60). Its similarity to the synonymous *ἱμείρομαι* (denominative from *ἵμερος*) is accidental. It may be a compound of *μείρομαι* *obtain*, which in the conative present could take the required meaning; or we may compare directly the root *smer* "remember." Debrunner, *Idg. Forsch.* xxi. 204, does not convince me. On the prepositional relic **ὀ-** see § 111.

ὄμνυμι (II. *β. b*) — **ὤμοσα**
swear
Only one non-thematic form (**ὀμνύναι**) survives: the present tense forms are from *ὀμνύω*.

ὁμοιόω (VII.) — **ὡμοίωσα**, **ὡμοιώθην** — **ὁμοιώσω**, **ὁμοιοθήσομαι** — **-ὡμοίωμαι**, **-ὁμοίωμαι**† So Heb 7[3] CD*al.*: see § 83 (5).
liken
Comp. **ἀφ-**

ὀνίνημι (II. *a. b*) — **ὠνάμην**
profit — Only opt. 1 sg. **ὀναίμην**: see § 88.

√*ὀπ* — **ὠψάμην** Only subj. — **ὄψομαι**, **ὀφθήσομαι**
see
ὀπτάνομαι†
ὄψησθε Lk 13[28], developed from fut.
ὤφθην
A suppletive of **ὁράω** and *βλέπω*, *q.v.*

ὁράω (VII.) — [**εἶδον** see √*Fειδ*] — [**ὠψάμην**, **ὤφθην**: see √*ὀπ*] — [**ὄψομαι**, **ὀφθήσομαι**: see √*ὀπ*] — **ἑόρακα**, **ἑώρακα**, **ἑωράκειν**
see
ἑώρων
ὁρῶμαι
-ὁρώμην (§ 83 (4))

VERBAL ὁρᾶτός
COMP. ἀφ-, ἐφ-, καθ-, προ-
A further suppletive in pres. stem active of simplex is **βλέπω**, which is already outstripping ὁρᾶν. The closeness of association between εἶδον and ὁράω is seen in forms like **ἀφίδω**, **ἔφιδε**, where the aspirate is carried on.

-ὀργίζω (VII.) **ὠργίσθην** **-ὀργιῶ**
anger
ὀργίζομαι
COMP. **παρ-**

ὀρθόω (VII.) **-ὤρθωσα** **-ὀρθώσω**
set upright **-ὠρθώθην** Lk 13[13] **ἀνορθώθη** ABDL *al.*: see § 83.
COMP. **ἀν-**, **ἐπι-δι-**

ὁρίζω (VII.) **ὥρισα** **-ὁριῶ** **ὥρισμαι**
define **ὡρίσθην** **-ὁρίσω**
-ὥριζον
COMP. **ἀφ-**, **ἀπο-δι-**, **προ-**

-ὀρύσσω **-ὠρύγην** **ὤρυξα**
dig (Mt 24[43] B *al.*, Lk 12[39] APQ *al.*). **-ὠρύχθην**
COMP. **δι-**, **ἐξ-**

-ὀτρῦνω (VII.) **-ὤτρῦνα**
incite
COMP. **παρ-**

ὀφείλω (VII.) **ὄφελον** (for **ὤφελον**—has become a particle: see *Prol.* 200 f.)
owe
ὤφειλον
ὀφείλομαι
COMP. **προσ-**

παίζω (VII.) **-ἔπαιξα**† **-παίξω**
play **-ἐπαίχθην**† **-παιχθήσομαι**†
ἔπαιζον
COMP. **ἐμ-**

παίω (I. *a*) **ἔπαισα**
strike

πάσχω (IV.) **ἔπαθον** **πέποιθα**
suffer
VERBAL **παθητός**
COMP. **προ-**, **συμ-**

πατάσσω (VII.) *strike*	ἐπάταξα	πατάξω	

A suppletive of τύπτω, *q.v.*

παύω (I. *a*) *stop*	ἔπαυσα	-παύσω	πέπαυμαι
	ἐπαυσάμην	παύσομαι	
παύομαι		-παήσομαι†	
ἐπαυόμην			

VERBAL -πα(υ)στός

COMP. ἀνα-, ἐπ-ανα-, συν-ανα-, κατα-

Ἀκατάπαστος is probably an instance of the change of αυ to ᾱ: see *Prol.* 47.

παχῡ́νω (VII.) *fatten*	ἐπαχύνθην		

πείθω (I. *a*) *counsel*	ἔπεισα	πείσω	πέποιθα
	ἐπείσθην	πεισθήσο-μαι	ἐπεποίθειν
ἔπειθον			πέπεισμαι
πείθομαι			
ἐπειθόμην			

VERBAL πιστός

COMP. ἀνα-

πεινάω (VII.) *hunger*	ἐπείνασα	πεινάσω	

This verb (inflected like τιμάω) has curiously parted from its twin διψάω, which keeps its future and aorist stems in -ησ, although they have both lost the η of pres. stem (διψῆν, πεινῆν). Debrunner (Blass[4] 43) suggests that association with κοπιάω fut. -άσω has affected it. In MGr it has pulled over διψῶ again (aor. ἐδίψασα).

-πείρω (VII.) *pierce*	-ἔπειρα		

COMP. περι-

πέμπω (I. *a*) *send*	ἔπεμψα	πέμψω	
	-ἐπεμψάμην		
-ἔπεμπον	-ἐπέμφθην		
πέμπομαι			

COMP. ἀνα-, ἐκ-, μετα-, προ-, συμ-

The punctiliar character of the root is in keeping with the rarity of its occurrence in the present stem.

πετάννυμι (II. *β*. *b*) *spread*	-ἐπέτασα		

COMP. ἐκ-

πήγνυμι (II. *β. b*) *fasten* COMP. **προσ-**	**ἔπηξα**			
-πιπλάω (VII.) *fill* COMP. **ἐμ-**	**ἔπλησα** **ἐπλήσθην**		**πλησθήσο-** **μαι**	**πέπλησμαι**

The simplex present *πίμπλημι* does not occur in NT.

πίμπρημι (I. *b*) *burn* **πίμπραμαι**	**-ἔπρησα**			

COMP. **ἐμ-** (**πιπρᾶσθαι**): so Ac 28[6] ℵ* (Bω **πίμπρασθαι**)

† *πιάζω* (VII.) *seize*	**ἐπίασα** **ἐπιάσθην**			
πιέζω (VII.) *press*				**πεπίεσμαι**

Like *ἀμφιάσαι* against *ἀμφιέσαι*, *πιάσαι* is said to be Doric: see Thumb in Brugmann *Gr.*[4] 78. Differentiated meaning seems to have set in, for *πιάσαι* (cf. MGr *πιάνω*) has the new force *seize*.

πικραίνω (VII.) *embitter* **πικραίνομαι** COMP. **παρα-**	**ἐπίκρᾱνα** **ἐπικράνθην**		**πικρανῶ**	
πίνω (II. *a*) *drink* **ἔπινον**	**ἔπιον** Inf. **πεῖν** (§ 38).	**ἐπόθην**	**πίομαι** (§ 85, see also *Prol.* 184 n.[3]).	**πέπωκα**

VERBAL (*ποτός*) whence noun **πότος**
COMP. **κατα-**, **συμ-**

πιπράσκω (IV.) *sell* **ἐπίπρασκον** **πιπράσκομαι**	**ἐπρᾱ́θην**			**πέπρᾱκα** **πέπραμαι**
πίπτω (I. *a*) *fall* **ἔπιπτον**	**ἔπεσον** (-*α*, § 88)		**πεσοῦμαι**	**πέπτωκα**

COMP. **ἀνα-**, **ἀντι-**, **ἀπο-**, **ἐκ-**, **ἐμ-**, **ἐπι-**, **κατα-**, **παρα-**, **περι-**, **προσ-**, **συμ-**

πλάσσω (VII.) *shape*	**ἔπλασα** **ἐπλάσθην**			

VERBAL **πλαστός**

πλατύνω (VII.) *broaden*	**ἐπλατύνθην**			**πεπλάτυμμαι**

πλέκω (I. *a*)	-ἐπλάκην	ἔπλεξα		
entwine				
-πλέκομαι				
COMP. ἐμ-				

πλέω (I. *a*)		ἔπλευσα		
sail				
ἔπλεον				

COMP. ἀπο-, δια-, ἐκ-, κατα-, παρα-, ὑπο-
For conjugation of present stem see § 84.

-πλήσσω	ἐπλήγην	-ἔπληξα		
(VII.)	-ἐπλἄγην			
strike				
-πλήσσομαι				
-ἐπλησσόμην				

COMP. ἐκ-, ἐπι-
Ac 13[12] ἐκπληττόμενος B 33: on this see § 43. The simplex passive aor. was used in Attic as suppletive for *τύπτω*: it was distinguished by its *η* from the form used in compound.

πλῦνω (VII.)		ἔπλῦνα		
wash (*clothes*)				
ἔπλυνον				

COMP. ἀπο-

πνέω (I. *a*)		ἔπνευσα		
breathe				

VERBAL -πνευστός
COMP. ἐκ-, ἐμ-, ὑπο-
For flexion of present stem see § 84.

-πνῖγω (I. *a*)	-ἐπνῖγην	ἔπνιξα		
choke				
-πνίγομαι				
ἔπνιγον				
ἐπνιγόμην				

VERBAL πνικτός†
COMP. ἀπο-, συμ-

ποιέω (VII.)		ἐποίησα	ποιήσω	πεποίηκα
make		ἐποιησάμην	ποιήσομαι	πεποιήκειν
ἐποίουν				πεποίημαι
ποιοῦμαι				
ἐποιούμην				

VERBAL -ποιητός
COMP. περι-, προσ-

The spellings without η are rare: thus ℵ in Lk 11^{42} ποῖσαι, but the same MS has ποιῆσαι normally. In earlier Greek and in papyri ποῶ is found, and papyri have forms without η. See p. 73.

ποιμαίνω (VII.) *shepherd* — **ἐποίμᾱνα** † — **ποιμανῶ**

πράσσω (VII.) *practise* — **ἔπραξα** — **πράξω** — **πέπρᾱχα**, **πέπραγμαι**

πρίω (I. *a*) *saw* — **ἐπρίσθην**
-ἐπριόμην
Comp. **δια-**

προφητεύω (VII.) *prophesy* — **ἐπροφήτευσα** — **προφητεύσω**
Later MSS augment προεφ.: see § 83 (2), (7).
ἐπροφήτευον

πταίω (I. *a*) *stumble* — **ἔπταισα**
Verbal **-πταιστός**

πτύσσω (VII.) *roll up* — **ἔπτυξα**
Comp. **ἀνα-**

-πτύω (VII.) *spit* — **ἔπτυσα** — **-πτῡσω**, **-πτυσθήσομαι**
-ἔπτυον
Comp. **ἐκ-**, **ἐμ-**

πυνθάνομαι (II. *a*. *a*) *ascertain* — **ἐπυθόμην**
ἐπυνθανόμην

-ῥαίνω (VII.) *sprinkle* — **-ῥέραμμαι**
Comp. **περι-**
The simplex may be original at Rev 19^{13} (pf. ptc. pass.): see WH *App.*^{2} 140. On the breathing see § 40.

ῥαντίζω (VII.) *sprinkle* — **ἐράντισα**, **ἐραντισάμην** — **ῥεράντισμαι** (On breathing see p. 100).

ῥαπίζω (VII.) *beat* — **ἐράπισα**

ῥάσσω (VII.) *strike*

An independent verb (only in Mk 9^{18} D 565), on which see Thumb in Brugmann *Gr.*^{4} 346.

ῥέω (I. *a*)　　**(ρ)ύην**　　　　**ῥεύσω**
flow　　subj. **-ρυῶ**
COMP. **παρα-**

ῥήγνυμι (II. *β*. *b*)　　**ἔ(ρ)ρηξα**　　**ῥήξω**
(§ 83 (9))

ῥήσσω (VII.)
break
ῥήγνυμαι
-ἐρησσόμην
COMP. **δια-**, **περι-**, **προσ-**

ῥιζόω (VII.)　　**-ἐρίζωσα**　　**-ριζωθήσομαι**　　**ἐρρίζωμαι**
root　　Only subj.
-ριζώσητε
-ἐριζώθην
COMP. **ἐκ-**

ῥιπτέω (VII.)　　**ἔριψα**†　　　　**ἔρ(ρ)ιμμαι**
cast　　　　　　see § 83 (8).
COMP. **ἀπο-**, **ἐπι-** (both with single ρ following)
The pres. *ῥιπτέω* is said to differ from *ῥίπτω* as *iacto* from *iacio* (*μετὰ σφοδρότητος ῥίπτω*): the latter does not occur in NT, the former once.

ῥύομαι (VII.)　　**ἐ(ρ)ρυσάμην**　　**ῥύσομαι**
deliver　　(§ 83 (9))
ἐρύσθην

ῥώννυμι　　　　　　**ἔρρωμαι**
(II. *β*. *b*)
strengthen

σαλπίζω (VII.)　　**ἐσάλπισα**†　　**σαλπίσω**†
trumpet
This is an instance of a new aorist and future coming from present (*σαλπίγγ-yω*→ *-ίζω* phonetically): cf. *σαλπίγξω*, etc.

σβέννυμι (II. *β*. *b*)　　**ἔσβεσα**　　**σβέσω**
quench
σβέννυμαι
VERBAL **-σβεστός**
Note phonetic spelling *ζβέννυτε* in 1 Th 5^{19} B*D_2*FG. All the present stem forms are still non-thematic.

σέβομαι (I. *a*) — **ἐσεβάσθην**
worship
VERBAL **σεβαστός**
In earlier Greek separate, but in Hellenistic the derivative verb is used as a suppletive, σέβομαι having no aorist in continued use.

-σείω (I. *a*) — **ἔσεισα** — **σείσω**
shake — **ἐσείσθην**
σείομαι
COMP. **ἀνα-, δια-, κατα-**

σημαίνω (VII.) — **ἐσήμᾱνα** †
signify
ἐσήμαινον

σήπω (I. *a*) — **σέσηπα**
rot

σκάπτω (VII.) — **ἔσκαψα** — **-ἔσκαμμαι**
COMP. **κατα-**

-σκέπτομαι (VII.) — **-ἐσκεψάμην** — **-σκέψομαι**
watch
COMP. **ἐπι-**
In Attic σκοπέω (only pres. stem in NT) was used as suppletive for the present stem. We find ἐπισκοποῦντες in Heb 12[15] in this sense, and in some papyri and inscriptions. It is perhaps significant that when interpolated (by A and the late MSS) in 1 Pet 5[2], it is a denominative from ἐπίσκοπος, and an entirely separate word.

σκληρύνω (VII.) — **ἐσκλήρῡνα**
harden — **ἐσκληρύνθην**
ἐσκληρυνόμην

σκύλλω (VII.) — **ἔσκυλμαι**
distress
σκύλλομαι

σπαράσσω (VII.) — **ἐσπάραξα**
convulse
COMP. **συν-**

σπάω (III.) — **-ἔσπασα** — **-σπάσω** — **-ἔσπασμαι**
draw — **ἐσπασάμην**
-ἐσπώμην — **-ἐσπάσθην**
VERBAL **-σπαστός**
COMP. **ἀνα-, ἀπο-, δια-, ἐπι-, περι-**

σπείρω (VII.) *sow* **ἔσπειρον** **σπείρομαι** COMP. **δια-**, **ἐπι-**	**ἐσπάρην**	**ἔσπειρα**		**ἔσπαρμαι**
σπεύδω (I. *a*) *hasten* **ἔσπευδον**		**ἔσπευσα**		
σπουδάζω (VII.) *be zealous*		**ἐσπούδασα**	σπουδάσω† (cl. -*ομαι*)	
-στέλλω (VII.) *send* **-ἔστελλον** **στέλλομαι** **-ἐστελλόμην** COMP. **ἀπο-**, **δια-**, **ἐξ-απο-**, **ἐπι-**, **κατα-**, **συν-**, **συν-απο**, **ὑπο-**	**-ἐστάλην**	**-ἔστειλα** **-ἐστειλάμην**	**-στελῶ**	**-ἔσταλκα** **-ἔσταλμαι**
στενάζω (VII.) *groan* COMP. **ἀνα-**, **συ-**		**ἐστέναξα**		
†**στήκω** (I. *a*) *stand* **ἔστηκον** A new present (MGr *στέκω*) formed from *ἕστηκα*—see *ἵστημι*.				
στηρίζω (VII.) *establish* VERBAL **-στηρικτός** COMP. **ἐπι-**		**ἐστήριξα** **ἐστήρισα** (Lk 9^{51} BCL *al.*, Ac 15^{32} CE, Lk 22^{32} ℵABL *al.*). **ἐστηρίχθην**	**στηρίξω** **στηρίσω**† (2 Th 3^{3} B)	**ἐστήριγμαι**
στρέφω (I. *a*) *twin* **-ἔστρεφον** **στρέφομαι** COMP. **ἀνα-**, **ἀπο-**, **δια-**, **ἐκ-**, **ἐπι-**, **κατα-**, **μετα-**, **συ-**, **ὑπο-**	**ἐστράφην**	**ἔστρεψα**	**-στρέψω** **-στραφήσομαι**	**ἔστραμμαι** **ἔστρεμμαι** †: see WH *App.*²177f.
στρώννυμι (II. *β*. *b*) *strew* **ἐστρώννυον** VERBAL -στρωτός COMP. **κατα-**, **ὑπο-**		**ἔστρωσα** **-ἐστρώθην**		**ἔστρωμαι**
σφάζω (VII.) *slay* COMP. **κατα-**	**ἐσφάγην**	**ἔσφαξα**	**σφάξω**	**ἔσφαγμαι**

-σχηματίζω (VII.) *fashion* -σχηματίζομαι Comp. μετα-, συ-	-ἐσχημάτισα	-σχηματίσω	
σχίζω (VII.) *split* Comp. δια-	ἔσχισα ἐσχίσθην	σχίσω	
σῴζω (VII.) *save* σῴζομαι ἐσῳζόμην Comp. δια-, ἐκ-	ἔσωσα ἐσώθην	σώσω σωθήσομαι	σέσωκα σέσω(σ)μαι Ac 4[9]—σται BDEP,—-ται ℵA, Eph 2[8],—-μένος P,—-σμένος rest.

The ι subscr. is best confined to pres.: see K.Bl. i. 544, and above, § 36, *d* (α).

ταράσσω (VII.) *disturb* ἐτάρασσον ταράσσομαι Comp. δια-, ἐκ-	ἐτάραξα ἐταράχθην		τετάραγμαι
τάσσω (VII.) -ἐτάγην *arrange* τάσσομαι Verbal τακτός	ἔταξα ἐταξάμην ἐτάχθην	-τάξομαι -ταγήσομαι	τέταχα τέταγμαι

Comp. ἀνα-, ἀντι-, ἀπο-, δια-, ἐν-, ἐπι-, ἐπι-δια-, προ-, προσ-, συν-, ὑπο-

-τείνω (VII.) *stretch* -ἔτεινον -τείνομαι	-ἔτεινα	-τενῶ	

Comp. ἐκ-, ἐπ-εκ-, παρα-, προ-, ὑπερ-εκ-. Simplex obsolete.

τελέω (VII.) *finish* τελοῦμαι Comp. ἀπο-, δια-, ἐκ-, ἐπι-, συν-	ἐτέλεσα ἐτελέσθην	-τελέσω τελεσθήσομαι	τετέλεκα τετέλεσμαι
-τέλλω (VII.) *accomplish ?* Comp. ἀνα-, ἐξ-ανα-, ἐν-	-ἔτειλα -ἐτειλάμην	-τελοῦμαι	-τέταλκα -τέταλμαι

The simplex occurs very rarely in early poetry. Its central meaning is quite doubtful: it is very probably a conflation of originally distinct roots.

-τέμνω (II. *a*) **-ἔτεμον** **-ἐτμήθην** **-τέτμημαι**
cut
VERBAL **-τμητός**
COMP. **περι-, συν-**

τήκω (I. *a*) **τακήσομαι**
melt So 2 Pet 3^{12} C, rest
τήκομαι mostly *τήκεται*.
See WH *App.*[2] 103, where Hort suggests *τήξεται* (quotable from one MS of Hippocrates) to account for the variants: Mayor seems to approve the emendation.

τίθημι (I. *b*) **θεῖναι** etc. (in-dic. wanting in NT). **ἔθηκα** **ἐτέθην** **θήσω** **-θήσομαι** **-τεθήσομαι** **τέθεικα** † **τέθειμαι** **-ἐτεθείμην**
set
ἐτίθουν **ἐθέμην**
τίθεμαι
-ἐτιθέμην
VERBAL **-θετός**
COMP. **ἀνα-, ἀντι-δια-, ἀπο-, δια-, ἐκ-, ἐπι-, κατα-, μετα-, παρα-, περι-, προ-, πρόσ-, προσ-ανα-, συν-, συν-επι-, συγ-κατα,- ὑπο-**
For the flexion see § 86 f.

The cl. **-τέ**-*θηκα* occurs in BGU II 388[1.43] (ii/iii A.D.), but the other form, formed after *ἀφεῖκα*, had long been current.

τίκτω (I. *a*. *a*) **ἔτεκον** **ἐτέχθην** **τέξομαι**
bear (child)

-τινάσσω (VII.) **-ἐτίναξα**
shake **-ἐτιναξάμην**
COMP. **ἀπο-, ἐκ-**

τίνω (II. *a*) **τείσω**
pay The cl. orthography—
COMP. **ἀπο-** usually written **τίσω**.

-τρέπω (I. *a*) **-ἐτράπην** **-ἔτρεψα** **-τραπήσομαι**
turn **-ἐτρεψάμην**
-τρέπομαι
-ἐτρεπόμην
COMP. **ἀνα-, ἀπο-, ἐκ-, ἐν-, ἐπι-, μετα-, περι-, προ-**

τρέφω (I. *a*) -ἐτράφην ἔθρεψα τέθραμμαι
nurture -ἐθρεψάμην
τρέφομαι
COMP. ἀνα-, ἐν-, ἐκ-
The root is *θρεφ*, which loses its first aspiration when the second is present.

τρέχω (I. *a*) [ἔδραμον]
run
ἔτρεχον
COMP. εἰσ-, ἐπι-συν-, κατα-, περι-, προ-, προσ-, συν-, ὑπο-
The suppletive is from √*δρεμ*: cf. δρόμος. The root is *θρεχ*, whence future *θρέξομαι*.

-τρίβω (I. *a*) -ἔτριψα -τρίψω -τέτριμμαι
rub -τρῐβήσομαι
-ἔτρῑβον
COMP. δια-, συν-

τυγχάνω (II. *a*) ἔτυχον τέτυχα† Heb 8^{6} א*AD*
happen τέτευχα *ib.* B
COMP. ἐν-, ἐπι-, παρα-, συν-, ὑπερ-εν τετύχηκα *ib.* P 33

-τυλίσσω (VII.) -ἐτύλιξα -τετύλιγμαι
wind
COMP. ἐν-

τύπτω (VII.) [ἐπλήγην] [ἔπαισα] [πατάξω]
strike [ἐπάταξα]
ἔτυπτον
τύπτομαι
For the suppletives see *παίω*, *πλήσσω* and *πατάσσω*: cf. for the cl. usage the excursus on "The Defective Verb *τύπτω*" in Sandys and Paley's *Demosthenes*, vol. ii. pp. 207–211.

ὑφαίνω (VII.)
weave
VERBAL ὑφαντός

√*φαγ* ἔφαγον φάγομαι †
eat
Suppletive to ἐσθίω, *q.v.*

φαίνω (VII.) ἐφάνην ἔφανα† φανοῦμαι
shine φανήσομαι
φαίνομαι
VERBAL -φαντός
COMP. ἀνα-, ἐπι-
In Rev 8^{12} 18^{23} *φάνῃ* is best thus accented, to mean "shine" rather than "appear" (*φανῇ*).

† -φαύσκω (IV.) -φαύσω

† φώσκω (IV.)

Comp. ἐπι-

dawn

-ἔφωσκον

The relations of these words are not quite clear. Ἐπιφαύσει might be the future of (ἐπι)φάϝω (φάε "shone" in Homer—still surviving in Aratus). The Homeric πιφαύσκω = "declare." Ἐπιφώσκω can be quoted from P Lond. 130[39] (=i. p. 134), a horoscope of ii/iii A.D.

φέρω (I. *a*) ἤνεγκον (not indic.) ἤνεγκα ἠνέχθην οἴσω -ἐνήνοχα

bear

ἔφερον

φέρομαι

ἐφερόμην

Comp. ἀνα-, ἀπο-, δια-, εἰσ-, ἐκ-, ἐπι-, κατα-, παρα-, παρ-εισ-, περι-, προ-, προσ-, συμ-, ὑπο-

On the question of aorist *Aktionsart* in ἔφερον see *Prol.*[3] 129, 247.

φείδομαι (I. *a*) ἐφεισάμην φείσομαι

spare

φεύγω (I. *a*) ἔφυγον φεύξομαι πέφευγα

flee

Comp. ἀπο-, δια-, ἐκ-, κατα-

φημί (I. *b*)

say

ἔφην

φάσκω (IV.)

ἔφασκον

Comp. σύμ-

Of φημί only φημί, φησί, φασί, and ἔφη are found.

φθάνω (II. *a*) ἔφθασα ἔφθακα

anticipate

Comp. προ-

φθέγγομαι (I. *a*) ἐφθεγξάμην

utter

Comp. ἀπο-

φθείρω (VII.) ἐφθάρην ἔφθειρα φθερῶ φθαρήσομαι -ἔφθαρμαι

corrupt

ἔφθειρον

φθείρομαι

VERBAL φθαρτός COMP. δια-, κατα-			
φορέω (VII.) *wear* VERBAL -φορητός	ἐφόρεσα	φορέσω	
φράσσω (VII.) ἐφράγην *shut*	ἔφραξα	φραγήσομαι	
φρυάσσομαι (VII.) *neigh* Middle in cl. Gr.	ἐφρύαξα †		
φυλάσσω (VII.) *guard* ἐφύλασσον φυλάσσομαι Comp. δια-	ἐφύλαξα ἐφυλαξάμην	φυλάξω	
φύω (VII.) ἐφύην † *grow* VERBAL -φυτός COMP. ἐκ-, συμ-			

In Mt 24^{32} = Mk 13^{28} we may accent ἐκφύῃ pres. (transitive) or ἐκφυῇ aor. (intrans.). Since this late strong aor. accounts for every other occurrence of φύω or compounds in NT, except φύουσα in Heb 12^{15}, there is a presumption in favour of it here, as it enables us to take both verbs as aorist. To parse ἐκφύῃ as aor. subj. act. is certainly wrong, for ἔφυν was obsolete and ἐφύην took its place.

φωτίζω (VII.) *illuminate*	ἐφώτισα ἐφωτίσθην	φωτίσω † φωτιῶ (Rev 22^{5} ℵ)	πεφώτισμαι
χαίρω (VII.) ἐχάρην *rejoice* ἔχαιρον COMP. συγ-		χαρήσομαι Χαροῦσιν in Rev 11^{10} TR is perhaps invented out of vg *gaudebunt.* Ἐπιχαρεῖ can be quoted from an Alexandrian inscription of ii/iii A.D., Preisigke *Sammelbuch* no. 1323.	
χαλάω (VII.) *let down*	ἐχάλἄσα ἐχαλάσθην	χαλἄσω	
χαρίζομαι (VII.) *grant*	ἐχαρισάμην ἐχαρίσθην †	χαρίσομαι † χαρισθήσομαι †	κεχάρισμαι

-χέω (I. *a*)	-ἔχεα	-χεῶ †	-κέχυμαι
-χύννω † (II. *a*)	-ἐχύθην	-χυθήσομαι	

pour

-ἔχεον
-ἔχυννον
-χέομαι
-χύννομαι
-ἐχυννόμην

There is difficulty as to the parsing of ἐκχέετε in Rev 16^{1} and συνέχεον Ac 21^{27}. That the active indic. present is nowhere χέω in NT proves nothing for impf., where there was not the same confusion with the future; and Luke is not likely to have altered aor. συνέχεαν so as to suggest an unintended impf. Moreover, he does use ἐπιχέων. In Rev the appearance of an uncontracted form ἐκχέετε (imper.) might, as WH *App.*^{2} 172 suggest, be aor. with termination of strong aor. But the syntactical argument they use is not very strong; and the open forms cited from LXX by WS 115 n.^{23} justify us equally in parsing this form as (iterative) present, considering the ways of the author of Rev.

Comp. ἐκ-, ἐπι-, κατα-, συγ-, ὑπερ-εκ-

χρήομαι (VII.)	ἐχρησάμην		κέχρημαι

use

ἐχρώμην

Verbal χρηστός

Comp. κατα-, συγ-

For flexion see § 85: the ordinary -άω flexion has considerably affected it.

χρηματίζω (VII.) *be called*	ἐχρημάτισα	χρηματίσω †	
χρηματίζω (VII.) *warn*	ἐχρηματίσθην		κεχρημάτισμαι

Two entirely distinct words, the former from χρήματα "business" —cf. our phrase "trading as X. & Co."; the latter from an equivalent of χρησμός "oracle."

χρίω (VII.)	ἔχρῑσα
anoint	-ἐχρῑσάμην (Rev 3^{18}, accenting ἔγχρισαι: cf. vg *inunge*).

Verbal χρῑστός

Comp. ἐγ-, ἐπι-

χρονίζω (VII.) *tarry*		χρονίσω† (Heb 10^{37}ℵ*D*) χρονιῶ (*ib.* A ω)	
χωρίζω (VII.) *separate*	ἐχώρισα ἐχωρίσθην	χωρίσω	κεχώρισμαι

χωρίζομαι

Comp. ἀπο-, δια-

ψάλλω (VII.) *sing*		**ψαλῶ**
ψεύδομαι (I. *a*) *lie*	**ἐψευσάμην**	
-ψύχω (I. *a*) *cool*	**-ἔψυξα**	**ψῠγήσομαι** †

COMP. **ἀνα-, ἀπο-, ἐκ-, κατα-**

-ὠθέω (VII.) *thrust*	**-ὦσα** †
	-έωσα (Ac. 7[45] ℵ*E)
-ὠθοῦμαι	**-ὠσάμην** †

COMP. **ἀπ-, ἐξ-**

PRINTED BY MORRISON AND GIBB LTD., EDINBURGH

PART III.

WORD-FORMATION.

§ 96. Our subject hitherto has been exclusively the form of words as isolated units, prepared to take their place in the combinations which make up speech. But we are not yet ready to pass on to Syntax, the study of principles governing these combinations: we have still to investigate important features in the history of the words themselves. We must go a step further back, and examine words before they are prepared for their place in a sentence by receiving inflexions of case or number, of person or mood. The larger part of this field must be excluded from our present survey. The Science of Language, or Grammar in the older and wider sense, is bound to concern itself with Semantics or Semasiology, the scientific investigation of the development of the meaning of words. In the same way it is bound to pass beyond Syntax, and study the phenomena classed under Rhetoric or Stylistic.

§ 97. But convenience demands an artificial limiting of what is involved in "Grammar"; and as we limit Syntax by the period or sentence, so we shall limit the study of single words within the provinces of Accidence and Word-formation. This latter division, upon which we now enter, will include the elements from which Semantics must start.

§ 98. There are two main divisions in the province before us, which we will take in retrograde order. First comes, then, the formation of Compounds, the combination of separate words within the history of the Greek language. Then follows the study of formative elements within words—comparative research into the function of prefixes and suffixes which ceased to be separate words (assuming that they ever were such) in a pre-historic stage of Indo-European speech. Under both these headings we shall have to deal separately with Nouns and Verbs.

WORD-COMPOSITION.

NOUNS.

§ 99. There is a marked difference between the languages of our family, and even between those which are closely related, in the extent to which noun-composition is employed. It is one of the most obvious differences between Greek and Latin, between German and English—the last pair fellow-members of one branch in the Indo-European family. English has less objection to compounds than Latin had; but we are familiar enough with the instinct that bids us coin our compounds in Greek rather than with native elements. We mentioned *Semasiology* just now. German philologists use *die Bedeutungslehre,* "meaning-science," where we invent a Greek combination and transfer it to our own tongue.

§ 100. The extreme example of proclivity towards compound-making is found in Sanskrit, where all sorts of relations are expressed by fitting words together, leaving their syntactical functions to be inferred. The Indian grammarians classified compounds with their usual acuteness, and our scientific accounts of them to-day are largely based upon the work of these early philologists. Macdonell (*Sanskrit Grammar,* p. 155) gives a good illustration: "Kālidāsa describes a river as 'wave-agitation-loquacious-bird-row-girdle-stringed,' while we should say 'her girdle-string is a row of birds loquacious because of the agitation of the waves.'" It will be noticed that Sanskrit has the advantage in brevity, but not in clearness. Greek, with its characteristic instinct of proportion, avoids the overdoing of this practice, especially in prose; and Hellenistic, as we might expect, restricts it somewhat more. Colloquial speech is not prone to multiply cumbrous words, and the more complex compounds are naturally avoided in the artless prose of everyday life.

§ 101. But it is possible to go too far in suspecting special culture when compounds are freely found. Within limits, a compound may be an actually simpler locution than its equivalent with the elements separated; and MGr vernacular shows that the genius of the language in respect of this resource has not changed. If we find Paul using a compound which we cannot trace elsewhere, we may provisionally allow him to have coined it without inferring any literary qualities in a man who can avail himself of such means of expressing a new thought. A modern peasant could do the same.

Classification. § 102. For the general principles of classification and the large literature thereon, reference may be made to Brugmann *Grundriss*[2] II. i. 35–40 and 49–120. A scientifically complete classification can only be made on comparative lines, and will not be attempted here, as we are not going beyond the compounds that occur in the NT. For our purpose we cannot do better than to apply with a few variations the classification devised by the Indian grammarians. We may quote Macdonell's summary (*Sanskrit Grammar*, p. 155): "The most convenient division is into the three classes of Co-ordinatives, Determinatives, and Possessives. The Determinatives, so-called because the former member determines (or qualifies) the latter, are of two kinds, Dependent and Descriptive. Possessives are secondary compounds, consisting chiefly of Determinatives turned into adjectives." The Sanskrit names for the classes, which will be given below, are with one exception typical examples of the class thus described.

Co-ordinatives. § 103. I. **Co-ordinative** Compounds (Skt. *Dvandva, i.e.* "couple") unite two or more words of the same class: thus Skt. *aho-rātram* "day and night." Numerals afford plentiful examples: *δώδεκα, duodecim, δεκαοκτώ, eighteen, twenty-one,* etc., may be compared with the forms in which *and* occurs, as the classical *τρεισκαίδεκα* or our *three and twentieth.* Apart from these there are very few examples of *Dvandva* in Greek[1]: the adverb[2] *νυχθήμερον* "by night and day" is the solitary NT instance.[3] *Ἀρτόκρεας,*

[1] [Mr. E. E. Genner cites *πλουθυγίεια health and wealth.* (Aristoph.[ter].)—Ed.]

[2] [So J. H. M. here: but see below, p. 283. "Substantivised neut. from **νυχθήμερος*," Brugmann *Grd.*[2] II. i. 99. Generally taken as direct obj. of *πεποίηκα* in 2 Co 11[25].—Ed.]

[3] The *vox nihili* **δευτερόπρωτος** might be said to belong to this class as probably as to any other: we may record it here simply because this is the first class named. Plummer's note on Lk 6[1] gives the various attempts made to explain it. It is an early Western interpolation. WH *App.*[2] 58 (*q.v.*) accept Meyer's explanation of its origin; Burkitt (*Gospel Hist.* 81 n.) supposes a dittography ϹΑΒΒΑΤΩΒΑΤΩ, from which "ΒΑΤΩ was erroneously expanded into *δευτεροπρώτῳ.*" Cod. *e* reads *sabbato mane*=*ἐν σαββάτῳ πρωί*: cf. Mrs. Lewis's conjecture of *πρωί* for *πρῶτον* in Jn 1[41], from a new reading of syr[sin] (*Exp T* xx. 229 ff.).

found in Persius 6[50] as a borrowed word, is taken by Brugmann to mean "bread and meat": it may be Hellenistic, or a survival from classical vocabulary. Brugmann notes that *Dvandva* is commoner in MGr: thus γυναικόπαιδα "women and children," μαχαιροπέρονα "knives and forks." It even appears in verbs, as ἀνεβοκατεβαίνω "pace up and down" (Thumb *Hdb.* 112). The papyri give us χορτάρακον (P Lond 1171[38]) (=iii. p. 178) (8 B.C.), which Grenfell and Hunt take as "hay and aracus," comparing κριθόπυρος (P Petr i. p. 78) "barley and wheat." (But see Mayser 468 on this. Kenyon takes it as "aracus for fodder.") Mayser 469 adds ναυκληρομάχιμος. We may fairly assume that the usage was known in Hellenistic.

Iteratives. § 104. II. Closely akin to these compounds are the **iteratives**, products of the reduplicating tendency which forms so many words in our own vernacular, and takes a large part in the history of the Indo-European verb-system. Unlike Sanskrit and Latin, Greek hardly ever fuses the two forms into one word, but the principle is not really affected. An exception is πέρπερος (whence περπερεύομαι), which is not attested till a later date than Latin *perperam* is found: it may quite possibly be borrowed from *perperus*. It comes from the pronominal *pero-* "other" (see below, p. 279, under πέρυσι), and the iteration produces elative force, "other than what should be"; cf. uses of ἕτερος. The reduplication produces *distributive* force in δύο δύο "two by two" (see *Proleg.* 97, and add P Oxy vi. p. 310 note), πρασιαὶ πρασιαί, συμπόσια συμπόσια, δεσμὰς δεσμάς: cf. Skt. *ékaikas* "each one," *yádyad* "what each time," Lat. *quisquis*, Avestan *nmāne-nmāne* "in each house." A modern Indian dialect like Gujarati may complete the case against Semitism! Emphasis of various kinds may be seen in πλέον πλέον, μᾶλλον μᾶλλον, *magis magis*, "more and more"; μέγας μέγας[1] (*Proleg. l.c.*) "very great"; ὅσον ὅσον (Aristophanes, LXX, Lk 5[3] D, Heb 10[37]) "only just so much as." The last is like our idiomatic phrase "only so-so": English iteratives like "tut tut!", "hear

[1] *Archiv* v. 163 cites an Egyptian inscr. of 29 B.C. with dedication θεῶι μεγάλωι μεγάλωι ὑψίστωι: O. Rubensohn regards it as referring to Jehovah, though it may or may not be from a Jew. The collocation μέγας μέγας was however specially Egyptian

hear!", "come, come!", "a red, red rose," will supply further illustration. See Delbrück, *Grd.* v. (iii.) 139 ff.

Dependent Determinatives. § 105. III. **Dependent Determinatives** (Skt. *Tatpuruṣa* "his man," abbreviated T.P.) form a very large class. In these the first element stands in a case relationship to the second. As in other compounds, the immense majority of instances show the bare stem in the first part. There are a few exceptions, of which we may name the following as NT words: νουνεχής (adv. in Mk 12[34]) *acc.*, ὁδοιπόρος (noun and verb in NT) *loc.*, ἄριστον (=ἀγέρι + στόν, *loc.* of obsolete noun=morning—cf. ἦρι Eng. *ere*—with p.p.p. of √ *ed* to eat), Διόσκουροι (*sons of Heaven*) Ac 28[11]; *gen.* A few specimens may be given to show these compounds in the various case relations: it should be premised that the selection of a case is often ambiguous.

Accusative.—θεοσεβής *God-worshipping,* γεωργός (=γη-οργός) *earth-working, tiller,* φωσφόρος *light-bringing, daystar,* κακοῦργος (=κακόεργος) *evil-doer* (hence by analogy παν-οῦργος *one who will do anything, knave*).

Genitive.—πατριάρχης *ruler of a clan* (πατριά), αἱματεκ-χυσία *shedding of blood*; οἰκοδεσπότης *lord of a house.*

Ablative.—διοπετής *fallen from heaven,* πατροπαράδοτος *handed down from our fathers,* ποδαπός (see *Prol.* 95, Hellen. ποταπός) *coming from whence?*

Dative.—ἀνθρωπάρεσκος *man-pleaser,* εἰδωλόθυτος *sacrificed to idols.*

Locative.—χείμαρρος *flowing in the winter,* γονυπετής *falling on the knees,* ὀφθαλμόδουλος *serving under the eyes.*

Instrumental.—ποταμοφόρητος *river-borne,* χειρόγραφον *written with the hand,* αἰχμάλωτος spear-captured, κιθαρῳδός (=κιθαρα-αοιδός) *singing with the harp,* θεοδίδακτος *God-taught.*

There are a great many compounds of this form which will easily be placed in one of the categories described above. Some words follow on which special notes are desirable. (As throughout this chapter, the original compound is given whenever it exists: in many cases the NT only shows a secondary derivative.)

Ἀλεκτοροφωνία is noted by Blass (*Gr.* 68) as "peculiar, there being no conceivable adjective from which it can be derived." It is no doubt genitivally dependent, *cock-crowing,* with its second element modelled on συμφωνία, etc. It is vulgar, as Blass observes.

Ἀλλοτριεπίσκοπος (1 Pet 4[15], vg *alienorum appetitor*) may very well be a coined word: of course such a statement only means that we have no other occurrences at present, and that the coining of such a compound is entirely according to usage in Greek of every kind. The elision of its is determined by ℵB and other authorities: for the *ἀλλοτριοεπίσκοπος* of the *a*-text MSS we might compare *ἱπποΐατρος* P Oxy i. 92 (iv/A.D.), Ramsay *C. and B.* ii. 662 (no. 627), *δειγματοάρτ(ης)* and *χωματοεπιμ(ελήτης)* in P Lond 1159[39f.] (=iii. p. 113) (Hermopolis, A.D. 145–7), the former also in P Oxy i. 63[8] (ii/iii A.D.). Probably the retention of the *o* was normal in freshly coined words at a rather later period than that of the NT Books: WM 124 n describes the other as "more correct." See further above, § 32.

Ἁρμολόγος may be tentatively given as the basis of **(συν)αρμολογέω**, though its authority (see LS) is *nil*, and the verb may be simply formed from analogy. It would mean *joint-gathering* (accus. dep.), with the verb *to fit together*.

Αὐτός forms sundry compounds that call for comment. In two of them the *αὐτός* is *nominative*, so that the words fall into the next class. In three it is instrumental, viz. **αὐθαίρετος** *self-chosen*, **αὐτόματος** *self-thought, spontaneous* (**-ματός* p.p.p. of √ *men* to think), **αὐτοκατάκριτος** *self-condemned*. Probably **αὐτόφωρος** is the same, *self-detected*: its usage (see Jebb on Soph. *Ant.* 51) depends on *φωράω* rather than on *φώρ*. The dative appears in **αὐτάρκης** *self-sufficient, content*: the vernacular use of the word practically lets the *αὐτός* go—see *Vocabulary s.v.* Also dative is **αὐθάδης** (*αὐτο-Fάδης*, from √ *sụād* of *ἥδομαι*, *ἁνδάνω*, *suavis* etc.) *self-pleasing, reckless*.

Βατταλογέω (Mt 6[7] ℵB—WH *App.*[2] 158) presumes an (unquotable) **βατταλόγος*, best perhaps taken as from **βατταλο-λόγος* by haplology. It is argued in *Vocabulary s.v.* that *βάτταλος*, the nickname of Demosthenes, may have meant *gabbler*: in that case Aramaic *battâl* (Wellhausen) may be only accidentally similar. *βατταρίζω* *stammer* is another possible source, for **βατταρο-λογέω* might suffer haplology after assimilation. The reading of D (gr.) *βλαττολ.* is akin to Latin *blatero* (i.e. **mlatero*, Eng. *blether*; the root perhaps in Skt. *mleccha* "foreign-speaking"). The uncertainty of the word's history makes it doubtful whether Class IV. or V. should not claim it.

Βλάσφημος probably shows the reduced form of the stem of *βλάβος*, thus *injury-speaking* (accus. dep.): see further *Vocabulary s.v.*

Γαζοφυλάκιον (Strabo p. 319) is derived by Blass (*Gr.* 68) from *γαζοφύλαξ* *treasure-warden* (gen. dep.).

Γλωσσόκομον (Jn 12[6] 13[29]) is *what holds* (*κομίζει*) *the mouthpiece of a flute* (*γλῶττα*—cf. Blass *ib.*). Phrynichus (Rutherford 181) tells us how the degenerate epigoni sacrificed the "correct" Attic *γλωττοκομεῖον*, and widened its use so as to describe a case for "books, clothes, money, or anything else." See *Vocabulary s.v.* for papyrus citations for the Attic form (still in W), and the shortened Hellenistic form.

Δεξιολάβος, a *ἁ.λ.* in Ac 23[23] (vg *lancearii*), is supposed to mean *taking* (a spear) *in the right hand* (instr. or loc. dependence). In military phraseology the spear was always connected with the right, as the shield with the left. It was certainly not a coined word, but as it does not re-appear till vii/A.D. we must suppose it a technical term of limited range.

Δημηγόρος public orator (whence -ρέω) starts best perhaps from *δῆμος ἀγείρειν contionem facere* (so accus. dep.), the connotation of a harangue coming from the conditions familiar from Homer down.

Εἰλικρινής (on breathing see WH *App.*[2] 151) is as yet unsolved. That the second element is from *κρίνω* seems clear, so that the meaning is —*tested*, —*discerned*, *sincere*. But neither the Homeric *εἰλίποδες* (*βόες*) nor Theocritus' *εἰλιτενής*, an epithet of a grass, seems to help us for the first element, and it must be left for the present.

Since *εὖ* is the neuter of an old adjective (Homeric *ἠΰς*, cf. Skt. *vasu* good, Zd. *vaṅhu*, O. Pers. *Dāraya-vahu* (Darius)=*possessing goods*), some of its cpds. may as well come here as in the other classes. Thus **εὐεργέτης** *benefactor* might be *bonorum factor*. But it is better to divide them between Classes IV. and V.

Θεοστυγής (see SH on Rom 1[30]) has sometimes been taken as accusatively dependent, *God-hating*; but there seems no reason for deserting the ancient evidence for *God-hated* (dative). Similarly the proper name **Θεόφιλος** means *God's beloved, dear to God* (gen. or dat.): the other meaning would be expressed by *μισόθεος*, *φιλόθεος* respectively. (As a Jewish name Theophilus appears in papyri: it carries on such OT names as *Jedidiah*.)

Θυμομαχέω —**θυμομάχος* is not found—seems to be instr. dep., *to fight with zest* or *heat*, so *to quarrel hotly*. So **λογομάχος** *fighting with words* (" speaking daggers ").

Θυρωρός=*θυρα-Fορός door-guardian* (*ὁράω*, Eng. *ware*) has gen. dependence. Cf. *κηπο-Fορός*, **κηπουρός**, *gardener*; **οἰκουρός** *house-guardian* (Tit 2[5] α-text). The 1st decl. nouns properly produced compounds in *-ωρός*, as *πυλωρός gate-guardian*, **τιμωρός** *honour-guardian, avenger*; but analogy sometimes produced in vernacular documents forms like *θυρουρός*.

Κενεμβατεύω " according to a probably certain conjecture, Col 2[18]" (Blass, *Gr.* 67) *ἀέρα κενεμβατεύων* for *ἃ ἑόρακεν ἐμβ*. The verb *ἐμβατεύω* is good vernacular, and, in the process of copying, might easily take the place of a ἁ.λ., which would probably be a coinage of Paul's own: a conjecture developed by such a succession of great scholars [1] is tempting. C. Taylor, to whom the conjecture in its final form is due, suggested that the phrase was based on the Rabbinic " fly in the air with nothing to rest on." Field's rather doctrinaire objection to a verb not found elsewhere, and not formed according to classical rules—which are far from " inviolable " in Hellenistic—would be easily turned by reading (with Peake) *κενεμβατῶν*, an existing word, and assuming that the common *ἐμβατεύειν*

---

[1] See its history in J. R. Harris's *Side-lights on NT Research* (1909), pp. 198 f.

ousted a rather rare expression. The new verb will mean *to invade the void* (accus. dep.), and with the internal accus. ἀέρα *to tread the empty air.*[1]

*Καραδόκος may perhaps be assumed as basis of (ἀπο)καραδοκία (see p. 299), but its formation is not at all clear. If δέκομαι (Att. δέχομαι) originally meant *to stretch out* (cf. Brugmann *Grd.*[1] II. 465), this (hypothetical) adjective *head-stretching* would supply a good basis for καραδοκέω *to expect eagerly*. See further on the noun (possibly a coinage of Paul—the verb is in Polybius) *Vocabulary s.v.*

Ναυᾱγός (ναῦς and Ϝάγνυμι[2]) must be interpreted on the same lines as its Latin synonym *naufragus*: accus. dependence is perhaps simplest, *one who has wrecked his ship*. **Ναύκληρος** is complex, as it combines ναύκληρος *with a ship as his portion* (a compound of Class V. below) with a dissimilated form of ναύκρᾱρος *ship-master*, from *κρᾱσρός *head* (κρᾱσ-πεδον, κρᾱνίον, Lat. *cerebrum* for *ceresrom*): there are semasiological difficulties here—see LS.

Οἰκουργός (ἁ.λ.), the true reading in Tit 2⁵, is a compound with locative dependence, *home-worker*, or it may be exactly parallel with γεωργός, which has accus.

Ὀρθοτομέω (2 Ti 2¹⁵) occurs in Pr 3⁶ 11⁵, of levelling or straightening a road—" cutting straight the path of Truth," for the pilgrims' progress thereon, would be an attractive meaning. But it is simpler to compare (with Grimm) καινοτομεῖν *to innovate*, where the second element has faded: ὀρθ. will then be *to direct, apply faithfully*, as men speak of " a *straight* talk." So practically vg *recte tractantem*, and RV.

Πατρολῴας and **μητρολῴας** in 1 Ti 1⁹ are spelt with ο (not α) by the best MSS: see WH *App.*[2] 159. The classical πατραλοίας seems to make *father-thrasher* (ἀλο(ι)άω) the meaning.[3] The levelling tendency of analogy has caused all the *r* nouns to substitute ρο in compounds for the ρα (*i.e.* ṛ) which was originally found (cf. Skt. *pitṛ-*, Goth. *broþru-*): here the tendency has even affected words in which the α belongs to the second element of the compound. This is simpler than Radermacher's suggestion (*Gr.*[1] 35, [2]37) that ὄλλυμι was in mind.

Πλεονέκτης should apparently mean *one who has more* (accus. dep.). But from the first it is *one who would have more*. It is difficult to see where the desiderative element came in: is the -έκτης really *ἕξ-της ? But cf. αἰσχροκερδής below, p. 284.

Πλήμμυρα may be placed here tentatively, on the assumption that the μμ (see § 41) only represents a popular connexion with πλήν, like πλημμελής.

---

[1] [This " probably certain conjecture " has been gravely discounted by Ramsay's discovery of the word ἐμβατεύω in inscrr. from Klaros as a t.t. of the Mysteries. His essay " The Mysteries in their Relation to St. Paul " (*Contemp. Review*, Aug. 1913, pp. 198 ff.) is republished in *The Teaching of Paul*, pp. 287 ff.). So now *Vocab.* 206*a*.—Ed.]

[2] The ᾱ is taken by Brugmann (*Grd.*[2] II. i. 92) as due to analogy of nouns that lengthened the vowel at the junction through contraction, as στρατᾱγός=*stṛto-ago-s*.

[3] For ω or ῳ replacing οι see p. 83. [WH spell both words with ῳ.—Ed.]

Boisacq regards πλη- as a gradation-doublet of πλω (πλώω, E. *flood*): μύρομαι, orig. *to flood*, supplies the second part. In that case the first element would be a primitive noun, accusatively or instrumentally dependent.

Πληροφορέω, which has no *πληροφόρος behind it, may come from the analogy of cpds. like **τελεσφορέω** (from τελεσφόρος *maturity-bringing*). The verb starts from *to bring in full* (accus. dep.). Its meanings in vernacular Greek may be seen in Deissmann *LAE* 82 f. ([2]86 f.), Milligan on 1 Th 1[5]: see also Lightfoot on Col 4[12].

Ποδήρης must mean *reaching to the feet* (dat. dep.), but its second element is not clear. The root of ἀραρίσκω is generally given, and may be right, though *feet-fitting* is not quite what we want. The -ήρης in ἀμφήρης, ἐπήρης, τριήρης *al.*, is connected with the root of our *row*, *rudder*, and is less suitable still.

Προσωπολήμπτης is one of the few genuine examples of "Jewish Greek." It is a natural Greek coinage from the phrase πρόσωπον λαμβάνειν (accus. dep.), which was a literal rendering of נָשָׂא פָּנִים—a notion not provided with a real equivalent in Greek. *Prol.* 13 gives an estimate of the place of such locutions in the language. The compound (with -ψία and -πτέω) serves as a good illustration of the fact that word-composition was a resource of language still very much alive in Hellenistic.

Σκύβαλον (Ph 3[8]) was a vernacular word, found in papyri. Wetstein gives a mass of passages from Κοινή literature, and one or two from earlier writers. The derivation from σκώρ is quite impossible phonetically. The alternative (based on Suidas), that it is a contraction of ἐς κύνας βαλεῖν, as σκορακίζω is formed from ἐς κόρακας, is not to be vetoed so decisively: it might be a popular abbreviation, in form anticipating partly the MGr στόν for ἐς τόν, etc. In that case we have a compound with quasi-dative dependence. Popular association with σκώρ might account for the predominance of the meaning *stercus*.

Σπερμολόγος *picking up seeds* (applied to a bird in Aristophanes and other writers) has accus. dependence: for the development of its meaning, see comms. on Ac 17[18].

Συκοφάντης (whence °τέω) *fig-showing* (accus. dep.) seems clear in its composition, but the meaning of the metaphor which thus describes an *informer* is still uncertain.

Φρεναπάτης *mind-deceiving* (accus. dep.), *conceited*. Blass (*Gr.* 68) notes its occurrence in P Grenf i. 1[i. 10] (ii/B.C.), a literary text.

Χειροτόνος (hence °έω) *stretching the hand* (Æschylus) has accus. dependence.

Χορηγός (χορός + ἀγός) *chorus-bringing* or *-leading*, originally used mostly of the equipment of a chorus (a λειτουργία at Athens), was early generalised to mean *one who supplies* the cost for anything. The irregular η (following ρ) is probably due to the analogy of other compounds in -ηγός, rather than to Ionic influence (see p. 68). (Cf. Brugmann *KVG* 304, 307, *Grd.*[2] II. i. 92.) In one of its meanings **ἀρχηγός** may belong here: see below, p. 277.

Descriptive Determinatives.

§ 106. IV. We come next to **Descriptive** Determinatives (Skt. *Karma-dhāraya*, a term of which the exact application is not certain —abbreviation K.D.). In these the first element is a noun, adjective, or adverb which describes the second element, standing to it in a predicate relation. We classify them naturally according to the character of the first element:

(*a*) Noun or adjective[1] or pronoun:—Αὐτόπτης *self-seer*, κωμόπολις *village-town* (a πόλις that is little more than a κώμη—Strabo, Mk 1³⁸), μεσότοιχος *middle wall, barrier*, ἀγριέλαιος *wild olive*, ὁλόκαυτος *burnt whole*. So in English *midsummer, ill-will*.

(*b*) A subdivision of (*a*) is required for compounds with numerals, like our *fortnight*: the Indian grammarians made a special class for these, called *Dvigu* (*two-cow*). In the nature of things these, if they belong to Class IV., can only be plural (except possible compounds of *one*, like the English t.t. *single-tax*: μονογενής *only born* might be classed here). Thus we have Latin *decemviri, centumviri*. Out of these arose a natural singular, not capable of analysis except by reference to its plural: thus *decemvir*=*one of a board of ten*. This is found in the NT τετραάρχης, *one of four rulers*. Compare the title δεκάπρωτος, found in papyri=*one of ten* πρῶτοι (cf. Ac 28⁷), δεκανός (whence our *dean*).

(*c*) A large class has an adverb as first element. It may be the negative ἀ-, ἀν- (n̥-, Lat. *in*-, Eng. *un*-, Skt. *a*-, *an*-: the reduced form of *nĕ*): so ἄγνωστος *unknown*, ἄσοφος *unwise*, etc. The second element might be a noun (like our *unfaith*): thus in Sophocles ἀμήτωρ=*one who is no mother*. But these compounds have in Hellenistic all become possessive (Class V.): ἀπάτωρ=*father unknown*,[2] *with no* recorded *father* (Heb 7³). *Εὖ* forms a good many compounds, as εὐεργέτης *well-doer, benefactor*; so δυσ-, as δυσβάστακτος *hardly borne* (cf. our *mis-trust*), etc. Many prepositional cpds. belong to this class (IV.*c*),

[1] An interesting observation is made by Brugmann *KVG* 362 as to fem. cpds. with -ο- at the juncture, like ἀκρόπολις. He regards these as dating from a time when the adj. did not take a fem. termination to suit grammatical gender.

[2] So in the papyri, for illegitimates: see *Vocabulary s.v.*

though Classes V. and VII. are responsible for the major part of them: thus πρόσωπον *what is towards the eyes, face*, προπάτωρ *forefather*, ἐπ-ενδύτης *overcoat*. We will reserve prepositional compounds until we can classify them together. (See §§ 110–129.)

We proceed to comment on special cases:

Class (a). Ἀκροβυστία is not completely explained. Ἀκροποσθία, a normal Descriptive cpd. from ἄκρος and πόσθη with a fresh suffix, is found in Hippocrates, and is obviously the original of the LXX word. When a word containing a *vox obscena* was taken from medical vocabulary into popular religious speech, it was natural to disguise it: a rare word βύστρα=βύσμα may supply the model.

Ἀκρογωνιαῖος presumes a (non-existent) ἀκρογωνία *extreme corner*.

Ἀκροθίνια, based on ἀκρόθινα (Pindar), *top heaps=top of a heap* (cf. Latin *summus mons*), *chief spoils*.[1]

Ἀρεοπαγίτης depends formally on a cpd. Ἀρε(ι)όπαγος, which never had any real existence: it was at a late period formed afresh from Ἀρεοπαγίτης (for which cf. Meisterh.[3] 61, also 43). Lobeck *Phryn.* 599 ff. successfully shows that in this and similar words the separate words were more in accord with Attic taste than the cpd.; but he totally fails in his attempt to eject the Descriptive altogether. His quotations illustrate that a locution containing two or three words was fused when a derived cpd. was wanted: cf. καλοκἀγαθία and other cpds., while καλοκἀγαθός never occurs till very late (ii/A.D.). On this see Brugmann *KVG* 306, who compares *terrimotium* from *terræ motus*, Ger. *langweilig* from *lange Weile* etc. So we make the compound *Free-Churchmanship* out of the separate *Free Church*.

Ἀρχηγός (cf ἀρχάγγελος, ἀρχιερεύς) may have as its first element ἀρχι: the ι is elided before -ᾱγός (ἄγω)—for the η see above under χορηγός (p. 275). The alternative ἀρχε- (see Cl. VI.) has probably affected this prefix, and when it precedes vowels we cannot tell which of the two to presume, in the case of early words: ἀρχι- monopolised the late formations. Since there are two distinct functions for the prefix, according as it means *chief* (Cl. IV.) or *ruling* (Cl. VI.), it is reasonable to conjecture ἀρχι- as original in the adjectival and ἀρχε- in the verbal function, with some natural mixture resulting. How far ἀρχι- is primitive we can hardly say. It was shown by Caland and Wackernagel (see the latter's *Altind. Gramm.* ii. 59 ff.) that from I.E. times -*i*- replaced the adjective suffix -*ro*- in the first part of cpds., and perhaps replaced other suffixes. Cf. καλλι- cpds. (as καλλιέλαιος) from καλός. In that case ἀρχι- will be either a primitive base-form, or made by analogy from ἀρχο-, the base of the noun ἀρχός. See Mayser 81. The great majority of the late ἀρχι-

---

[1] [Mr. E. E. Genner points out that the new LS gives ἄκροθις as a subst. (like ἀκρόπολις) from a iv/B.C. inscr. See Rüsch, *Gr. d. delph. Inschriften*, i. 216: ἀκρόθις *Erstlingsgabe*: τὰν ἀκρόθινα D[47].—ED.]

cpds. belong to Cl. IV. The old word ἀρχηγός shows fluctuation in meaning between *originator* and *leader*, according as the force of ἄρχεσθαι and ἄρχειν respectively predominates. The former may really go back to ἀρχή+ἀγος, *beginning-leader*, a cpd. of Cl. III.: the latter is Cl. IV., *supreme leader*. See *Vocabulary s.v.*

Αὐθέντης (whence **αὐθεντέω** *be master of, govern*) is a contracted form of the Sophoclean αὐτοέντης (=αὐτο-έντης from root of ἀνύειν, Skt. *sanoti*, Lat. *sons*, our *sin*). The verb is branded as vulgar by Atticists, and is accordingly good vernacular, in the same sense as in 1 Tim 2^{12}. Latin and English join in giving the verb the nuance of our word *perpetrate*. The curious meaning " murderer " in classical writers comes from an entirely different word, derived from αὐτο-θέντης: see *Vocabulary s.v.* It is classed with αὐτόπτης as a cpd.

Δημιουργός, from δᾱμιοϝεργός, is as old as Homer. It seems to start from *public worker*, which developed in two different directions into (1) *craftsman*, (2) *magistrate* (in some Doric cities). Under (1) the idea of *skill* grew stronger—perhaps from the contrast of a publicly recognised workman, contrasted with one who only works for himself—and it becomes in philosophy a name for the Creator: cf. Philo *De Somn.* 13 fin. (p. 632 M.), where it is contrasted with the higher title κτίστης. It is natural to think that the author of Heb 11^{10} was at least semiconscious of this.

Ἱεράπολις and **Νεάπολις** are printed *divisim* by WH: in Col 4^{13} the MSS cannot help us, in Ac 16^{11} CD* are quotable (with the mob) for the cpd. form. Blass's " sic divisim antiquiores " is a useless remark, since Luke was not an " antiquior." On the whole, however, the oldest uncials may be allowed to decide, though the tendency to fuse these phrases into cpds. was strong by this time. Μεγαλόπολις, for example, occurs in Strabo (i/B.C.). Ramsay (*C. and B.* ii. p. 681) shows that *Hieropolis* was the local name, and a sign of imperfect Hellenisation.

[**Καλοδιδάσκαλος** in Tit 2^3, being a ἁ.λ., might be taken as *noble teacher*; but this would probably be *καλλιδιδάσκαλος, and the other cpds. of διδάσκαλος belong to Cl. III.]

Κράσπεδον is an old cpd., apparently of this class, from the stem to which κέρας, κάρα and κρά(σ)νιον belong: *utmost edge* seems the meaning.

Λειτουργός, from λήϊτο-εργός (Blass *Gr.* 8), is later in its attestation than its formal derivatives (**-έω** and **-ια**). Λήιτον occurs in Herodotus (vii. 197) for a set of public offices: this connotation would suggest a clerk in government service as the oldest meaning. It is curious to note how far it has diverged from the very similar δημιουργός.

Μεσημβρία, from μέσος and an ablaut form of ἦμαρ, ἡμέρα, answers to our *mid-day*.

Μεσουράνημα, *mid-heaven*, in Rev 8^{13}, is from the verb μεσουρανέω *to culminate*, of heavenly bodies crossing the meridian, but the presumable base *μεσούρανος is not quotable, and may never have existed.

Νεομηνία *new-moon*, or rather the *day of the new moon*, is a derivative rather than a direct Descriptive cpd.

Νεόφυτος *new plant*, or *newly planted*, might equally well be put with (*c*) below.

Πανήγυρις, like some other cpds. of πᾶς, loses the τ of the stem by the influence of the neuter πᾶν, but keeps the original ᾰ. *General assembly* represents the meaning.

Πανοικεί is the locative of an unused *πανοικός, which would mean *whole house*: cf. πανστρατιᾷ, πανοικίᾳ. Πανοικεί comes under the ban of the Atticists (Lobeck *Phryn.* 514). No doubt it was formed on the analogy of other locatives in -εί (ἀμισθεί etc.), by substituting οἶκος for οἰκία; nor need we suppose that such formations were ever used in the nom. or other cases, being called into being only for the adverb.

Πέρυσι is another locative without other cases in use, but it is of prehistoric antiquity. Its first element is the primitive pronoun *pero-* = *other*, Skt. *para-* : cf. πέραν, *perendie, perperam*, Eng. *far* etc. : the second is the locative of *ụet* (cf. Fέτος, *vetus*)=year, with weak grade. The Skt. *parut* has the same meaning, and only differs by the absence of the locative suffix -*i*.

Πρῶτος forms a good many cpds. of this class, as in NT **πρωτοκαθεδρία, πρωτοκλισία, πρωτοστάτης**. **Πρωτότοκος** *first-born* forms the further noun **πρωτοτόκια** (pl.). Πρωτοτόκος = *bearing a firstborn* is an older word, which is still quotable in ritual language of iii/ii B.C. (*Syll.* 615[16], or *Syll.*[3] 1024[16] ὗν ἐνκύμονα πρωτοτόκον). Isidore of Pelusium (Lightfoot *Col.* p. 150) proposed to use this for the crux in Col 1[15], *qs.* "the *first author* of all creation"; but his admission that he was innovating must be noted, and Lightfoot's exegesis may be maintained—see also Peake *EGT in loc.*

Σαρδόνυξ, χρυσόλιθος, χρυσόπρασος and the cpds. in **ψευδο-** (exc. two of Cl. V.) are words of this class that need no comment.

Σήμερον is an adverb (accus.) like πέρυσι. Its termination is an adj. suffix; and the σ- represents a pronoun κịo- "this," compared by Brugmann *KVG* 401 with O.E. *hiu-diga* (Ger. *Heute*) "to-day." Hence *σσήμερον, Attic *ττήμερον, whence the initial consonant was reduced.

[**Σκληροκαρδία** might belong to this class, if=" hard heart." It is better taken as Possessive (Cl. V.) in origin, =*hard-heartedness*.]

Συροφοινίκισσα in Mk 7[26] ℵALΔ stands against Σύρα Φοινίκισσα Bω and Σύρα Φοίνισσα W *al.*—the last probably an Atticist correction. Συροφοῖνιξ occurs in Lucian (cf. also Juvenal)—see Grimm-Thayer—and is the natural antithesis to Λιβυφοῖνιξ.

Φθινοπωρινός (Jude [12]: see J. B. Mayor's excursus, pp. 55 ff.) is a time-adjective (p. 358 below) from φθινόπωρον, which is a *double* cpd. of this class. **Ὀπώρα** = *late season* (ὥρα orig. =*spring*, but generalised): its first part is the ὀπ- of ὀψέ, ὀπίσω, ὄπισθεν, the association with which has ejected the φ that would be regular. In usage this season opened as early as July; and a new word was needed to describe the autumn proper. The adj. φθινάς and cpds. in φθινο- show that the present-stem *φθιν-* was accompanied by an adj. base (perhaps merely analogical) containing the *ν*. The season is therefore *ὀπώρα φθίνουσα* (like *μηνὸς φθίνοντος*, of the days following the 20th). So *ἰσημερία ἡ φθινοπωρινή* (Aristotle)=*the autumnal equinox*. *Pomifer autumnus* finds these trees *ἄκαρπα*.

Χαλκολίβανος, ἁ.λ. in Rev 1[15] and 2[18], is explained by Hort as " brass-like *λίβανος*," *i.e.* amber, and so " the glowing metal named from amber by this name as well as by *ἤλεκτρον*." If this view of the word be taken, it is a noun of the Descriptive class. See Hort's note, also Swete's *in loc.*

Ψευδής forms **ψευδάδελφος, ψευδαπόστολος, ψευδόμαρτυρ, ψευδοπροφήτης, ψευδόχριστος.**

Class (b). On the whole it seems best to transfer to the next class all the remaining nouns under this head, as being essentially adjectival. Thus **δίδραχμον** is (*an amount*) *of two drachmæ*; **διετές** is the neuter of an adj.=*lasting two years*; **ἡμίωρον** is (*a space*) *of half an hour*. The only exception then will be the *τετραάρχης* type described above.

Class (c). Descriptive compounds in which the first element is an adverb—a term which of course includes prepositions—need not be catalogued in full. The prepositional cpds. will be reserved for the next chapter, so that we may bring together all the combinations in which the several prepositions are concerned. First come the cpds. made with the negative prefix. In the great majority of cases this was from I.E. times *n̥*, the weak grade of *nĕ*, which in Greek became *ἀ-*, as **ἄ-γνω(σ)τος** =*i(n)-gnotus*, *unknown*; **ἄκων** (*ἀ-Fέκων*)=*un-willing*; or *ἀν-* before vowels, as **ἀν-άξιος**=*un-worthy*. That *nĕ* in the high grade could he compounded with nouns, adjectives and participles is proved by such formations as *ne-fas*, *nēmo* (*ne-hemo*), our *naught* (=*not one wight or whit*—see Skeat *E.D.*). Even verbs were once capable of taking this prefix: there is no essential difference between *ne-scio*, *nōlo* (*ne-volo*) and *οὐκ οἶδα*, *οὐ θέλω*, except that the former have become one word. A restriction of *n̥* to nouns, adjectives and participles had established itself in I.E. times; **ἀ-δύνατος**, *im-potens*, *un-witting*, are normal; but we do not find *ἀ-δύναμαι*, *im-possum*, or the like. In Greek this restriction excluded even participles when they still belonged to a verb system —*ἄκων* is found, but not *ἀδυνάμενος*.[1] (The verbal in *-τος* does not originally belong to the verb system proper: see *Prol.* 221 f.) One class of words still maintains (according to Brugmann *KVG* 310) the old *nĕ*, viz. words where there is *ă*, *ĕ*, *ŏ* in Anlaut, which sometimes took *nĕ* instead of *n̥*. Thus *νήκεστος* from *νε*+*ἀκεσ-* (*ἀκέομαι*) etc.: from these forms, with initial *νη-* (*νᾱ-*) as the result of contraction, came such words as *νή-πιος* (=*-πF-ιος*, cf. *νη-πύτιος*)[2] *unintelligent, infant*. This account is not wholly satisfactory as an explanation of the prefix *νᾱ-* or *νη-*, but no other is forthcoming that will do as well, unless we revert to the theory

[1] There are rare exceptions, like *ἀπιστεύσας* in P Oxy ii. 237 v.5 (A.D. 186).

[2] The old etym. *νη-*+*Fέπος word* is impossible, as an uncontracted form must have occurred in Homer.

of the long vowel *n* producing *νā*. Among the Cl. IV. cpds. with ἀ- we need only name one or two.

Ἄγνοια may be from ἀγνώς, if we may assume this to combine an earlier *ἀγνωός with the stem in -τ- (gen. ἀγνῶτος): **ἀγνοέω** presumes the same.

Ἀδημονέω is a problem imperfectly solved. T. W. Allen (*CR* xx. 5) takes it from ἀδήμων (Hippocrates, 1 cod.), the negative of a presumed δήμων *prudent*, traceable in proper names, as Dor. Δᾱ́μων, familiar in pastoral poetry. This he takes from δέδαε, that is √ δασ (perh. from *dems*—Skt. *daṁsiṣṭha*), *δάσμων becoming δάμων regularly. We might take the original meaning of ἀδήμων to be *bewildered*: cf. the association o ἀδημονῶν and ἀπορῶν in Plato (see LS).

Ἀόρατος, not ἀν-, because of the *F* in *F*οράω (cf. Eng. *ware*).

Ἄσωτος *not salvable, past saving, dissolute*: on this connotation of the -τος verbal see *Proleg*. 222.

Other cpds. may be taken as they come. **Ἀγανακτέω** is not completely explained, but it may possibly depend on an (unused) Descriptive *ἀγαν-άκτης *greatly angry*: ἄγαν is supposed to be a reduced form of μέγας (cf. *ingens*, both thus from *m̥gn̥t*), and the second element I should tentatively regard as an agent noun from √ αχ (ἄχομαι) *grieve*.

Διχοτόμος (whence **διχοτομέω** *cut in two*) is from δίχα *a-two*: its derivatives are from the active paroxytone, but the adj. appears earlier as διχότομος passive =" hewyne in to " (*Chevy Chase*).

Δυσ- cpds. are primitive: in Skt. we have not only the prefix *duṣ* but also the noun *doṣa, harm*. Cf. also Gothic prefix *tuz-*. Of doubtful history is **δύσκολος** (*morose*, in NT simply *difficult*). Osthoff (*IF* iv. 281), on βουκόλος, makes probable the existence of an I.E. √ *qel* (with pure velar) " to keep, tend," found with an extension in our *hold*. The synonymous *qᵘel* of Latin *colo* would serve equally well, since εὔκολος (with υ preceding the labiovelar—see Giles *Manual*² 132) would determine the form of its correlate (*δύσπολος otherwise). The meaning seen in *colo* (e.g. *patronum* or *deum*) would suit the Greek very well: δύσκολος would be one who ἄνθρωπον οὐκ ἐντρέπεται, so *disagreeable*.

Over against these δυσ- compounds stands the more numerous family of **εὖ**. This adverb performs the same function as the Skt. *su-*, but it does not seem possible to equate them. It is assigned by the best authorities (see Boisacq *Lex*. 298 f.) to a primitive *esu-s*, which makes Gaulish *Esogen(us)* (Welsh *Owen*[1])=Εὐγένιος. *Su-* appears in **ὑ-γιής**, from √ *gᵘi̯ē live*, whence ζῆν and βίος. (Cf. also the probably Iranian proper name which in O. Pers. would be *U-frāta*, **Εὐ-φράτης**, *qs*. *εὔπλητος well-filled.) **Εὐαγγέλιον** depends on the Descriptive εὐάγγελος *well-reporting, good-news-bringer*. Though its application to the news itself instead of the messenger's reward or the thanksgiving to the gods is not found in classical

[1] [Mr. E. E. Genner observes that Welsh *Owen* is commonly derived from *Eugenius* direct, as *Emrys*=*Ambrosius*, where an " Ancient British " etymology seems impossible.—Ed.]

Greek, the more general sense of this derivative is current in ordinary Hellenistic and may be independent: it may even be a Descriptive taken directly from *εὐ-αγγελία*, with the decl. changed. [**Εὐδοκία** seems to start from *εὐδοκέω*, which will be treated under Cl. VII.] *Εὐωχέω* (whence **συνευωχεῖσθαι**) may be classed here if it originates in a cpd. *εὔωχος* (not found): this would be from *εὖ+-οχος* (gradation of *ἔχω*), with the vowel lengthened in composition on analogy (cf. on *χορηγός*, p. 275)—the meaning would be *treating well*. Other cpds. of *εὖ* belonging to Cl. IV. are **εὐάρεστος** *well-pleasing*, **εὐγενής** *well-born* (or Cl. V. *having good* " *birth* "—see p. 287), **εὔθετος** *well-placed*, **εὐλαβής** *handling well, cautious, reverent*, **εὐμετάδοτος** *readily distributing*, **εὐπάρεδρος** *assiduous*, **εὐπειθής** *obedient*, *εὔπορος* *well-faring* (hence °**ρέω** and °**ρία**), **εὐσεβής** *pious*, **εὐχάριστος** *grateful*, **εὔχρηστος** *serviceable*. **Εὐποιΐα** need not imply a non-existent *εὔποιος* *well-doing*, but may be formed on analogy. *Εὐτράπελος* *versatile*, hence *witty* and (*in mal. part.*) *ribald* (whence °**λία**) comes from *τρέπω*: the adj. **τράπελος* is not found, but is guaranteed by its Latin equivalent *torculus* (*tr̥qᵘelos*)—both=*turning*, but they are applied in different ways (Brugmann *Gr.*[4] 231).

Εὐπερίστατος, ἁ.λ. in Heb 12[1], is a well-known crux. To the material given in Westcott's note need be added only the fact that in vernacular Greek (see Deissmann *BS* 150) *περίστασις* often means *distress, evil circumstances*: we sometimes use *circumstances* with the same suggestion. This is what Theophylact was thinking of in explaining *εὐπ.* " because of which one easily falls into distresses (*περιστάσεις*)." I do not quite understand Westcott's objection to Chrysostom's " what can easily suffer *περίστασις* i.e. *removal*." " The cpd. could not lose the -*ι*-: it must be formed from *στατός*." No doubt, but we should expect *περίστατος* and °*σις* to have kindred meanings. We are at liberty to give the verbal in -*τος* either active or passive force, the root being intransitive (*Proleg.* 221 f.). From the form it does not seem that there is any fatal objection to (1) *easily avoided*, (2) *admired* (lit. *well-surrounded*), (3) *easily surrounding, besetting*, or (4) *dangerous* (lit. *having easy distress*). This last (Theophylact's) implies that *τὸ περίστατον* got the sense of *περίστασις in malam partem*, so that the cpd. becomes a Possessive (based on Cl. IV.*a*).

Εὐθυδρόμος (whence °*έω*) may be put here as a cpd. of *εὐθύ*, *straight-running*. But as in other cases where an adj. seems used adverbially, we might get the same result by applying the Possessive, based on a Descriptive *straight run*.

Ἡμιθανής=*half dead*: we can hardly class this with the numeral cpds.

Μογίλαλος *speaking with difficulty*, and **παλιγγενεσία** *re-generation*, are both simple exx. of the present class.

Ταλαίπωρος has in the first place a form from the root of *τάλας* etc. which seems to recur in the Gothic *þulains, patience*: cf. *ταλαίφρων* beside *ταλάφρων*. The *πωρός* presumed for the second half—apparently the gradation of πηρός *disabled*—does not show itself outside the notes of ancient scholiasts and grammarians, who may be etymologising.

Τηλαυγής *far-shining* or *far-discerned*, according as αὐγή or αὐγάζω is to guide our interpretation of the second part.

Possessive. § 107. V. **Possessive** Compounds are called in Skt. *Bahu-vrīhi* (B.V.), a term which illustrates the class: as a K.D. it would mean "much rice," but it has developed instead the possessive sense, "having much rice." These cpds. can be based on any of the foregoing classes, a distinction being made in the earliest times by change of accent. Thus in Skt. *rāja-putrá* (Rajput)=*king's son*, a T.P. (Cl. III.); *rājá-putra*=*having a king for son*, a B.V. So in Greek θηρο-τρόφος=*feeding wild beasts* (Cl. III.), while θηρό-τροφος=*having wild beasts as food* (Cl. V.). Brugmann (*Grd.*[2] II. i. 75) shows that the accenting of the *first* element in a Possessive cpd. goes back to I.E. though comparatively few traces are left in Greek: this is a natural consequence of the Greek restriction of the accent to the last three syllables of a word, a restriction unknown to Skt. and to Germanic in its earliest stages. Brugmann, however, insists that the Possessive class is not to be regarded as secondary: it is as old as the other classes.

Based on Cl. I.—Possessives related to Cl. I. can hardly be illustrated from the NT, unless we treat νυχθήμερον as the adverbial acc. of an adj. =*including a day and a night*. Here as in many other Possessives the line separating this class from others is rather unreal.

On Cl. III.—Ἄγραυλος (whence °λέω) is perhaps best taken as=*with dwelling* (αὐλή) *in the fields*: it might, however, be Cl. IV.

Αὐτόχειρ is probably based on a Cl. III. noun *hand of himself*, hence *with his own hand*.

Cpds. ending in -ώδης (γραώδης *anile*, δαιμονιώδης *devilish*, θειώδης *of brimstone*, πετρώδης *rocky*) belong to this class if Wackernagel is right (see Giles *Manual*[2] 349) in comparing this suffix with that which meets us in εὐώδης (whence °δία) *fragrant*, from √ *od* of ὄζω, *oleo*, *odor*. Θειώδης thus=*having scent of brimstone*, and the suffix lost its special limitation through its likeness to the -ῴδης produced by contraction of -ο- with -ειδής (from εἶδος).[1]

On Cl. IV.—The great majority of Possessives in the NT are closely connected with the Descriptives, from which it is often impossible decisively to separate them.

[1] [See also p. 376 below, and Debrunner's note, *Wortb.* 195 n.[1].—Ed.]

To IV. (*a*) belong the following :—**Αἰσχροκερδής** *having base gain.* As in the case of *πλεονέκτης* above, there is a desiderative tone imported, for the word is normally *turpi-lucri-cupidus* (as Plautus renders it).

[**Αἰσχρολογία** is best taken from *αἰσχρολόγος*, which may be analysed *turpia loquens*, Cl. III., or *having foul speech*, Cl. V. So **ματαιολόγος** *idle talker*.]

Ἀλλογενής *of another γένος*, and **ἀλλόφυλος** *of another φυλή*.

Ἀριστόβουλος (pr. name)=*having excellent counsel.*

Βαρύτιμος=*having heavy price.*

*Βραδύπλοος may be assumed for **βραδυπλοέω** *having a slow voyage.* (Here as in other such cases we do not assume that the postulated word really existed : when an analogy was started, words would often skip a stage.)

Ἑτερόγλωσσος=*using a strange language.* [The other two cpds. of ἕτερος seem to belong to Cl. III., viz. *ἑτεροδιδάσκαλος* (whence °**λέω**) *teacher of strange things*, and *ἑτερόζυγος* (whence °**γέω**) *yoked to a stranger.*]

Ζώπυρον (whence °**ρέω**)[1] *spark*, or *bellows*, seems to be from *ζώς*, =*what has live fire* : hence the verb means *kindle to flame.*

Ἱεροπρεπής *having sacred seemliness, reverent*, might be Cl. III. (dat. dependence) *beseeming what is sacred.* **Μεγαλοπρεπής** *having great seemliness, majestic*, belongs here.

Κακοήθης (whence °**θεια**)=*having evil nature, malicious.*

Μακροχρόνιος *having long time*, has an additional adjective suffix -*ιος*—a superfluity not uncommon in these cpds., both in Greek and Skt.

Μετριοπαθής (whence °**θέω**) is the antithesis of *ἀπαθής*,=*μέτρια τὰ πάθη ἔχων*. So **ὁμοιοπαθής** *with like nature.*

Three cpds. of *ὀλίγος* come here, viz. **ὀλιγόπιστος** *Little-faith*, **ὀλιγόψυχος** *little-souled, Faint-heart*, and *ὀλίγωρος* (whence °**ρέω**, from *ὥρα*) *little-caring.*

Ὅλος forms **ὁλόκληρος** *having parts entire*, and **ὁλοτελής** *having entire completeness.* Like the last is **παντελής**.

From the base *ὁμό-* (whence *ὁμοῦ*, *ὅμοιος* etc.,=E. *same*—gradation form of *sem-* (*εἷς*) and *sm̥* (*ἅ-παξ* etc.)) come *ὁμόθυμος* (whence °**μαδόν**) *one-minded* ; *ὁμόλογος* (whence °**γέω**, °**γία**) *having one speech*, and so *agreed* (or *same-speaking*, Cl. III.) ; *ὅμορος* (whence **συνομορέω**) *having same boundary* ; **ὁμότεχνος** *having same trade* ; **ὁμόφρων** *of one mind.* With the last cf. **σώφρων** *having sound mind* and *ὑψηλόφρων* (whence °**φρονέω** (*high-minded*). We find in papyri *ὁμότυπος*, *having one impression*, i.e. *duplicate* copy.

Ὀρθόπους (whence °**ποδέω**) *having straight feet.*

Πάνοπλος (whence °**ία**) *having full armour.*

[**Παντοκράτωρ**, if it means *having all strength*, belongs here. But

[1] [*ἀναζωπυρέω* 2 Tim 1⁶. Simplex not in NT.—Ed.]

the termination is probably adjectival, a gradation variant of κρατερός, so that the cpd. goes into Cl. IV., *All-mighty.*]

Πιθανολόγος (whence °ία) *having persuasive speech*, has the same doubtful classification as the other -λογος cpds.

Πολλαπλασίων *having many folds, manifold*, has extra suffix -ιος, and the individualising -ων: its base πλατ is from *pl̥t*, whence our *fold*. Other cpds. of πολύς have the base πολυ-. So πολυλόγος (whence °ία) *much-speaking*; πολυμερής (adv. only) *having many parts*; πολυποίκιλος *having much varied*; πολύσπλαγχνος *having much compassion* (so εὔσπλαγχνος); πολυτελής *having great cost*, so πολύτιμος; πολύτροπος (adv. only) *having many ways*.

Πραϋπαθής (whence °θεια) *having gentle nature*: cf. the other cpds. of πάθος.

Ῥᾳδιουργός (whence °γημα and °γία)=*having easy* (and so *reckless*) *works*: it might equally well be Cl. III. *doing reckless things*, or Cl. IV. *reckless worker*.

Σκληροτράχηλος *stiff-necked* is like σκληροκαρδία (see above, p. 279).

Σκυθρωπός=*with gloomy face*.

Σῶς, from σάϝος (=*tvavos*, cf. Skt. *tuvi* "strong"), answers in meaning to *sanus*, "sturdy." It forms a good many proper names, as Σωσθένης from σθένος: Σώπατρος *having a healthy father* (or, *having his father safe*), will be a name given by the father because of auspicious omen for himself. Σώφρων=*healthy minded*: cf. other cpds. of φρήν above, p. 284.

Χρυσοδακτύλιος=*having gold* δακτύλιον (*ring* or *rings*).

Ψευδής or its root makes in this class ψευδολόγος *with false speech* (but cf. above) and ψευδώνυμος *with false name*.

To IV. (*b*) belong the following (as explained above):

One (1) *sm̥*, weak grade of *sem* (εἷς=*sems*, μία=*smia* etc.).

Ἀδελφός, like ἄλοχος etc., has lost its breathing: there was a powerful analogic influence in ἀ- privative, and probably also in ἀ- from *n̥*, the reduced form of the prep. *en*. It is *sm̥-gᵘelbhos* "having one womb."

[Ἀκέραιος has been plausibly explained as *sm̥-k̑erə-i̯os* "having one growth," differing only in gradation from Lat. *sin-cērus*. But the etymology has been disputed by such authorities as Brugmann and Osthoff: it may be safer (with Boisacq *Dict. Étym.* 35) to interpret *undamaged* (cf. κεραΐζω etc.), or again *unmixed* (κεράννυμι).]

Ἀκόλουθος (whence °έω) is *sm̥*+κέλευθος *path*, so *having one way, on the same way*.

Ἅπας, Skt. *çaçvant* (=*sa-çvant* by assimilation), is a stronger form of πᾶς.

Ἁπλοῦς (cf. διπλοῦς, Lat. *duplus*, Ger. *Zweifel* ("*double* mind," doubt)) has a somewhat doubtful second element (see Hirt *Gram.* § 372). Perhaps the element *plo* (seen in Latin) is increased by different suffixes, -*vo*- in Gk. -πλόϝος, -*to*- or -*tio*- in Greek -πλάτιος (διπλάσιος, πολλαπλασίων) and Gothic *ainfalþs* (our -*fold*), -*k*- in Lat. *simplex*. A further element is seen in ἅπαξ, presumably a case (which, is not certain) of a cpd. = *having one thrust* (πήγνυμι *fix*): cf. Ger. *einfach*.[1]

(2) Μόνος gives us μονόφθαλμος *with one eye*. Μονογενής (see above) might also be classed as meaning *of single birth*.

Two takes in Greek cpds. the form δι- (=δϝι-, formed in prehistoric times on analogy of *tri-*; cf. Lat. *bi-* = *dui-*, etc.). So δί-δυμος *twin* (cf. ἀμφί-δυμος *entered on both sides*, νήδυμος *enfolding* (sleep): the root is that of δύω—see Brugmann in *IF* xi. 283,[2] and below, p. 305, on ἐνδύνω)—δίδραχμος *of two drachmae* (see p. 280), διετής *of two years* (*ib.*), διθαλάσσιος (with added suffix) *with two seas*, δίλογος *double-tongued*, διπλοῦς *double* (see above), δίστομος *two-edged* (στόμα as in Heb 11[34] *al.*), δίψυχος *with two selves*.

Three is τρι-, in τρίβολος (*three-pointed*, so as a noun) *caltrop*, τρίκλινος (whence ἀρχιτρ.) (a room) *with three couches*, τρίμηνος *three months long*, τρίστεγος *with three storeys*, or *belonging to the third storey* (a noun in Ac 20[9]).

Four occurs in its most reduced form (q^u*tvr̥*, πτρα-) in τράπεζα *four-footed* (table). Less primitive cpds. show τετρα- (q^u*etvr̥*, cf. Gothic *fidur-*): so τετράγωνος *four-cornered*, τετράμηνος *four months long*, τετραπλοῦς *fourfold* (see above), τετράπους *four-footed*. A curious analogy-product results from this last: the association of domestic animals and slaves in the household gave birth to ἀνδράποδα to stand by τετράποδα—in such a sense the word was first wanted in the collective plural: cf. the 3rd decl. dat. ἀνδραπόδεσσι in its earliest occurrence, *Iliad* vii. 475. (Hence ἀνδραποδίζω "to kidnap," and noun ἀνδραποδιστής.)

Eight from Hesiod down makes cpds. in ὀκτα- (cf. πεντα-, ἑξα-, following ἑπτά etc.). So the NT ἁ.λ. ὀκτα-ήμερος (Ph 3[5]) *on the eighth day, eight days old*.

Ten appears in Δεκάπολις (sc. χώρα) *having ten cities*:[3] cf. Ἑπτακωμία, a district named in a i/B.C. papyrus (*Archiv* v. 38).

Twelve makes δωδεκάφυλος *having twelve tribes*.

Forty, like 2 and 100, forms a cpd. with ϝέτος *year*, τεσσαρακονταετής *forty years old*.

Hundred, besides ἑκατονταετής, makes ἑκατονταπλασίων *hundredfold*. The base follows τριάκοντα etc.

To IV. (*c*) belong many cpds. with ἀ- privative, of which only a few need be named.

Ἄβυσσος (βυσσός *bottom*, cf. βυθός), sc. χώρα, *the bottomless* place.

---

[1] Brugmann (*IF* xi. 283) thinks πλόος *voyage* was used in a metaphor—like ὁ δεύτερος πλοῦς "a second string to my bow"—and then extended when its meaning was forgotten.

[2] Brugmann thinks the meaning was obscured in prehistoric times, like that of ἁπλοῦς. May not the connexion he himself makes with νηδύς *womb* have helped the specialising of its meaning?

[3] Cf. for this ellipsis τὴν δεκάπληγον (sc. τιμωρίαν) P Par 574[3037].

Ἀγενής *having no "birth"* (in the conventional sense), so *ignoble*: opposite of **εὐγενής**.

[**Ἀκριβής** may be mentioned simply to say that its etymology is not known: for some guesses see Boisacq.]

Ἀληθής from √ of λήθω, λανθάνω, *having no mistake, true.*

Ἄνους *mindless* (whence **ἄνοια**): cf. εὔνους etc.

Ἀνωφελής *profitless*, from ὄφελος: for the lengthening of the ο, cf. Boisacq, 732.

Ἀπρόσκοπος *without* προσκοπή, is either active *not causing to stumble*, or passive *not stumbling, void of offence.*

Ἀργός, originally ἀϝεργός, =*without work.*

[Ἀσελγής (whence **ἀσέλγεια**) is of unknown origin. The popular etymology connecting it with θέλγω is probably responsible for the spelling ἀθελγία in BGU iv. 1024[v. 17] (iv/v A.D.).]

Ἄστοχος (whence °**έω**) *having no aim.*

Ἀσχήμων, from σχῆμα with its final *-m̥n̥* replaced by the long grade *-mōn*, =*without* due *form, unseemly.*

Ἄτοπος *having no place, strange*: in Hellenistic developed into *wrong.*

Ἀφελής (whence °**λότης** *simplicity*) seems rightly connected with φελλίς, φέλλια (pl.)—the form is imperfectly preserved—=*stony ground*: ἀφελής appears in Aristophanes as an epithet of a *smooth* plain.

Ἀχρεῖος (the derivative **ἀχρειόω** drops ι in NT) is formed from χρή, a primitive noun=*use*, with suffix -ιος: cf. Ion. ἀχρήϊος.

One word needs adding that is formed with *nĕ*, viz. **νῆστις** *having no eating* (*ἔστις from √ *ed*), *hungry.*

Passing from the negative words, we come to miscellaneous items.

Δυσ- forms δυσέντερος (which may be assumed as base of °ρία, °ριον), *having the* ἔντερα *wrong*: the word is late, and was very likely remade. Also δύσφημος (see below).

Εὖ forms a good many, of which we can name without comment **εὐγενής** *well-born* (see on **ἀγενής**), **εὔθυμος** *good-tempered, cheerful*, **εὔκαιρος** *well-timed*, **εὔκοπος** *with easy labour, easy*, εὔνους (whence **εὔνοια, εὐνοέω**) *good-minded, friendly*, εὔοδος *with prosperous path* (whence °**δόω** *make prosperous*), εὐπρόσωπος (whence °**πέω**) *with fair show, specious*, **εὔσημος** *having easy signification, intelligible*, **εὔσπλαγχνος** *kind-tempered, compassionate*, **εὐσχήμων** *respectable* (see on ἀσχήμων above), **εὔτονος** (τείνω), *well-strung, vigorous*, εὔφρων (whence **εὐφραίνω** and **εὐφροσύνη**) *happy-minded, merry*, εὔψυχος (whence °**χέω**) *of good courage*), εὐώδης (whence °**δία**) *well-smelling.* **Εὔδιος** (fem. used as noun) contains the weak grade of Ζεύς (*di̯ēu̯s*, the personification of the bright sky)=*having fair sky.* **Εὔφημος** by etymology means *with good* φήμη, *with auspicious sound*, as opposed to δύσφημος (whence °**μία** and °**μέω**) *inauspicious.* The words were not without a wider use, and in 2 Co 6[8] presumably bear this: in Ph 4[8] a suggestion of the earlier association may well survive. **Εὐώνυμος** *well-named* is a conspicuous example of εὐφημισμός: the *left* hand, which in Greek augury was unlucky, was called ἀριστερά *better* or εὐώνυμος *lucky* in the hope that it might answer to its name.

Verbal.

§ 108. VI. A name for the next class is not easy to find: we may call it **Verbal,** *faute de mieux.* Its characteristic is that the determining element governs the other as a verb does. This does not prevent its having the characteristics of a noun or adjective. Since in Composition we deal mostly with stems that will serve Noun or Verb equally, the line is not easy to draw; and there is a whole class, the Determinatives with accus. dependence, which has been dealt with above, but must be noted as logically coming here.

(A) Verb Second.

The class is divided according as the verbal element stands first or second. *A.* Cpds. with verbal element in the second place include (1) a few in which a group of noun+governing verb has been contracted into a single word. Thus ζωγρέω starts from ζωὸν ἀγρεῖν "to take alive": the stem—*casus indefinitus* as Hirt describes it, since it will stand in any case relation or none—is substituted for the full word. As Hatzidakis suggests (*Einl.* 227),[1] we have a trace of this mode of word-formation when a second element with verbal function is reduplicated for the perfect, without regard to its history: ἱπποτετρόφηκεν occurs in Lycurgus (iv/B.C.), though τροφέω does not exist, and if it did would govern an accus. This class of course is only treated here because we must register exceptions to the general rule that cpd. verbs, if not formed by joining a "proper" preposition to an existing verb, can only come into being through a cpd. noun or adjective.

It is likely enough that there are some other exceptions not provided for in our general theory. Thus such a word as ἀποκεφαλίζω, used in secular Hellenistic (Philodemus, Arrian), but not found earlier than in LXX, may be got from a presumed *ἀποκέφαλος *having the head off.* But the analogy of our own *behead* (*by*+*head*) suggests the probability of a direct coinage without this intermediary: the preposition then plays

[1] [Hatzidakis cites "Lykurg. 139 nach allen Codicibus." Mr. E. E. Genner, who points out that the latest Teubner emends it to the correct form, contests the attribution to Lyc. himself.—Ed.]

the part of a verb (cf. ἄνα *up!*), and the cpd. gains resemblance to those in Class B below. (See, further, § 109.)

(2) The bulk of the cpds. in this division are the Cl. III. words in which the second element has a strongly verbal force—such as φωσ-φόρος, *Luci-fer, light-bringer.* This noun is in fact an agent noun, or sometimes an action noun, as we have *day-spring.* It is largely a matter of indifference whether we do or do not transfer here a considerable number of the Cl. III. words, and not only those with accus. dependence. *Cave-dwelling* and *cave-inhabiting* cannot be classed apart, though *cave* in the first represents a locative and in the second an accusative. Brugmann notes (*Grd.*[2] II. i. 63) that *agri-cola* may be taken either as a Verbal cpd.=*agrum colens* or as a Determinative=*agri cultor.* It will not be necessary to deal further with this class, as the principle of it may be borne in mind while placing the Determinatives.

(B) Verb First.

B. Cpds. with the verbal element standing first. There are two formations of this order which come down from I.E. times, though they are not productive of new formations in Hellenistic. In (1) the verb stands in the same form as the imperative: thus Ἀρχέ-λαος *ruling the people*—the same sense can be obtained from a Cl. III. form, as πολιτ-άρχης. In (2) the form coincides with the stem of an action-noun in *-ti*, as μεμψί-μοιρος *complaining of one's lot.* These action-nouns supply infinitives in Vedic Skt., and in Latin they can govern an accus. (cf. *hanc tactio* in Plautus). Brugmann (*Grd.*[2] II. i. 64) regards them as infinitives with imperative function, so that both classes start from an exclamatory phrase. Such a noun as our *skinflint* could obviously arise from a sarcastic imperative turned into a nickname: cf. *lie-a-bed, cut-throat, knock-kneed* (with adj. suffix), *tumble-down, forget-me-not,* as varied exx. of the way such cpds. could originate.

The form of words in the first division has been largely affected by the strength of the tendency to make *o* the vowel at the juncture. This goes with the fact that some pure noun-stems acquire in composition a strongly verbal meaning. *Μῑσο-, νῑκο-, τῑμο-, φίλο-* are not verbal bases at all: the verbs connected with them are secondary derivatives. Strictly speaking, φιλάδελφος=*having a loved brother*, Cl. IV. This classification will not suit the other three bases named: it seems best to suppose that since φιλάδελφος so clearly meant φιλῶν ἀδελφόν (or -ούς), analogy formed μισάδελφος as its opposite, and so the type grew. So Aristophanes coined Βδελυκλέων to match his Φιλοκλέων. We will include words of these types with the rest which agree with them syntactically. In some words the elision of the vowel makes it doubtful whether we have the old type or the new.

(1) NT words of the first form are as follows:

Ἄγρυπνος (whence °νέω °νία) is supposed by Wackernagel to mean originally *sleeping in the field* (Cl. III.), like ἄγραυλος, ἄγροικος; but the meaning *sleepless* is established from the first, and the connexion is strained. I prefer to take a base ἀγρο- from the noun ἄγρα *chase*, and give it a verbal meaning, which may very well differ from that of the independent derivative verbs ἀγρεύω and ἀγρέω. *Chasing sleep* is sufficiently near to *chasing sleep away*.

Ἀρχέλαος has been already mentioned, the only NT word to preserve the primitive ἀρχε- form (ἀρχέκακος etc.). See above, p. 277, for this family. There are two words in which the first element is necessarily verbal, **ἀρχισυνάγωγος** and **ἀρχιτρίκλινος**: had these been formed in the earliest period, they would perhaps have had ἀρχε-.

Βερνίκη is a Macedonian name also found in the form Βερενίκη, answering to Greek Φερενίκη *carrying off the victory*.[1]

Ἐθελοθρησκία, the well-known crux in Col 2[23], may be paralleled with the conjectural **ἐθελοταπεινοφροσύνη** which Hort would restore in v.[18] for the almost unintelligible θέλων ἐν ταπεινοφροσύνῃ: Peake practically approves. If so, the ἐθελο- prefix tinges ταπεινοφροσύνη in v.[23] as well. Our *would-be* gives the sense adequately: Paul's meaning will be rather like that of Jas 1[26]. For other ἐθελο- cpds. see LS: note the survival of the older form with initial ε, not found in Hellenistic with the verb θέλω.

Μυωπάζω (2 Pet 1[9], practically ἁ.λ.) is formed from μύωψ (Aristotle—μυωπός in Xenophon)=*short-sighted*, *i.e.* one who *screws up* (μύει) *his eyes* to see. For the formation see J. B. Mayor *in loc.*

Νικᾱνωρ and **Νικόδημος** and **Νικόλαος** are names of almost the same signification, based on the verbal νῑκο-, *conquering*, on which see above. [**Νικόπολις** is better referred to Cl. III., *city of victory*.]

Πείθαρχος (Æsch., whence °χέω)=πειθόμενος ἀρχῇ, *obedient to command*: cf πειθάνωρ, where likewise the noun is in dat. dependence.

Τιμόθεος=τιμῶν Θεόν: on the τῑμο- prefix see above. The name is classical, like its correlative Θεότιμος (Cl. III.), which might also mean *God-honoured* (instr. dep.).

[1] The second ε was lost by "Kretschmer's Law"—see p. 64.

The large φιλο- class has been also dealt with: it forms an immense number of cpds. in later Greek, some 15 of which occur in NT (reckoning only words with different second element). [**Φιλόφρων** (also adverb) is the only clear Cl. IV. word, =*having friendly temper.*]

(2) From the second class we have but few:

Ἀλέξανδρος (pr. name) may be put here because of the antiquity of words like ἀλεξίκακος: either ἀλέκω or ἀλέξω (Skt. *rakṣ*) will account for the form, which=*defending men.*

Ἀνεξίκακος *forbearing evil*, from ἀνέχομαι, is formed in the same way.

Δεισιδαίμων shows stem assimilated as usual to sigmatic aorist: the root (*dṷei̯* to fear) has no -σις noun in Greek. *Fearing the* δαίμονες is the meaning: whether this comes nearer to *religious* or to *superstitious* is a question of usage.

Λύω gives us the only others (**μεμψίμοιρος** having been dealt with above). **Λυσανίας** (pr. name) from ἀνία=*destroying trouble.* Λυσιτελής (whence °**λέω**) *paying expenses*, and so *profitable.* The υ is long, so that we have another ex. of the assimilation to the aorist stem: in λύσις of course it is short. That new cpds. could be made in this class may be illustrated from the Alexandrian tribe Σωσικόσμιος (as in P Strass 52[2]–151 A.D.),[1] called after the Emperor (Hadrian ?) as *σωσίκοσμος=σώζων τὸν κόσμον. Schubart (*Archiv* v. 99 n.) mentions also two other tribes in Alexandria (both i/A.D.), Φυλαξιθαλάσσειος and Αὐξιμητόρειος, and (p. 101) Αὐξισπόρειος.

Based on Prepositional Phrases.

§ 109. VII. Last we may define a class of prepositional cpds. which have apparently been developed directly from a phrase: the exx. will be treated under the head of their respective prepositions in the next section. It is clear that we cannot force into previous classes such a word as **πρόσκαιρος** *temporary*, which is simply πρὸς καιρόν run into a single word and declined afresh. Often we have more complex suffixes added, as **καθημερινός** *daily*, from καθ' ἡμέραν, **ἐνύπνιον**=τὸ ἐν ὕπνῳ *dream.* Similarly we find verbs made in this way, as **κατακρημνίζειν**= *to cast* κατὰ κρημνοῦ—**ἀποκεφαλίζειν**=ἀπο(κόπτειν)τὴν κεφαλήν.

Closely akin to these are two formations in which the first part is an adjective, but the second part is dependent on it, instead of agreeing with it. **Μεσοποταμία** (properly an adj.) is ἡ ἐν μέσῳ τῶν ποταμῶν χώρα: cf *mediterraneus*, and our *midland*, if it means "what is in the midst of the land"—of course it might be "land which is in the midst." The ἴσος cpds. have a dative dependence: **ἰσάγγελος**=ἴσος ἀγγέλοις—

[1] [Cf. P Oxy iii. 513[48] (184 A.D.).—Ed.]

the only other two in the NT (**ἰσότιμος** and **ἰσόψυχος**) belong to Cl. IV.

Like ἰσάγγελος are ἰσοπλάτων (Anthology) *equal to Plato*, ἰσόνειρος (Aeschylus) *like a dream*, ἰσομάτωρ (Theocritus) *like one's mother*, ἰσολύμπιος (Philo) *like the Olympians*, ἰσοκιννάμωμος (Pliny) *like cinnamon*, ἰσόθεος (Homer down) *godlike*, ἰσοβασιλεύς (Plutarch) *equal to a king*, ἰσάδελφος (Euripides) *like a brother*, etc. The formation was still capable of being made afresh in Hellenistic, and if Lk 20[36] gives us a new coinage, it is so entirely according to analogy and the practice of other writers that we cannot treat it as the basis of any inference as to Luke's Greek.

Εὐδοκέω (and -ία) stands apart as a new verb made with an adverb. There is no reason why we should postulate an adj. *εὔδοκος*: the verb has probably come straight from *εὖ δοκεῖ* "it pleases me well," fused into a closer union by usage. Laws of speech were made for men, and not men for the laws.

PREPOSITIONS.

§ 110. The part played by Prepositions in Word-composition is of such peculiar importance that it will be well to make a separate section of it, gathering here all that must be said of their formation and history, and their functions in composition. Their use with nouns must be reserved for the Syntax under the Cases; and we shall also have to return under Verb-syntax to some of the phenomena of perfectivising (*Prol.* 111 f.). It will be convenient to anticipate the Syntax by indicating the cases with which the prepositions are found in the NT: the Gen. will have *, the Dat. †, the Accus. ‡.

It is usually assumed that Prepositions are simply Adverbs, separated from their class by special uses. Many of them are obviously specialised cases of nouns: some of the oldest, however, have no link with existing cases, unless it be the *casus indefinitivus* which is used in noun-composition. Delbrück's most important discussion, in his chapter on Prepositions in *Grd.* III. (i.), makes it clear that in their origin they were not Adverbs at all in the ordinary sense. Their oldest use was as *Praeverbia*, and their function as prepositions "governing" cases was derived from this, as was also their rare use as simple adverbs. If this is so—and the facts of Vedic Sanskrit and Homeric Greek unite with scattered indications from less primitive idioms to make it extremely probable—the old grammarians followed a right instinct when they classed Prepositions as "Proper" and "Improper." The latter are ethnic developments, not used in verb compounds, but only in the later function in association with nouns. There were even *praeverbia* which never became "prepositions" at all. These, as retaining only what we regard as the most primitive force, we may take as our first class, dealing next with the Prepositions, and finally with the "Improper" Prepositions, as latest in development.

In distinguishing below (*a*) *Composita* proper and (*b*) compound nouns—often only seen in verbs derived from them—we note Delbrück's argument that noun compounds began as mere adjuncts to Composita formed from the same verbal root. Even as late as Hellenistic this class is far more numerous than that which contains real nouns. Compounds belonging to Class VII. are apparently the earliest to arise. With these I have put the verbs of this class, as described above (p. 291). Miscellaneous derivatives go together in a class (*c*), where especially are found the compound prepositions (like our *be-neath*, Lat. *s-uper*=(*e*)*x-uper*, ἔναντι etc.): in many of these we cannot strictly use the term *compound*, as the word is only a stereotyped phrase, starting from separate words in syntactical relation. These are as old as Homer, *e.g.* μετέπειτα, and are greatly extended in Hellenistic.

I. PRAEVERBIA.

Praeverbia. § 111. Hardly any of this class leave any traces in Greek, except those (forming our next section) which developed the use with cases, whether or no this use was in existence in the proethnic period. Thus we have no trace of Skt. *sam* "together" (Av. *ham*, also in Lith.-Slav.), *ni* "down" (Av., and our *nether*, be*neath*: also cf. *ne*-st and Lat. *nīdus*=*ni*-zd-os), *vi* "apart" (Av., and Ger. *wider*), *ava* "off" (Av., Lat. *au*-, and Slav.), *ud* "out" (ὕβρις—cf. βρι-αρός, ὕστερος, *utter*), *ati* "beyond" (also prep. in Skt., and adverb in ἔτι, Lat. *et*). Only one of these is at all conspicuous in Greek, viz. ὠ-, Skt. *ā* (also preposition).[1] It is well seen in ὠκεανός Skt. *āçayāna* "surrounding," which seems

[1] Brugmann *Dem.* 142 sees it in Lat. *id-ō-neus*, Goth. *it-a*, also *þan-a* etc. (τόν + ὠ).

thus to be a participle of *ὤκειμαι "lie around." Ὠρύομαι (cf. Lat. *rūmor* etc.), ὠφελέω (? Skt. *phala* "fruit, profit"), ὀδύρομαι (whence ὀδυρμός) and ὀκέλλω (ἐποκέλλω late MSS in Ac 27[41]), compared with their simplicia δύρομαι and κέλλω, οἴγω (whence ἀνοίγω) from ὀϝείγω, ὀδύνη (perh. from δύη ?), ὀμείρομαι (?√ *smer* "to remember," "bethink"—Lat. *memor* etc.), ὄνειδος (?√ *neid, neit,* cf. Ger. *Neid,* O.E. *nīþ*). The shortened ὀ- may point to gradation: cf. ἐ- against ἠ- (below). The general sense of the prefix seems to be directive. But the whole of this entry is decidedly charged with uncertainty. The compounds with other prepositions will be seen in III. below. A cognate preverb ἠ (cf. Lat. *ē*) may account for ἤ-θελον. (See p. 188.)

II. PREPOSITIONS.

Proper Prepositions.

§ 112. The Proper Prepositions are here discussed in their function as *praeverbia,* and in the probably derived use as forming noun compounds. The latter may be assumed to be of the IV.*c* class (p. 280 above) unless otherwise stated. Under each preposition (*a*) contains preverbial uses, (*b*) noun compounds, and both nouns and verbs of Cl. VII. (p. 291), while (*c*) contains adverbial compounds or phrases that have become stereotyped as single words.

Ἀμφί

1. Ἀμφί *on both sides,* obsolete in Hellenistic as a preposition.[1] Latin *ambi-,* OHG *umbi* (Ger. *um*), Skt. *abhítas* "on both sides," make its meaning clear, as does its connexion with ἄμφω *ambo.* Brugmann (*KVG* 468) regards it as a compound, the second part of which is compared with Eng. *by* (Ger. *bei*), and Skt. *abhi,* Av. *aiwi.*

(*a*) Ἀμφιβάλλω in NT is the verb of ἀμφίβληστρον, but in its oldest use was especially applied to putting on clothes: the dual idea suggested to us by the symmetrical shape of our garments applied less obviously in ancient times. The only other verb compound in NT is that for clothing, in its literary form ἀμφιέννυμι (Mt 6[30]) and vernacular ἀμφιάζω (Lk 12[28]).

(*b*) The original dual meaning survives in the place-name Ἀμφίπολις *on-both-sides-*(the-river)*-town.* In ἀμφίβληστρον the meaning *casting-net*

---

[1] It is a *dual* word, and disappears before περί for reasons explained in *Prol.* 57, 77–80.

is as old as Hesiod, and the separate manipulation of the net's two ends makes the ἀμφί appropriate. But ἄμφοδον (*a road round*) is like most of the compounds not much concerned with duality.

'Ανά

§ 113. 2. ‡'Ανά *upwards*, as an independent word accented ἄνα (not in NT). It is found in Avestan *ana*, Gothic *ana*, Slav. *na*, where the original *up* is only partially visible: Lat. *an-helare* shows it well. *Over*, of space covered, *on* (as in the English cognate), and *up to*, of a goal attained, are developments reached in other languages than Greek. See Delbrück *Grd.* III. (i.) 734.

(*a*) 71 composita are found in NT. Of these 13 show the local force *up* only: ἀναβαίνω *go up*, ἀναζώννυμι *gird up*, ἀνακράζω, ἀναφωνέω and ἀναστενάζω *cry* (*groan*) *up* (*i.e.* the sound is fetched *up* by a deep respiration), ἀναπληρόω *fill up*, ἀνέχομαι *hold oneself up, endure* etc. In 26 ἀνά answers to Lat. *re*(*d*) in its rather different senses *again* and *back*. 'Αναζάω *live again, revive*, ἀναγεννάω *regenerate*, ἀνακαινίζω and -όω and ἀνανεόω *renew*, ἀνανήφω *become sober again*, ἀνοικοδομέω *rebuild* show the former: ἀνασταυρόω *crucify afresh*, which in classical Greek shows ἀνά=*up*, illustrates the close connexion of all these meanings. For *back* cf. ἀναχωρέω *retire*, ἀνίημι *relax*, ἀνακυλίω *roll back* etc. A few of these answer to the English prefix *un*- (Goth. *and*-, ἀντί), which reverses an action: ἀνακαλύπτω=*re-velo, un-cover*, ἀνακύπτω (*qs. un-stoop*) *lift oneself up*, ἀνασκευάζω (*qs. disfurnish*[1]) *unsettle*. In some verbs these various meanings of ἀνά exist side by side: thus ἀναπέμπω *send up* or *send back*, ἀνίστημι *raise up* or (*make stand again*) *restore to life*, ἀναβλέπω *look up* or *regain sight*. Naturally there are ambiguous cases: thus Delbrück (*Grd.* III. (i.) 738) makes ἀνέχω=hold *back, restrain*.

A difficulty is raised by ἀναγινώσκω, which in the Κοινή has always the peculiar Attic meaning *read* (generally *read aloud*). In Homer ἀναγνῶναι=*recognise*, and once or twice in Herodotus. But in the latter there is a transitive meaning *persuade*, found in pres. and 1st aorist. It looks as though a transitive force, *cause to understand*, came from the compound and developed independently in Attic and in Ionic: it may even be proethnic (not of course in the developed sense), since *anakunnan* in Gothic means *read*.[2] There are other verbs in which ἀνά either gives or preserves a causative force. 'Αναμιμνήσκω *remind* and ἀναφαίνω (nautical term) *sight* are transitive in the simplex; but not ἀναθάλλω

---

[1] [Mr. E. E. Genner questions the meaning "disfurnish," and observes that ἀνασκ. τὴν τράπεζαν in the Orators is just like our "reconstruct" a company (euphemism for bankruptcy).—Ed.]

[2] But only in 2 Co 1^{13} 3^2, where there is paronomasia with other cpds. of γινώσκω. Elsewhere ἀναγινώσκω is *ussiggua*. This rather weakens the inference.

make to bloom, revive, nor (practically) **ἀνατέλλω** *make to rise.* The antithesis of ἀνά has this causative force among its functions (see **κατά** below), and it seems possible that ἀνά may have developed it.

In a considerable number of ἀνά compounds we may recognise a distinctly perfective force. As was shown (*Prol.* 112) by evidence from English, perfective force may coexist with the local force of the preposition, there being always a more or less strong tendency to make compounds perfective. Ἀνά is not one of the more markedly perfective prefixes, but such compounds as *eat up, grow up, fill up, upset, done up* (ptc.) illustrate how naturally it may take this function. The following NT verbs may be classed under this heading:—**ἀναδείκνυμι** (*show up*), **ἀναδέχομαι** (cf. *taking up* an acquaintance); **ἀναδίδωμι** (*hand in* documents), **ἀνατίθεμαι** (sim.); **ἀναζητέω** (cf. our *hunt up* references), **ἀναθεωρέω, ἀνακρίνω, ἀνετάζω, ἀνευρίσκω**; **ἀναζωπυρέω** (*make burn up*), **ἀνάπτω**; **ἀναιρέω** (*take up, remove, destroy*), **ἀναλύω** (*break up*), **ἀναλίσκω** (probably=ἀνα-Ϝᾰλίσκω, so *take up, spend*); **ἀνακεφαλαιόω** (*sum up*); **ἀναμένω** (cf. *stay up for*); **ἀναπείθω** (*seduce*—the perfective suggests success: cf. *Prol. l.c.*), **ἀνασείω** (*shake up*); **ἀνοίγω** (our *open* is akin to *up*); **ἀνατρέφω** (*bring up*); **ἀνήκω** (*come up, arrive,* hence *belong, befit*).

(*b*) Many of the nouns simply attach themselves to the verbs described above. For the local meaning add **ἀνάγαιον** *upper room,* perhaps formed by antithesis from κατάγαιον [1] *cellar*; the doublets **ἀνάθεμα** and **ἀνάθημα**, votive offerings hung up on a temple wall; **ἀνάπειρος** (cl. ἀνάπηρος), i.e. *maimed* all the way *up*; ἀνάστατος (whence the vernacular verb **ἀναστατόω** *upset*), with the suggestion of ἄνω κάτω *upside-down* in it.

Ἀναλογία is of a different formation, coming from the phrase ἀνὰ λόγον *proportionately*: it belongs to Cl. VII.

(*c*) On **ἄνω** see § 130 *s.v.* ἔξω: hence **ἄνωθεν, ἀνώτερος, ἀνωτερικός** and **ὑπεράνω** (an impr. prep.).

Ἀντί § 114. 3. ***Ἀντί** *in front, opposite,* is found in most of the I.E. dialects: Skt. *ánti* "over against, near (adv.)," Lat. *ante* "before," Goth. *and* "along, on," Lith. *añt* "on, to." Cf. also ἄντα, Goth. *anda-* (as *anda-bauhts*=**ἀντίλυτρον**). The local meaning which (with the consequent temporal) occupied the whole field in Latin appears in some Greek dialects.[2] Thus Cretan ἀντὶ μαιτύρων "*before* witnesses." It survives freely in composition. We may note the verb ἀντάω (whence **ἀπαντάω** etc.) as formed from ἄντα: cf. our verb *to face,* also there is the adj. ἀντίος (Homeric), whence **ἐναντίος, ὑπεναντίος.**

[1] Class. ἀνώγαιον is not quite clear (see pp. 70, 76).

[2] And even (very rarely) in Hellenistic.

(*a*) *Opposite* is the obvious starting-point in all the 20 composita of the NT. Ἀντιπαρέρχομαι *pass by on the other side* shows it in the simplest form. Ἀνθίσταμαι (Lat. *antisto* "excel," Goth. *andstandan* "oppose") develops "oppositeness" into "opposition": so ἀνταγωνίζομαι, ἀντιλέγω (ἀντεῖπον), ἀντιδιατίθεμαι, ἀντικαθίστημι, ἀντίκειμαι, ἀντιπίπτω, ἀντιστρατεύομαι, ἀντιτάσσομαι. *Reciprocal* action appears in ἀνταναπληρόω, ἀνταποδίδωμι, ἀνταποκρίνομαι, ἀντιβάλλω, ἀντικαλέω, ἀντιλοιδορέω, ἀντιμετρέομαι: in classical and Κοινή Greek the same sense attaches to ἀνθομολογέομαι, but in its NT occurrence, as in LXX, this is modified by the context—thanksgiving *in return for* benefits. Ἀντέχομαι and ἀντιλαμβάνομαι go together: perhaps the local force survives, to express grasping while squarely facing the object.

(*b*) Putting aside, as before, the nouns that answer to verbs given above, there are not many left. The original local force appears in *ἀντόφθαλμος* (only Hesych.) which may perhaps be presumed for ἀντοφθαλμέω: it might, however, be a Cl. VII. verb from *ἀντ' ὀφθαλμῶν.*[1] *Opposition* appears in ἀναντίρητος, ἀντίδικος, ἀντίθεσις; *reciprocity* in ἀντάλλαγμα, ἀντίλυτρον, ἀντιμισθία, where is implied the *equivalence* of the object to that against which it is set. Equivalence in a different way is implied in ἀντίτυπος, ἀνθύπατος (=*pro consule*), ἀντίχριστος, which last is not "an opponent of Christ" but "one who assumes the guise of Christ" in order to seduce His people, just as ἀνθύπατος is "one who holds the power of a consul." The proper name Ἀντίπατρος, Ἀντίπας should probably be classed here: cf. Ἄντανδρος in BGU iv. 1134[6] (B.C. 10).

(*c*) The only adverbial derivatives of *ἀντί* appear in the list of Improper Preps.

Ἀπό

§ 115. 4. *Ἀπό, *off, away*: as an independent word accented ἄπο (not in NT). Skt. *ápa*, Av. *pa*, Lat. *ab* (cf. *a*perio) and *po* (in *po*-situs al.), Goth. *af* etc.: cf. also the adverbs ἄψ *abs* (for the -s see pp. 164, 329). The meaning is practically the same all over the field, all the uses of the word starting from the notion of *separation.*

(*a*) 90 composita occur in NT, in about 40 of which the local force described above is clearly visible (with perfective force in some). Some of them are proethnic: thus ἀποτίθημι, ἄπειμι (*abeo*), ἀποβαίνω, ἀφίστημι, ἀπάγω may be recognised in at least two other. I.E. languages. The common meaning *off* or *away* produces different *nuances* according to the meaning of the verb root. Sometimes the starting-point is the subject, sometimes the object: ἀπαγγέλλω *bring news* (*from*) starts at one

[1] For this use is not unknown in Hellenistic, where the verb arose: see *ἀντί* in the Syntax. But the other is perhaps more likely, as in compounds this local sense is obviously active.

end, ἀποδέχομαι *welcome* and ἀπεκδέχομαι *wait for* (see ἐκ) at the other. Ἀπεῖπον=*renounce* (cf. Goth. *afaikan* and *afqiþan*, both translating ἀπαρνεῖσθαι). In ἀποβλέπω and ἀφοράω looking *away* to an object suggests concentration: we might as well class them as perfective. Ἀποθησαυρίζω *store away* has likewise practically perfective force, and so ἀπολούομαι and ἀπονίπτομαι *wash away*, ἀπομάσσομαι *wipe off*, ἀφίημι and ἀπολύω *release, dismiss*, ἀποφεύγω *flee away, escape* (φεύγω=*flee*), ἀφορίζω and ἀποδιορίζω *separate off*, ἀφυπνόω *fall off to sleep*. Ἀπό is, as we saw in *Prol.* 112 ff., one of the most conspicuous of perfectivising prefixes: quite one-third of the NT composita have perfective force more or less clearly recognisable. It will be well to continue the list, premising that the similar use of the cognate *off* enables us generally to translate literally:—ἀπάγχομαι and ἀποπνίγω (cf. choke *off*, and ἔπνιγεν simplex in Mt 18²⁸), ἀπαλλάσσω (starting from the idea of a *complete* change[1]), ἀπαλλοτριόω (cf. *abalienare*), ἀπαντάω and ἀφικνέομαι,[2] ἀπαρνέομαι (cf. *abnego*), ἀπεκδύομαι, ἀπέχω (as used in receipts[3]), ἀπογράφομαι (? write oneself or one's family *off*), ἀποδείκνυμι (cf. show *off*), ἀποθλίβω (unless comparable with ἀποδέχομαι above), ἀποθνήσκω and ἀπόλλυμι and ἀποκτείνω, ἀποκλείω (shut *off*), ἀποκυέω (contr. κυέω=*be pregnant*), ἀπορφανίζω and ἀποστερέω, ἀποστυγέω, ἀποτελέω, ἀποτολμάω (carry daring *to its limit*), ἀφομοιόω (finish *off* the likeness). In ἀφυστερέω the perfectivising preposition apparently produces transitive force. There remain two other developments of the local ἀπό. In several verbs we render *back*. Ἀπαιτέω is to *demand back* one's own, ἀποδίδωμι to *give back* what belongs to another, ἀπολαμβάνω to *receive back*, ἀποτίνω to *pay back*, ἀπονέμω to *dispense back, assign*, so also ἀποκαθιστάνω to *establish back, restore*, ἀποκρίνομαι to *decide for oneself back, reply*, ἀποκαταλλάσσω to *effect a thorough change* (perfective κατά) *back, reconcile*. In another class the ἀπό reverses the verb's action:—ἀπαλγέω *have pain off, be past feeling*, ἀπελπίζω *cease hoping*, ἀποδοκιμάζω *disapprove*, ἀποκαλύπτω *take off covering, unveil*, ἀποστεγάζω *unroof*, ἀποφορτίζομαι *unburden*, ἀποψύχω *cease breathing, faint*.

(*b*) Some twenty of the noun compounds of ἀπό go with verb compounds accounted for under (*a*). Among these ἄφιξις *departure* alone need be specially mentioned, as having a peculiar meaning, divergent from that of its verb ἀφικνοῦμαι *arrive*: see *Prol.* 26 n. The noun ἀπαύγασμα (Wis 7²⁶, Heb 1³) comes from ἀπαυγάζω, where we have to choose between ἀπό=*from, away* and ἀπό=*back*, between *radiance* and *reflexion*, sunlight and moonlight. Philo's usage is divided. The Greek Fathers are unanimous for *radiance*: see Westcott's citations *in loc.* The Biblical use—*effulgence*, φῶς ἐκ φωτός—seems to me fairly certain,

[1] Note the very common Hellenistic use of the pf. ptc. ἀπηλλαχώς=*dead*.

[2] Cf. *Prol.* 247 on the late development by which ἀπέρχομαι was similarly transferred to the goal.

[3] *Prol.* 247.

though the RV should have given a marginal alternative, as the question is exegetical rather than grammatical or lexical, and on the latter grounds the choice is quite open. Other words showing local ἀπό are **ἀποστασία** (cf. **ἀφίσταμαι**), **ἀποστάσιον** (cf. **ἀφίστημι** and see *Vocabulary s.v.*), **ἀποτομία** (from ἀπότομος=*ab*ruptus), **ἀφορμή** (what one starts *from*). A partitive sense is given by the prefix in **ἀπαρχή** (something to begin with taken *from* the whole). **Ἀπελεύθερος** *freedman* (**ἐλεύθερος**=*freeman*) connotes reparation from a former master: **ἀπολύτρωσις** *redemption* is parallel. Ἀπό is *back* in **ἀπολογέομαι** (like **ἀποκρίνομαι**), but there is a difficulty about the formation, as ἀπόλογος, from which it would seem to come, has not the meaning *defence* (an argument *back*). Our classing the word in (*a*) is forbidden not by the fact that λογέω does not figure in our dictionaries, which might be accidental: it does not seem that the word, even if it existed (which is very unlikely), gave birth to ἀπολογεῖσθαι as a genuine compound. Either (1) we must assume that ἀπόλογος once existed, probably as an adjective, and went out of use in this sense after producing **ἀπολογία** and **ἀπολογέομαι**—a fairly easy supposition. Or (2) we might suppose the verb formed directly from ἀπό and λόγος, just as ἀποδιδόναι λόγον might have been the correlative to αἰτεῖν λόγον (1 Pet 3^{15}): this would bring the word in line with **ἀποκεφαλίζω** and others below. It should be added that LS would take ἀπό as *away*, in the sense of repelling an accusation from oneself. **Ἀπαρτισμός** *completion* comes from the perfective verb ἀπαρτίζω, and **ἀπόχρησις** from ἀποχράομαι *use up*. **Ἀπελεγμός** *disrepute* is like ἀποδοκιμάζω; in **ἀπόλαυσις** from ἀπολαύω *enjoy* the prep. points to the source from which the enjoyment comes. Similarly **ἀποκαραδοκία** is parallel with **ἀποδέχομαι** (above): for the second element see above, p. 274.

(*c*) There are a few compounds that derive from a phrase (Cl. VII.). **Ἀποκεφαλίζειν** was explained above (p. 288). **Ἀπόδημος** (whence **ἀποδημέω**) is simply ἀπὸ δήμου. The formation was still capable of use for new words, as **ἀποσυνάγωγος**—much as we could coin verbs like *un-church* as the need arises. Ἄφεδρος, a Κοινή word found in LXX (whence **ἀφεδρών**) is from ἀφ' ἕδρας (LS *s.v.* ἕδρα iii.). A verb formed like ἀποκεφαλίζω is **ἀποστοματίζω**, which is in earlier Greek exactly like *extemporise*, even to the verbal suffix (*extempore* applied to speech is ἀπὸ στόματος).[1] In NT the meaning is factitive—to force to extemporise, to heckle.

Ἀπέναντι appears among the Improper Prepositions. **Ἀπάρτι**, or if preferred **ἀπ' ἄρτι** (WH)—the Greeks would hardly have recognised the difference—is no true compound, for ἀπό practically governs ἄρτι as a case (cf. ἀπὸ τότε). It is only named here to distinguish it from the classical ἀπαρτί *exactly* (glossed ἀπηρτισμένως, τελείως, ἀκριβῶς), or (as some said) *on the contrary*, which was a real compound, with different

[1] Thayer-Grimm is quite wrong in postulating στοματίζω, which neither does nor can exist.

accent. LS recognise the Hellenistic meaning in Aristophanes and Plato (Comicus), which is of course just the one kind of Attic wherein a Κοινή formation might be foreshadowed.[1] But see the discussion in Lobeck *Phryn.* 20 f.

Διά

§ 116. 5. *‡Διά *through*, orig. *between through*, is apparently cognate with Lat. *dis-* (Ger. *zer-*). This equation is simple and satisfactory, the only divergence being that Greek has added *-a* (*δισ-ά): Brugmann *KVG* 478 thinks the analogy of μετά has been working. The question is whether we may identify this *δισ(ά) with the δίς or δί- which comes from I.E. *du̯i*, our *twice* (cf. *between* for connexion of meaning). Greek would of course leave this quite open. But I.E. *du̯is* is *bis* in Latin and **twis-* in Gothic (Ger. *zwischen*). It is proposed to postulate I.E. doublets *du̯is* and *dis*, postconsonantal *u̯* disappearing under presumable *sandhi* conditions. See the evidence in Brugmann *Grd.*[2] I. 259, where the proof of a sound-change in proethnic I.E. is regarded as indecisive. There seems to me a balance of probability in favour of our regarding this dropping of *u* as proethnic rather than independent: perhaps in either case we may accept it for the several dialects, and so connect διά with the numeral *two*. Hirt *Gram.* 219 notes on διά, "es steht wohl für δ(ϝ)ισα." Outside Greek this adverb does not become a preposition.

Διά forms 79 composita in NT: it is noteworthy that 200 out of 343 occurrences of these are in the Lucan Books. The διά compounds offer rather special difficulties, from the fineness of the distinctions between the classes in which we may place them.[2] The survey of the whole field shows us that the etymological connexion with *two* justifies itself by usage. To represent it graphically, we have two points or areas (A) (B) set over against one another, and the preposition is concerned with their relations and the interval between them. *Per*, *trans* and *inter*, as well as *dis*, will describe different relations, while our own *through and through* (*per*) comes with equal naturalness: *per* covers the intervening space in passing from

[1] [The new LS remarks after the Hellen. citations, "This is not an Att. use, hence Pl. Com. I. 43 must be incorrectly interpr. by" *Anecdota Graeca* (ed. Bekker.) 79.—Ed.]

[2] Winer's monograph (part v. of his *De Verborum Compositorum in N.T. usu*, 1843) is still most valuable, though of course needing supplement now.

A to B, *trans* only considers the reaching of B from A, while *inter* stops on the road, and *dis* still more emphatically dwells on the interval as a gulf fixed between them. *Dis* accordingly coincides only with part of *διά*'s area, and does not so often include the perfectivising force which is conspicuous in *διά* compounds. This is well brought out by the opposite meaning of διαζώννυμαι (perfective) *gird right round* and *discingor* un*gird*: the sense of reversal can attach to *διά* (not in NT), as the equation *διαζεύγνυμαι*=*disiungor* will show. In the attempted classification below we have alternative possibilities presented to us in many cases. We can in some of these only come to a tentative choice, depending generally upon the relative antiquity of meanings attaching to the word in question, where a meaning appears to be derived from earlier developments of the word itself, rather than from independent application of varying uses of *διά* to the word with which it is compounded.

(*a*) We may take first composita in which *διά*=*per*. These are almost necessarily perfective, though the original force of the prefix is retained, for they describe the carrying of action *through* to a definite result. *Spatial διά* may be seen in διαβαίνω *et sim.* (five others), describing some sort of a journey to a goal. Διηγέομαι is the same used metaphorically; διασῴζω is to *bring safely through*, and διαφεύγω, διαφυλάσσω, διατηρέω are similar. Διανύω and διατελέω, διαπρίω (metaph.) and διορύσσω and διυλίζω, διαγγέλλω and διαφημίζω and διαγογγύζω, διακαθαίρω and διακαθαρίζω all show space traversed; διακούω, διαμένω, διατρίβω, διανυκτερεύω, with *temporal διά*, may be reinforced with διαγρηγορέω if it means *remain awake throughout* (but see below). Διαυγάζω (ultimately from αὐγή, the Hellenistic for *ἕως*) has probably local *διά*, of dawn breaking *through*: here Latin has *dis* (*di*lucesco). But it is obviously not far from διαβλέπω, which we might class as a pure perfective. *Temporal διά* more in the sense of *inter* is seen in διαγίνομαι *intervene* (of time) and διαλείπω (-λιμπάνω in Ac 8[24] D).

Trans will perhaps be the closest equivalent for *διά* in διαβάλλω=*tra*duco, *durch*ziehen, as it were to *toss across*: Winer compares *διασύρω* (*pull to pieces*) which would suggest *dis* also for *διαβάλλω*, *qs.* "throw to the winds." Winer compares διαχλευάζω *ver*spotten, which I would rather put below. Διερμηνεύω is *trans*late. *Through* has passed into *thoroughly* in the pure perfectives διαπραγματεύομαι (*Prol.* 118), διαφθείρω, διασείω (? *give a thorough shaking to*, hence *extort by intimidation*—Lat. *concutio*), διεγείρω, with which we might class διαγρηγορέω if taken as in RV *text* Lk 9[32] (with ingressive aorist). Διακατελέγχομαι (ἁ.λ. in Ac 18[28]) might be taken as a sort of double perfective, a combination of *διελέγχομαι* *confute* and *κατελέγχομαι* *convict*; but Blass is probably right in classing it with **διαλέγομαι** (see below). In **διακωλύω** Winer would make *διά* express "intercipiendi et arcendi notionem": he compares *ver*-hindern against hindern, and *διακλείειν* *inter*cludere. It is perfective in any case: Mt 3^{14} is "John was for stopping him altogether." **Διασαφέω** (common in earlier vernacular Κοινή) raises a difficulty in that *σαφέω* does not seem to have existed, though *ἀποσαφέω* is found, another perfective: it is likely that these two composita were formed at once from *σαφής* (cf. *σαφηνίζω*), the simplex being skipped. In that case we can enter it still as a proper compound verb, with perfective *διά*: we may compare our verb *clear up* from the Middle English adj. *clear* (nearly a century older than the verb *clear* in the *N.E.D.*). Next to these exx. of perfective *διά* we might put some in which the prefix may be rendered *thoroughly*, but there does not seem to be perfective force. **Διαβεβαιόομαι** *affirm strongly*, **διαμαρτύρομαι** *solemnly declare*, **διισχυρίζομαι** *confidently assert*, only differ from the simplicia by the equivalent of *σφόδρα*, no achieved result being implied. So **διαπονέομαι**, **διαπορέω**, **διαταράσσω** (*per*turbo).

There remain the compounds in which *διά*=*dis*, *between* or *to and fro*. The force of *dis* is easily recognised in **διαγινώσκω** and **διακρίνω** (where the middle *distinguish for oneself* naturally develops into *hesitate* by stressing the *dis*-), in **διαδίδωμι**, **διανέμω**, **διαιρέω**, **διαμερίζω**, **διαρρήσσω**, **διασπάω**, **διαχωρίζω**, **διαρπάζω**, **διασπείρω**, **διασκορπίζω**, most of which are perfectives. So also **διαφέρω**=*differo*, **διαστρέφω** *dis*tort, **διατίθεμαι** =*dispono*, **διαστέλλω**=*dis*crimina *facere* (whence to give *express* commands), **διατάσσω** (*sim.*), **διαλύω**=*dissolvo*, **διικνέομαι** penetrate *between*, **διίστημι** *put asunder* (**διαστῆναι** *intervene* or *depart*), **διανοίγω** (Winer compares with Ac 7^{56} Virgil's *video medium* discedere *caelum*). In **διενθυμέομαι** we think of "This way and that dividing the swift mind." **Διαχειρίζω** *administer* (possibly coloured by the common business phrase *διὰ χειρός*) seems to have been developed into a euphemism for *kill* (as our *settle* is sometimes, or *despatch*). In the rest the mutual relation of the A and the B is indicated by *mediating* *διά*, as we might call it: **διαλέγομαι**, **διαλαλέω**, **διαλογίζομαι**, **διερωτάω** recall the two parties in a conversation, **διανεύω** the same for a dumb show, **διαχλευάζω** perhaps is similarly conditioned by the flinging of ridicule at another party. So **διαλλάσσω** is to make a (favourable) change in people who are at variance (**διαμαχόμενοι**): *διαλύω* is similarly used in papyri; **διαδέχομαι** applies to one official who succeeds another.

(*b*) Some 20 noun compounds of *διά* are connected with verbs accounted for in (*a*), and the prefix is similarly explained. Sometimes, however, the noun happens to fall into a different class, attaching itself to a use of the verb which does not occur in NT. Thus **διαστολή** *difference* has the *dis* still very marked, which has become latent in **διαστέλλω**: the verb has the corresponding force in Polybius. **Διαταγή** has the *mediating* *διά*, not seen in the verb. In **διαυγής** *transparent* (cf. *διαφανής*—printed in Rev 21[21] TR without any authority) *διά* is much clearer than in **διαυγάζω.** **Διάλεκτος**=*ἡ διάλεκτος γλῶττα*, with verbal adj. in two terminations: *διά* expresses very well the language of ordinary *intercourse.*

Passing to nouns without congeners in (*a*), we must pause on the old crux **διᾱκονος** (°-*νέω*, °*νία*). It is curious that the latest scientific opinion has been swinging back to the recognition of this as a *διά* compound after all, with *ᾱ* (Ion. *διήκονος*) affected by **διηνεκής** (*q.v.*) and its class. (See Brugmann *ap.* Boisacq *s.v.*). In that case we can connect with the older word *ἐγκονέω* (Homer, in ptc.) and recognise a metaphor from the games (cf. *ἀκονιτί* etc.): the starting-point would be *ἐν κόνι* as an imperative, **διακονέω** (which would thus come before its noun) being like this a compound of Class VII. (above, p. 291). I set this down with some reserve. **Διηνεκής** may be taken next, as in any case containing *διά*=*per*. Thumb observes (*Dial.* 117) that the *η* is Doric as well as Hellenistic: Attic *διᾱνεκής* will thus (like *διᾱκονος*?) be due to the special Attic sound-law that made *η pure* into *ᾱ*.[1] Like *ποδηνεκής* *reaching to the feet*, *δουρηνεκής reaching a spear-throw*, this comes from √ *enek̑* which makes part of the system of *φρέω* (cf. the two roots combined in our *br-ing*). The *η* is from the rule that lengthened the vowel at the junction, in compounds whose second element had vowel *anlaut*. **Διάδημα** goes with **διαζώννυμαι**: the dual character of *διά* is dropped like that of *ἀμφί* in **ἀμφιέννυμι** (p. 294). **Διέξοδος** if taken according to RV will have *διά*=*dis*—the streets that come out of the town and fork there. See *Vocabulary s.v.* **Διόρθωμα** and °**σις** are from *διορθόω* to correct right *through* (constantly used of what we should call *proof-reading*). **Διατροφή** goes with the perfective verb *διατρέφω* (*per* temporal), but the perfective sense is hardly visible. On the other hand, **διαπαρατριβή** (ἁ.λ. in 1 Tim 6[5]) is a perfective from *παρατριβή collision* (Polybius), with temporal *per*. Finally comes **διανόημα** from *διανοέω*, like **διενθυμέομαι** above, and **διάνοια**: the formation of this last is probably influenced by **ἄνοια**, *δύσνοια*, **ἔννοια**, where there were adjectives with possessive force (*e.g.* *ἄνοος*) to start the abstract.

(*c*) **Διόπερ** and **διότι** are the only words in this class, and of course they are only conjunctions formed out of phrases—*δι' ὅπερ* and *δι' ὅτι*, *for which reason*—and not compounds at all. *Διότι* has come in Hellenistic to be often a mere synonym of *ὅτι that*, used by Polybius, for example, in order to escape hiatus: in NT=*because* or *for*.

[1] [See, however, the new LS *s.v.* Mr. E. E. Genner points out that the "Attic" form only occurs in the *Hippias Major* (twice on one page), where the MSS are not unanimous, whilst *διηνεκής* occurs in the *Laws*, where they are unanimous.—Ed.]

Εἰς

§ 117. 6. ‡Εἰς *into* is for ἐνς, which still survived in Cretan before vowels, its *sandhi*-form ἐς coming before consonants: in Hellenistic ἐς was obsolete, only appearing in NT in ἔσω and ἔσοπτρον. It should not be treated separately from ἐν, of which it is a variant found in Greek alone, being formed on the analogy of ἐξ for use with verbs of motion. Some dialects (Boeotian, Thessalian and N.W. Greek—see Thumb *Dial.* 55, 184) used only ἐν. Its compounds are naturally few by comparison, though they go back to Homer: *ineo* is more original than εἴσειμι, *infero* than εἰσφέρω.

(*a*) Ten εἰς composita are left in NT. *Going into* (*leap, run*) accounts for half of them. Εἰσάγω and εἰσφέρω *bring into*, εἰσκαλέομαι *invite into*, are all simple. In εἰσακούω alone has there been any obscuration: as early as Homer the εἰς developed the simplex *hear* into *attend to*. It is not unlike εἰσδέχομαι receive *into* (one's house), *welcome*. Nine of these verbs only occur 50 times in NT all told, and εἰσέρχομαι (191 times) is the only common one.

(*b*) Two compounds of εἰσάγω, ἐπεισαγωγή and παρείσακτος, give nothing to discuss under the εἰς heading. Εἴσοδος *incoming* (in various senses) is often in Hellenistic associated with ἔξοδος: the former goes back to Homer, the latter to Herodotus and Attic. Ἔσοπτρον, always so spelt, illustrates the fact that the *sandhi* distinction of εἰς and ἐς was lost early (from Pindar down) in this word: on √ ὀπ see *Prol.* 111, and on the suffix -τρον below, p. 369.

(*c*) Ἔσω (whence ἐσώτερος and ἔσωθεν) is dealt with below, p. 330.

Ἐν

§ 118. 7. †Ἐν *within* has been mentioned under εἰς. It is found with the same meaning in Lat. *in*, Goth. *in*, and in Keltic and Slavonic, etc. Greek has besides ἐνς (εἰς) the form ἐνί, but not (like Skt., Lat., Keltic and Germanic) the derivative *enter* (*n̥tér*). It is possible that the reduced form *n̥* (found in Lithuanian) may account for some compounds with initial ἀ-: thus ἀτενής (whence ἀτενίζω) suggests *intendo* more naturally than the prefix *sm̥* (ἀκολουθέω, etc.). See above, under ἀ-, p. 285. Ἐν is by far the commonest of prepositions in NT (*Prol.* 98), but in forming compounds falls behind ἀνά, which is nearly extinct as a preposition. This illustrates very well the independent development of the two uses of these adverbs which we call prepositions: the facts presented in this chapter make it easy to understand how prepositions which one language uses largely are only adverbs in another.

(*a*) Fifty-five composita occur in the NT, which seem about equally divided between the forces of εἰς and ἐν. It will not be necessary to mention many of them, as in most the choice between *into* (*on*) and *in* is easy, or may be left indeterminate. Those that need a note may be taken as we come to them. **Ἐγκαλέω** does not intrinsically differ from **εἰσκ.**; but one may "call in" a person for various purposes, and ἐγκ. was early specialised *in malam partem*, calling a man in to accuse him. In all languages doublets tend to be utilised for different meanings. So **ἐνδέχομαι**=*admit to oneself* (with **ἀνένδεκτος**): **εἰσδέχομαι** and **εἰσκαλέω**, as is natural in compounds of the more sharply defined εἰς, have meanings coming directly from their constituents without later development. **Ἐγκαταλείπω** will serve as a type of some others: **καταλείπω** *abandon* (perfective) is supplemented with ἐν, pointing to the plight *in* which the victim is left. **Ἐγκομβόομαι** is not a quite certain compound, as its simplex does not occur in extant literature: we depend on Suidas citing Epicharmus and a later comedian. It is presumably to *gird* something *on oneself*. **Ἐμβριμάομαι** seems to connote strong feeling *within oneself*. **Ἐμπαίζω**=*il*lūdo, **ἐμπίπλημι**=*im*pleo, **ἐμπλέκω**=*im*plico. **Ἐμπορεύομαι** is in form a compound, but according to its meaning has nothing to do with **πορεύομαι**: it would indeed be more correct to exclude it from the list of composita. Its meaning is entirely determined by **ἔμπορος** (see below), but had there been no *πορεύομαι*, the verb would more probably have been *ἐμπορέω*: on this ground we may keep it here. The same may perhaps be said of **ἐνδοξάζομαι**, which I suspect was partly influenced by **ἔνδοξος**—**δοξάζω** *extol* is common in Hellenistic but very rare in classical Greek. Probably both forces acted, for the compound is late: the ἐν has distinct force in one of its occurrences at least. **Ἐνορκίζω** likewise owes its ἐν not so much to significant composition (**ἐν** + **ὁρκίζω**) as to the association with *ἔνορκος* *iuratus* (*ἐν ὅρκῳ ὤν*, Cl. VII.). **Ἐνάρχομαι** is supposed by Lightfoot to retain a trace of its classical connotation, the initial act of a sacrifice. But in Polybius and LXX it is simply *begin* (*qs.* make a start *upon* an act), and it does not seem that the technical force survived. In its two Pauline occurrences, as in those of its cpd. **προεν.**, it is directly contrasted with **ἐπιτελεῖν** (perfective), which marks the last step as the other marks the first. **Ἐνδείκνυμαι** (cf. *indĭco*) suggests completer demonstration than the simplex—laying the "index" finger, as it were, *on* the object. With **ἐνδύνω** (*ἐνδύω* is not found in NT) we may couple **ἐνδιδύσκω**, an alternative present stem. The ἐν is simple, but the semasiology is hard. The meanings *clothe* and *sink* are not easy to correlate, and both of them are found in Skt., in separate roots which can equally well answer to the

Greek:[1] we may perhaps make *dū-ịó* aor. *édūm* (Skt. *upā-du*) the I.E word for *clothe*, and *dusnó* (cf. Skt. *doṣā* "in the evening") *sink down, set, penetrate*, whence **δυσ-μή**. The two must have been confused in Greek from the first. With **ἔνειμι** *insum* we join **ἔνι** (common in Hellenistic), which is simply the alternative form of *ἐν* with the substantive verb understood and meaning specialised.[2] **Ἐνέχω** has the *ἐν* rather obscured by development. When=*en*tangle, hold *in*, the prefix is clear (cf **ἔνοχος**): the three Biblical passages (so far unparalleled) for **ἐνέχω** c. dat.=*press on, set upon*, may be most simply explained by Hesychius' *ἔγκειται*, with intrans. use of *ἔχω* and *ἐν*=*against*—others assume an ellipse (*χόλον* or simply *νοῦν*). **Ἐνίστημι** (only intr. tenses) answers to *insto* (*ἐν* practically=*εἰς*). **Ἐγκαινίζω** *innouo* (P Par 16[24] (B.C. 127), as well as LXX). **Ἐγκόπτω** must be the opposite of **προκόπτω**, which is perhaps a metaphor from path-making, *cut* one's way *forward*: this will be *cut into* the path, *hinder*. **Ἐγκρίνω**=*judge* or *reckon among*. **Ἐνοχλέω** is probably *bring annoyance upon*. **Ἐντέλλομαι** is difficult, the relation between simplex and cpd. being far from clear: moreover, the associated nouns **ἔνταλμα** and **ἐντολή**, by their form clearly primitive, have no uncompounded form at all. Unless we make the influence of *ἐντέλλω* on them rather improbably strong, the root should be I.E. *tel*, not *q^uel*, from which other uses of *τέλλω* certainly come: can we compare *intuli*, and make **ἐντέλλομαι**=*bring one's influence to bear upon* a man? **Ἐντρέπομαι** is apparently *turn towards* (*in bonam partem*), so *regard*. **Ἐντυγχάνω** (whence in a special sense **ἔντευξις**) *fall in with, meet*.

(*b*) The main points requiring settlement under this heading concern the recognition of compounds belonging to Class VII. Nearly a score of nouns and adjectives attach themselves to verbs occurring in NT, and either explained above or omitted as self-evident. Nearly all the rest, however, will need some comment. **Ἐγκάθετος** (from *ἐγκαθίημι let down into*)=*suborned*. **Ἐγκρατής** (°**τεια** °**τεύομαι**)=*having strength within, self-controlled*.[3] **Ἔγκυος** (*κύος*) *having fœtus within*. **Ἐμβατεύω**,[4] which in the absence of any *βατεύω* must come in this class, raises some difficulty, in that *ἐμβάτης*, its presumed noun original, begins to appear in literature nearly a century later than the verb, and then in a sense which cannot help us. But *ἐπεμβάτης*, *mounted*, is classical, and so are *ἐπιβάτης* and *ἐπιβατεύω*, which between them probably formed **ἐμβατεύω** directly: the sense in Hellenistic is always *enter upon* (also class.), of

[1] Latin *ind-uo* and *ex-uo* can have no etymological connexion with *ἐνδύω*, for all the similarity of form and meaning. It is possible, however, that *induo* may be a conflation of *ind-euo* (*endo*, our *into*) and *in-duo*=*ἐνδύω*.

[2] Its development in mediæval Greek may be seen in Dieterich *Unters.* 225 ff. The MGr *εἶναι*=*ἐστί* is *ἔνι* with the vowels assimilated to those of *εἶμαι* and *εἶσαι* (*sum, es*).

[3] But its opposite **ἀκρατής** suggests the possibility of its being a Cl. VII. cpd.—see below.

[4] Very often *ἐμβαδεύω* in papyri: cf. Wilcken, *Ostr.* i. 190 f.

taking possession. (See also above, p. 273, on κενεμβατεύω.) **Ἐμφανής** (whence **°νίζω**) resembles ἐναργής, which differs from ἀργής apparently in the suggestion of *inherent* light that makes the compound more emphatic: the Greek sense of the word we have just used is another case in point—cf. ἔμφασις in LS *s.v.* III. **Ἐνδεής** *having want within* presumes (like ἐπιδευής, ὑποδεής) a neuter noun *δέϜος *want.* **Ἐνδώμησις** (so ℵ*A in Rev 21^{18}: see p. 73, and WH *App.*^{2} 159)[1] *building in*, from δωμάω (√*dem* with long grade). **Ἐνέδρα** (whence **°ρεύω**) *sitting within* (in hiding), exactly as the independent Lat. *insidiae.* **Ἔννοια** is apparently from ἔννους (see on **διάνοια** above) *having mind within, intelligent.* But as the opposite of ἄνους, we might as well put ἔννους below. **Ἐνταφιάζω** (whence **°σμος**) is from ἐντάφιος *funereal*, which is most naturally explained as an adj. from the root of ἐνθάπτω *bury in*: Class VII., however, (τὰ ἐντάφια *obsequies*=τὰ ἐν ταφῇ), is quite possible, though less probable. **Παρεμβολή** *army, camp*, or *barracks*, seems originally to have meant *troops drawn up for battle*, cf. **παρεμβάλλω**. This specialisation of meaning is said to have started in Macedonia. In Attic at any rate an entirely different use appears, *insertion*, depending on ἐν *in*, while the other is linked with ἐμβάλλω *attack* (ἐν=*against*).

(*c*) There is a considerable proportion of Class VII. compounds made with ἐν. Indeed, it is quite an open question whether a good many of the compounds classified above may not have originated rather like those to be described now. Compounds of ἐν are largely found as antithetic to those in ἀ- privative, which have the meaning *without* . . . (lit. *having no* . . .). So **ἄνομος** *without law* is opposed to **ἔννομος** *under law* in 1 Co 9^{21}, **ἄτιμος** *without honour* to **ἔνδοξος** *with glory* in 1 Co 4^{10} (**ἔντιμος** elsewhere). These must be interpreted as adjectives directly formed from ἐν νόμῳ, ἐν δόξῃ, ἐν τιμῇ. So **ἔμφοβος** (opp. **ἄφοβος**), **ἐνάλιος**, ἔνδημος (whence **°μέω**, opp. ἀπόδημος), **ἔνδικος** (opp. **ἄδικος**), **ἔννυχος** (only adv.—the χ for κτ=χτ represents a simpler form of the root), **ἔντρομος**, **ἐντόπιος** (with further suffix, like **ἐνάλιος**), and so **ἐνύπνιον** (ἐνύπνιος from ἔνυπνος). Some others need detailed treatment. **Ἔγγυος** goes with ἐγγύη *security*, which is probably from an old word for *hand* (cf. γύαλον, Lat. *vola*, Av. *gava-*), like ἀμφίγυος and ὑπόγυος, so=what is put in the hand. **Ἐγκακέω** is best taken as ἐν κακῷ εἰμί "in a bad way," ill, enfeebled: this depends mostly on a physical connotation of κακός, while **ἄκακος** depends on the moral, and so does ἐγκακέω itself in Polybius (iv. 19. 10). **Ἐγκρατής** (etc.—see under *b*) might be reckoned here because of its opposite **ἀκρατής** *without self-control.* Since κράτος suggests the possession of strength, as βία the using of it, ἐν κράτει (ὤν)=*self-controlled* involves only the specialising reference to *moral* κράτος. **Ἐλλογάω** (or **-έω**—see §§ 84–5)=ἐν λόγῳ τίθημι, according to the very common use of λόγος=*accounts*: so *imputo, put to the account of.* There is no connexion with ἔλλογος *rational*

[1] *Syll.* 583^{30} (=*Syll.*^{3} 996^{30}) (i/A.D. ?), *BCH* xvii. 78 (no. 1^{8}).

(cf. ἔννους), the opposite of ἄλογος, from ἐν λόγῳ in the other sense. Ἐναντίος (and ὑπεν.) is probably a cpd. of ἀντίος (p. 296). But while ἔναντι and such compounds (p. 329) are correlative adverbs whose contents are added together ("within opposite," etc.), the similar-seeming adj. must be explained differently, though in this case the closely parallel compounds affected one another. Ἐναντίος = ἐν ἀντίῳ (ὤν). For the relations of this group see Wackernagel *Hellenistica* pp. 1 ff. Ἐνθυμέομαι (-ησις) comes directly from ἐν θυμῷ (ἔχω): the negative ἄθυμος (whence °μέω) starts from a different association of θυμός, with εὔθυμος as antithesis. Ἐνεργός (whence °γέω and its derivative °γημα) appears to be from ἐν ἔργῳ *active*, or *productive*, as opposite of ἀργός *inactive* or *barren*. The formation of its later equivalent ἐνεργής is not perfectly clear: the derivative ἐνέργεια speaks for an original *-es-* stem, but its record is not good enough to claim antiquity. Has it been formally assimilated to its like-sounding adj. ἐναργής *clear*? On the whole group see J. A. Robinson's important excursus, *Ephes.* pp. 241–7. Ἐνιαυτός *year*, originally *anniversary*, is taken by Prellwitz as starting from ἐνὶ αὐτῷ (sc. I suppose ἤματι, "on the same day"). But see Brugmann *Gr.*[4] 195 n.[1], and below, p. 372. Ἐνωτίζομαι = ἐν ὠτὶ (ἔχω) is formed directly, in complete independence of ἐνώτιον *earring* (Attic ἐνῴδιον—Meisterhans[3] 79).

Apart from the cpds. named in § 130, the following adverbs are connected with ἐν. Ἐνθάδε *here* or *hither* (the two being confused in Hellenistic) is from ἔνθα, with suffix -θα, which may be compared with Skt. *kúha* (*where?*), *ihá* (*here*): Brugmann *KVG* 455 gives this doubtfully, and (*ib.* 456) denies the equation ἔνθα = *inde* (as far as the *in-* goes). The suffix -δε = Eng. *to* in origin and meaning. Ἔνθεν has the ablative suffix -θεν. Ἐντεῦθεν has suffered a shifting of aspiration in Attic: Ionic ἐνθεῦτεν is original. Brugmann *Demonstr.* 104 n. shows how the flexion of οὗτος produced a whole series by analogy—ἐνθεῦτεν came from ἔνθεν as τηλικαῦτα from ταῦτα etc.

Ἐξ

§ 119. 8. *Ἐξ, ἐκ, *out*. The primitive form was *eĝhs*, as Brugmann (*KVG* 179) shows from Locrian ἐχθός (Att. ἐκτός by anal. of ἐντός) and ἔσχατος (from *eĝhs-qo-* becoming *eĝsgho-*): the by-form ἐκ (also ἐγ) is due to the dropping of σ between two mutes (see Brugmann *Gr.*[4] 148 f.). Latin and Gaulish *ex* are among the cognates, which confirm the meaning given: in the Keltic branch *ex* (Ir. *ess*) is only used in compounds, which illustrates its large proverbial use in Greek.

(*a*) Ninety-four composita with ἐξ are found in NT. We can recognise *out* in about fifty of them very clearly, and in many more with an easy adaptation: naturally the prefix has, like its English equivalent, a considerable range of meaning. In cpds. where the local force is marked, there is nearly always perfective action: indeed, it is only when *out* is weakened, and *from, forth* or *off* gives the sense, that we have exceptions. Thus ἐκκρέμομαι *hang from,* i.e. *upon*: ἐκτείνω *stretch out* and ἐκπετάννυμι *spread out* are the nearest NT exx. to go with it, but even here ἐκ shows the action of the verb carried as far as it will go, so that we may class both verbs as perfective. The simplest local sense is seen (as with ἀπό etc.) in verbs of *going*—ἔξειμι and ἐξέρχομαι, ἐκβαίνω, ἐκπορεύομαι etc., or allied conceptions, as ἐκπέμπω, ἐκβάλλω, ἐκκολυμβάω, ἐκκομίζομαι, ἐκπηδάω and ἐξάλλομαι, ἐκπλέω, ἐκσῴζω (Ac 27[39]), ἐκτινάσσω, ἐκφεύγω, ἐξανίστημι and ἐξεγείρω, ἐξαιρέω, ἐκκλάω, ἐκκόπτω, ἐξορύσσω, ἐκχέω (-χύννω), ἐξωθέω etc., involving removal *out of* one place into another. Local force of slightly varying kinds (literal or metaphorical) is seen in ἐξαγγέλλω and ἐξομολογέω; ἐκλαλέω let *out,* divulge; ἐκνήφω of sobriety attained *out of* drunkenness; ἐκπνέω and ἐκψύχω (strongly perfective); ἐξαιτέομαι *beg surrender of* (removal *from* present position), ἐξαγοράζομαι *ransom* (*from* bondage [1]); ἐκμάσσω wipe *out* and ἐξαλείφω smear *out,* ἐκκαθαίρω clear *out*; ἐκνεύω (perhaps a metaphor from driving a horse); ἐξίστημι (orig. *displace*—ellipsis of φρενῶν or the like accounts for specialised meaning); ἐκδίδομαι let *out* (but act. in sense *surrender,* in the verbal ἔκδοτος); ἐκκαίω (of fire blazing *out*—the perfective force (metaph.) is very clear in Rom 1[27] as compared with the simplex of the same metaphor in 1 Co 7[9]), ἐκλάμπω to shine *out*; ἐκπορνεύω; ἐκλείπω is primarily "leave *off*"; ἐξορκίζ (verb purely perfective in NT occurrence=*adjure, bind* by an oath, but elsewhere like its noun ἐξορκιστής *exorcise,* get an evil spirit *out* by potent words); ἐκτίθημι (ἔκθετος) as in Ac 7[19. 21]; ἐκλεγομαι *eligo,* choose *out* of a larger number; ἔξεστι (ἐξουσία, °ἄζω) it is *out, i.e.* open, allowed, which comes curiously near its apparent opposite ἔνεστι in its classical meaning *it is possible.*

In a very few cases ἐξ may be rather intensive (*out and out*) than perfective. Ἐκθαμβέομαι and ἐκθαυμάζω might be described as perfective in that they denote a *complete* astonishment, but a perfective does not differ from a non-perfective merely by the addition of *very.* Ἐκμυκτηρίζω primarily may be only "scoff *bitterly,*" but might be called perfective as much as καταγελάω *laugh to scorn.* Ἐκταράσσω is *graviter turbare*—but *conturbare* (Vulg.) is perfective. Ἐκπειράζω (τὸν θεόν or equiv.[2]) might suggest the daring of the act, or we might find in it the effort to put to a *decisive* test. It would not be difficult, indeed, to trace in all of these a nuance that would bring them among the perfectives. Ἐκδύω may be noted here as a verb which, though perfective

[1] So J. A. Robinson even in Eph 5[16] (see note there), Col 4[5]=redeeming what has fallen into bad hands. For other views see Peake and Lightfoot on Col. *l.c.*

[2] In Dt 8[2. 16] God putting Israel to a *thorough* test. This may be the meaning in Lk 10[25], or the Evangelist may be using instinctively of Jesus a word normally used of God.

already, forms a further perfective: it might imply only the putting off of certain garments, while **ἀπεκδύομαι**, like its noun *ἀπέκδυσις*, connotes complete stripping, of oneself or another in one's own interest (Col. 2$^{11. 15}$ 3^{9}).

The following are the perfectives in which the local force of *ἐξ* has wholly or nearly disappeared. We take first those on which some comment is wanted. 2 Co 4^{8} **ἀπορούμενοι** *ἀλλ' οὐκ* **ἐξαπορούμενοι**, *perplexed*, yet not *unto despair*,[1] is a specially good example of perfective action. **Ἐκζητέω** always seems to denote that the seeker *finds*, or at least exhausts his powers of seeking (Heb 12^{17}): so **ἐξεραυνάω, ἐξετάζω** (rare simplex *ἐτάζω*—*h* in Arcadian, suiting its probable connexion with √ *es* to be—akin to *ἐτεός* and *ἔτυμος*, so *verify*). The Hellenistic verbs **ἐξουθενέω** and **ἐξουδενέω** (NT and BGU iv. 1117^{31} (13 B.C.—reading not certain)) are good exx. of the continued vitality of this word-forming process. Thackeray shows (*Gr.* 105) that the former was coined first, during the vogue of *οὐθείς* (see p. 111), and *ἐξουδενόω* later, when *οὐδείς* had begun to reassert itself: **ἐξουδενέω** is due to mixture. Independent of both is Plutarch's *ἐξουδενίζω* (see above, § 46): the forming of compounds on the basis of the neuter *οὐδέν* goes back to Plato's *οὐδένεια*. We have then three separate verbs for "making nothing of, despising," formed from *ἐξ* and the word for *nihil* without intervention of a simplex verb. Probably *ἐξ* was appropriate not only for the needed perfective force, but also to make the transitive clear—a function these prefixes often tend to achieve. **Ἐκδέχομαι** in its NT sense (so Sophocles and Herodotus) is a little obscure. Jebb (on *Philoct.* 123 *σὺ μὲν μένων νυν κεῖνον ἐνθάδ' ἐκδέχου*) notes: "*ἐ., excipe.* The idea of the compound is, 'be ready for him,'—prepared to deal with him the moment that he appears." This fits the perfective idea when we remember the present-stem action (*Prol.* 114): *qs.* "go on with the act of 'receiving' *till he comes.*" (We may compare the way in which **μέλλειν** *to be about to* gets from the durative present the sense of *delaying.*) **Ἐξηγέομαι** is in NT always "*explain,*" *set forth,* as already in (post-Homeric) classical Greek. The comparison of cognate words (Lat. *săgio, săgax,* Goth. *sokyan,* Eng. *seek,* Ir. *saigim,* with same meaning) shows that the metaphorical application in *ἡγέομαι* was there from the first: *ἡγεῖσθαί τινι* would be *explore for, blaze a path for.* Ἐξηγεῖσθαι then is the perfective: cf. **ἐκζητέω** (above) and **ἐκθέσθαι** *exponere.* **Ἐξισχύω** in Eph 3^{18} c.inf. is a striking perfective—"be strong enough" to apprehend, a strength exerted till its object is attained. **Ἐκριζόω** is in form a compound, and of course perfective. But the meaning *uproot* cannot be deduced from a combination of *ἐκ* and **ῥιζόω**, and we must explain it as we explained **ἐμπορεύομαι** above (p. 305): its meaning is determined by *ἐκ ῥιζῶν* (*ἀναιρεῖν*), just as *eradicare* is really short for *ex radicibus evellere.* It is therefore virtually a cpd. of Class VII. Most of the other perfectives

[1] So (virtually) first AV. The earlier vss. take **ἀπ.**=*be poor*, but represent the antithesis correctly.

need only be named. Ἐκδαπανάω spend *out*, spend wholly; ἐκδιηγέομαι tell right through *to the end*; ἐκκεντέω to give a *deadly* stab; ἐκλανθάνομαι *quite* forget; ἐκλύομαι faint *off* (lit. be dissolved outright); ἐκπληρόω fill *up*, as we say; ἐκπλήσσομαι, much like ἐκφοβέω, and ἐκταράσσω above—our use of *strike* for a mental impression will illustrate; ἐκτελέω (cf. ἐξαρτίζω) finish *off*; ἐκτρέφω rear *up*, in our idiom, decidedly perfective—*nourisheth* is too weak in Eph 5^{29}, and *nurture* (RV) in 6^{4}; ἐξακολουθέω follow *out*; ἐξαπατάω of *successful* deceit[1]; ἐξολοθρεύομαι destroy *utterly*.

(*b*) There are some twenty-five noun cpds. which attach themselves to verbs accounted for in (*a*), and only a few remain. Local ἐξ is recognisable in διέξοδος (see διά), ἔκγονος, ἐκκλησία (orig. a *summoned* assembly), ἔκτρωμα (ἐκτιτρώσκω), ἐξέραμα, ἔξοδος, ἐξοχή (ἐξέχω) of *out*standing prominence. Perfective ἐξ appears in ἀνεξιχνίαστος (cf. the ἐκζητέω class above), ἔκδηλος, ἔκτρομος (only ℵD in Heb 12^{21}—probably assimilated to ἔκφοβος in context, on which cf. ἐκφοβέω).

(*c*) To Class VII. belong the following. Ἔκδικος in earlier Greek is ἐκ (*i.e.* ἄνευ) δίκης, *exlex*, but as early as the Batrachomyomachia shows the distinct meaning *avenger*: see Milligan *Thess.* 50. This may possibly be derived from another use of ἐκ, seen in the recurrent formula in legal papyri, καθάπερ ἐγ δίκης "just as *after* a legal decision": ἔκδικος would thus be one who carries out a sentence. There is, however, the alternative possibility that the classical compositum ἐκδικάζω *avenge* has influenced the meaning of ἔκδικος (with its deriv. °κέω °κημα). Ἔξυπνος (hence °νίζω)=ἐξ ὕπνου (γενόμενος). Συνέκδημος (see σύν) is a compound of ἔκδημος=ἐκ δήμου (ὤν), like ἀπόδημος.

Perfective ἐξ appears strengthening an adverb in ἐκπερισσῶς (ὑπερεκπ. 1 Th 5^{13} BDG—see ὑπέρ). Ἔκπαλαι is like ἀπὸ τότε, no real compound: cf. ἐξαυτῆς (really two words). Ἐξάπινα (earlier ἐξαπίνης, with ending assimilated to adverbs) and ἐξαίφνης are no doubt similar phrases, but the second element is not clear: αἶψα is likely enough for the second word, but will not suit the first. For ἔξω and its derivatives and ἐκτός, see § 130.

Ἐπί

§ 120. 9. *†‡Ἐπί (independent accent form ἔπι), *near*, *on*, *up to*, appears in three gradation forms, answering to I.E. *opi* (ὄπι-θεν, Lat. *op-*, *ob*), *epi* (ἔπι)—Skt. *ápi*, Av. *a*ⁱ*pi* may be either; and *pi* (πιέζω Skt. *pīḍayati*= *pi-zd-* √ *sed* (*sedēre*); also πτ-υχή whence ἀνα-πτύσσω, from *pi*+*ugh*, Skt. *pyukṣṇa*).

(*a*) As many as ninety-nine composita with ἐπί occur in NT, a total only exceeded by κατά and σύν, the main perfectivising prefixes. Accord-

[1] Conative force may be added in present stem—see *Prol.* 114.

ing to some scholars,[1] a contributory cause for its great frequency in all periods of the language was its inheriting much that belonged to another preposition, akin to Skt. *abhi*, Zd. *aiwi*, Eng. *by*. The hypothesis explains one or two forms like ἐφίορκος, and Delbrück brings up a good many parallels between ἐπί compounds and Skt. *abhi-* compounds: there is also the advantage of a slightly easier explanation of the range of meaning found in the ἐπί family. But it cannot be said that the phonetic argument for the conflation has much weight; and the hypothesis, which is opposed by Brugmann, must remain only a possible one at best. We may still observe (with Brugmann *KVG* 467) that in Latin *ob* has taken over some of the functions of *obhi*: *bhi*, though actually derived from *opi*; and similar mixtures may have occurred in isolated cases elsewhere without demanding the fusion postulated by Delbrück.

In many of the verbal ἐπί cpds. we can trace a clear local sense, and these are clearly the oldest. Delbrück (*Grd.* III. (i.) 675) gives some which may have been compounded before the ethnic period. Closely akin to these are the composita in which the preposition may be described as *directive*, indicating the concentration of the verb's action upon some object: in these cases the simplex will be general and the compositum special in its force, the one may be abstract and the other concrete. The exx. which Dean Robinson chooses for his "directive" sense are "ἐπαινέω, ἐπιδείκνυμι, ἐπιζητέω, ἐπικαλέω, ἐπικηρύσσω, ἐπικρατέω, ἐπικρύπτω, ἐπιμέλομαι, ἐπιμιμνήσκομαι, ἐπινοέω (*excogitare*), ἐπιχορηγέω," as well as ἐπιγινώσκω, the special subject of his well-known excursus (*Ephes.* 248 ff.). We may add to the class ἐπαγγέλλομαι, ἐπαγωνίζομαι, ἐπαθροίζομαι, ἐπαίρω, ἐπαισχύνομαι, ἐπαιτέω, ἐπακολουθέω, ἐπακούω and ἐπακροάομαι, ἐπανάγω and the other cpds. in ἐπ-ανα- (with *hostility* implied in ἐπανίσταμαι), ἐπαρκέω, ἐπαφρίζω, ἐπεγείρω (hostile), ἐπεῖδον, ἐπεισέρχομαι, ἐπεκτείνομαι, ἐπερωτάω, ἐπέχω (in some forces), ἐπιβάλλω (or local), ἐπιβαρέω, ἐπιβλέπω and ἐπισκέπτομαι and ἐπισκοπέω, ἐπιγίνομαι, ἐπιδέχομαι, ἐπιδίδωμι, ἐπιδύω, ἐπικαλύπτω, ἐπίκειμαι (or local), ἐπικέλλω, ἐπικρίνω, ἐπιλαμβάνομαι, ἐπιλανθάνομαι, ἐπιλέγω and ἐπονομάζω, ἐπιλέγομαι (*choose*), ἐπιλείπω, ἐπιλείχω, ἐπιλύω, ἐπιμαρτυρέω, ἐπιμένω, ἐπινεύω, ἐπιπλήσσω, ἐπιποθέω, ἐπισκευάζομαι, ἐπιστέλλω, ἐπιστηρίζω, ἐπιστρέφω, ἐπισυνάγω, ἐπισυντρέχω, ἐπισχύω, ἐπισωρεύω, ἐπιτάσσω, ἐπιτελέω, ἐπιτρέπω, ἐπιτυγχάνω, ἐπιφαίνω and ἐπιφαύσκω and ἐπιφώσκω, ἐπιφέρω, ἐπιφωνέω, ἐπιχρίω.

Two more members of this class require a special note. Ἐπίσταμαι is an old compound not very easily analysed: it seems to be ἐπι-στάμαι (not duplicated—cf. φημί, ἐφάμην) with meaning "put oneself in position for." Our *understand*, Ger. *verstanden*, will show that the root *stā* is capable of application to the mind. It was no longer felt to be a compound verb. Ἐπιτιμάω comes from a meaning of the simplex not found in NT=*lay penalty on*, and so *censure*. In many of these, which

[1] Especially Delbrück *Grd.* III. (i.) 675 f., 679.

account for some three-quarters of the total, the line is hard to draw as against the purely local force, which I have restricted almost entirely to verbs of motion with ἐπί=*to* or *upon*. It will be seen at once that the directive force as understood here is much wider than is implied in the exx. given by Robinson. We might subdivide, but the general nexus is clear enough. The only compounds left now are a few in which ἐπί means *in addition*, a natural development of *upon*: thus **ἐπενδύω, ἐπιγαμβρεύω** (make a *new* marriage connexion), **ἐπιδιατάσσομαι, ἐπιδιορθόω.**

(*b*) About one-third of the noun compounds of ἐπί in the NT attach themselves to composita accounted for in (*a*). Only one of these needs separate mention, **ἐπιούσιος**, the well-known crux in Mt 6^{11}=Lk 11^{3}. That this ἁ.λ. was a coinage by the author of the Greek Q may be safely assumed, after Origen. If so, the scholarship of its origin does not justify our laying too much stress on considerations which would weigh with us if Luke himself or even Matthew were responsible, still less some Atticist scholar. Jerome's *supersubstantialis*[1] is therefore not finally discredited by the objection against the non-elision of ι: ἐπιούσιος would thus become a Class VII. cpd. rather like **ἐπουράνιος** (see below), from ἐπί *upon* and so *above*, and **οὐσία**. The only meaning quotable for this noun from NT and papyri is *property* or *estate*, which is not hopeful; and even if it is found in an abstract sense in magical documents, this is most improbable in a context so simple and direct as the Lord's Prayer. Lightfoot's argument[2] has not been superseded by later literature (see WS i. 136); and we may perhaps agree with Schmiedel in the "sicherlich" with which he put down **ἡ ἐπιοῦσα** as the true etymon. Ἔπειμι (*obire* etymologically) is to *come close after*, tread on the heels of, as it were; and its participle was current, as the NT itself shows, to express the *immediately* following day. In the evening it would mean the same as **ἡ αὔριον**, but in the morning (see esp. the opening of Plato's *Crito*) it is a day earlier than this. The immediacy is quite sufficient reason for the translator's being dissatisfied with τὸν τῆς αὔριον or the like as a rendering of the Aramaic before him: he followed a right instinct in coining a new adjective from the common word for "the coming day." That such scholars as Delitzsch and Keim (*ap.* Lightfoot *op. cit.* p. 226) should have imagined inconsistency with Mt 6^{34} only proves that the succession of Martial's *Graeci quibus est nihil negatum* is not yet closed. The only serious alternative to the above account of ἐπιούσιος is that proposed by Debrunner, and epitomised by himself in his Blass *Gr.*[4] 75. He makes it a substantivising of ἐπὶ τὴν οὖσαν (ἡμέραν) "for the current day": for this use of ὤν cf. *Prol.* 228. He compares ἐπιμήνιος (Polybius) "for the current month," ἐφημέριος etc.; but modestly claims only a preference for this over the derivation from ἡ ἐπιοῦσα. The lamented

---

[1] Origen seems to have started the idea. Jerome meant by his word, he tells us, *super omnes substantias, extra omnia*, and so *praecipuus, egregius, peculiaris.*

[2] *On a Fresh Revision*[3], p. 217 ff. But see below.

Albert Thumb accepted Debrunner's view whole-heartedly: a pencilled note from his hand on this page, which he saw on a visit to me a few months before his death, refers to Brugmann-Thumb 675 for his endorsement of it. On the other hand, Deissmann[1] holds to the Lightfoot theory, rightly laying stress on the fact that ἡ οὖσα without ἡμέρα expressed has not been found. He even suggests that the later ἡμερούσιος, and ἐφ- and καθ-ημερούσιος, found in papyri and the anti-Christian writer Proclus, are modifications of ἡμερίσιος based on ἐπιούσιος as an "already existing vernacular word" used by the evangelists.[2] Origen's ignorance of it is met by Deissmann with the remark that he need not have known all the popular vocabulary of the Mediterranean littoral. Whether this be tenable or not, I should give my own vote for ἡ ἐπιοῦσα with much the same degree of preference as Debrunner himself shows in voting for ἐπὶ τὴν οὖσαν. On the legitimacy of the hiatus involved in Debrunner's theory, see above, § 38.

Directive ἐπί may be recognised in the following, with the same latitude of application that we found in the verbs:—Ἐπανόρθωσις (like the composita of ἐπί+ἀνά in (*a*)), ἐπάρατος and ἐπικατάρατος (ἀρᾶσθαι might be cursing at random—the cpd. has an object in view), ἔπαυλις (perhaps formed from αὖλις by influence of ἐπαυλίζομαι), ἐπεισαγωγή (ἐπεισάγω=introduce as a substitute), ἐπήρεια (papp.) whence ἐπηρεάζω (ἀρειή in Homer=*violence*), ἐπιβουλή, ἐπιεικής and °κεια (Ϝείκω—pf. ϜέϜοικα—in Homer=*suit* or *agree*—cpd. suggests the environment which is "suited"), ἐπιθυμέω °μία °μητής (the stage *ἐπί-θυμος="having one's θυμός *towards*," is apparently passed over—cf. ἐνθυμέομαι above), ἐπίκουρος whence °ρία, and °ρειος from the proper name (√ *qers*=*run*—cf. *curro, horse*, and the Keltic original of *car*), ἐπίνοια (see on διάνοια and ἔννοια above), ἐπισιτισμός (from °ίζομαι, get σιτία *for* definite people), ἐπισφαλής (directing danger *to* certain objects), ἐπιφανής and °νεια (ἐπιφαίνω has been dealt with, but this comes from a technical sense—a divine being *manifested to* human eyes in human form), ἐπόπτης and °τεύω (√ *oq*ᵘ οπ=*see*—cf. ἐφορᾶν, ἐπιβλέπειν etc.), ἐφευρετής (from °ρίσκω, to find or invent *for* a purpose).

Local ἐπί may be seen in ἐπίσημος=*with* σῆμα *upon* it, the opposite of ἄσημος, and in ἐπιγραφή and ἐπίθεσις, the verbs of which belong to (*a*). Ἐπίλοιπος, left *over*, has the sense *added to*. The name Ἐπαφρόδιτος (with short form Ἐπαφρᾶς[3])=*having Aphrodite upon* him: in earlier Greek this was *venustus* (Horace's *Veneris muneribus potens*), but later represented *felix*, from the Venus-throw of the dice—so as epithet of Sulla. Ἐπίορκος (°κέω) raises various difficulties. Its frequent appear-

---

[1] Ἐπιούσιος, in *Ntliche Studien Heinrici dargebracht* (1914), pp. 115–9.

[2] [Deissmann's guess finds support by the discovery of the word ἐπιουσί[ων] in an old housekeeping book given in Preisigke, *Sammelbuch*, Nr. 5224. See also Deissmann, *LAE*² 78, n. 1.—Ed.]

[3] Not implying any necessary identification of the persons.

ance in the Κοινή as ἐφίορκος[1] (*Prol.* 234) was explained by Thumb (*Spir. Asp.* 72) as due to contamination of ἔφορκος and ἐπίορκος: he compares ἐφὶ ἱερέως on an inscription. Against Osthoff's conjecture—accepted by Delbrück—that the I.E. *ebhi* (Skt. *abhi*, Eng. *by*) underlies it, there is the fact that ἐφίορκος is late: Phrynichus is right, from his point of view, when he bans it as un-Attic, and thereby evidences its prevalence in his own day. Delbrück (*Grd.* III. (i.) 676) defines it hesitatingly as concerning " the oath by which one presses on a person and compels him " ; but this does not explain the *false* oath. Is *against* the force of ἐπί here, whether drawn from *epi* or *ebhi* ?

(c) The remaining compounds are of Class VII. Ἐπιτήδειος as a difficult word may be mentioned first. Brugmann *Dem.* 140 ff. suggests that ἐπιτηδές, from which it is the adj., starts from ἐπὶ τὸ ἧδος=*good for that* (purpose), τό being demonstrative and ἧδος a rare Homeric noun=ὄφελος: he compares *idoneus* (see p. 293 *n.*[1]). Ἐπάναγκες is presumably neuter of *ἐπανάγκης, which might even be ἐπ' ἀνάγκης used as an adj. unaltered: in any case it starts from it. (Ἐπάναγκος occurs also in papyri and inscriptions, even as early as the Gortyn Law—see v. Herwerden *s.v.*) Ἔπαρχος (whence °χ(ε)ία) is from ἐπ' ἀρχῆς, ἐπίγειος from ἐπὶ γῆς, ἐπίδημος (whence °μέω, παρεπίδημος) from ἐπὶ δήμῳ, ἐπιθανάτιος=ἐπὶ θάνατον κείμενος, ἐπικεφάλαιον (Mk 12[14] D k and two important cursives)=τὸ ἐπὶ κεφαλὴν πρασσόμενον, ἐπουράνιος=ἐπ' οὐρανοῦ ὤν, and ἐφήμερος (°ρία) is from ἐφ' ἡμέραν. Verbs in this class are ἐπιστομίζω from ἐπὶ στόμα (θεῖναι) like the proverb βοῦς ἐπὶ γλώσσῃ, and ἐπιχειρέω=χεῖρα θεῖναι ἐπί τι: in neither case does a noun compound intervene. Both are ancient words.

Ἐπάνω=ἐπί+ἀνά+ῶ (see § 130, *s.v.* ἔξω). Ἐπαύριον is a true compound, ἐπί giving the force of succession: its form echoes its primary, the adverb αὔριον. Ἐπέκεινα, *to your* side, is from ἐπ' ἐκεῖνα. Ἐφάπαξ might just as well be written as two words, like ἐπὶ τρίς, at any rate for the meaning *at once* (1 Co 15[6]): when=*once for all* it is more like a compound, a directive strengthening of ἅπαξ in the same sense.

Κατά

§ 121. 10. *‡Κατά is taken by Brugmann (*KVG* 479) as an extended form of *ko* or *kom*, found in Latin *cum* and *co-*, in Keltic, and in κοινός=κομι̯ός: Gothic *handugs* " wise " (√ *dhē* θη), *qs.* " capable of mental synthesis." Κάτα (so accented as an independent word) is for κm̥-τα, with second element as in μέ-τα. Its nearest connexions are Irish *cēt-*, Old Welsh *cant*=*along, by, with.* Brugmann defines its earliest use as " along something so as to remain in connexion

[1] So Mt 5[33] ℵ, 1 Ti 1[10] D*P: in LXX three times, in B, A and C respectively (Thackeray 126). If it is Western (WH *App.*[2] 151), it is only another instance of Western agreement with the most genuine Κοινή.

and contact with the object." The kindred Latin *contra* illustrates one development, *against*, but the meaning *down* can hardly be said to be explained. It is noteworthy that neither *down* nor *against* survives in MGr.[1] As the word had of course a long history in pre-Homeric Greek beyond our reach, the obscurity of its semasiology is not strange. Most probably the key should be found in the antithetic development of *ἀνά* and *κατά*, which with acc. come very near: such antithesis as *ἀνὰ ῥόον* and *κατὰ ῥόον* might be very productive.

(*a*) **Κατά** forms 107 composita in the NT, falling thus only a little short of *σύν*, the other great perfectivising preverb. It will be noticed that Latin *co-*, *com-*, which conspicuously performs this function in Italic, is related to *κατά* in form and to *σύν* in meaning. To this class belong fully two-thirds of the *κατά* compounds: we cannot always, however, classify with confidence, and the ambiguous elements in the word's history cause difficulty. There are some clear instances of local force: thus **καταβαίνω, καθίημι, κατανεύω** and **κατασείω** (when compared with *ἀνανεύω*), **κατάγω, καταπλέω, κατατρέχω, κατέρχομαι.** In others this meaning could be recognised if the centrality of the meaning *down* could be accepted. **Καθέζομαι** and **κατάκειμαι,** for example, are rendered *sit down, lie down,* **καταπίπτω** *fall down,* **καταπατέω** *tread down*; but we may ask pertinently how it is possible to sit, lie, fall or tread in any other direction—even if it be allowed that we may "sit up" and even "lie up"! It is better to regard them as simply perfective, the preverb (whether *down* or *over* or *together*) bringing the action of the verbal root to a definite result. In another class of verbs *κατά* seems to be represented by *against*, as often when placed with a genitive as a preposition. Thus **καταβραβεύω, καταγινώσκω, καταγωνίζομαι, καταδυναστεύω, κατακρίνω, κατακυριεύω, καταλαλέω, καταμαρτυρέω, καταναρκάω, κατασκοπέω, καταστρηνιάω, καταφρονέω, κατεξουσιάζω, κατισχύω,** alike differ from their simplicia in that they indicate action unfavourable to an object. (The bringing in of an object, where the simplex had been intransitive, is found not infrequently, but it is not easy to connect it causally with the preverb: further instances are **καταργέω** *put out of action*, from **ἀργέω** *be out of action*, **καταπονέω, κατασοφίζομαι, κατακληρονομέω, κατακαυχάομαι, καταγελάω.**) In a good many of the verbs classed as perfective we could easily reach that sense through *κατά*=*down*, and in others by the "hostility" connotation: it is less easy to find compounds where we might recognise the meaning which Brugmann regards as most original. **Κατακολουθέω** and **καταδιώκω** describe following right over an intervening space till the quarry is reached: **καταντάω** and perhaps **κατευθύνω** are not very different, nor is the ἁ.λ. **κατεπέστην** ("make a dead set upon").

[1] Thumb *Hdb.* p. 106.

(*b*) About 40 compound nouns or adjectives found in NT attach themselves to the verbs under (*a*), as derivatives or as parallel formations. On ἀκατάπαστος as a negatived verbal from *καταπαύω* see § 37. Καθηγητής from *καθηγέομαι deduco* goes into the perfective list, as does καταπέτασμα from *καταπετάννυμι*, unless that is to be compared with καταχέω pour *over*. Κατόρθωμα is from *κατορθόω*, where *κατά* has produced a transitive verb. Κατατομή *mutilation* is linked with perfective *κατατέμνω* (we say "cut *up*"). Κατάρα against the more general ἀρά has the *κατά* of hostility, and so κατάθεμα, κατήγορος (-ωρ, °ρέω, °ρία) and καταδίκη. Κατήφεια, of quite uncertain etymology, seems to contain *κατά*=*down*. Κατάδηλος and κατάλοιπος have the intensive *κατά*. Κατείδωλος is (naturally enough) ἁ.λ.: the special Jewish use of *εἴδωλον* is sufficient to explain this. But it is coined (by Luke or some Jewish predecessor) in accordance with analogy: cf. *κάθαλος full of salt*, *κάτοξος drenched with vinegar* (both New Comedy), *κατάγλωττος talkative* (Epictetus), *κατάδενδρος densely wooded* (Nymphodorus—of an uncertain date B.C.).

(*c*) Κατακρημνίζω=*cast κατὰ κρημνοῦ*, καθημερινός from *καθ' ἡμέραν daily*, καταχθόνιος=*κατὰ χθονὸς ὤν*, belong to Cl. VII.[1] Compound prepositions or adverbs include κάτω (with κατώτερος), ὑποκάτω, κατενώπιον, καθεξῆς. Adverbial phrases which are always or often written as single words are καθ' ὅ, καθ' ἅ, καθ' ἅπερ, καθ' ὅτι, κατὰ μόνας, καθ' ὅλου: it makes no real difference whether we make them one word or two. Καθώς=*καθ' ὥς* belongs to the same category as ἐκ τότε etc. (Brugmann *Gr.*[4] 524).

Μετά

§ 122. 11. *‡ Μετά has been already noted as an extension of *μέ* with the same element that we find in *κα-τά*. The I.E. *me* seems to have produced *medhi*, whence *medhi̯os*=μέσος, *medius*, *mid*, Skt. *madhyas*, etc.: the Germanic preposition seen in Goth. *miþ*, Ger. *mit*, might equally go back to **metí*. The Greek form with -*τα*, accented *μέτα* as an independent word, has apparently no parallel, since the Iranian *mat* "with" must be compared with *ἅμα* because of its obvious link with Skt. *smat*: see Brugmann *Grd.*[2] II. ii. 856. Μέ-χρι(ς) and the dialectic *μέστα*, *μέσποδι*, *μέττ' ἐς*, *μέσφα*, with the early compound μεταξύ, belong to the family. It is possible to conjecture that *metí* was the oldest form, accounting for Germanic and Greek alike: in that case **μές* (cf. the dialect forms above) may be its surviving repre-

[1] **Καθολικός, from καθ' ὅλου, does not occur in NT, though appearing in late MSS.**

sentative, like πρός from προτί, and μέτα may be due to the analogy of κάτα. As to its meaning, it seems to start from *amid*, as we may see in μετέχω "possess *among others*, share." The common sense of *change* is assigned by Brugmann-Thumb *Gr.* 509 to the local idea of an intervening space (*medium*) which is crossed: they compare Lat. *interesse* "differ." As a preposition the primary force is *with*, in various senses, which alone survives in MGr.,[1] except for phrases of *manner*: *after*, coming from the idea of crossing over the "mid" space to the other side, is of course common in Hellenistic, but leaves no trace to-day.

(*a*) Μετά forms 21 verb compounds in NT. Of these 16 have the idea of *change*, answering often to Latin compounds with *trans-*, which supports the explanation of this force of μετά given above from Brugmann. I include μεταμέλομαι here, though Grimm finds the sense of "*after*thought": there seems no reason for placing it and μετανοέω in different classes, and the latter indicates "change of mind" beyond question. "Sharing" action (like German cpds. in *mit-*) accounts for μεταδίδωμι, μεταλαμβάνω, μετέχω. Μετακαλοῦμαι and μεταπέμπομαι, "call for" and "send for," have the sense which appears with μετά c. acc., action crossing over a space to a goal.

(*b*) Some 16 noun compounds of μετά are found, if we include μετέωρος on account of its derivative μετεωρίζομαι. Of these 11 are derivatives of verbs included under (*a*), while μετοικεσία may be added as very near to μετοικίζω. Μεθόριον (Mk 7[24] ANω) is a literary word (μετά *between*) foisted on Mark by copyists. Μεθοδεία comes from μεθοδεύω, and this from μέθοδος, where μετά is like that in μεθέπω "follow *after*, up." Μέτωπον is apparently the part "between the eyes" (cf. μεσόφρυον). Μετέωρος (cf. Lesbian πεδ-ἄορος—from ἀϝείρω) is like μετάρσιος (from αἴρω): in μεταίρω the idea of *removal* is clear, so that "lifted *across*" a gulf of air will be the starting-point.

(*c*) Μετέπειτα *afterwards* is a very early example of μετά=*after*, occurring as it does in Homer. Cf. the note above, p. 293, on this early (non-Attic) justification of Hellenistic combinations like ἀπὸ τότε, etc.

Παρά

§ 123. 12. *†‡ παρά makes itself conspicuous by retaining prepositional use with all three cases: it has, however, a very limited range in MGr. It belongs to a family with the common element *per*, including περί (loc.), πάρος (gen. abl.), παραί=Lat. *prae* (dat.), πέρᾱν, πρό, πρω-, πρός (=προτί): our own *for*, be*fore*, *from* and *fro*,

[1] Thumb *Hdb.* 104.

Latin *pro, prae, per, por-*, may be mentioned among words quotable from all I.E. dialects. The root of what may well have been a primitive noun can probably be recognised in *πόρος*, our *fare*, *πείρω* "pierce": "going *across*" (cf. *πέραν*) is the central idea. From the adj. **peros* we have in Greek the acc. fem. πέραν *to the other side* (c. gen.), *πέρα* instr. *beyond*: see Brugmann *Grd.*[2] II. ii. 872 f. Πάρα itself—whose independent accent is unoriginal, like that of *κάτα*—is presumably an instr. case-form, but such identifications of prehistoric words are of course only conjectural. It answers to Skt. *purā*, Av. *para* "before," Alban. *para*, OIr. *ar*, Goth. *faúra*, all= "before," in time or place. Gothic *faúr* may answer in form to the alternative *πάρ*, Lat. *por-*: (*παράγων*) *παρὰ τὴν θάλασσαν* is in Wulfila *faúr marein*, (*ἔπεσε*) *παρὰ τὴν ὁδόν faúr wig.* "Close to, beside" is apparently the oldest Greek meaning; but new developments branch out: *beside* gives *mis-*, *stealthily* (*qs.* entering by a *side* way), and sometimes diverges into *onward*, with metaphorical application.

(*a*) Παρά forms 53 or 54 verbal cpds. in NT, a fair proportion of which are not very easy to define in relation to the preverb's earliest meanings. The simplest are those where we may represent the *παρά* by "beside, close to." Thus παρακαθεσθεῖσα in Lk 10^{39} is like 9^{47} *ἔστησεν αὐτὸ παρ' ἑαυτῷ*. Παραβάλλειν *compare* (Mk 4^{30} ADω—a plausible reading), παράκειμαι, παρακολουθέω *follow closely*, παραμένω, παρατηρέω *watch closely*, παρατίθημι, παραχειμάζω, παρίστημι, παροικέω, are fairly clear. Others have the idea of motion affecting the sense, so that we compare the uses of *παρά* c. acc. Παραβιάζομαι (in Luke)=*βιάζομαι παρ' ἐμαυτόν*, παραγίνομαι=*come near*, πάρειμι=*am near*, παρατυγχάνω=*chance* (to be) *near*; παρακαλέω (in Ac 28^{20}) *call to one*; παραδίδωμι *hand on to*; παρακύπτω *stoop close to*; παρασκευάζω *prepare ready*—almost identical with *σκευάζω* but suggesting a "presentation" of the prepared object. The idea of going *past* does not come naturally out of the general sense of *closeness*, and may go back to earlier elements (cf. *praeter*). So παραβαίνω, παρέρχομαι, παράγω, παραπλέω, παραπορεύομαι, παραρρέω, παραφέρω, παροίχομαι. *Aside*, developing into *mis-*, is recognised in παραθεωρέω *overlook*, παραιτέομαι *deprecor* (*qs.* "ask *aside*"), παρακούω *mis-hear*, *ignore* (also with *παρά close=overhear*), παραπίπτω *fall aside*, παραλογίζομαι *mis-calculate*. Others have the ablatival connotation: παραδέχομαι, παραιτέομαι (in Mk 15^{6}), and παραλαμβάνω suggest the source (*παρά τινος*) as παραδίδωμι does the recipient (*παρά τινι*). A kind of dative idea attaches to παραινέω and παρακαλέω, where *παρά* suggests an intimacy with the object. Παραγγέλλω is *pass a message on*, with the same idea of "onward motion" that we saw in παραδίδωμι, etc. "On one side" may possibly be the meaning in **παρακαλύπτω** and **παραλύομαι**. The "onward" nuance seems to produce **παραζηλόω**, **παραπικραίνω**, **παροξύνω**, **παροργίζω** and **παροτρύνω**. **Παρακαλέω** and **παραμυθέομαι** with the sense "comfort" may be attached better to the idea of *intimacy*, speaking "to the heart." "Sideways" and so "stealthily" is seen in the παρ-εις- cpds. of ἄγω, δύω and ἔρχομαι: the last, with **παρεισφέρω**, has also the meaning *besides*. **Παρεμβάλλω** as a military word, said to be Macedonian—*i.e.* coined especially in Philip's or Alexander's army—must be left uncertain, as a t.t. which might have originated in conditions we cannot trace. On **παραφρονέω**, **παραδειγματίζω** and **παρομοιάζω**, see (*b*).

(*b*) Twenty-six noun compounds of παρά in NT are formed from verbs already occurring there. Among these we should notice **παρουσία**, in which the RV marginal note ("Gr. *presence*") would suggest that the idea of "*motion* towards" is to be excluded: outside evidence for the technical meaning "royal visit" shows that *advent* is as literal a rendering as *presence*, which occurs in some places. The simple locative force may be seen in **εὐπάρεδρος** (cf. **παρακαθέζομαι**), παράδειγμα (from παραδείκνυμι show two things *side by side*) whence **παραδειγματίζω**,[1] **παραλλαγή** (*deviation*), **παράσημος** (marked *on the side*), **παρεπίδημος** (staying *with*), **παρηγορία** (cf. note on **παραμυθέομαι**, °ιον above), **πάροδος** (journey *past*), **παροιμία** (cf. *obiter* dictum, τὸ παρ' οἶμον), **πάροινος** (=παρ' οἴνῳ ὤν), **παρόμοιος** (strengthened ὅμοιος, παρά as elsewhere=*beside* in comparison) whence **παρομοιάζω**,[2] **παροψίς** (*side*-dainty—with transference to the dish, the converse change to that in our *dish* when used of the food). **Παραβολεύομαι**, from παράβολος *venturesome* (cf. class. παραβάλλομαι in same sense), has the verbal part expressing the energy of βάλλειν, instead of being static as in **παραβολή**. Hence παρά describes motion along, like that of an object flung into a rushing stream. **Παραφρονία** from παράφρων=having the mind *awry*: **παραφρονέω** might be a cpd. of φρονέω, "to think awry," but is more probably from παράφρων.

(*c*) **Παράδοξος**=παρὰ δόξαν ὤν, and παράνομος (whence **-ία**)=παρὰ νόμον ὤν, are obvious Class VII. forms, with παρά (c. acc.)=*contrary to*. **Παραθαλάσσιος**=παρὰ θαλάσσῃ ὤν, and **παράλιος**=παρὰ ἁλὶ ὤν, show the ordinary locative sense of παρά. **Παραχρῆμα** is a phrase adapted unchanged for adverbial use. In **παραπλήσιον**, **παραπλησίως** and **παραυτίκα** the addition *close by* intensifies the force of an adverb which invites an element of this kind.

---

[1] The simplex **δειγματίζω** is apparently later than the cpd. in emerging, and is best taken as a popular derivative from **παραδειγματίζω** on the basis of the existing δεῖγμα. But that the verb does not emerge till the papyri is not positive proof that it did not exist. [See also *Vocab.* 138.—Ed.]

[2] The simplex, if it really exists, is secondary to the cpd.

Περί

§ 124. 13. *‡ Περί (πέρι) answers exactly in form and meaning to Skt. *pári*, Av. *pairi*, "around"; Lat. *per*, Goth. *fair-*, Lith. *per̃*, less obviously connected in meaning, remind us that the semasiology will not be wholly easy to follow. Brugmann (*Grd.*[2] II. ii. 865) notes that the divergence dates from I.E. times. He gives the meanings of the preverb as *hinüber, über etwas hinaus—Übergang in ein anderes Verhältniss, in eine andre Form, zu Entgegengesetztem, Umänderung, besonders zum Schlechten—hindurch—umher, herum, um—durch und durch, allseitig, sehr.* But in Greek, as he and Thumb observe (*Gr.*[4] 511 f.), *around* covers most of the ground: its development was connected with that of ἀμφί, and in dialects and *Κοινή* the preposition came near ὑπέρ.

(*a*) There are 32 περί verbs in NT (33 if we accept περιραίνω from ℵ* in Rev 19[13]), of which about four-fifths show the meaning "round, about." Περιάπτω *kindle* is not quite clear: perhaps it is enough to compare περιαστράπτω and περιλάμπω and point to the way the flame runs "round." Περιβάλλω *clothe* illustrates the link with ἀμφί (cf. ἀμφιέννυμι): so περιζώννυμι (=Lith. *pérjosti*). Περιρήγνυμι *tear off* (clothes) is correlative. Περιπατέω *walk about* links itself with Lat. *perambulare*. So does περιφέρω *bear about* with *perfero*. To other headings we assign the following. Περιαιρέω *remove* is taken by Grimm to include (2 Cor 3[16], Ac 27[40]) the idea of something *enveloping* or *lying on both sides*; but it is better to make it intensive (see above). Περιεργάζομαι (cf. περίεργος) implies *overdoing* a thing, with the pejorative nuance included under Brugmann's second heading (above): cf. *perverto, perdo, perimo*. Περιέχω (in 1 Pet 2[6], and vernacular sources) has a curious intransitive force, *is contained*: the active *include* is easy, and the intransitive use appears to follow the analogy of οὕτως ἔχει etc. Cf. περιοχή *period*. Περιίσταμαι *avoid*, a Κοινή use, is somewhat difficult: it may belong to the second category again, of "passage into another relation," whence *shift round*, mid. intransitively with acc. of objec shunned. Περιλείπομαι *remain over, survive*, περιποιέομαι *make survive for oneself, gain*, have the force seen in περισσός. Περιμένω is like *pervenio*, Goth. *fairrinnan* (=ἐφικνεῖσθαι): περί is *hindurch*. Περιπείρω *pierce through*, like *perforo* etc. Περιπίπτω is apparently *fall amid*, a kind of passive to περιβάλλω. Περισπάομαι *distract* is like our "pull about." Περιφρονέω *despise* is compared by Brugmann with Skt. *paricakṣ* (*cakṣ*—see—cf. περιορᾶν) *overlook, disregard*.

(*b*) Ten noun compounds in NT are linked with verbs included under (*a*). This includes εὐπερίστατος, the difficult ἁ.λ. discussed above, § 106.

Περικάθαρμα and περίψημα (*ψήω, ψάω, *wipe*), start from "cleaning, wiping *round*." Περικρατής = having κράτος over, lit. *around*. Περίλυπος is intensive, *having excessive sorrow*. Περίοικος *having house around*—like περίχωρος—is really independent of περιοικέω, but is counted among the ten above. Περιούσιος[1] is said to be a Biblical coinage (LXX), like ἐπιούσιος in NT, to render a Hebrew word meaning "special possession." Can we get the meaning *special, superior*, out of περιουσία *superiority* ? It seems desirable to connect it with the quite common noun if at all possible.

(*c*) Περικεφαλαία is a Cl. VII. noun = τὸ περὶ κεφαλήν (cf. προσκεφάλαιον). Πέριξ appears to be the nom. sing. of an old adj. formed directly from περί with suffixal κ: so περισσός (= *perikyos*) and its derivatives.

Πρό

§ 125. 14. * Πρό, for the cognates of which see on παρά *ad. init.*, answers to Skt. *prá*, Av. *frā*, Lat. *prŏ-*, OIr. *ro-*, Goth. *fra-*, Ger. *ver-*, E. *for-*, Lith. *pra*: its original and still normal sense is *forwards, before*, of either time or place. Lat. *prō*, *prōd-*, is closely related, and in many cpds. takes the place of *prŏ-*. The I.E. preverb seems to have been used with special frequency: its close attachment to the verb is marked by the rule that in double or treble cpds. containing *pró* this always comes last—*e.g.* ὑπεκπροφυγών (Hom.), Skt. *ánu prá eti*, etc. (This rule is primitive, but extinct fairly early: five NT cpds. violate it.) Significant also is the frequency of cpds. which seem to have I.E. antiquity, such as *pró* g^{u}*em* (Gk., Lat., Goth.), *pró bher* (Ar., Gk., Lat., Goth., Slav.).

(*a*) Πρό forms in NT 49 verbal cpds., in 28 of which it more or less clearly implies *before*, of time, and in about 11 *before*, of place: in προγράφω, προέρχομαι, and προοράω both occur. Besides these we have verbs in which *forward* or *forth* would suit better, whether in local sense, as προπέμπω, προτείνω, προφέρω, or metaphorically, as προκαλέομαι, προλέγω (in some disputed places), προτίθεμαι = *propono*, προτρέπομαι. In προαιρέομαι we have the idea of *preference* (cf. πρὸ πάντων), in προΐσταμαι[2] that of *protection* or *care*. (Προτάσσω is counted in the list on the strength of one occurrence in D*.) The problem of προεχόμεθα in Rom 3[9] does not turn on the προ-: see the Verb-syntax.

(*b*) Five noun compounds are linked with NT verbs accounted for

[1] See J. B. Lightfoot, *Fresh Revision* (1891), pp. 260 ff.

[2] Brugmann-Thumb (p. 514) prefers *forward*, i.e. *openly*; but does this suit the following genitive so well ?

under (*a*). *Before* in time or space appears in πρόγονος, πρόδρομος, προθεσμία, πρόκριμα, προπάτωρ; *openly* in πρόδηλος, *forward* in πρόβατον (whatever the second element), πρόθυμος (=having mind *forward*, ready), προπετής, πρηνής (if=*headlong*[1]). Προδότης *traitor*, from προδίδωμι=*prodo*, seems to start from *forth*, *away*: we use *give away* in the sense of *betray*. Πρόφασις is *saying* or *showing in front of*, *i.e.* an excuse to *cloak* the reason. Προφήτης has *representative* force, an interpreter speaking *for* the divinity. According to Brugmann (*Gr.*[4] 158) we should place here the problem-word πρό-σφατος, the second element of which is an isolated by-form from the root of φθάνω: this is obviously commended by the meaning.

(*c*) Πρό has a comparative πρότερος: πρῶτος if for πρώϝ-ατος is from a cognate and not directly formed. To Cl. VII. belong προαύλιον=τὸ πρὸ αὐλῆς ὄν, and πρόχειρος (whence °ρίζομαι)=πρὸ χειρῶν ὢν or ἔχων, with πρό local in both cases. Προσάββατον from πρὸ σαββάτου has πρό temporal. Πόρρω may be remotely connected.

Πρός

§ 126. 15. *†‡ Πρός is less conspicuous as a preverb than as a preposition. Its oldest Greek form is προτί=Skt. *práti*, but the dialects show also a synonymous ποτί (Doric) and πός (Arkad.-Cyprian). The Ar. *pas-cā* ("after"), Lat. *pos-t*, Lith. *pàs* ("near, to"), Alb. *pas* ("after"), may prove *pos* as well as *poti* to be pre-Greek, in which case we have an additional force to explain the survival of πρός (=*proty*, the *sandhi*-form before vowels) over προτί. Like Greek, Aryan had both *prati* and *pati*, the former surviving in Indian, the latter in Iranian: whether there was any distinction of meaning we cannot tell. Both seem to have been local adverbs="over against." *Πός* survived in the *Κοινή* of Phrygia, but otherwise only πρός is found in our period. For all these statements see Brugmann-Thumb *Gr.* 514 f. Outside Aryan there is hardly any sign of προτί: Brugmann (*Grd.*[2] II. ii. 877) would find its gradation doublet *preti* in Lat. *pretium*, and Lettish *pret* ("against"), also Pamphylian περτί. He suggests that *po-s* and *po-ti* may be extensions of (*a*)*pó*, as *pro-ti* of *pro*: for the element *-ti* cf. ἀντί, *me-tí* (?—see under μετά), ἔτι. *Direction* and *addition* are the general headings under which the Greek meanings fall.

[1] Which is improbable for the one NT occurrence, since Bp. Chase's argument for πρησθείς *swollen* as the meaning in Ac 1[18]: see *JTS* xii. 278 and Harnack's endorsement in *ThLZ* xxxvii. 235.

(*a*) There are 44 composita with πρός in NT, if we include **προσαχέω** (Ac 27[27] B*) and **προσεγγίζω** (Mk 2[4] ACDω). In all but about 8 of these the πρός is directive, answering to the meaning of πρός as preposition c. acc. In **προσαιτέω** and **προσδέομαι** we should express the force better by πρός c. abl., where the case implies *from* and πρός adds "*to* oneself." Sometimes the prepositional equivalent would be rather πρός c. loc., as **προσμένειν τινί**=μένειν πρός τινι. Other cpds. have πρός=*in addition*, a meaning which it held in its use as an adverb without a case: so **προσαναπληρόω, προσαπειλέομαι, προσδαπανάω, προσεάω, προσεργάζομαι, προσοφείλω, προστίθημι.** One of the directive cpds. deserves a note, **προσεύχομαι**, an old word which is markedly appropriated in NT for Christian prayer: contrast **εὔχομαι** in Ac 27[29]. The vivid sense of πρὸς τὸν θεόν accompanying it made it the natural word.

(*b*) Sixteen noun cpds. in NT are linked with verbs accounted for under (*a*). **Ἀπρόσιτος** from πρόσειμι *go to*, **πρόσχυσις** from προσχέω *pour on*, may be added. A pure noun cpd. is **προσφιλής** *dear to, pleasing.* **Προσευχή** was probably secondary to the verb **προσεύχομαι**, with εὐχή as a starting-point. **Πρόσωπον** (with its derivatives) goes with **μέτωπον**, and on its analogy will mean the part "up to the eyes."

(*c*) Nouns of Cl. VII. are **πρόσκαιρος** from πρὸς καιρόν, **προσκεφάλαιον** from πρὸς κεφαλήν, **πρόσπεινος** from πρὸς πεῖναν. **Ἔμπροσθεν** from ἐν and πρόσθεν: see under Improper Prepositions, § 130.

Σύν

§ 127. 16. † **Σύν**, which as a preverb has a most extended use in Greek, has no clear cognates outside: μεταξύ is witness to two older by-forms, ξύν and ξύ. It may be assumed that ξύν (cf. Ion. ξῦνός=κοινός in formation and meaning, being ξύν and κομ- with adj. suff. -*y*ος) is the older form, but the phonetic conditions which caused the κ to vanish are not cleared up: ξύλον and ξύλινος have initial σ- in a few Attic inscrr. of iv/B.C.[1] For the possibility of a Slavic cognate see Boisacq *s.v.* ξύν. It is conceivably a primitive Greek compound of ἐξ (reduced by gradation as in Lat. *s*-uper and *s*-ub) and *su* which may be recognisable in Lith. *sù* "with," unless this is capable of representing *ksu* by itself: see Brugmann *Grd.*[2] II. ii. 897. The restrictions of σύν when used as a preposition are obvious—note that they are not shared when the word becomes a preverb.

(*a*) The proper meaning of σύν being *together*, it is capable (like the synonymous Latin *com*-) of making pure perfectives, under which heading we may class about 24 of the 123 σύν compounds in NT.[2] The rest con-

[1] Meisterhans[3] 92.

[2] The total includes συνελαύνω (Ac[1] AEPω) and συγκατανεύω (Ac[1] D).

tain *σύν*=*with*, or various shades of meaning included under *together*. The perfectives reckoned in the above total are **συλλαμβάνω** (*con*cipio), **συλλογίζομαι** (*col*ligo), **συναρπάζω** (*com*primo), **συνευδοκέω** (in 1 Cor $7^{12f.}$—elsewhere *joint* approval), **συνέχω**, **συνθλάω**, **συνθλίβω**, **συνθρύπτω** (cf. *con*fringo etc.), **συγκαλύπτω** (*conceal*), **συγκάμπτω**, **συγκινέω** (*com*moveo), **συγκλείω** (*con*cludo), **συγκύπτω**, **συνοράω**, **συμπεριλαμβάνω**, **συμπίπτω** (*con*cĭdo), **συμπληρόω** (*com*pleo), **συμπνίγω**, **συντελέω**, **συντέμνω** (*con*cīdo), **συντηρέω**, **συντρίβω**, **συγχέω** (**-χύννω**) (*con*fundo), **συσπαράσσω** (*con*vello). Some of these have the ordinary force of *σύν* in some of their uses; and in other cases the line between perfective *σύν* and non-perfective is not easy to draw. A few of these latter call for note. **Συμβαίνω** (cf. *con*tingo) seems to start its special sense from the idea of *coincidence*, and **συμφέρω** from *contributory* action. **Συναλλάσσω** when compared with the nearly synonymous **καταλλάσσω** might be treated as an instance of *σύν* perfective; but it seems to derive its force mainly from the idea of *intercourse*. **Συνελαύνω**, in the one place where NT MSS show it (Ac 7^{26}, where the tense alone suffices to make the reading impossible), must be *com*pello=drive *together*, of two parties. **Συνίημι** and **συνιστάνω** (=*exhibit*) seem to contain the idea of a mental "synthesis." **Συλλυπέομαι** in Mk 3^{5} is difficult, since the word in its earlier record involves *sympathy*, which is somewhat forced here: can it be perfective=*utterly* distressed? **Συγχράομαι** might almost be called an equivalent of *χρᾶσθαι*=*deal with*; but the sociative *σύν* seems to be consciously present, and there is no specially perfective force visible.

(*b*) In noun cpds. *σύν* acts very much as in verbal. There are 18 words and groups in NT closely connected with verbs found there: **σύγχυσις**, **συνοχή**, **συντέλεια**, **συντόμως**, **σύντριμμα** belong to the perfectives, and the rest to the *com-* class. (**Συντέλεια** of course is from *συντελής*, but its Hellenistic meaning, *consummation*, appears to spring from association with **συντελέω**.) Definitely verbal cpds. are **συναγωγή** (which has become concrete from abstract) and its cpd. **ἐπισυναγωγή**, **συγγνώμη** (from **συγγιγνώσκω** *pardon*)—the special meaning seems to spring from the idea of *sympathy*, **συγκυρία** (from *συγκυρέω coincide*), **συνδρομή** (cf. **συντρέχω**), **συνείδησις** (a Hellenistic derivative from **σύνοιδα**=*con*scio), **σύνεσις**, **συνετός** and **ἀσύνετος** (from **συνίημι**), **συνωμοσία** (from **συνόμνυμι**=*con*iuro), **συστατικός** (from **συνιστάνω**=*com*mendo), and **ἀσύνθετος** (from **συντίθημι**). Of purely noun character are a good many of Cl. V. (based on IV.*c*), as **συγγενής** *having common race*, **σύμμορφος** *having same form*, **σύμφωνος** (whence °**έω** etc.), **σύμψυχος**, **συμπαθής** (whence °**έω**), **σύζυγος**, **σύμβουλος**, (**συνέδριον** from) *σύνεδρος*, **συνεργός**, (**συνήθεια** from) *συνηθής*, **σύντροφος** (*τροφή*), **σύνδεσμος**, etc. Others again are Descriptives (IV.*c*), as **συγκληρονόμος**, **συγκοινωνός**, **συμμαθητής**, **συμμιμητής**, (**συμπόσιον** from) *συμποτής*, **συναιχμάλωτος**, **σύνδουλος**, **συνέκδημος**, **συστασιώτης**. Note the pleonasm in **συμμέτοχος**.

(c) Apart from μεταξύ (see above), there seem to be no compound adverbs containing σύν; nor are there any Cl. VII. formations in NT.

Ὑπέρ

§ 128. 17. *‡ Ὑπέρ was in proethnic speech the antithesis of *n̥dheri* (*under*, Lat. *infer-us*, *infrā*, Skt. *ádharas*, Av. *adairi*, perh. ἀθερίζω "to slight"). The alternative form with the locative suffix *-i* appears in Skt. *upári* (also Iranian). Lat. *s-uper* (a compound), Gaulish *Ver*(cingetorix etc.), Goth. *ufar*=*over*, and Armen. *i ver*, illustrate it further. The meaning is uniform throughout the wide field, viz. *over*, passing into *across*, *beyond*. Ὕπερ is still capable of adverbial use in the NT period (2 Cor 11[23]). For the curious fact that the I.E. *uper(i)* and *upo*, which are obviously kin, should in Greek and other languages have antithetic meanings, see under ὑπό.

(a) Only 14 verb cpds. of ὑπέρ occur in NT; but it is conspicuously capable of forming new ones in this period. Thus it is very likely that Paul coined ὑπερνικάω. In this word and in ὑπεραυξάνω, ὑπερπερισσεύω, ὑπερπλεονάζω, ὑπερυψόω (all Pauline) the preverb simply magnifies, as in *overjoyed* (ὑπερχαίρω). Elsewhere, as usually in our own *over-* cpds., there is the sense of *excess*: so ὑπεραίρομαι, ὑπερβάλλω (cf. *overshoot*), ὑπερεκτείνω, ὑπερεκχύννομαι, ὑπερφρονέω (cf. *overweening*). Ὑπερβαίνω= go *beyond*, *transgress*; ὑπεροράω=*overlook*, *neglect*; ὑπερεντυγχάνω= intercede *for* (ὑπέρ τινος); ὑπερέχω=*sur*pass. It is characteristic of Paul's temperament that only $\frac{3}{25}$ occurrences of ὑπερ- cpds. in NT lie outside the *corpus Paulinum*.

(b) Ὑπερβολή and ὑπεροχή are parallel in meaning with their verbs in (a) above. Ὑπερήφανος="*over*bearing" is generally assumed to contain ὑπέρ (or ὕπερος) and the root of φαίνω, but the -η- (for ᾱ, as Pindar shows) is not thus satisfactorily explained.[1] Nor is ὑπερῷον, from the adj. ὑπερώιος=*upper*, the suffix of which is obscure. Ὑπέρογκος *with excessive swelling* is a Descriptive based on a Cl. IV.c cpd.

(c) Ὑπέρακμος, from ὑπὲρ ἀκμήν *beyond prime*, belongs to Cl. VII. Ὑπερέκεινα, which is guaranteed to be good Κοινή by the strictures of Thomas Magister, is simply ὑπὲρ ἐκεῖνα turned into one word: so the earlier ἐπέκεινα. In ὑπερεκπερισσοῦ a compound adverbial phrase has been heightened as in ὑπερεκπερισσῶς, ὑπερλίαν and ὑπερπερισσῶς a simple or compound adverb. Ὑπεράνω is rather different, as the former element prevails and makes the whole an improper preposition differing little from ὑπέρ c. gen.: cf. ἐπάνω.

[1] Wackernagel *Dehnungsgesetz* 42 makes it=ὑπερ-ᾱφ-α-νος, with the vowel of √ αφ lengthened at the juncture: cf. κατηφής and derivatives.

Ὑπό

§ 129. 18. *† Ὑπό=Lat. *sub*, *sup-* (like *super*, somewhat doubtfully explained as for *x-upo*, *x-uper*, from *ex*), Skt. and Av. *upa*, Gaulish *Vo*(retus etc.), OIr. *fo*, Goth. *uf*, Ger. *auf*. The adv. *ὕψι* (superl. ὕψιστος) and noun ὕψος seem to have affected the originally distinct ὑψηλός, for **ὑξηλός* (cf. Gaul. *Uxello*dunum 'Hightown'). These cognates, together with ὑπέρ, need to be brought in here to account for the meaning: add *up*=O.E. *uppe*, OIcel. *upp*, probably from proto-Germanic *upn*, Skt. *upan*-ayati (Brugmann *Grd.*[2] II. ii. 911). The original idea accordingly seems to be "upwards from below": cf. also Goth. *iup* (I.E. *eupn-*) "upwards," Lat. *sus*que deque "up and down," *sus*tineo "hold up." Brugmann also compares *aufsteigen*, *succingere*, for the idea of motion from below. In that case it was possible, in languages which like Greek and Latin had lost the I.E. antithesis of *over* and *under* (*uperi*, *n̥dheri*—see above by the disappearance of the latter, that the starting-point of *upo* should be isolated, and *ὑπό sub* become the antithesis of *ὑπέρ super*. This is essentially Brugmann's explanation (*op. cit.* 912). Note that Goth. *uf* renders *ὑπό* c. acc., as in Mt 8[8].

(*a*) The 27 *ὑπό* cpds. occurring in NT can mostly be paralleled with Latin words containing *sub*. The idea of "submission" accounts for ὑπακούω,[1] ὑπείκω, ὑπέχω, ὑποτάσσω; that of "underhand" for ὑποβάλλω, ὑποκρίνομαι.[1] *Under* in the literal sense gives ὑποδέομαι and ὑποστρωννύω (cf. Aryan, Lat., Goth., OIr., for an identic cpd.). Motion *ὑπό τι* may explain ὑποδέχομαι, ὑποστρέφω, and perhaps originally ὑπάγω, ὑποχωρέω, but *ὑπό* leaves no sensible force but *away*, or even *back*, in the last three named. Ὑπαντάω=come *up* to; ὑπάρχω spring *up*, arise; ὑποδείκνυμι, ὑπομιμνήσκω and ὑπονοέω (cf. *sug*gest) convey the idea of thoughts making their way *up* into the mind; ὑποζώννυμι gird *up*, cf. *suc*cingo, ὑπολαμβάνω =take *up*, in various senses; ὑπολείπω (-λιμπάνω)=leave *behind* (*qs.* at the bottom); ὑπομένω=*under*go, sometimes=tarry *behind*, as in *ὑπολείπω*; ὑποπλέω=sail *under*, close up to, and so ὑποτρέχω; ὑποπνέω =*suf*flo, breathe *softly*; ὑποστέλλω=draw *back* (cf. on *ὑποχωρέω* above)—note that Wulfila renders *ufslaup* in Gal 2[12].

(*b*) Ὑπακοή and ὑπήκοος, ὑπάντησις, ὕπαρξις, ὑπόδειγμα, ὑπόδημα, ὑπόκρισις and -κριτής, ὑπόλειμμα, ὑπόμνησις, ὑπομονή, ὑπόνοια, ὑπο-

---

[1] In both of these verbs the sense of *ὑπό* has continued to work in the later development. *Ὑπακούω* was originally only to "answer" the door, *ὑποκρίνομαι* (in Attic—developed from "answer") to "play a part": in both we recognise originally the local sense found in *ὑποχωρέω*.

στολή, ὑποταγή and **ἀνυπότακτος** are accounted for above, under their allied verbs in (*a*). **Ὑπηρέτης** (whence **-έω**) was originally a t.t. of the galley (cf. ἐρέσσω), as ὑπηρεσία still shows in classical writers, but it early lost its special connotation and became an "*under*ling" in general. **Ὑπολαμπάς** (Ac 20[8] D)=*window* is a very rare word (see LS, and add *Syll.* 588[219] (*Syll.*[3] om.) [ii/B.C.]): apparently a screen *under* which the light shines. **Ὑπόστασις** in its various meanings runs parallel with its Latin equivalent *substantia*, an underlying foundation being implied. **Ὑποτύπωσις** is like **ὑπογραμμός**, both suggesting a copy traced over a pattern below. **Ὑπεναντίος** is a stronger form of **ἐναντίος**, with ὑπό as in **ὑπαντάω**: the opponent "comes up against" one.

(*c*) Nouns of Cl. VII. are **ὕπανδρος**=ὑπ' ἀνδρὶ οὖσα, **ὑπόδικος**= ὑπὸ δίκῃ ὤν, **ὑποζύγιον**=ὑπὸ ζυγῷ ὄν, **ὑπολήνιον**=ὑπὸ ληνῷ ὄν, **ὑποπόδιον** =ὑπὸ ποσὶν ὄν, and ὑπώπιον (whence **ὑπωπιάζω**)=τὸ ὑπ' ὠπί, the cheek just under the eye. All come from the meaning *under*, as used (in class. Gk.) with locative. **Ὑποκάτω** down *under* is the only compound adverb —see the improper prepositions.

III. IMPROPER PREPOSITIONS.

Improper Prepositions. § 130. † **Ἅμα** is an old instr. case of *sem* (εἷς),=*sm̥ma*: Lat. *unā* has a similar history. **Ὁμοῦ** is a case of *ὁμός (=*same*), which only differs in gradation, but it is not used prepositionally. The meaning is that of *simul* (a derivative of the same root), *with one* thing, *together*.

* **Ἄνευ** *without* is of doubtful history. It has been connected by Wackernagel with Lat. *sine*, by others with Goth. *inu* (Ger. *ohne*). So Brugmann-Thumb, *Gr.* 523.

* **Ἄντικρυς** (Attic—other dialects are without the -ς, for which see under ἄχρι(ς)) *opposite*. Clearly a cpd. of ἀντί: its second element has been assigned to the root of κάρα, *qs.* "having the head (face) opposite": this is not perhaps a great improvement on the older derivation from κρούω. WH accentuate proparoxytone: Blass (p. 20) gives Attic ἄντικρυς= *downright*, but accentuates this late preposition on analogy of Attic (κατ)αντικρύ.

* **Ἀντιπέρα** *opposite* has the later form without final ν: it is a cpd. prep.—see below for its elements.

* **Ἀπέναντι** *opposite*: see ἔναντι below.

* **Ἄτερ** *without* probably came into the *Κοινή* mainly from

Ionic, which would account for its limited use there [LXX, NT and papp. once each]. It is generally taken as=Eng. *sunder*, I.E. *sn̥tér*. The aspirate destroyed by Ionic psilosis is plausibly recognised in *ἅτερος*, the older form of ἕτερος (cf. Attic *θἅτερον*) =*separate* ("*sundry*"). *Sine* and perhaps ἄνευ will be cognate.

* Ἄχρι(ς) *until* is a phonetic doublet of μέχρι(ς) : *α* (=*m̥*) is the weak grade of *με*. The final -ς, which had become functionless in the prehistoric period and came into Hellenistic perhaps through the influence of Epic language, appears to a very limited extent in the NT as in LXX and papyri, and never before a consonant. See Thackeray 136, WH *App.*² 155 : for its history Brugmann *KVG* 456. There is no visible difference between *ἄχρι* and *μέχρι*. Brugmann gives the Armenian *merj* "near" as a cognate.

*† Ἐγγύς *near* (cpve. ἐγγύτερον) is the neuter of an obsolete adjective in -*ύς* with an -ς added which has the same history as that in *ἄχρις*, *οὕτως*, *εὐθύς* etc. No very safe guess has been made as to its etymology.

* Ἐκτός *outside* is a derivative of *ἐξ* : the -*τος* is a suffix with ablative force as in Lat. *coelitus*, Skt. *nāmatas*, etc. See Brugmann *KVG* 455, also 180, where Locrian *ἐχθός* is noted as older, *ἐξ* being for **ἐχς* (cf. ἔσχατος).

* Ἔμπροσθεν *in front of* is a combination of *ἐν* with *πρόσθεν*, that is *πρός* + ablative suffix -*θεν*.

* Ἔναντι *in the presence of* has two further compounds ἀπέναντι and κατέναντι, which secured a place in *Κοινή* literature, while *ἔναντι* itself appears in a very old Cretan inscription, and in LXX and one or two inscriptions and papyri of the Hellenistic period. Wackernagel (*Hellenistica*, pp. 3–6) shows that it came into Hellenistic from Doric Greek. The Attic was *ἐναντίον, which held a stronger position in the *Κοινή* than an element drawn from the less influential dialect. It is acc. of the adj. ἐναντίος (see p. 308). Ἀπέναντι has the same three adverbs as the French *en avant*, but in a different order. (Note that *ἔναντι* was for Grimm presumably a Jewish coinage !)

* Ἕνεκεν, less frequently ἕνεκα, also εἵνεκεν (*quater*) *because of*. On the variant forms cf. Thackeray 82 f., 135, Mayser 241 f., Crönert 114, Schwyzer 35 f., Nachmanson 18 f., WS 50. The NT order of frequency matches that found in the *Κοινή* sources : it does not seem possible to trace much system in the use of

variants due originally to dialect mixture. The Attic was ἕνεκα, which was invaded by ἕνεκεν as early as iv/B.C. (end): see Meisterhans[3] 215 f., who shows that in ii/B.C. it has almost driven out ἕνεκα even in Attica. Thumb *Dial.* 359 gives εἵνεκα and ἕνεκε (Erythrae al.) ἕνεκε (Ephesus al.) as the Ionic forms. It is derived from *ἕνϝεκα, and the second element is a case-form of √ ϝεκ- (whence the ptc. ἑκών). Brugmann (*Gr.*[4] 524) compares Armen. *vasn* with same meaning as ἕνεκα, but notes that its morphology is not clear.

* Ἐντός *within*, Latin *intus*: see ἐκτός above.

* Ἐνώπιον *before, in presence of* (cpd. κατενώπιον), an adverb from the old adjective ἐνώπιος, a derivative of the phrase ἐν ὦπα (acc.) *to the face*, which became stereotyped as an adverb. It was only moderately common in the *Κοινή*, but attained currency among Biblical translators as a conveniently literal equivalent of לִפְנֵי: see *Prol.* 99. In legal papyri it gains a separate currency by its equivalence to Lat. *coram*.

* Ἔξω *outside*, whence (cpve. ἐξώτερος and) the similarly used ἔξωθεν, is best, I think, treated as a compound of ἐξ and the obsolete adverb *ὤ, Skt. *ā*, possibly a gradation variant of either (Lat.) *ā* or *ē*: traces of it are probably visible in ὠ-κεανός, ὠ-ρύομαι, ὀ-κέλλω, ὀ-δύρομαι al. Cf. ἔσ-ω, ἄν-ω, κάτ-ω, ὀπίσω. So now Brugmann *KVG* 465.

* Ἐπάνω *above, upon*, a compound of ἐπί and ἄνω (see above).

* Ἐπέκεινα *beyond*, lit. *to that* (side), ἐπ' ἐκεῖνα. Cf. ὑπερέκεινα.

* Ἔσω (whence ἐσώτερος and ἔσωθεν adv.) *inside*. The classical alternative εἴσω (more correct, since εἰς is phonetically the form before vowels) has rather strangely yielded in Hellenistic to ἔσω, though ἐς is there obsolete (above, p. 304). For -ω see above *s.v.* ἔξω.

* Ἕως *until*, also of space *as far as* (as ὡς in MGr, Thumb *Hellen.* 125). It answers (except in the final -ς) to Skt. *yāvat* "so long as," with correlative *tāvat*: in Homer these were presumably ἆϝος and τᾶϝος (Doric τᾶς, ἇς), but they are affected by Ionic spellings. Ἕως is accordingly from the stem of the relative ὅς, with a possessive suffix (Brugmann *KVG* 667): its passage from conjunction to preposition (in and after Aristotle) is traced by Brugmann (*Gr.*[4] 496) to the analogy of μέχρι, which already combined these functions.

* Μεταξύ *between* is most simply taken as a mere compound of

μετά and ξύν : cf. νύ by the side of νῦν. (So Brugmann *Gr.*[4] 521).

* Μέχρι(ς) *until* : see ἄχρι(ς) above.

* Ὄπισθεν and ὀπίσω *behind, after.* The older form ὄπιθεν seems to be an ablative from the noun base whose accus. is seen in κατόπιν. But at the same time *ὄπι belongs with gradation to ἔπι (ἐπί)—cf. ὀπ-ώρα, ὀψέ, Latin *op* (*ob*) and our *after* : its weak grade is seen in πι-έζω. The form of both these "improper" preps. has been affected by the antithetic πρόσω and πρόσθεν : πρόσσω (=*proty-ō*, with ō as in ἔξω above) produced its opposite ὀπίσσω as early as Homer, and ὄπιθεν was modified in the same period, surviving only in poetry (see ἔμπροσθεν above). An alternative account in Brugmann *Grd.*[2] II. ii. 729 seems less probable.

† Παραπλήσιον *near to*, neuter of an adj. compounded of παρά and πλησίος : see πλησίον below.

* Παρεκτός *except* : see ἐκτός above.

* Πέρᾱν *beyond* is closely connected with πέρᾱ (cf. ἀντιπέρα above) : they are case-forms of a pronominal adjective common in Skt. (*para=other*)—cf. πέρυσι (p. 279), *perendie*, Eng. *far*. See under περί among the Prepositions proper.

* Πλήν *except* is connected by Brugmann (*Gr.*[4] 523—see *KVG* 479) with πλησίον : πλήν τινος *qs.* "prope ab aliqua re." The final -ν, as in other cases (πέραν al.) may be accus. or instrumental ultimately. The root appears to be *seq*ᵘ, as in ἕπομαι *sequor* : *socius* and *secus* show the same divergence as πλήν and πλησίον.

* Πλησίον *near* (Dor. πλᾱτίον), from √ *pelā* "draw near" hence πέλας with accent on first syllable of root, and πλᾱτίος accented later. The word is of course the adverbial accus. of an adj.

* Ὑπεράνω *above*, a compound of ὑπέρ and ἄνω (see above).

* Ὑπερέκεινα *beyond*, lit. *beyond that* (side), ὑπὲρ ἐκεῖνα. Cf. ἐπέκεινα.

* Χάριν *for the sake of, on account of*, accus. of χάρις, exactly like our *thanks to*, except for the case governed.

Χωρίς *apart from* has a suffix parallel with that in ἅλις, Megarian ἄνις (=ἄνευ), which may possibly be akin to the plural instrumental ending (λόγοις etc.). The root seems to be found in χώρα χῶρος "empty space" and (with different grades) χῆρος "empty of" and Skt. *hitvā* "without." The meaning *apart* comes easily from an instr. of such a noun. See Solmsen *Gr. Wortf.* 175 f.

*Μακράν is a preposition in P Oxy i. 113[18] (ii/A.D.), but in NT has ἀπό after it. It is only the acc. sg. fem. of μακρός, with presumably ὁδόν understood. Conceivably the consciousness of words like this may have prompted the new improper preposition *ὁδόν *by way of* in the "translation Greek" of Mt 4[15] (not LXX).[1]

SUFFIXES.[2]

WORD-FORMATION BY SUFFIXES.

§ 131. We must now turn our attention to the second main division in the province of word-formation, namely, the study of formative elements within words. In the structure of the individual word we can generally distinguish between (*a*) the root, (*b*) the formative suffix (or suffixes), (*c*) the case suffix in the noun, or the personal suffixes in the verb. In addition to these there is sometimes (*d*) a prefix (or prefixes) at the beginning of the word. (For illustration, reference may be made to Giles, 26 ff.) In this section we are concerned primarily with the formative suffix, for notes have already been supplied under the heading Composition on the origin and meaning of such prefixes as we meet with in the vocabulary of the NT. Here, again, it is necessary to deal separately with nouns and verbs.

THE FORMATION OF NOUNS AND ADJECTIVES.

Root Nouns. § 132. A preliminary distinction must be made between root nouns and those nouns and adjectives which contain a formative suffix. Root nouns are those in which the case suffixes are attached to the bare root, that is, to something which is incapable of further analysis. They are generally monosyllabic, and are often found as the

[1] [See further, Appendix, p. 459.—ED.]

[2] Dr. Moulton's MS ends with § 130. The chapter on Suffixes has been written by the Editor. See Preface.

second member of a compound noun. It is usual to classify them as they preserve two or more ablaut grades in the case forms, or as they show the same grade throughout.

(*a*) To the former class belong:

Πούς, gen. *ποδός*. Dor. *πώς*. Skt. *pắt, padáș*. Lat. *pēs, pedis*.

Εἷς, gen. *ἑνός*. In Cret. *ἕνς* and neut. *ἕν* the *m* of **sem-* has become a according to phonetic law (see Brugmann *Gr.*[4] 86, 88). The weak form of the stem appears (**sm̥-*) in *ἅμ-α* (*simul*), *ἅ-παξ* (Skt. *sa-kṛ́t*) and (**sm-*) in *μ-ία* and *μ-ῶνυξ*.

Φρήν, *φρεν-ός*. Derivation uncertain. For conjectures see Boisacq.

Ζεύς (see above, p. 142).

Χιών originally an *m*-stem (Brugmann *Gr.*[4] 88), cf. Lat. *hiem-s*.

Βοῦς, Skt. *gāúș*. The weakest grade of the stem **gᵘu-* is seen in *ἑκατόμ-βη* (cf. Skt. *śata-gu-*=having 100 kine) and possibly in *βόσ-πορος*.

(*b*) To the second class belong:

Ὗς (Lat. *sus*), **ἰχθύς, ὀφρύς, ὀσφύς** (for accentuation see above, p. 141), **ναῦς** (from **νᾱυς*, Skt. *nāú-ș*. See above, p. 142), **χείρ** (p. 138), **ἅλς** (p. 132) (Lat. *sal*), **θρίξ** (p. 130).

(For full treatment see Brugmann *Grd.*[2] II. i. 130–146.)

Formative Suffixes.

Suffixes. § 133. Whether the suffixes which play so important a part in the stem formation of Greek nouns ever had a separate existence in the prehistoric stage of the original Indo-European language we cannot say. In O.E., *dōm* meaning judgment was a separate noun, though it also appeared as a suffix in such words as *cynedōm* (kingdom), *freodōm* (freedom). In the same way O.E. *līc*, which meant body or corpse (as preserved in the words lych-gate and lyke-wake) became the very common suffix -ly, so that manly or man-like means "having the body or form of a man."[1] Analogy is a tempting form of argument, but in the absence of convincing evidence, we must leave the question of the sometime separate existence of the Greek suffixes unanswered, and confine our attention to their function in the historical period of the language. The Indian grammarians distinguished between rim-p ary and secondary suffixes used in noun formation, primary being those attached to a root or to a verbal stem, secondary those added to a noun stem. Thus *-τορ-* in *δώ-τορ-ες* was primary,

[1] See Giles[2], 246 ff.

-ιο- in πάτρ-ιο-ς secondary. Modern philologists (*e.g.* Giles[2], 245) apply these terms differently, using primary of a suffix which is added directly to a root, and secondary of a suffix which is added to an existing stem which already contains a suffix. Thus -νο- in ἐαρι-νό-ς is secondary because it follows the locative case ending of the noun. For our treatment of the subject, however, the distinction may be ignored for reasons given by Brugmann (*Grd.*[2] II. i. 124 f.).

A. Vowel Suffixes.[1]

(1) *-o- and -ā-.*

1. *Nouns in -ος.*

-ος § 134. This -o- was originally the second syllable in dissyllabic light bases, and in the primitive I.E. period served a noun function, *e.g.* λύκο-ς (Skt. *vṛ́ka-s*)<I.E. **u̯l̥qᵘó-s*; ζυγό-ν (Skt. *yugá-m*); also adjectivally, *e.g.* νέ(F)ος (Skt. *náva-s*). The ablaut relation o/ε appears in the vocative λύκε (Skt. *vṛ́ka*, Lat. *lupe*). The suffix -o- was then attached to bases which had the accent originally on the first syllable. In the same way the -ā-, originally the second syllable of dissyllabic heavy bases, appears to have been extracted and given an extended use as a feminine suffix in the I.E. period.

The most important use of the -o- suffix is in connexion with verbal roots. Two classes of nouns are thus formed, according to the accent; the barytones are *nomina actionis*, and the oxytones *nomina agentis.*

(*a*) *Nomina actionis* are γόμος, δρόμος, πλό(F)ος, πόνος (πένομαι), σπόρος, τόκος, τρόμος, τρόπος, φόβος (φέβομαι), φόνος, φόρος: and with hanged meaning λόγος, νόμος, ὄγκος (ἐνεγκ-εῖν), τάφος (θάπτω), τοῖχος.

(*b*) *Nomina agentis* are τροφός, τροχός.

Both classes became important in providing the latter member for compound nouns and adjectives. The NT provides examples in χιλί-αρχος, ἀρχ-ηγός, πρό-δρομος, οἰκο-δόμος, δεξιο-λάβος (δεξιο-βόλος, L in Ac 23[23]), ἔμ-πορος, ὁδοι-πόρος (>ὁδοιπορέω), ἱερό-συλος.

For the accentuation of such compounds see below, p. 392 N.2.

Compounds, not only from verbal stems, but from nouns with various stem-endings, often took this suffix. See below, Adjectives in -ος.

2. *Nouns in -α, -η.*

Verbal abstract nouns in -ᾱ́ (-ή), formed directly from the

[1] An obelus (†) before a word in the chapter on Suffixes marks it as not appearing before Aristotle.

root, were inherited at an early stage, and were still in active formation during the historical period :

-α (-η) *E.g.* ἀρχή, βολή (βαλ-εῖν), δίκη (cf. δείκ-νυ-μι, Skt. *diç-*, *dik*, Lat. *dīco* and *judex* (**ious-dic-s*)), δοχή (δέχ-ομαι), κλοπή (*κλεπ-ἰω), νομή (νέμ-ω), πνοή (πνέω), ῥιπή (ῥίπτω<*Fρῖπ-ἰω), ῥοπή (ῥέπω; for ῥιπή, 1 Co 15[52] DG), σπορά (σπερ- or σπαρ-), σπουδή (σπεύδ-ω), στεγή (στέγω, cf. Skt. *sthagati*, Lat. *tego*), στολή (στέλλω), σφαγή (σφάζω<*σφαγ-ἰω), ταφή (θάπτω, ταφ-εῖν), τροπή (τρέπω), τροφή (τρέφω), φθορά (φθείρω<φθερ-ἰω), φυγή (φυγ-εῖν), χαρά (χαρ-ῆναι).

Note.—The transition from the abstract to the concrete is specially noticeable in ἀκοή, which is often used for the organ of hearing as well as for the object heard, and γραφή (see *Vocab. s.v.* for its common use in papyri as "document of contract," and its use in Aristeas and NT for "Scripture").

From the classical age all kinds of verbs gave rise to such formations, especially those ending in mutes, and more particularly those whose stems ended in mediae or aspirates, *e.g.* ἁρπαγή, διδαχή, καταλλαγή, παραλλαγή, ταραχή.

A few back-formations in -η are of special interest.

†Ἀγάπη, a shortened form of ἀγάπησις, just as συναντή (3 K 18[16], 4 K 2[15] 5[26]) and ἀπαντή (3 K 20[18]) are back-formations from συνάντησις and ἀπάντησις. (See *Vocab. s.v.* and supplementary note in *Exp T* xxvi. 139.)

†Οἰκοδομή, shortened in the same way from οἰκοδόμησις, appears first in Aristotle, and is frequently found in the Κοινή, both literary (see Lobeck *Phryn.* 487 ff.) and vernacular (see *Vocab. s.v.*), for οἰκοδόμημα; -ᾱ- is also used to represent the feminine equivalents to masculines in -ος : *e.g.* θεός : θεά, ἀδελφός : ἀδελφή. In this the adjectival type -ος, -ᾱ, -ον was followed.

3. *Adjectives in -ος.*

(*a*) Simplicia: ἀγαθός, βάρβαρος, ἐνεός ("*étym. inconnue,*" Boisacq), ἔρημος, κωφός, λεῖος, λοιπός, μάρμαρος, μόνος, μωρός, νόθος, ὀλίγος, πειθός, σοφός, στενός, φίλος, χαλεπός, χωλός.

(*b*) Compounds: ἄναλος, πρόγονος, ἀργός (see pp. 158, 287), δύσκολος, ἔγκυος, ὅμιλος (see below, n. 1), ἄπειρος, ταλαίπωρος, †ἄραφος (for ἄραπτος, see p. 371), ἄσπονδος, †τρίστεγος, δίστομος, ἄστοργος, ἱερόσυλος, αὐτόφωρος.

Note.—1. ὅμιλος (which owes its place in NT text (Rev 18[17]) to cursive 1, the sole MS used by Erasmus for the Apoc.—a rdg. also found in Hipp.) is given a note here because it has not been included in the ὁμο- cpds. in § 107 (p. 284). Sütterlin 61 suspects that it is a cpd. Boisacq

(p. 700) derives from *ὁμο-μιλ- by syllabic haplology and cft. Skt. *miláti to come together, join, mēlá-ḥ meeting*, Lat. *mīles -itis* (*mīl-it-ēs* " *ceux qui marchent en troupe* ").

2. Adjectives formed from composita generally took the suffix most appropriate to the second member of the cpd. But when the first member was a particle or a preposition an -ᾱ- stem gave way to the suffix -ο-. This usage spread to most cpds. ending in -α- stems, and consonantal stems also showed a strong preference for the convenient suffix -ος. See Debrunner *Wortb.* 71 ff., and p. 289 above.

(2) *-ιο- and -ιᾱ-.*

1. *From adverbs and locatives in -ι- we have—*

-ιος § 135. **Ἄρτιος** (ἄρτι), **πρώιος** (πρωΐ) and so by analogy **ὄψιος** (ὀψέ), **ἐνάλιος** (ἐν ἁλί) and **παράλιος**, **δεξιός** (cf. δεξι-τερός). So **ἀΐδιος** (for the locative ἀεί see *Vocab. s.v.*).

Under this head should also come **μέσος** (cf. Lat. *medius*, Skt. *mádhyas*. Brugm. *Grd.*[2] II. i. 164 relates this to **me-dhi*, μετά and Skt. *á-dhi*) and **ἄλλος** (**ali̯o-s*, Lat. *alius*, from **ali*, cf. Lat. *ali-ter*).

2. *Verbal adjectives.*

E.g. **ἅγιος** (ἅζομαι, Skt. *yájya-s*), **ἄξιος** (*ἀγ-τι-ος, Boisacq, *s.v.*), σφάγιος (>**σφάγιον**, σφάζω=*σφαγι̯ω). In this way comes **μανία** (μαίνομαι<I.E. **mn̥i̯-ó-*).

In I.E. there were a number of adjectives in (ι) ι̯ο with verbal force (see Brugm. *Grd.*[2] II. i. 183 ff.), and this tendency has not been without effect in Greek, though the suffix did not prove a fruitful source for adjectives.

3. *Denominative adjectives.*—This very numerous class consists of adjectives formed from the stems of nouns by means of the suffix -ιος with the meaning " of, or belonging to."

Thus †**δοκίμιος** (<δοκιμή<δόκιμος<δέκομαι), **τίμιος** (<τιμή), **κόσμιος** (<κόσμος).

The suffix is thinly disguised by contraction in **θεῖος** : θεός, **πεζός** (πεδ-ι̯ος, cf. Skt. *padyás*) : πούς.

This came to be the appropriate adjectival suffix in cpds., *e.g.* **καταχθόνιος**, **μακροχρόνιος**.

-τήριος From such regular formations as **σωτήριος** the new suffix -τηριο- was extracted, which appears in **ἱκετήριος**, and in the neuter nouns in -τήριον given in § 137 below. Apart from a rather numerous list of derived substantives (represented in NT by †**ζευκτηρία** and **σωτηρία**), this suffix soon worked itself out, and was displaced by -τικός. Thus we have **κριτήριον**, but **κριτικός** (see p. 379).

-σιος The addition of -ιος to various -t- stems produced -σιος (K. Bl. ii. 292), **ἑκούσιος** : ἑκοντ-. In this way -σιος came to be the regular adjectival formation corresponding to the verbal adjectives in -τος, *e.g.* **θαυμάσιος** : θαυμαστός, and to the denominative nouns and *deverbativa* in -της, *e.g.* **δημόσιος** : δημότης (<δῆμος), **γνήσιος** : γνησιότης (<γίγνομαι).

NOTE.—1. Debrunner *Wortb.* 143) observes that this -σιος has become specially attached to compounds, since the verbal adjectives in -τος favoured the compounds, and the *nomina agentis* in -της were originally also peculiar to the compounds ; in particular the fem. noun in -σία thus came into sharp contrast with -σις in the simplex verb. Thus **γνῶσις : ἀγνωσία, δόσις : †μισθαποδοσία, κρίσις : †δικαιοκρισία, στάσις : †ἀποστασία.**

2. **Φιλιππήσιος** (Ph 4[15]) does not, of course, belong to this group, but has the Gr. -ιος added to the -*e*(*n*)*s*- stem of the Lat. -*ensis*. For the loss of -*n*-, see above, p. 106. Ramsay (*JTS* i. 116) says this suffix is only used in Gr. to reproduce a Lat. name, as Μουτουνήσιος for *Mutinensis*. The ordinary Gr. was Φιλιππεύς or -ηνός. Possibly the remembrance of Homeric Ἰθακήσιος (Bl[5]-D 6 n. 6) may be a factor.

-αῖος With ᾱ- stems -ιος combines to form -αῖος (rarely -αιος as δίκη : **δίκαιος**); thus we have **ἀγοραῖος, ἀναγκαῖος, ἀρχαῖος, †ἀκρογωνιαῖος** (see § 106 (*a*) and *Vocab.*), **ἑδραῖος, κρυφαῖος, σπουδαῖος, ὡραῖος.**

Brugmann (*Grd.*[2] II. i. 194) finds the explanation in the contraction of *-ασιο- to -αιο- in the three words κνεφαῖος, γεραιός, γηραιός (the accent in the last two following that in παλαιός). The rest would then be formed by false analogy. Brugmann's earlier explanation (*Gr.*[3] 181, retained by Thumb in *Gr.*[4] 212) rests on the loc. sing. -αι+-ι̯ο-. At any rate the locative meaning so evident in **ἀγοραῖος**, θυραῖος and πυλαῖος gave the meaning "belonging to a place" to -αῖος, and it was added in this sense to ο- stems. Thus in class. Gr. we find νησαῖος and χερσαῖος. This predominant meaning may account for its wide use in gentilic names. In addition to those given above on p. 150, the NT supplies **Ἀθηναῖος, Βεροιαῖος, Δερβαῖος, Κυρηναῖος.** For **δευτεραῖος** and **τεταρταῖος** see p. 176 above (also W. Bauer *HNT ap.* Jn 11[39]).

-αιός In **παλαιός** and **κραταιός** the suffix -ος is added to the adverb πάλαι and to κραται (cf. κραταί-πους).

-αιος Like **δίκαιος** (δίκη) the following are proparoxytone : **βίαιος** (: βία), **μάταιος** (< μάτην < μάτη), **βέβαιος** (<βαίνω, cf. βέβα-μεν), **ἀκέραιος** (accented as almost all compounds with ἀ-). For the noun **προσκεφάλαιον** see above, § 126 (*c*).

-ιαῖος **Ταλαντιαῖος** represents a class of adjective in which the suffix -ιαῖος stands for measure, weight or value. Kühner-Bl. ii. 292 f. suggests an origin in -ι- stems, σταδιαῖος, ὀργυιαῖος, though these first appear in Hellenistic. Μηνιαῖος is early ;

for its frequent use in papyri of monthly accounts see Mayser *Gr.* i. 448, and add Wilcken *Archiv* ii. 126 and P Oxy xii. p. 48.

-ειος The suffix -ειος represents the convergence of two formations.

(*a*) -ειος <*-εσιος, attached to ς- stems.

E.g. **τέλειος** : τέλος (τελεσ-ιος), **ἐπιτήδειος** (<adv. ἐπιτηδές, see above, § 120), **Ἄρειος** : Ἄρης.

(*b*) -ήϊος (Hom.) <*ηϝ-ιος attached to stems in ευ- : υ.

In this way arose **βασίλειος** (: βασιλεύς), **ἀστεῖος** (: ἄστυ).

Οἰκεῖος (: οἰκεύς, Hom.) would be popularly attached to οἶκος after οἰκεύς had become obsolete. With the help of this analogy the rapid extension of the suffix to other stems can be explained.

Ἀνθρώπειος has its natural counterpart in **γυναικεῖος**. So also we find **αἴγειος** (: αἴξ), †**ἐπάρχειος** (ἔπαρχος), **ἐπίγειος** (see above, § 120), **μεγαλεῖος**, **ἀχρεῖος** (for deriv. see above, § 107, also Boisacq 1070).

-οῖος This suffix, according to Brugmann (*Gr.*[4] 212), originates in loc. sing. in -οι+ιο and is found in ποῖος, τοῖος, ἀλλοῖος etc. with παντοῖος conforming to type.

It is represented in NT by **ὁποῖος** and **ὅμοιος**.

The locative derivation is disputed by Hirt *Hdb.* 255. Debrunner *Wortb.* 144 derives the suffix from *ο-οιϝος, and regards it as originally a *Kompositionshinterglied* with the meaning "kind," "sort."

-ῷος Two examples in NT.

Πατρῷος (in Hom., Hes. and Herod. always πατρώιος; see LS. From stem πατρωϝ-. Brugmann *Grd.*[2] II. i. 206).

Ὑπερῷος (an adjectival ending added to ὑπέρ, following πατρῷος, μητρῷος), represented by the neut. noun **ὑπερῷον**. See p. 326.

(3) *Nouns in -ία.*

-ία § 136. Several important groups call for consideration.

1. *Names of Countries.*—Many of these are back-formations from national names. **Συρία** < Σύριος < Σύρος; **Ἀχαΐα** < Ἀχαιός; **Φρυγία** < Φρύγιος < Φρύξ will serve as examples of many more in NT.

2. *Abstract Nouns.*—The normal type is found in **ἐλευθερία** (<ἐλευθέριος<ἐλεύθερος), **ξενία** (<ξένιος<ξένος), **σωτηρία** (<σωτήριος< σωτήρ). So with **ἡσυχία**, **παρθενία**, †**σκοτία**, **φιλία**.

But a far larger number are formed straight from nouns, or from adjectives in -ος without the intervention of an adj. in -ιος, *e.g.*:

from adjectives in -ος, **δειλία**, **ἐλαφρία**, **κοινωνία**, **μαλακία**, **μωρία**, **πικρία**, **πονηρία**, **ῥυπαρία**, **σοφία**;

from nouns, **ἀγγελία** (ἄγγελος), **ἡγεμονία** (ἡγεμών), **ἡλικία** (ἧλιξ), **κυβία** (κύβος), **μαγία** (μάγος);

from verbs, **ἁμαρτία** (°άνω, ἁμαρτ-εῖν), **μαρτυρία** (°έω);

from compounds, *e.g.* †ἐπιχορηγία (°γέω), †κενοδοξία (†κενόδοξος). So ἀγρυπνία, †ἀντιμισθία, ἐπαρχ(ε)ία, †ἐφημερία, φιλαδελφία, (§ 108), φιλανθρωπία, φιλαργυρία, φιλονεικία.

Compounds in -ια are formed direct, *e.g.* ἀναλογία (from prepositional phrase, see § 113), †ἐθελοθρησκία (§ 108).

(4) *Nouns in -εία.*

-εία Abstracts in -εία are formed either from nouns in -ευς (originally through the mediation of an adjective in -ειος, for -ήϊος), or from verbs in -εύω.

Thus βασιλεία<βασίλειος<βασιλεύς.

All the other abstracts in -εία found in the NT are derived from verbs in -εύω (-εύομαι): viz. ἀλαζονεία*, ἀρεσκεία*, δουλεία, ἐριθεία*, ἑρμηνεία*, θεραπεία, †θρησκεία, ἱερατεία*, κολακεία*, λατρεία, †λογεία, †μεθοδεία*, μοιχεία, νηστεία, †οἰκετεία, παιδεία, †περισσεία, πολιτεία, πορεία, πορνεία, πραγματεία*, πρεσβεία, †προφητεία, στρατεία, φαρμακεία*, φυτεία.

NOTE.—1. Those nouns marked above with an asterisk (*) are spelt by WH in the shortened form -ία (*App.*[2] 161). This is due to the itacistic tendencies of the scribes in the age of the great uncials. See above, pp. 57, 76 f. and *Proleg.* 47.

2. The transition from abstract to result is seen in some words, *e.g.* φυτεία *planting* in Xen., LXX, but *plant* in Mt 15[13] (as in inscrr.); to collective concrete in θεραπεία (Lk 12[42]), οἰκετεία (Mt 24[45]), πρεσβεία (Lk 14[32] 19[14]). Θρησκεία hovers between *worship* and the *ritual of worship* (see *Vocab.*). Μεθοδεία used *in malam partem* in Eph 4[14] 6[11], as in Polyb. and LXX. See J. A. Robinson *in loc.* *Vocab. s.v.* shows that in papp. the word reverted in meaning to *method.*

3. For ἀρεσκεία and ἐριθεία see p. 57. That the former is derived from ἀρεσκεύω is clear from the bad sense in which it is used by class. writers and in literary Hellenistic. For vernacular support of Philo's use in good sense, as in NT, see *Vocab.* 'Εριθεία<ἐριθεύομαι *to work for hire,* <ἔριθος *day labourer, worker for hire. Selfishness* rather than *factiousness* was the original meaning, labouring for one's own interests rather than devotion to public service. So in the 3 NT passages. See Kennedy *EGT ap.* Phil 1[16], and *Vocab.*

4. The word λογεία was rescued by Deissmann (*BS* 142 ff., 219 f., *LAE*[1] 103 ff., [2]104) from Grimm's class of "biblical words," and the discovery of its verb λογεύω *to collect* (see Wilcken *Ostr.* i. 255 n.[1], 493 f.) removes its derivation from doubt. For further instances of this word, so common in the papp. and yet entirely absent from literary sources, see *Vocab. s.v.* Προφητεία is Hellenistic, with very slight support until we come to papp. and inscrr., for which see *Vocab. s.v.*

-ίας Masculine nouns in -ίας originate from abstracts in -ᾱ.

Thus νεανίας, the only NT member of this class, is derived, acc. to Debrunner (*Wortb.* 145), from *νεανία *youth* (abstract), which then gave *youth* (concrete collective) from which the individualised masc. form in -ίας came.

(5) *Nouns in -σ-ία.*

-σία Abstracts in -σια are derived in the same way as the adjectives in -σιος (*-τιος); see above, § 135.

(*a*) From composita came ἀγνωσία, ἀθανασία, ἀκαθαρσία, ἀκρασία, ἀπιστία,[1] †ἀκαταστασία, ἀσωτία,[1] †ἀφθαρσία, †αἰχμαλωσία, †μισθαποδοσία, †προσωπολημψία, †αἱματεκχυσία, ὁρκωμοσία, νομο-, νου-, †ὁρο-, †υἱο-θεσία, †κενοδοξία, †δικαιοκρισία, †ὀλιγοπιστία,[1] εὐεργεσία, εὐχαριστία, †παλινγενεσία, πλεονεξία, †πρωτοκλισία, παρρησία, διχοστασία, ἐκκλησία, μετοικεσία, †ἀποστασία, συνωμοσία.

(*b*) The only simplicia to come under this heading are θυσία and κλισία.

(*c*) Seven abstracts from verbs in -άζω (-άζομαι) complete the list: γυμνασία, δοκιμασία, ἐργασία, ἑτοιμασία, †ὀπτασία, παραχειμασία, φαντασία.

Note.—1. Παραχειμασία, from *αζω (see § 123), a verb used by Polyb. ii. 54. 5. The simplex χειμασία is also used in the same context of winter quarters, upon which Capes remarks: "The word is used by Herod. of the haunts of birds (ii. 22. 6), but only reappears in the later language."

2. For fuller treatment see Fraenkel *ZVS* xlv. 160 ff.

(6) *Neuter Nouns in -ιον.*

-ιον § 137. This extremely large class of nouns requires systematic treatment, both because of the common belief that its fundamental characteristic is the diminutive meaning, and on account of its prolific extension from the Hellenistic age onwards. It is necessary to separate nouns which do not originate with the diminutive connotation from those that do.

[1] For phonetic reasons the τ- remains unchanged in these words.

1. *Nouns in -ιον (other than diminutives).*

Here we may follow the same classification as in § 135 above when dealing with adjectives, for the substantivised neuter of such adjectives probably marks the starting-point of this development.

1. *Adverbs and locatives in -ι* do not seem to have contributed nouns to our NT vocabulary.

2. *Adjectives.*—(*a*) Verbal adjectives (as in I.E.) are responsible for a number of *nomina actionis*. In some of these the verbal force is strongly felt throughout the history of the word; in most the concrete meaning superseded the abstract at an early stage. Closely associated with these are many denominatives in -ιο- themselves formed from *nomina actionis* and *nomina agentis*. Other nouns are formed directly from verbs without the intervention of any adj.: *e.g.* †προσφάγιον and †σιτομέτριον. For extra-biblical use, see *Vocab. s.vv.* The noun may have come to represent the *result* of the action, as in λόγιον, εὐαγγέλιον, †θεμέλιον; or its *object*, as σφάγιον; or its *instrument*, as ἱμάτιον, †ὀψώνιον (see *Vocab. s.v.* for history and meaning), παραμύθιον. Sometimes the subjects of the action are expressed collectively, as in συμπόσιον, συνέδριον, †συμβούλιον (see Deissmann *BS* 238 and *Vocab. s.v.* for this late word), and by analogy, †πρεσβυτέριον.

This varying relation of the noun to the verbal action is sometimes reflected in the different uses of the same word. †Γεώργιον in 1 Co 3[9] (a rare word, see J. Weiss *in loc.*) seems to = *husbandry, tilth*, as in LXX[ter]; whereas in Pr 24[5. 30], as in Strabo, it = *field*. So μαρτύριον.

(*b*) Very near to these in meaning are adjectival abstracts in -ιον expressing a state or attribute.

The change in relation to verbal action may account partly for the two meanings of αἴτιον in Ac 19[40] (= *cause*) and in Lk 23[4. 14. 22] (= *crime*). So Petersen *Gr. Dim.* 27, "τὸ αἴτιον 'the cause,' with the distinct idea of activity, must have been originally conceived as 'the blame-worthiness,' for it comes from the adj. αἴτιος, 'blame-worthy.'"

The transition from abstract to concrete is seen in δαιμόνιον, *divinity* (<δαιμόνιος, *divine*). From a vague meaning of "divine power," a personal denotation was evolved. The limitation in Attic (as in magic, see *BS* 281 and *Vocab. s.v.*) to inferior deities is probably due to influence of diminutives in -ιον. See below, § 138.

(*c*) Compound adjectives. We may note specially two kinds:

α. prepositional compounds, in some of which the adjective survives, *e.g.* μεθόριον, ὑποζύγιον; but not in all, *e.g.* ἐνύπνιον (see above, § 109), προαύλιον (§ 125 (*c*)).

β. numerical compounds, and those signifying a part of the simplex. Cpds. of ἡμι- and ἀκρο- are common. In the NT we find †ἡμιώριον (Rev 8[1] ℵP 046), ἀκροθίνιον (§ 106), †μεσονύκτιον.

3. *Denominatives.* (As some of these are formed from *nomina actionis* they have been referred to under 2 (*a*) above.)

The infinite variety of meanings connoted by this suffix forbids an exhaustive classification. The main groups come under the following headings:

(1) *Appurtenance.*

(*a*) *Place.*

a. The primitive is *nomen agentis*. The derivative denotes the place connected with the person. Ἐμπόριον (<*ἔμπορος*), †τελώνιον (<*τελώνης*). (Cf. *δεκατώνης* : *δεκατώνιον* iv/B.C.)

A special group is formed from *nom. agentis* in -*τηρ*, of the type *δικαστήρ* : *δικαστήριον*. The termination -*τήριον* was then detached and applied to *nomina agentis* in -*της*. Thus †ἀκροατήριον, δεσμωτήριον, κριτήριον, οἰκητήριον (κατ-).

β. The sanctuary of a god or hero. Ἀπόλλων : Ἀπολλώνιον, Νύμφη : Νυμφαῖον. So Ἀσταρτεῖον 1 K 31[10].[1] On this analogy †εἰδώλιον (an idol's temple, 1 Co 8[10]).

(*b*) *Instrument* or *Means.*

a. Sometimes the primitive is not extant, *e.g.* ἱμάτιον (<*ἷμα <**Fίσμα*< √**u̯is*), "that which is used for winding about or surrounding." πηδάλιον (<*πηδόν*=*blade of oar*), †γαζοφυλάκιον (see above, § 105).

β. Primitive is a *nomen agentis* in -*τηρ* (-*της*).

Αἰσθητήριον (see *Vocab. s.v.*), θυμιατήριον, †θυσιαστήριον, †ἱλαστήριον (Deissmann *BS* 124 ff.), μυστήριον, σωτήριον, τεκμήριον (see *Vocab. s.v.*), φυλακτήριον (see below, § 150), *καυ(σ)τήριον* (<†καυστηριάζω).

(*c*) *Vessels and utensils, household effects.*

These really form one congeneric group with words like ποτήριον, †ὑπολήνιον, †ὑποπόδιον. The primitive of τρύβλιον is not extant.

(*d*) *Herd of domestic animals. E.g.* ποίμνιον (=*herd of sheep* : *ποιμήν*). See below, p. 346.

(*e*) *Part of the whole designated by the primitive. E.g.* κράνιον : *κάρανον* =that which belongs to the head, *the skull.* †βαΐον (*palm branch* : *βαΐς*).[2]

(*f*) *Indefinite plurals in -ια.* Ὅρια=what belongs to the boundary, *limits, frontier.* Φορτία=the things belonging to the load (<*φόρτος*=*load*), then φορτίον=*load.* Χωρία=what belongs to a particular country (*χώρα*), *regions.* Then χωρίον, a particular place, or, as in Mk 14[32], *an enclosed piece of ground* (RVmg).

(*g*) A word that comes under none of these headings is †δυσεντέριον (Ac 28[8] ℵAB, see p. 125). Can this late form of the word be influenced by *μεσεντέριον*, one of "a large number of words beginning with *μεσο-* which are of a heterogeneous semantic character" (Petersen, *op. cit.* 37)? For its derivation see p. 287 above.

---

[1] Cf. P Gurob 22[10] Μιθραίου, [22] Ἀφροσιδίου, [37] Ἑρμαίου, [43] Σαχμιείου, [45] Νεφθιμιείου (iii/B.C.).

[2] The new LS accents *βάϊον* (*βάϊς*).

-τήριον NOTE.—1. Under (*a*), (*b*) and (*c*) we see examples of -*τήριον* as a suffix. Ὁρμητήριον (found in Xen., Isocr. and Dem. and more freely in Hellenistic authors), *πολεμητήριον* (Polyb.), show that in Attic and literary Hellenistic the suffix was already productive in the formation of new words. For new words appearing in Ptolemaic papyri see Mayser *Gr.* i. 439 f. For later words, cf. *ἀπαντητήριον* (*inn*) in PSI iii. 175[5] (A.D. 462). Ἁγνευτήριον occurs in the Gospel fragment P Oxy v. 840[8. 13].

2. Some nouns in -*τήριον* pass from the local meaning in the later language, *e.g.* *βουλευτήριον*, *council chamber* in class. Gr., becomes *senate* in Polyb. ii. 50. 10; cf. Dion. H. 2. 12.

Κριτήριον, which is used with both the instrumental and the local meanings in Plato (so papp. and inscrr.)=*tribunal* Jas 2[6], but *law-suit, cause* 1 Co 6[2. 4] (see J. Weiss *in loc.*).

(2) *Material, substance.*

This can be illustrated from the NT by **ἀργύριον** (*ἄργυρος*) *silver, silver coin, money*; **χρυσίον** (*χρυσός*) *gold, piece of gold, money, golden ornament*; **χαλκίον** (*χαλκός*) *brazen vessel* (Mk 7[4]); **κεράμιον** (*κέραμος*) *earthenware vessel*; **βιβλίον** (*βίβλος, βύβλος*) that which is made of papyrus pith, a *papyrus roll, book*; **σχοινίον** *rope*, that which is made of reeds (*σχοῖνοι*); **ὀθόνιον** (*ὀθόνη*) that which is made of linen, *linen cloth, bandage, swathing band*; **σιτίον** (*σῖτος wheat*) *grain* (generally used in plur.=*food, provisions*); **κηρίον** (*κηρός*=bees-wax) *honeycomb* (Lk 24[42], EKMΘ).

(3) *Category.*

This class of words with the connotation " belonging to the category of," " having the nature of," Petersen divides into those in which -*ιον* has a " generalising " nature, under which **θηρίον** would come, and those in which the suffix has a " specialising " force. Under the latter heading must come **σανδάλιον** (from a root of Semitic origin) *a shoe of the sandal kind*; †**τετράδιον** (see above, p. 176); **ζῷον** (which is adjectival in origin and has no noun primitive).

(4) *Similarity.*

NT examples are †**κεράτιον** (*κέρας horn*) *carob-pod* (Lk 15[16]), **κολλούριον** (p. 78) (*κολλύρα*=*κόλλιξ*, a *bread-roll*) *eye-salve*, because put up in small cakes (see *Vocab. s.v.*), †**πτερύγιον** (*πτέρυξ*) anything like a wing—in architecture, a *turret*, a *pinnacle, battlement* or *pointed roof*.

†**Τοπάζιον**, a word of uncertain derivation, in which the root is almost certainly Semitic (see Cheyne in *EBi. s.v.*), possibly owes its suffix to the influence of *ὀνύχιον* (*ὄνυξ*) " that which is like a nail," " a gem streaked with veins," an *onyx*, *ἀνθράκιον* (*ἄνθραξ*) a kind of jewel that is like charcoal. Under this heading of Similarity come the names of quite a number of articles of dress and ornament.

Under the influence of such words as *δελφίνιον* (: *δελφίς*) the -*ιον* suffix came to be used as the normal ending for plant names. In this way probably we can account for the two forms †**ἀψίνθιον** (Rev 8[11] א*

and ἄψινθος (Rev 8^{11} A *et al.*); see above, p. 123. Here also should come in †ζιζάνιον (for its Semitic root see Lewy, *Fremdwörter*, 52).

-εῖον As with adjectives in -ιος, the nouns in -ιον provide a subdivision in -ειον. Here, again, we notice the convergence of two formations, those deriving from s- stems and those from nouns in -ευς, or verbs in -εύω (see above, p. 339).

(*a*) **Ἀγγεῖον** (: ἄγγος). See *Vocab.* for variety of meaning in papyri. **Δανεῖον** (: δάνος <*δανός=Skt. *diná-s.* See Brgm. *Gdr.*[2] II. i. 256, 526).

(*b*) **Βραβεῖον** (: βραβεύς), **πανδοχεῖον** (: πανδοχεύς), **ταμεῖον** (: ταμεύω); for spelling see above, p. 89.

This suffix before long was appended to other stems, as we are reminded by **σημεῖον** (: σῆμα) and **μνημεῖον** (: μνῆμα).

Θεῖον (Hom. θέειον sulphur fumes) *brimstone* (<*θϜεσ-ειον : <I.E. **dhụos* breath); an adj. "emitting vapours, fumes," from a noun *θεός or *θεόν (θϜεσός, -όν) "breath, fume." So Boisacq 337; *q.v.* for connexion with θεός and θύω.

NOTE.—This termination was added to various stems in the classical age to betoken a *place* (especially for the carrying on of business), *e.g.* χαλκεύς : χαλκεῖον, κάπηλος : καπηλεῖον, Μοῦσα : Μουσεῖον. In Hellenistic it proves a fertile source for such nouns as the papyri show, *e.g.* †γραφεῖον (="writings" in Clem. *ad Cor.* 28^{3}), †ἀγορονομεῖον and μνημονεῖον different names of the same notarial office (see *Archiv* vi. 104), ἀρχεῖον †καταλογεῖον. For all these terms see Mitteis, *Papyruskunde*, II. i. 59 ff.

A notable instance comes in a schedule of water rates, P Lond 1177^{60} (A.D. 113) (=iii. p. 183), where a Jewish place of prayer †εὐχεῖον is mentioned in the same connexion as a προσευχή or synagogue.

2. *Diminutives in -ιον.*

Diminutives in -ιον. § 138. This term is here used to include words with a "deteriorative" and "hypocoristic"[1] significance, as well as those which connote relative smallness of size. The entire class has probably arisen from the use of the suffix (see above, p. 343) to connote similarity to the type represented by the primitive noun. The original meaning is then "a kind of," "something like."

NOTE.—1. The question whether the diminutive suffix is inherited from I.E. or was developed in Greek within the class. period is still open.

[1] The ancient Greek grammarians coined the word ὑποκοριστικά (from ὑποκορίζεσθαι="to speak as a child (κόρη)") for words formed to express tenderness, and so smallness and even disparagement. It seems better to restrict its use to the original meaning.

Brugmann (*Grd.*[2] II. i. 676) states that -(*i*)*i̯o*- was a diminutive suffix in I.E. times. But his earlier view (*Gr.*[3] 180, retained by Thumb in ed.[4] 212) was that this development in the use of the suffix was post-Homeric. The absence of diminutives proper in Homer might of course be deliberate, but the total absence of "faded diminutives" is significant. Two strong arguments in favour of the post-Homeric origin of diminutives are: (*a*) The dim. meaning is only found in the historic Gk. -*ιον*, never in words such as *πέζον* (<*πεδ-yον*) or those in which the dissyllabic -*ιον* is merged in a diphthong, as -*αιον*, -*ειον*, -*οιον*; thus this function may be presumed to have developed after -*dy*-, -*ασι*-, -*εσι*-, -*οσι*-, had become -*ζ*-, -*αι*-, -*ει*-, -*οι*-. (*b*) The accentuation of *παιδίον*, which was the principal pattern of diminutives and one of the oldest. Παῖς <*πάϝις* was still often dissyl. in Homer (*πάϊς*), and the diminutive, if formed in early Homeric times, would be accented on the antepenult (*παΐδιον* >*παίδιον*). This suggests that *παιδίον* and all words modelled thereupon must be later at least than the earlier parts of Homer. See Petersen *Greek Diminutives in -ιον*, from which this account is abridged.

2. The accentuation of "diminutives" seems to defy precise definition. Petersen (*ib.* 12 ff.) suggests "trisyllabic substantives in -*ιον*, if all connexion with the adjectival types from which they are derived has faded from the mind, have a tendency to accent the penult if they are dactylic, but the antepenult if they are tribrachs." But in view of the conflicting analogical influences at work both in early and later times he cannot make use of accent in his treatment of the semantic development of the -*ιον* diminutives.

Diminutives, which are found sparsely in tragedy, abound, as might be expected, in comedy. During the Hellenistic period the intimate language of the home and the speech of the lower social strata forced its way up into the vocabulary of literature. Words which originated in the nursery and the streets lost their hypocoristic meaning or became "faded diminutives," in many cases superseding the primitive noun. (See p. 346, Note.)

In the NT the following classes of diminutives in -*ιον* are represented:

Persons.—**Παιδίον** (*παῖς*), **θυγάτριον** (: *θυγάτηρ*), †**τεκνίον** (1 Jn *passim*) (: *τέκνον*), **κοράσιον** (: *κόρη*). In all of these the hypocoristic use is specially evident in the vocative.

Animals.—**Στρουθίον** (: *στρουθός*), **προβάτιον** (: *πρόβατον*), **ἀρνίον** (: *ἀρήν*), **νοσσίον** (: *νοσσός*).

Parts of the body.—†**Ὠτίον** (: *οὖς*).

Geographical terms.—†**Νησίον** (: *νῆσος*).

Food.—†**Ψιχίον** (=*ψίξ*) ἀ.λ. in Mk 7[28] (‖ Mt 15[27]), †**ψωμίον** Jn 13[26ff.] (elsewhere Marcus vii. 3, Diog. L. vi. 37 and papp.). By this time **παιδίον** and προβάτιον are faded diminutives, for no consideration of size distinguishes them from their primitives.

Ποίμνιον might seem to show a survival of hypocoristic use in Lk 12[32], but the addition of τὸ μικρόν proves that there is no consciousness of diminutive force (see p. 342).

Ὠτίον is a faded hypocorism and has "passed from the language of nurses and lovers into universal use. Both ὠτίον and ὠτάριον are never used when the ear is thought of as an organ of hearing, nor in a figurative sense, but only when the outer ear is distinctly in mind" (Petersen *ib.* 183).

NOTE.—Petersen cites Plut. *Ages.* 13 in proof that ἐπιστόλιον was a true diminutive. But its fairly common use in papyri without any such suggestion, *e.g.* P Fay 122[5] (*c.* 100 A.D.), P Lips 69[3] (118 A.D.), shows how easily the diminutive became a substitute for the primitive. Vogeser illustrates this tendency in the later vernacular and cites many passages where μικρόν is added (*Gr. Heiligenleg.* 42 f.). The full development of this tendency is seen in MGr. (See Thumb, *Hellen.* 178, 220, *Handb.* 62.)

3. *Conglutinates with -ιον.*

-ίδιον § 139. -ίδ-ιον is a suffix which probably takes its rise from stems in -ιδ-, *e.g.* ἀσπίδ-ιον (: ἀσπίς). The suffix was then applied to other stems, as in κλινίδιον (: κλίνη). The uncertainty whether some words in -ίδιον had primitives in -ι- or -ιο- (*e.g.* in NT πινακίδιον <πινάκιον or <πίναξ may have given rise to the suffix -διον which appears in ἰχθύδιον (: ἰχθύς).

At the side of -ίδιον there appears a suffix -ΐδιον, as in βιβλΐδιον (<*βιβλι-ίδιον<βιβλίον), οἰκΐδιον (<*οἰκεΐδιον<οἰκία, but also assignable to οἶκος). In this way some have explained ἰχθῦδιον : ἰχθύς.

Further examples are ἀγρίδιον (*Mart. Polyc.* 5[1]), βιβλίδιον (Herm. *Vis.* iii. 1[4]; Ignat. *Eph.* 20[1]), ξιφίδιον (*Mart. Polyc.* 16[1]), ἐπιστολίδιον (P Hamb 89[4]; PSI i. 93[15]). Thumb *Dial.* 376 quotes Pollux x. 116 to show that Aristoph. used λυχνίδια for λύχνα. Cf. P Ryl ii. 239[21], ὀναρίδιον μικρόν. See also Mayser *Gr.* i. 428 for productivity of this suffix.

-άριον Stems in -αρ- provided a number of diminutives in -άριον which was then regarded as an independent suffix, and used to form a large number of diminutives, *e.g.* γυναικάριον (: γυνή), κλινάριον (: κλίνη), κυνάριον (: κύων), ὀνάριον (: ὄνος), ὀψάριον (: ὄψον), παιδάριον (: παῖς), πλοιάριον (: πλοῖον), †ὠτάριον (: ὠτίον).

NOTE.—1. The freedom with which this suffix was used in coining fresh words is seen from such a formation as κερβικάριον (Herm. *Vis.* iii. 1[4]) (<Lat. *cervical*<*cervix*), ξυλάριον (3 K 17[12] and papp.; see *Vocab.* 434 f.), μοσχάριον (LXX and PSI vi. 600[4]).

2. The decline and disappearance of the diminutive force in these -άριον formations becomes evident from their use in the papyri. Thus κοσμάριον (P Hamb 10[42] χρυσᾶ ἐν κοσμαρίοις μναιαῖα), φερνάριον (BGU iv. 1102[19] where the amount of the dowry is quite substantial), ᾠάρια (BGU iii. 781 v.[6]). Οἰνάριον preserves a diminutive meaning in Epict. *Ench.* 12 (ἐκχεῖται τὸ ἐλάδιον, κλέπτεται τὸ οἰνάριον), but the deteriorative force found in Demosth. *c. Lacr.* 32 is retained in P Flor ii. 160[3], according to Comparetti's note "a light wine, or of inferior quality," though there is nothing to indicate this in the context. See note in P Par p. 414 and additional ref. given in Witk.[2] p. 27 n. In MGr the process is complete, as λιοντάρι shows (see Thumb *Handb.* 338).

Not to be confused with these are the Latin loan words, in which *assarius* and *denarius* are given this common neuter ending, ἀσσάριον, δηνάριον, σουδάριον (*sudarium*, see *BS* 223), which, with σικάριος, is simply transliterated. For papp. see *Vocab. s.v.* For further creations under Latin influence see Vogeser, *Gr. Heiligenleg.* 41.

These secondary suffixes can be yet further combined, as in †βιβλαρίδιον (Rev 10[2, 8ff.]), †βιβλιδάριον (Rev 10[2] C, 10[8] ℵ, 10[9] 046). Βιβλίδιον and βιβλάριον (Rev 10[9] A*) have also some MS attestation. In Herm. *Vis.* ii. 1[3], βιβλαρίδιον and βιβλίδιον are used together synonymously.

(7) -εο-.

-εος The simple suffix -εος (<*-ε̯ιος), which in Attic contracts to -οῦς (see above, pp. 120, 121, 156 for irregularities in NT), forms a group of adjectives of material, represented by ἀργυροῦς, χρυσοῦς, χαλκοῦς, σιδηροῦς. The transition from material to colour, *e.g.* πορφυροῦς, may have been helped by the secondary meaning of χρυσοῦς = golden.

The old connexion between -*e̯io*- and *i*- stems, which is absent from these adjectives, appears in a few nouns which bear trace of adjectival origin, *e.g.* ὀστέον (cf. Skt. *ásthi*), and ὄρνεον (<ὄρνις). In the same way the stem of στερεός appears in στέρεθος (Brugm. *Grd.*[2] II. i. 199).

Two masc. nouns in -εος seem to come in here.

Θυρεός in its Hom. meaning "door-stone" shows its derivation from θύρα more clearly than in its Hellenistic meaning of "shield" (Polyb. Plut. Eph 6[16]).

†Φωλεός (Mt 8[20] ‖ Lk 9[58]) occurs first in Arist. For derivation see Boisacq, *s.v.*

(8) -ι̯ᾰ.

§ 140. Widely productive at an early stage of the language for the formation of feminines to adjectives and nouns, this suffix now survives in longer suffixes in -*a* impure used for forming the feminine of third declension adjectives and participles with three terminations, *e.g.* -ουσα (=-οντι̯α) etc. See § 65 above.

Φέροντ-, φέρουσα (=φερόντι̯α), cf. Skt. *bhárant-*, *bhárant-ī*.
In γλῶσσα (=*γλωχι̯α) the suffix is added directly to a root.

1. *Nouns in* -ειᾰ.

-ειᾰ Feminine nouns in -εια are almost all regularly formed feminines of the εσ-stem adjectives (<*-εσ-ι̯α). As a separate feminine was not used for these adjectives, the feminine was used substantivally.

From adjectives in -ης we have ἀκρίβεια, ἀλήθεια, ἀναίδεια*, αὐτάρκεια, συγγένεια, ἐπιείκεια* (§ 120), εἰλικρίνεια* (§ 105), ἐνέργεια, κακοήθεια*, συνήθεια, ἐγκράτεια, εὐλάβεια, ἀ-, θεο-, εὐ-σέβεια, ἐπιμέλεια, κακοπάθεια,* †πραϋπάθεια,* ἀπείθεια, εὐπρέπεια, ἀσέλγεια (§ 107), ἀσθένεια, ἀσφάλεια (§ 107), συντέλεια (§ 127 (*b*)), †ἐκτένεια, ἐπιφάνεια, κατήφεια; to these must be added ἀπώλεια, βοήθεια, ὠφέλεια*, which are verbal derivatives.

Three more which come from -ες- stems have yielded to the influence of the -ία class, viz. ἀηδία (Lk 23[12] D, see *Vocab. s.v.*), ἀφειδία, εὐωδία. The same influence affected the orthography of other words. See p. 78 above, also WH *App.*[2] 161, where the words marked * are spelt -ία, ἀκριβία, ἀπειθία (in Heb.) and ἐκτενία being treated as doubtful.

Originally a similar suffix (<*-εϝ-ι̯α or *-ηϝ-ι̯α) was used to form a few feminine titles to nouns in -εύς, whilst -εία̅ (the fem. of adj. -ειος) served for abstract nouns, *e.g.* βασιλεύς, king; βασίλεια, queen; βασιλεία, kingdom. But in the Tragedians -ις has already displaced -εια, and in Hellenistic the Macedonian suffix -ισσα established itself and spread widely from βασίλισσα to other feminine titles (see Mayser *Gr.* i. 255, and below, p. 349).

2. *Nouns in* -αινα.

-αινα This suffix, so largely used in Greek for feminines from -*n*- stems (*-n̥-i̯ă >*-αν-ι̯α, >-αινα), is only represented in NT by †γάγγραινα, the name Τρύφαινα, and the adj. μέλαινα.

The origin of the suffix is seen in such a word as τέκτων : τέκταινα (=*τεκταν-ι̯α) (cf. Skt. *tákṣan-* : *takṣn̥-ī*). Then through similarity of nom. in -ων, this became fem. suffix for nouns with οντ- stem. The suffix was detached and appended even to -ο stems, specially for names of persons and animals, *e.g.* λέων : λέαινα, λύκος : λύκαινα.

Γάγγραινα may be derived from γόγγρος (so Boisacq), or may come directly, with reduplication, from γραίνω = γράω, to gnaw.

(9) -τρ-ια.

-τρια †**Μαθήτρια** is the only NT example of this form of the feminine of *nomina agentis* in -της (< -τηρ, see § 150).

To Mayser's instances (*Gr.* i. 444), βεβαιώτρια and προπωλητρια, we may add ἀγοράστρια, P Thead 1[11] (A.D. 306), BGU iii. 907[11] (*c.* 185 A.D.).

(10) -ισσα.

-ισσα This suffix (from *-ικ-ι̯α) arose with such examples as *Κίλιξ* : *Κίλισσα*, but was widely used in the Hellenistic period under the influence of the Macedonian court. See (8) above.

Βασίλισσα (see *Vocab. s.v.*), **Φοίνισσα** (Mk 7[26] D), **Φοινίκισσα** (*ib.* B *et al.*), **Συροφοινίκισσα** (*ib.* ℵAL *et al.*).

The papyri furnish further exx. of this fem. formation, *e.g.* πατρώνισσα IGSI, 1671, P Oxy iii. 478[27] (A.D. 132), ἀρτοκόπισσα (new fem. of ἀρτοκόπος) P Oxy viii. 1146[8, 9] (early iv/A.D.). Mayser (i. 255, 451) cites ἱέρισσα from numerous Ptolemaic papp., and the two adjectives μελανοσπαλάκισσα (*iron-grey*) and ψακάδισσα (*dappled*) from a register of cavalry horses, P Petr ii. 35, col. 1[7, 9] (*c.* 240 B.C.).

(11) -ισσος.

-ισσος The proper name **Νάρκισσος** preserves a plant name showing the same suffix as κυπάρισσος. See *Vocab. s.v.*, and for the suffix -σσος, Kretschmer *Einl.* 405 ff.

(12) -ευ-.

-εύς (*a*) From the earliest period this was freely used as a denominative suffix to indicate a person specially concerned with the thing denoted by the primitive. It thus came in time to mark a trade or profession.

Our examples are **ἁλιεύς**, †**βυρσεύς**, †**γναφεύς** (see p. 108), **γραμματεύς**, **ἱερεύς**, **ἱππεύς**, **κεραμεύς**, **φαρμακεύς** (only in inferior MSS of Rev 21[8]), **χαλκεύς**.

(*b*) In a few words we have trace of an early formation from a verb, **γονεύς** (< γέν-εσθαι) and **φονεύς** (< √φεν. cf. Hom. ἔ-πε-φν-ε).

(c) In compound formations this suffix is almost confined to prepositional compounds (for reasons shown by Debrunner *Wortb.* 152 f.). †Καταγγελεύς is a NT example. Πανδοχεύς is an exception. Συγγενεῦσιν as read in some MSS in Mk 6[4], Lk 2[44], is really from the adjective *συγγενής*—an instance of popular heteroclisis, see above, p. 138.

(d) *Ethnica* were generally formed by substituting *-εύς* for suffix in name of city or country, *e.g.* Θεσσαλονικ-εύς (*-η*), Κολόσσ-εύς (*-αι*), Λαοδικ-εύς (*-ία*), Ταρσ-εύς (*-ός*).

From names in *-εια*, both *-ειεύς* and *-εύς* (*-ειεύς* >*-εεύς* >*-εύς*) were formed in Attic, *e.g.* *Δεκέλεια*, *Δεκελειεύς* and *Δεκελεύς*; in Hellenistic almost always *-εύς*, *e.g.* Ἀλεξανδρεύς, Ἀντιοχεύς.

(e) Νηρεύς (Rom 16[15]), a personal name, possibly marking one of Nero's freedmen; see Rouffiac 91 for inscriptional evidence of widespread occurrence in Galatia and Athens. The name, of course, is as old as Homer.

(13) *-eu̯- : -u-.*

-υς (a) *-eu* is represented by the solitary noun πῆχυς (p. 141) and the adjectives on p. 160 above.

(b) *-u-*. For nouns see p. 141.

B. Nasal Suffixes.

(1) *-mo-*, *-mā-*.

1. *Nouns in -μός, -θμός, -σμός.*

-μός § 141. This suffix originates in an I.E. abstract suffix which appears in different stages of development in Gr. While it is used primarily to form verbal abstracts, that meaning is often lost in the concrete.

(a) In λιμός *hunger*, λοιμός *plague*, the underlying root has vanished though both may perhaps be related to Lat. *lētum* (=*death*).

(b) It is attached to primary verbal stems in a number of words, such as ἁρμός (probably from √ seen in *ἀραρίσκω*), βρυγμός (*βρύχω*), βωμός (<*βā-*, cf *ἔ-βη-ν*), †ὑπογραμμός (*γράφω*), διωγμός (*διώκω*), †ἐλεγμός (*ἐλέγχω*, also ἀπελεγμός fr. *ἀπ°*), ὀδυρμός (*ὀδύρομαι*), οἰκτιρμός (*οἰκτείρω*), †ἐμπαιγμός (*ἐμπαίζω*), σεισμός (*σείω*, cf. *σέ-σεισ-μαι*, *ἐ-σείσ-θην*), φραγμός (*φράσσω*), ψαλμός (*ψάλλω*).

(c) Its more typical use is with denominative verbal stems, *e.g.* †ἁρπαγμός, στεναγμός, στηριγμός.

-σμός (d) Far more usual is the extended form of the suffix, *-σμός*, which is specially attached to the denominatives in *-ίζω*, *-άζω* and *ύζω*, with dental stems.

From *-ίζω* come **†ἁγνισμός, -αρτισμός (†ἀπ-, †κατ-), †βαπτισμός, βασανισμός** (Alexis in Athen., 4 Macc), **θερισμός, †ἱματισμός** (see *Vocab.*), **†Ἰουδαϊσμός, †καθαρισμός, λογισμός, μακαρισμός, μερισμός (δια-), †ὀνειδισμός, †παροργισμός, †πορισμός, †ῥαντισμός, †σαββατισμός** (see Moffatt *ICC*, *ap.* Heb 4[9]), **ἐπισιτισμός** (from Xen. down), **†ἀφανισμός, †σωφρονισμός, †φωτισμός, χρηματισμός, †ψιθυρισμός.**

From *άζω*, **†ἁγιασμός, ἀσπασμός, †ἐνταφιασμός, πειρασμός, †παραπικρασμός.**

From *-ύζω*, **†γογγυσμός** (see Rutherford *NP* 463), **κατακλυσμός** (see *Vocab.*).

Then the suffix passed over to nasal and other verbs whose perf. pass. ended in *-σμαι* as with the *-ζω* verbs, *e.g.* **ἱλασμός** (*ἱλάσκω*, cf. *ἱλάσ-θητι*), **†μιασμός** (*μιαίνω*), **†μολυσμός** (*μολύνω*), **παροξυσμός** (*παροξύνω*), **†κυλισμός** (2 Pet 2[22] BC) (*κυλίνδω*, later form *κυλίω*, p. 246).

Δεσμός exhibits this suffix as early as Homer (*δέω, δέ-δε-μαι*).

Note.—For papyrus nouns in *-μός*, see Mayser *Gr.* i. 435 ff., and for the very large class of new formations in *-ισμός* cf. *δειγματισμός* PSI iv. 358[8. 21]; *ἐμπυρισμός* PSI iv. 338[7. 15] (*v.* Intr.), 339[7] (all iii/B.C.).

-θμός.

(*e*) In the termination *-θμός* we have the root determinative[1] *-dh-* combined with the suffix *-μός*.

Ἀριθμός where the root is *ἀρι-*, as found in *νήριτος* (=*numberless*), **†βαθμός** (see p. 112, *Vocab. s.v.*) from the root *βα-* (seen in *βαίνω* <**βαμιω* <**g^u m-iō*) *βη* (*ἔ-βη*), **κλαυθμός** from *κλαίω* (fut. *κλαύ-σ-ομαι*).

-μος

(*f*) Several nouns in *-μος* go back to a very early stage in the language.

Ἄνεμος (I.E. *anēi*, *to breathe*, cf. Skt. *áni-ti*).

Δῆμος (√ *dā(i)*, cf. Skt. *dāti*, *to cut, divide*) originally meant the *portion of territory* belonging to a community, then a *canton*, finally the *people* (see Boisacq 182).

Κάλαμος (I.E. **k°l°mo-s*, see Boisacq 397).

Κέραμος (I.E. **qer°mo-s*, cf. Lat. *crĕmo* from √ **qer* or **qar*, cf. Lat. *carbo* (**car-dho*), see Boisacq 436).

Κόσμος (<**κονσμο-ς* I.E. **kens-*=*to make authoritative announcement*, cf. Lat. *censeo*=*to judge*; see Boisacq 500).

Κῶμος (opinion is divided between I.E. **qō(i)mo-s* from a supposed √ *qōi*=*to meet*, suggested as root of *κώμη*, and I.E. **k̂ō[i]-mo-s*, cf. Skt. *çiçāti*=*to share with one*, Boisacq 544).

Μῶμος probably connected with *ἀμύμων*, for which Hirt suggests I.E.

---

[1] For root-determinatives see Brugmann *KVG* 296 f., Hirt *Handb.*, 202 ff., Debrunner *Wortb.* 3 f. The term is applied to a consonant coming between the root (or base) and the suffix, differing from the former in that it contributes nothing to the meaning of the word, and from the latter in that it is not used in the formation of groups of words (cf. *τρέμειν, τρέσσε, trepidus*, where *μ, σ, p*, belong neither to the root nor to the suffix).

mōum (see Boisacq 57). For vowel gradation see Hirt *Hdb.* 89. On the interesting Biblical history of the word see Hort *Comm. on 1 Pet.* p. 77.

Πόλεμος. Uncertain derivation. See Boisacq *s.vv.* πελεμίζω, πάλλω. With these should also come:

Ποταμός (Lesb. πόταμος)<I.E. **petā-*, *to move rapidly, fly, tumble* (cf. ἐπτάμην), cf. also I.E. **pet-* **pete-*, Skt. *pát-man*, πέτομαι (ἐπτόμην).

2. *Nouns in -μή.*

This formation is closely parallel to that in -μός, and was used for verbal abstract nouns, many of which became concrete.

(*a*) The verbal root is evident in γνώμη, δέσμη (for accent and meaning see *Vocab. s.v.*), δραχμή (<δράσσομαι, but for other theory see *Vocab. s.v.*), δυσμή (<δύνω. First=δύσις *setting*, then=*west*), μνήμη, ῥύμη (<ῥύομαι. For its Hellenistic meaning=*street*, see Rutherford *NP* 487–8), στιγμή (<στίζω <*στιγ-ɩ̯ω), τῑμή (<τίω, τίνω), φήμη (<φημί).

(*b*) The suffix -σμή is half concealed in αἰχμή (whence αἰχμάλωτος), which comes from **aik̂smā*, and ὀσμή (cf. ὀδμή, p. 112) from ὄζω.

(*c*) Other nouns are †δοκιμή (see *Vocab. s.v.*), ζύμη (<*ζῡσμᾱ or ζῡμᾱ, I.E. **jū(s)-mā*, "juice," "pottage," see Boisacq, *s.v.*), κᾰλᾰ́μη (see under 1 (*f*)), ὁρμή (<I.E. **ser-*), πυγμή (see Boisacq, *s.v.* πύξ), which seems to be concrete (=*fist*) in the difficult passage Mk 7[3]. The verbal force is prominent in Barn 12[2] (*fighting, fight*).

Θέρμη (=θέρμ-η) is not in place in this group.

3. *Adjectives in -μος.*

§ 142. These are mainly denominatives and compounds.

(*a*) †Ὑπέρακμος (for derivation see p. 326 above). For meaning, however, of this ἀπ. λεγ. see J. Weiss *ap.* 1 Co 7[36], where the comparative force of the adjective is taken to be modal rather than temporal. So D. Smith (*L. and L. of St. Paul*, 268 n. 6) favours "*exceedingly lusty*" rather than "*past the flower of youth*," and cites ὑπερακμάζω=*excel in youthful vigour* (Athen. 657 D). Ἀπόδημος, †δίδραχμος, ἄζυμος, πρόθυμος, ἄμωμος (see *Vocab. s.v.*), ἡδύοσμος, ἄσημος (also εὔ-σ°, ἐπί-σ°, παρά-σ°), δίστομος, †σύνσωμος, ἄτιμος (also βαρύ-τ°, ἔν-τ°, †ἰσό-τ°, πολύ-τ°), βλάσφημος, and εὔφημος, εὐώνυμος, and ψευδώνυμος.

(*b*) Δίδυμος (Boisacq derives from *δι-, cf. δίς "deux fois" +δυ-μος "apparenté de façon peu claire à duo"; cf. ἀμφίδυμος "double." Brugmann *IF* xi. 283 n. suggests influence of νήδυμος), ἔρημος (<I.E. *erē*=*separate*, cf. ἀραιός, *scarce*, Lat. *rarus*), †ἤρεμος (1 Ti 2[2], see LS, and for vernac. use see *Vocab.*). The derivation of ἕτοιμος is obscure. (See under (4) below.)

(*c*) †Ἄθεσμος (2 Pet 2^7 3^{17}, see Mayor *in loc.* and *Vocab.*) <θεσμός for Laconian θεθμός. For analogical invasion of σ (from -σμός group) into conglutinates in -θ-μός see Brugmann *Grd.*[2] II. i. 252.

(*d*) Ἕβδομος represents a distinct suffix -μο-, cf. Lat. *septimus*, and see Brugmann *Grd.*[2] II. i. 225 f.

4. *Adjectives in* -(σ)ιμος.

Those in -ιμος begin with adjectives in which -μος was added to an *i*- stem; thus πρώϊμος (: πρωΐ), ὄψιμος (: *ὀψί) were formed from adverbs (for πρόϊμος, the correct rdg. in Jas 5^7, see p. 73; Ruth. *NP* 124); noun stems are recognisable in the Homeric κάλλι-μος and φαίδιμος (where -ι- represents an *r*- suffix φαιδρ-ός), and thus the ending -ιμος came to be detached and given as a new suffix.

Examples in the NT are δόκιμος and ἀδόκιμος, σπόριμος, φρόνιμος, ὠφέλιμος. We may compare the proper name Τρόφιμος.

The same suffix -μος joined to *ti*- stems, *i.e.* to verbal abstracts in -σις, produced the suffix -σιμος, which has become very productive in late and MGr. (Brugmann-Thumb *Gr.* 219). For papyri, see Mayser *Gr.* i. 449.

Thus βρώσιμος, θανάσιμος, χρήσιμος. Cf. proper name Ὀνήσιμος (with the play upon words in Philem [11]).

Note.—1. Debrunner *Wortb.* 155 suggests that from -ι stems the suffix passed naturally to the verbal abstracts in -σις in which the Attic effacement of the ι- character (declension -εως, -ει etc.) favoured a further transference to other verbal nouns (*e.g.* μάχιμος : μάχη), and then to nouns other than verbal (*e.g.* νόμιμος (-ως) : νόμος). (See also Solmsen *Gr. Wortf.* 49.)

2. Ἕτοιμος (earlier ἑτοῖμος) might possibly come here, but Boisacq's verdict seems against this (" mot obscur ; formation isolée ").

(2) *-men-*, *-mon-* (-μα, -μην, -μων).

1. *Neuters in* -μα.

§ 143. This very productive class of neuter nouns originates in I.E. *-mn̥*, which is widely represented in many branches of the parent language.

In Greek it appears as a dental stem, but the close connexion of -μα with *-men-* is seen both in comparison with Latin (*e.g.* ὄνο-μα, -ματος, *no-men*, *-minis*) and in the continuance of the *n*- stem in verba derivatives in -μαίνειν (see § 167) and in the cpds. in μων (see p. 355).

It is found with :

(*a*) Primary verbal stems : Ἅρμα, βῆμα, βλέμμα, ἐπί-βλημα, βρῶμα, γράμμα, δεῖγμα, δέρμα, διάδημα, ὑπόδ°, δόγμα, †δόμα, †ἔν-δῠμα, δῶμα, θαῦμα, †ἀνά-θεμα, ἀνά-θημα, θρέμμα, ἴαμα, κάλυμμα, καῦμα, κέρμα, κλέμμα, ἔγκλημα, κλῆμα, κλίμα, †πρόσ-κομμα, κρίμα, κτῆμα, κῦμα, λεῖμμα, †κατά-λυμα, μίγμα, μνῆμα, ὄμμα, πλάσμα, πλέγμα, πνεῦμα, †πόμα, πρᾶγμα, πτύσμα, πτῶμα, ῥῆγμα, ῥῆμα, σπέρμα, στέμμα, διάστημα, στίγμα, σχῆμα, τάγμα, †ἔν-ταλμα, τραῦμα, τρῆμα, σύν-τριμμα, †ἔκ-τρωμα (Rutherford *NP* 288 f.), χάσμα, χρῆμα, †περί-ψημα (§ 124 (*b*)).

NOTE.—In Hellenistic a great preference is shown for the short penultimate in such words as *κλίμα, κρίμα, πόμα*, which had already come in as doublets to *κλῖμα, κρῖμα, πῶμα*, under the influence of the feminine abstracts in *-σις* (*δόμα: δόσις* etc.) and the verbal adjectives in *-τος*. See (*θέτος*) above, p. 57, also Brugmann *Gr.*[4] 222. The two forms ἀνάθημα (*votive offering*) and ἀνάθεμα (*curse*) were both preserved for the convenient distn. of meanings: see *Proleg.* 46, *Vocab. s.vv.*

(*b*) Denominative verbal stems: Ἐπ-άγγελμα, αἴνιγμα, αἴτημα, †αἰτίωμα (for class. *αἰτίαμα*, see *Vocab. s.v.*), †ἀλίσγημα, ἀντάλλαγμα, ἁμάρτημα, †ἄντλημα, †βδέλυγμα, βούλημα, †γένημα, γέννημα, †ἀ-γνόημα, ἀ-δίκημα, δικαίωμα, δώρημα, †ἑδραίωμα, ἕλιγμα, †ἐξ-έραμα, †ἐνέργημα (see Capes *Ach. L.* p. 248), ῥᾳδιούργημα, ἐπ-ερώτημα, ζήτημα, †ἥττημα (see Lightfoot, Lietzmann, J. Weiss *ap.* 1 Co 6[7], and *Vocab. s.v.*), †θέλημα, θυμίαμα, †ἱεράτευμα, †περι-κάθαρμα, †ὁλο-καύτωμα, καύχημα, κήρυγμα, μίσθωμα, νόημα, νόσημα, οἴκημα, ὁμοίωμα, ὅρāμα, δι-όρθωμα (Ac 24[2] ℵAB 33), κατ-όρθωμα (*ib.* ω), ὅρμημα, †μεσουράνημα, ὀφείλημα, ὀχύρωμα (Xen.), πάθημα, †περίσσευμα, πλήρωμα, ποίημα, πολίτευμα, ἀ-σθένημα, σκήνωμα, στερέωμα, στράτευμα, τρύπημα, †ὑστέρημα, ὕψωμα, φίλημα, φρόνημα, φύρāμα, χάραγμα.

-σμα (*c*) The suffix takes the form *-σμα* with *-ίζω, -άζω* and other dental stems: from *-ίζω* come †βάπτισμα, κτίσμα, νόμισμα, ῥάπισμα, †σχίσμα, †χάρισμα;

from *-άζω*, †ἀπαύγασμα, σέβασμα, σκέπασμα, †ἀπο-σκίασμα, φάντασμα, †χόρτασμα;

from other dental stems, πλάσμα (*πλάσσω*<*πλαθ̯ω*), ψεῦσμα (*ψεύδομαι*).

Thence the suffix spreads (as with *-σμός*, p. 351) to nasal stems and stems of other verbs with perf. pass. in *-σμαι*: πτύσμα (*πτύω*), χάσμα (*χάσκω* or *χαίνω*), χρίσμα (*χρίω*), κέλευσμα (*κελεύω*), κλάσμα (*κλάω*), κύλισμα (*κυλίνδω*: °μα, 2 Pet 2[22] ℵAKLP), μίασμα (*μιαίνω*), †καταπέτασμα (*καταπετάννυμι*); also *μέθυσμα* (Herm. *Mand.* viii. 3: *μεθύσκω*).

(*d*) A few words of uncertain derivation remain:

Αἷμα<**αἶhμα*, **αἶσμα*, cf. Skt. *iṣ- iṣás*, "juice," "drink," "power."

Ὄνομα cf. Skt. *nā́ma*, Lat. *nomen*; Brugm. *Grd.*[2] II. i. 234; Boisacq, *s.v.*

Στόμα. See *Grd.*[2] I. 383; Boisacq, *s.v.*

Σῶμα probably <*_tu̯ōmn̥t_, "swelling." I.E. *_teu̯ā-_ which is seen in σῶος (*τϝω-ϝος) σάος (τϝα-ϝο-ς) etc. Boisacq, _s.v._

Χεῖμα (**χείμαρρος**), see χειμών.

NOTE.—1. Although the close verbal connexion of these nouns in -μα is evident throughout the history of the language, in its earlier stages there was at the same time a tendency to use these formations for all kinds of _nomina actionis_, and another to lose the verbal conception in the most concrete of nouns. In the classical, and still more in the Hellenistic period, a differentiation of meanings was observed in the use of the several formations: -σις then expressed the verbal abstract (cf. Latin _-tio_), -μός generally indicated the state, and -μα the result of the action (see, however, pp. 350, 374). Debrunner (_Wortb._ 157) points out other factors which played their part. Thus phonetic sympathies gave a preference for -ημα over -ημός, whilst -ισμός was preferred to -ισμα. The NT list shows 35 nouns in -ημα as against one only in -μος, δῆμος, which goes back to very early times (see above, § 141 (_f_)), and 23 nouns in -ισμός against 8 in -ισμα. He also finds distinctions due to the period, dialect and style of Greek writers.

2. Thumb (_Hellen._ 216) calls attention to the productivity of this suffix in the Κοινή, and attributes it to Ionic influence. Where Attic uses ἀπόκρισις, ἔγκλισις, νίκη, νόσος, the Κοινή prefers ἀπόκριμα, ἔγκλιμα, νίκημα, νόσημα. He also remarks that outside the Κοινή this formation is most common in poetry, and specially in the Tragedians.

3. See Capes _Ach. L._ p. 247, for relation between σύστασις in Polyb. ii. 42. 1 and σύστημα _ib._ 41. 15.

4. See Helbing _Gr._ 113 ff. for LXX nouns in -μα. To his list Wackernagel _ThLZ_ xxxiii. 641 adds ἀνάστεμα, ἀνταπόδομα, ἀφαίρεμα, ἀπόδομα, διάταγμα, δόμα, εὕρεμα, ἕψεμα, ζέμα, κάθεμα, παράθεμα, σύστεμα. See also Thackeray _Gr._ 80.

5. For words in -μα in papyri, see Mayser _Gr._ i. 433 ff., to which add, _e.g._, ἀγώνισμα C P Herm 121[10], κατόρθωμα 125 ii.[4], τέλεσμα 127[10], δαπάνημα BGU iv. 1126[18], ὕδρευμα BGU iv. 1130[12].

2. _Masculines in -μην and -μων._

These suffixes were specially used in the formation of _nomina agentis_ and adjectives.

Λιμήν, ποιμήν, †ἀρχι-ποιμήν.

†Ἀρτέμων (: ἀρτάω), **χειμών** (=χεῖμα), **δαίμων** (<*_dᵊi_, cf. δαίομαι), **ἡγεμών** (: ἡγέομαι), **Φιλήμων.**

Adjectives: **Ἐλεήμων, οἰκτίρμων, ἐπιστήμων, ἀσχήμων, εὐσχήμων** (: σχῆμα).

(3) _-mi-._

-μις A small group of nouns may be mentioned here. Θέμις (>**ἀθέμιτος**) cf. Av. _dāmi-_ (Brugmann _Gr._[4] 219, _Grd._[2] II. i. 254), and probably **δύναμις.**

(4) *Other Suffixes in -n-.*

§ 144. *-en, -on.*

For these nouns with their various ablaut grades, see above, pp. 134–6, also Brugmann *Gr.*[4] 219 f.

-ην and -ων

It has been observed (J. Wright *Comp. Gr. Gr.* 130) that this suffix was specially used in the formation of nouns denoting (1) animate objects and (2) parts of the body.

Under these headings come:

(1) Ἀρήν (see p. 135), ἄρσην; γείτων, κύων, τέκτων, τρυγών. To this group δράκων, λέων, θεράπων originally belonged, as the feminine forms *-αινα* (=*-αν-ι̯α*) show.

(2) The only NT words which represent this class are φρήν, σιᾱγών. Perhaps βραχίων may come in here.

(3) A very old use of the suffix *-ων* (gen. *-ωνος*) was to represent the possession of a quality or characteristic signified by the primitive noun. Examples of this usage are not here in evidence, but an extension of it is seen in the formation of surnames, nicknames, and, indirectly, in the patronymics in *-ίων*.

We may quote Τίμων, Σίμων, Ἡρῳδίων. For other names in *-ων*, see above, p. 146.

(4) There is uncertainty about the origin of place-names in *-ών* (gen. *-ῶνος*) and words indicating locality.

To this class belong ἀμπελών, †ἀφεδρών, κοιτών, μυλών (Mt 24[41] D *et al.*), †νυμφών, πυλών. For Ἐλαιών see above, pp. 151 f., for Κεδρών (so in Josephus) see above, p. 149.

(5) For the comparative suffix see above, pp. 165 ff.

(6) For derivation of αἰών see *Vocab.* 16*b*.

(5) *-no-, -nā-.*

1. *-νος, -νη.*

-νος, -νη

§ 145. As primary suffix in nouns and adjectives.

(*a*) Nouns, *e.g.* αἶνος, ἀμνός, θρόνος, καπνός, οἶνος, πόρνος, ὕπνος, χρόνος; ζώνη, κλίνη, πλάνη, σκηνή, φάτνη, φωνή; δεῖπνον, κρίνον, τέκνον.

(*b*) Adjectives, esp. verbal adjectives, *e.g.* ἁγνός, δεινός, πτηνός, σεμνός, γυμνός, πυκνός.

-s-no- is disguised in λύχνος (<*λυκσνο-ς), τέχνη (<*τεκσνα).

Ἴχνος (<*iksmno-*, see Brugm. *Grd.*[2] II. i. 265, 245) belongs to the stems in *-σ*, see below, § 158.

-νᾰ

-να is found in a few back-formations from verbs. Thus μέριμνα from *μεριμνάω*; cf. *ἔρευνα* from °*άω*, *γέννα* from *γεννάω*. So Solmsen, *Wortf.* 39 f., 238, following Wackernagel *KZ* xxx. 300, 314.

2. *-ανος, -ανη, -ανον* is used in the formation of a number of nouns and adjectives.

αν-ος, -η, -ον

(*a*) κλίβανος, οὐρανός, στέφανος; βοτάνη, δαπάνη, σαργάνη; δρέπανον, λάχανον, πήγανον, φρύγανον.

(*b*) ἱκανός, ὀρφανός.

Note.—According to Solmsen *Wortf.* 257 f., ἔχιδνα is a substantivised adj. in *-δνος* (cf. Μακεδνός=Μακεδανός), **ἐχίδνη* becoming ἔχιδνα under the influence of *δράκαινα.*

3. *-εινός* arises from *-νος* added as a secondary suffix to neuter stems in *-es* (*-εινός=-εσ-νο-ς*). Thus ἐλεεινός : *ἔλεος*, ὀρεινός : *ὄρος*.

-εινός

In φωτεινός the same suffix has been transferred to the stem of the Attic *φῶς* (*φωτ-*) from *φαεινός* (<**φαϝεσνος*): *φάος*.

Analogy played a larger part in the formation of *σκοτεινός* either in the direct influence of *φωτεινός* or through the influence of the neut. *φῶς* in changing *ὁ σκότος* to *τὸ σκότος* in the early classical period. See, however, Brugmann's theory (p. 126 above).

Πετεινός (<*πέτομαι*) and ταπεινός (for deriv. see Boisacq) are probably analogical formations.

Note.—1. As **εσ-νο-ς* has produced this group, so **ασ-νο-ς* is not altogether unfruitful, as evidenced by σελήνη (Attic for Lesb. *σελάννᾱ*), which is the substantivised fem. of **σελ-ασ-νο-ς* : *σέλας*.

2. WH *App.*[2] 161, "Adjectives that in the best MSS have *-ινός* for *-εινός* are *ὀρινός, σκοτινός, φωτινός*."

4. *-όνη* is a suffix used in words to denote tools, instruments etc., as βελόνη (perhaps also ὀθόνη), and also (with a different accent) to form abstracts, *e.g.* ἡδονή.

-όνη

The derivation of *ὀθόνη* is uncertain. Some trace it to **Ϝεθόνη* (accounting for its form by vocalic assimilation). Cf. Zd. *fra-vaδəmnā*, Fr. *vêtue*, A.S. *woéd*. Others find evidence of Semitic origin, and cf. Hebr. אֵטוּן *yarn*. See Boisacq 687, 1119. Its use by Luke, as also that of *βελόνη*, is remarked by Hobart, pp. 218, 61.

5. *-υνος, -ύνη.*

-υνος, -ύνη

Originally an extension of the *-νο-* suffix to *u-* stems, this never became productive in the formation of nouns.

Of the four which occur in the NT, **αἰσχύνη** is a back-formation from *αἰσχύνω* which was formed from the much older *αἶσχος*.

Βόθῦνος (< √*bhed*(*h*), *bhod*(*h*)) is a rare and late equivalent for *βόθρος* and is probably influenced by the cognate *βαθύς*.

In **κίνδῦνος** and **ὀδύνη** the -*u*- has not been explained, but for the latter see the suggestion in § 111.

6. -συνος, -σύνη.

-συνος, σύνη The adjectival suffix -*συνος*, of obscure origin, was never fruitful except in the formation of abstract nouns in -*σύνη*.

Starting from such adjectival formations as *δουλόσυνος*, an extended form of *δοῦλος*, the suffix -*σύνη* was added to nouns ending in -*ος*, to nouns and adjs. in -*ης*, to adjectives in -*ων* and even to nouns in -*ις*, which were all treated as *o*- stems.

In the NT we have:

Δικαιοσύνη (: *δίκαιος*), †**ἐλεημοσύνη** (: *ἐλεήμων*).

Ἀφροσύνη, **εὐφροσύνη** **σωφροσύνη**, †**ταπεινο-φροσύνη** (: °*φρων*).

Ἀσχημοσύνη, **εὐσχημοσύνη** (: °-*σχήμων*).

-ωσύνη **Ἱερωσύνη** (<*ἱερεωσύνη* Attic <*ἱερηF-οσύνη*) : *ἱερεύς*, became in Hellenistic a model from which -*ωσύνη* was conveniently applied to avoid a series of short vowels, *e.g.* †**ἀγαθωσύνη**, †**ἁγιωσύνη**, †**μεγαλωσύνη**.

For frequency in Hellenistic see *Vocab.* *s.v.* *ἀγαθωσύνη*, and for NT see SH *Romans*, p. 404.

7. *Temporal Adjectives in -ινός.*

-ινός § 146. These can be traced to locatives or adverbs in -*i* (see Brugmann *Grd.*² II. i. 270). Thus *ἐαρινός* : *ἔαρι*, **πρωϊνός** : *πρωί*. In the class. age -*ινός* was applied to other stems, **ἑσπερινός** (which appears in Xen.) superseding the earlier *ἑσπέριος* formed regularly from *ἕσπερος*. The detached suffix was then used analogically for all kinds of time descriptions; *e.g.* †**ὀρθρινός** (: *ὄρθρος*) Lk 24[22] for earlier form *ὄρθριος* (*ib.* E *et al.*), also Herm. *Sim.* v. 1[1] (see Lobeck *Phryn.* 51), and **ταχινός** (: *τάχα*).

†**Καθημερινός** (<*καθ' ἡμέραν*, § 109; see p. 158) survives in MGr *καθημερνός*.

Φθινοπωρινός, see above, § 106, and Mayor on Jude [12].

Cf. *νυκτερινός*, quoted from papp. in *Vocab.* 432a; also Clem. *ad Cor.* 20[9], *καιροὶ ἐαρινοὶ καὶ θερινοὶ καὶ μεταπωρινοὶ καὶ χειμερινοὶ ἐν εἰρήνῃ μεταπαραδιδόασιν ἀλλήλοις*.

8. *Adjectives of material in -ινος.*

-ινος A large group of adjectives signifying material, origin or kind was formed with the suffix -ινος, in prehistoric times originating with *i- stems*, but from Homer onward found used with all kinds of stems.

The NT supplies ἀκάνθινος, †ἀμαράντινος, ἀνθρώπινος, βύσσινος, δερμάτινος, ἐλεφάντινος, †θύϊνος, †κόκκινος, κρίθινος, λίθινος, †μύλινος, ξύλινος, ὀστράκινος, πύρινος, σάρκινος, τρίχινος, ὑακίνθινος, ὑάλινος.

To these may be added σάρδινος (Rev 4^{3} P *et al.* for σάρδιον) and †σμαράγδινος, the adjective in each case being used with λίθος (understood).

Two oxytones obviously belong to this rather than the preceding class:

Ἀληθινός the only adjectival derivative in this group, from ἀληθής.

Πεδινός (<πεδίον) which probably follows the accent of its antonym ὀρεινός (see 3. above).

The activity of this suffix in late Greek (cf. οὐθαμινός P Flor ii. 170^{7} (iii/A.D.); ὑαμινός, (see Herwerden *Lex. s.v.*) suggests a possible explanation of the form συκάμινος (see above, p. 153).

9. -ῖνος, -ανός, -ηνός.

-ῖνος Ethnica and adjectives signifying "belonging to," which have the suffix -ῖνος, may have originated, as Debrunner (*Wortb.* 162) following K.Bl. ii. 296 suggests, in words formed from the names of Greek towns in S. Italy and Sicily, and were therefore of Latin origin (*e.g.* Ἀκραγαντῖνος, Ταραντῖνος).

In NT we have Ἀλεξανδρῖνος (which, however, in the best MSS is Ἀλεξανδρινός), Ἐφεσῖνος (296 and another cursive *ap.* Rev 2^{1}), and the unquestionably Latin Λιβερτῖνος.

-ανός, -ηνός -ανός and -ηνός, which were not native to Greece, came to be used from the time of Alexander as ethnica, for Asiatic towns and districts. Thus Ἀδραμύττειον : Ἀδραμυττηνός (WH Ἀδραμυντηνός), Ἀσία : Ἀσιανός, Γερασά : Γερασηνός, Δαμασκός : Δαμασκηνός, Ναζαρά : Ναζαρηνός. Also Μαγδαλά : Μαγδαληνή. Used as nouns for place-names, Ἀβειληνή, Μελιτήνη (Ac 28^{1} B), Μιτυλήνη.

10. -ιανός.

-ιανός Latin is also responsible for the extended suffix -ιανός. Stems in -*i* took the normal Latin termination -*anus* to denote a follower of a party leader. The partisans of C. Marius were thus termed *Mari-ani*, those of Cn. Pompeius *Pompei-*

ani. It was an easy transition to *Cæsar-iani*. Thus Χριστιανός, Ἡρῳδιανός.

NOTE.—R. S. Radford, "The Suffixes -ānus and -īnus" in *Gildersleeve Studies*, 1903, pp. 95 ff., shows (after Schnorr v. Carolsfeld, *Archiv f. lat. Lex.* i. 177–194) that the formation was so regularly from the nomen in -ius (or -ia stems, cf. *Fimbrianus*) that "from the second half of the Augustan period on new formations are made only in -iānus." On p. 98 he catalogues "extension of the purely Roman suffix -ānus (-iānus) to other than Roman words." Thus *Herculanus*, cf. *Plautaneus*, *Trophonianus* (Cic.), *Thyonianus* (Cat.), *Hannibalianus*, *Hasdrubalianus* and many others. The suffix when added to names of persons makes a possessive, closely allied to gen. for cases of adoption, but more restricted than corresponding gen. and tending to recur in set phrases. He cft. "the Clayton-Bulwer treaty," etc. [Germ. *-sche*]. Varro says (LL 9. 42, 71 Sp.) from *Faustus* should be *Faustinus*, *Faustianus* could only rightly be from *Faustius*. But Cato says *Quirinianus*. Cicero avoids these new forms in the orations and philosophical works, and uses them twice only in his letters. From -ōn- base he has *Pisonianus* and *Neronianus* in or. and phil. The suffix -īnus was practically obsolete in the silver age. The conclusion is "that the possessive adjectives in -anus are later formations of the language, and that the gentile adjective (*Titius*, *Aelius*) originally possessed a much broader, perhaps a wholly unrestricted, use. This older usage was always retained in the ritualistic language, in the poets and in the authors of archaic tendencies."[1]

C. Liquid Suffixes.

(1) *l- Suffixes*.

1. *-lo-*, *-la-*

-λος, -λη § 147. The simple suffix -λος, -λη was not fruitful, though a number of words survive.

Nouns: Αὐλός, ἆθλος (ἀ-Ϝεθ-λος) (>ἀθλέω), ζῆλος, ξύλον, ὅπλον (<I.E. *sop-lo-m), σπήλαιον (cf. Hom. σπέος), σπίλος, στύλος (Skt. *sthurá-s*).

Ὀμίχλη, φυλή.

Adjectives: Βέβηλος, δειλός, δῆλος (<*δειηλος), δοῦλος, στρεβλός (>στρεβλόω), τυφλός, φαῦλος.

NOTE.—Βέβηλος, an old t.t. of religion, from √ βη- in βαίνω, means accessible and so *profane*, as opposed to ἄβατος, inaccessible and so *sacred*. Σπίλος Boisacq (p. 693) connects with κηλίς, Lat. *cālīgo*, *squālus*, <I.E. *sqᵘā, or else from I.E. *spōi- *spī-. Rutherford *NP* 87, identifies with σπιλάς [<I.E. *spēi-, *spī=*to be pointed*, cf. Lat. *spīna*, *spīca*, *pinna* (*pitnā), Boisacq, p. 896 f.], and "tracks σπίλος *rock* through

[1] Mr. E. E. Genner calls attention to such formations as Ἀττικιανός from "Atticus."

an easy gradation of meanings historically consecutive from the beginning to the close of Greek literature. Originally meaning rock, it came to signify successively *porous rock, rotten-stone, clay,* and *clay-stain,* till Paul could employ it metaphorically as in Eph 5[27], and Dion. H. apply it to men with the meaning *dregs of humanity.*"

2. -αλο-, -ελο-, -ιλο-.

These are more numerous.

-αλος Nouns : **Αἰγιαλός, διδάσκαλος, ὕαλος** (see Thumb in *DAC* i. 553b) : **κύμβαλον, πηδάλιον, †σκάνδαλον, †σκύβαλον** (<I.E. **squb-*, see Boisacq *s.v.*, but see § 105 for derivation, which removes it into class of cpds.) : **ἀγκάλη** (<ἄγκος), **κεφαλή** (cf. Gotha *gibla,* OHG *gebal*), **κρεπάλη**, σπατάλη (>**†σπαταλάω**), **φιάλη**.

Adjectives : **Ἁπαλός** (cf. Lat. *sapere,* and ὀπός *juice*), **μεγάλ-η**.

-ελος **Ἄγγελος, ἄμπελος, μυελός ; ἀγέλη, νεφέλη** (Lat. *nebula*) ; εὐτράπελος (>°**λία**, § 106).

-ιλος. **Ὀργίλος, ποικίλος : κοιλία** (<κοῖλος <*κόϝιλος, cf. Lat. *cavus*).

NOTE.—**Αἰγιαλός.** Hirt *IdgF* (1917) xxxvii. 229 f., starting from Hesych. αἶγες· τὰ κύματα· Δωριεῖς (also Artem. *Oneirocrit.* ii, 12), leaps to αἴξ=*shore.* Then in such a line as Hom. *Il.* iv. 422 ἐν αἰγιαλῷ may originally have been ἐν αἰγὶ ἁλός, *i.e.* " on the shore of the salt-flood." If this association was frequent, they flowed together into one word, at least in pronunciation. We should then have a connexion which was transformed into αἰγιαλῷ, to form again a nom. from this, αἰγιαλός.

Σκάνδαλον, Moulton *Exp T* xxvi. 331, connects with Skt. *skand* "leap," " spirt," Lat. *scando,* O.Ir. *scendim* " I spring," and holds that σκάνδαλον existed before σκανδάληθρον (Arist. *Acharn.* 687), though not occurring in literature.

Κρεπάλη (for spelling see p. 81) possibly connected with κραιπνός *swift, impetuous.* So Boisacq 506, who, however, rejects the theory of a primitive *κραπνιος, related to καρπάλιμος, and is unconvinced by the etymology *κρᾱι- *head* + πάλη.

3. -ᾱλό-, -ηλό-, -ωλό-.

These productive adjectival suffixes, in which -ᾱλός came to be specially appended to stems with corresponding verbs in -ᾶν, and -ηλός to stems with similar verbs in -εῖν, are not represented in N.T.

-ηλος The later use of -ηλος to form *nomina agentis* has provided κάπηλος (whence °**λεύω**), **τράχηλος** (properly "carrier," so Brugmann *Gr.*[4] 231. For another derivation see Boisacq, *s.v.*) The detached suffix is appended without any semantic reason in **ὑψηλός.**

-ωλός -ωλός is represented in **ἁμαρτωλός** and **εἴδωλον.**

4. *-υ(λ)λο-.*

-υλος The diminutive conception which was always closely related to the *-lo-* suffixes and is specially evident in the mass of Latin diminutives in *-ulus, -ellus, -illus,* comes out in Greek, specially with words in *-υλος* and *-υλλος.* In proper names this suffix generally marks either a pet name or an abbreviation of a compound appellative.

Δάκτυλος (<**δατ-κ-υλο-* <**dn̥t-qo-*, cf. MHG *zint*, Germ. *Zinke, Zacke*), acc. to Brugmann (*IF* xi. 284 ff., *Gr.*[4] 159, *Grd.*[2] II. i. 484), originally meant "little tooth."

Σταφυλή (<I.E. **stm̥bh-*), see Boisacq 90, 91, 903.

†**Βήρυλλος** (Rev 21^{20}, so also in Tob 13^{17} B). For the form *βηρύλλιον* (Ex 28^{20}) see above, p. 343.

Τέρτυλλος=Lat. *Tertullus*, dim. of *Tertius.*

Τρωγύλιον. For this "Western and Syrian" reading in Ac 20^{15} see WH *App.*[2] 98. For spelling see WS 47, and Ramsay *CRE* 155.

5. *-αλέος.*

-αλέος It is curious that this extended suffix which was widely used in the Κοινή (Br.-Thumb *Gr.* 231) does not appear in NT except in inferior MSS for *νηφάλιος* (see p. 76).

6. *-αλις.*

-αλις This seems to be a feminine suffix in names of animals, in **δάμαλις** (perh. through masc. *δαμάλης*, where √ is *δαμ-* (cf. Ir. *dam*<Celt. **damo-s*), **πάρδαλις** (masc. *πάρδος* <I.E. **pr̥da*, cf. Skt. *pŕ̥dāku-ḥ*). So also **μοιχαλίς** (LXX, *Test. XII Patr.*, Plut.; for Attic *μοιχάς*, see Lobeck *Phryn.* 452).

Quite distinct is **σεμίδᾱλις**, cf. Lat. *simila* (**sem-*). Possibly from I.E. *sem-* <**bhs-em-* (: *ψωμός*), cf. **bhas- to pound*, which fits the meaning *fine wheat.* This rare word (Rev 18^{13}) in addition to citations in Gr.-Th. is found Justin M. *Ap.* i. 37 and papp. (see *Vocab. s.v.*).

(2) *r- Suffixes.*

§ 148. The most important words with ***r- suffixes*** are the *nomina agentis* in *-τηρ* and *-τωρ* (see §§ 150, 152) and the related formations in *-τρος, -τρον* (see § 152), which are dealt with below.

1. *-ro-, -ra.*

-ρος, -ρα This suffix was partly connected with the *-ρ* in the nom. and acc. sing. of neuters, *e.g.* **ἄνυδρος** : *ὕδωρ*, **ἄλευρον** : **ἀλεϝαρ*, and with the suffix *-er*, *e.g. αὔρα* : *ἀήρ*.

Nouns: Ἀγρός, ἄγρα, ἄκρον, αὔρα, ἀφρός, δῶρον, ἕδρα, (ἔνεδρα, see above, p. 125), ἔχθρα, κλῆρος, κόπριον, κοπρία, λεπρός, λέπρα, μῆρος, νεφρός, ὄμβρος, πέτρα, πήρα, πλευρά, πρῷρα, σταυρός (Brugm. *Grd.*[2] II. i. 351), τέφρον (τεφρόω), χώρα.

Adjectives: Αἰσχρός, ἄνυδρος, ἄφεδρος (>†ἀφεδρών, see § 115), ἐλαφρός, ἐρυθρός, ἐχθρός, λαμπρός, μακρός, μικρός, νεκρός, νωθρός (see *Vocab. s.v.*), ξηρός, πενιχρός (see *Vocab. s.v.*), πηρός (ἀνάπηρος), πικρός, σαπρός, σκληρός, σύνεδρος (>συνέδριον), ὑγρός, χλωρός, ψυχρός.

2. -ᾰρο-, -ερο-, -ορο-, -υρο- (principally with adjectives). See Brugmann *Grd.*[2] II. i. 347 f.

-αρος, -αρα Κιθάρα; ἱλαρός, καθαρός, λιπαρός, ῥυπαρός, χλιαρός.

-ερος, -ερα Ἑσπέρα, ἡμέρα; πενθερός, πενθερά; βλαβερός, ἱερός, καρτερός (whence °ρησις), φανερός, φοβερός.

With different accentuation, ἐλεύθερος (ἐ- prothetic vowel, Brugmann *Gr.*[4] 173, cf. Lat. *līber*. Boisacq 242, derives from *ἔλευθος, *generation, people*, cf. O. Slav. *ljudĭje*).

-ορος Βόρβορος (2 Pet 2[22], a classical word found elsewhere in bibl. Gr. only in Jer (LXX) 45[6]): λοίδορος.

For the -Ϝορος cpds. (*e.g.* θυρωρός) see § 105. Θεωρός (>°ρέω) belongs probably to that group; see below, p. 391.

-ῠρος Ἄχυρον; ἄργυρος (Skt. *árjuna-s, bright, white*), ὀχυρός (ὀχύρωμα), ψίθυρος (†ψιθυρισμός).

3. -ᾱρο-, -ηρο-, -ῡρο-.

As with -*lo*- suffixes, combination with stems ending in long vowels (*e.g.* ὀδυνηρός : ὀδυνάω, ὀδύνη) formed a class to which adjectives derived from other stems were added by false analogy.

-ᾱρος Φλύᾱρος (φλύω).

-ηρος Αὐστηρός (αὔω, *dry up*, <*αὐσι̯ω, Lat. *haurio, haustum*), αὐχμηρός (αὐχμός, *drought*), ὀκνηρός (: ὀκνέω, ὄκνος), πονηρός (: πονέομαι, πόνος). Τολμηρός (>τολμηροτέρως) formed regularly from τολμάω. The origin of the noun σίδηρος is unknown.

-ῡρος, -ῡρα Αγκῦρα (ἀγκών), κολλύρα (>κολλύριον, see p. 78): ἰσχυρός (ἰσχῦς).

4. -ήρ, -ωρ.

For ἀήρ see Brugm. *Grd.*[2] II. i. 339, ἀνήρ, *ib.* 332 f.

-ήρ, -ωρ †Κατήγωρ is a Hellenistic back-formation from κατήγορος (see Thumb *Hellen.* 126, and Brugmann-Thumb *Gr.* 210 n.[3], also p. 127 above).

5. For -τερος, see below, § 153, p. 369.

6. *-dhro-*, *-dhrā-*, and *-dhlo-*, *-dhlā-*.

This suffix seems to be related on one side to the *-ro-*, *-lo-* suffixes, and on the other to those in *-tro-*, *-tlo-* (see § 152 below). Brugmann (*Grd.*[2] II. i. 377) regards this *-dh-* (as in -θμός, § 141 above) as probably a root determinative.

-θρος, -θρον, -θρα **῎Ολεθρος** (ὄλλῡμι, <ὀλ-νῡ-μι), **ὄρθρος**, σκυθρός (>**σκυθρωπός**) <*σκυσθρός (by dissimilation) : σκύζομαι, **φόβηθρον** (Lk 21[11] BDW, see pp. 110, 369), **κολυμβήθρα** (: κολυμβάω).

There is no NT example of -θλο-, but γενέθλιον (*Mart. Polyc.* 18[3]) is a derivative of γένεθλον and appears in disguise at Mk 6[21] D (see p. 112).

D. Suffixes with Labial Stops.

1. -π-.

-ψ § 149. Apart from ποταπός (see *Prol.* 95 and pp. 112, 271 above), stems in -π- are **κώνωψ**, **μώλωψ**, **ὕδρωψ** (**ὑδρωπικός**) (genitives in -ωπος), **σκόλοψ** (gen. -οπος), **λαῖλαψ** (gen. -απος). (See further Sturtevant, *Cl. Phil.* vii. 425 ff.)

As **ἄνθρωπος** has not been dealt with among the cpds., it may be mentioned here. Boisacq rejects the old derivation ἀνήρ + ὤψ (which leaves the -θ- unexplained), preferring <*ἀνδρ-hωπο-ς "having the appearance of a man," where the second element is related to the Gothic *saiƕan*, to see, Lat. *signum*<**seq*[u]*no-m*.

2. *-bho-*, *-bha-*.

-φος **῎Εριφος** is the sole representative in the NT of the old class of animal names in -φος (cf. ἔλαφος).

We may note three other words. **῎Εδαφος** <*ἐδ-, √*sed*), by the law which forbids successive aspirates under the influence of ἕδος has passed from the masc. type to the neut. with stem in ἐδαφε(σ)- (Brugm. *Grd.*[2] II. i. 390). Κόλαφος is preserved in †**κολαφίζω**. **Ψῆφος** *pebble*, polished by the churning of the waves, suggests connexion with I.E. **bhs*[e]*-bh-* >Skt. *bhas-*, "to pound," "crush." The same root appears in ψάμμος (=sand). See Boisacq, *s.vv.*

E. Suffixes with Dental Stops.

(1) The *-t- Suffixes.*

1. ***Nomina agentis*** in -τήρ, -τωρ, -της.

§ 150. The original distinction between these suffixes was that simple verbs formed *nomina agentis* in -τήρ or -τωρ, and noun compounds in -της. Compound verbs followed the usage of the simplex when the preverb was felt to be an integral part of the verb; otherwise they took -της. Ionic-Attic very early substituted -της for -τηρ, with the result that in Hellenistic -της is left in possession.

-τήρ A few of those in -τήρ, -τωρ, mostly religious and legal terms, survive: **σωτήρ, φωστήρ,** *φυλακτήρ* (preserved in **φυλακτήριον**).

-τωρ †**Κοσμοκράτωρ,** †**παντοκράτωρ** (see § 107), †**κτήτωρ, πράκτωρ, ῥήτωρ. Σπεκουλάτωρ** is a Latin loan word. Οἰκήτωρ occurs in Clem. *ad Cor.* 14[4]. **Οἰκητήριον** is witness for the earlier -τήρ. **᾿Αλέκτωρ** (superseded in Att. by ἀλεκτρύων, but reappearing in Κοινή: see Rutherford *NP* 307 f. and *Vocab. s.v.*) should come here, if Kretschmer (*KZ* xxxiii. 560) is right in deriving it from ἀλέξω. See Boisacq 43.

NOTE.—For difference of accent in -τήρ and -τωρ see Brugmann *Grd.*[2] II. i. 331.

-της, τής The vast majority of these *nomina agentis* are formed in -της.

From verbs in -άω: **᾿Ακροατής, κυβερνήτης, πλανήτης, τολμητής.**

From verbs in -έω: **Αὐλητής, ἐπιθυμητής,** †**καθηγητής,** †**καταφρονητής, μετρητής, μιμητής, ποιητής,** †**προσαίτης** (a late word—Plut., Lucian—by haplology for προσαιτήτης, see Hirt *Handb.* 172), †**προσκυνητής** (NT ἁ.λ. Jn 4[23]. See *Vocab. s.v.* and *LAE*[1] 99 f. ([2]101), for probable pre-Christian use), †**συνζητητής** (NT ἁ.λ. 1 Co 1[20], elsewhere only in the citation in Ignat. *Eph.* 18[1]).

From verbs in -όω: **Ζηλωτής,** †**λυτρώτης** (LXX, Philo, Just. M., *Act. Thom.*), †**τελειωτής** (ἁ.λ. in Heb 12[2]—apparently coined by the author).

From verbs in -εύω: **Βουλευτής, ἑρμηνευτής,** †**ὀλοθρευτής** (ἁ.λ. in 1 Co 10[10]; for form see p. 71), **παιδευτής.**

From verbs in -άζω: †**Βιαστής** (NT ἁ.λ. in Mt 11[12]. A late form for βιᾱτάς, common in Pindar. Wetst. cites from Eustath. and Aretaeus alone. Gr.-Th. quotes Philo *Agric.* 19, where Cohn and Wendland print *divisim*, βίας τῶν), **δικαστής,** †**στασιαστής** (for class. στασιωτής).

From verbs in -ίζω: **᾿Ανδραποδιστής** (see p. 286 for derivation of this class. word; in NT only 1 Ti 1[10]), †**βαπτιστής** (NT and Joseph.; see *Vocab.* 102 *b*), **βασανιστής,** †**δανιστής** (for form, see p. 77), †**῾Ελληνιστής,** †**ἐξορκιστής** (apart from NT ἁ.λ. Ac 19[13], only found in Joseph., Lucian, and eccles. writers), †**εὐαγγελιστής** (NT and eccles., but see *Vocab. s.v.* for inscr. possibly non-Christian), **θεριστής,** †**κερματιστής** (see N. 1 below), †**κτίστης** (NT ἁ.λ. 1 Pet 4[19]; see *Vocab. s.v.* for use in Κοινή), **λῃστής, μεριστής** (NT ἁ.λ. Lk 12[14]. To Pollux and eccles. add Κοινή exx. in *Vocab. s.v.*), †σαλπιστής (for class. σαλπιγκτής, Lob. *Phryn.* 191), ὑβριστής, ψιθυριστής.

From verb in -ύζω: †Γογγυστής (NT ἁ.λ. Jude [16]; elsewhere only LXX, Sym., Theod.).

From other verbal stems: †Γνώστης (in which σ is inserted before τ as in δυνάστης and ψεύστης), †διώκτης (NT ἁ.λ. 1 Ti 1[13], elsewhere *Did.* 5[2], Barn. 20[2], Sym. But the LXX cpd. ἐργοδιώκτης is "profane," as shown by a iii/B.C. papyrus: see *Vocab.* 166*a*), †δότης (ἁ.λ. 2 Co 9[7] (LXX), for class. δοτήρ; see *Vocab. s.v.* for pre-Christian inscr. ἐκδότης), †ἐμπαίκτης (only LXX semel, 2 Pet 3[3], Jude [18]: see Mayor *Commentary, in loc.*), ἐπενδύτης (see n. 2 below), ἐφευρετής, κλέπτης, κριτής, μαθητής (cf. με-μάθ-η-κα), νομοθέτης (a T.P. cpd., see § 105), ὀφειλέτης, παραβάτης, †πλήκτης, †προσωπολήμπτης (§ 105), προφήτης, ὑπηρέτης (§ 129 (*b*)).

NOTE.—1. Κερματιστής (peculiar to NT and related writings) is formed from °ίζω, a classical verb for *to cut small,* which gained the meaning in Hellenistic *to coin into small money* (Anth.), *to exchange* (for papp. see *Vocab.*); †κολλυβιστής, a late word (Rutherford *NP* 499, common in papp., see *Vocab.*), has no corresponding verb, and must owe its form to analogy, probably with κερματιστής. The noun κόλλυβος is of Semitic origin.

2. As with nouns in -τήρ, we can trace an easy transition from *nomen agentis* to instrumental meaning in some words, *e.g.* ἐπενδύτης, μετρητής.

2. *Derivatives in -της from nouns.*

§ 151. The denominatives include ναύτης, πρεσβύτης. The suffix is found after a variety of stems, some of which have given rise to complex suffixes which were freely used in the production of analogy formations. Thus:

- -έτης: from stems in -ο-, οἰκέτης (οἰκότης only found in vulgar curse tablet, Meisterhans[3] 117), †συμφυλέτης (for Attic φυλέτης, from φῦλον or φυλή). So εὐεργέτης (see below, under cpds.).
- -ώτης: from -ο- stems, δεσμώτης, ἰδιώτης: from -α stems, στρατιώτης, †συνηλικιώτης (for class. ἡλικιώτης).
- -ίτης: from -ι- stems, πολίτης. By analogy μεσίτης and a group of appellatives which τεχνίτης and τραπεζίτης (WH -είτης) represent in the NT. These two influences may account for Ἀρεοπαγίτης (§ 106). The common ethnica in -ῑτης are naturally reinforced by the Semitic ethnica in ִי (fem. ִית), though the spelling -είτης is better supported (WH *App.*[2] 161). See the list above, p. 150.

Νικολαΐτης, a follower of Νικόλαος—an easy extension of the idea of "membership" that constitutes the preceding classes. Μαργαρίτης may (through its association with precious stones) be quoted as the one NT example of a class of nouns with this suffix used of kinds of stone (*e.g.* πυρίτης, αἱματίτης; cf. Lat. *anthracites* (Pliny)).

3. *Compounds in -της.*

The large class with *-στάτης* as second member of the compound is represented by **ἐπιστάτης** and **πρωτοστάτης** (a K.D. cpd., § 106). So **αὐτόπτης** (a K.D. cpd. § 106) and **ἐπόπτης** (§ 120) represent another group. Three T.P. cpds. (§ 105) are **ἀρσενοκοίτης** (from *ἄρσην, κοιτή*), **οἰνοπότης**, †**φρεναπάτης**. Probably to the same class belongs **χρεοφειλέτης** (for form see p. 73, also Lob. *Phryn.* 691).

NOTE.—The accentual variations within these groups call for some notice. Brugmann (*IF* ix. (1898) 368 n.[2]) draws attention to the correspondence between the masculines *κλέπτης, γυμνήτης* etc., with their penultimate accent, and the abstracts *βλάστη, ἀήτη* etc., just as *κριτής* etc. correspond to the abstracts *ἀκτή, μελετή* etc. But the connexion is not shown. The fullest treatment is in Fraenkel, *Geschichte der griechischen Nomina agentis*, ii. 199–215. Debrunner *Wortb.* 175 f., while suspecting that the ancient grammarians added to the confusion by unreliable transmission in individual words as well as groups, offers the following general rules. Derivatives in *-της* from nouns are barytone, also the old *nomina agentis* in *-της*, and the compounds, together with a few uncompounded formations as *ἱκέτης* and *κλέπτης*. Oxytone are those formations in *-της* which have taken the place of an earlier *-τήρ*. Thus *οἰκέτης, πολίτης, δεσμώτης, ἐπόπτης, οἰνοπότης*; but *βουλευτής*. Other factors, however, may break through this partition. Thus the Hellenistic *δότης* (for Homeric *δοτήρ*) is under the influence of *-δότης*, so often the final member in cpds. (*e.g.* *μισθαποδότης*). On the contrary, *κριτής* (also *ὑποκριτής*), which replaced Dor. *κριτήρ*, maintained a sturdy independence of *δικαιο-κρίτης* etc. because of its legal use. It will be seen that generally those formed directly from a verb are oxytone.

4. *Abstract nouns in -της.*

Abstracts in -της

§ 152. These are nearly all formed from adjectives in *-ο-*, with the result that the suffix *-ότης* is regularly attached to the consonantal stems as well.

From nouns in *-ο-* : †**Θεότης**, †**ἀδελφότης** (note extension of meaning to concrete and collective sense. See *Vocab.*).

From adjectives in *-ο-* : †**Ἁγιότης**, †**ἁγνότης**, **ἁδρότης**, **αἰσχρότης**, †**γυμνότης**, †**ἀδηλότης**, †**θειότης**, **ἱκανότης**, †**ἱλαρότης**, **ἰσότης**, **καθαρότης**, **καινότης**, †**κυριότης**, **λαμπρότης**, †**ματαιότης** (see *Vocab.*), †**μεγαλειότης**, **νεότης**, **ὁμοιότης**, **ὁσιότης**, **παλαιότης**, **σεμνότης**, **σκληρότης**, **τελειότης**, †**τιμιότης**, **χρηστότης** : **ἁπλότης** (from *-όος*).

†**Ἀφελότης** (from *-ης*, for which see § 107) appears in the Κοινή together with class. *ἀφέλεια*, *e.g.* Vett. Val. p. 240[15]. (See *Vocab. s.v.*)

Πιότης (from *πίων*), †**ἑνότης** (from *εἷς* gen. *ἑνός*).

From adjectives in -ύς: **Βραδυτής**, **†εὐθύτης**, **πραΰτης**.

NOTE.—For the accent in **βραδυτής** see Br.-Th. *Gr.* 180 and Debr. *Wortb.* 184 n.[1]. The distinction seems to rest upon an I.E. principle of accentuation. In Att. and Hellen. there was a tendency to assimilation, *e.g.* Att. κουφοτής : τραχυτής. Hellen. γλυκύτης etc. : νεότης.

5. *Other nouns in -τηρ.*

-τηρ These fall into three groups:

(*a*) Closely connected with *nomina agentis*, already discussed under 1, are a number of terms for instruments, tools, etc. (cf. words in -τρον (under 6. below).

†Νιπτήρ.—This word for basin, found first in Jn 13[5], and elsewhere only in writings influenced by the Johannine narrative of the foot-washing, is formed from the late verb νίπτω (class. νίζω): cf. κρατήρ, κρητήρ fr. κεράννυμι. **Στατήρ** (Skt. *sthātār*, Lat. *stator*, I.E. **sthā-*, cf. √ *sta-* of ἵστημι), used first of a weight, then of a coin. The connexion with *nomina agentis* is here traceable.

Χαρακτήρ (χαράσσω), originally a tool for engraving, then of the die or mould, then of the stamp or impress, as on a coin or seal; so Heb 1[3].

(*b*) Terms of relationship: **Θυγάτηρ**, **μήτηρ**, **πατήρ**. On the "relative" force of -τηρ cf. under 7. below.

(*c*) A few other nouns of various meaning:

Ἀστήρ (Skt. *stár-*, Lat. *stella* <**stēr-lā*. The *a-* in Gr. and Arm. *astl* is not prothetic. I.E. **astēr*, gen. *strós*. Boisacq, *s.v.*).

Γαστήρ.—Brugmann (*IF* xi. 272 n.) suggests connexion with γέν-το "he held," γέμω "I am full of anything," γέμος, γόμος etc. For the σ he compares Skt. *vasti-*, *vaniṣṭhú-*, Lat. *vē(n)sīca*; Germ. *wanst*, Lat. *venter*.

NOTE.—Brugmann (*Gr.*[4] 180) suspects that the recessive accent in **μήτηρ**, **θυγάτηρ**, for *μητήρ, *θυγατήρ (Skt. *mātā*, *duhitā́*), is due to the influence of the vocative μῆτερ, θύγατερ, in the same way that personal names prefer the recessive accent on that account. (See p. 59 above.)

6. *Nouns in -τρος, -τρα, -τρον.*

-τρος, -τρᾱ, -τρον These are closely related to the *-ter-*, *-tor-* suffix of the *nomina agentis*.

(*a*) -τρος, a most unproductive suffix, is represented in NT only by **ἰᾱτρός** (: ἰᾱτήρ, Ion. ἰητήρ).

(*b*) -τρᾱ is seen in **μήτρα**, *womb*, where the instrumental force is evident.

(*c*) -τρον is common in names for implements. Debrunner (*Wortb.* 176 f.) traces three stages in use of this suffix: (α) instrument, (β) locality, (γ) payment.

Under (α) we have **ἄγκιστρον** (Mt 17[27], Ignat. *Magn.* 11[1]), **ἄροτρον**, **ἀμφίβληστρον** (§ 112, 1 (*b*)), **ἔσοπτρον** (§ 117), **κέντρον**, **λουτρόν**, **μέτρον**, **φόβητρον** (Lk 21[11]. So most MSS, see above, pp. 110, 364. Both suffixes are old, but this spelling was preferred because of dissimilation of aspirates. Bl-D § 35, 2). Under (β) **θέατρον** (so Ac 19[29.31]; then *spectacle* as in 1 Co 4[9]). Under (γ) **λύτρον** and **ἀντίλυτρον**.

NOTE.—1. The accent of *λουτρόν*, like that of another Homeric word *δαιτρόν*, distinguishes it from almost every other noun in *-τρον*. (For the group of cognates, *λουτρών* and *λουτήρ*, with which it is so closely allied in meaning, see J. A. Robinson *ap.* Eph 5[26].)

2. The papyri show that *-τρον* was still active. Thus for (α) *ἐγκοίμητρον* "counterpane," P Petr ii. 9[20]; for (γ) the very common *φόρετρον* "cost of carriage," *e.g.* P Ryl ii. 209[5] (ii/A.D.).

7. -τερος.

-τερος § 153. This was confined in the historical period to the formation of the comparative of adjectives, but the suffix *-tero-* was used at a much earlier stage to indicate ideas that were relative rather than absolute. The I.E. comparative in *-tero-* did not stand for an intensification of the positive, but represented a comparison. So the form in *-tero-* expressed no absolute property of a thing, but a relationship. Pairs of correlatives or opposites were thus formed,

E.g. **ἀριστερός**—*δεξιτερός* (cf. Lat. *sinister*—*dexter*).
ἡμέτερος—**ὑμέτερος** (cf. Lat. *noster*—*vester*).
ὀρέστερος—*ἀγρότερος* ("on the hills"—"on the plain").

Streitberg (*IF* xxxv. 196 f.) contends that the suffix *-ter-* is to be explained in the same way. It is seen at once in the terms for family relationship *πατήρ*, *μήτηρ*, *θυγάτηρ*, *φράτηρ*, which all point to the character of one person in relation to another. We can understand why such nouns should be provided with the same suffix as the so-called comparative formations. It is but one step further to claim that the same holds good of the *nomina agentis*. These originally were concerned with ideas which had no unqualified but only a relative meaning, and would be unthinkable except in some external connexion. Just as the term "father" involves a relationship to another person, "child," so "giver" (*dātar-*, *δοτήρ*, *δώτωρ*) implies relationship to a second party. Thus the suffix *-ter-* is appropriate here also.

Comparatives. See above, pp. 165–7. The ordinal *δεύτερος* is of the same formation.

Pronouns: Ἀμφότερος, *ἕτερος*, see p. 182 above. Πότερος, *which of two*, survives in NT only in adverbial form, **πότερον**, *whether*, Jn 7[17].

The adj. **ἀλλότριος** owes the secondary suffix *-ιο-* to its original antonym *ἴδιος*. The primary suffix *-τρ-* is the weak grade of *-τερ-*. For similar ablaut changes see Brugmann *Gr.*[4] 228, *Grd.*[2] II. i. 165, 329.

8. *Nouns and adjectives in -τος, -τη, -τον.*

§ 154. These suffixes were chiefly used in the parent I.E. to form verbal adjectives and ordinal numerals. In Greek the verbal connexion is less strong than in some cognate languages, and *-τος* is not the mark of the perf. pass. partic. (cf. Lat. *-tus*), but is free from tense and voice connexions (*Proleg.* 221). The verbal attachment was weak enough to allow the suffix to be added to noun stems.

-τος (*a*) *Verbal adjectives.* For formation see pp. 188, 224, and for accent, p. 224.

These may be grouped conveniently under the conjugation classes (*supra* 184 f., *infra* 381 ff.). Often the neg. adj. alone occurs.

From verbs in I. *a.* (*a*): †'Αδιάλειπτος (see *Vocab. s.v.*), †ἀκατάλυτος, †ἀκατάπαστος (p. 253, *Vocab. s.v.*), †ἀκατάσχετος, *ἀκώλυτος* (-ως, *Vocab. s.v.*), ἄμεμπτος, ἀμεταμέλητος, ἀνεκτός, †ἀνένδεκτος, ἄπιστος, †ἀπόδεκτος, ἄπταιστος (Xen. and later), γραπτός, †δεκτός (*Vocab. s.v.*), ἐκλεκτός, †ζεστός, †θεόπνευστος (p. 255, *Vocab. s.v.*), †παρείσακτος (*Vocab. s.v.*), πιστός (*Vocab. s.v.*), †πνικτός, †προσήλυτος (p. 237, also *Vocab. s.v.*), †συνεκλεκτός.

(*b*) 'Απρόσιτος.

I. *β.* (*b*) 'Ακατάστατος (Hippocr. and Hellen. writers), †ἀμετάθετος, ἀνεύθετος, ἀσύνετος, ἐγκάθετος, ἔκδοτος, ἔκθετος, εὔθετος (§ 106), *μετάδοτος* (εὐμετ°, § 106), *παράδοτος* (†πατρο-°, § 105), *περίστατος* (εὐπ°, § 106), συνετός.

II. *a.* (*a*) 'Αναμάρτητος, ἀνεπίλημπτος, †ἀπερίτμητος, *ποτός* (>noun, πότος, p. 254).

(*b*) Δυνατός, whence ἀδύνατος (§ 106).

II. *β.* (*a*) 'Αμετακίνητος, πρόσφατος (§ 125).

(*b*) Ἄκρατος, ἄρρωστος (Hippocr. and Hellen.), ἄσβεστος, *στρωτός* (λιθό-°).

III. †'*Απερίσπαστος* (†-ως).

IV. (*a*) 'Αρεστός, εὐάρεστος (*Vocab. s.v.*), *-βρωτός* (†σητό-, †σκωληκό-), παθητός. *Μεθυστός*>ἀμέθυστος (in Plut. = "not drunken," then used for a remedy against drunkenness, and so of the stone (*ἡ ἀμέθ.*)).

(*b*) Ἄγνωστος (§ 106), †ἀκατάγνωστος, γνωστός, διδακτός.

(*c*) Αἰχμάλωτος (<*αἰχμή* and *ἁλίσκομαι*, a T.P. cpd., § 105), θνητός.

There are no verbals from verbs in Classes V. and VI. Those in the next Class follow the subdivision of verbs in *yo* : *ye* given below, § 160.

VII. From verbs in *-άω.* 'Αγαπητός, †ἀρτιγέννητος, ἀνεξεραύνητος, ἀμώμητος, ἀόρατος (§ 106), γεννητός, ὁρατός. From *χρήομαι*, χρηστός (p. 265).

in -έω. †Ἀγενεαλόγητος, †ἀλάλητος, †ἀμετανόητος, †ἀναπολόγητος, ἀναρίθμητος, ἀνέγκλητος, †ἀνεκδιήγητος, †-ἀνεκλάλητος, ἀνόητος, ἀόρατος (§ 106), ἀρκετός, αὐθαίρετος, †ἀχειροποίητος, δυσνόητος, Ἐπαίνετος, ἐπιπόθητος, †εὐλόγητος, κλητός, παράκλητος, †ποταμοφόρητος, (for papp. see *Vocab. s.v.*), στυγητός, χειροποίητος.

in -όω. Μισθωτός.

in -ύω. -θυτός (†εἰδωλόθυτος, ἱερόθυτος), -φυτός (ἔμφυτος, νεόφυτος).

in -εύω. Ἀπαίδευτος, ἀσάλευτος, †δυσερμήνευτος, †λαξευτός, σιτευτός.

in -αίνω. †Ἀμάραντος, ἀμίαντος, ἀπαράβατος (Ruth. *NP* 367. For meaning, see Westcott *ap.* Heb 7^{24} and *Vocab. s.v.*), ἀπέραντος, ἄφαντος (see *Vocab. s.v.*), ὑφαντός.

in -ίνω (-*n*- *yo*). Ἀδιάκριτος, †ἀκατάκριτος, ἀνυπόκριτος, Ἀσύνκριτος, †αὐτοκατάκριτος.

in -ύνω. †Ἀνεπαίσχυντος.

in -αρω, -είρω. Ἀκάθαρτος, φθαρτός, ἄφθαρτος. (Here also may come ῥητός (-ῶς), ἄρρητος, ἀναντίρητος. See p. 235.)

in -λλω. Ἀπόβλητος.

in -πτω. †Ἄγναφος (=ἄγναπτος, see *Vocab. s.v.*), †ἀκατακάλυπτος, ἄμεμπτος, ἄνιπτος, ἄραφος (= °πτος), κρυπτός.

in -σσω. †Ἀνυπότακτος, ἄτακτος, †βδελυκτός, πλαστός, τακτός.

in -άζω. †Ἀνεξιχνίαστος, ἀπαρασκεύαστος, †ἀπείραστος, †δυσβάστακτος (for guttural form, see p. 230 and *Vocab.* pp. 106, 173), θαυμαστός, σεβαστός.

in -ίζω. †Ἀστήρικτος, ἀθέμιτος (for older ἀθέμιστος), †ἀστήρικτος, ἀχάριστος, εὐχάριστος, †σιτιστός; also ἄσωτος (-ως, § 106). But ἀθέμιτος (for older ἀθέμιστος) from θέμις. Χριστός is from χρίω.

Note.—1. The general rule for accentuation is that verbal adjectives in -τος are oxytone when uncompounded, or when compounded with a preposition if they denote possibility (three terminations). Otherwise the compounds are proparoxytone (and of two terminations). But as the passive meaning can so easily pass over into that of possibility, we often find paroxytones with two terminations for oxytones with three terminations. For exceptions to these rules see K.Bl. i. 538. Schmiedel (WS 69) explains ἐκλεκτός as derived direct from ἐκλέγω (with no corresponding simplex), so also εὐλογητός from εὐλογέω. This probably explains συνετός. Συνεκλεκτός is influenced by its simplex above. For ἀπόδεκτος and ἐκλεκτός, *supra*, p. 58.

2. Ἀμέθυστος and διάλεκτος preserve their adjectival force, as is shown by their feminine gender, due to the supply of λίθος and γλῶσσα respectively.

(*b*) *Nouns, abstract and concrete.*—The masc., fem., and neut. of these verbal adjectives often came to be used as abstract nouns. Many, however, have the concrete meaning.

a. **Θάνατος, κονίορτος, κοπετός, μαστός** (see p. 110 above, **νότος** (see Boisacq, *s.v.* *νάω*), **πλοῦτος, πότος, πυρετός, ὑετός, φόρτος, χόρτος.** *Στρατός* (<*στόρνυμι*) is represented in NT by compounds (*e.g.* **στρατηγός, στρατολογέω**). **Σῖτος** (<**ψῖτος* : *ψίω*=*pound.* So Prellwitz. Boisacq gives this with alternative etymologies), **ἐνιαυτός** (<Hom. *ἐνιαύω*=*rest in.* Hence original meaning was *solstice, i.e.* place of rest in the sun's progress. See Boisacq *s.v.*, and Brugmann *IF* xv. 89 ff., xvii. 319 f.).

-τή *β.* **Ἀρετή, βροντή** (*βρέμω*), **γενετή, κοίτη, κρύπτη, τελευτή,** *μελετή* (Barn. 10^{11}). **Ἑορτή** possibly belongs to this group if the derivation <**Ϝε-Ϝορ-τᾱ* is right. (See Boisacq *s.v.*)

-τόν *γ.* **Ἑρπετόν** (*ἕρπω*), **πρόβατον** (*προβαίνω*), **λεπτόν** (*λέπω*) ; **ἄριστον** rightly comes in here, <**ἆρι*<**ἀ*[*ι*]*ερι* (a locative form=*in the morning*) and **ἐστόν* <*ἔδω* (=*eat*). See Brugm. *KVG* 453, and, for loss of *ε* by ablaut, *ib.* 143. *Ποτόν drink* occurs in *Did.* 10^{3}, Ignat. *Tral.* 2^{3}, *Ep. Diogn.* 6^{9}.

(*c*) *Suffix -ωτός.*—A special variety is the suffix *-ωτός*, originally belonging to the verbal adjective closely associated with verbs in *-όω* (see IV. (*c*) above), and then attached to other stems, even to nouns, in the sense of "supplied with."

-ωτός **Λιβανωτός** (<*λίβανος*) may come under this heading, if in Rev 8^{3} it=*censer*, a view which Charles supports (*ICC in loc.*). See, however, *Vocab. s.v.* **Κιβωτός** is a word of Semitic origin and uncertain etymology.

In later Greek the fem. form *-ωτή* is fairly common as an elliptical subst. with the meainng "made of" or "coming from." Thus **μηλωτή** *sc.* *δορά*) *coat of sheepskin* (<*μῆλον sheep*). See Mayser *Gr.* i. 454, Jannaris *Gr.* 297.

(*d*) *Superlatives and Ordinals.*—For the -*τος* suffix in the formation of superlatives see above, §§ 67–69, and for the closely related ordinals see § 72.

The suffix *-to-* appears chiefly in ordinals, *e.g.* *ἕκτος* (Skt. *ṣaṣṭháḥ*) Lat. *sextus*). From *ἔνατος, δέκατος* etc., *-ατος* became detached as a distinctive suffix and is found in two superlatives, *πρῶτος* and *ἔσχατος* (see p. 167). How the once productive superl. suffix *-τατος* arose is not clear. Brugmann (*Gr.*^{3} 202) suggested *φέρτατος*=*φέριστος* as the explanation, but this is dropped in ed.^{4} (p. 238). Others account for it by comparing the Hom. ὕστατος with Skt. *uttamás* and assuming that -ταμο- became -τατο- under the influence of -τος in -ιστος. So Hirt *Handb.* 294. The suffix -ιστος goes back to I.E. (cf. Skt. *-iṣṭha-*, Goth. *-ista-*), and is composed of *-is-*, weak grade of the suffix *-i̯es-* (cf. Lat. *magis*), and the *-to-* already mentioned.

9. -τῐ, -τεί.

Under this heading we find in NT only the group of adverbs in -ιστί, for which see p. 163.

10. *Nomina actionis in -ti-.*

-σις § 155. A very productive suffix from the I.E. period in the formation of primary verbal abstracts (*nomina actionis*) of the feminine gender.

For the change of τ to σ before ι and ε at a primitive stage of the language, see Brugmann *Gr.*[4] 118.

This suffix was originally added to the weak grade of the roots or bases (as with the verbal adjectives in -τος). In time, however, with the gradual passing of the ablaut distinction in many verbs, and partly under the influence of other forms of the verb, and of other verbal nouns, the suffix was attached also to the strong grade of ablaut. Thus βάσις, δόσις, but in Hellenistic ῥεῦσις came in for the earlier ῥύσις. It is therefore worthy of notice that ῥύσις is the form in the NT.

(1) Formed by adding suffix directly to root or base:

Αἵρεσις (ἀν-, δι-, καθ-), βάσις (ἔκ-, κατά-, παρά-), βρῶσις, γένεσις, γνῶσις (ἀνά-, διά-, †ἐπί-, †πρό-), δόσις (ἀνταπό-, παρά-), δύσις (<δύνω=*set*), ἔγερσις, †ἔλεγξις, †ἔλευσις, ἕξις, θλίψις, ἴασις, καῦσις, κλῆσις (παρά-, πρόσ-), κρίσις (ἀνά-, ἀπό-, διά-, †κατά-, ὑπό-), κτίσις, λῆμψις (ἀνά-, ἀντί-, μετά-, πρόσ-), λύσις (ἀνά-, ἐπί-), ὅρασις, ὄρεξις, ὄψις, πόσις, πρᾶξις, πτῶσις, ῥύσις, στάσις (ἀνά-, ἀποκατά-, ἔκ-, ἐξανά-, ἐπί-, †ἐπισύ-, ὑπό-), τάξις, φάσις (πρό-), φύσις, χρῆσις (†ἀπό-).

In the following words the suffix is added to the compound verbal stem (as was the case with most of the compounds just given in brackets). They are put in a separate list as the simplicia are not found in NT:

Ὕπαρξις, ἀνάβλεψις, †ἀνά-, ἀπό-, ἔν- δειξις, †ἀπέκ-, ἔν- δυσις, (<°δύω), ἄν-, ἄφ-, πάρ-, σύν- εσις, †κατάσχεσις, ἀντί-, ἀπό-, ἐπί-, μετά-, †περί-, πρό-, †συνκατά- θεσις (θέσις in Herm. *Vis.* iii. 13[3]), ἄφιξις, ἀπόλαυσις, ἀνά-, ὑπό- μνησις, †κατάνυξις, ἄνοιξις, ἀνά-, κατάπαυσις, ἔντευξις, †ἀνά-, †πρόσ-, σύγ- χυσις.

(2) This suffix was then attached to denominative verbal stems, especially when the existing noun from which the verb was derived did not convey the abstract verbal meaning.

Thus from verbs in -άω:

†Ἀγαλλίασις (see below, p. 385), ἀπ-, συν-, †ὑπ- άντησις, γέννησις, †ἐνδώμησις (pp. 73, 307), †καύχησις, κοίμησις, κυβέρνησις.

From verbs in -έω:

Ἀγανάκτησις, †ἀθέτησις, †ἄθλησις, †αἴνεσις, δέησις, διήγησις, †ἐκδίκησις, ἐνθύμησις, †ἐπιπόθησις, †ἔσθησις (but see p. 133), ζήτησις, κατοίκησις, κίνησις, †παρατήρησις, ποίησις, †προσκαρτέρησις, πτόησις, †συμφώνησις, †ὑστέρησις, φρόνησις.

The short vowel in the penult of αἴνεσις, as the long vowel in θέλησις (<θέλω), is probably due to the influence of the aor. ᾔνεσα, ἐθέλησα (see Brugm. *Gr.*[4] 239).

From verbs in -όω:

†Ἀνακαίνωσις, βεβαίωσις, †βίωσις, δι-, ἐπαν- όρθωσις, δικαίωσις, †ἐκπλήρωσις, †ἐρήμωσις, †κατασκήνωσις, †λύτρωσις, †μόρφωσις, †νέκρωσις, ὁμοίωσις, πύρωσις, πώρωσις, ταπείνωσις, τελείωσις, †ὑποτύπωσις, †φανέρωσις, †φυσίωσις.

From other verbal stems:

Κόλασις (: -άζω), †κατάρτισις (: -ίζω), †ἀποκάλυψις (: -πτω), αἴσθησις (: αἰσθ-άνο-μαι), αὔξησις (: αὐξ-άν-ω, fut. αὐξήσω), ἅλωσις (: ἁλίσκομαι, fut. ἁλώσο-μαι), συνείδησις (: σύνοιδα, fut. -ειδήσω), †πεποίθησις (: πείθω, πέποιθα).

Notes may be given on three words.

Ἅλυσις *chain* is of uncertain etymology, and may have no connexion with these *nomina actionis*.

Πεποίθησις. "Substantives in -σις from the perfect stem were not used by Attic writers" (Rutherford *NP* 355).

Συνείδησις (see above § 127). For history of this word see Norden *Agnostos Theos*, 136 n.[1]. It is noteworthy that with one doubtful exception Epictetus prefers the participle τὸ συνειδός (cf. Bonhöffer, *Epiktet u. das NT*, 156).

(3) The old form of the suffix -τις survives in a few old words only. Πίστις (=πίθ-τις), νῆστις *fasting*, where νη is the result of contraction, high grade *nĕ* coming before *ĕ* in Anlaut, √*ed-*, see above, p. 287.

The masc. μάντις (Herm. *Mand.* xi. 2) was originally fem. abstract (cf. Lat. *hostis*. Brugmann *Gr.*[4] 239).

NOTE.—1. -σις nouns in Hellenistic no longer represent action merely, but also result. Thus κτίσις *creation* or *creature*, γνῶσις the result of insight, as well as insight itself.

2. "-σις is apparently concrete in αἴτησις C P Herm 73 ii[3], but οἰκοδόμησις in 83[9] is *nomen actionis*; so πλάκωσις 94[18], δήλωσις 101[10]. But κτῆσις 101*b*, οἴκησις 119 iii[17], σύμπτωσις often, κράτησις 119 iv[29], βεβαίωσις [31], μέτρησις v[23], ἄθλησις verso iii[13] [are concrete]. Ἀξίωσις *ib.*[20] less clear. Πρᾶξις, legal execution (BGU iv. 1115[33] etc.). Thumb (*Dial.* 373) says -σις and -μα were signs of Ionic influence in Attic prose."—J. H. M.

(2) *The -d- Suffixes.*

§ 156. Though originating in the I.E. period, this suffix had a specially extended use in Greek.

1. *Nouns in -αδ-, -ιδ-.*

-ας (-αδ-) 1. As a root determinative it appears in such formations as *παρα-στά-ς, -άδος*, which became a model for formations in *-άς, -άδος*. Thus **ἰκμάς** (Lk 8^{6}, see *Vocab.*), **λαμπάς, σπιλάς** (Jude ^{12}: see Mayor *in loc.*), **στιβάς** (Mk 11^{8}, see Swete *in loc.* For *στοιβάς* and *στυβάς* see p. 76 above). **Δορκάς**, a woman's name, means "gazelle," and is an instance of a form modified by popular etymology, *ζορκάς* (=I.E. **i̯ork-s*) being conformed to supposed connexion with *δέρκομαι*.

2. Patronymics and place-names are represented by **Ἡρῳδιάς, Τιβεριάς, Τρῳάς**, and **Ἑλλάς**.

3. For the numerals **μυριάς** and **χιλιάς**, see above, pp. 169, 176.

-δ-απος 4. The old class to which *ποδαπ'ς, ἀλλοδαπός* etc. belonged is represented in the NT by **ποταπός**, which has been modified by popular etymology under the influence of *πότε*. (See *Proleg.* 95.)

-ις (-ιδ-) 5. The ethnica in *-ίς* are represented only by **Ἑλληνίς** (: masc. *Ἕλλην*), and **Ἑβραΐς** (a peculiar form for the more usual *Ἑβραϊκός, ή, όν*), which is found twice in the LXX (4 Mac 12^{7} 16^{15}, *ἡ Ἑ. φωνή*) and in the NT in Acts *ter* (*ἡ Ἑβ. διάλεκτος*).

Σαμαρεῖτις in Joseph. = the region of Samaria, but in Jn 4^{9} is the fem. of *Σαμαρείτης*.

6. Feminine appellatives in *-ις* are **†συγγενίς** (from m. *-ής*), **†μοιχαλίς** (Hell. form of Att. *μοιχάς*, see above, § 147, from m. *μοιχός*), **†πορφυρόπωλις** (from m. *-ης*).

7. A diminutive meaning may be traced in **θυρίς** (: *θύρα*), **κεφαλίς** (: *κεφαλή*), **πινακίς** (Lk 1^{63} C^{3}D)). Cf. Plummer *in loc*: 'All four forms, *πίναξ, πινακίς, πινάκιον*, and *πινακίδιον*, are used of writing-tablets, and *πινακίδα* is *v.l.* here. But elsewhere in NT *πίναξ* is a "dish" or "platter."'

8. Apart from these groups we have a large number of nouns with the *-ις* termination. **Ἀκρίς, ἀσπίς, ἀτμίς** (cf. *ἀτμός*, <*ἄω* = to blow), **†βολίς** (Heb 12^{20} (LXX) *minusc. pauc.*), **ἐλπίς, κλεῖς, λεπίς, μερίς, παῖς** (<*πάϝις*), **παγίς, ῥαφίς, ῥυτίς, σανίς, σφραγίς, σφυρίς** (see above, p. 109).

Ἴασπις, a word of Phœnician origin (see Boisacq, and cf. Hebrew יָשְׁפֵה). **Ἶρις** <**ϝῖ-ρι-ς*, I.E. **u̯ī-ri-s*.

Παροψίς (see above, § 123). The Atticists condemned the use of this word in the derivative sense (see *NP* 265).

Πατρίς, originally poet. fem. of *πάτριος*, then subst. (=*ἡ πατρία γῆ*), Σύρτις, Λωΐς.

9. -*τις* has become the regular feminine for *nomina agentis* in -*της*, *e.g.* προφῆτις, προστάτις, and for denominatives in -*της*, *e.g.* πρεσβῦτις.

2. *Conglutinates with -αδ-, -ιδ-.*

-ίδιον These are represented in the NT only by the neuter nouns in -*ίδιον*, for which see above, p. 346.

3. *Nouns in -δον-.*

-δων (-δον-) The sole NT representative of this formation is χαλκηδών. Found in Rev 21[19] alone in Biblical Greek, it is the name given to a copper silicate found in the mines near Chalcedon. The place name itself is a derivative of *χαλκός copper*.

It is doubtful whether *σινδών* should come under this heading. It seems to be an Oriental loan word; cf. Hebr. סָדִין "linen wrapper."

4. *Adjectives in -ώδης.*

These have been given in § 107 above (p. 283) under compounds. The fondness of Hermas for words of this formation is striking: *ἐρημώδης* (*Sim.* ix. 26[1]), *κροκώδης* (*Sim.* vi. 1[5]), *μαστώδης* (*Sim.* ix. 1[4]), *πυροειδὴς καὶ αἱματώδης* (*Vis.* iv. 3[3]), *κρημνώδης*, *ἀκανθώδης*, *τριβολώδης* (*Sim.* vi. 2[6]), ἀκανθώδης (*Mand.* xii. 1[3. 4] *et al.*).

(3) *The -θ- Suffixes.*

See above, p. 364.

F. Suffixes with Guttural Stops.

(1) *The -k- Suffixes.*

1. *Primary nouns in -κη.*

-κη § 157. A few words have this as a primary suffix, *e.g.* θήκη, νίκη.

νίκη<*νῑ- according to Osthoff *MU* iv. 223 f., who cft. Skt. *nī-ca-ḥ*. But this is very doubtful; see Boisacq 671.

2. *Adverbs in -ιξ, -αξ.*

-ιξ, -αξ Πέριξ (§ 124 (*c*)) and ἅπαξ (p. 286) are nom. sing. of adjectives petrified as adverbs (cf. *ἀναμίξ*, *πατάξ*, Brugmann *Gr.*[4] 207).

3. *Nouns with stems in -ακ-, -εκ-, -ηκ-, -υκ-, -ικ-.*

Nouns in -αξ, -ηξ, -υξ, -ιξ Ἄνθραξ, θώραξ, κόραξ, πίναξ, φύλαξ, χάραξ; in -εκ-: ἀλώπηξ; in -ηκ-: σκώληξ; in -υκ-: κῆρυξ (for accent, see above, p. 57); in -(α)ικ-: γυνή; in -ικ-: Φῆλιξ, Φοῖνιξ, φοῖνιξ, χοῖνιξ.

The history of the relation between γυναικ- and γυνή is uncertain, but that it goes back to prim. I.E. is shown by Armen. *kanai-*. The accent in γυναικός may be derived from the monosyllabic *βναικ- (*βναικός). See Brugmann *IF* xxii. 171 ff., *Gr.*[4] 242. For etymology of ἀλώπηξ, see Brugmann *Grd.*[2] II. i. 474.

4. *Denominative adjectives and nouns in -κο-.*

-κος, -κη, -κον Φυσικός (φύ-σι-ς), ἁλυκός (ἅλς), μαλακός; φάρμακον; φυλακή.

Ἁλυκός is supplanted in Hellenistic by ἁλικός, really a distinct word. See above, p. 80, and *Vocab. s.v.* (Apart from Jas 3[12] the classical form is found in the Bible only in the name for the Dead Sea, Num 3[12], Deut 3[17].)

Φάρμακον<*φαρμα<**bhr̥men-*. So Brugm. *Grd.*[2] II. i. 485. See, however, Thumb in Brugm. *Gr.*[4] 241 n.[4], and Boisacq 1015 n.[1]

Μαλακός<I.E.**m°l -qó-s*, <*melā^x-*, to *grind, pulverise* (see Boisacq, *s.vv.* μαλθακός, μύλλω, βλάβη). For the meaning of this word in 1 Co 6[9] see Deissmann *LAE* 150 ([2]164) n.[4], *Vocab. s.v.*

5. *Denominative adjectives in -ιακός*, formed from nouns in

-ιακός -ιο-, -ια, on the analogy of -ιάς : -ίς, -ιάδης : -ίδης, -ιάζειν : -ίζειν.

†Κυριακός (κύριος), †οἰκιακός, are both Hellenistic formations.

For the contemporary use of κυριακός=*imperial*, and for the origin of the use of ἡ κυριακή=*Lord's day* in Rev 1[10], see Deissmann *BS* 217 ff. *LAE* 362 ff. ([2]358 ff.), and *Vocab.* 364.

Οἰκιακός (Mt 10[25. 36] only in Gr. Bible), a Κοινή formation found in papp. (see *Vocab.*) in the sense of a *member of a household.* Οἰκειακός, read v.[25] by CDMU (v.[36] UΓ), is a late formation from οἰκεῖος, meaning *his own.* (Found in Plut. *Cic.* 20).

6. *Denominative adjectives in -ικός* (after -ιος the most

-ικός productive of adjectival suffixes in Greek), from prim. I.E. *-iqo-*, as in Skt. *paryāyiká-s* (=strophic) from *paryāyá-s* (=strophe), cf. Lat. *modicus* : *modus.*

(*a*) In Homeric period these were mostly ethnica, which continue to be formed in this way.

Ἀχαϊκός, Γαλατικός, Ἑβραϊκός, Ἑλληνικός, Ἰουδαϊκός, Ἰταλικός, Λευιτικός, Ποντικός, Ῥωμαϊκός.

Φοινίκη (p. 149) and Σαμοθράκη (-θρᾴκη, BE) are of a different formation.

(*b*) The extension of this suffix in the classical period probably arose with such words as φυσικός, μαντικός, where the suffix -κός was attached to an -ι- stem.

The idea of "belonging to" is seen in βασιλικός. (For the meaning in Jn 4[46] see Bauer *in loc.*, in Jas 2[8] see Hort *in loc.* and Deissmann *LAE* 367 n.[3] ([2]362 n.[5]). For the stem see Fraenkel *ZVS* xlv. 222 f.). The suffix, which was a favourite with the Ionian sophists, came into common use with the Attic writers in the latter part of the fifth century B.C.,[1] where the meaning of "pertaining to," "with the characteristics of," became prominent. In the NT list we have †ἀρχιερατικός, †ἐθνικός, εἰρηνικός, ἱππικός, κεραμικός (see note 2 below), κοσμικός, †λειτουργικός (see *LAE* 70, [2]76), λογικός (see *Vocab. s.v.* For Rom 12[1] see Lietzmann *HNT in loc.*; for 1 Pet 2[2], Hort *in loc.*), μουσικός, †μυλικός, νομικός, †ὀνικός (NT, papp., inscrr., see *Vocab. s.v.*), πατρικός, προβατικός, σιρικός (by vowel assimilation for σηρικός, see Mayser *Gr.* i. 150, WH *App.* 158, above p. 72;—really an ethnic adj. from οἱ Σῆρες), Στοϊκός, τυπικός, (†-ῶς), †τυφωνικός, ὑδρωπικός, †χοϊκός.

From compar. adjectives come ἀνωτερικός, †νεωτερικός, and from adv. καθόλου, καθολικός (in the titles of Cath. Epp. in late MSS. See Mayor *Comm. James* ed.[2] cclix).

Κοινωνικός, originally "social," later acquired the meaning "ready to go shares" (so 1 Ti 6[18]), and thus approximates to a nuance found in some of the adjectives in -τικός (see below (*c*)).

Σαρκικός, ψυχικός, πνευματικός, σωματικός form an important group.

NOTE.—1. The distinction in meaning between adjectives in -ικός and those in -ινος is generally maintained, the former connoting . . . -*like*, and the latter *made of* . . . . It corresponds to that found in the English suffixes -*y* and -*en*: *e.g. leathery, leathern, earthy, earthen.* "The termination -ινος denotes a *material* relation, while -ικός denotes an *ethical* or dynamic relation, to the idea involved in the root" (Plummer *ap.* 1 Co 3[1], where σαρκίνοις is deliberately chosen in distinction from σαρκικοί in v.[3]). The true reading is preserved in ℵABC*D* 33; σαρκικοῖς (D[3]EFGLP) is an obvious correction. The same contrast with πνευματικός has led to the substitution of -ικός for -ινος in Rom 7[14] (ℵ[c]LPω); a similar misunderstanding is answerable for -ικῆς (ϛ) in Heb 7[16]. On the other hand -ικός is right in Rom 15[27], 1 Co 3[3] (*bis*) (-ινοι D*FG) 9[11], 2 Co 1[12] (-ίνῃ FG) 10[1], 1 Pet 2[11]. In 1 Co 3[4] ℵ[c]LP have

[1] Fraenkel, *ut supra*, 205 f., gives statistics showing the relative frequency in Euripides compared with Sophocles, in Thucydides : Herodotus, and in Isocrates : Isæus. It is specially common in Plato, Xenophon, and Aristotle, and in scientific terminology.

σαρκικοί, where *ἄνθρωποι* is the true reading. (See Westcott *ap.* Heb 7[16] for true distribution of these words.) For confusion of meaning in these suffixes see *Vocab. s.v.* *ξύλινος*.

2. **Κεραμικός** *earthen* (<*κέραμος* *clay*) is to be distinguished from *κεραμεικός* *of a potter* (<*κεραμεύς*). It was a late form, deprecated by Phrynichus (see Lob. 147), for class. *κεραμεοῦς*, which was already undergoing change in Hellenistic (-*μαῖος*, Polyb., -*μειος* Plut.). Fraenkel shows (*ib.* 221) how closely *κεραμεικός* and -*ικός* approximated in meaning. In view of P Lond 121[867] (=i. p. 112) *ἀπὸ τρόχου* [*κε*]*ραμικοῦ* and Ps 2[8] *ὡς σκεῦος κεραμέως*, Rev 2[27] (*σκεύη κεραμικά*) is probably an itacism (see above, 76 f.).

3. The form **ἀρχιερατικός** follows the classical *ἱερατικός*, which is influenced by the verb *ἱερατεύω*, although there is no verbal stress in the adjective.

4. **Ἡλίκος**, **πηλίκος**, *τηλίκος* (**τηλικοῦτος**) preserve a suffix -*λι*- (cf. Lat. *qualis, talis*) to which the secondary suffix -*κος* is attached.

-τικός

(*c*) From *nomina agentis* in -*της* were formed many adjectives in -*τικός*, in which the verbal force was strongly present. These verbal derivatives took the same suffix with either an intransitive or a causative force.

Thus **αἱρετικός** *capable of choosing* (Plato) and so *factious* (Tit 3[10], where the current use of *αἵρεσις*=*secta, factio*, has coloured the meaning, see Parry, *Comm. in loc.*), †**διδακτικός** *apt at teaching* (1 Ti 3[2], 2 Ti 2[24]), elsewhere only in Philo. The class. *διδασκαλικός* appears even in Vett. Val., and survives in MGr (see *Vocab.*). **Κριτικός** *able to discern*, †**παραλυτικός** the late and vernacular word (probably formed on the analogy of *ἀναλυτικός*, *διαλυτικός*, *ἐκλυτικός*, from Arist. onwards—for exx. see Fraenkel *ib.* 216) always used by Mt and Mk, whereas Lk retains the medical term *παραλελυμένος*, **συστατικός** (<*συνίστημι*) post-classical in sense of "constructive," and more often, as in 2 Co 3[1] a t.t. for *commendatory* (letter), †**προφητικός** (<*προφήτης*), apart from Rom 16[26], 2 Pet 1[19] and Patrr., only in Philo and Lucian.

Note.—1. **Βιωτικός** (<*βιόω*) as first used by Aristotle=*fit to live, lively*, and shows analogy with most words in this group. But its regular use in Hellenistic (Polyb., Diod., Philo, Plut., Artem.), condemned by Phryn. (Rutherford *NP* 459), appears in Lk 21[34], 1 Co 6[3], where it is adj. corresponding to *βίος* (see Lightfoot *Notes* 211, Field *Notes* 171). This meaning of "worldly," "secular," "business," "everyday" can be illustrated from the unliterary as well as the literary Κοινή (papp. Vett. Val. etc., see *Vocab. s.v.*)

2. †**Πιστικός**, that *crux interpretum* in Mk 14[3], Jn 12[3], if a Greek word, is either (*a*) from *πιστός* (<*πείθω*) *fit to be trusted, genuine*, though elsewhere of persons, as in Artem. *On.* ii. 32, 66, iii. 54, where=*faithful*

(applied to woman); or (*b*) from *πιστός* (<*πίνω*)=*ποτός*, *liquid.* If a loan-word, John Lightfoot's conjecture (*Hor. Hebr.* ii. 446), followed by Merx (*ap.* Mk 14[3]), is possible, that we have a transliteration of the Aramaic פיסתקא, *pistaca.* So that the ointment was *unguentum balaninum.* Against this must be set the difficulty of the Syriac translator. Abbott (*J.V.* 252), following Wetstein, who quotes abundant instances of *σπικάτου* as the name of an ointment (<*spica*, cf. Vulg. *spicati*), suggests that an early Galilean tradition, finding in the original some form of *σπικάτου*, played upon it by saying " not *σπικάτου* but *πιστικόν*." W. C. Allen (*Comm. on Mk.* 168) supposes *σπικάτου* transliterated into Aramaic and misread by the Greek translator. (See also *Vocab. s.v.*)

7. *Nouns in -ίσκος, -ίσκη.*

-ίσκος, -ίσκη A frequent diminutive suffix, represented in NT only by †βασιλίσκος, νεανίσκος, παιδίσκη.

Βασιλίσκος, which D reads in Jn 4[46. 49], a diminutive precisely corresponding to our *princelet.* So Polyb. iii. 44. 5, Dittenb. *OGIS* 201[1. 10] (quoted by Bauer *in loc.*).

Παιδίσκη. The deteriorative force of this diminutive is constant in the NT. Cf. Meyer, *Ostr.* 57[6] (A.D. 192) and Deissmann's note, *LAE* 186 ([2]200) n.[7] " *παιδίσκη* meaning as in the NT a ' female slave.' "

The formation of a diminutive *νεανισκάριον* (Epict. ii. 16. 29) shows that νεανίσκος was a " faded diminutive."

(2) *The -g- Suffixes.*

1. *Nouns in -αγ-, -υγ-, -ῑγ-.*

-αγ-, -υγ-, -ῑγ- This group was no larger in Greek than in the cognate languages; see Brugmann *Grd.*[2] II. i. 506 ff. Ἅρπαξ (for ἁρπαγή, see p. 335), πτέρυξ (for πτερύγιον, see p. 343), μάστιξ.

2. *Nouns in -γγ-.*

-γγ- A group of words denoting a hollow or a musical instrument is represented in the NT by λάρυγξ, σάλπιγξ, φάραγξ.

(3) *The -χ- Suffixes.*

-χ- To this small miscellany belong στόμαχος, θρίξ, ὄρνιξ (see p. 130).

G. Stems in -σ-.

Stems in -ος : -εσ-.

-ος (-εσ-). § 158. (*a*) *Nouns*. For this class see p. 138 above. Of the sixty-two nouns found in the NT notes are required for very few.

†Γλεῦκος first appears in Arist. For vernacular use of this NT ἀπ. λεγ. in Ac 2[13], see *Vocab. s.v.*

Ἔλεος and σκότος; see above, pp. 126 f.

Νῖκος. An old word, as Lobeck *Phyrn.* 647 shows. Wackernagel, *Hellenistica* 27, suggests that νεῖκος, a poetical word in Attic, and alive in Ionic for Herodotus (=*contention*), passed into the Κοινή with the meaning *victory*, through confusion with νίκη.

Στρῆνος. This ἀ.λ. in NT at Rev 18[3] first appears in the New Com. See Lobeck *Phryn.* 381, Kennedy *Sources* 41.

(*b*) *Adjectives.*—For this class see p. 162.

THE FORMATION OF VERBS.

§ 159. In considering the formation of verbs by suffixes we have to do with present stems, and shall follow the classification set forth above on pp. 184 f. Under most of the headings a classified list of verbs occurring in the NT will suffice without further comment. Class VII., however, is very rich in types, and was specially productive in the Hellenistic period. These types must be discussed in greater detail. As a general rule the simplex preceded by a hyphen is given for composita. If the *Prœverbia* do not follow within brackets, they may be found by reference to the List of Verbs, § 95.

I. *a*. Person suffixes added to root.

(*a*) With thematic vowel:

-ἄγχω, ἄγω, ἀλείφω, ἀνοίγω, ἄρχω, βλέπω, βούλομαι, βρέχω, βρύω, γράφω, δέομαι (p. 195), δέρω, δέχομαι, διώκω, -δύω, -εἴκω, ἐλέγχω, ἕλκω, ἐμέω (p. 236), -ἕπομαι, ἐρείδω, ἐρεύγομαι, ἔρχομαι, εὔχομαι, ἔχω, ζέω (p. 195), ἥκω, θέλω, θλάω, θλίβω, θραύω, καθεύδω, λάμπω, λέγω, λείπω, λούω, λύω, μέλλω, -μέλομαι, μέμφομαι, μένω, -νέμω, νήφω, -οἴχομαι, παίω, παύω, πείθω, πέμπω, πλέκω, πλέω (p. 195), πνέω (p. 195), -πνίγω, πρίω, πταίω, ῥέω (p. 195), σέβομαι, -σείω, σήπω, σπεύδω, στήκω, στρέφω, τήκω, τρέπω, τρέφω, τρέχω, τρῖβω, φείδομαι, φέρω, φεύγω, φθέγγομαι, -χέω (p. 195), ψεύδομαι, -ψῦχω.

NOTE.—In συνθλάω the simplex θλα(σ)-ω may be from *dhṛsát>Skt. dṛsát, mill-stone (cf. δειράς), see Boisacq 347 n.[1].

(b) Without thematic vowel:

Εἰμί, -εἶμι, ἐπίσταμαι, κεῖμαι, κρέμαμαι, φημί.

NOTE.—Κρύβω (περι°) is a late formation, following the analogy of τρίβω: ἔτριψα. (See Thumb in Brugmann Gr.[4] 375 n. 1.)

I. β. Reduplicated forms.

(a) Thematic:

Γίνομαι (class. γί-γνομαι, see p. 232), πίπτω (*πĭ-πτω), τίκτω (*τι-τκω).

(b) Unthematic:

Δίδωμι, -ἵημι, ἵστημι, κίχρημι, τίθημι; (with nasal inserted) πίμπρημι.

II. With formative suffix in -n-.

a. (a) Suffix νο : νε or ανο : ανε.

(i) Added to root: Δάκνω, δύνω, ἱστάνω (p. 241), κάμνω, -κτέννω (p. 245), πίνω, τέμνω, -χύννω. Αἰσθάνομαι, ἁμαρτάνω, αὐξάνω, βλαστάνω (but see p. 231), †ὀπτάνομαι (for this late present, a back-formation from ὤφθην, see pap. instances in Vocab. s.v.).

(ii) Added to root with nasal inserted: Θιγγάνω, λαγχάνω, λαμβάνω (p. 247), λανθάνω, λιμπάνω, μανθάνω, πυνθάνομαι, τυγχάνω.

(b) Suffix νη : νᾰ added to root. Δύναμαι, ὀνίνημι (p. 251).

β. (a) (i) Suffix ννο : ννε. Δεικνύω.

(ii) Suffix νϜο : νϜε. Τίνω, φθάνω.

(iii) Suffix νεϜο : νεϜε. -ἱκνέομαι, κινέω (<I.E. *qī-, cf. Lat. ac-cītus), προσκυνέω (κυνέω=*κυ-νεσω <*κυ-νε-σ-μι, according to Johansson, followed by Boisacq. Brugmann (Grd.[2] II. iii. 276), however, follows Wackernagel in deriving Skt. cumba-ti "kissed" from *cunva-ti, which supports Ϝ as against σ).

(b) Suffix νῡ : νῠ added to root. Ἀμφιέννυμι, δείκνυμι, ζώννυμι, κεράννυμι, -κτέννυμι (p. 245), -μίγνυμι, -ὄλλυμι (*ὀλ-νῡ-μι), ὄμνυμι (p. 251), πέταννυμι, πήγνυμι, ῥήγνυμι, ῥώννυμι, σβέννυμι, στρώννυμι.

III. With formative suffix in so : se.

Αὔξω (cf. Lat. aug-eo), κλά-(σ)-ω, σεί-(σ)-ω, σπά-(σ)-ω.

IV. Suffixes in *sko* : *ske*.

(*a*) Added to simple stems: **Ἀρέσκω, βόσκω, γηράσκω, μεθύσκομαι, πάσχω** (=πάθ-σκω), **φάσκω, -φαύσκω, -φώσκω** (for relation between these last two words, and possible derivation of former, see above, p. 263).

(*b*) Added to reduplicated stem: **Βιβρώσκω, γι(γ)νώσκω, διδά(κ)σκω, -διδύσκω** (ἐν-), **μιμνήσκω, πιπράσκω.**

So also **ἱλάσκομαι**, according to Boisacq, p. 373, <*σι-σλᾰ-σκομαι.

(*c*) With ι before the suffix: **Ἀναλίσκω** (but see p. 228 above), **γαμίσκομαι, εὑρίσκω, -θνῄσκω.** To these we may add the ἀπ. λεγ. σταυρίσκω, *Ev. Petr.* ii. 3.

Note.—1. According to J. Wright (*Comp. Gram.* 290), in such verbs as ἁλίσκομαι and εὑρίσκω the -ι- was the weak grade form of an original long diphthong -*ēi*-, -*ōi*. Such presents as Attic θνῄσκω and μιμνῄσκω were formed by analogy.

2. The inceptive meaning which is so prominent in Latin verbs in -*sco* is rarely traceable in Greek. Μεθύσκω, which in the active is used as a causative of μεθύω, means, in the middle, "to get drunk." But that cannot always be pressed, as 1 Th 5[7] shows. (See Milligan *Commentary in loc.*). Γαμίσκω is used in a causative sense in Lk 20[34], and is equivalent to γαμίζω in v.[35].

V. Suffixes in *to* : *te*.

See above, p. 185, where it is shown that these may be ignored.

VI. Suffixes in θο : θε.

This small class is represented by **†ἀλήθω, ἔσθω, †κνήθω, νήθω** (see LS), πλήθω, πρήθω. The present stems πλήθω, πρήθω are not found in NT. **Ἀλήθω, κνήθω** and **νήθω** are Hellenistic forms for ἀλέω, κνάω and νέω (Rutherford *NP* 90, 134, 240).

VII. Suffixes in *yo* : *ye*.

§ 160. For this very large class of verbs it will be convenient to discuss word-formation under different headings from those of the divisions suggested on p. 185.

i. *Vocalic yo- presents.*

These consist of 1. άω; 2. έω; 3. όω; 4. ίω; 5. ύω; 6. εύω.

1. *Verbs in άω.*

-άω

(*a*) A few root verbs, ἐάω (etym. uncertain, Boisacq, *s.v.*), ἰάομαι (<*ἰσᾱ-ι̯ο-), κτάομαι (cf. pf. κέ-κτη-μαι, κτῆ-μα, Skt. *kṣáyati*), and, with suffix -*m*-, κοιμάω (c. κοίτη, κεῖμαι).

(*b*) Denominatives from *ā*- stems supply the majority.

Βοάω, δαπανάω, διψάω, θεάομαι, καταράομαι (<κατάρα), **καυχάομαι, κολλάω,** ναρκάω (**κατα-**), **νικάω, ὀδυνάω** (see *Vocab.*), **ὁρμάω, πεινάω, πειράω, σιγάω, σιωπάω,** †**σπαταλάω** (once in Polyb., in LXX and late writings), **συλάω** (<σύλη or σῦλον, both used mostly in plur.), **τιμάω, τολμάω, τρυγάω, τρυφάω,** φυσάω (**ἐμ-**), **χολάω.** To these may be added **ὁράω** for which Sütterlin (p. 10) postulates *ὁρα (cf. φρουρά and Germ. **warō*).

(*c*) **Ἀγαπάω, γεννάω,** †**ἐραυνάω** (see p. 86), **ἡττάομαι, μεριμνάω, πλανάω** are not derived from the corresponding nouns in -*ā*, which are back-formations or "noms postverbaux"; see pp. 335, 356 *supra*. For ἐραυνάω see Solmsen *Gr. Wortf.* 50, who also (pp. 48 f.) derives μεριμνάω from *μερίμων <*μέριμος (cf. μάχιμος etc.). Γεννάω, ἐρευνάω, and πλανάω had originally an -*n*- suffix, but were later taken over into the -*ō*- conjugation. Ἡττάομαι (<ἥττων) has replaced *ἡττόομαι (cf. Ion. ἑσσόομαι) under analogy of νικάομαι. (See further, p. 107.)

(*d*) Conformity to type influences many verbs, especially when a considerable group already exists with the same general meaning.

Thus the large group of verbs of *sound* in -άω is represented in NT by βριμάομαι (**ἐμ-**)[1] and **μυκάομαι** (<I.E. **mūk*-, extension of *mū*-, an onomatop. word, Sütterlin 25). Another drawn from *agriculture*, and represented in (*b*) above by **τρυγάω**, supplies us with **ἀλοάω** (<ἅλως (Att.), †**ἅλων**), **ἀμάω, λικμάω** (<λικμός). *Sickness*, and unhealthy desire, furnish another group, as **χολάω** in (*b*). This may possibly account for the LXX μοιχάω, NT **μοιχάομαι** (Xenophon and Hellenistic), which replaces the class μοιχεύω (see *Vocab.*).

Analogy accounts also for the following: **Ἀτιμάω**, Mk 12⁴ D (<ἄτιμος), follows τιμάω (<τιμή); ἀντάω (**ἀπ-, ὑπ-**) <adv. ἄντα (see § 114) conforms to the pattern πειράω: πεῖρα, so περάω (**δια-**) <adv. πέραν. **Μωμάομαι** (<μῶμος) may be influenced by λωβάομαι (λώβη).

(*e*) A few verbs in -άω apparently come under none of these headings: **Ἀριστάω** (<ἄριστον), **ἐμπιπλάω** (pp. 205, 254), **ἐμπιπράομαι**, Ac 28⁶ ℵ* (p. 254), **κολυμβάω** (<κόλυμβος), **μασάομαι** (Aristoph. and Hellen.) <*μαθι̯αομαι <*μαθι̯α, I.E. **mn̥th-i̯a* (Boisacq, *s.v.*), πηδάω (**ἐκ-**) <πηδόν <I.E. **pēd*, which has the long grade of **ped*, the root found in πέδη, πέζα, πέδον, πούς; also **χαλάω** (deriv. uncertain, Boisacq, *s.v.*), **ψηλαφάω** (see Boisacq, *s.v.* ψάλλω).

[1] See § 163 (3) (*c*) below. The new LS maintains this distinction between βριμάομαι and °όομαι, as between sound and feeling.

(*f*) †**Ἐλεάω** is a later form of **ἐλεέω** (p. 235, and for confusion of flexions, pp. 195, 197, 198). **Προσδοκάω**, though simplex is *δοκέω*. †**Ἐλλογάω**, a Κοινή word, is an instance of a verb in *-άω* formed from a prep. phrase (see § 118 and *Vocab. s.v.*). **Γελάω** (<*γελασ-ιω, cf. γέλως) is an example of a consonantal *yo-* present.

-τάω (*g*) There is really no justification for treating verbs in *-τάω* as a distinct class. The only possible example in NT of a frequentative force is in **σκιρτάω** (: σκαίρω), though it is doubtful whether there is any connexion between this ending and that of the Lat. frequentatives (e.g. *dictare* : *dicere*). As the *nomina agentis* in *-της* regularly form their verbs in *-τέω*, that noun formation supplies no reason for a separate group here. The presence of *τ* in the stems of several *ᾱ-* nouns gives us †**βλαστάω** (p. 231), **μελετάω**, **τελευτάω**. **Φρεναπατάω** (<φρεναπάτης) follows the analogy of **ἀπατάω**. **Ἐρωτάω** (<*ἐρϜ-ωτ-) is connected with *ἐρέω* (*ἐρέϜω*); see Boisacq 278.

-ιάω (*h*) Some verbs in *-ιάω* are simply denominatives from stems in *-ια*; *e.g.* **δειλιάω**, **κονιάω**, †**προαιτιάομαι** (ἁ.λ. Rom 3^{9}. Its simplex <*αἰτία* is common in class. Gr.). Others are affected by the clearly marked groups in *-ιάω* (Sütterlin 29 ff., and see (*d*) above), *e.g.* †**ἀγαλλιάω** (for class. *ἀγάλλω*), **ἀροτριάω** (<*ἄροτρον*), **θυμιάω** (*to burn incense*, distinguished from **θυμόω**, *to be angry*. The latter accords with the only meaning attaching to the Gr. word *θῡμός*, whereas *θυμιάω* goes back to the original and literal sense found in Skt. *dhūmáḥ*, I.E. **dhū-mó-s*), **κοπιάω** (<*κόπος*), **στρηνιάω** (a word first found in the Mid. Comedy, see Lobeck *Phryn.* 381, Rutherford *NP* 475) <*στρῆνος*.

(*i*) For **ζήω**, **χρήομαι**, the only two remaining verbs in the class *-ήω*, see p. 195.

2. *Verbs in -έω.*

-έω § 161. The principal classification follows the distinction between verbs derived from simple noun stems, and those derived from compound nouns (and adjectives). In early Greek these verbs were more commonly formed from simple nouns in *-ος*. The proportion gradually changed, until in the Hellenistic period the overwhelming majority of new formations came from compounds.

Sütterlin (p. 63) examines and corrects v.d. Pfordten's tables, and with 1160 verbs in *-έω* shows the following ratio of new formations in (*a*) Homer, (*b*) Classical, (*c*) Post-classical authors—

From simplicia, (*a*) 50, (*b*) 30, (*c*) 10.

From compounds, (*a*) 20, (*b*) 450, (*c*) 600.

A. Verbs in -έω from simplicia.

(*a*) Denominatives in -έω (I.E. *-*e-i̯ŏ*) corresponding to stems ending in -*o*-, where the -*e*- represents the $^o/_e$ gradation.

Ἀθλέω (ἆθλος), ἀντλέω (fr. °λος=*hold of ship*, then *bilge-water*) *to bale out*, thence simply *to draw* (water), ἀργέω (°γός<ἀ-, ἔργον), ἀριθμέω (°μος), αὐλέω (°λος), γαμέω (°μος), δειπνέω (°νον), †δεσμέω (°μος) read by CD and late uncials at Lk 8^{29} for δεσμεύω (ℵBL 33) late and rare, δωρέομαι (°ρον) (LXX -έω, as less often in class.), θορυβέω (°βος), θρηνέω (°νος), θροέω (°οος), καρτερέω (°ρυς<κάρτος, Ep. and Ion. for κράτος), κοινωνέω (°νός), κοσμέω (°μος), λοιδορέω (°ρος), μετρέω (°ρον), μιμέομαι (μῖμος), (παρα-)μυθέομαι (μῦθος), νοέω (νόος, νοῦς), νοσέω (°σος), οἰκέω (°κος) (so ἐν-, κατ-, ἐνκατ-, συν- : but παρ- and περι- probably from cpds., see below, p. 389), ὀκνέω (°νος), ὁμιλέω (°λος) (for meaning see *Vocab. s.v.*, and for ὅμιλος, see above, p. 335), ὁμορέω (†συνομορέω a ἁ.λ. in Ac 18^7; συνόμορος is only found in later eccles. writers), from ὅμορος (see above, § 107, p. 284), is found as early as Hdt. and occurs in Plut. See also *Syll.*^{2} 641^{16}, ed.^{3} 1044^{16}), ὀχλέω (°λος), πατέω (<πάτος<**pn̥to-s* [cf. πόντος, Skt. *pánthāḥ*, Lat. *pons -tis*] <I.E.**pent(h)* : see Boisacq 803), πλουτέω (°τος), (ἐπι-)ποθέω (°θος), πολεμέω (°μος), (δια-, κατα-) -πονέω (°νος), στοιχέω (°χος), (ἀπο-)στυγέω (°γος), τηρέω (possibly[1] from τηρός, which is only found in Aesch. *Supp.* 248. It may come from I.E. **qu̯ē-* : cf. Skt. *cāyati*, "perceive, watch"; O. Slav. *čają* <**kĕją*, "wait, hope"; Boisacq, *s.v.*), ὑμνέω (°νος), ὑστερέω (°ρος), φθονέω (°νος), φιλέω (°λος), φλυαρέω (°ρος), φοβέω (°βος), φρουρέω (°ρος), χωρέω (°ρος), ὠνέομαι (ὦνος).

Note.—1. αἰνέω (αἶνο-ς) belongs to this group, as Hom. ᾔνησα shows. The later form ᾔνεσα (cf. fut. αἰνέσω) is due to its antonym νεικέω (<νεῖκος, neut.).

2. Ποιέω is denominative from *ποι-Fό-ς (so Boisacq, *s.v.*), which, as Sütterlin (p. 41) observes, only survives in cpds., *e.g.* ἀρτοποιός, *baker*.

(*b*) A few deverbativa in -έω (I.E. -*é-i̯ō*) with traces of frequentative force. †Γρηγορέω, a Hellen. back-formation from pf. ἐγρήγορα of ἐγείρω, πορθέω (<πέρθω), ῥιπτέω (<ῥίπτω, cf. *iacto* : *iacio* : see p. 257, also Brugmann *KVG* 536), σκοπέω (acc. to Brugmann-Thumb *Gr.* 360, this corresponds to σκέπτομαι as an iterative. See above, p. 258, for the denominative ἐπισκοπέω in 1 Pet 5^2 (Aω)), φορέω, frequentative of φέρω (but see Debrunner *Wortb.* 95 for φορέω<φόρος).

(*c*) Denominatives in -έω (<*-εσ-i̯ο) from *s*- stems. A few of these preserve traces of their origin outside the present tense, *e.g.* τελέω, aor. ἐτέλεσα, f. τελέσω. Most of them have conformed to the *-*e-i̯ó* type.

---

[1] Mr. E. E. Genner observes that the word τηρός in Aesch. *Supp.* 248 is almost certainly corrupt. [Sidgwick's textual note in the *OCT* is "ἢ τηρόν *ex* ἤτηρον *ut videtur factum* M."—Ed.]

('Απ-)ἀλγέω, (ἐπι-, κατα-)βαρέω, a later form of βαρύνω, ἐλεέω (see above, pp. 195–7, 235, 385), θαμβέω, θαρρέω later form of θαρσέω, κρατέω, μισέω, πενθέω. All these are formed from neuter nouns in -ος, -εσ-.

NOTE.—Βαρέω and θαμβέω are Ionic contributions to the Κοινή.[1]

(*d*) Denominatives from other stems.

'Απειλέω (ἀπειλή), †ἐλαττονέω (ἐλάττων). See *Vocab. s.v.* for other occurrences of this rare word. 'Ιστορέω (ἵστωρ<*Ϝιδ-τορ-). For the history of the meaning of this word (ἁ.λ. in NT Gal 1[18] =*to visit*) see Burton *ICC in loc.*, 59 *Vocab. s.v.* Λυπέω (: λύπη following ἀλγέω : ἄλγος), μαρτυρέω (μάρτυς, -υρ-), φρονέω (φρήν, φρεν-), φωνέω (: φωνή, following ἀΰτέω : ἀϋτή, and other primary verbs of sound).

(*e*) A number of verbs in -έω remain, which are not formed from compounds, but for which a Greek simple noun is not quotable. Some are root verbs, but not all:

Αἱρέω, "l'étymologie de αἱρέω est incertaine; l'initiale n'a pas été Ϝ." Boisacq, *s.v.*

Αἰτέω, formerly connected with αἰκίζω, Skt. *yâcati*, Goth. *aihtrōn*, and derived from base *aịeqᵘ*. For Buck's phonetic objections to this, see Boisacq, *s.v.*

†'Αλισγέω, a late verb (LXX[ter]), is attested by †ἀλίσγημα (Ac 15[20]). Boisacq notes "le groupe -σγ- est énigmatique; rapport possible avec ἀλίνειν."

'Αρκέω, cf. Lat. *arceo, arx, arcānus*, from base *areq* "to avert," "repel." Brugmann (*Grd.*[2] II. iii. 339) derives from Skt. *rákṣa-ti* "to arm," "deliver" <*(*a*)*leq-s*(*o*)-.

'Αρνεομαι, possibly connected with Arm. *uranam* "to refuse," from **ōr*.

'Ασκέω. Uncertain etym. Boisacq quotes theory deriving word from *ἀ-σκός<*ἀν-σκος, and cft. ἀνακῶς *carefully* <κοέω.

†'Ενειλέω (Mk 15[46], εἰλέω *Ev. Petr.* vi. 24) for classical ἐνείλλω (Thuc.). See *Vocab. s.v.*

Ζητέω<*δ̯ιᾱτεi̯ω. Cf. Skt. *yátati* "to fix," *yátatē* "to make an effort."

Καλέω, weak and strong grades seen in καλέ-σαι, κέ-κλη-μαι, Lat. *călō, -āre, clāmor, clāmo.* I.E. **qalā-* and **qel* (ᵉ)-. See Boisacq, *s.v.*

---

[1] See Thumb *DAC* i. 555 *a*. "Words like ἀπαρτίζω (in ἀπαρτισμός), ἔκτρωμα, κοπάζω (of the wind), ὄλυνθος, σανδάλιον, σκορπίζω, etc., in the LXX or NT are of Ionic origin. The Ionic element includes, further, the so-called poetical words of the Κοινή, *i.e.* Hellenistic words which formerly were to be found only in the poets, but which from the fact of their occurrence in papyrus texts concerned with matters of everyday life, and partly also from the fact of their survival in MGr, are now seen to have belonged to the colloquial language. They include, *e.g.*, βαρέω, ἐντρέπομαι, θαμβέω, μεσονύκτιον, πειράζω, ῥάκος, ὠρύομαι, in the LXX and the NT, and ἀλέκτωρ, βαστάζω, ἔριφος, φαντάζω, φημίζω, in the NT. Words of this class were imported first from the literary Ionic of the earlier period into the language of poetry, and then again from the vernacular Ionic of the later period into the Κοινή, and there was no direct link of connexion between the two processes."

(Ἐκ-)κεντέω to *prick, stab, goad,* cf. κοντός *pole* (Lat. *contus*), Skt. *çnáthati, çnatháyati,* "to pierce."

Λᾱκέω (see p. 246 and *Vocab. s.v.*), cf. Lat. *loquor* (<**laquor*, **laq-u̯o-*). I.E. **l̥ᵊq-*, extension of **l̥ᵊ*, reduced form of **lā*(*i*)- "to cry." See, further, Boisacq, *s.v.* λαίειν.

Λαλέω, onomatop. cf. Skt. *lalalla.* The original sense of *to chatter* had quite left the word in NT times. See *Vocab. s.v.*, where a number of exx. from papp. "all bear out the usual distinction that while λέγω calls attention to the substance of what is said, the onomatopoetic λαλέω points rather to the outward utterance."

Μυέω from √ μῦ, μύ, a sound made with closed lips. J. A. Robinson, *Ephesians* 234, casts doubt on the derivation from μύω as that, when used simply, always means to close the eyes, not the lips. For the fading of technical meaning from μυέω and μυστήριον in later Greek, see *Vocab. s.v.*

Ὀρχέομαι. Cf. Skt. *r̥ghāyáti* "to tremble," I.E. **ergh-* (see Boisacq, *s.v.*).

Πτοέω from √ πτω-, πτᾱ-, πετ- <**pet-* seen in πέτομαι, πίπτω, in πτάξ, πτώξ, πτώσσω (see Boisacq 823,—also Sütterlin 84, on late date of πτοία from which verb has sometimes been derived).

Πωλέω <I.E. **pel-*. Cf. Skt. *pánatē* (**pr̥natē* <*pl̥-n-*).

(Ἀπο-) στερέω. Root uncertain. Boisacq cft. MIr. *serbh* "theft."

(Ἀπ-, ἐξ-) ωθέω. Cf. Skt. *vadh-* "to strike," <IE **u̯edh-* **u̯odh-* **u̯ōdh-* (see Boisacq, *s.v.*).

Ὠφελέω (see above, § 111, and Boisacq 732, 1085).

B. Verbs in -έω from compounds.

§ 162. (*a*) Denominatives corresponding to stems in *-o-*.

Many of these are verbs in -φορέω, -ποιέω, -λογέω, -εργέω, which were very productive verbal endings in later Gr. (For tables of relative frequency in class. and post-class. writers, see Sütterlin 49).

The most noticeable groups in the NT vocabulary are those in—

-αγωγέω: **†δουλαγωγέω, †συλαγωγέω, †χαλιναγωγέω** (only Jas[bis], Lucian[bis]: °γος first appears in Chryst.), **†χειραγωγέω** (Ps-Anacr., LXX, *Ev. Petr.* x. 40).

-αρχέω: **πειθαρχέω** (§ 108, p. 290) represents for the NT this very large group, whilst for **†τετρααρχέω**, which has °**χης** for its cognate in NT, we may either postulate a form in -ος, or account for the verb by analogy (see Sütterlin 79).

-γονέω: **ζωογονέω** (see *Vocab. s.v.* for LXX and NT meaning, *to preserve alive,* as against class. use=*to endue with life,* **†τεκνογονέω.**

-δημέω: **ἀποδημέω** (§ 115, p. 299), **ἐκδημέω, ἐνδημέω, ἐπιδημέω** (§ 120, p. 315).

-εργέω: **†ἀγαθοεργέω** (1 Ti 6[18]: the rare contracted form **ἀγαθουργέω** appears in Ac 14[7]), **ἐνεργέω** (§ 118, p. 308), **συνεργέω, γεωργέω**

(§ 105, p. 271), †ἱερουργέω, λειτουργέω (§ 106), συνυπουργέω (elsewhere found only in Hipp. *Art.* 824, and Lucian *Bis Accusat.* 17) is an instance of the tendency in later Gr. to coin double cpds. Ὑπουργέω (<°γός) is common in class. Gr., though °γός is not found before Xenophon.

-ηγέω : ὁδηγέω, χορηγέω (see § 105, p. 275).

-ηγορέω : †ἀλληγορέω (<°ρος, acc. to v. d. Pfordten *Gr. Denom.* 35, but, °ρος not given in LS.[1] For verb see Burton *Gal* (*ICC*) 254 f.), δημηγορέω (§ 105, p. 273), κατηγορέω.

-θετέω : †ἀθετέω (see *Vocab. s.v.*) is from °τος, with which we may compare νομοθετέω (<°της) and νουθετέω, for which a primitive °τος is not extant.

-θυμέω : ἀθυμέω, εὐθυμέω (§ 118, p. 308), †μακροθυμέω.

-λογέω : ἀπολογέομαι may possibly come in here, but see § 115, p. 299, and Sütterlin 52. †βατταλογέω (§ 105, p. 272), γενεαλογέω (found as early as Hdt., whereas °γος is not quotable until Dion. H. Cpds. formed with λογέω were very numerous, so that analogy probably plays its part), εὐλογέω (given by v. d. Pfordten 54 as from °λος, but as the meaning of the adj. is *reasonable*, and of the verb *to praise, bless*, the cpd. of εὐ and λέγειν may simply follow the common type of -λογέω verbs, esp. its antonym), κακολογέω (<°γος), ὁμολογέω (§ 107, p. 284), ἁρμολογέω (†συν- see § 105, p. 272), †στρατολογέω (2 Ti 2^4).

-μαχέω : in †θυμομαχέω and λογομαχέω (ἁ.λ. 2 Ti 2^{14}) the first constituent is instrumental (see § 105, p. 273), whereas in θεομαχέω (Ac 23^9 HLP) and †θηριομαχέω (<°ος not °ης, see Sütterlin 79) it is dative.

-νομέω : κληρονομέω, οἰκονομέω, παρανομέω.

-οικέω : Unlike the cpds. of οἰκέω mentioned above, παροικέω and περιοικέω are derived directly from πάροικος, περίοικος. This is clearly seen in the former by the changed meaning of the verb in Hellenistic corresponding to the changed meaning of the adj. from *neighbouring* to *foreign, alien*. (For πάροικος in Hellenistic see Deissmann *BS* 227 f.)

-ποιέω : ἀγαθοποιέω, †εἰρηνοποιέω, ζωοποιέω, κακοποιέω, †καλοποιέω, †μοσχοποιέω (ἁ.λ. Ac 7^{41}), †ὀχλοποιέω (ἁ.λ. Ac 17^5). A special note may be given to ὁδοποιέω (from Xenophon), which is read in Mk 2^{23} by BGH 13 etc. It is tempting to adopt this rdg. with WH mg., and so avoid the incorrect use of the active for the middle. But the avoidance of the term in the Synoptic parallels,

[1] The new LS cites the *Etymologicum Gudianum*, 515. 42. Mr. E. E. Genner tells me that this medieval glossary, based on material of the early Byzantine age, quotes, *s.v.* συνήγορος, παρήγορος and ἀλλήγορος as parallel forms.

and the evidence of confusion between act. and mid. in the papyri (see *Prol.* 159), raises a doubt. For the word see *Vocab. s.v.*

-*πορέω*: **ἀπορέω, εὐπορέω, ὁδοιπορέω.**

-*τομέω*: **διχοτομέω** (§ 106, p. 281), †**λᾱτομέω** (elsewhere in LXX, Justin M., Diod., <°*μος* [<*λᾶς, τέμνω*] only found in LXX and Josephus), †**ὀρθοτομέω**, a direct formation on analogy of other cpds. in -*τομέω*. See above, § 105, p. 274.

-*φημέω*: **βλασφημέω** (§ 105, p. 272), **δυσφημέω** (§ 107, p. 287).

-*φορέω*: **εὐφορέω** (<°*ρος*, which started with the passive sense of *bearable*, and then developed the active meaning, *fruitful, productive*, common in the medical writers (Hobart 144), and in Hellenistic. See further Sütterlin 42), **καρποφορέω**, †**πληροφορέω**, which follows the analogy of **τελεσφορέω** (§ 105, p. 275), **τροποφορέω** (Ac 13^{18} ℵBC²Dω) also found as a v.l. in Deut 1^{31} B*; its existence (=*φέρω τὸν τρόπον*) is attested by Cicero *Att.* xiii. 29. 2. In the absence of °*ρος* we must regard the verb as a direct formation. †**Τροφοφορέω** (*ib.* AC*E 33) is the reading of BᵃAF in Deut 1^{31}, and the word occurs without *v.l.* in 2 Mac 7^{27}. The adj. °*ρος* is not found before Eustathius.

A number of these verbs in -*έω* were formed from noun compounds having *ἀ*- privative or *εὐ*- as a prefix. In addition to those given above, we find in the NT **ἀγνοέω** (<**α-γνοο-ς*, <**γνα-Fο-ς*, cf. Lat. *cognitus*, <*-*gna-to-s*, see Brugmann *Grd.*² i. 203; but see above, § 106, p. 281), **ἀδικέω** (as in class. Gr. both intrans. and trans., whereas †**ἐκδικέω** (<°**κος**) is only used transitively. The latter verb is only found in Κοινή. For papyrus exx. see *Vocab.*). **Ἀδυνατέω** (Xen., Plat., Arist.) from °**τος** has given us the analogous †**δυνατέω** from °**τός**, a verb found in Philodemus the Epicurean philosopher of i/B.C., elsewhere only in Paul (Rom 14^4, 2 Co 9^8 13^3). †Ἀκαιρέω (Diod. †-**έομαι**, N.T. ἁ.λ. Phil 4^{11}, Herm. *Sim.* ix. 10^5) is a Hellenistic derivative from the class. *ἄκαιρος*, opposed to †**εὐκαιρέω**, which is a good Κοινή word (Polyb., Plut., papp.) condemned by Phrynichus and Photius (Rutherford *NP* 205), who prefer *εὖ σχολῆς ἔχειν* (°**ρος** and °**ρία** are sound Attic, but not in the sense of *σχολαῖος* and *σχολή*). See *Vocab. s.vv.*, as also for remaining words in this group, **ἀπιστέω**, †**ἀστατέω** and **ἀτακτέω**. †**Εὐαρεστέω** is used by Hellenistic writers alone (so °**τος** can be quoted from inscrr. and papp. in addition to the "bibl. and eccl." citations. *Vocab. s.v.*). **Εὐνοέω** (§ 107, p. 287).

The remaining verbs in this class are:

Ἀγραυλέω (§ 107, p. 283), **ἀγρυπνέω** (§ 108, p. 290), **αἱμορροέω** (<°*ροος*, where the first element in the word is instrumental in case relationship; see T.P. cpds., § 105), **ἀκολουθέω** (§ 107, p. 285), †**ἀντοφθαλμέω** (unless this vb. should be placed in class (*e*) below. See above, § 114 (*b*), p. 297), **βραδυπλοέω** (<*°*πλοος*, see § 107, p. 284), **διακονέω** (<°**νος**, but see § 116, p. 303, for another possibility), **ἐπιορκέω** (§ 120, p. 314), †**ἑτεροδιδασκαλέω** (§ 107, p. 284), †**ἑτεροζυγέω** (<°*γος*) occurs first in 2 Co 6^{14} (see § 107,

p. 284), †εὐθυδρομέω (Philo and NT; for °μος see § 106, p. 282), †εὐπροσωπέω (§ 107, p. 287), εὐχαριστέω (for meaning of this verb in Hellenistic, see Milligan, *Thess.* p. 5, and *Vocab. s.v.*, also Deissmann *LAE*[1] 132 n.[3], 168 n.[2] ([2]135 n.[3], 179 n.[5])), †εὐψυχέω (§ 107, p. 287), εὐωχέω (συνευωχοῦμαι, first in Arist. See § 106, p. 282), (ἀνα-)ζωπυρέω (<ζώπυρον, § 107, p. 284), θεωρέω (<°ρος <*θεᾱ-ορος, *-Fορος, cf. ὁράω, O.E. *warōn, ware*), ἱεροσυλέω, †κατακληροδοτέω (Ac 13[19] minusc. pauc. for °νομέω "from missing active sense of κληρονομ.," (Knowling *EGT in loc.* See *Vocab. s.v.* for use elsewhere), †κληρονομέω, †λιθοβολέω, μεγαλαυχέω (Jas 3[5] ℵC[2]KL, written *divisim* in other MSS; both verb and °χος as early as Aeschyl.), ναυαγέω (for ναυᾱγός see § 105, p. 274), ξενοδοχέω (spelt in Attic with κ for χ, as all the cognate words, see Rutherford *NP* 362), οἰκοδομέω, ὀλιγωρέω (for °ρος see § 107, p. 284), στενοχωρέω, ταλαιπωρέω (§ 106, p. 282), τιμωρέω, φιλοτιμέομαι (for these φιλο- and τιμο- cpds., see § 108), χειροτονέω (§ 105).

(*b*) Denominatives corresponding to *nomina agentis* in -ης, -της.

There is one doubtful example only of verbs formed from first declension nouns in -ης, τετρααρχέω (see under (*a*) above).

As already seen in § 150 above, noun compounds show a strong preference for the ending -της when forming *nomina agentis*. Eleven of these supply verbs in -έω in the NT. In most cases the nouns have been discussed above, and the references are accordingly given: Ἀγανακτέω (§ 106), †αὐθεντέω (§ 106), †γονυπετέω (§ 105), εὐεργετέω (§ 106), νομοθετέω (see (*a*) above), †οἰκοδεσποτέω (§ 105), πλεονεκτέω (§ 105), †προσωπολημπτέω (§ 105), συκοφαντέω (§ 105), ὑδροποτέω, ὑπηρετέω (§ 129 (*b*)).

(*c*) Denominatives from compound adjectives in -ης (-ες-).

But for the absence of any surviva' in the *s*- conjugation, we might relate this group to the *-*es*-*i̯o*- class in A (*c*). As it is, we can infer that before the Homeric period these verbs conformed in all ways to the predominating class of -*o*- stems.

Ἀμελέω, ἀπειθέω (for meaning, see *Vocab. s.v.*), ἀσεβέω and its opposite εὐσεβέω, ἀσθενέω, εὐλαβέομαι, κακοπαθέω (first in Xenophon), and the other -παθέω cpds., †μετριοπαθέω (§ 107) and συνπαθέω (§ 127), λυσιτελέω (§ 108), διασαφέω, which appears to have been formed straight from σαφής, without the intervention of *διασαφής (§ 116).

(*d*) Denominatives from adjectival compounds in consonantal stems.

Of stems in -ον- the -φρονέω cpds. are as old as Homer. In NT this formation supplies παραφρονέω (§ 123 (*b*)), σωφρονέω (§ 107, pp. 284–5), ὑψηλοφρονέω (§ 107). In addition there are two ἀ- cpds., ἀδημονέω (§ 106), ἀσχημονέω.

Of stems in -ρ- ψευδομαρτυρέω (§ 106).

Of stems in -δ- †ὀρθοποδέω (§ 107).

(*e*) Compound verbs in -έω formed directly on the model of those grouped under (*b*).

This flexibility in verb formation goes back to very early times, for **ζωγρέω** and **ἐπιχειρέω** appear in Homer and **ἐνθυμέομαι** is very common in class. writers. Still greater freedom was shown at a later stage in the language, for the remaining seven verbs in this list are purely Hellenistic.

†**Ἀντοφθαλμέω** (Polyb., see Capes, *Achaean League*, p. 262), possibly a Class VII. verb[1] from ἀντ' ὀφθαλμῶν (§ 114 (*b*)).

Ἐνθυμέομαι, from ἐν θυμῷ (ἔχω), see § 118 (*c*), and, for meaning, *Vocab. s.v.*

†**Ἐνκακέω** (Polyb.) for ἐν κακῷ εἰμί. See § 118 (*c*) for derivation and meaning.

†**Ἐξουδενέω** (LXX and pap.). See above, §§ 46, 119, and *Vocab. s.v.*

Ἐπιχειρέω, a verbal cpd. of Class VII. above (§ 109)=χεῖρα θεῖναι ἐπί τι, without the intervention of a noun cpd.: see § 120 (*c*).

†**Εὐδοκέω** (Polyb., Diod., LXX), a new verb made with an adv. (p. 292).

Ζωγρέω, Class VI. above, from ζωὸν ἀγρεῖν (§ 108).

†**Κακουχέω** (Plut.[1] LXX*bis*, common in papp., esp. in marriage contracts, see *Vocab. s.v.*, though the derivative noun °ια is found as early as Aeschyl.) seems to belong to Class VI. A (§ 108).

†**Τεκνοτροφέω** (1 Ti 5[10]. Elsewhere Arist., Epict.), Class VI. A.

†**Χρονοτριβέω** (Ac 20[16]. Elsewhere Arist., Plut., and late writers), Class VI. A.

NOTE.—The distinction of class in these verbs in -έω corresponds broadly to a difference in meaning, which again lies in the nature of the nominal types from which the verbs are formed. The compounds are adjectival in meaning, and the derivative verbs have the force of "to be what the adjectival word stands for." The simple nouns, on the other hand, stand rather for things or abstractions. Other compounds are virtually *nomina agentis*, and the derived verbs have what at first sight appears to be a factitive force, though it actually comes under the general meaning "to be so and so." The distinction is not absolute, and the following considerations may be observed.

1. Verbs in -έω from simplicia sometimes admit the meaning "to be what the noun represents." *E.g.* in class. authors, **διακονέω, καρτερέω, κοινωνέω, λαλέω, λοιδορέω, μιμέομαι, σκοπέω, τηρέω, ὑστερέω, φλυαρέω.** Sütterlin 49 attributes this in **τηρέω** and **σκοπέω** to their being primitive formations, whereas **φλυαρέω** is from a *nomen actionis* °**ρος**. In NT we have also †**δυνατέω** and its predominantly Hellenistic negative **ἀδυνατέω.**

2. The factitive appearance of some verbs in -έω from cpds. involves a question of accent. A good example is †**λιθοβολέω.** The rule is that when a T.P. cpd. is a transitive, or active, verbal in -ος, it accents the penult if this is short, otherwise the last syllable. But if the last part is intransitive, or passive (in meaning), the accent is recessive (see Goodwin, *Gr. Gr.*[2] 194). Thus λιθο-βόλος *thrower of stones*, λιθό-βολος *pelted with stones.* The verb corresponds to the former only. Similarly **διχοτομέω** follows the active meaning of διχοτόμος. Of course this

[1] The classification here referred to is set forth in § 102 above.

uncertainty as to the accent of the nominal cpd. sometimes leads to ambiguity in the force of the derivative verb.

3. A number of Possessive (B.V.) cpds. give rise to ambiguity in their derivatives. Thus, **εὐθυμέω** in class. writers is both trans. and intrans.; in NT always intrans. **Εὐπορέω** class. both trans. and intrans.; in NT intrans. =*to be well off*. Similarly **ταλαιπωρέω** in its NT occurrence (Jas 4[9]) has the intrans. meaning, though exx. can be quoted from class. writers and LXX to support an active sense =*to weary, distress.*

4. Occasionally an unambiguous adjective results in a verb with double meaning. Thus *στενόχωρος narrow* gives °**ρέω** =(1) intr. *to be straitened* (LXX), *anxious* (Hipp.); (2) trans. *to straiten, compress* (LXX, Diod., papp.). So in NT the pass. =*to be straitened.* (See *Vocab. s.v.*)

Similarly with simplicia. **Θόρυβος**, *uproar*, gives °**βέω**; (1) *to make an uproar*; (2) *to throw into confusion.*

5. In Hellenistic there are numerous examples of a tendency, already traceable in the class. age, to give an active sense to the verb, though its corresponding adjective is passive. Thus the good Κοινή verb †**ἀθετέω** *to annul, cancel*, comes from *ἄθετος*, which is found in the passive sense *null, void, set aside.*

6. Note the transitive force produced by the perfectivising preposition *ἀπο-*, in †**ἀφυστερέω**, *to keep back* (Jas 5[4]), see § 114.

7. The deponent verb **φιλοτιμέομαι** may owe its form to the inherently middle force of the word in its classical (but not Hellenistic) sense of *to be ambitious*; or, as Sütterlin (p. 44) and Debrunner (*Wortb.* 99) suggest, it may follow the example of other verbs of desire, *e.g. βούλομαι, ὀρέγομαι.*

3. *Verbs in -όω.*

όω § 163. This class of verbs, if not peculiar to Greek, must have arisen at a very late stage in the I.E. parent language. We have already seen that *ā*-stems gave rise to *-άω* verbs, and *-o-* stems to *-έω* verbs.

The origin of the *-όω* verbs may probably be traced to three or four influences.

(*a*) The analogy of the instrumental *-άω* verbs would play a part. Thus, *πέδη a fetter, πεδάω to fetter, σκέπη a cover, σκεπάω to cover*, from which the transition was easy to *στέφανος, στεφανόω*. This tendency would be strengthened by the parallel formations *μῆνις* : *μηνίω, μέθυ* : *μεθύω.*

(*b*) Apart altogether from the denominative verbs and their tense system, there was a direct formation of denominative adjectives, *e.g.* Lat. *barba* : *barbātus, aeger* : *aegrōtus.* So in Greek we have *κοντός* : *κοντωτός provided with a rowing pole* (though this adj. is not attested before Diod.). Brugmann (*KVG* 532) postulates *μισθός* : *μισθωτός*, and derives from this μισθωθῆναι, μισθώσω, ἐμίσθωσα, and finally μισθόω. (See also *Grd.*[2] II. iii. 206 and *Gr.*[4] 357.)

(*c*) Where there are pairs of nouns derived from the same root and closely related in meaning, one ending in an -ᾱ- stem and the other in an -ο- stem, a verb in -όω may well have arisen from the noun in -ος corresponding to the already existing verb in -άω. Thus χολή : χολάω, χολός : χολόω. (See Sütterlin 99.)

(*d*) Dr. Giles finds the beginning of this series in -όω " with denominatives like ῥιγόω from *ῥιγώς (gen. *ῥιγόος, cf. Lat. *rigor*), ἱδρόω from ἱδρώς (=**su̯idrōs*, cf. Lat. *sūdor*=**su̯oidōs*)" (*Manual*[2] 442 n.).

Whatever the origin, this type became very common in forming verbs from -*ο*- stems with a factitive or an instrumental meaning. There are 96 verbs in -*όω* in the NT, together with 25 additional compound verbs. Of these about three-fourths are derived from *ο*- stems (in about equal proportions from nouns and adjectives), 7 from *α*- stems, 9 from 3rd Decl. nouns, 4 from adjectives with consonantal stems, and a few from prepositional and other phrases.

(1) Denominatives from -*ο*- stems.

Many of these were normal in the classical period, some few are only found in the late classical writers, others first appear in prose in the *Κοινή*, whilst the considerable batch of fresh formations shows that this suffix was actively creative. Attention need only be called to the following :—

†Ἀκυρόω (<ἄκυρος common in legal phraseology. *Vocab. s.v.*).

†Ἀναλόω. (Back-formation, see p. 228.)

†Ἀνακαινόω (first in Paul, for class. °ίζω (as in Heb 6[6] and LXX). See *Vocab. s.v.*).

†Ἀναστατόω. (See § 113. A vernac. word found in LXX, NT and papp. *Vocab. s.v.*).

†Ἀφυπνόω. (Late verb. In Anth. trans. *to wake from sleep*. Elsewhere, as in Lk 8[23], *to fall asleep*. For this meaning see § 115 and *Vocab. s.v.*)

†Βεβηλόω. (First in LXX. See *Vocab. s.v.* °λος.)

†Δεκατόω. (Sütterlin 108 would derive this from ἡ δεκάτη (μερίς), but the adj. in -τος would account for the Hellenistic suffix -όω in place of class. °τεύω. Note, however, " the rare ἀποδεκατόω (without var. Mt[1], Lk[1], Heb[1]) is replaced by the rarer ἀποδεκατεύω (ℵ*B), Lk 18[12] " (WH *App.*[2] 178). A reason for the new coinage is suggested in *Vocab. s.v.*

†Ἐντυπόω. (Hellenistic, though the simplex appears in Plato.)

†Ἐπιδιορθόω. (Almost peculiar to Tit 1^{5}, is the common διορθόω cpded. with ἐπι- = *in addition*. See § 120.)

Θεμελιόω. (First in Xen. In MGr θεμελιώνω.)

Θυμόω. (Act. in LXX only. In class. and in the one NT occurrence, pass. = *to be angry*.)

†Ἱκανόω. (Act. in NT. Elsewhere pass., *e.g.* P Tebt i. 20^{8}.)

†Κατιόω. (Apart from Jas 5^{3} only found in Sir. and Epict.)

†Καυσόω (for class. καυματίζω. See Mayor, *ap.* 2 Pet 3^{10}.)

Κεφαλαιόω. If this rdg. is right in Mk 12^{4} (ἐκεφαλαίωσαν), κεφάλαιον has given rise to a verb with a totally different meaning. Lobeck (*Phryn.* 95) points out that κεφαλή > κεφαλίζειν, *caput percutere*, λαιμός > λαιμίζειν, ῥάχις > ῥαχίζειν and adds "*alia huius significationis terminatio est in verbis* γναθοῦν, *i.e.* εἰς γνάθους τύπτειν, γυιοῦν, κεφαλαιοῦν *in Ev. D. Marci* xii. 4." But as κεφάλαιον does not mean *head*, but *sum total*, or *chief point* (whence ἀνακεφαλαίοω, *to sum up*, see J. A. Robinson *Ephes.* 145), there is much to be said for the rdg. of ℵBL, ἐκεφαλίωσαν. The verb would then be †κεφαλιόω, formed from κεφάλιον, a Hellenistic diminutive of κεφαλή. For further suggestions see *Vocab. s.v.*

Κημόω. Only in Xen. before Paul, who in 1 Co 9^{9} (κημώσεις B*D*FG, φιμώσεις ℵACω) substitutes this verb for φιμόω, which our MSS of the LXX read in the pass. cited. (Lietzmann (*HNT in loc.*) thinks Paul here gives the true text of the LXX.)

†Κολοβόω (first in Arist.), from κολοβός = *maimed, mutilated*. For vernacular use of cognates of this verb see *Vocab. s.v.*

Λυτρόω. Class. but well established in vernac. See *Vocab. s.v.*

†Ματαιόω. LXX and Paul (Rom 1^{21}). Act. only in Jer 23^{16}, where intrans. (= *to pretend*).

†Νεκρόω. See *Vocab. s.v.* νεκρός.

Παλαιόω. In act. peculiar to LXX and NT, but pass. in Hipp., Plat., Arist.

Πωρόω. Factitive verb in medical and Hellen. writers. Metaph. meaning peculiar to LXX and NT. (For confusion with πηρόω in some MSS, see J. A. Robinson *Ephes.* 271.)

Ῥυπόω. A rare class. verb given in NT lexicons on strength of T.R. in Rev 22^{11}. Ῥυπωσάτω seems to be without MS warrant. According to v. Soden and R. H. Charles the alternatives are ῥυπανθήτω (ℵ, 94, 2017), ῥυπαρωθήτω (205), ῥυπαρευθήτω (046 *et al.*) ῥυπασάτω (2029).

Σαρόω. For σαίρω, which was in common use in Tragedy. But even this was condemned as un-Attic by Phrynichus (Rutherford *NP* 156), who requires παρακορέω, as κόρημα for σάρον. Lobeck (*Phryn.* 83) remarks "σαροῦν *improbat Phryn., non* σαίρειν."

The explanation may be that σαρόω had completely displaced σαίρειν=*sweep* by this time, the latter being only still used in the sense of *to grin*.

†**Σημειόω.** For σημαίνω (2 Th 3[14]. See Milligan *in loc.*).

Σπαργανόω. From σπάργανον *a swathing-band.* Lk is preceded by the medical writer Hipp. as well as by Arist. It is also used by Plut.

†**Σπιλόω.** A Hellenistic derivative from the word σπίλος, which in late Gk. came to mean a *stain* (Rutherford *NP* 87 and Lobeck *Phryn.* 28).

Σταυρόω. In class. *to fence with a palisade*; in Polyb. and NT=to *crucify*.

Στερεόω. A factitive verb, not found before Xen.

†**Ταρταρόω.** ἁ.λ. in 2 Pet 2[4], though the cpd. κατα° is found in Sext. Emp. and other late writers.

†**Φραγελλόω.** From φραγέλλιον=Lat. *flagellum* by consonantal dissimilation (§ 42). Only NT and eccles. Sütterlin 120 curiously derives from °λη.

(2) Denominatives from -*a*- stems.

These are **ζημιόω** (though Sütterlin 123 derives from *ζήμιος on the ground that the fem. abstracts in -ια are probably all secondary formations, see above, § 136), **ζυμόω**, †**μορφόω** (Hellenistic, as also is **μετα°**. †**Συμ°** is ἁ.λ. in Ph 3[10] (ℵ^c D^c EKL), where συμμορφίζω is correct rdg. See below, § 173), **ῥιζόω** (class., but †**ἐκριζόω** LXX and NT only. **᾿Εκ°** is only in form a cpd. See § 119 and *Vocab. s.v.* Note the different senses in which the two verbs are factitive), **σκηνόω** (class., but **ἐπι°** Hellenistic, **κατα°** Xen. and Hell.), †**τεφρόω** (ἡ τέφρα *ashes*), †**φυσιόω** (<φῦσα *bellows.* NT and eccles. for class. °ιάω).

(3) Denominatives from other stems.

Stems ending in -*es*-.

From nouns, **σκοτόω** (possibly from ὁ σκότος, then attributed to τὸ σκότος, hence by analogous formation), **ἑλκόω**, **κυρόω**, †**σθενόω** (a word only known from 1 Pet 5[10], and its mention in Hesych.), **ὑψόω** (though this may be influenced by its antonym ταπεινόω <ταπεινός). From adjectives, **ἀκριβόω**, **πληρόω** (but Sütterlin 117 connects this with -o-stem, and cft. Lat. *plerus*).

Consonantal stems, **πυρόω**, †**χαριτόω**.

From comparatives, **ἑσσόω** (2 Co 12[13] ℵ*BD*, see above, p. 107, and *Vocab. s.v.* ἡττάομαι), **ἐλαττόω**. Debrunner (*Wortb.* 103) traces these verbs in -όω back to the neut. ἔλαττον, which resembles the neut. of -o-abjectives.

For †**ἐξουδενόω** (Mk 9[12] AC), °**θενόω** (*ib.* ℵ69) see §§ 46, 119, and *Vocab .s.v.*

The dominant force of these verbs in -όω was instrumental or factitive, and as words tend to fall into groups under the stress of similarity of meaning, this kind of relationship was a determining factor in the history of the growth of this class.

Instrumental conception shown in various ways, *e.g.*—

(*a*) *To present*, or *reward with*; *to injure*, or *punish with*:

Σημειόω, θανατόω, μαστιγόω, νεκρόω, σταυρόω, †ταρταρόω, τυφλόω, †φραγελλόω. Perhaps we may extend to **κημόω, φιμόω, μισθόω, στεφανόω, †χαριτόω** (*to endue with* χάρις, see J. A. Robinson *Ephes.* 227).

(*b*) *To treat with* kindness, or with eagerness, with evil, with guile etc.;

†δολιόω (LXX and NT. See *Vocab. s.v.*), **ζηλόω, ζυμόω, κακόω.**

(*c*) *To give expression to* personal feelings:

θυμόομαι, which may have influenced **ἐμβριμόομαι** (for the form see above, pp. 198–201; for the derivation, Debrunner in *IF* xxi. 53; for this group of words, Sütterlin 125).

The *Factitive* conception is evident in a number of groups, *e.g.*—

(*a*) Words meaning *to make strong* etc.:

†ἱκανόω, †κραταιόω (late form for °τύνω, see *Vocab. s.v.* κραταιός), and †ἰσχυρόω (LXX, Herm. *Mand.* v. 2[8]), from -*o*- stems, are accompanied by **†δυναμόω** (*Vocab. s.v.*), **†σθενόω.**

The group, which is quite Hellenistic, may have originated in such pairs of contrasts as ἀσθενέω (*to be weak*): ἀσθενόω (*to weaken*—as early as Xen. *Cyr.* I. v. 3), καρτερέω : καρτερόω. On the other hand, the group may have started with the class. **βεβαιόω.**

(*b*) A contrast of meaning may have produced **ὑψόω** (from an -*es* stem) to match **ταπεινόω**, and **πληρόω** against **κενόω.** (See, however, above, under (3)).

(*c*) A very important variety of the factitive meaning is found in a group of verbs in -όω, derived from adjectives of *moral* as distinguished from *physical* meaning. Here the meaning is *to regard as, to treat as*, not *to make.* Thus **ἀξιόω** (see Lightfoot *Notes on Epp.* 105), **δικαιόω** (see Evans *ap.* 1 Co 6[11] cited by S and H *Romans* 30).

4. *Verbs in -ίω.*

-ίω § 164. This small class of denominatives from ῐ-stems was almost confined to Homer. There are on representatives in the NT, and the noun μῆνις which is found in Hermas (*Mand.* v. 2[4]), has produced a verb μηνιάω (*Sim.* ix. 23[3]) according to the later formation. (See § 160 (*h*) above.)

Two verbs **ἐσθίω** and **κυλίω** are later forms of ἔσθω and κυλίνδω, as shown on pp. 238, 246.

5. *Verbs in -ύω.*

-ύω § 165. A small class of denominatives in υ- stems is represented in the NT by **ἀρτύω** from *ἀρτύς*, which Hesych. gives as Ion. for *ἀρθμός*, cf. Lat. *artus*. (The same root as in *ἄρτι*, *ἀραρίσκω*.) For the transition from original meaning *to prepare* to later meaning *to season*, see *Vocab. s.v.* and Wakernagel's important note in his review of Mayser *Gram.* i. (*ThLZ* xxxiii. 36, n.[1]). **Δακρύω, ἰσχύω, μεθύω** <*μέθυ, wine*).

Two other verbs **κωλύω** and **μηνύω** are of doubtful etymology (see Boisacq *s.vv.*) ; *κωλύω* probably belongs to Class I. *a.* (*a*) above.

In the following the suffix *-yo* is added to a root :

Θύω (<**dhu̯-i̯i̯o*), **-πτύω** (**ἐκ-, ἐμ-**) (*[*s*]*pi̯ū-i̯ō*, Lat. *spuo*), **φύω** (Lesb. *φυίω* <**φυι̯ω*), **ῥύομαι** (<**Fρῡ-*, **u̯rū-*, see Boisacq 846).

Two other stems are represented by compounds. **Καμμύω**, a syncopated form of *καταμύω*, is a Κοινή word (see Ruth. *NP* 426 f.). For **ὠρύομαι** see above, pp. 330, 387 n.[1]. Its root (I.E. *(*e*)*rĕu-*=" cry ") is quite distinct from that of *ῥύομαι* above.

6. *Verbs in -εύω.*

§ 166. The denominatives were first formed from the stem of nouns in -ευς. Strict phonetic law would require a verb in *-είω* from *-ηF-ι̯- or -*εF-ι̯-, but the influence of the nom. sing. -ευ-ς, and perhaps the analogy of other tenses (cf. *καίω*, **καFι̯ω* : *ἔκαυσα*) determined the form -εύω. Thus *-αίω* : *-αυσα* : *-αύω* : : *-είω* : *-ευσα* : *-εύω*.

As the suffix -ευς in a noun stands for one holding a professional rank or vocation, so the corresponding verb in *-εύω* marks the exercise of that profession. Thus **βασιλεύω, βραβεύω, ἑρμηνεύω, ἀγρεύω, †ἁλιεύω**. This type became very productive at an early stage of the language and spread to other stems than nouns in -ευς, largely under the influence of semantic analogy. No doubt the relation *ἵππος* : *ἱππεύς* : *ἱππεύειν* partly accounts for the freedom with which this suffix was added to stems in -ος.

The following groups are specially noteworthy :—

(*a*) Domination, oversight, rank :

Βασιλεύω (which **βραβεύω** regularly follows) gives by example **ἡγεμονεύω** (˚*μων*), **†θριαμβεύω, καταδυναστεύω, κελεύω, κυριεύω** (**κατα**˚), **παιδεύω, πρεσβεύω, ἐπιτροπεύω, †ἀνθυπατεύω** (Ac 18[12] HLPSs, *Mart. Polyc.* 21), **ἀγγαρεύω** (for this " interesting old Persian word," and the noun *ἄγγαρος* in Aesch., see *Vocab. s.v.*). So perhaps **ἐποπτεύω** (<˚**της**, originally *overseer*).

(*b*) Correlative to these are verbs for subjection, obedience and service, especially religious service, thus leading on to verbs which mark the exercise of religious functions:

Δουλεύω, λατρεύω, νηστεύω, †ἱερατεύω (see Hort *Comm. 1 Pet.* 109), **μαντεύομαι, †μεσιτεύω, παρεδρεύω** (1 Co 9[13], "kultischer Terminus," Lietzmann *HNT in loc.* See also *Vocab. s.v.* Προσ° is read by KL and later MSS), **προφητεύω**. For **μαθητεύω** see note below.

(*c*) Verbs connected with hunting, snaring, etc.:

Ἀγρεύω, θηρεύω, ἐνεδρεύω (§ 118), **†ἁλιεύω, †παγιδεύω** and possibly also **φονεύω** and **†ὀλοθρεύω** (late form of ὀλεθρεύω). Κατατοξεύω (Heb 12[20 (LXX)]) finds its way into T.R. on the strength of "nonnulli minusc."

(*d*) A number of these verbs mean "to play the part of," "to act as" the man denoted by the corresponding noun:

Καπηλεύω (°λος), *to play the huckster, to deal in for purposes of gain.* For pap. illustrations in support of RVmg., see *Vocab. s.v.* So **μαγεύω** *to play the magus, deal in magic*; πολιτεύω, in LXX and NT always °**τευομαι**, *to act the citizen, live one's public life*; **πυκτεύω** (°της) *act like a boxer, fight*; **†γυμνιτεύω** (spelling, p. 72), *to be scantily clad* (as in Dio Chrys.; but in Plut. and Dio Cass. *to be light-armed*, where we may possibly trace a noun γυμνίτης formed after ὁπλίτης; see Brugmann *Gr.*[4] 237). The meaning "to behave as" is clear in **μοιχεύω** (°χος), **πορνεύω** (°νος).

Many of the verbs in -εύω fall naturally into none of these groups. They are either factitive, or connote the possession of a quality, or represent an action. In some instances we find the relationship of quality passing to that of action.

The *factitive* meaning is evident in—

Δεσμεύω *to bind* (°μός), **σαλεύω** *to shake* (°λος *a trembling*), **†σωρεύω** (°ρος a heap) *to heap on, overwhelm*, **φυτεύω** *to plant*, **†ἀποδεκατεύω** (see °όω above, § 163).

The possession of a *quality* is conspicuous in—

Ἀληθεύω *to be truthful*, hence *to deal truly* (Field, *Notes* 192, *Vocab. s.v.*), **εἰρηνεύω, ζηλεύω** (late and rare for -όω), **μνημονεύω, περισσεύω** (passes from the intr. to the trans., see Lightfoot *Notes* 48, Milligan *Thess.* 44), **πιστεύω** (passes from the intr. to the trans., but in the NT the activity of faith is strongly present in the word), **πτωχεύω, συμβουλεύω** (< °λος). The cpd. **†φιλοπρωτεύω**, ἁ.λ. in 3 Jn[9], is from φιλόπρωτος (Polyb., Plut., Artem.), the simplex **πρωτεύω** (LXX, Col 1[18]) is later class. (Plat., the Orators etc.).

The idea of *action* appears in the following:

Ἀγορεύω *to speak in the ἀγορά* (contr. °ράζω, § 172 (*d*)) lost its specific meaning, and its cpd. **προσαγορεύω**=to *address, hail* (so Heb 5[10], see Moffatt *ICC in loc.*). See *Vocab. s.v.*, and for use of ἀγορεύω and cpds., Rutherford *NP* 326 ff. **Διανυκτερεύω**, a Hellenistic coinage (Xen.), following διημερεύω which occurs once in Plato, afterwards in Hellen.

authors. Ἐμβατεύω (see § 118 (*b*), *Vocab. s.v.*), †ἐπιγαμβρεύω (see § 120, *Vocab. s.v.* γαμβρός), κινδυνεύω, κυκλεύω (rather rare word for common °έω, °όω, Jn 10[24] (B), Rev 20[9], see WH *App.*[2] 178, also *Vocab. s.v.*), μνηστεύω (as old as Homer, <μνηστήρ <μνάομαι. See Boisacq 641), Πορεύω in class. Gk. was used with a transitive force, but only the far more common °εύομαι survives (with its 8 cpds.) in the NT. Its synonym ὁδεύω was an early poet. word which reappeared in Hellen. prose. Πεζεύω (poet. until Xen.). The cpd. †αἰχμαλωτεύω (<°τος, [2] 105) probably followed the analogy of φυγαδεύω (Debrunner in Blass *Gr.*[5] 65). Lobeck (*Phryn.* 442) observes "Extrema Graeciae senectus novum palmitem promisit αἰχμαλωτεύειν."

Although the active ending -εύω could, and did originally, convey the idea of "being or behaving, or acting as ——," the influence of other classes of verbs where this condition is expressed by the middle (*e.g.* ἄχθομαι, αἰδοῦμαι) led to the formation of *deponents in* -εύομαι:

Ἐγκρατεύομαι (<°τής, § 118 (*c*)), ἐμπορεύομαι (<°ρος, assumed this form through mistaken connexion with πορεύομαι, see § 118 (*a*)). †Περπερεύομαι (<°ρος, § 104) is first met with in 1 Co 13[4]; elsewhere only in Marcus. Πραγματεύομαι (<πράγματα, *business*) *to trade*, a common commercial term in papp. See *Vocab. s.v.* †Παραβολεύομαι (<παράβολος, § 123 (*b*), according to the true rdg. Phil 2[30], rather than †παραβουλεύομαι (CKLP), see Kennedy, *EGT in loc.*). †Ῥυπαρεύομαι (read by 046 *ap.* Rev 22[11], see under ῥυπόω above, § 163). Στρατεύομαι (στρατός, army in camp) *to serve as a soldier, make war.* Depon. only is found in NT, though -εύω is occasionally used in class. authors. In later Hellen. active used transitively=*enlist.* †Χρηστεύομαι (from °τός) not found earlier than 1 Co 13[4].

Note.—In several of these verbs we observe the transition from intr. to trans. use:

Ἐμπορεύομαι *to travel as a merchant* (Jas 4[13]), 'then, with a transitive force "to import," "purchase," "traffic in," "make gain or business of,"' Mayor, *ap.* 2 Pet 2[3]. This meaning of *to exploit* occurs in Polyb. xxxviii. 10, where the active form is used. †Θριαμβεύω *to celebrate a triumph* (so in Plut. *e.g. Tib. Grac.* 21, *C. Grac.* 17). Then, as in NT, *to lead in triumph.* So Col 2[15], 2 Co 2[14] (on which see Lietzmann *HNT in loc.*, with parallels from Plut., also *Vocab. s.v.*). †Μαθητεύω, intr. *to be a disciple* (Mt 27[57] ABL. So Plut.), and trans.=*to make a disciple* (Mt 28[19], Ac 14[21]); -εύομαι, depon.=*to be a disciple,* (Mt 13[52] 27[57] ℵCD, 1. 33, 17).

ii. *Consonantal yo- presents.*

These consist of A. *-n-i̯o-*, (1) *αἴνω*, (2) *-ύνω*.

B. *-r-i̯o-*, *-l-i̯o*, (1) *-αίρω*, *-είρω*, *-ῦρω*, (2) *-άλλω*, *-έλλω*, *-ίλλω*, *-ύλλω*. C. *-πτω*, *-σσω*. D. *-ζω*, (1) *-άζω*, (2) *-ίζω*, (3) *-ύζω*. (4) *-έζω*, (5) *-όζω*.

A. Verbs in *-n-i̯o-*.

1. *-αίνω*.

-αίνω § 167. These denominatives were formed from a variety of stems. Starting with stems containing, or ending in, *-n-*, the suffix was extended under the influence of analogy to other groups of words.

Thus:

(*a*) To stems with *-n-*: **Ποιμαίνω** (from *ποιμεν-* <**-mn̥-i̯*), **εὐφραίνω** (from *εὐφρον-*), **βασκαίνω** (fr. *βάσκανος* <**βακ-σκ-ανο-ς*); **κερδαίνω** (present stem not found in NT) may come from **κέρδων* (>*'Ακέρδων* prop. name, also Lat. *cerdo, -ōn-is*), see *IF* xxi. 20.

This applies also to neuters in *-μα* (<**-mn̥-*; cf. *ὄνομα*, Lat. *nomen*): **Σημαίνω** (from *σῆμα* <I.E.* *dhi̯ā-mn̥*), **θερμαίνω** (probably from a neut. **θέρμα*), and **λυμαίνομαι** (from **λῦμα**, not *λύμη*, see *IF* xxi. 22).

(*b*) The suffix is often added to stems in *-ρος*. Debrunner (following Brugmann *Grd.*[2] II. i. 347, 578) recalls the interchange of the *n-* and *r-* suffixes in I.E., and thus accounts for the partiality of the *ro-* and *lo-* stems for *-αίνω* (*IF* xxi. 31).

Μωραίνω from **°ρός**, **ξηραίνω** from **°ρός**, **πικραίνω** from **°ρός**, illustrate this partiality, whilst **μιαίνω** from **μιαρός** is an example of the interchange of *n-* and *r-*.

(*c*) Certain verbs are treated by Brugmann (*Gr.*[4] 349) as instances of the *i̯o* extension of a nasal present. To this class belong:

Μαραίνω (cf. Skt. *mr̥-n̥ā́-ti*)<I.E. **merāˣ-* (*grind*), **mere-* (*die*) identical in Lat. *morior*, *βροτός*; *mer-n̥-i̯o* >*μαραίνω* (Boisacq).

Ὑφαίνω <**u̯ēbh-n̥-i̯o* >*ὑφ-ανi̯ο* >*ὑφαίνω*.

(*d*) The analogic spread of this suffix in verbal formation was aided by certain groups of words. We need only consider the bearing of this upon NT vocabulary. In the factitive group *μελαίνω* (from *μελαν-*) quite naturally led to **λευκαίνω** from *λευκός*, whilst **θερμαίνω** set the fashion for a whole group of words of which **ξηραίνω** is our only example. Under the influence of **μιαίνω** the Homeric *ῥυπόω* gave place to **ῥυπαίνω** (Xen., Arist.), with the result that an adj. **ῥυπαρός** was formed on the reverse analogy of *μιαρός*: *μιαίνω*. One may hazard the suggestion that **πικραίνω** was influenced by *γλυκαίνω*, which Brugmann (*IF* xxxviii. 125 f.) has explained as a substitute for *γλυκύνω* by the principle of "prohibitive dissimilation." *Γλυκαίνω* is the one verb from a *-υ* stem which joins the *-αίνω* class; contrast its synonym *ἡδύνω*. In the intransitive group there are a number of words representing a state of mind or character, to which, in the class. age, **μωραίνω** belonged (see Note below), and others representing a bodily condition, *e.g.* **ὑγιαίνω** from **ὑγιής**.

NOTE.—As was the case with -εύω verbs, we see a change from active to middle, and from trans. to intr., in the following:

Μωραίνω (1) class. *to be foolish.* (2) In LXX and NT, factitive, *to make foolish* (1 Co 1^{20}), **-ομαι**, *to become foolish* (Rom 1^{22}), *to become tasteless* (Mt 5^{13} ‖ Lk 14^{34}).

Πικραίνω *to make bitter* (Rev 10^{9}), **-ομαι** *to show bitterness* (Col 3^{19}).

2. -ύνω.

-ύνω § 168. Verbs in -ύνω stand in close relation to adjectives and nouns with υ- stems. But since some adjectives in -ύς were related to neut. nouns in -ος, the verbal suffix -ύνω came to be attached to other stems in -ος where no such adjectives in -ύς were to be found.

(*a*) In **ἀμύνω** and **πλύνω** we have primary verbs, where -υν- is part of the stem (see Debrunner *IF* xxi. 73).

(*b*) Adjectives in -ύς furnish us with **βαθύνω**, **βαρύνω**, **βραδύνω**, **εὐθύνω**, (**παρ-**)ὀξύνω, **παχύνω**, **πλατύνω**; and **πληθύνω** may have been formed from the Homeric noun *πληθύς*.

(*c*) **Αἰσχύνω** comes from *αἶσχος*, which had no corresponding adj. in -ύς, (**αἰσχύνη** being a back-formation from the verb).

(*d*) **Βαθύνω** and **πλατύνω** became patterns for a group of words represented by **μεγαλύνω**, **μηκύνω**, and possibly **πληθύνω**. **Παχύνω** probably led the way for **σκληρύνω** (from **σκληρός**).

(*e*) **Μολύνω** is closely connected with *μέλας* (<**μέλανο-ς*), cf. Skt. *maliná-s*, I.E. *melno-s*. Ὀτρύνω (**παρ-**) is really a compd., <**ὀ-τρυ-ν-ιω* <**ὀ* (see § 111 above, and Brugmann *Grd.*^{2} II. ii. 817), and *τρυ* (cf. Skt. *tvar-*, Brugmann *ib.* i. 260, 311).

(*f*) Other -*n-yo-* verbs: **Κρίνω** (*κρι-ν-ιω*), **ἐλαύνω** (see p. 235. Solmsen, *Gr. Wortf*, 51 <*ἐλα-υν-ιω* <*ἐλα-Fων*, *nomen agentis* from *ἐλα-* in *ἐλά-σαι*, *ἐλα-τήρ* etc.).

B. Verbs in -*r-i̯o*, -*l-i̯o*-.

-αίρω § 169. (1) In -αίρω we have two primary verbs **αἴρω** and **χαίρω**, and the denominative **καθαίρω** (from **καθαρός**).

-είρω In -είρω almost all the verbs are primary, thus, **ἐγείρω**, **κείρω**, **σπείρω**, **φθείρ**

For **ὀμείρομαι** see p. 251 above.

Οἰκτείρω is another spelling for *οἰκτιρω*, which Brugmann *Grd.*^{2} II. i. 358 derives from **οἰκτι-ρο-* (cf. *οἰκτίζω*) after the type *ὀλοφῡ-ρο-μαι*.

-ύρω In -ύρω we have two primary verbs, **πτύρομαι** and σύρω, and the denominative **μαρτύρομαι**.

-άλλω, -έλλω (2) The only verbs in -άλλω in the NT are primary, viz. ἅλλομαι, βάλλω, θάλλω, ψάλλω. The same applies to verbs in -έλλω, viz. **μέλλω, στέλλω, τέλλω**, except **ἀγγέλλω**, which is a denominative from ἄγγελος. For ὀκέλλω see pp. 243 and 294.

In -ίλλω and -ύλλω we have only the primary verbs **τίλλω** and **σκύλλω**.

C. Verbs in -πτω and -σσω.

-πτω 1. § 170. It is an open question whether any of the -πτω verbs (except denominatives as χαλέπτω <χαλεπός, none of which occur in the NT) were originally -ι̯ο- verbs. The NT list consists of **ἅπτω, βάπτω, βλάπτω, θάπτω, θρύπτω, καλύπτω, κάμπτω, κλέπτω, κόπτω, κρύπτω, κύπτω, νίπτω, ῥάπτω, †ἐπιράπτω, ῥίπτω, σκάπτω, σκέπτομαι, (ἐπισκ°**, late form of ἐπισκοπέω), **τύπτω**.

Of these **βλάπτω** and **νίπτω**, whose roots ended in a labiovelar (for βλάπτω cf. Skt. *marc-*, νίπτω < √*neig*ᵘ-), must belong to the -το- class, for **neig*ᵘ-ι̯ō> νίζω (cf. *peq*ᵘι̯ō> πέσσω). Similarly with those whose roots ended in φ, viz. **βάπτω** (ἐβάφην), **θάπτω** (√*dhm̥bh-*), **κρύπτω** (κρύφα), **σκάπτω** (ἐσκάφην, σκάφος), where the similarity of the aorist forms (ἔκρυψα : ἐκάλυψα) reacted on the form of the present. The remaining verbs in the list may quite well have come from stems in -ι̯ο. **Σκέπτομαι** may be <*σκεπι̯ομαι <*σπεκι̯ομαι (=Lat. *specio*, Skt. *páśyāmi*). See Brugmann, *Gr.*[4] 343 f., also Debrunner *IF* xxi. 207 ff., Hirt *Handb.* 378 f.

-σσω 2. § 171. Verbs in -σσω are almost all from guttural stems and most are primary.

(*a*) *Guttural stems.*—Primary: **Δράσσομαι** (>δράγμα, **δραχμή**), **-μάσσω** (**ἀπο-, ἐκ-**), **πράσσω** (from *πρᾱκ(ο)-, cf. πέρᾱ, πέρᾱ-ν, *Grd.*[2] II. i. 481), **ταράσσω** (ταραχ-), **τάσσω** (ἐ-τάγ-ην), **φράσσω** (*φρακι̯ω), **πλήσσω** (*πλᾱκι̯ω, cf. **πληγή**), **ῥήσσω** (according to Wackernagel, *Hellenistica* 24, Fraenkel, *Nom. Ag.* ii. 40 f.) supplanted ῥήγνυμι (*to break*) in the Hellen. age, under the influence of ἔπληξα : πλήσσω. There was a distinct verb, Att. ῥάττω, Hellen. ῥάσσω Ion. ῥήσσω (*to throw, strike, dash*). Debrunner (Blass *Gr.*[4] 61) suggests that the two verbs coalesced in the Κοινή, and it is significant that the latter meaning fits the verb better in Mk 9[18] (where, in fact, D reads ῥάσσει) and Lk 9[42], also in the cpd. προσέρηξεν, Lk 6[48]. For derivation of **ῥάσσω** see *Vocab.* s.v. ῥήγνυμι. **Φρίσσω** (cf. **φρίξ**), **νύσσω, ὀρύσσω** (*ὀρυχι̯ω), **πτύσσω** (cf. πτύξ, -υχός. For etym. see Boisacq 824). Denominative: **Πατάσσω** (πάταγος), **φυλάσσω** (**φύλαξ**), χαράσσω (χάραξ), which is represented in NT by its derivative **χάραγμα, ἀλλάσσω** probably from the adv. ἀλλάξ (Debrunner *IF* xxi. 219), **ἑλίσσω** (see above, p. 236), **βδελύσσω** (βδελυρός, cf. Aesch. βδελύκτροπος), **κηρύσσω** (**κῆρυξ**).

(*b*) *Dental stems.*—Primary: **Πλάσσω** (**πλαθι̯ω*, following the -χ-ι̯ω type in present, but aor. **ἔπλασα, ἐπλάσθην**. See Brugmann, *Gr.*[4] 119, Anm.[8]). Denominative: **πυρέσσω (πυρετός)**.

(*c*) **Ἐντυλίσσω** was formed from the prepositional phrase *ἐν τύλῳ* under the influence of **ἑλίσσω** (see Debrunner *IF* xxi. 235, *Wortb.* 115); for its rarity and meaning see Abbott *JV* 346 f. and *Vocab. s.v.* By back-formation a simplex *τυλίσσω* was made (see LS *s.v.*).

(*d*) **Σπαράσσω** (<I.E. **spereg-*) is taken by Debrunner (*IF* xxi. 224) as a -*ζω* verb, which follows the analogy of *ταράσσω* in the present (Aor. also **ἐσπάραξα**); *τινάσσω* (**ἀπο-, ἐκ-**) of uncertain etymology; **φρυάσσω** (like its cognate *φριμάσσομαι*) a lengthened form, related to *φρέαρ* (<**φρῆϝαρ* <I.E. **bhrēu̯r̥-*); *αἰνίσσομαι* (>**αἴνιγμα**) from *αἶνος*. The origin of the -*ίσσομαι* is unexplained.

D. Verbs in -*ζω*.

1. -*άζω*.

-άζω § 172. This suffix originated in the attachment of -*ι̯ω* to stems in -*αδ*-, thus **λιθάς** (*λιθαδ-*) **λιθάζω**. In a few instances a guttural stem was so used, *e.g.* **ἅρπαξ** (*ἁρπαγ-*): **ἁρπάζω**. The use was extended to neuter nouns with stems in -*ατ*-, *e.g.* **ὄνομα** : **ὀνομάζω**, and then to nouns in -*ā*- stems, *e.g.* **ἀγορά** : **ἀγοράζω**. In time -*άζω* was a suffix that could be added to any stem, though it is generally easy to trace the influence of semantic analogy.

(*a*) How productive this suffix became may be judged from the fact that out of about 70 verbs in -*άζω* in the NT only two are derived from stems in -*αδ*-, the second being **φράζω** (<*φραδ-ι̯ω*, see Brugmann *Grd.* II. iii. 182; cf. *φραδή, ἀρι-φραδ-ής*). **Σεβάζομαι** probably came from *σέβας*, which has not stem in -*αδ*-, but see p. 258 above; and *σκεπάζω* (whence °**σμα**) from *σκέπας, -αος*.

(*b*) **Κράζω** and **σφάζω** are the only other verbs (cf. **ἁρπάζω**) from guttural stems, though a confusion of flexion is found sometimes in the conjugation. See *Proleg.* 56, § 95 above, and *Vocab. s.vv. ἁρπάζω, βαστάζω*.

(*c*) Like **ὀνομάζω** are **θαυμάζω** (*θαῦμα*), **χειμάζω** (*χεῖμα*), **δελεάζω** (*δέλεαρ, -ατος*).

(*d*) From nouns in -*ā* we have **ἀγοράζω** (see Rutherford *NP* 214), **ἀκμάζω, ἀλαλάζω,** *ἀναγκάζω, αὐγάζω* (see *Vocab. s.v.*), **βιάζω, δικάζω, δοξάζω** (§ 118), **ἐξουσιάζω, ἑορτάζω, ἐπηρεάζω** (see § 120), **θηλάζω, κραυγάζω, πειράζω** (poet. and late prose for °*ράω*), **παρρησιάζομαι,**

σεληνιάζομαι (Mt 4[24] 17[15]. A "late and rare" word. To reff. given in lexicons add Vett. Val. 113[10], and °*σμός*, 127[6. 30]), *σκευάζω* (**παρα-**), *σκιάζω* (**ἐπι-, κατα-**), **σπουδάζω**, *-στεγαζω* (**ἀπο-**), **σχολάζω**, **τυρβάζω** (Lk 10[14] AP), **χλευάζω** (see Solmsen 246 n.[1]).

(*e*) From nouns and adjectives in *-(ι)ος, -(ι)ον*: **Ἐνυπνιάζω, ἐργάζομαι, θορυβάζω, †καυ(σ)τηριάζω, κοπάζω** (*κόπος*), **σινιάζω** (*ἁ.λ.* in Lk 22[31] for Attic *σήθω*; probably both *σίνιον* and its verb belong to the colloquial *Κοινή*), **ὑπωπιάζω** (from *ὑπώπιον*, but **†μυωπάζω** from *μύωψ*, see § 108 above, and Mayor *Jude and* 2 *Pet* 95 n.[1]), **χορτάζω** (for history of word see Lightfoot *ap*. Phil 4[13]).

†Ἁγιάζω (on this new word coined (or appropriated) by Jewish piety see *Vocab. s.v.*), **ἀτιμάζω, γυμνάζω, δοκιμάζω, †ἐνταφιάζω** (§ 118), **ἑτοιμάζω, ἡσυχάζω, νηπιάζω** (1 Co 14[20], elsewhere only Hipp., for *νηπιαχεύω* (Hom.), *νηπιάχω*), **†παρομοιάζω** (Mt 23[27], elsewhere only eccles.; for this and for the simplex read by B, 1, see § 123), **†πυρράζω** (Mt 16[2], from **πυρρός**; elsewhere only in Byzantine authors. In LXX and Philo *πυρρίζω*. The *-άζω* form may possibly be due to the accompanying verb), **†στυγνάζω** (LXX, NT, late). To these should be added **διστάζω** from **διστος*, cf. Skt. *dviṣṭhaḥ* (*uncertain*), **ἐξετάζω** (whence also *ἐτάζω* (Wis 2[19]) and **†ἀνετάζω**) from *ἐτεός* (<**ἐτεϝος*) *true, real*: see *Vocab.* 42*a*, **κολάζω** from *κόλος docked* (<I.E. **qolā-*).

(*f*) From adverbs: **Διχάζω** (*δίχα*), **πλεονάζω** (*πλέον*).

(*g*) From verbs: **Ἀμφιάζω** (on the form and spelling, see p. 228). "The back-formation *ἀμφιέζω* (from the aor. of *-έννυμι*) is an obvious first step towards **ἀμφιάζω**, which shows the influence of the large class of *-άζω* verbs" (*Vocab.* 28*a*). For derivation direct from *ἀμφί* see p. 68. **-βιβαζω**, causative of *βαίνω*, mostly in cpds. (in NT only a cpd. with **ἀνα-, ἐμ-, ἐπι-, κατα-, προ-, συν-**), from *βα-* < √*g ā-* in Skt. *jigāti*, cf. Lac. 3 pl. *βίβαντι* and Hom. ptc. *βιβὰς* (=*striding*). **Δαμάζω** (according to Debrunner *Wortb.* 122 n.[1]) is a back-formation from *ἐδάμασα* the aor. of the older present stem *δάμνημι*. **Στενάζω**, originally a frequentative of *στένω*. **Φαντάζω** from *φαίνω*.

(*h*) A few verbs come under none of the above headings:

Ἀσπάζομαι is derived from *ἀ* <**n̥* (cf. prep. *ἐν*, § 118), and √*seqᵘ*, seen in the Hom. *ἔννεπε* (<**ἐνσεπε*) *ἕσπετε* (<**ἐν-σπετε*), Lat. *inseque.*

Βαστάζω (for meaning and flexion see *Vocab. s.v.*), cf. Lat. *gero* (<**geso*), *gesto, to carry.*

Νυστάζω and its cognate *νύσταλος* from I.E. **sneudh-* <**snā*, cf. Lat. *nāre.*

†Πιάζω (see pp. 69, 254) from I.E. **pι-s(e)-d-*, cf. Skt. *pīḍáyati* (**pi-zd-*). See Boisacq, *s.v.*

NOTE.—1. Semantic analogy may account for a few groups of words in *-άζω* related by common meaning rather than by similarity of stem:

Thus for *utterance of sound*, ἀλαλάζω, κράζω, κραυγάζω, στενάζω:
for *reviling, ridiculing, reproaching*, ἀτιμάζω, χλευάζω, ἐπηρεάζω:
for *testing, judging, separating*, δικάζω, διχάζω, δοκιμάζω, ἐξετάζω, πειράζω, σινιάζω:
for *numerical relationships*, following μονάς: μονάζω (a verb found in Barn 4[10], Herm. *Sim.* ix. 26[3]), δυάς: δυάζω etc., διχάζω, διστάζω, πλεονάζω:
for *mark of age*, ἀκμάζω, νηπιάζω:
for *state of health*: the related pair ὑγιαίνω: ὑγιάζω represented the intrans. and the factitive conceptions. Hence *νοσαίνω: νοσάζω.

The obsolescence of νοσαίνω led to the use of the passive -άζομαι, to mark the possession of a disease. Hence †σεληνιάζομαι from which by analogous formation Deissmann (*LAE* 251, [2]256) accounts for δαιμονιάζομαι, in Wesseley *Zauberp.* (=P Par 574) [86. 3007].

2. The termination -άζω does not always carry a transitive meaning. This is seen specially when it is attached to -ο- stems, for -όω here has a prescriptive right to the factitive meaning. Rutherford *NP* 284 says, " Verbs in -άζω from adjectives in -ος are rare at the best, and though ἀτιμάζω, διπλασιάζω and one or two more bear a transitive meaning, the majority of such words are neuter." The famous crux βιάζομαι is discussed fully in *Vocab. s.v.*

2. -ίζω.

-ίζω

§ 173. The origin and extended use of this most productive suffix is closely parallel to that of -άζω.

(*a*) From stems in -ιδ-.

Ἀγκαλίζομαι (ἐν-), the simplex poetical, from ἀγκαλίς, Homeric for ἀγκάλη (Lk 2[28]). †Ἐναγκαλίζομαι (LXX and Plut.) may be an old poet. word which survived only in vernacular. Mt and Lk avoid it when used by Mk 9[36] 10[16]. For meaning see *Expos.* IX. ii. 300. †Βολίζω (*Vocab. s.v.*), ἐλπίζω, ἐρίζω, μερίζω, ῥαπίζω (for origin and meaning, see Rutherf. *NP* 264; Field *Notes* 105), ῥιπίζω (see Hort *ap.* Jas 1[6]), σφραγίζω, φροντίζω. So παίζω is from πάϜις. Αὐλίζομαι might conceivably come from αὖλις (Hom.), but is generally derived from αὐλή. Κομίζω from κομίδη (Brugmann *Grd.*[2] II. iii. 231: cf. Skt. *çama-ḥ* (<I.E. **k̂omo-s*) *çámī*, Boisacq 489. For various meanings of the word see *Vocab. s.v.*).

(*b*) Other stems with nominatives in -ις follow this type, with the mixed declension of ἔρις (acc. ἔριν and ἐρίδα) as a possible link (so Debrunner *Wortb.* 128).

Κιθαρίζω, ὑβρίζω, χαρίζομαι, and, through similarity of declension (see p. 140), †πελεκίζω (<πέλεκυς. See Lob. *Phryn.* 341).

(*c*) Guttural stems supply **μαστίζω** (Ac 22[25], Ep. and late prose for **μαστιγόω**), **σαλπίζω**, **στηρίζω** (for mixed conjug. see p. 259), **φλογίζω** (<φλόξ, though possibly belonging to the class (*h*) below).

(*d*) From *-a-* stems come **αὐλίζομαι**, **ὀργίζω**, †**σμυρνίζω** (Mk 15[23], *mingle with myrrh.* Elsewhere only Diosc. *be like myrrh.* In very late writers, *embalm*), **διυλίζω** (both simplex and cpd. are late—from ὕλη, *sediment*), **φημίζω** (see p. 387 n.[1]), †**φυλακίζω**.

(*e*) From (*a*) nouns and (*β*) adjectives, in -ος (-ον). (*a*) **Ἀφρίζω**, †**ἀνεμίζω** (elsewhere only schol. on *Od.* xii. 336. For class. ἀνεμόω. See Hort *ap.* Jas 1[6], also Mayor, who shows that James has a fondness for verbs in -ίζω), **βασανίζω** (βάσανος, *touch-stone*), **βυθίζω**, †**γαμίζω** (see N. 2 below), **εὐαγγελίζω** (§ 106), †**εὐνουχίζω**, †**θεατρίζω** (first occurs Heb 10[33], but ἐκθ° twice in Polyb.), **θησαυρίζω**, †**ἱματίζω** (*Vocab. s.v.*), †**κατοπτρίζω** (κάτοπτρον, *mirror*), **κεντρίζω** (Xen.), †**κολαφίζω** (not found earlier than NT, from κόλαφος, vernac. for κόνδυλοι, *knuckles*, see Lobeck *Phryn.* 175), †**κρυσταλλίζω** (ἁ.λ. Rev 21[11]), **λογίζομαι**, **μυρίζω** (Ion. and Comed. also pap.), **νομίζω**, **ξενίζω**, -οικίζω (**κατ-**), Jas 4[5] ℵBA (see N. 2 below), †**μετοικίζω** (<μέτοικος, Arist.), **ὁπλίζω**, †**ὀρθρίζω** (LXX and Lk 21[38] for class. ὀρθρεύω. Hellen. acc. to Moeris, see Thumb *Hellen.* 123), **ὁρίζω**, **ὁρκίζω** (sound Attic in spite of Phrynichus, as Demosth. *Fals. Leg.* 278 shows. See Rutherford *NP* 466 f., Lob. *Phryn.* 560 f.), ὁρμίζω (**προσ-**), **πλουτίζω**, ποντίζω (**κακα-**), πορίζω (whence †°**σμός**), **ποτίζω**, **ῥαβδίζω**, †**σκανδαλίζω** (only LXX and NT, see Thumb *Hellen.* 123, Helbing *Gr.* 127), **σκορπίζω** (an Ionic word, found in a fragment of Hecatæus, elsewhere only in Hellen. writers for Att. σκεδάννυμι, see p. 387 n.[1]. Rutherford *NP* 295: from σκορπίος, an engine for throwing missiles, hence *to scatter*), **σπλαγχνίζομαι** (Thumb *ib.*, Helbing *ib.*, *Vocab. s.v.*), **τραχηλίζω** (Xen.; for meaning see Moffatt *ICC ap.* Heb 4[13]), **τυμπανίζω** (Eupolis and Hellen., originally *to beat a drum*, τύμπανον, later *to beat to death*, see Moffatt *ap.* Heb 11[35]), **φορτίζω**, **χρονίζω**, **ψηφίζω**, **ψωμίζω**.

(*β*) **Ἁγνίζω**, **ἀθροίζω** (from ἀθρόος, *assembled in a crowd*, ἀ copulative (see § 107) for ἁ under the law forbidding successive aspirates, and θρόος, *noise*<I.E. **dhreu-*, **dhrū-*), †**αἰχμαλωτίζω** (from °τος, see § 105), ἀρτίζω (†**ἐξ- κατ-**), †**ἐνορκίζω** (§ 118), **ἐξυπνίζω** (§ 119), ἰσχυρίζομαι (**δι-**, § 116), †**καθαρίζω** (for class. καθαίρω, see *Vocab. s.v.*), **ἀνακαινίζω** and †**ἐνκαινίζω** (see *Vocab. s.vv.*), **κουφίζω**, **μετεωρίζομαι** (§ 122 (*b*), *Vocab. s.v.*), ὀρφανίζω (**ἀπ-**), **προχειρίζω** (§ 125), **σοφίζω**, †**συμμορφίζω** (Ph 3[10] ℵABD, 33; nowhere earlier), σῴζω, †συνετίζω (fr. συνετός), Herm. *Mand.* iv. 2[1], *Ep. Diogn.* 12[9], (first found in Arist.).

(*f*) From other 3rd Declension nouns and adjectives.

Stems in -ες- supply **γεμίζω** (unless this belongs to class (*h*) below), **δανείζω** (for spelling, see p. 77), **ἐθίζω**, †**ἐδαφίζω** (Arist. For meaning see Field *Notes* 74), **θερίζω**, **ὀνειδίζω**, †**σκοτίζω**. Ἁλίζω (**συν-**) (<ἁλής, ἀ-Ϝαλής, cf. ἀολλής: see Solmsen *Gr. Wortf.* 20), †**ἀσφαλίζω** (see *Vocab. s.v.*), **ἀτενίζω**, **ἀφανίζω**, and **ἐμφανίζω** (see pp. 236, 307).

Stems in -ον-, -ων-. **Ἀγωνίζομαι**, **δαιμονίζομαι**, †**κλυδωνίζομαι** (Eph 4^{14}. Elsewhere only Is 57^{20}, Joseph., Vett. Val.), **σωφρονίζω**.

Stems in -ματ-. †**Δειγματίζω** (Mt 1^{19} ℵ^{a}BZ 1, Col 2^{15}. See p. 320 n.[1]. For other exx. of this rare word see *Vocab. s.v.*), †**δογματίζω** (see *Vocab. s.v.*), †**καυματίζω**, **μετασχηματίζω** and **συνσχηματίζω**, **τραυματίζω**. **Χρηματίζω** covers two entirely distinct words: (*a*) *to be called*, <χρήματα (<χρῶμαι, <*χρη-ιομαι) *business*, hence *to do business under the name of X*, *to bear the name of*; (*b*) *to warn*, <χρῆμα (<χρῶ, <*χρη-ιω)=χρησμός (<χρήζω), *oracle*.

Stem in -ωτ-. **Φωτίζω**.

Various stems supply †**ἁλίζω** (from ἅλς, ἁλός: Mk 9^{49}, Mt 5^{13}, Ignat. *Magn.* 10^{2}, LXX; first in Arist.), **ἀνδρίζω**, **μακαρίζω** (<μάκαρ), **μυκτηρίζω** (<μυκτήρ, *nose*), *to sneer at*, *mock* (see *Vocab. s.v.*), **διαχειρίζω** (§ 116 (a)).

(*g*) From adverbs: **Λακτίζω** (<λάξ, *with the foot*), *to kick*. **Νοσφίζω** (<νόσφι, *apart*, *aside*) has in the two NT occurrences (Ac $5^{2.3}$, Tit 2^{10}) a special middle force, *to purloin*, supported by the papyri (see *Vocab. s.v.*). This poet. word first appeared in prose in Xen. *Cyr.* IV. ii. 42, and is frequently found in Hellen. authors (as Wetstein shows). **Χωρίζω** (<χωρίς). †**ἐγγίζω** (<ἐγγύς) not very common in papyri (see *Vocab. s.v.*).

(*h*) From verbs: **Γνωρίζω** from the same verbal root as γι-γνώ-σκω, but with the *r* that appears also in γνώριμος, *norma* (<**gnōrimā*), then *gnārus* (<**ĝn̄*-), *narrō* (<**gnārō*), *ignōrō* (Boisacq *s.v.*). The original causative force is largely lost, but is to be recognised in all its NT occurrences, even Phil 1^{22} (see *Vocab. s.v.*). **Ἐρεθίζω** (ἐρέθω), †**προσοχθίζω** (Heb 3^{10} (LXX) late form, rare outside the LXX, for προσοχθέω), **πρίζω** (πρίω); **χρῄζω**, *to need*, is closely related to χράω, but both are derived from an old noun χρή (see § 107 under ἀχρεῖος; also Boisacq p. 1069). **Φλογίζω** (if from φλέγω, but possibly it comes from φλόξ, and belongs to class (*f*) above).

The most common type of verbal derivative, as the ending -τίζω shows, is formed from the verbal adj. in -τος. These verbs are generally intensive or iterative. NT examples are **αἱρετίζω** (αἱρέομαι, °ρετός) (Hipp. and inscrr. Polybius does not use the verb, but its deriv. °τιστής=*partisan*), **βαπτίζω** (βάπτω, βαπτός), †**ῥαντίζω** (ῥαίνω, ῥαντός).

(*i*) The productivity of this suffix may be seen from the freedom with which new verbs were coined from prepositional phrases. This began in the class. period, *e.g.* σκορακίζω=ἐς κόρακας (βάλλω), but grew considerably in later Greek. In the NT we have **ἀποστοματίζω** (see § 115, *Vocab. s.v.*), but **ἐπιστομίζω** (see § 120, for form cf. ἐνστομίζω in P Par 574^{2174}), both of classical origin, †**ἀποκεφαλίζω** (see §§ 108, 109), †**ἐνωτίζομαι** (§ 118), †**ἐξουδενίζω** (Lk 23^{11} W, see § 119), which are all Hellen., **κατακρημνίζω** (see §§ 109, 121) first appears in Xen.

As an example of new formations in papp. cf. ἐπιβωμίζω PSI iv. 435[8] (258 B.C.).

(j) A few root verbs end n -ίζω and may be given here:

ἵζω (**καθίζω**)<**si-zd-ō* or **s$_e$d-i̯o* < √*sed*, cf. ἕζομαι.

κτίζω, cf. Skt. *kṣēti*, *kṣiyáti* (see Boisacq *s.v.*).

σχίζω, cf. Skt. *chid-*, *chinátti*, *chinttē*, *to cut*, *split*, Lat. *scindo*, pf. *scidi* (see Boisacq *s.v.*).

τρίζω (Mk 9[18] τρ. τ. ὀδ. *to grind the teeth*), a word found from Homer onwards for the utterance of any sharp sound, from I.E. *(*s*)*trei-g-* with **strei-d-* in Lat. *strīdēo*.

NOTE.—1. This suffix was freely used in coining words on the analogy of groups with similar meaning. Thus (*a*) **Ἰουδαΐζω** follows the well-known type of "imitatives," μηδίζω, λακωνίζω and even φιλιππίζω, *to ape the Mede*, *to imitate the Spartan manners*, *to side with Philip*, to which we may add ἑλληνίζω (>°**ιστής**) *to Hellenise*, *to speak Greek*. (*b*) The suffix was commonly used for the celebration of a festival; thus σαββατίζω (LXX, Logion in P Oxy i. 1, °**σμός** Heb 4[9]) follows the example of πανηγυρίζω (<**πανήγυρις**). In this way may have arisen **γαμίζω** (on which see N. 2 below), after the type παννυχίζω. (*c*) The only other group that calls for mention here is that of verbs describing a sound, whether vocal or instrumental. In the NT **κιθαρίζω**, σαλπίζω, **τυμπανίζω**, originated thus: see (*c*) above.

2. The meaning of a verb in -ίζω often depends on the context, as Rutherford observes (*NP* 179). Sometimes the instrumental force is obvious, as in **ῥαβδίζω**, or the factitive, as in **γεμίζω**, or the causative, as in **ποτίζω**; but the lists given above show with how many verbs such a ready decision is impossible. Consistency in verb formation was sometimes hindered by the previous appropriation of a suffix to another root. An instance of this occurs in 1 Co 14[7], where **αὐλέω** and **κιθαρίζω** are parallel. Here the verb expected, αὐλίζω, had been coined from the root αὐλή as early as Homer, with an entirely different meaning (see (*a*) and (*d*) above). An important point arises over the distinction of meaning between a verb in -ίζω and a cognate formation. Sometimes the primary distinction between intrans. and trans. is maintained, as in **σωφρονέω** and **σωφρονίζω**, **πλουτέω** and **πλουτίζω**. On the other hand, although **καθέζομαι** and **κάθημαι** were available for the intrans. sense, **καθίζω** is *intrans.* in more than 20 passages and causal in only 3, unless we add Jn 19[13] as evidently interpreted by Justin M. (*Ap.* i. 35) and *Ev. Petr.* iii. 7. The compounds of **καθίζω** are all used intransitively (**ἀνα-** Lk[1] Ac[1], **ἐπι-** Mt[1], **περι-** Lk[1]), with the exception of **συν-**, which is intrans. Lk 22[55] ℵAB, but trans. Eph 2[6]. The meaning of **γαμίζω** in 1 Co 7[38] has an important bearing upon exegesis. The verb is not found outside the NT, and here only in the active. It has generally been assumed that **γαμίζω** must stand in causative relation to **γαμέω**, but apart from exx. given above, we have the pairs ὑστερέω : ὑστερίζω, κομέω : κομίζω, to remind us that this

distinction is not invariably observed. Lietzmann *HNT in loc.* cites χρονίζω, ἐλπίζω, ἐρίζω, ὑβρίζω as intrans. verbs with this suffix, and calls attention to the tendency in Hellenistic towards the intrans. use of trans. verbs (so Radermacher *Gr.*[1] 18 f. [2]22 f.). He follows Wendland in conjecturing that itacistic pronunciation, *ἐγάμησα=ἐγάμισα*, may have led to the confusion. It is significant that in the only other passages where the word occurs, Mk 12[25] (and ||s), Lk 17[27], γαμίζεσθαι means no more than *γαμεῖσθαι*.

3. -ύζω.

-ύζω

§ 174. This suffix was mostly used in onomatopœic formations, as γογγύζω (papp., Epict., Marcus, as well as LXX and NT; classed as Ion., not Att., by Phrynichus; see *NP* 463 and *Vocab. s.v.*), ὀλολύζω (see *Vocab. s.v.*), κατακλύζω from κλύδων (common in papp., *Vocab. s.v.*).

4. -έζω.

-έζω

Ἀμφιέζω (see pp. 228, 294, and 405 above). Καθέζομαι (from √*sed). Πιέζω (see above, p. 254 and *Vocab. s.v.*).

5. -όζω.

-όζω

The primary verb ὄζω (cf. *ὀδ-μή*), and the denominative ἁρμόζω (cf. *ἁρμόδ-ιος*) the Hellen. spelling for Att. -ττω; see Lobeck *Phryn.* 241, and, for other reff., *Vocab. s.v.*

APPENDIX

SEMITISMS IN THE NEW TESTAMENT

SYLLABUS

SEMITISMS IN THE NEW TESTAMENT

THE right of such an essay to a place in a volume dealing with Accidence and Word-formation is obviously open to challenge. It may be defended on two grounds. First, it will be highly convenient when such constructions call for treatment in the volume on Syntax to be able to refer to their systematic classification in the present context, and thus to save space where compression is most needed. Secondly, the student who has found multitudinous references to this subject scattered through every part of the *Prolegomena*, both in the main text and in numerous additional notes, and who has felt the inadequacy of the brief survey in the Introduction to this volume, will rightly expect a more detailed and methodical investigation at the earliest possible place in this Grammar. To the Editor there is the additional and sufficient reason that such was the design of Dr. Moulton himself.

Before entering upon this survey, however, it seems necessary to remind the reader that in some respects Dr. Moulton's attitude to the subject of Semitisms in the New Testament was slightly modified after the first edition of the *Prolegomena* appeared. His main concern was to support Deissmann in his contention that the New Testament was written in no Judaeo-Greek jargon but in the *lingua franca* of the first century. He would have quoted, with some exegetical freedom, the saying of a second-century writer, "The Christians use no strange variety of dialect." [1] But while he maintained this thesis to the end, a comparative study of the successive editions of the *Prolegomena*, of the articles in *Cambridge Biblical Essays* and Peake's *Commentary on the Bible*, and of the Introduction to the present volume of the Grammar, will reveal a progressive tendency to do full justice to the influence of translation where Semitic originals may be posited with good reason. It must be remembered that Wellhausen's *Einleitung in die drei ersten Evangelien* only came into the author's hands when the proofs of *Prolegomena* were in an advanced stage.[2] But the cumulative evidence set forth in that book, supported by Syriac parallels to which his attention was drawn by Dr. Rendel

[1] *Ep. ad Diognetum*, 5[2]: οὔτε γάρ που πόλεις ἰδίας κατοικοῦσιν οὔτε διαλέκτῳ τινὶ παρηλλαγμένῃ χρῶνται οὔτε βίον παράσημον ἀσκοῦσιν.

[2] See *Proleg.*[1] xii f. Additional notes were inserted at once at pp. 4 n.[3], 11 n.[1], 14 n.[3], 58 n.[1], 91, 94 n.[1], 97 also n.[4], 139 n.[1], 163 n.[2], 213, 224, 226[bis] 231, 233, 235, 236[bis], 237, 240, 241 f. In the 2nd and 3rd editions further points were considered on pp. 244, 247, 249.

Harris, unquestionably restrained the ardour of the "grammatical anti-Semitism" with which Dr. Moulton has so often been charged.[1] Some years later, after reading *Studies in the Apocalypse*, he wrote with reference to the grammatical anomalies of the Book of Revelation, "Dr. R. H. Charles has recently shown how many of its mannerisms are due to a literal transference of Semitic idioms."[2] None the less Dr. Moulton insisted that many locutions which suggest Semitic idiom to the specialist in Hebrew or Aramaic fall within the range of late vernacular Greek, and he was careful to distinguish between pure Semitisms and those to which that title can only be given in a secondary sense.[3] The importance of these "secondary Semitisms" is best seen when we "are seeking for evidences of Semitic birth in a writer whose Greek betrays deficient knowledge of the resources of the language." A subtler test than that of pure Semitisms is found "in the *over-use* of locutions which can be defended as good Κοινή Greek, but have their motive clearly in their coincidence with locutions of the writer's native tongue."[4] This statement of the case satisfies two such able critics of "Deissmannism" as Professor G. C. Richards[5] and the late Canon C. F. Burney.[6]

One further point must be mentioned, though obviously this Appendix is not the place for its full discussion. In an additional note to the second edition of *Prolegomena*,[7] Dr. Moulton hinted at the possibility that Aramaic-speaking populations in Egypt may have infected the Κοινή of that country. In the preface to the third edition[8] this matter was examined in reply to criticisms offered along this very line by Drs. Redpath, Swete and Nestle. Dr. Moulton's fullest answer, supported by the weighty authority of Dr. A. S. Hunt, is to be found in *Cambridge Biblical Essays*.[9] Quite recently the argument has reappeared in two forms. Canon Burney[10] has attempted to turn Deissmann's flank by quoting the word μαγδωλοφύλαξ from the very papyrus letter written by two pig merchants at Arsinoe which Deissmann had used as an example of the paratactic style of sources where no Semitic influence can be predicated. Now this word contains the same root as the Hebrew מִגְדָּל, and is unquestionably Semitic, as Drs. Grenfell and Hunt show in their notes

[1] Père Lagrange has phrased it happily: "Il n'en est pas moins vrai que lorsqu' un helléniste ouvre le NT, en particulier les évangiles, il se trouve transporté dans les tentes de Sem. L'exagération de quelques hellénistes a été, reconnaissant chaque objet comme déjà vu dans le domaine de Japhet, de prétendre qu'il en venait toujours" (*S. Luc*, p. xcvi).

[2] Peake's *Commentary on the Bible*, 592 *b* (art. "The Language of the New Test.").

[3] *Supra* 14–18. This should be borne in mind in qualifying two footnotes by Dr. Charles (*ICC*) *Revelation*, i. pp. x, n.[1], cxliii, n.[1]. *Vide supra*, 33 f.

[4] *CBE* 474.

[5] *JTS* xxi. 286.

[6] *Aramaic Origin of Fourth Gospel*, 7.

[7] P. 242.

[8] Pp. xvi ff.

[9] Pp. 468 ff.

[10] *Aram. Orig.* 5 f.

on the document.[1] But then so was Μαγδῶλα, the name of a village in the Fayum. Yet the reader who ransacks the volume of papyri found at Magdola[2] will find as many Hebraisms there as he would find Gallicisms in a bundle of letters written by a farmer of Ashby-de-la-Zouch. It is in vocabulary that the Egyptian papyri show any such influence. Even here, as Schubart remarks,[3] but few foreign loan-words are to be found. There are several Semitic and Persian terms, even fewer Latin words than we have in the Gospels, in spite of the large number of Romans and Italians living in Egypt, and, most remarkable of all, the native Egyptian languages have contributed practically nothing.[4]

The other form of the argument emphasises the ubiquity of the Semitic stock.

"Some dialect of the Semitic family was spoken in nearly all the eastern regions subdued by Greeks and Romans. . . . The mixing of languages in the different provinces at this time will tend to explain the peculiar terms and formulae found in Aramaic and Greek inscriptions and papyri dating from the Imperial age. Many of these linguistic idioms may still be properly called 'Semitisms,' though no longer found exclusively in the LXX and the NT. We may reject the notion of a 'Judaeo-Greek' dialect, but the Greek received something of its prevalent form 'by its passage through the Semitic mind.' . . . The Greek papyri show how Semitic influence was perpetuated in Greek-speaking regions. Many 'Semitisms' silted through into the Κοινή, and became naturalised in the Greek vernacular." [5]

This appears to be an overstatement for which no adequate evidence has yet been adduced. If, however, it were to be fully substantiated, this would be a striking confirmation of Deissmann's claim that the Greek of the New Testament is essentially the spoken Κοινή of the world of

---

[1] P Fay 108[13].

[2] *Papyrus Grecs de Lille*, tome ii.

[3] *Einführung in die Papyruskunde*, 188 f.

[4] Thackeray dealt with this question, *Gr.* 20. See also Mayser *Gr.* i. 35–43. Later writers confirm the statements of Thumb *Hellen* 107–120.

[5] J. Courtenay James, *The Language of Palestine*, 70 ff. Unfortunately this argument is confused by the introduction of NT Semitisms. On the main issue, however, Mr. James has not made his position clear. He appears to agree with Harnack and Moulton that some natural productions of the Κοινή more or less accidentally coincide with Semitic forms. Six examples are given. "But even in these instances the prominence and frequency of such words and phrases must be attributed to a nearer or more remote Semitic influence." Five other constructions equally attested are then given as neither natural developments of the Greek, nor accidental coincidences with Hebrew or Aramaic. "These and many other forms found in Greek inscrip. and papyri could scarcely have come into the Κοινή except through Semitic." A complete list of such forms, with accurate information as to date and provenance, would provide a valuable test for Mr. James's theory. Meanwhile, it is difficult to recognise any principle behind the classification observed in n.[3] and n.[4] on p. 72.

Hellenism. The only difference would be that whereas the one school finds this unity in the comparative absence of distinctive Semitisms, the new school would have to concede this identity by postulating Semitism as a widespread characteristic of popular Hellenistic. Fortunately we have not to choose between these alternative routes to the same goal. We have rather to inspect every trace of possible Semitic influence in the Greek of the New Testament in order to determine the degree of probability that any book has reached us through a Semitic medium, whether near or more remote.

The method of treatment will be as follows. As far as possible all passages will be tabulated which Semitic scholars have claimed as obvious or possible Semitisms. They will be classified under grammatical headings, the passages under each heading being arranged in four groups, distinguished by numbers in bold type thus: **1.** the Synoptic Gospels and Acts, **2.** the Johannine writings, **3.** the Pauline Epistles, **4.** the remaining Epistles. The distribution of these constructions throughout the New Testament can thus be seen at a glance. The distinction between Hebraism and Aramaism will be observed wherever it should be recorded, and separate notice will be taken of passages where a difficulty in the Greek might be resolved by reference to a hypothetic Semitic original. Evidence will be offered, where it is available, of parallel usage in literary Greek, or in the Κοινή. To this extent the Appendix may serve as a fairly comprehensive and critical survey of the present stage of the discussion. It is an attempt to assemble the data upon which students will form their own judgments.

A. GENERAL STYLE AND STRUCTURE OF SENTENCE.

1. Position of the Verb in the Sentence.

An important consideration urged by Wellhausen (*W*[1] 18 f., [2]10 f.) is the Semitic order of words. He claims that in Mark, with few exceptions, the verb is followed by the subject. This argument has been seriously discounted by Lagrange (*S. Marc*, lxxxviii) on three grounds: (*a*) This order is Hebrew and Arabic rather than Aramaic and Assyrian (*e.g.* in Aram. portions of Daniel the verb more often follows than precedes the subject). (*b*) Whilst the verb does more often precede than follow the subject, if those instances are taken into account where, under the form of a participle, the subject really precedes, the balance is changed. A statistical examination of Mk 1–2 shows the subject after the verb 27 times, the subject before the verb 18, sentence beginning with participle 18. Moreover, in the Passion narrative the verb is far less often before the subject. (*c*) In Greek the verb is often enough put before the subject, with the same rule as in Semitic, of leaving it in the sing. when it has two subjects. However vaguely Semitic the order of words may be in Mark, it does not in this respect give the un-Greek impression of 1 Maccabees.

Strangely enough, Wellhausen, as we have already observed (p. 32 above), does not attribute the priority of the verb in the word order of the Fourth Gospel to Aramaism, but rather to general imitation of the Biblical style, an explanation, which, in Prof. Torrey's opinion, "has not the least plausibility" (*HTR* xvi. 323). Burney is silent upon the question.

Strong support comes from E. Norden, for the judgment of such a Hellenist as the author of *Die antike Kunstprosa* carries great weight. "Placing the verb first is, next to parallelism of clauses—the two are very often combined—the surest Semitism of the NT, especially in those instances in which this position comes in a series of clauses. That has struck me specially in Luke among the Synoptists, although in other respects he inclines more to the Hellenic side. But he shows a greater preference than the others for a flowing style of narrative, in which there was naturally more opportunity for this position of the verb" (*Agnostos Theos* 365). Lk 1[57ff.] is cited as illustrating the Semitic style of narrative, both by the position of the verb, and by the linking of parallel clauses with *καί*. The second half of the Magnificat is given as an instance of the priority of the verb without the repetition of *καί*. Of course the Hebraic style of these first two chapters of Luke is undeniable. The initial place of the verb in the series of clauses (bound by the common relative pronoun ὅς) in the credal hymn of 1 Ti 3[16] is declared to correspond with its Hebraic parallelism of thought (*ib.* 257). So also the distinctive position of the imperatives in the Lord's Prayer is compared with the style of Jewish prayers, as in Is 37[17-20], Sir 36[1-17].

But the subject calls for more exact treatment than this, and Thumb's section on "Wortstellung," appended to Brugmann's *Gr. Gr.*[4] 658 ff., is a useful corrective. Thumb points out a distinction observed in MGr between the order of words in a principal sentence and in a subordinate clause, and thinks that in the Κοινή this distinction was beginning to assert itself. "In dependent clauses without exception the verb follows immediately upon the introductory particle, or is separated from it only by the negative or the conjunctive pronoun, and practically without exception the verb follows upon an interrogative word and a relative" (*Handb.* 202). We have therefore to give special attention to the place of the verb in principal clauses. Here he rejects the rule for classical Greek given in K-G ii. 595: "the subject takes the first place, the predicate the last, and the object comes before the predicate." Delbrück, with more caution, says, "We have the general impression that the position is a matter of freedom" (*Grd.* v. (iii.) 65). Emphasis could, of course, be gained by putting any word out of its usual order. The fullest investigation so far is that by Kieckers (see above, 32 n.), who examines the place of the verb in principal clauses (excluding direct imperatives) in a selection of passages from several classical and Hellenistic prose authors. For this purpose he has taken 20 pages from Herodotus, Thucydides, Polybius, and the Chronicle of Theophanes, 20 also from Xenophon (10 from the *Anabasis* and 10 from the *Hellenica*). Five pages are also taken from each of the four Evangelists. The position of the verb is classified according to its occurrence in the initial (I), middle (M), end (E) position. The results are :

	I	M	E
Herodotus	47	165	71
Thucydides	54	149	82
Xenophon, *Anab.* . . . *Hell.* . . .	34 16 —50	95 89 —184	45 48 —93
Polybius	22	127	29
Matthew	37	51	20
Mark	40	66	24
Luke	63	55	31
John	71	48	25
Theophanes	50	167	77

This high ratio of verbs in the initial position in the Gospels is largely due to the considerable number of verbs of saying, which in accordance with regular Greek usage stand at the beginning of their sentence. Kieckers proves (p. 64) by numerous examples how very common this is in the simple narrative of Herodotus. It is very rare in the more dignified style of Thucydides, where important political speeches are generally introduced with more elaborate phraseology. Brugmann (*KVG* 683) states that the initial position of the verb is usual throughout I.E. speech, at the beginning of a narrative, or in the carrying on of the narrative in a recital consisting of a series of clauses. This order in narrative is less common in Skt. and Gr. than in Germ. and Slav., but more common than in Lat. When all allowance has been made for these factors, the predominance of initial position in Luke and John is remarkable.

2. Parallelism.

The questions raised under this head can hardly be treated in a Grammar of NT Greek. A reference to the principal authorities must suffice. It has long been recognised that much of the teaching of Jesus falls into the poetical style of Hebrew poetry and Wisdom Literature. See C. A. Briggs' "The Wisdom of Jesus the Messiah" (*Exp T* viii. 393–398, 492–496, ix. 69–75). Burney (*JTS* xiv. 414 ff.) showed that the Parable of the Last Judgment if turned into Hebrew is a rhythmical structure which is largely lost when rendered into Aramaic. But in his posthumously published work, *The Poetry of our Lord*, an elaborate proof is attempted that very much of the teaching, when translated into Aramaic, conforms to the various metres of the poetry of the OT. It is for Semitic scholars to say how far a valid argument can be built upon such data for the contention that Mt preserves the teaching of Jesus as given in Q better than Lk. Inasmuch as the teaching of Jesus, and the original record of it, is assumed throughout this Grammar to have been in Aramaic, and since the Semitic colouring of our Greek documents in these very parts is not in dispute, no more need be said. For the influence of the LXX upon Paul's most exalted passages, and for a study of parallelism in the Epistles, see J. Weiss *Festschrift f. B. Weiss*, P. Wendland *Die urchristlichen Literaturformen* 355 f., and the appendix on "Semitischer und hellenischer Satzparallelismus," in E. Norden *Agnostos Theos* 355 ff.

3. Tautology.

A Semitic colouring is seen in the continual repetition of an idea by (*a*) a subordinate clause, or (*b*) a co-ordinate parallel sentence. Thus:

(*a*) Mk 7^{13} (cf. Mt 15^{6}), Mk 12^{23} (cf. Mt 22^{28}), Mk 13^{19} (cf. Mt 24^{21}).

(*b*) Mk 2^{19} (cf. Mt 9^{15}), Mk 4^{30} (D *ἐν ποίᾳ παραβολῇ παραβάλωμεν*) (cf. Mt 13^{31}, Lk 13^{18}), Mk 11^{28} (=Mt 21^{23}=Lk 20^{2}), Mk 12^{14} (cf. Mt 22^{17}, Lk 20^{22}).

Archdeacon Allen, who gives a much fuller list (*Exp T* xiii. 329), shows that in all these examples Mt has pruned some of the redundancy. The faithful rendering of the Aramaic teaching of Jesus is responsible for many "symmetrical tautologies" in non-Marcan sources (W^{1} 18), *e.g.* Mt 6^{6}, Mt 6^{24} (=Lk 16^{13}), Mt $7^{3ff.}$ (=Lk $6^{41ff.}$), Mt $7^{7f.}$ (=Lk $11^{9f.}$), Mt $7^{13f.}$, Mt 11^{12} (toned down in Lk 16^{16}). There is, of course, no violence to Greek idiom in these instances.

A special form of tautology is that accompanying the adverbial use of the relative pronoun (which is often attracted into another case):

1. Mt 27^{9} *τὴν τιμὴν τοῦ τετιμημένου ὃν ἐτιμήσαντο ἀπὸ υἱῶν Ἰσραήλ.* Not from LXX of Zech 11^{12}; probably from Testimonies. See J. R. Harris, *Testimonies*, i. 58 f. Also McNeile, Lagrange, Allen *in loc.*
2. Jn 17^{26} *ἡ ἀγάπη ἣν ἠγάπησάς με.*
3. 1 Th 3^{9} *ἐπὶ πάσῃ τῇ χαρᾷ ᾗ χαίρομεν.*

   1 Co 7^{20} *ἕκαστος ἐν τῇ κλήσει ᾗ ἐκλήθη ἐν ταύτῃ μενέτω.*

   Eph 1^{6} *χάριτος ἧς ἐχαρίτωσεν*, 1^{19} *ἐνέργειαν ἣν ἐνήργηκεν* (cf. 3^{20}, Col 1^{29}), 2^{4} *ἀγάπην ἣν ἠγάπησεν*, 4^{1} *κλήσεως ἧς ἐκλήθητε.*

   (Eph 3^{19} 4^{4}, 2 Ti 1^{9} illustrate a different tautology.)

Dr. J. Rendel Harris, who called attention to this characteristic of Eph. (letter to J. H. M., Dec. 28, 1913), also suggests that some of these "Aramaisms" have been corrected, and that 1^{8} *τὸ πλοῦτος τῆς χάριτος ἧς ἐπερίσσευσεν*, had *ὅ* for *ἧς*, 1^{9} *εὐδοκίαν ἣν προέθετο* was originally *πρόθεσιν ἣν προέθετο*, 3^{11} *κατὰ πρόθεσιν . . . ἣν ἐποίησεν* was *ἣν προέθετο* (the pleonasm having been resolved in two different ways).

He further urges large elements of Aramaism in 2 Peter.

4. 2 Pet 3^3 ἐμπαιγμονῇ ἐμπαῖκται, 2^{12} ἀδικούμενοι μισθὸν ἀδικίας, 2^{13} ἡδόνην ἡγούμενοι τὴν ἐν ἡμέρᾳ τρυφήν (regarding the almost meaningless ἡγούμενοι as a substitute for the pleonastic ἡδόμενοι). "The whole sentence is pleonastic and Aramaic."[1] P. Wendland also (*Die urchristl. Literaturformen*, 369 n.[2]) observes that 2 Pet 2^{12} 3^3 give an impression of Semitism not found in the parallels in Jude.

In view, however, of Epict. i. 29. 49, ταῦτα μέλλεις μαρτυρεῖν καὶ καταισχύνειν τὴν κλῆσιν ἣν κέκληκεν (ὁ θεός) . . . ; it seems needless to label this idiom Semitic.

4. Parataxis.

Under this heading we must bring :—

(*a*) **Co-ordination of clauses with the simple καί, instead of the use of participles or subordinate clauses.**—This is far more common in Mk than in either Mt or Lk. As a characteristic of John, see Burney *Aram. Orig.* 56.

Wellhausen (*W*[1] 21, [2]25), who regards B as more reliable than D for particles, shows that δέ has often been substituted for Mk's καί by the other evangelists or by copyists in all Gospels. He further claims that there is evidence in the MSS of resolved, or imperfectly resolved, parataxis in a number of passages, *e.g.* D retains parataxis Mk 3^{21} (ἤκουσαν καὶ ἐξῆλθον), similarly 4^{36} 8^{10} 10^{22}. Also Lk 22^{32} σὺ δὲ ἐπίστρεψον καὶ στήρισον. In Mk $6^{7.12}$ B retains parataxis where D has participle. D sometimes links a participle and a finite verb with καί. *E.g.* Mt 26^{14} πορευθεὶς . . . καὶ εἶπεν, Lk 9^6 ἐξερχόμενοι . . . καὶ ἤρχοντο. There are many such instances in the D text of Mark, but, as Lagrange has shown (*S. Marc*, p. lix), these are cases (Mk 5^{27} 7^{25} 11^2 $14^{1.63}$) where καί has been inserted to correspond with the number of Latin words in *d* (16^{14} *d* is missing).

For bearing of this upon general question, see *Proleg.* 12.

Milligan (*Vocab. s.v.* καί) thinks it "impossible to deny that the use of καί in the LXX for the Heb. ו influenced the Johannine usage." Lagrange, in view of the slight trace of LXX influence on Jn, suggests Aramaic for Heb. For the hypotactic force of καί from Aristotle to MGr, see Thumb *Hellen.* 129, and for examples of some of the following usages, Thumb *Handb.* 184.

(*b*) **The co-ordinate use of subjunctive after** (α) **an imperative, or** (β) θέλειν.

E.g. (α) Mk 1^{44} ὅρα μηδενὶ εἴπῃς (but see *Vocab.* 455 *b*).
Mt 7^4 ἄφες ἐκβάλω (but see *Prol.* 175. Common in Epict., *e.g.* i. 9. 15, ἄφες δείξωμεν αὐτοῖς; ii. 18. 24, ἄφες ἴδω τίς εἶ).

[1] In the absence of any textual warrant one must resist the tempting suggestion to read 2 Pet 2^{12} ἐν φθορᾷ φθαρήσονται.

(β) Mk 10[36] τί θέλετέ με ποιήσω ὑμῖν (אB, numerous *v.ll.*), Mk 10[51] (=Mt 20[32]=Lk 18[41]), Mk 14[12] (=Mt 26[17]=Lk 22[9]), Mk 15[12] (ADΘ), Lk 9[54], Mt 13[28].

Plummer *ICC Luke*, p. 264, who notes that ἵνα is not inserted when the first verb is in the second person, and the second verb in the first person, cft. Soph. *OT* 650. In class. Gr. common with βούλομαι, which is largely replaced by θέλω in NT. Cf. Plato *Gorg.* 521 *d*, βούλει σοι εἴπω; Xen. *Memor.* II. i. 1, βούλει σκοπῶμεν; 10, βούλει σκεψώμεθα; cf. Lat. *vis maneamus?* See *Prol.* 185. Cf. BGU i. 38 (ii/iii A.D.) τί θέλεις ἀπενέγκω αὐτῷ.

There is therefore nothing Semitic in Jn 18[39] βούλεσθε οὖν ἀπολύσω ὑμῖν τ. βασ. τ. Ἰουδαίων;

(*c*) **The conditional parataxis of the imperative.**—Wellhausen discovers a Semitic locution when two imperatives linked by καί represent the protasis and apodosis of an implied condition (*W*[1] 25).

1. *E.g.* Mk 8[34] (=Mt 16[24]=Lk 9[23]) ἀπαρνησάσθω ἑαυτὸν καὶ ἀράτω τὸν σταυρὸν αὐτοῦ καὶ ἀκολουθείτω μοι (=*then he will be my disciple*), Lk 7[7] εἰπὲ λόγῳ, καὶ ἰαθήτω ὁ παῖς μου (=Mt 8[8] . . . καὶ ἰαθήσεται). A less striking example is the imperatival protasis followed by καί and the future; *e.g.* Mt 7[7] (=Lk 11[9]), Lk 10[28] τοῦτο ποίει καὶ ζήσῃ. Wellhausen adds Mt 12[33] with the remark, "The καί introduces the apodosis, and after this the nominative would have been used more fittingly—καὶ ὁ καρπὸς αὐτοῦ καλός. He recognises, however (*W*[2] 13), that this idiom, "*Divide et impera*," "Give a dog a bad name and *hang him*,"[1] is found in all languages. It is certainly good Greek, as in Soph. *El.* 1207, πιθοῦ λέγοντι, κοὐχ ἁμαρτήσει ποτέ. For other exx. see K-G ii. 248. [MGr.—R. McK.]

Burney describes this as less characteristic of Aram. than of Hebr., "except where the sequence is clearly to be regarded as the *result* of the preceding imperative." For examples in Hebr. and Aram., see *Aram. Orig.* 95. He cites:

2. Jn 1[30] ἔρχεσθε καὶ ὄψεσθε. 16[24] αἰτεῖτε καὶ λήμψεσθε. Elsewhere we find—

Rev 4[1] ἀνάβα ὧδε, καὶ δείξω σοι.

4. Jas 4[7. 8. 10].

(*d*) **The temporal use of καί in parataxis.**—(*W*[1]. 20. In [2]13 recognised as quite good Greek.)

1. *E.g.* Mk 15[25] ἦν δὲ ὥρα τρίτη καὶ ἐσταύρωσαν αὐτόν.
Lk 23[44] καὶ ἦν ἤδη ὡσεὶ ὥρα ἕκτη καὶ σκότος ἐγένετο.
19[43] ὅτι ἥξουσιν ἡμέραι ἐπὶ σὲ καὶ περικυκλώσουσίν σε.
Mt 26[45] ἰδοὺ ἤγγικεν ἡ ὥρα καὶ ὁ υἱὸς τοῦ ἀνθρώπου παραδίδοται.

---

[1] We might add "*Wait and see*" (=ἐὰν μείνητε, ὄψεσθε) in its historic use in the British House of Commons.

On this see *Proleg.* 12 n.[2]. Thumb, in Brugmann *Gr.*[4] 640, cft. Xen. *Anab.* II. i. 7: καὶ ἤδη τε ἦν περὶ πλήθουσαν ἀγορὰν καὶ ἔρχονται . . . κήρυκες, and deprecates the suggestion of Hebraism. Bauer (*Lex.* 611) gives several reff. to classical authors. [Common in MGr.—R. McK.]

We may add an interesting example from Tob 1^{8}א (on which see D. C. Simpson *OA* i. 181, 203): ὅτι ὀρφανὸν κατέλιπέν με ὁ πατὴρ καὶ ἀπέθανεν ("Because my father left me an orphan *when* he died").

Other possible instances in the NT are:

2. Jn 2^{13} 4^{35} 7^{33}.

4. Heb 8^{8} (LXX).

(*e*) **The consecutive use of καί in parataxis** (closely related to (*c*) and (*f*). (See Lagrange *S. Matthieu* p. xc f., *S. Jean* p. cvii, Burney *Aram. Orig.* 68. For *Waw apodosis*, see Ges-K, § 143 (*d*), Kautzsch *Aram. Gr.* § 69. 1, Marti *K.Gr.* 105 f.)

1. Mt 6^{4} καὶ ὁ πατήρ σου . . . ἀποδώσει σοι.
   8^{21} ἐπίτρεψόν μοι ἀπελθεῖν καὶ θάψαι (contr. Lk 9^{57} ἀπελθόντι θάψαι).
   Lk 2^{21} καὶ ὅτε ἐπλήσθησαν ἡμέραι . . . καὶ ἐκλήθη τὸ ὄνομα αὐτοῦ Ἰησοῦς.
2. Jn 5^{10} 6^{57} 11^{48} 14^{16}. Lagrange cft. Plato *Phaed.* 59e, καὶ ἥκομεν καὶ ἡμῖν ἐξελθὼν ὁ θύρωρος εἶπε.

The clearest instances are in the Apocalypse. See Charles *ICC* i. 101, 265, ii. 16.

Rev 3^{20} א 046. ἐάν τις ἀκούσῃ τῆς φωνῆς μου . . . καὶ ἐλεύσομαι πρὸς αὐτόν. . . .
10^{7} ὅταν μέλλῃ σαλπίζειν, καὶ ἐτελέσθη τὸ μυστήριον τοῦ θεοῦ. . . .
$14^{9.\,10}$ εἴ τις προσκυνεῖ τὸ θηρίον . . . καὶ αὐτὸς πίεται ἐκ τοῦ οἴνου. . . .

3. Phil 1^{22} εἰ δὲ τὸ ζῆν ἐν σαρκὶ τοῦτό μοι καρπὸς ἔργου, καὶ τί αἱρήσομαι; οὐ γνωρίζω. (But if . . . , *then* what shall I choose?)

Radermacher (*Gr.*[2] 223) accepts this reading and punctuation, but counts it vernacular rather than translation Greek. [MGr.—R. McK.]

(*f*) **Interrogative parataxis,** where καί introduces (α) a temporal apodosis (*W*[1] 20, [2]13), closely related to (*e*); or (β) a paradox (Burney *Aram. Orig.* 67).

(α)

1. *E.g.* Mt 18^{21} ποσάκις ἁμαρτήσει . . . ὁ ἀδελφός μου καὶ ἀφήσω αὐτῷ;
   26^{53} . . . ὅτι οὐ δύναμαι παρακαλέσαι τὸν πατέρα μου καὶ παραστήσει μοι . . .;
   Lk 14^{5} τίνος ὑμῶν υἱὸς ἢ βοῦς εἰς φρέαρ πεσεῖται καὶ οὐκ εὐθέως ἀνασπάσει αὐτόν . . .;
   24^{26} οὐχὶ ταῦτα ἔδει παθεῖν τ. χριστὸν καὶ εἰσελθεῖν . . .;
3. Rom 11^{35} (LXX).

(β)

2. Jn 2^{20} τεσσεράκοντα καὶ ἓξ ἔτεσιν οἰκοδομήθη ὁ ναὸς οὗτος, καὶ σὺ ἐν τρισὶν ἡμέραις ἐγερεῖς αὐτόν; So 3^{10} 8^{57} 9^{34} 11^{8}.

Lagrange adds 12^{34} ἡμεῖς ἠκούσαμεν ἐκ τοῦ νόμου . . . καὶ πῶς λέγεις σύ . . . ; with the comment that this interrogative phrase beginning with καί, "and yet" (often ironical), was quite good Greek. Cf. Eur. *Medea* 1398, κἄπειτ' ἔκτας ; [MGr.—R. McK.]

For καί adversative see below, under *Conjunctions* (p. 469).

(*g*) **Circumstantial clauses introduced by** καί. (See *W*[1] 19, *Ev. Marci* 36, *Ev. Lucae* 110. Ges-K § 156). [Common in MGr.—R. McK.]

1. Mk 1^{19} καὶ προβὰς ὀλίγον εἶδεν Ἰάκωβον . . . καὶ Ἰωάννην τ. ἀδελφὸν αὐτοῦ, καὶ αὐτοὺς ἐν τῷ πλοίῳ καταρτίζοντας τὰ δίκτυα.

4^{27} καὶ καθεύδῃ καὶ ἐγείρηται νύκτα καὶ ἡμέραν, καὶ ὁ σπόρος βλαστᾷ καὶ μηκύνηται.

Lk 19^{44} καὶ ἐδαφιοῦσίν σε καὶ τὰ τέκνα σου ἐν σοί (*i.e.* the enemy will beleaguer the city while her children are in her—not only the regular population, but all Jews from far and near who have fled to the metropolis). But Torrey (*C. H. Toy Studies*, p. 283 n.) shows from Nah 3^{10}, Hos 10^{14} 14^{1}, that these words are the object of the verb, not a circumstantial clause.

Charles (*ICC* i. p. cxlviii; ii. 120, 417, 431) thus explains καί (= *seeing that*) in three passages in the Apocalypse:

2. Rev 12^{11} καὶ αὐτοὶ ἐνίκησαν αὐτὸν διὰ τὸ αἷμα τοῦ ἀρνίου.

18^{3} καὶ οἱ βασιλεῖς τῆς γῆς μετ' αὐτῆς ἐπόρνευσαν.

19^{3} Ἀλληλουΐα· καὶ ὁ καπνὸς αὐτῆς ἀναβαίνει εἰς τοὺς αἰῶνας τῶν αἰώνων.

(*h*) On καὶ εὐθύς in Mark (=οὖν in John)=*Waw Consecutive*, see Burkitt *Ev. da-Mepharreshe*, ii. 89, Burney *Aram. Orig.* 68 n.

On parataxis as a test of Semitism, see also E. Norden *Agnostos Theos* 367, with Deissmann's reply *LAE*[2] 132 n. Radermacher (*Gr.*[2] 218) cites many parallels from later Greek writers, and concludes that this was a feature common to the popular speech in Hebrew and Greek.

5. Casus Pendens, followed by Resumptive Pronoun.

This is not to be confused with the construction in which the subject of an interrogative sentence is put first for emphasis or clearness, *e.g.* Mk 11^{30} τὸ βάπτισμα τὸ Ἰωάνου ἐξ οὐρανοῦ ἦν ἢ ἐξ ἀνθρώπων ;

The *casus pendens* is generally, but not always, the nominative; the resumptive pronoun may be in any case. This usage is specially frequent with participial clauses. Here, again, D seems to preserve the construction in several passages where most MSS have smoothed away the irregularity.

1. Two OT citations can be illustrated from the Hebrew original:

Mk 12^{10} (=Mt 21^{42}=Lk 20^{17}) λίθον ὃν ἀπεδοκίμασαν οἱ οἰκοδομοῦντες, οὗτος ἐγενήθη εἰς κεφαλὴν γωνίας. (Cited from Ps 117(118)[22].)

אֶבֶן מָאֲסוּ הַבּוֹנִים הָיְתָה לְרֹאשׁ פִּנָּה׃

Here the Greek syntax is obviously unaffected by the Hebrew. It is otherwise in Mt 4^{16} ὁ λαὸς ὁ καθήμενος ἐν σκότει φῶς εἶδεν μέγα, καὶ τοῖς καθημένοις ἐν χώρᾳ καὶ σκιᾷ θανάτου φῶς ἀνέτειλεν αὐτοῖς. (Cf. Is 9^{2}.)

הָעָם הַהֹלְכִים בַּחֹשֶׁךְ רָאוּ אוֹר גָּדוֹל יֹשְׁבֵי בְּאֶרֶץ צַלְמָוֶת אוֹר נָגַהּ עֲלֵיהֶם׃

For *Casus pendens* in Synoptic Gospels see *W*^{1} 19 f., ^{2}11 f.

Other examples are:

Mk 1^{34} D καὶ τοὺς δαιμόνια ἔχοντας ἐξέβαλεν αὐτὰ ἀπ᾽ αὐτῶν (where Wellhausen suspects an original οἱ δαιμόνια ἔχοντες).

Mk 6^{16} 7^{20} 13^{11}.

Mt 5^{40} καὶ τῷ θέλοντί σοι κριθῆναι καὶ τὸν χιτῶνά σου λαβεῖν (D ὁ θέλων τὸν χιτῶνά σου λαβεῖν), ἄφες αὐτῷ καὶ τὸ ἱμάτιον.

10^{11} D ἡ πόλις, εἰς ἣν εἰσέλθητε εἰς αὐτήν, ἐξετάσατε τίς ἐν αὐτῇ. . . .

*12^{36} πᾶν ῥῆμα . . . ἀποδώσουσιν περὶ αὐτοῦ λόγον.

17^{14} D καὶ ἐλθὼν πρὸς τὸν ὄχλον προσῆλθεν αὐτῷ ἄνθρωπος γονυπετῶν. . . .

13$^{20. 22. 23}$ (=Lk 8$^{14. 15}$) 13^{38} 15^{11} 19^{28} 24^{13} 25^{29} 26^{23}.

*Lk 12^{48} παντὶ δὲ ᾧ ἐδόθη πολύ, πολὺ ζητηθήσεται παρ᾽ αὐτοῦ, καὶ ᾧ παρέθεντο πολύ, περισσότερον αἰτήσουσιν αὐτόν.

Here the *casus pendens* is in the dative by inverse attraction of the relative.

21^{6} ταῦτα ἃ θεωρεῖτε, ἐλεύσονται ἡμέραι ἐν αἷς οὐκ ἀφεθήσεται λίθος ἐπὶ λίθῳ ὃς οὐ καταλυθήσεται.

Cf. the parallels Mk 13^{2}, Mt 24^{2}, in which the *casus pendens* has been absorbed by making it the object of βλέπειν.

Other examples are Lk 12^{10}* 13^{4} 23$^{50-52}$, Acts 7^{40} (LXX).

* *N.B.*—Passages in which the suspended clause contains πᾶς.

2. For *casus pendens* in Johannine writings, see Burney *Aram. Orig.* 34, 63 ff., 151; Torrey *HTR* xvi. 322 f.; Lagrange *S. Jean* cx f.; Charles *ICC* i. pp. cxlix, 53.

Jn 1^{12} ὅσοι δὲ ἔλαβον αὐτόν, ἔδωκεν αὐτοῖς. . . .

Burney cites also 1$^{18. 33}$ 3$^{26. 32}$ 5$^{11. 19. 36. 37. 38}$ 6$^{39. 46}$ 7^{18} 8^{26} 10$^{1. 25}$ 12$^{48. 49}$ 14$^{12. 13. 21. 26}$ 15$^{2. 5}$ 17$^{2. 24}$ 18^{18}. Of these, 6^{39} 15^{2} 17^{2} have πᾶς in the suspended clause.

1 Jn 2^{24} ὑμεῖς ὃ ἠκούσατε ἀπ᾽ ἀρχῆς, ἐν ὑμῖν μενέτω.

Rev 2^{26} 3$^{12. 21}$ ὁ νικῶν δώσω αὐτῷ. 6^{8} ὁ καθήμενος ἐπάνω αὐτοῦ, ὄνομα αὐτῷ ὁ Θάνατος. In oblique cases 2$^{7. 17}$ 6^{4} 21^{6} (046).

Lagrange shows that in several of the examples from Jn there is a degree of emphasis which accords with classical usage, and he regards them not as translation Greek but as locutions which would come naturally to those accustomed to the vigorous rather than varied Semitic idiom. But he recognises a Semitic locution when a pronoun resumes the clause introduced by πᾶς (*S. Jean*, p. cxi).

Closely allied to this construction is one in which πᾶς is used with a participle in an introductory circumstantial clause, though no resumptive pronoun follows (*W*^{2} 11). Such hyperbaton, however, is not unclassical. *E.g.* Lk 6^{47} πᾶς ὁ ἐρχόμενος πρός με . . . ὑποδείξω ὑμῖν τίνι ἐστὶν ὅμοιος. (In Mt 7^{24} the πᾶς ὁ ἐρχόμενος becomes subject of ὁμοιωθήσεται, and the syntax is more precise. Wellhausen suspects a similar correction of an original *nominativus pendens* in the gen. abs. of Mt 13^{19}).

The Hebrew construction (see Ges-K § 116 *w*) may be illustrated by 1 Sam 2^{13} כָּל־אִישׁ זֹבֵחַ זֶבַח וּבָא נַעַר הַכֹּהֵן, which, rendered quite literally into Greek, would be πᾶς θύων θυσίαν, ἤρχετο ὁ παῖς τοῦ ἱερέως. (The LXX, with a different verse division, reads καὶ τὸ δικαίωμα τοῦ ἱερέως παρὰ τοῦ λαοῦ παντὸς τοῦ θύοντος, καὶ ἤρχετο τὸ παιδάριον τοῦ ἱερέως . . .). In 1 Sam 3^{11} the same construction is rendered by gen. abs. in LXX.

Closely akin to this is

Sir 31^{21} *θυσιάζων ἐξ ἀδίκου, προσφορὰ μεμωκημένη, καὶ οὐκ εἰς εὐδοκίαν μωκήματα ἀνόμων.*

(RV 34^{18} He that sacrificeth of a thing wrongfully gotten, his offering is made in mockery,
And the mockeries of wicked men are not well-pleasing.)

Box and Oesterley (*O.A.* i. 435) supply an original זבח מעול מנחת תעתעים, pointing זֶבַח מְעַוֵּל, where the Greek translator read זְבַח מֵעָוֶל, and rendering "The sacrifice of the unrighteous man is a mocking offering."

The *casus pendens*, followed by resumptive pronoun, is said by Radermacher (*Gr.*^{2} 21 f.) to appear quite early in Greek literature and to be common in the later language. His examples from Hom. *Od.* xii. 73 and Xen. *Cyrop.* I. vi. 18 are not parallel, but the Silco inscr. (*OGIS* 201$^{19f.}$) is near enough: οἱ δεσπόται τῶν ἄλλων ἐθνῶν οὐκ ἀφῶ αὐτοὺς καθεσθῆναι εἰς τὴν σκιάν. Quite a crop of instances has been gathered from Aelian *De Nat. Anim.* e.g. i. 48, ὁ κόραξ, ὄρνιν αὐτόν φασιν ἱερόν. Cf. i. 19. 55, ii. 51.

For other instances see K-G i. 47. 660. (The two cited by Mr. G. R. Driver, Lucian, *Dial. Mort.* xii. 5, Epict. *Ench.* 42, are not parallel.) A good papyrus example is BGU ii. 385^{7} (ii/iii A.D.) καὶ ὁ ἐνιγών (*i.e.* ἐνεγκών) σοι τὴν ἐπιστολήν, δὸς αὐτῷ ἄλλην. See also Thumb *Hellen.* 131, and, for survival in MGr, *Handb.* 32. [Dr. McKinlay shows that the idiom is so thoroughly vernacular that, out of 27 instances cited by Burney in Jn, Pallis retains 25 in his *Romaic Gospels*. There is no parallel in MGr to the *nom. pend.* with part., but the constr. was common in Med. Gr.]

6. Constructions with καὶ ἐγένετο.

These are (*a*) καὶ ἐγένετο ἦλθε, (*b*) καὶ ἐγένετο καὶ ἦλθε, (*c*) ἐγένετο ἐλθεῖν. See *Proleg.*^{3} 15 ff. for detailed treatment.

Thackeray (*Gr.* 50 ff.) shows that with a single exception LXX uses (*a*) and (*b*) only. His statistical table proves that (*b*) predominates in LXX as does its equivalent in Hebr., but this predominance is accounted for by the slavish imitation of the Hebr. in the later historical books. The first two books of the Pentateuch and the prophetical books prefer (*a*). Both (*a*) and (*b*) seem to have been "experiments of the translators, which must be classed as Hebraisms," but the asyndetic form (*a*) "was rather more in the spirit of the later language, which preferred to say, *e.g.*, 'It happened last week I was on a journey,' rather than 'It was a week ago and I was journeying.'" We notice further that while the translator of 1 Mac uses (*a*) three times and (*b*) five times, the free Greek of 2–4 Mac avoids both and retains the classical *συνέβη* c. infin. (as in Gen $41^{13.}$ 42^{38}).

The following tables (based partly upon the references supplied in Hawkins *HS* 37) will illustrate what has been written in *Proleg.* about the distribution of these constructions in the Gospels and Acts.

(*a*) καὶ ἐγένετο (†ἐγένετο δὲ) ἦλθε.

	Temporal Clause.			
	ἐν τῷ c. infin.	*ὡς* c. aor. ind.	*ὅτε* c. aor. ind.	Other Time Determination.
Mark .	4^{4}	..	..	1^{9}
Matthew .	..	..	7^{28} 11^{1} 13^{53} 19^{1} 26^{1}	..
Luke . .	1^{8}† 2^{6}† $9^{18.\ 33}$ $11^{1.\ 27}$† 17^{14} 18^{35}† $24^{30.\ 51}$	$1^{23.\ 41}$ 2^{15} 19^{29}	..	1^{59} $2^{1.}$† ^{46} 7^{11} $9^{28.}$† ^{37}† 11^{14}† 20^{1}
Acts . .	..	..	..	[4^{5} D] [1]

(*b*) καὶ ἐγένετο (†ἐγένετο δὲ) καὶ ἦλθε.

	Temporal Clause.			
	ἐν τῷ c. inf.	*ὡς* c. aor. ind.	*ὅτε* c. aor. ind.	Other Time Determination.
Mark . .	..	..	..	..
Matthew .	..	..	..	9^{10}
Luke . .	$5^{1.}$† ^{12} 9^{51}† 14^{1} 17^{11} 19^{15} $24^{4.\ 15}$	..	..	5^{17} 8^{1} $^{22.}$†
Acts . .	[2^{1} D] [1]	..	..	[? 5^{7}†] [1]

[1] See *Proleg.*[3] 16 n.[2] 70. 233.

(c) ἐγένετο δὲ (*καὶ ἐγένετο) ἐλθεῖν.

	Temporal Clause.			
	ἐν τῷ c. inf.	ὡς c. ind.	ὅτε c. ind.	Other Time Determination.
Mark . .	—	..	..	2^{23*} [2^{15} γίνεται without temp. cl.].
Matthew .	..	..	..	..
Luke . .	3^{21}	..	..	3^{21} (gen. abs.) $6^{1.6.12}$ 16^{22} (without temp. cl.)
Acts . .	9^3 19^1	..	..	4^5 $9^{32.37.43}$ 11^{26} 14^1 16^{16} [$21^{1.5}$] $22^{6.17}$ 27^{4*} (καὶ οὕτως ἐγ. without temp. cl.) 28^8 (without temp. cl.) ^{17}.

These constructions are thus distinctively Lucan, with a marked contrast between the Third Gospel and Acts, which becomes still more striking when we observe that in the latter Luke not only uses (*c*) almost entirely to the exclusion of (*a*) and (*b*), but also avoids the more Hebraic form of the time clause. Twice the familiar ἐν τῷ c. inf. occurs (once in the Palestinian narrative, once in the later story), four times a prepositional phrase indicates the time, four times a participial construction is used, twice an accus. of time duration modifies the infin., and twice there is no temp. clause at all. In other ways the construction tends to depart from the Hebraic pattern. In 9^3 the formula is changed to ἐν δὲ τῷ πορεύεσθαι ἐγένετο: it is hardly recognisable in 21^1 ὡς δὲ ἐγένετο ἀναχθῆναι ἡμᾶς . . . ἤλθομεν, or in 21^5 ὅτε δὲ ἐγένετο ἐξαρτίσαι ἡμᾶς τὰς ἡμέρας . . ., still less in 10^{25} ὡς δὲ ἐγένετο τοῦ εἰσελθεῖν τὸν Πέτρον (with which Plummer *ICC Luke*, p. 45, after J. R. Lumby, cft. *Acta Barn.* 7, ὡς δὲ ἐγένετο τοῦ τελέσαι αὐτοὺς διδάσκοντας).

The classical word συμβαίνω is used for γίνομαι in this sense once in Acts, possibly because γίνομαι has already appeared in the sentence: Ac 21^{35} ὅτε δὲ ἐγένετο ἐπὶ τοὺς ἀναβαθμούς, συνέβη βαστάζεσθαι αὐτὸν ὑπὸ τῶν στρατιωτῶν. This is good vernacular Greek also, as we see from Tob 3^7 א ἐν τῇ ἡμέρᾳ ταύτῃ συνέβη Σάρρᾳ . . . καὶ αὐτὴν ἀκοῦσαι ὀνειδισμούς. . . . The equivalence of the two verbs in this sense in the Κοινή can be illustrated from papyri. Thus P Par 49^{29} (ii/B.C.) παρακαλέσας αὐτὸν ἀπόστειλον πρὸς ἐμέ, γίνεται γὰρ ἐντραπῆναι, where Witkowski (*Ep. Priv.*[2] 71) remarks, "γίνεται c. inf. = συμβαίνει c. inf.

Cf. Atticum ἔστιν c. inf. ut Plat. *Rep.* i. 331c . . . et ἔστιν ὥστε 'fieri potest, ut; fortasse' Sophocl." See *Vocab.* 126*a* for pap. exx. of ἐὰν γένηται c. inf.='if it should happen that' and σοὶ γίνοιτο c. inf. With these may be compared P Petr ii. 13(19)[10] (iii/B.C.) as corrected by Wilamowitz (=Witkowski[2] p. 19) ἀ[λλ'] ἔσται καὶ Θεύδωρον καταλειφθέντα ταὐτὸ ποιεῖν. Thackeray also calls attention to γίνεται εὑρεῖν='it is possible to find' in Theognis, and Xenophon's use of ἐγένετο ὥστε or ὡς=' it happened that.'

Dr. G. G. Findlay (letter to J. H. M., December '09) remarks: "The instances of ἐγένετο (δὲ) with infin. in the non-Palestinian parts of Ac seem worth considering separately, as evidence that the usage was not mere Hebraism. It is curious there is *no* non-Biblical ex. Ac 20[16] seems decisive evidence of the native (or thoroughly naturalised) stamp of the idiom."

[(*a*) Common in MGr (with συνέβη, συνέβηκε), see Pallis's *Romaic Gospels.*

(*b*) Found occasionally in MGr dialects.—R. McK.]

7. Co-ordination of the Participle or Infinitive with the Finite Verb.

(In addition to authorities cited below, see full treatment by Burney *JTS* xxii. 371–6.)

Driver *Hebrew Tenses* § 117, "It is a common custom with Hebrew writers, after employing a participle or infinitive, to *change the construction,* and, if they wish to subjoin other verbs which logically should be in the partcp. or infin. as well, to pass to the use of the finite verb. Thus Gen 27[33] הַצָּד צַיִד וַיָּבֵא, ὁ θηρεύσας θήραν καὶ εἰσενέγκας (lit. ὁ θηρεύσας θήραν καὶ εἰσήνεγκε)."[1] The bearing of this upon the grammar of the Apocalypse was first shown by Archdeacon Charles (*Studies in Apoc.* 89 ff., *ICC Revelation* i. pp. cxliv ff.), but Burney (*Aram. Orig.* 96) extends the usage to cover two examples in the Fourth Gospel, and quotes Dn 4[22] to show that the construction is found in Aramaic also.

On the other hand Holden, in his note on Xen. *Cyrop.* II. iii. 8, cites 9 passages from the *Cyrop.* in which there is a transition from the participial construction to that of the *verbum finitum.* (The other eight are I. iii. 5, II. iii. 17, 21, III. iii. 9, IV. ii. 10, V. iii. 30, iv. 29, VIII. ii. 24). Cf. also Shilleto on Thuc. I. 57, 58, "The return from the subordinate to the primary construction in Greek is too well known to require more than a passing illustration. . . . IV. 100, ἄλλῳ τε τρόπῳ πειράσαντες καὶ μηχανὴν προσήγαγον (inst. of προσαγαγόντες). Plat. *Theaet.* 144c, ἀνδρὸς . . . καὶ ἄλλως εὐδοκίμου καὶ . . . κατέλιπεν (inst. of καταλιπόντος or ὅτι κατέλιπεν). Examples of this sort might be multiplied to any

[1] Dr. R. H. Charles *ICC Rev.* i. p. cxlv, wrongly refers to this for a literal translation in LXX. Even the reading of A εἰσήνεγκας does not secure that.

amount." For numerous examples see K-G ii. 100.[1] For later Greek see Jannaris *Gr.* § 2168*b*.

N.B.—In all these citations the participle is used for the *verbum finitum*, and in the great majority it is in the nominative.

The NT occurrences are:

(*a*) **Participle.**

1. None.
2. Jn 1[32] *τεθέαμαι τὸ πνεῦμα καταβαῖνον . . . καὶ ἔμεινεν ἐπ' αὐτόν.*
   5[44] *πῶς δύνασθε ὑμεῖς πιστεῦσαι, δόξαν παρ' ἀλλήλων λαμβάνοντες, καὶ τὴν δόξαν τὴν παρὰ τοῦ μόνου θεοῦ οὐ ζητεῖτε* (ℵ *ζητοῦντες*);
   2 Jn [2] *διὰ τὴν ἀλήθειαν τὴν μένουσαν ἐν ἡμῖν, καὶ μεθ' ἡμῶν ἔσται.*
   Rev 1[5. 6], *τῷ ἀγαπῶντι ἡμᾶς καὶ λύσαντι ἡμᾶς . . . καὶ ἐποίησεν ἡμᾶς βασιλείαν.*
   1[18] 2[2. 9. 20. 23] 3[9] 7[14] 14[2-3] 15[3]. [Charles (*ICC* i. p. 15) adds 20[4], treating *οἵτινες* as an editorial gloss.]
3. Col 1[26] *τὸ μυστήριον τὸ ἀποκεκρυμμένον ἀπὸ τῶν αἰώνων καὶ ἀπὸ τῶν γενεῶν, νῦν δὲ ἐφανερώθη.*

Of these examples R. H. Charles rejects Jn 1[32] in agreement with Abbott *JG* 335 ("the meaning is 'it abode once for all,'" *i.e.* aor. ind. in contrast with pres. ptcp.). J. H. Moulton disallows Col 1[26], accepting the punctuation in WH, and Burney dismisses Rev 1[18] 20[4] on the ground that the Hebrew construction requires that the finite verb should express the proper sequence of the ptcp., and not describe an event actually prior in time to its antecedent.

The extreme frequency of this construction in Rev marks it as a Hebraism there. Moreover, Dr. Charles has strengthened his case by giving instances in which the ptcp. is in an oblique case.

4. Heb 8[10] 10[16] (both LXX) are not pressed, for reasons given by Charles *Studies in Apoc.* 90 n.[1].

(It is quite possible that a similar Aramaic construction lies behind the awkward Greek in Lk 10[8] *καὶ εἰς ἣν ἂν πόλιν εἰσέρχησθε καὶ δέχωνται ὑμᾶς, ἐσθίετε. . . .* R. H. Charles observes the loose construction in 1 Co 7[13] *γυνὴ ἥτις ἔχει ἄνδρα ἄπιστον καὶ οὗτος συνευδοκεῖ* (=*καὶ συνευδοκοῦντα*) and suggests an idiomatic Hebrew background. But this could be paralleled in class. Gr. from Homer downwards, e.g. *Od.* ii. 114. See Monro *Hom. Gr.* 247, K-G ii. 432 f.)

Two papyrus examples may be given. BGU iii. 846[14] (ii/A.D.) *Ἤκουσα παρὰ το[ῦ υἱ]οῦ μου τὸν εὑρόντα σαι ἐν τῷ Ἀρσαινοείτῃ καὶ ἀκαίρως πάντα σοι διήγηται.* P Ryl ii. 153[40] (A.D. 138–161) "If anything happen to my son being childless and intestate," *ἢ καὶ τέκνα μὲν εἴχοντι ἐπιμεταλ(λ)άξῃ δὲ καὶ τὰ τέκνα* "or if he has children, in the case of the decease of those children . . ." [Pallis renders Lk 10[8] literally.—R. McK.]

---

[1] The construction illustrated by these examples from class. Greek is not close enough to that found repeatedly in Rev to discount Hebraism in the instances cited below.

(*b*) **Infinitive.**

The solitary instance of the resolution of the infinitive into a finite verb in the following clause is claimed by Charles for

2. Rev 13^{15} *καὶ ἐδόθη αὐτῷ δοῦναι πνεῦμα τῇ εἰκόνι . . . καὶ ποιήσῃ,*

on the ground that the sense demands this co-ordination of *ποιήσῃ* with *δοῦναι* rather than with the intervening *ἵνα λαλήσῃ ἡ εἰκών.*

Cf. Tob 2^4 ℵ *καὶ . . . ἔθηκα μέχρι τοῦ τὸν ἥλιον δύειν καὶ θάψω αὐτόν* (*om.* BA, *-τω* P Oxy). D. C. Simpson *OA* i. 206. : " An instance of the resolution of an infin. into a finite verb in Hebraistic style, and of its rejection or modification in a subsequent recension."

B. THE SEVERAL PARTS OF SPEECH.

1. Pronouns.

(*a*) **Definite Article.**

(*a*) *Unusual insertion of the article.* " Peculiar to Hebrew (cf. analogous examples in Biblical Aramaic, Dan 2^{14} 3^2 *et al.*) is the employment of the article to denote a single person or thing (primarily one which is as yet unknown, and therefore not capable of being defined) as being present to the mind under given circumstances. In such cases in English the indef. art. is mostly used." Ges-K *Heb. Gr.*^{28} § 126, *q.* Wellhausen's examples (*W*^{1} 26, ^{2}19) support his assertion that Codex D preserves many Semitisms which have been pruned away in other MSS (see *Proleg.* 242). With one exception, Mk 10^{25} *διὰ τῆς τρυμαλίας τῆς ῥαφίδος* (where Mt and Lk have dropped the def. art. before each genitive), all the examples are peculiar to D, viz. Mk 3^{26} *τὸ τέλος,* 8^{11} *τὸ σημεῖον,* 9^{36} *τὸ παιδίον,* 12^6 *τοῖς γεωργοῖς,* Mt 10^{29} *τοῦ ἀσσαρίου,* 14^{11} *ἐπὶ τῷ πίνακι.*

See *Proleg.*^{3} 81. 236.

(*β*) *Omission of the article* (*W*^{1} 26, ^{2}11), see *Proleg.*^{3} 81. 236.

1. Blass^2 150 called attention to illustrations of the Semitic rule which drops the art. with a noun in construct state, and quoted many examples, especially from the Hebraic songs in Lk. In prepositional phrases Debrunner (Bl-D § 259) recognises Greek usage. Wellhausen notices the omission of article with noun in construct state preceding a definite noun, Mt 12^{42} (=Lk 11^{31}), and compares two relics of this construction in D, Mt 10^{13} *εἰρήνη ὑμῶν,* Lk 11^{19} *υἱοὶ ὑμῶν,* emphasising " the extraordinary importance of this unpretentious Semitism."

In view of this, W. C. Allen's claim that Mk 3^{28} *τοῖς υἱοῖς τῶν ἀνθρώπων* is a pure Aramaism seems questionable (*Exp T* xiii. 330. See also his *Comm. on Mk.* p. 50, " *τ. υἱ. τ. ἀνθ.*=בני נשא. Cf. Dn 2^{38} (Θ), where LXX substitutes *ἀνθρώπων* for *οἱ υἱοὶ τῶν ἀνθρώπων* "). But see below, p. 441.

The evidence of D in this matter is of dubious value considering the long list of omissions and additions of the article furnished by Von Soden (*Die Schriften des NT,* I. ii. 1309), who comments on the remarkable uncertainty of its treatment of the article and attributes the omissions partly to scribal blunders.

2. Torrey (*HTR* xvi. 323) finds "traces" of this Semitism in six phrases in John:

Jn 1[49] σὺ εἶ ὁ υἱὸς τοῦ θεοῦ, σὺ βασιλεὺς εἶ τοῦ Ἰσραήλ (for ὁ βασιλεύς).
4[6] ἦν δὲ ἐκεῖ πηγὴ τοῦ Ἰακώβ.
5[27] υἱὸς ἀνθρώπου.
5[29] εἰς ἀνάστασιν ζωῆς . . . εἰς ἀνάστασιν κρίσεως.
6[68] ῥήματα ζωῆς αἰωνίου ἔχεις.
9[5] ὅταν ἐν τῷ κόσμῳ ὦ, φῶς εἰμι τοῦ κόσμου (contr. 1[4] 8[12]).

For the qualitative force of the anarthrous nouns in the last two exx., see *Proleg.* 82.

(*b*) **Personal Pronouns.**

(*a*) *Redundant use to strengthen definition of noun* (*W*[1] 27, [2]19).

1. Mk 5[16] D αὐτῷ τῷ δαιμονιζομένῳ.
6[17] αὐτὸς γὰρ Ἡρώδης.
6[18] D αὐτὴν γυναῖκα τοῦ ἀδελφοῦ σου.
6[22] AC αὐτῆς τῆς Ἡρωδιάδος.
Mt 12[45] D αὐτοῦ τοῦ ἀνθρώπου ἐκείνου (but not in || Lk 11[26]).

In Mt 3[4] αὐτὸς δὲ ὁ Ἰωάνης may mean "John in his person," or "As to himself, John . . ." [Perhaps simply "John." So Med. and MGr. —R. McK.]

In Mk 6[22] W. C. Allen suggests that whether αὐτῆς or αὐτοῦ (אBDL) be the original reading, the word is due to mistranslation of בְּרַתַּהּ דְּהֵרוֹדְיָא or of בַּת הֵרוֹדְיָא, the daughter of Herodias (*op. cit.* 330, also *Mark, in loc.*). In the former explanation דְּ the sign of the genitive has been confused with the Aramaic demonstrative pronoun. (Cf. Stevenson *Aram. Gr.* pp. 24 and 18).

2. Jn 9[18] τοὺς γονεῖς αὐτοῦ τοῦ ἀναβλέψαντος.
[13] ἄγουσιν αὐτὸν πρὸς τοὺς Φ. τόν ποτε τυφλόν. (Burney *Aram. Orig.* 85, who quotes Pal. Syr. in support of these Aramaisms, adduces 9[18] as a parallel to Mk 6[22], and 9[13] as reproducing "another peculiarly Aram. idiom," viz. "the anticipation of the direct object of a verb by a pronominal suffix.")

(*β*) *Unusual frequency of the oblique case of the unemphatic personal pronoun*, e.g. οἱ μαθηταὶ αὐτοῦ, δύο ἐκ τῶν μαθητῶν αὐτοῦ (for class. οἱ μαθηταί, δύο μαθηταί). [Idiomatic in MGr.—R. McK.]

Wellhausen (*W*[1] 29, [2]22) was here following Blass (§ 48, 2), who found the reason for this in the Semitic usage where these pronouns are easily attached as suffixes to substantival and verbal forms. But the evidence from the Κοινή given in *Proleg.* 85 is accepted by Debrunner (Bl-D § 278) as partial explanation. In addition to papyrus examples given in *Proleg.* and *Vocab.* 94, we may add P Iand 9[40] (ii/A.D.) σοῦ τὸ πορφυρ[ιν ἐπί σε ἀ]νέ[πεμψα], on which editor remarks, "persaepe pronominis genetivus sic collocatur, velut P Oxy vii. 1064^{6} (iii/A.D.) *εἰδώς σου τὸ σπουδαῖον.* Seiungitur etiam a substantivo uno pluribusve verbis, velut BGU ii. 523^{18} *οἶδάς μου γὰρ τὴν πρὸς ἐμὲ καὶ σὲ φιλίαν.*"

(γ) *Confusion of personal and demonstrative pronouns.*

It is hardly necessary, with Wellhausen (^{1}30, ^{2}23), to posit a Semitic identity of pronouns as in any way the cause of a Lucan peculiarity. That Luke writes, 10^{21} *ἐν αὐτῇ τῇ ὥρᾳ*, where Mt 11^{25} has *ἐν ἐκείνῳ τῷ καιρῷ*, or again in 12^{12} when Mt 10^{19} and Mk 13^{11} have *ἐκείνῃ*, can hardly be accounted for by fidelity to an Aramaic original, when we observe this use of *αὐτὸς ὁ* by Luke when Semitic sources are not in question, *e.g.* Acts 16^{18} 22^{13}. Other examples of this mannerism are Lk 2^{38} 7^{21} 20^{19}. For distribution of *αὐτὸς ὁ* in NT see Hawkins *HS*^{2} 16. For Hellenistic parallels to the Lucan idiom see *Proleg.* 91 and *Vocab.* 94.

(δ) Burney (*ut supr.* 80 ff.) accounts for the great frequency of *the unemphatic use of the personal pronouns in the nominative* in John by the Semitic idiom by which the pronoun marks the subject of the participle. This may well be a "secondary Semitism" in John, as in the LXX.

(*c*) Reflexive Pronouns.

The attempt (*W*^{1} 30, ^{2}23) to find the general want of these pronouns reflected in the Gospels is sufficiently discussed in *Proleg.* 87. To what is said there about substitutes for the reflexive pronoun we may add that Mk 2^{8} shows the equivalence of *διαλογίζεσθαι ἐν ἑαυτοῖς*, and *διαλ. ἐν ταῖς καρδίαις ὑμῶν*, which is a Semitism of vocabulary to be expected in sayings of Jesus or in passages which echo the language of the Old Testament.

The substitution of *ἑαυτούς* for *ἀλλήλους* in D (*e.g.* Lk $24^{14.\ 17.\ 32}$) proves nothing, for it is not constant, and the reciprocal use of the reflexive pronoun is, apart from NT usage, common in papyri; *e.g.* BGU iv. 1101^{4} (i/B.C.) *ἐπεὶ συνόντες ἑατοῖς ἔτ[η . . .] ἐχωρίσθημεν ἀπ' ἀλλήλων*, 1110^{11} *συνχωροῦμεν πρὸς ἑατοὺς ἐπὶ τοῖσδε*, and so 1157^{14} (i/B.C.).

(*d*) Indefinite Pronouns.

A Semitic origin is claimed (*W*^{1} 27, ^{2}20) for three substitutes for *τις*, where the indef. art. would be used in English.

(*a*) Εἷς.

1. From Mt, Hawkins quotes (*HS*^{2} 30) 8^{19} 18^{24}(?) 21^{19}, 26^{69} ("Perhaps also 9^{18}, which, if *εἷς* is the right reading, would correspond to *εἷς τῶν* in Mk 5^{22} as 26^{69} does to *μία τῶν* in Mk 14^{66}." The difficulty of *εἰσελθών* is shown by the corrections *προσελθών* ℵ^{b}B, *τις προσελθών* LG). To these add Mk 10^{17} 12^{42} 14^{47} (ℵAL), Lk 5^{3} D (*εἷς ἐν πλοῖον*). Torrey (*CDA* 7) would add Ac 12^{10} (here improbable).

2. Rev 8^{13} 9^{13} 18^{21}.

Radermacher (*Gr.*^{2} 76 n.^{3}) cites Strabo (p. 230) *ἐπηγγείλατο ἕνα ἀγῶνα* ἱππικόν. For εἶς c. part. gen. (*e.g.* Lk 5$^{12. 17}$ 15^{15})=τις see *Prol.* 96 f., *Vocab.* 187, where papyrus evidence is supplied. See also Bl-D § 247 who denies weakening in classical exx. In MGr ἕνας is indef. art., Thumb *Handb.* 328.

(β) ἄνθρωπος, corresponding to Aram. נָשׁ, which, in the st. abs. is used for *quidam*, and is put before and after nouns. This, of course, is also very common in Hebrew, and is sometimes reproduced in LXX, *e.g.* 1 Ki 17^{10} אִשָּׁה אַלְמָנָה = γυνὴ χήρα (whence Lk 4^{26}).

Thackeray (*Gr.* 45) observes this use of ἀνήρ and ἄνθρωπος, and while noting a similar use in Aristoph. regards it as Hebraism in OT.

Possible examples of ἄνθρωπος with another noun in this indef. sense are:

1. Mt 11^{19} (=Lk 7^{34}) 13$^{28. 45}$ D ^{52} 18^{23} 20^{1} 21^{33} 22^{2}.

Simple ἄνθρωπος=τις.

3. 1 Co 4^{1} 7^{26} 11^{28}.

But Epict. iii. 23. 15 is quite parallel to this Pauline use. (For Greek usage see new LS, *s.vv.* ἀνήρ, ἄνθρωπος; *Vocab.* 44.

(γ) The plur. of indef. pron. often expressed by ἀπό or ἐκ c. gen. (=Hebr. and Aram. מִן), *e.g.* Mk 9^{37} 6^{43}, Mt 23^{34} (=Lk 21^{16}).

But in Κοινή ἀπό and ἐκ c. gen. had largely replaced part. gen. (*Proleg.* 72. 102, P Iand 8^{6} note), and even in class. Gk. the part. gen. was not unknown as subj. or obj. of a verb, *e.g.* Xen. *Hell.* IV. ii. 20, Πελληνεῖς δὲ κατὰ Θεσπιᾶς γενόμενοι ἐμάχοντό τε καὶ ἐν χώρᾳ ἔπιπτον ἑκατέρων. See further WM 253, Brug.-Th. 442, Jannaris § 1313, Bl-D § 164. Buck (*Gr. Dial.* 195) remarks that part. gen. as *subj.* is found in Av., Lith., and once in Umbrian.

(δ) The negative of the indef. pron. assumes some unusual forms.

(i) Εἷς . . . οὐ. Mt 10^{29} ἓν ἐξ αὐτῶν οὐ πεσεῖται is claimed as "unadulterated Semitism" (W^{1} 31, ^{2}24). It may be an extension of the usage found in Mt 5^{18}, Lk 11^{46}, for which parallels in Dem. *c. Onet.* i. 33, Xen. *Anab.* v. vi. 12, are given in Bl-D § 302. [Med. Gr.—R. McK.]

The emphatic οὐδὲ . . . εἷς is sufficiently attested in classical and Hellenistic Gk., and οὐδείς ἐστιν ὅς is acknowledged (*W*^{2} 24) to be "certainly not unGreek," though Wellhausen compares it with Syr. *lait de.*

(ii) Πᾶς . . . οὐ, for Hebrew and Aramaic כל . . . לא.

To what has been written by Moulton in *CR* xv. 442, add reff. given above, p. 22 n.^{3}. D. S. Sharp cites Epict. iii. 22. 36, πᾶσα ψυχὴ ἄκουσα στέρεται τῆς ἀληθείας. R. Law (*Tests of Life*, 379), commenting on 1 Jn 2^{19}, "It seems questionable whether this is a Hebraism, as is usually said. The explanation of the idiom probably is, not that πᾶς was used in a consciously distributive sense, but that, in vernacular Greek, the negative was attached in sense to the verb, where we attach it to the nominative ('all are-not'='none are'). The attachment of οὐ to what seems to us the wrong word is not unusual in Greek [*e.g.* in Aristoph.

Vesp. 1091, πάντα μὴ δεδοικέναι=μηδὲν δεδοικέναι.—J. H. M.], and is invariable in the common οὔ φημι τοῦτο εἶναι=I say that this *is not* so." [Rare in Med. Gr.—R. McK.]

1. Mk 13^{20} (=Mt 24^{22}) οὐκ ἂν ἐσώθη πᾶσα σάρξ.
Lk 1^{37} οὐκ ἀδυνατήσει παρὰ τ. θεοῦ πᾶν ῥῆμα. (Not a quot. from LXX or Heb. of Gen 18^{14}.)
Ac 10^{14} οὐδέποτε ἔφαγον πᾶν κοινόν.

2. Jn 6^{39} ἵνα πᾶν ὃ δέδωκέν μοι μὴ ἀπολέσω ἐξ αὐτοῦ. (See also p. 424.)
11^{26} πᾶς ὁ ζῶν καὶ πιστεύων εἰς ἐμὲ οὐ μὴ ἀποθάνῃ εἰς τὸν αἰῶνα.
12^{46} ἵνα πᾶς ὁ πιστεύων εἰς ἐμὲ ἐν τῇ σκοτίᾳ μὴ μείνῃ.
1 Jn 2^{21} πᾶν ψεῦδος ἐκ τῆς ἀληθείας οὐκ ἔστιν. (In the similar construction in $2^{19.\,23}$ $3^{6.\,9}$ 4^{3} 5^{18} the πᾶς is positive, and the οὐ negatives the verb.)
Rev 7^{16} οὐδὲ μὴ πέσῃ ἐπ' αὐτοὺς ὁ ἥλιος οὐδὲ πᾶν καῦμα.
18^{22} καὶ πᾶς τεχνίτης πάσης τέχνης οὐ μὴ εὑρεθῇ ἐν σοὶ ἔτι.
21^{27} καὶ οὐ μὴ εἰσέλθῃ εἰς αὐτὴν πᾶν κοινόν.
22^{3} καὶ πᾶν κατάθεμα οὐκ ἔσται ἔτι.

(Charles has not included this construction in his list of Hebraisms.)

3. Rom 3^{20}=Gal 2^{16} (=Ps 143^{2} LXX for: כִּי לֹא יִצְדַּק לְפָנֶיךָ כָל־חָי).
Eph 4^{29} πᾶς λόγος σαπρὸς ἐκ τ. στόματος ὑμῶν μὴ ἐκπορευέσθω.
5^{5} ὅτι πᾶς πόρνος . . . οὐκ ἔχει κληρονομίαν.

4. 2 Pet 1^{20} ὅτι πᾶσα προφητεία γραφῆς ἰδίας ἐπιλύσεως οὐ γίνεται.
Cf. *Didache* 2^{7} οὐ μισήσεις πάντα ἄνθρωπον. *Protev. Jac.* vi. 1, πᾶν κοινὸν καὶ ἀκάθαρτον οὐκ εἴα διέρχεσθαι δι' αὐτῆς.

WM 215 observes that "this Hebraism should in strictness be limited to the expression οὐ (μὴ) . . . πᾶς; for in sentences with πᾶς . . . οὐ (μή) there is usually nothing alien to Greek usage."

For the latter Radermacher (*Gr.*[2] 220) cites Dion. H. *Ep. ad Pomp.* 756 R, οὐκ ἀπὸ τοῦ βελτίστου πάντα περὶ αὐτῶν γράφων. Wackernagel, *Vorlesungen* ii. 274, cft. Propertius ii. 28. 13, ***semper, formosae, non nostis parcere verbis,*** "niemals versteht ihr."

(*e*) The Relative Pronoun.

(*a*) The Hebrew construction by which indeclinable אֲשֶׁר is followed by a pronoun or pronominal suffix is paralleled in Aramaic by the use of דְּ or דִּי indecl.

1. The passages which have been claimed as examples of this Semitism (see Blass *Gr.*[2] 175, Bl-D § 297, *W*[1] 22, [2]15, Burkitt *Ev. d. M.* ii. 75) are Mk 1^{7} (=Lk 3^{16}. Note Mt corrects, also Luke in Ac 13^{25}), 7^{25} (Note ℵB omit αὐτῆς). Mt 10^{11} D, ἡ πόλις εἰς ἣν εἰσέλθητε εἰς αὐτήν, 18^{20} D, παρ' οἷς οὐκ εἰμὶ ἐν μέσῳ αὐτῶν. Lk 8^{12} D, ὧν ἔρχεται ὁ διάβολος καὶ αἴρει ἀπὸ τῆς καρδίας αὐτῶν τὸν λόγον.

Mt 3^{12} (=Lk 3^{17}) is normal Greek, as Burney *Aram. Orig.* 85 n. seems to allow.

The conjecture that Lk 10^{41} should read, in the absence of all textual evidence, ἧς (for ἥτις) οὐκ ἀφαιρεθήσεται αὐτῆς (=she has chosen the better part from which she shall not be taken away) was offered in *W*^{1} 22, but is withdrawn in the 2nd ed.

Of the same kind is Mk 13^{19} θλίψις, οἵα οὐ γέγονεν τοιαύτη (*N.B.*—Mt corrects, θλίψις μεγάλη, οἵα οὐκ ἐγένετο). Hawkins *HS*^{2} 134 points out that this does not occur "in Dn 12^1 (either LXX or Theod.), which is here being referred to. See, however, Gen 41^{19}; and compare ἥτις τοιαύτη in Ex 9^{24} and 11^6. Somewhat similar is Mark's οἵα . . . οὕτως in the best texts of 9^3."

Cf. Ac 15^{17} (LXX).

2. Burney (*Aram. Orig.* 85) cites Jn 1^{27} 1^{33} 13^{26} 18^9 (also 9^{36}, see (β) below. 18^9 is doubtful).

   In the Apocalypse Moulton notes six examples: Rev 3^8 $7^{2.9}$ $13^{8.12}$ 20^8 (to which Charles adds, ὅπου . . . ἐκεῖ $12^{6.14}$, and ὅπου . . . ἐπ' αὐτῶν 17^9).

3. Philem [12] is not an instance, since αὐτόν is emphatic, with the following clause in apposition.

4. 1 Pet 2^{24} ℵ*LP οὗ τῷ μώλωπι αὐτοῦ. (See *Prol.*^{3} 237.)

Moulton discussed the question in *Proleg.*^{3} 94 f., 237, 249. In *Einl.* 150 f. he cites, after Helbing (*Gr.* p. iv), P Oxy i. 117 (ii/iii A.D.) ἐξ ὧν δώσεις τοῖς παιδίοις σου ἓν ἐξ αὐτῶν, but quotes Wackernagel (*ThLZ* xxxiv. 227) as thinking that the equivalence of MGr ποῦ clauses and such sentences as οἷς ἐδόθη αὐτοῖς is not proved. (See Psichari, 182 f.).

Thackeray (*Gr.* 46) finds the construction in all parts of the LXX, where it "undoubtedly owes its *frequency* to the Hebrew original. But the fact that it is found in an original Greek work such as 2 Mac (12^{27} ἐν ᾗ . . . ἐν αὐτῇ) and a paraphrase such as 1 Esdras ($3^{5.9}$ $4^{54.63}$ 6^{32}) is sufficient to warrant its presence in the Κοινή." We may add that sometimes, as in Is 1^{21} ἐν ᾗ . . . ἐν αὐτῇ, the construction is used in the Greek with no corresponding use in the Hebrew (see Ottley *Isaiah* i. p. 41, ii. p. 108).

Canon Box has shown how this Semitism has infected the Latin of 4 Ezra: *e.g.* 4^{28} *de quo me interrogas de eo.* Cf. also 4^4 $6^{14.29}$ 13^{26} (*OA* ii. 547).

A common classical usage, when a relative clause is continued by a clause co-ordinate with it, is to abandon the relative construction in the second clause and to replace the relative by a personal or demonstrative pronoun (cf. Xen. *Cyrop.* III. i. 38, IV. i. 15, V. ii. 15). Mr. G. R. Driver (*Orig. Lang.* 4) quotes, for the extension of this idiom "to single-limbed relative clauses," Soph. *Phil.* 315 (MSS), οἷς Ὀλύμπιοι δοῖέν ποτ' αὐτοῖς. Callim. *Epigr.* 43, ὧν ὁ μὲν αὐτῶν. *Anth. Pal.* vii. 72, ὧν ὁ μὲν ὑμῶν. For further exx. see Radermacher *Gr.*^{2} 217, and Jannaris § 1439. We may add Clem. *ad Cor.* 21^9 οὗ ἡ πνοὴ αὐτοῦ ἐν ἡμῖν ἐστίν. [Med. Gr.—R. McK.]

(β) The same particle דְּ (דִּי) can also introduce a subordinate clause and may be rendered by ὅτι, or ἵνα. (See below, pp. 469 f.)

1. It has been suggested that sometimes these particles in the Greek text mistranslate the Aramaic relative. Thus W. C. Allen (*Exp T* xiii. 330 and *Comm. in loc.*) explains Mk 8[24] ὅτι ὡς δένδρα ὁρῶ περιπατοῦντας, where ὅτι = דְּ = οὕς. So *W*[1] 22, [2]15, explains Mk 4[22] οὐ γάρ ἐστιν κρυπτόν, εἰ μὴ ἵνα φανερωθῇ (=*nisi quod reveletur*=*quod non reveletur*). The parallels in Mt 10[26] and Lk 12[2] (ὃ οὐκ ἀποκαλυφθήσεται), and Lk 8[17] (ὃ οὐ μὴ γνωσθῇ καὶ εἰς φανερὸν ἔλθῃ) support Wellhausen.

We may, however, cite Epict. *Ench.* 51, ποῖον οὖν ἔτι διδάσκαλον προσδοκᾷς, ἵνα εἰς ἐκεῖνον ὑπερθῇ τὴν ἐπανόρθωσιν ποιῆσαι τὴν σεαυτοῦ; where Melcher (*De Sermone Epicteteo* 85) observes "Att. εἰς ὅντινα ὑπερθήσῃ."

So Epict. i. 24, 3, οὐδεὶς δὲ δειλὸν κατάσκοπον πέμπει, ἵν', ἂν μόνον ἀκούσῃ ψόφου καὶ σκιάν ποθεν ἴδῃ, τρέχων ἔλθῃ τεταραγμένος . . . (Att.: ὅστις . . . ἐλεύσεται, vel πρόσεισιν . . .).

Moulton (*Einl.* 332 n.) accepted Wellhausen's explanation of Mk 4[41] (retained in Mt 8[27], slightly changed in Lk 8[25]), τίς ἄρα οὗτός ἐστιν, ὅτι καὶ ὁ ἄνεμος καὶ ἡ θάλασσα ὑπακούει αὐτῷ; where ὅτι is used only to avoid ᾧ . . . αὐτῷ. Lagrange, however (*S. Marc*, p. xc), cites Plato *Euthyph.* 2 *a*: τί νεώτερον, ὦ Σώκρατες, γέγονεν, ὅτι σὺ . . . διατρίβεις;

There seems less reason to follow Wellhausen in taking ὅτι=ὅς in Mt 11[29], or in reversing the process in Mt 11[10] ("still more than a prophet is this, for about him (דַּעֲלוֹהִי) is it said").

2. Burney (*Aram. Orig.* 75 f., 101 ff.) discovers many such mistranslations, supporting his contention in some instances by quoting the Syriac or Arabic versions:

ἵνα for relative:

Jn 1[8] 5[7] 6[30, 50] 9[36] 14[16].

Rev 19[15] is quite parallel to Jn 6[50].

ὅτι for relative:

Jn 8[45] 9[17] (? 1[16]).

N.B.—The converse is suspected by Burney (*ib.* 29, 34) in Jn 1[4, 13], with Torrey's strong endorsement (*HTR* xvi. 328):

Jn 1[4] punctuating ὃ γέγονεν ἐν αὐτῷ ζωὴ ἦν, and taking ὃ γέγονεν = דַּהֲוָא, the result is "inasmuch as in Him was life."

1[13] supporting the poorly attested *qui natus est* by showing that in Aramaic the final ו alone distinguishes the sing. verb from the plur., whilst the next sentence begins with וְ (καί). "Who believe on His name, inasmuch as He was born, not . . ."

In neither instance is there any necessity for this explanation of the relative pronoun.

Mr. G. R. Driver (*ut supr.* 3) remarks (*a*) that if this usage is due to Semitic influence, it is strange that the Hebr. אֲשֶׁר is never so rendered in the LXX; (*b*) in no case in Jn is this translation necessary; (*c*) in every case (exc. 1[8] and 1[16]) the constr. occurs in words presumably spoken originally in Aramaic. The last observation tells against Burney's theory that Jn was (mis-)translated from a written Aramaic original, but not against the possibility that we have here a genuine Aramaism.

Lagrange (*S. Jean*, p. cix) shows that in the Ancyra inscr. (Cagnat iii. 188) the Lat. *ex quo . . . darentur* is rendered, ἵνα ἐξ αὐτοῦ . . . δίδωνται, whilst in two other passages ἵνα represents *ut*. This, coupled with the examples given above from Epictetus, shows that by this time ἵνα was used in Greek as equivalent to a relative. We may therefore speak of this use in Jn as a secondary Semitism.

(γ) The indeclinable particle דְּ is suspected by Burney (*ut supr.* 101 ff.) to lie behind the difficult syntax of the relative pronoun in this characteristic group of passages in the Fourth Gospel.

2. Jn 10[29] ὁ πατήρ μου ὃ δέδωκέν μοι πάντων μείζων ἐστιν. (ὃ ℵB*LW, ὅς A. μείζων ℵLW, μεῖζον AB).

17[11] τήρησον αὐτοὺς ἐν τῷ ὀνόματί σου ᾧ δέδωκάς μοι.

[12] ἐγὼ ἐτήρουν αὐτοὺς ἐν τῷ ὀνόματί σου ᾧ δέδωκάς μοι. (ᾧ ℵABCLW, οὓς D[2], ὃ D*).

Cf. 17[24] Πατήρ, ὃ δέδωκάς μοι, θέλω ἵνα ὅπου εἰμὶ ἐγὼ κἀκεῖνοι ὦσιν μετ' ἐμοῦ.

17[2] ἵνα πᾶν ὃ δέδωκας αὐτῷ δώσει αὐτοῖς ζωὴν αἰώνιον. Burney suggests πᾶν ὃ = כֹּלָא דְּ Aramaic for "all who," "every one who," "all which"; so Hebr. כֻּלּוֹ "the whole of it," with plur. reference, cf. Ex 14[7].

6[37] πᾶν ὃ δίδωσίν μοι ὁ πατὴρ πρὸς ἐμὲ ἥξει.

[39] ἵνα πᾶν ὃ δέδωκέν μοι μὴ ἀπολέσω ἐξ αὐτοῦ, ἀλλὰ ἀναστήσω αὐτὸ τῇ ἐσχάτῃ ἡμέρᾳ.

Cf. 1 Jn 5[4] ὅτι πᾶν τὸ γεγεννημένον ἐκ τοῦ θεοῦ νικᾷ τὸν κόσμον, which shows that the neut. πᾶν is used as a collective pronoun.

In none of these instances does Lagrange so much as suggest Aramaic; the attraction of the relative is offered as the explanation of 17[11. 12]. Mr. G. R. Driver does not dispute the Aramaic origin of the idiom, but observes that in every case the passage is attributed to Jesus, and is not evidence of an Aramaic Gospel translated into Greek, but of the Aramaic of the *ipsissima verba* of our Lord.

(δ) By this ambiguous use of דְּ Burney accounts for the Lucan variation οἱ βλέποντες for the Matthaean ὅτι βλέπουσιν . . . ὅτι ἀκούουσιν, . . . דְּחָזַיִן דְּשָׁמְעִין in Mt 13[16. 17] = Lk 10[23. 24] (*The Poetry of our Lord*, 145).

(*f*) Distributive Pronouns and Pronominal Adjectives.

(*a*) The absence in Hebrew and Aramaic of special words corresponding directly to ἄλλος or ἕτερος, involves the use of certain Semitic idioms to express the idea *alter . . . alter*. (See G-K § 139 (*c*).)

These are:

(1) אִישׁ with אָחִיו or רֵעֵהוּ as correlate. Gen 13[11] (LXX ἕκαστος ἀπὸ τοῦ ἀδελφοῦ αὐτοῦ).

(2) זֶה . . . זֶה Ex 14[20] (LXX καὶ οὐ συνέμιξαν ἀλλήλοις), Is 6[3] (LXX ἕτερος πρὸς τὸν ἕτερον).

(3) הָאֶחָד . . . הָאֶחָד 2 Sam 14[6] (LXX καὶ ἔπαισεν ὁ εἷς τὸν ἕνα ἀδελφὸν αὐτοῦ).

(4) The substantive repeated Gen 47[21] (LXX ἀπ' ἄκρων ὁρίων Αἰγύπτου ἕως τῶν ἄκρων), cf. Dt 4[32] 28[64].

(2) and (3) are both found in 1 Sam 14[4] מִזֶּה . . . מִזֶּה (LXX ἔνθεν . . . ἔνθεν) and הָאֶחָד . . . הָאֶחָד (LXX τῷ ἑνὶ . . . τῷ ἄλλῳ).

Thackeray (*Gr.* 45) observes: "The rarity of phrases like ἕτερος τὸν ἕτερον (still found in the Pentateuch, Isaiah and the early chapters of Ezekiel) is partly due to the tendency in the Κοινή to abandon words expressive of duality. But it is noticeable that the use of ἀνήρ=ἕκαστος is practically confined to one group of books," in which "ἕκαστος, which is freely used in other parts of the LXX, is either wholly or nearly unrepresented."

1. In the Synoptic Gospels (1) and (2) are not represented, but the idiom of (3) may possibly be found in Mk 15[27], Mt 20[21] 24[40f.] 27[38], Lk 18[10] D, εἷς Φαρισαῖος καὶ εἷς τελωλωνης (*sic*), and (4) in Lk 11[17] οἶκος ἐπὶ οἶκον πίπτει, Mk 13[2] (=Mt 24[2]=Lk 21[6]) λίθος ἐπὶ λίθῳ, Mt 23[34] ἀπὸ πόλεως εἰς πόλιν. (*W*[1] 30, [2]23.) "From city to city," however, is quite idiomatic English and is not necessarily Hebraic. A closer parallel than this seems to be Lk 17[24] ὥσπερ γὰρ ἡ ἀστραπὴ ἀστράπτουσα ἐκ τῆς ὑπὸ τὸν οὐρανὸν εἰς τὴν ὑπ' οὐρανὸν λάμπει.

2. (3) is found in Jn 20[12],

3. and in Gal 4[22].

But in both exx. ἕνα . . . καὶ ἕνα is probably due to the gradual disappearance of μὲν . . . δέ in Hellenistic.

See Bl-D, § 247. 3, and for vernacular use, *Vocab.* 187. [(4) Med. and MGr.—R. McK.]

(β) Closely akin to the idiom of (3) above is 1 Ki 22[13] כִּדְבַר אַחַד מֵהֶם *Let your speech be like the speech of the rest of them.* This has been cited (*W*[1] 30, [2]23) to explain Mk 6[15] ὅτι προφήτης ὡς εἷς τῶν προφητῶν, *A prophet as another prophet, like any other prophet.* Moffatt translates, *It is a prophet like one of the old prophets.* Lk 9[8] corrects, ὅτι προφήτης τις τῶν ἀρχαίων ἀνέστη.

(γ) For "*the rest*" as compared with a single example of a class, Hebrew and still more Aramaic use כֹּל.

Thus Gen 3[1] "The serpent was more subtle *than any other beast of the field,*" מִכֹּל חַיַּת הַשָּׂדֶה.

Gen 43[34], "And Benjamin's mess was five times as much *as any of the rest of theirs,*" מִמַּשְׂאֹת כֻּלָּם.

This use of πᾶς may possibly be seen (so *W*[1] 31, [2]23) in Mk 4[13], Lk 3[20. 21] 13[2. 4], though in Lk 3[20. 21] the explanation is far-fetched. [MGr sometimes uses ὅλος in much the same way.—R. McK.]

2. Numerals and Distributives.

Semitic influence has been suspected in—

(a) The use of Cardinals for Ordinals in dating Incidents. Cf. Gen 1[5] יוֹם אֶחָד (LXX, ἡμέρα μία). So in Aramaic (Kautzsch *Gr.* 122, Marti *Gr.*[2] 82, Dalman *Gr.*[2] 131). See *Proleg.* 95 f., 237.

1. Cf. Mk 16[2], Lk 21[1], τῇ μιᾷ τῶν σαββάτων.
   Mt 28[1] εἰς μίαν σαβ.
   Ac 20[7] ἐν τῇ μιᾷ τ. σαβ. [Plummer (*ICC*, p. 407) suggests this meaning (unnecessarily) in Lk 17[22] ὅτε ἐπιθυμήσετε μίαν τῶν ἡμερῶν τοῦ υἱοῦ τ. ἀνθρώπου ἰδεῖν.]
2. Jn 20[1. 19]. [Charles unnecessarily suggests this in Rev 6[1]. See *ICC* i. p. cxlviii.]
3. 1 Co 16[2].

See however p. 174, *Proleg.* 96, and for MGr, Thumb *Handb.* 82. [Med. Gr.—R. McK.]

(b) The use of Cardinals for Adverbials.

1. Mk 4[8. 20] εις τριάκοντα καὶ εν ἑξήκοντα καὶ εν ἑκατόν.

"The MSS offer many variations and combinations of εις and εν. But whatever be original, it is no doubt due to over-scrupulous translation of חד," W. C. Allen (*Exp T* xiii. 330), who cites Dn 3[19] חַד־שִׁבְעָה *seven times*, and Gen 26[12] (Targ. Onk.) עַל חַד מְאָה, *one hundredfold.* "The writer of the First Gospel has avoided the Aramaism by substituting ὃ . . . ὃ . . . ὃ" (*Comm. Mark*, 79).

(c) Distributives expressed by Repetition, either of the Cardinal Number or of the Noun itself.—The former is literally reproduced in LXX, *e.g.* in εἷς εἷς 1 Chr 24[6], δύο δύο Gen 6[19], ἑπτὰ ἑπτά Gen 7[3]. (This is also Aramaic, Dalman *Gr.*[2] 135.) The latter *e.g.* in 2 Chr 34[13] ἐργασίᾳ καὶ ἐργασίᾳ (= לַעֲבוֹדָה וַעֲבוֹדָה, *in every department of work*). Sometimes κατά is combined with this reduplication, *e.g.* κατ' ἐνιαυτὸν ἐνιαυτόν 1 K 7[16], κατὰ μικρὸν μικρόν Dt 7[22], κατὰ φυλὰς φυλάς Zech 12[12].

1. The NT supplies δύο δύο Mk 6[7]; συμπόσια συμπόσια, πρασιαὶ πρασιαί Mk 6[39f.]; δεσμὰς δεσμάς Mt 13[30] Epiph.; ἀνὰ δύο δύο Lk 10[1] B *al.*; εἷς κατὰ εἷς (Mk 14[19]) is claimed as a hybrid confusion between the Aram. חַד חַד and the vulgar Greek καθεῖς.
3. 2 Co 4[16] ἀλλ' ὁ ἔσω ἡμῶν [ἄνθρωπος] ἀνακαινοῦται ἡμέρᾳ καὶ ἡμέρᾳ is regarded as Hebraism by Bl-Debr. § 200. 1. = יוֹם וָיוֹם (contrast Heb 3[13] καθ' ἑκάστην ἡμέραν).

See *Proleg.*[3] 21 n.[3], 97, for the significance of these locutions, with the important additions made by Moulton in *Einl.* 156 f. (See also § 104 above.) Psichari (183 ff.) adduces MGr examples to support Thumb's denial of Hebraism (*Hellen.* 128, *Handb.* 83). Wackernagel (*ThLZ* xxxiv. 227), however, recognises a Semitism in Mk 6[39f.]. G. and H. point out on P Oxy

vi. 940[6] (vi/A.D.) that σου μίαν μίαν means *together with you*, and is not distributive in that passage. The new LS cites Soph. *Frag.* 201, μίαν μίαν (=κατὰ μίαν).

3. Adjectives and Adjectival Substitutes.

In Hebrew the wide use of the construct state largely took the place of the adjective. Greek has many corresponding uses of the genitive case of a noun to mark description, material etc. The two most characteristically Semitic idioms are (1) the genitive of an abstract noun in place of an adjective of quality, and (2) the use of υἱός with a following genitive of origin or definition.

(1) The so-called "Hebraic Genitive" is an extension of the construction found in Greek poetry, as shown in *Proleg.*[3] 74, 235. In the LXX Thackeray regards it as "partly but not altogether due to literal translation" (*Gr.* 23). The same may be said of the NT instances. To the classical instances referred to in *Proleg.*[3] (*ut supra*), Radermacher (*Gr.*[2] 109, 111) adds Herodotus iv. 136 αἵ τε ἡμέραι ὑμῖν τοῦ ἀριθμου διοίχηνται. From late Greek he cites Demosth. *In Midiam* 93 ("an interpolated document of the Hellenistic age") ἡ κυρία τοῦ νόμου (*the legal limit*—contrast ἡ κυρία in § 84, the equivalent Attic term); Marcellinus *Vit. Thuc.* 57, λόγοι εἰρωνείας (as well as λόγοι εἰρωνικοί), pseudo-Chion *Ep.* 16. 3, ἀπεχθείας ἔργον, and, in view of Pauline parallels, pseudo-Hippocr. *Ep.* 10. 6 σῶμα σοφίης. Thumb (Brugmann *Gr.*[4] 677) dissents from Wackernagel's assumption that MGr ἄνθρωπος τῆς μπιστοσύνης, *a trustworthy man*, is a Hebraism.

1. Mk 2[26] (=Mt 12[4]=Lk 6[4]) οἱ ἄρτοι τῆς προθέσεως a t.t. from the OT.
   Lk 4[22] οἱ λόγοι τῆς χάριτος, 16[8] οἰκονόμος τῆς ἀδικίας, [9] μαμωνᾶς τῆς ἀδικίας, 18[6] κριτὴς τῆς ἀδικίας.
   Ac 6[11] ℵ*D ῥήματα βλασφημίας, 8[23] χολὴ πικρίας, 9[15] σκεῦος ἐκλογῆς.
2. Rev 13[1] 17[3] ὀνόματα βλασφημίας.
3. Rom 1[26] πάθη ἀτιμίας, 8[21] τὴν ἐλευθερίαν τῆς δόξης κ.τ.λ., 12[20] (LXX) ἄνθρακες πυρός. Possibly Eph 1[14] 4[22] (see p. 485).
   Phrases with σῶμα. Rom 6[6] τὸ σ. τῆς ἁμαρτίας, 7[24] τὸ σ. τοῦ θανάτου, Ph 3[21] τὸ σ. τῆς ταπεινώσεως ἡμῶν, τὸ σ. τῆς δόξης αὐτοῦ, Col 1[22] 2[11] τὸ σ. τῆς σαρκὸς (αὐτοῦ).
   Phrases with ἡμέρα, Rom 2[5] ἡμ. ὀργῆς, 2 Co 6[2] ἡμ. σωτηρίας (LXX), cf. 1 Pet 2[12] ἡμ. ἐπισκοπῆς (LXX). These are rooted in the language of the OT, but they can only be termed Secondary Semitisms.
4. Heb 12[15] ῥίζα πικρίας (LXX Dt 29[18] AF; see Bl-D § 165).
   Jas 1[25] ἀκροατὴς ἐπιλησμονῆς. Perhaps νόμον τέλειον τὸν τῆς ἐλευθερίας (*ib.*) and τὸ πρόσωπον τῆς γενέσεως αὐτοῦ ([23]) come under the same head.

Debrunner (Bl-D § 165) includes Ac 1[18], 2 Pet 2[15]. But μισθὸς (τῆς) ἀδικίας is an objective genitive. (Cf. Ezek 14[4] ἡ κόλασις τῆς ἀδικίας αὐτοῦ, 44[12] εἰς κόλασιν ἀδικίας.)

(2) The use of υἱός or τέκνον with genitive in metaphorical sense.

Thackeray (*Gr.* 41) observes that in LXX "this Hebraism is mostly confined to the literal group: the Hexateuch, Isaiah and Chronicles generally avoid it." Wellhausen sees in this a common mark of genuinely Aramaic style (cf. Arabic *dhu*), W^1 27. NT instances are:

1. Mk 2[19] (=Mt 9[15]=Lk 5[34]) υἱ. τ. νυμφῶνος; 3[17] υἱ. βροντῆς.
Mt 23[15] υἱ. γεέννης.
Lk 10[6] υἱ. εἰρήνης, 16[8] 20[34] οἱ υἱ. τ. αἰῶνος τούτου, 20[36] υἱ. τ. ἀναστάσεως.
Ac 4[36] υἱὸς παρακλήσεως.
2. Jn 17[12] ὁ υἱ. τ. ἀπωλείας.
3. 1 Th 5[5] υἱ. φωτός, 2 Th 2[3] ὁ υἱ. τ. ἀπωλείας.
Rom 9[8], Gal 4[28] τὰ τέκνα τ. ἐπαγγελίας.
Eph 2[2] 5[6] υἱ. τ. ἀπειθείας (whence imported into text of Col 3[6] in inferior MSS), 2[3] τέκνα ὀργῆς, 5[8] τέκνα φωτός, Col 1[13] τ. υἱ. τ. ἀγάπης αὐτοῦ.
4. 1 Pet 1[14] τέκνα ὑπακοῆς, 2 Pet 2[14] κατάρας τέκνα.

N.B.—Οἱ υἱοὶ τ. πονηροῦ (Mt 13[38]), υἱ. διαβόλου (Ac 13[10]), as also τὰ τέκνα τοῦ διαβόλου (1 Jn 3[10]), hardly come under this heading.

Deissmann (*BS* 161) accepts these in **1** and **2** as translation-Greek. Of those in **3** and **4** he says, "In no case whatever are they un-Greek; they might quite well have been coined by a Greek who wished to use impressive language. Since, however, similar terms of expression are found in the Greek Bible, and are in part cited by Paul and others, the theory of analogical formations will be found a sufficient explanation."

(3) The phrase ὁ υἱὸς τοῦ ἀνθρώπου, a literal translation of the Aramaic בַּר אֱנָשָׁא, was quite unintelligible except on Palestinian soil. Apart from its frequent use in all the Synoptic Gospels (on the lips of Jesus), it is found in—

1. Ac 7[56].
2. Jn 1[52] 3[13. 14] 6[27. 53. 62] 8[28] 9[35] 12[23. 34] 13[31].

The phrase υἱὸς ἀνθρώπου occurs 3 times. In Jn 5[27] the anarthrous form is probably due to the writer's sense that the title is here used qualitatively. In Rev 1[13] 14[14] the wording is doubtless influenced by the LXX of Dn 7[13].

On the whole subject see Dalman *WJ* 234–267.

4. Degrees of Comparison.

(*a*) The absence of degrees of comparison in Semitic languages (other than Arabic) may account, according to Wellhausen, for the use of the positive adjective in some passages in the Gospels. (See W^1 28, ^{2}21, and Moulton's discussion in *Einl.* 124 f.)

1. Mk 10[25]. Clement of Alex. reads εὐκόλως for εὐκοπώτερον. Τάχιον (D) suggests an independent smoothing of εὐκόλως.

Mt 22^{36} ποία ἐντολὴ μεγάλη, a less idiomatic rendering of the Aramaic (from Q ?) than πρώτη πάντων in Mk 12^{28}. Note that Mt 22^{38} μεγάλη καὶ πρώτη ἐντολή is quoted by Justin M. *Ap.* i. 16 as μεγίστη.

Lk 5^{39} ὁ παλαιὸς χρηστός ἐστιν, according to Wellhausen (*Das Ev. Luc.* 19), must be taken as comp. or superl. Plummer (who regards χρηστότερος, AC vg, as a corruption) and Lagrange defend the positive interpretation.

Mk $9^{43. 45. 47}$ καλόν . . . ἤ, whilst in ^{42} μᾶλλον is inserted.

(*b*) The comparative particle is sometimes used after a verb as though by itself it meant " more than."

1. Mk 3^4, Lk 15^7.
Lk 17^2 λυσιτελεῖ αὐτῷ . . . ἢ . . . (contrast Mt 18^6 σύμφερει αὐτῷ ἵνα, Mk 9^{42} καλόν ἐστιν αὐτῷ μᾶλλον εἰ . . .).

W[2] 21 acknowledges that this is found in Plut.
For classical instances see WM 302, Riddell, Plat. *Apol.* p. 183, K-G ii. 303. [Rare in Med. and MGr.—R. McK.]

3. 1 Co 14^{19} θέλω . . . ἤ. Cf. the agraphon in Justin M. *Ap.* i. 15, θέλει γὰρ ὁ πατὴρ ὁ οὐράνιος τὴν μετάνοιαν τοῦ ἁμαρτωλοῦ ἢ τὴν κόλασιν αὐτοῦ. Gildersleeve (*in loc.*), cft. Eur. *Tel.* fr. 714 N[2]:

σμίκρ' ἂν θέλοιμι καὶ καθ' ἡμέραν ἔχων
ἄλυπον οἰκεῖν βίοτον ἢ πλουτῶν νοσεῖν.[1]

(*c*) For reduplication to express the *elative* force of the adjective, see Moulton's treatment, § 104 above; Delbrück *Grd.* v. (iii.) 139 ff. Wetstein (*ap.* Heb 10^{37}), cft. Aristoph. *Vesp.* 213 τί οὐκ ἀπεκοιμήθησαν ὅσον ὅσον στίλην; For numerous parallels see Radermacher *Gr.*[2] 68 n.[1]. [MGr. —R. McK.]

1. Lk 5^3 D ὅσον ὅσον for ὀλίγον.
4. Heb 10^{37}, which may be an echo of Is 26^{20}, μικρὸν ὅσον ὅσον, in introducing the citation from Hab $2^{3f.}$.

Conybeare and Stock (*Selections from LXX*, 77) refer to σφόδρα σφόδρα, Ex $1^{7. 12}$, Num 14^7, Ezek 9^9, Jdth 4^2; σφόδρα σφοδρῶς Gen 7^{19}, Jos 3^{16}; θιμωνιὰς θιμωνιάς Ex 8^{14}, ἄνω ἄνω . . . κάτω κάτω Dt 28^{43}. They observe, " In all the above instances the kind of intensification involved is that of a repeated process."

(*d*) For the comparative use of παρά see below, *under* B 8.

(*e*) The superlative idea was sometimes expressed in Hebrew by adding לֵאלֹהִים to the adjective. This could be rendered literally in the LXX by the " dative of the person judging." Thus Jon 3^3, πόλις μεγάλη

---

[1] Mr. E. E. Genner tells me that this passage is cited by two authorities, one of which gives μᾶλλον instead of βίοτον.

τῷ θεῷ, *an exceedingly great city.* Two possible instances are found in NT:

1\. Ac 7[20] ἀστεῖος τῷ θεῷ, *exceedingly fair.*
3\. 2 Co 10[4] δυνατὰ τῷ θεῷ *divinely strong* (Moffatt). In this passage more probably *dat. commodi.* For the former see *Prol.* 104, also p. 166 above.

(*f*) A well-known Hebrew equivalent for the superlative קֹדֶשׁ קָדָשִׁים has sometimes been discovered in—

2\. Rev 19[16] βασιλεὺς βασιλέων, κύριος κυρίων.
3\. 1 Tim 6[15] ὁ βασιλεὺς τῶν βασιλευόντων καὶ κύριος τῶν κυριευόντων.
4\. Heb 9[3] σκηνὴ ἡ λεγομένη ἅγια ἁγίων.

The last is Hebraic, but is introduced as a stereotyped t.t. In the other two, βασ. βασ. means "ruler over kings." Cf. P Leid. W[xiv. 9] (ii/iii A.D.) ἔνδοξο ἐνδοξοτάτων, δαίμων δαιμώνων, ἄλκιμε ἀλκιμωτάτων, ἅγιε ἁγίων. P Par 51[24] (=UPZ i. p. 360, ii/B.C.) ἐλθέ μοι θεὰ θεῶν. For MGr, Thumb (*Handb.* 33) gives γεναῖκα τῶν γεναικῶν "a queenly woman," σκλάβος τῆς σκλαβιᾶς "a vile slave."

5. Adverbs and Adverbial Locutions.

"Adverbs derived from adjectives are certainly common in later Syriac, but are not properly Semitic" (*W*[1] 28, [2]21).

Various substitutes are employed:

(1) In Hebrew "the infin. absol. occurs most frequently in immediate connexion with the finite verb of the same stem, in order in various ways to define more accurately or to strengthen the idea of the verb" (G-K § 113 *l*). This is extremely rare in pure Aramaic.[1] In the LXX there are two main forms adopted by the translators for rendering this idiom. Leaving on one side the purely Greek constructions, in which an adverb replaces the infin., or the infinitive is dropped without replacement, and on the other the solitary instance of barbarously literal employment of the Greek infinitive (Jos 17[13] B), Thackeray (*Gr.* 48 f.) shows that the translators had recourse to—

(*a*) Finite verb with dat. of the cognate noun. So Gen 2[16] βρώσει φάγῃ=אָכֹל תֹּאכֵל, [17] θανάτῳ ἀποθανεῖσθε=מוֹת תָּמוּת.

Possible NT examples:

1\. Lk 22[15] ἐπιθυμίᾳ ἐπεθύμησα.
Ac 2[30] ὅρκῳ ὤμοσεν (not citation, but in introducing LXX quotation), 4[17] (EP syr[hl], Chrys.) ἀπειλῇ ἀπειλησώμεθα, 5[28] παραγγελίᾳ παρηγγείλαμεν, 23[14] ἀναθέματι ἀνεθεματίσαμεν.

Also the following in LXX citations: Mk 7[10]=Mt 15[4], Mt 13[14], Ac 2[17]. With qualifying adjective, Mk 5[42] ἐξέστησαν εὐθὺς ἐκστάσει μεγάλῃ, Lk 1[42] ACD ἀνεφώνησεν φωνῇ μεγάλῃ (κραυγῇ ℵBL). (With this BGU ii. 427[22], καὶ βεβαιώσει πάσῃ βεβαιώσει, has been compared. But this stereo-

[1] See Dalman *WJ* 34. Torrey (*CDA* 33) disputes the rarity.

typed formula which occurs in scores of contrasts is not parallel to any of these examples, but rather to Eph 1³.)

2. Jn 3²⁹ χαρᾷ χαίρει. (Jn 18³² 21¹⁹ must not be placed under this heading.)

4. Jas 5¹⁷ προσευχῇ προσηύξατο.

See the discussion in *Prol.*³ 75 f. 245, and more fully in *Einl.* 118 n.¹, where P Oxy i. 5¹⁶ (early Christian document iii/iv A.D.) is mentioned, ὅτι δοχῇ δεκτικόν ἐστιν. Radermacher (*Gr.*² 129) adds Anderson-Cumont Grégoire *Studia Pontica* III. 71*a*. 1. βιώσασα βίῳ, and calls attention to the many parallels in the language of Attic tragedy and the Old Comedy, *e.g.* φόβῳ ταρβεῖν, φόβῳ δεδιέναι, φύσει πεφυκέναι, νόσῳ νοσεῖν. He rightly sees the Semitic influence only in the extension of such expressions in the NT.

(*b*) Finite verb with participle of the same verb or a verb of kindred meaning. Thus Gen 3¹⁶ πληθύνων πληθυνῶ = הַרְבָּה אַרְבֶּה. The only decisive NT examples are in quotations from LXX:

1. Mt 13¹⁴ (=Mk 4¹²) βλέποντες βλέψετε (LXX).
Ac 7³⁴ ἰδὼν εἶδον (LXX).

3. [1 Co 2¹ (so Wendt on Ac 7³⁴). But the only possible meaning is "When I came".] Eph 5⁵ ἴστε γινώσκοντες. (See *Prol.*³ 245, also *supra*, 22 and 222.)

4. Heb 6¹⁴ εὐλογῶν εὐλογήσω σε καὶ πληθύνων πληθυνῶ σε (LXX).

Canon Box (*OA* ii. 547) calls attention to the extreme frequency of this Hebraism in 4 Ezra as one of the reasons for postulating a Hebrew original behind the Latin text. He instances 4² *excedens excessit cor tuum*, 4²⁶ *festinans festinat*, 5³⁰ *odiens odisti*. Another example illustrates (*a*) above: 4³⁷ *mensura mensuravit tempora et numero numeravit tempora*.

See discussion in *Prol.* 76 [1] and *Einl.* 118.

A good Κοινή instance is P Tebt ii. 421¹² (iii/A.D.) καὶ μὴ σκύλῃς τὴν γυναῖκά σου ἢ τὰ παιδία, ἐρχόμενος δὲ ἔρχου ἰς Θεογονίδα, "but in any case came to Theogonis." (The editors' trans. "when you come," misses the pleading note of the urgent appeal.) See Goodspeed *AJT*, xii (1908), p. 249 f. With this cf. instances of redundant participles in class. Gr. given by K-G ii. 99. (Radermacher *Gr.*² 210, cft. Schol. Dem. *c. Androt.* 17, ἀποδρὰς ᾤχετο, and Bekker *Anecd.* 425: 5 ἀπιὼν ᾤχετο· συνήθης ὁ πλεονασμὸς τοῖς Ἀττικοῖς.) This may explain Eph 5⁵. In the LXX Hebraism is undeniable.

(2) The cognate accusative of the abstract noun is sometimes used in the LXX, where the Hebrew uses a similar construction to strengthen the force of the verb, *e.g.* Gen 27³³ ἐξέστη δὲ Ἰσαὰκ ἔκστασιν μεγάλην σφόδρα. The construction is common to Hebrew and Aramaic. But

---

[1] Against the parallel from Aeschylus given there, Mr. C. D. Chambers wrote (letter, Aug. 1921), "The passage in *P.V.* would only be even remotely parallel if it ran, μάτην βλέποντες, μάτην ἔβλεπον, οὐ κλύοντες οὐκ ἤκουον."

ἐφοβήθησαν φόβον μέγαν (see Mk 4[41]) is only given twice in H-R (Jon 1[10], followed v.[16] by ἐφ. φόβῳ μεγάλῳ, 1 Mac 10[8]) as against φοβεῖσθαι σφόδρα twenty times.

Examples in NT of this intensive use, resembling the Semitic construction:

1. Mk 4[41] *ἐφοβήθησαν φόβον μέγαν.*
   Mt 2[10] *ἐχάρησαν χαρὰν μεγάλην σφόδρα.*
2. Rev 16[9] *ἐκαυματίσθησαν καῦμα μέγα.*

(3) The adverbial use of an auxiliary verb (*W*[1] 28, [2]21).

(*a*) The clearest instance is the use of προστιθέναι (προστίθεσθαι) for the Hebraic הוֹסִיף (c. infin.)=πάλιν. Thackeray (*Gr.* 52 f.) shows that in LXX it takes three forms: (*a*) προσέθετο λαβεῖν, (*β*) προσέθετο καὶ ἔλαβεν, (*γ*) προσθεὶς ἔλαβεν. (*a*), with 109 examples, and (*β*), with 9, are direct imitations of the Hebrew; (*γ*), with only 6 instances, is nearer to classical types.

Varieties of the same Hebraism appear in the Latin text of 4 Ezra (see G. H. Box, in *OA* ii. 548), *e.g.* 5[32] *adiciam* (*dicere*) *coram te,* 8[55] *noli ergo adicere inquirendo,* 9[41] *adiciam dolorem,* 10[19] *adposui adhuc loqui.*

(*a*) is represented in NT by—

1. Mk 14[25] D οὐ μὴ προσθῶ πεῖν (*al.* οὐκέτι οὐ μὴ πίω).
   Lk 20[11. 12] προσέθετο πέμψαι (not D)=Mt, Mk πάλιν ἀπέστειλεν.
   Ac 12[3] προσέθετο συλλαβεῖν καὶ Πέτρον is rather similar, but see Bl-D § 435, and cf. Clem. *ad Cor.* 12[7] καὶ προσέθεντο αὐτῇ δοῦναι σημεῖον.

(*γ*) Lk 19[11] προσθεὶς εἶπε (cf. *Apoc. Petr.* 4 προσθεὶς ἔφη).

See *Prol.*[3] 233, *Einl.* 3, *Vocab.* 551.

Also Schmidt *De Eloc. Joseph.* 514–7, Crönert in Wessely *Studien* iv. 3, Deissmann *BS* 67 n., Burney *Aram. Orig.* 14.

Helbing (*Gr.* p. iv) disputes that (*a*) is necessarily Hebraistic and cft. Pseudo-Callisthenes II. 41 (end), οὐκέτι οὖν προσεθέμην ἀδύνατα ἐπιχειρεῖν, also P Grenf i. 53[29]. (But the obscure Greek of this iv/A.D. letter only furnishes a parallel in Crönert's rdg., προστεθείκαμεν ἐάν.)

(*b*) Wellhausen offers two other examples (*W*[1] 28, [2]21).

Mk 14[8] προέλαβεν μυρίσαι. W. C. Allen (*Comm. Mark* 169) regards constr. as unclassical, as προλαμβάνω has nowhere else the sense of "anticipating" the action of a subsequent verb. He refers to Joseph. *Ant.* vi. 13. 7, xviii. 5. 2; *B.J.* i. 20. 1; Ignat. *Eph.* 3[2], but thinks they are not parallel. He concludes that, while the phrase is not impossible Greek, it is probably a translation of Aram. root קדם. Mt 26[12] avoids προέλαβεν. Lagrange (*S. Marc, in loc.*) thinks this on a par with the Attic φθάνω c. inf. (rare in Att. but frequent in later writers) and cft. Jos. *Ant.* xviii. 9. 7 φθάσας ὑπαντιάζειν. But he admits the striking resemblance to Aramaic and compares syr[sin] קַדְּמַת בַּסְמַת.

Mk 6[20] ACDω lat syr ἀκούσας αὐτοῦ πολλὰ ἐποίει *he listened to him often.* Debrunner (Bl-D § 414) agrees, but W. C. Allen and

Lagrange prefer ἠπόρει (אBL boh) as giving better sense ("car aveo ἐποίει ce qui suit est absolument banal"). Strangely, neither commentator recognises a possible Semitism.

The two exx. under (*b*) are not found in the LXX, but Thackeray's comment on the adverbial use of all such auxiliary verbs may apply. "The classical language had used verbs like λανθάνειν and φθάνειν with a participle in a similar way: in the later language the participle with (προ)φθάνειν was replaced by an inf.: the constructions given above may be regarded as a sort of extension of this use" (*Gr.* 54).

Πολλά *adverbial* (*W*[1] 28).

"The frequent πολλά as an adverb may be due to translation of the Aramaic שַׂגִּי. Cf. Dn Θ 2[12] שגיא = πολλή, 5[9] 6[15. 24] = πολύ" (W. C. Allen *Exp T* xiii. 330). Marti (*Gr.*[2] 92*) gives שַׂגִּיא, pl. fem. שַׂגִּיאָן *much*; adv. *very*, Dan. Pap. El. I. 2 [=Strasb. 2]. Dalman (*Gr.*[2] 102) says, "Peculiar to the Galilean dialect is a special preference for the ending in ן. This accounts for the form סגין *very* for סגי."

The NT occurrences of πολλά adverbial are given by Hawkins *HS*[2] 35 thus:

1. Mk 1[45] 3[12] 5[10. 23. 38. 43] 6[20] 9[26] 15[3]. He regards all other instances as accusatives.
3. Rom 16[6. 12], 1 Co 16[12. 19].
4. Jas 3[2].

The free use of the adverbial accus. in Greek removes this from the category of Semitisms. See LS *s.v.* πολύς. The disproportionate use of πολλά in the second Gospel is a Marcan mannerism which may be due to Aramaic influence.

Πάλιν *and* εὐθύς *as conjunctions.*

Πάλιν, a favourite Marcan word (in narrative, Mt 6, Mk 26, Lk 2), is sometimes an inferential conjunction, not merely *again*, but *further*, *thereupon*, and has been claimed as a translation of the Aramaic *tub* (Dalman *Gr.*[2] 213, תוב תובן *ferner noch*). So *W*[1] 28, [2]21, endorsed by Souter *Lex. s.v.* But in many even of the Marcan instances, the meaning is really iterative, and where the meaning is inferential it is unnecessary to go back to Aramaic. "Might not πάλιν come to have the same secondary meaning as 'again' in English, *i.e.* 'however'? See P Oxy xiv. 1676[20]" (Moffatt *Expos* viii. 20. 141). [Med. and MGr. —R. McK.]

Εὐθύς (εὐθέως) is not only extremely frequent in Mark, but is sometimes an inferential conjunction (*e.g.* Mk 1[21. 23. 29. 30] "So then"). Hawkins *HS*[2] 12) gives the relative occurrences in the Gospels as Mt 18, Mk 41, Lk 7, Jn 6; in narrative Mt 12, Mk 34, Lk 1. Dalman (*WJ* 28) equates the temporal εὐθύς (-έως) with Aram. מִיַּד, which, however, is far less common. Lagrange (*S. Marc* p. xcii) suggests that its other meaning resembles אֱדַיִן or בֵּאדַיִן, which occurs often in Daniel (see Marti *Gr.*[2] 57*).

Burkitt (*Ev. da-Meph.* ii. 89) suggests influence of Hebr. ו consec. But Mk's freedom from Hebraisms weakens this contention. Dalman is doubtless right in saying the excessive use of this adverb in Mark depends on "the particular predilection of the author, and is due probably to Greek rather than Jewish-Aramaic influence."

Temporal use of ἰδού.

This has been claimed as an Aramaism (*W*[1] 29, [2]21) representing Aramaic הָא (neither Marti (*Gr.* 67) nor Dalman (*Wörterb.* 107) quotes any such use).

1. Lk 13[16] *ἣν ἔδησεν ὁ Σατανᾶς ἰδοὺ δέκα καὶ ὀκτὼ ἔτη.*
13[7] *ἰδοὺ τρία ἔτη* [*ἀφ' οὗ* om. ΑΧΔ . . . min syr[sin vg hl]] *ἔρχομαι.*

This corresponds to the Hebrew use of זֶה (Ges-K § 136, *b*. 3), which is often translated literally by *ταῦτα* in LXX, *e.g.* Gen 31[41] זֶה־לִּי עֶשְׂרִים שָׁנָה בְּבֵיתֶךָ LXX, *ταῦτά μοι εἴκοσιν ἔτη ἐγώ εἰμι ἐν τῇ οἰκίᾳ σου.* So Num 14[22], Judg 16[15], Zech 7[3](*ἤδη*). But this temporal זֶה is sometimes rendered *ἰδού*.

Deut 2[7] *ἰδοὺ τεσσαράκοντα ἔτη Κύριος ὁ θεός σου μετὰ σοῦ.*
8[4] *οἱ πόδες σου οὐκ ἐτυλώθησαν ἰδοὺ τεσσαράκοντα ἔτη.*
Gen 27[36] *ἐπτέρνικε γάρ με ἰδοὺ* [R *ἤδη* A] *δεύτερον τοῦτο.*

It is noteworthy that where this *nominativus pendens* occurs in Mk 8[2] (to which D adds *εἰσίν, ἀπὸ πότε*) *ἤδη* is the word used.

The papyrus instance, BGU iii. 948, given in *Proleg.*[3] 11 n.[1], is very close to Lk 13[16], which, however, may well be an instance of Luke's adoption of LXX language.

6. Verbs.

(i) Voice.

The Passive is used less freely in Aramaic than in Greek. Wellhausen looks for evidence of Aramaic influence in three directions (*W*[1] 25, [2]18). (*a*) Aramaic avoids passive when the subject of the action is named. Hence comparative rarity of passive with *ὑπό* in Mk.

M-G show *ὑπό* after passive verb as follows:

1. Mk 7 times, Mt 22, Lk 22, Ac 36.
2. Jn 1, 3 Jn 1, Rev 2.
3. Rom 3, 1 Co 12, 2 Co 10, Gal 4, Eph 2, Phil 2, Col 1, 1 Th 2, 2 Th 1, 2 Tim 1.
4. Heb 8, Jas 4, 1 Pet 1, 2 Pet 5, Jude 2.

(*b*) Impersonal use of 3rd plur. act. in place of passive. This is usual in Hebrew (G-K § 144 *g*) as well as Aramaic (Kautzsch *Aram. Gr.* § 96. 1 (*c*)).

1. Mk 6[14] 10[13] 13[26] 15[27]; Mt 1[23] 5[15] 7[16] 24[9].
Lk 6[44] 12[20. 48] 14[35] 16[9] 17[23] 18[33] 23[31]; Ac 3[2]. [Lk 12[11] may be detached from its context in Q. Cf. Mt 10[19].]

2. Jn 15^6 20^2, Rev 12^6.
3. 1 Co 10^{20} BDG. [An echo of several passages in LXX.]
4. Heb 10^1 (see *Proleg.* 58 f.).

(*c*) The use of an intransitive verb in place of the normal Greek passive

1. Mk 4^{21} 7^{19} (contr. Mt 15^{17}) 9^{43} (contr. v.^{47}) 14^{21}.
Mt 17^{27} 8^{12} (contr. Lk 13^{28}).
Lk 4^{41} 8^2.

(W. C. Allen, *Exp T* xiii. 330, found in ἔρχεται Mk 4^{21} a mistranslation of the Aphel or Ittaphal of אתא "bring" or "be brought." Lagrange, *S. Marc* p. xcvi, proposes that the text should read הַיְתִיו 3rd plur. Aph. as in Dn 5^3, and that the ה was mistaken for the interrogative particle.)

Archdeacon Allen has strengthened the case for Mark's Aramaism by giving a list of thirteen places where Mt. has changed an active or middle verb in Mk. into a passive (*ICC, Matthew* p. xxiii).

The three groups of data given above vary in value. The statistics of (*a*) are not very convincing, especially as the free use of ὑπό after a pass. verb is found in reported sayings of Jesus; (*b*) is more weighty, as this use is uncommon in Greek apart from λέγουσι, φασί. [Yet note that in all the exx. from the Gospels under (*b*) Pallis preserves the idiom. The passive is rarely used in MGr.—R. McK.]

(ii) The Infinitive.

In the LXX the influence of the prep. לְ has given the infin. a very wide range. Thackeray (*Gr.* 24) observes the great extension of the inf. with τοῦ, and an enlarged use of the " epexegetic infinitive."

As examples of the former cf. Gen 18^{25}, 2 Sam 19^{21}, 1 Chr 11^{18}. For the latter cf. Dt 29^4 καὶ οὐκ ἔδωκεν Κύριος ὁ Θεὸς ὑμῖν καρδίαν εἰδέναι καὶ ὀφθαλμοὺς βλέπειν καὶ ὦτα ἀκούειν.

Moulton (*Einl.* 346) denies that such infinitival constructions in the NT owe anything to Semitism, except in those books where actual translation from Hebrew or Aramaic is in evidence.

(*a*) τοῦ *c. inf.*—To the full treatment accorded to this construction in *Proleg.* 216 f. little need be added here. Hawkins (*HS*^{2} 48) classifies all the NT uses, and adds, " the telic use of τοῦ with the infinitive remains a decidedly Lucan characteristic."

Radermacher (*Gr.*^{2} 189) recognises its moderate employment in correct Greek (as also by Mt and Mk), but remarks on the frequency and freedom of the use in Lk, Ac, and Paul as resembling the " Jewish-Greek " of the LXX. For class. reff. see Stahl *Synt.* 675, K-G ii. 40. Thumb (*Dial.* 373) recognises ultimate Ionic influence on Attic.

Only one NT example deserves examination as direct Semitism.

2 Rev 12^7 καὶ ἐγένετο πόλεμος ἐν τῷ οὐρανῷ, ὁ Μιχαὴλ καὶ οἱ ἄγγελοι αὐτοῦ τοῦ πολεμῆσαι μετὰ τοῦ δράκοντος.

Charles (*ICC*, i. 322) rejects Moulton's explanation (*Proleg.* 218), and shows that this is a literal translation of a Hebrew construction,[1] already followed by the LXX in several passages. *E.g.* Hos 9^{13} Ἐφράιμ τοῦ ἐξαγαγεῖν = אֶפְרַיִם לְהוֹצִיא, *Ephraim must bring forth*; Ps 25^{14} καὶ ἡ διαθήκη αὐτοῦ τοῦ δηλῶσαι αὐτοῖς = וּבְרִיתוֹ לְהוֹדִיעָם׃ (Vulg. *et testamentum ipsius ut manifestetur illis*); 1 Chr 9^{25} ἀδελφοὶ αὐτῶν . . . τοῦ εἰσπορεύεσθαι κατὰ ἑπτὰ ἡμέρας = אֲחֵיהֶם לָבוֹא לְשִׁבְעַת הַיָּמִים *their brethren had to come in every seven days.* So Eccles 3^{15} ὅσα τοῦ γίνεσθαι = אֲשֶׁר לִהְיוֹת. "Thus in the Hebrew the subject before לְ and the infin. is in the nom., and the Greek translators have literally reproduced this idiom in the LXX." The original Hebrew is then taken to be מִיכָאֵל וּמַלְאָכָיו לְהִלָּחֵם בַּתַּנִּין *Michael and his angels had to fight with the Dragon.* (*N.B.*—א, 046 omit τοῦ.) Charles claims that the same use of the infinitive (this time without τοῦ) accounts for the reading of A in 13^{10} εἴ τις ἐν μαχαίρῃ ἀποκτανθῆναι, αὐτὸν ἐν μαχαίρῃ ἀποκτανθῆναι, and suspects that αὐτόν is a corruption of αὐτός. The Hebrew would be אֲשֶׁר בַּחֶרֶב לָמוּת הוּא בַּחֶרֶב לָמוּת.

Apart from the uncertainties of the text in this passage, this is a useful parallel, as it enables Dr. Charles to meet an obvious objection to his claim that τοῦ πολεμῆσαι is a Hebraism. For τοῦ c. inf. does not seem the most literal translation of לְ c. inf. He gives (*ICC*, i. 356) a list of the various attempts made by the LXX to reproduce this Hebrew idiom. Ps 32^{9} (אB) is a close parallel to Rev 13^{10} (A). For the Hebrew constr. and a full list of examples see G-K § 114 *h-k*, Driver *Tenses* § 204. Guillemard, *Hebraisms in the Greek Testament*, p. 3, *ap.* Mt 2^{6}, quotes the Heb. and LXX of Mic 5^{1}. "An apt example of the practice almost universal, in that version, of rendering לְ with infinitive, after neuter or passive verbs, by τοῦ with Greek infinitive; to the loss very often of all intelligibility or sense: *e.g.* 2 Sam 19^{21}, Gen 18^{25}, 1 Chr 11^{18}. The translators appear to have concluded that a Greek idiom, which was the appropriate interpretation of the Hebrew idiom under certain conditions, was always to be employed as its equivalent: and so have introduced into their version renderings which are otherwise inexplicable. And to this we owe, in great measure, the strange and startling instances of the τοῦ with infinitive, occasionally met with in the NT."

With the one exception of Rev 12^{7} this sweeping assertion is disproved by the analysis given in *Proleg.* 216 ff. "The general blurring of the expressions which were once appropriated to purpose";

[1] This gerundival use of לְ with the infinitive is common to Aramaic and Syriac as well as Hebrew, and Burkitt (*Ev. da-M.* ii. 66) has pointed out that Jn 9^{30} in syr^{sin} is a good example of the infin. used without a finite verb to express "must." The alleged Aramaised Greek of Jn is free from the in] fection that might be looked for, since the Syriac *hādē lemetdammārû bah* is a translation of ἐν τούτῳ γὰρ τὸ θαυμαστόν ἐστιν.

the tendency to substitute ἵνα c. subj. for a noun clause leading to the similar use of τοῦ c. inf. in a few cases; the original adnominal use of the genitive of the articular infinitive: these account not only for the examples dealt with in that analysis, but also for the six LXX passages (viz. Lk 4^{10}, Ac 13^{47}, Rom 11^{10}, Gal 3^{10}, Heb 10^{7}, 1 Pet 3^{10}. The LXX is not accountable for this construction in the Pauline mosaic of Rom 11^{8}).

See also Radermacher *Gr.*² 188 ff., D. Emrys Evans *CQ* xv. 26 f. (*Vide infra*, pp. 484 f.)

(*b*) *The simple infinitive* (*a*) *in jussive sense*, corresponding to late Hebrew independent infin. c. לְ.

1. Lk 24^{47} καὶ κηρυχθῆναι ἐπὶ τῷ ὀνόματι αὐτοῦ μετάνοιαν. Thus *W*¹ 23, *Das Ev. Lucae*, 141. The sense precludes the dependence of the infin. on οὕτως γέγραπται, as seen by syr^sin and arm., which substitute ἔδει for γέγραπται, and by AC²fq vg., which insert καὶ οὕτως ἔδει after γέγραπται. But possibly the infin. depends, by zeugma, on the εἶπεν of v.^{46}. See (β) below.

2. Rev. 13^{10} A. See (*a*) above.

(β) *After* εἶπεν. This is not set forth in G-K or in Driver *Tenses*, but W. C. Allen (*Mark*, p. 50) shows that in late Heb. and Aramaic אָמַר = *command*, was followed by לְ c. infin., and is represented in LXX or Θ by εἶπεν c. infin. Thus 1 Chr 21^{17}, 2 Chr 1^{18} 14^{3} $29^{21.\,27.\,30}$ $31^{4.\,11}$ 35^{21}, Esth 1^{10} 6^{1}, Dn 2^{2} Θ 2^{46} Θ 3^{19} Θ 5^{2}.

1. Mk 5^{43} καὶ εἶπεν δοθῆναι αὐτῇ φαγεῖν.
8^{7} καὶ εὐλογήσας αὐτὰ εἶπεν καὶ ταῦτα παρατιθέναι.
Lk 12^{13} εἰπὲ τῷ ἀδελφῷ μου μερίσασθαι μετ᾽ ἐμοῦ τὴν κληρονομίαν.

Allen grants that the usage in Mt 16^{12} and Lk 9^{54} is not quite parallel.

3. Rom 2^{22} ὁ λέγων μὴ μοιχεύειν μοιχεύεις;

But Lk 12^{13}, Rom 2^{22} (cf. Mt $5^{34.\,39}$) are sufficiently close to P Fay 109^{3}, cited in *Vocab.* 372*a*, to remove them from this category. For Mk 5^{43} see Bl-D § 392 (4). We may add that the simple inf. in jussive sense after λέγω and εἶπον is quite classical: *v.* LS.

(*c*) ἐν τῷ *c. infinitive.*—Regularly used in LXX to render בְּ c. inf. According to Dalman, *WJ* 33, the Targums copy the Hebrew idiom, in Biblical Aramaic the kindred construction of כְּ c. inf. is used (Dan 6^{21}), but the construction was wanting in spoken Aramaic.

The NT occurrences are:

1. Mk 4^{4} (=Mt 13^{4}=Lk 8^{5}) 6^{48}.
Mt $13^{4.\,25}$ 27^{12}.
Lk $1^{8.\,21}$ $2^{6.\,27.\,43}$ 3^{21} $5^{1.\,12}$ $8^{5.\,40.\,42}$ $9^{18.\,29.\,33.\,34.\,36.\,51}$ $10^{35.\,38}$ $11^{1.\,27.\,37}$ 12^{15} 14^{1} $17^{11.\,14}$ 18^{35} 19^{15} $24^{4.\,15.\,30.\,51}$.
Ac 2^{1} 3^{26} 4^{30} 8^{6} 9^{3} 11^{15} 19^{1}.

3. Rom 3^{4} (LXX) 15^{13}, 1 Co 11^{21}, Gal 4^{18}.

4. [Heb 2^{8} $3^{12.\,15}$ 8^{13}. But none of these clearly temporal.]

Mk 4[4] and the majority of the Lucan examples are found in καὶ ἐγένετο constructions (see tables p. 426 above). All the above passages use ἐν τῷ c. inf. in the temporal sense (including Lk 12[15], see Moulton *Einl.* 342 n.[1]) except Ac 3[26] 4[30], Ro 15[13] and those from Hebrews.

The treatment of this construction in *Proleg.* 14, 215 was slightly modified in *Proleg.*[3] 249 (*Einl.* 341) under the influence of E. A. Abbott, who wrote (Nov. 1907): " Of course ἐν τῷ c. infin. =*consisting in*, etc., would be allowable in Attic. But I confess I go with Blass in thinking that ἐν τῷ c. inf. =*during* is non-existent or very rare in Thucydides." The instinctive feeling of two such scholars as Dr. Abbott and Dr. Henry Jackson led to the transference of this " Hebraism " to the category of " possible but unidiomatic Greek." This, of course, does not apply to Ac 3[26] 4[30] or the examples in Hebrews, which do not depart from classical usage. Moffatt's rendering of Rom 15[13] " with all joy and peace in your faith," confirms us in removing this also from the class of Semitisms. The remarkably large number of examples in Luke and Acts is one more evidence of the great influence of the LXX on the style of Luke.

That the temporal sense of ἐν τῷ c. inf. is not impossible Greek seems to be shown by Soph. *Ajax* 554 ἐν τῷ φρονεῖν γὰρ μηδὲν ἥδιστος βίος.

(iii) The Participle.

(*a*) *The Use of the Participle in Periphrastic Tenses.*—See the very full discussion of this question in *Prol.* 226 f., where the periphrastic imperfect is recognised to be a secondary Semitism in the Synoptics and Acts (cc. 1–12), inasmuch as these books are *based on* direct translations from the Aramaic. Blass's treatment (*Gr.* 202 ff., Bl-D § 353) is on the whole accepted (as also by Thumb *Hellen.* 132). The construction is classical enough in itself (see K-G i. 38 ff.), but with a certain emphasis, that justifies its use in John and Paul, but can hardly be maintained elsewhere in the NT. Moulton's papyrus examples of ἔσομαι c. perf. part., and of the periphrastic pluperf. are supplemented in *Einl.* 358, and more might be given. Here we must only stop to note Mt 24[29] πεσοῦνται as a correction for the more vernacular ἔσονται πίπτοντες of Mk 13[25]. [Med. but not MGr, though found in Laconian dialect.—R. McK.]

Restricting our survey to the periphrastic imperf. we notice that this is fairly frequent in the LXX (see Conybeare and Stock, *Selections*, p. 69). The construction is found in Hebrew, though its frequent use is a mark of the later writers, and of the decadence of the language (Driver *Tenses*, § 135 (5)). In Aramaic, however, this analytic tense often supersedes the imperfect. In Biblical Aramaic the periphrastic tense rather emphasised the duration or the repetition of the verbal action or condition (Kautzsch *Aram. Gr.* § 76 (*f*), Marti *Gr.*[2] § 102 (*d*)). Duration was emphasised by this use in the Aramaic of the Babylonian Talmud (Margolis *Gr.* § 58 (*f*)). The same construction is rarely used in the Targums, but is common in the Palestinian Talmud, though generally to bring out the thought of duration, repetition or habit (Stevenson *Aram. Gr.* § 22 (2)).

In the NT we find the imperf. of *εἰμί* with the present partic. as follows:

1. Mk 1^{12} $2^{6.\ 18}$ 4^{38} $5^{5.\ 11}$ 9^{4} $10^{22.\ 32(bis)}$ $14^{4.\ 40.\ 49.\ 54}$ $15^{40.\ 43}$.
   Mt 7^{20} 8^{30} 19^{22}.
   Lk $1^{10.\ 21.\ 22}$ $2^{33.\ 51}$ $4^{20.\ 31.\ 38.\ 44}$ $5^{1.\ 16(bis)\ 29}$ 6^{12} 8^{40} 9^{53} 11^{14} $13^{10.\ 11(bis)}$ 14^{1} 15^{1} 19^{47} 21^{37} $23^{8.\ 53}$ $24^{13.\ 32}$.
   Ac $1^{10.\ 13.\ 14}$ $2^{2.\ 5.\ 42}$ $8^{1.\ 13.\ 28}$ $9^{9.\ 28}$ $10^{24.\ 30}$ 11^{5} $12^{5.\ 6.\ 20}$ 14^{7} $16^{9.\ 12}$ 18^{7} 21^{3} $22^{19.\ 20}$.
2. Jn $1^{9.\ 28}$ 2^{6} 3^{23} 10^{40} 11^{1} 13^{23} $18^{18.\ 25.\ 30}$.
3. (2 Co 5^{19}),[1] Gal $1^{22.\ 23}$, Phil 2^{26}.
4. 1 Pet 2^{25}.

The most important results from an analysis of these data are Mt's almost complete avoidance of this locution when following Mark's narrative, Luke's rejection of it in every instance where a Marcan parallel allows comparison, and yet the freedom with which it occurs in the Lucan writings. It is so often introduced by Luke when absent from the Marcan source that one hesitates to suggest its frequency in cc. 1, 2, in "Proto-Luke," and in Ac 1–12 as evidence of fidelity to Aramaic originals. (Lagrange *S. Luc.* p. cv, observes that most of the examples in the Gospel accord with Greek usage.)

Blass finds in most of the Johannine passages that *ἦν* "has a certain independence of its own." It is strange that though Burney devotes a page and a half to a list of the instances of this usage in the Aramaic of Daniel, it is merely to show that the LXX and Theodotion generally translate by the imperfect, whereas he is silent about the 10 instances that might possibly be adduced from the Fourth Gospel.

A similar construction in which *ἐγένετο* is joined with a present participle appears in Mk 1^{4} $9^{3.\ 7}$ (to be changed by Mt every time). Archd. Allen (*Exp T* xiii. 328 f., *ICC*, *Matthew* xxii.) quotes Dn 1^{16} and La 1^{16} as evidence of its use in LXX or Theod. to render the same idiom in Biblical Aramaic. The construction only comes once in the Apocalypse, here with *γίνομαι*.

Rev 3^{2} *γένου γρηγορῶν*.

(*b*) *Redundant use of Participle.*—For the various forms of this Semitic pleonasm see Dalman *WJ* 20 ff.; *W*[1] 17, [2]14; Lagrange *S. Matthieu* p. xcv, *S. Marc* p. lxxxvii, *S. Luc* p. cvi; W. C. Allen *Exp T* xiii 330; Burney *Aram. Orig.* 52 ff.

It is hard to say when the participle is really pleonastic, but a Semitic flavour clings to the following examples:

(*a*) *Ἐλθών* (*ἐρχόμενος*), *ἀπελθών*, *πορευθείς*, coupled with finite verb. [Med. and MGr.—R. McK.]

1. *Ἐλθών.* Mk 5^{23} 7^{25} 12^{42} $14^{40.\ 45}$ 16^{1}, Lk 15^{25}.
   Ἀπελθών. Mt $13^{28.\ 46}$ 18^{30} $25^{18.\ 25}$.

---

[1] I include 2 Co 5^{19} in spite of the disclaimer in *Prol.* 227. Of recent commentators Windisch agrees with Moulton, but Plummer, Bousset and Lietzmann treat *ἦν* . . . *καταλλάσσων* as a periphrastic imperfect.

Πορευθείς. Lk 7^{22} (=Mt 11^{4}) 13^{22} 14^{10} 15^{25}. (In 8^{14} the Syr. versions have not translated πορευόμενοι.)

[Ac $16^{37.\ 39}$ ἐλθόντες emphatic.]

3. Eph 2^{17} ἐλθὼν εὐηγγελίσατο might possibly come into this class, but ἐλθών is probably significant. (See E. Haupt in Meyer's *Kommentar, in loc.*)

N.B.—This construction, corresponding to the redundant הָלַךְ and בּוֹא in Hebrew, which is also Jewish-Aramaic, is absent from John.

(β) Ἀφείς, καταλιπών (with verb of departure).

1. Mk 4^{36} 8^{13} 12^{12} 14^{50}.
Mt 13^{36} 16^{4} 21^{17} 22^{22}.
N.B.—Jewish-Aramaic rather than Hebrew. It is absent from Luke and John.

(γ) Ἀναστάς or ἐγερθείς (followed by verb of motion).

1. Mk 1^{35} 2^{14} 7^{24} 10^{1}.
Mt 9^{9} 1^{24} $2^{13.\ 14.\ 20.\ 21}$ $9^{7.\ 19}$.
Lk 1^{39} $4^{29.\ 38.\ 39}$ 5^{28} $15^{18.\ 20}$ 17^{19} 23^{1} (24^{12}) 24^{33}.
Ac 5^{6} 8^{27} 9^{39} $10^{20.\ 23}$ 22^{10}.
N.B.—This idiom is common to Hebrew and Aramaic (see Dalman *loc. cit.*). It is absent from John.

(δ) Ἀποκριθεὶς εἶπεν.

This locution is of interest apart from the element of redundancy. It is strictly redundant (in the sense that nothing has been said to which an answer is needed) only in a few places, viz. Mk 9^{5} 11^{14} 12^{35}, Mt 11^{25} 12^{38} (? 15^{15}) 17^{4} 28^{5}. It deserves mention here because of its extreme frequency in the Synoptic Gospels, and its close resemblance to the common Hebrew idiom וַיַּעַן וַיֹּאמֶר. This Hebrew construction is copied by the LXX and the Targums and in Biblical Aramaic עָנֵה וְאָמַר is often found. But Dalman goes on to say that in later Jewish Aramaic this formula is quite unknown. "Direct speech is introduced by the simple אמר. . . . The word for 'answer' in Galilean-Aramaic אֲגִיב is rarely used. . . . אֲתִיב, the word for 'answer' used by Onkelos, appears to be as yet a learned term for 'making good an objection.' Probability supports the view that the formula in question was unknown in genuine Aramaic." This statement is the more significant in view of the following data. The locution is found (sing. or plur. with an occasional λέγει, ἔφη or ἐρεῖ).

1. Mk 15 times, but with a high proportion of λέγει for εἶπεν.
Mt 45 „
Lk 38 „
Ac 5 „ (4^{19} 5^{29} $8^{24.\ 34}$ 25^{9}).

2. In John the participial construction is not found once, but, as Burney shows, ἀπεκρίθη (-θησαν) occurs at asyndeton opening 65 times (and with ἀποκρίνεται once), whilst the verb with a connective particle opens a sentence 11 times. Mk 12^{29} is the only other instance of ἀπεκρίθη as an asyndeton opening. Burney's conclusion is remarkable. "It is difficult to resist the conclusion that ἀπεκρίθη καὶ εἶπεν is a literal rendering of the Aramaic עֲנָה וְאָמַר and ἀπεκρίθησαν καὶ εἶπαν of עֲנוֹ וְאָמְרִין, for which, as we have seen, they stand in Theodotion's Daniel." But in 38 instances ἀπεκρίθη (-ησαν) introduces the words spoken without further verb.

In other words, the first three Evangelists have modelled themselves here on the familiar language of the LXX, whereas John in 26 passages follows the example of the Aramaic part of Daniel, and in the remaining 38 passages uses the ordinary Hellenistic word, betraying his Aramaic cast of thought only by asyndeton.

(ε) Ἐλάλησεν (εἶπεν) λέγων.

1. Mk 8^{28} 12^{26}, Mt $23^{1f.}$ 28^{18}, Lk 14^{3} $24^{6f.}$, Ac 8^{26} 26^{31}.
2. Jn 8^{12}.

(For the indeclinable use of λέγων (λέγοντες) = לֵאמֹר in Rev 4^{1} $5^{11.\,12}$ $11^{1.\,15}$ 14^{6}, see Charles *ICC, in loc.*)

The Hebrew וַיְדַבֵּר . . . לֵאמֹר is also imitated in Biblical Aramaic twice (Dn 6^{22}, Ezr 5^{11}), and in the Targums, but Dalman denies its place in the later Jewish-Aramaic dialects. On the other hand, Lagrange (*S. Matth.* p. lxxxix) finds it a dozen times in the Elephantine papyri and accepts it as commonly spoken, but not very pure Aramaic.

For the constant introduction of oratio recta by *dicens* in 4 Ezra, esp. *dixit dicens*, 11^{37} 12^{40}, see G. H. Box in *OA* ii. 548.

Other participial uses, such as καθίσας, ἑστώς, σταθείς, are less pleonastic than idiomatic, and belong to the category of Semitisms of vocabulary rather than of grammar. See Dalman *WJ* 22 f., *Proleg.*[3] 230, 241. To the same class belongs Mt 5^{2}, καὶ ἀνοίξας τὸ στόμα αὐτοῦ ἐδίδασκεν αὐτοὺς λέγων, on which see Bornhäuser *Die Bergpredigt*, 6 ff.

Wellhausen accounts for the wealth of pleonastic verbs in these constructions by the lack of compound verbs in Semitic languages, which necessitated the use of a special root to express every shade of meaning.

(ζ) Ἀρξάμενος. [See *Proleg.*[3] 182, 240 (*Einl.* 287), *Vocab.* 82 *b*.]

1. Mt 20^{8}.
   Lk 23^{5} 24^{47}.
   Ac 1^{22} 10^{37} 11^{4}.
2. [Jn] 8^{9}.

Torrey's claim (*CDA* 25) that this is an Aramaic idiom in Acts is disputed by J. W. Hunkin (*JTS* xxv. 401) on the ground of the papyri usage, also of its occurrence in Xenophon and Plutarch. See further ἤρξα(ν)το c. infin., below under iv (*a*).

(iv) Indicative Mood.

(a) *Redundant Auxiliary Verb.*

This characteristic of Hebrew and Aramaic has already been dealt with under the Participle, and we there saw that in 26 instances John substitutes the indicative for the participle so familiar to us in the Synoptic formula *ἀποκριθεὶς εἶπεν*. The Johannine *ἀπεκρίθη καὶ εἶπεν* is not the only example of a redundant verb in the indicative. The most striking example is *ἄρχομαι*.

1. Ἤρξα(ν)το *c. infin.*
   Mk 1^{45} 2^{23} 4^{1} $5^{17.\,20}$ $6^{2.\,7.\,34.\,55}$ $8^{11.\,31.\,32}$ $10^{28.\,32.\,41.\,47}$ 11^{15} 12^{1} 13^{5} $14^{19.\,33.\,65.\,69.\,71}$ $15^{8.\,18}$.
   Mt 4^{17} $11^{7.\,20}$ 12^{1} $16^{21.\,22}$ $26^{22.\,37.\,74}$. [Also in other tenses, in sayings of Jesus, 18^{24} and 24^{49}, and in 14^{30}.]
   Lk 4^{21} 5^{21} $7^{15.\,24.\,38.\,49}$ 9^{12} $11^{29.\,53}$ 12^{1} $14^{18.\,30}$ $15^{14.\,24}$ $19^{37.\,45}$ 20^{9} 22^{23} 23^{2}. [Also in other tenses, in five passages from sayings of John the Baptist or of Jesus, 3^{8} 12^{45} $13^{25.\,26}$ 14^{9}.]
   Ac 1^{1} 2^{4} 18^{26} 24^{2} 27^{35}.
2. Jn 13^{5}.

This cannot be called a Hebraism, for though it is found fairly often in the LXX a glance at H-R shows that it has no fixed Hebrew original. Sometimes it represents a word with a definite meaning (*e.g.* Hiph. of יָאַל), often the Hiph. of חָלַל, sometimes (*e.g.* Gen 2^{3}) it is without warrant in the Hebrew, and occurs quite freely in books without a Hebrew source.

On the other hand, it is claimed that its use in Mark is due to the use of שָׁרֵי in Aramaic as an auxiliary verb. See W. C. Allen, *Comm. Mark*, 49 f., who points out (*a*) all the 26 instances in Mk are in narrative, and not one has special emphasis. (*b*) Mt omits all but 6 of Mk's instances, probably from the perception that the word was Aramaic rather than Greek. (*c*) Luke's use is remarkable. He retains only 2 of Mk's cases. Of the remaining 25, 12 are in sayings, 13 occur in narrative, 5 of which occur in passages with Marcan parallels. His conclusion is that the frequency in Mk is due to translation from Aramaic, in Luke partly to the Aramaised Greek of his sources, partly to a feeling that (especially in "began to say") such phrases were quite natural in Greek. I venture to add that its comparative frequency in the LXX may have inclined Luke to its use, as was possibly the case with *ἀποκριθεὶς εἶπεν* (see above, pp. 453 f.).

G. H. Box (*OA* ii. 548) accounts for the very frequent use of *incipere* c. infin. in 4 Ezra as a literal rendering of Heb. הוֹאִיל, and cft. the similar use of *ἄρχεσθαι* in the Gospels.

Radermacher[1] calls attention to a parallel to *ἤρξατο λέγειν* in the vulgar Latin *coepit dicere, c(o)epimus ascendere, ubi coeperit lucescere.*

---

[1] *Idg. F.* xxxi. *Anz.* 6 (his valuable review of Moulton's *Einleitung*). The point is not mentioned in the recent 2nd ed. of his *Neutestamentliche Grammatik.*

The fullest treatment that this idiom has received is by J. W. Hunkin *JTS* xxv. 390–402, "*Pleonastic*" *ἄρχομαι in the New Testament.* Here Dalman's examples of the Aram. שָׁרֵי and post-Biblical Hebrew הִתְחִיל are examined closely, the former being found to carry the ordinary meaning, whilst the latter is sometimes semi-pleonastic. Test. Levi (Charles's ed. pp. 249 f.) is quoted in Aramaic and Greek in support and Enoch lxxxix. 42–49 (which is based on an Aramaic original) is shown to favour this locution strongly. Archd. Hunkin then adduces numerous parallels from Xenophon and two from Aristophanes. This leads him to the conclusion: "The above parallels are quite sufficient to show that the usage of ἄρχομαι with the infin., as we have found it in Mt or Lk, is no indication that either St Matthew or St Luke was acquainted with Aramaic. Nor does it necessarily suggest that any of the documents used by St Matthew or St Luke was originally written in that language. . . ." The loose and somewhat pleonastic way in which "begin" is used by Mark, and in some of the Lucan records of the speeches of Jesus, is admitted to be due to Aramaic.

(*b*) *Tense.*

(**a**) *Historic Present and Imperfect as renderings of Aramaic participle.*

a. Historic Present.—The proportionately high frequency of this in Mark has been claimed as an Aramaism by W. C. Allen, and in John by Burney. [MGr.—R. McK.]

The statistics (given by Hawkins *HS*[2] 144 ff., Burney *Aram. Orig.* 87) are as follows:

1. Mk 151 (of which 72 are words signifying speaking, *e.g.* λέγει, φησίν).
   Mt 93 „ 68 „ „ „
   Lk 9 „ 6 „ „ „
   Ac 13 „ 11 „ „ „
   [*N.B.*—Of Mt's 93 examples, 21 are retained from Mk, and 15 occur in Parables.
   Of Lk's 9 examples, 5 come in Parables.]
2. Jn 164 (of which 121 are words signifying speaking, *e.g.* λέγει, φησίν).

It is evident that both Mt and Lk regarded this as a vulgarism to be removed when possible (see *Proleg.* 121), but Thackeray, *Schweich Lectures*, 20 ff., has shown strong reason for denying that it is due to Aramaism. Taking the first three books of each of the four leading historians he finds the historic present in Herod. 206 times, Thuc. 218, Xen. 61, Polyb. 40. Thus in the classical age it was common to the literary style and to vernacular, whereas in Hellenistic it was increasingly regarded as vernacular. Hawkins (*HS*[2] 213) shows that out of 337 instances in the LXX, 232 occur in the four books of Kingdoms, of which 151 are found in 1 Kgd. Thackeray's thorough examination shows that in Mk as in 1 Kgd the historic present tends to come at or near the beginning of a paragraph. The exceptions are specially dramatic, as Mk $15^{24.\ 27}$ (pictorial). Verbs of (*a*) saying, (*b*) seeing, (*c*) coming and going, (*d*) bringing and sending, are conspicuous. The tense as a rule is dramatic in the sense that it serves to introduce new scenes in the drama. Cf. stage directions, "*Enter* . . .," "*Scene* . . ." "*Loquitur* . . ." He considers Archd. Allen's claim for Aramaism in the Marcan use quite untenable. "Would he maintain that 1 Samuel lay before the Greek translator in Aramaic ?"

Allen pointed out (following Nöldeke, *Syr. Gr.* 190)[1] that in Syriac this participial expression of action described as taking place is practically limited to the verb "to say" (*Exp T* xiii. 329).

β. Imperfect.—Stevenson *Aram. Gr.* 56. In Palestinian Talmud and Midrash "the use of participles in place of perfect tenses in narratives of past events is very characteristic." "In Old Test. Aramaic the participle . . . is a very frequent alternative to a perfect in narratives of past events. It is also used as a progressive tense descriptive of events in the present or the past, and in stating general truths." In the Targums participles often represent Hebr. imperfects, but not to the same extent as in the Palestine Talmud and not in the same uses.

Allen (*ut supr.* also *ICC, Matthew,* p. xxiii) observes that there are about 220 imperfects in Mark, about 30 of which Mt changes to aorist. He finds a striking parallel in Theodotion's version of Daniel (which contains 149 verses from Hebr. and 206 from Aram.). "In rendering Hebr., Theod. uses about 9 imperfects; in rendering Aram., about 64. Of these 64 about 4 correspond to perf., about 12 to imperf., but about 27 to a part., and about 21 to a part. with הָיָה. That is to say, a literal translator, where he had an Aram. partic., or partic. with הָיָה, thought it natural to render them by imperfects."

To estimate the force of this argument we must examine the other historical books in the NT. Hawkins's figures for the imperfect (excluding ἔφη, and with Burney's correction of that for John) are:

Mt 79, Mk 222, Lk 252, Ac 314, Jn 165,

and he adds the explanation that the smaller proportion in Mt and Jn is partly due to the larger amount of discourse in proportion to narrative which they contain (*HS*² 51).

If we adapt these figures to an average per WH page, the results are:

Mt 1·16, Mk 5·4, Lk 3·5, Ac 4·5, Jn 3·1.[2]

A further test reduces the significance of this argument for Aramaic. "I find that in Milligan's *Selections from the Greek Papyri* there are 22 impf. to 111 aor.; in Mk 1, 19 : 39; in Mt 3 and 4, 7 : 29, in Polybius (7 pages in Wilamowitz *Lesebuch*) 37 : 54; and in Appian (6 pp. in *do.*) 90 : 25. So Appian here uses impf. seven times as much as Mk does, and Polybius 1½ times." (Note by J. H. M.)

---

[1] Nöldeke *Syr. Gr.*² 200: "Die Erzählung verwendet das Part. act. (als Praes. histor.) fast nur bei *'âmar*, aber dies *'âmar*, *'âmᵉrâ*, *'âmᵉrîn*, *'âmᵉrân*, 'er, sie sagte'; 'sie sagten' ist sehr häufig."

[2] Burney counts 118 cases in Jn 4–12, *i.e.* 4·37 per WH page.

(b) *Future for Imperative.*

Lagrange (*S. Matthieu*, p. xcv) traces this use in the Gospels to the Semitic use of the imperfect for both jussive and future, calling attention to the alternation of imperatives and jussives in Dan 4^{11-13}.

Thus he accounts for Mt 5^{48} *ἔσεσθε* (Lk 6^{36} *γίνεσθε*), 6^{5} *οὐκ ἔσεσθε*, $20^{26.\,27}$ *ἔσται* (so Mk $10^{43.\,44}$, but Lk 22^{26} *γινέσθω*), 23^{11} *ἔσται* (so Mk 9^{35}).

On the other hand, Mt 21^{3} (=Lk 19^{31}) *ἐρεῖτε*, where Mk 11^{3} has imper. *εἴπατε*.

(c) *Aorist for Present.*

In *Proleg.* 134 f. reason was given for regarding a number of NT examples, which seem to come under this heading, as either epistolary or gnomic aorists, or else as instances of the very old use (ordinary in early Sanskrit) of the aorist of the proximate past.

Two instances stand apart from the others.

Mk 1^{11} (=Mt 3^{17}=Lk 3^{22}) *ἐν σοὶ εὐδόκησα*. This may be explained as summary aorist (referring to the "30 blameless years," so G. G. Findlay), or the aor. of indefinite time reference, or else as the aor. of proximate past (the Dove the sign). All these are fully in accord with Greek usage. Notice, however, the allusion to Is 42^{1} בְּחִירִי רָצְתָה נַפְשִׁי, LXX, *ὁ ἐκλεκτός μου, ὃν εὐδόκησεν ἡ ψυχή μου* (B *προσεδέξατο αὐτὸν ἡ ψ. μου.*), quoted again (with *ὁ ἀγαπητός* for *ὁ ἐκλεκτός*) in Mt 12^{18}. Here the Hebr. perf. (*delighteth*, רָצָה is stative) is represented by Greek aor. Allen (*ICC*, *Matthew* 29) says, "The aor. *εὐδόκησα* is modelled on the aorists of the LXX in this passage, which were probably interpreted as implying the divine election of Israel, and so here the divine election of the Messiah."

Mt 23^{2} *ἐπὶ τῆς Μωϋσέως καθέδρας ἐκάθισαν οἱ γραμματεῖς καὶ οἱ Φ.* One naturally remembers Ps 1^{1} with the three perfects יָשַׁב עָמַד הָלַךְ rendered in the LXX by three aorists *ἐπορεύθη, ἔστη, ἐκάθισεν*; cf. Ps 122^{5}. For the whole subject see Driver *Tenses* §§ 12, 35.

Prof. G. C. Richards, reviewing *Proleg.* in *JTS* x. 284, wrote: "Is it ingressive, 'they came to sit,' effective, 'they seated themselves,' or constative, 'they sat'? It would be very inappropriate to call it gnomic. Wellhausen claims it as an Aramaism. Is it not probable that he is right, and that a limited number of verbal forms in the NT will defy analysis on Greek lines?" To which Moulton replied (*Einl.* 220 n.[1]): "I am not sure of this, although, as often shown, I am in no way opposed to the assumption of 'translation-Greek.' It may be translated by 'they seated themselves,' an act of indefinite time reference in the past, as every rabbi in turn claimed this *ex-cathedra* authority on beginning his life-work; the tense is then natural. It is ingressive, and expresses the self-assertion of the would-be Moses more vigorously than the present could; and it is iterative, for it applies to many individual scribes."

Wellhausen[1] admits that *ἐβάπτισα* Mk 1^{8} (=*βαπτίζω* Mt 3^{11}, Lk 3^{16}) and *ἐδίστασας* Mt 14^{31} are rather different, as they refer to an action

---

[1] See W^{1} 25, ^{2}18.

completed in a moment, or, as we should prefer to describe the tense, "the aorist of the thing just happened" (proximate past).

7. Nouns.

The peculiar idioms in the treatment of nouns come more conveniently under other headings. One or two special uses are mentioned below.

(1) *Casus Pendens*: see above, A 3.

(2) *Accusative Case*: see under adverbial expressions, B 5. A special instance of alleged Hebraism is Mt 4^{15} *ὁδὸν θαλάσσης* for דֶּרֶךְ הַיָּם. But see W. C. Allen (*ICC in loc.*), who shows that it is not from LXX, but probably due to careless copying from some other version.

(3) *Genitive Case*: see under adjectival substitutes, B 3.

A Hebraic use of the genitive after a perf. pass. part., or a verbal adj., has been suspected in such passages as:

1. Mt 25^{34} *οἱ εὐλογημένοι τοῦ πατρός* (בָּרוּךְ יהוה, LXX *εὐλογητὸς κυρίου*, or *εὐλογημένος ὑπὸ κυρίου*).
   Lk 2^{27} *τὸ εἰθισμένον τοῦ νόμου*. [But is quite class. =*τὸ ἔθος τοῦ νόμου*.]
   Mt 11^{11} (=Lk 7^{28}) *ἐν γεννητοῖς γυναικῶν* (cf. Job 14^{1} 15^{14} 25^{4}, *γεννητὸς γυναικός*, יְלוּד אִשָּׁה and contr. Gal 4^{4} *γενόμενον ἐκ γυναικός*).
2. Jn 6^{45} (LXX) *καὶ ἔσονται πάντες διδακτοὶ Θεοῦ* (=Is 54^{13} לִמּוּדֵי יהוה).
3. 1 Co 2^{13} *οὐκ ἐν διδακτοῖς ἀνθρωπίνης σοφίας λόγοις, ἀλλ' ἐν διδακτοῖς πνεύματος*.

If in some of these we must acknowledge the influence of the LXX, we can also see an extension of a use common in poetry, *e.g.* Soph. *Ajax* 807 *φωτὸς ἠπατημένη*, Eur. *Or.* 497 *πληγεὶς θυγατρός*. See K-G i. 376.[1]

(4) *Dative Case*: see under adverbial substitutes, B 5. A few special uses remain for treatment.

(*a*) Dat. of agent after pass. part. is claimed by Wellhausen as Aramaic, "as *amandus mihi*, or rather *amatus mihi*" (*W*[1] 25, [2]18). Nöldeke (*Syr. Gr.*[2] § 279) attests the fondness of Syriac for this construction. The one NT example is Lk 23^{15} *ἐστὶν πεπραγμένον αὐτῷ*. It is not easy to see why Lk should have preserved the Roman procurator's statement in Aramaised Greek. But the numerous examples of the dat. of the agent after a perfect passive given by K-G i. 422 show that it was perfectly good Greek. Cf. Thuc. i. 51, 118; Hdt. vi. 123; Isoc. iv. 4; Lys. xxiv. 4; Xen. *Anab.* I. viii. 12, VII. vi. 32; *Cyr.* VII. ii. 15, and more closely Dem. *c. Aphob.* 1: *δεῖ διηγήσασθαι τὰ τούτῳ πεπραγμένα περί ἡμῶν*. Cf. Kälker 279: "Dativus, qui cum passivo conjungitur, eadem notione qua *ὑπό* c. genit., saepissime a Polybio usurpator: *e.g.* i. 13. 3." P Petr ii. 13(19)^{13} (iii/B.C.) (=Witk. 8^{13}) *οὐθέν σοι μὴ γενηθῆι λυπηρόν, ἀλλὰ πᾶν ἐ[μοὶ ἔστ]αι πεφροντισμένον τοῦ σε γενέσθαι ἄλυπον*.

---

[1] With Jn 6^{45}, 1 Co 2^{13}, Mr. E. E. Genner cft. Soph. *El.* 343–4 *νουθετήματα κείνης διδακτά*, and such phrases as *τὰ πεπολιτευμένα αὐτῶν* in the orators.

(*b*) Dat. after ἔνοχος, claimed by Wellhausen as "ungriechisch." (*W*[1] 33 f. omitted in ed.[2]). Mt 5[22] ἔνοχος ἔσται τῇ κρίσει.

J. C. James, *Language of Palestine* 72 n.[4], observes: "It is equivalent to יִתְקְטֵיל אִתְקְטָלָא Onk. Gen. 26[11], LXX θανάτῳ ἔνοχος ἔσται." But θανάτου has the best MS support, and it is not easy to see what bearing the Hebrew original מוֹת יוּמָת, or the Aramaic of Onkelos, has upon the alleged Semitism of the Greek idiom. Moulton has shown conclusively (*Einl.* 378 n.[1] *Vocab.* 217) that this, as well as other NT uses of ἔνοχος, accords with Greek usage.

(*c*) Dr. Charles explains the difficult dative in Rev 21[8] τοῖς δὲ δειλοῖς καὶ ἀπίστοις . . . τὸ μέρος αὐτῶν as a reproduction of the Hebrew idiom by which לְ introduces a new subject (*ICC* i. p. cxlviii, ii. 216 n.[1]). Viteau *Étude* ii. 41 f., cft. 2 Es 10[14] καὶ πᾶσι τοῖς ἐν πόλεσιν ἡμῶν . . . ἐλθέτωσαν.

8. Prepositions and Improper Prepositions.

The *extensive* use of many prepositional phrases in LXX is recognised by Thackeray as due to Hebrew influence.

Ἀπό and ἐκ in constructions influenced by מִן.

(*a*) Thackeray (*Gr.* 46) notes that in LXX ἀπό c. gen. is thus used instead of acc. after αἰσχύνεσθαι, εὐλαβεῖσθαι, λανθάνειν, προσέχειν, τρέμειν, ὑπερηφανεύεσθαι, ὑπεροπᾶν, φοβεῖσθαι, φυλάσσεσθαι.

NT instances are:—

1. Mt 7[15] 10[17] 16[6. 11. 12] (=Lk 12[1]), Lk 20[46] προσέχειν ἀπό.
 Mt 10[28]=Lk 12[4] μὴ φοβηθῆτε ἀπὸ τῶν. . . . Hawkins (*HS*[2] 64) observes that against this NT example the LXX contains the idiom 49 times, 25 of them with ἀπὸ προσώπου, out of about 440 occurrences of the verb.
 Mk 8[15] 12[38], βλέπειν ἀπό (see p. 31 above).
 Lk 12[15] φυλάσσεσθε ἀπό. (Cf. Xen. *Cyr.* II. iii. 9, *Hell.* VII. ii. 10.)

2. 1 Jn 5[21] φυλάξατε ἑαυτὰ ἀπὸ τ. εἰδ.
 2[28] μὴ αἰσχυνθῶμεν ἀπ' αὐτοῦ ἐν τῇ παρουσίᾳ αὐτοῦ.

W[1] 32 attributes φεύγειν and φοβεῖσθαι ἀπό to Semitic influence, but *W*[2] 25 concedes that they can also be Greek. So κρύπτω ἀπό is as old as Homer (*Od.* xxiii. 110) (Bl-D § 155. 3). For ἀπὸ προσώπου, however, see below. Mr. Emrys Evans touches upon this idiom in a paper upon Case-Usage in the Greek of Asia Minor (*CQ* xv. 28). He cites *C. and B.* ii. p. 565 (no. 466), ἐὰν δέ τις μὴ φοβηθῇ τούτων τῶν καταρῶν. By the side of this ablatival genitive he sets *Pelagia* x. 12 (Usener, p. 12), μὴ δειλιάσῃς ἀπ' αὐτοῦ, and concludes that the NT construction is a development quite natural to Greek—a "secondary" Hebraism. [Προσέχω and φυλάσσω ἀπό in Med. and MGr, βλέπω ἀπό in Med. Gr, φοβοῦμαι ἀπό in MGr, which prefers φοβ. c. acc.—R. McK.]

(*b*) Mt 11[19]=Lk 7[35] δικαιοῦσθαι ἀπό is taken as Aram. מִן קֳדָם =Hebr. מִפְּנֵי by Wellhausen (*W*[1] 32, [2]25). But it seems far better to take this ἀπό (as so often in the Κοινή) as=ὑπό, marking the agent after a passive verb.

(*c*) The causal use of ἀπό has been explained thus. (For ἀπό in LXX =causal מִן, cf. Gen 9[11], Ps 76[7].) *W*[1] 32, [2]25 cites from Synoptics:

1. Mk 2[4] D ἀπὸ τοῦ ὄχλου (for διὰ τὸν ὄχ.).
   Mt 18[7] οὐαὶ ἀπὸ τῶν σκανδάλων, 14[26] 28[4] ἀπὸ τοῦ φόβου [add 13[44] ἀπ τῆς χαρᾶς αὐτοῦ].
   Lk 22[45] ἀπὸ τῆς λύπης, 24[41] ἀπὸ χαρᾶς [add 19[3] ἀπὸ τοῦ ὄχλου, 21[26] ἀπὸ φόβου].
   Ac 11[19] ἀπὸ τῆς θλίψεως, 12[14] ἀπὸ τῆς χαρᾶς, 22[11] ἀπὸ τῆς δόξης.
2. Jn 21[6] ἀπὸ τ. πλήθους τ. ἰχθύων.
4. Heb 5[7] ἀπὸ τ. εὐλαβείας.

This usage is classical (see LS). For vernacular examples see Kuhring 35 f., *Vocab.* 58 f. For parallels to Mt 18[7] see *Prol.*[3] 246. [Med. and MGr.—R. McK.]

(*d*) A special kind of ablative use appears in—

1. Mt 27[24] ἀθῷος ἀπό, Ac 20[26] καθαρὸς ἀπό [cf. Gen 24[41] ἀθῷος ἀπό (ἐκ)= נָקִי מִן], for which abundant parallels from papyri are given by Kuhring 52 f. See also Vogeser *Spr. d. gr. Heiligenlegenden* 26.
   Lk 24[31] ἄφαντος ἐγένετο ἀπ' αὐτῶν, claimed as a Hebraism by Psichari *Essai* pp. 204 ff. See *Vocab.* 95*b*.

(*e*) The partitive use of ἀπό after ἐσθίειν.

Mk 7[28]=Mt 15[27]. McNeile *Comm. in loc.* "The Hebraic ἐσθίειν ἀπό (אָכַל מִן), frequent in the LXX, is not found elsewhere in NT; cf. ἐσθ. ἐκ." It is an instance of the more general use of ἀπό or ἐκ c. gen. to replace the partitive gen. in later Greek. Cf. MGr. δειπνάω ἀπὸ χῶμα, *I eat* (*of*) *earth* (Thumb *Handb.* 102). [Very common in MGr.—R. McK.]

(*f*) The phrase ἀπὸ μιᾶς Lk 14[18], has been claimed as a literal translation of Aramaic מִן חֲדָא "all at once," "suddenly." See above, p. 28. Moulton asks (*Einl.* 15 n.[1]), "But why μιᾶς fem.? Simply because it is a Greek idiom." Blass (*Gr.* 140 f., Bl-D § 241, n. 6) regards it as a stereotyped phrase, "with one mind or voice," and cft. Aristoph. *Lysistr.* 1000, ἀπὸ μιᾶς ὑσπλαγίδος (strictly of runners in a race, who rush off together at the fall of the single rope). Plummer *ICC in loc.* supplies γνώμης for an "expression unique in Gr. literature," and cft. Philo (*De Spec. Legg.* ii. p. 311), ἀπὸ μιᾶς καὶ τῆς αὐτῆς γνώμης. For the Semitic use of the fem. see G-K, § 122 *q*. I cannot trace the Aramaic idiom in the grammars of Marti, Kautzsch, or Dalman, or in Dalman's *Wörterbuch*. But the Syriac *mechᵉdâ* supplies that meaning.[1] Moulton (*op. cit.*)

[1] As Mr. C. R. North informs me.

adds: "My thesis does not in the least deny the Aramaic origin: I only protest that the translation is quite idiomatic." It appears that such idioms are not uncommon in Med. Gr. and in MGr. For one example (in a story from Epirus) see Thumb *Handb.* 240, τὸ βράδυ ἐχτύπησαν τὸ κούτσουρο ὅλοι ἀπὸ μνιὰ καὶ τὸ ἔκαναν κομμάτια, also p. 244. [Med. and MGr.—R. McK.]

Διά.

Mt 11[2] πέμπειν διά=שְׁלַח בְּיַד, Hebr. and Aram. So *W*[1] 31. The idiom is seen more clearly in Mk 6[2] διὰ τῶν χειρῶν, Ac 2[23] ἔκδοτον διὰ χειρὸς ἀνόμων, where Torrey (*CDA* 6) observes that the same Aramaic words are rendered παραδίδοται εἰς τὰς χεῖρας τῶν ἁμαρτωλῶν in Mk 14[41]. See, however, *supra*, p. 29, *Vocab.* 145 f., where it is said that διὰ χειρός c. gen. is based on בְּיַד, but is not a literal translation. "It is obviously modelled upon the vernacular phrase διὰ χειρός, of money paid 'directly.'"

Εἰς.

(*a*) Εἰς c. acc. in place of predicative nom. (esp. with εἶναι, γίνεσθαι, λογίζεσθαι) or predicative acc. ("Semitic influence unmistakable," Bl-D, § 157. See *Oxf. Heb. Lex.* p. 512).

Moulton (*Proleg.* 71 f.) discounts Hebraism, "for the vernacular shows a similar extension of the old use of εἰς expressing destination," but he allows Semitic influence in some of the passages, adding examples (p. 76) from non-Semitic sources. For further examples see Radermacher *Gr.*[2] 21 and D. Emrys Evans *CQ.* xv. 24 f. [Med. Gr.—R. McK.]

Johannessohn (*Kasus und Präp.* 4) gives examples of this LXX rendering of לְ, and others where LXX thus renders Hebr. nominative. But his most significant results show that whereas the predic. nom. with εἰμί and γίνομαι is common in all four books of Mac., εἰς c. acc. is used instead of the predic. nom. in 1 Mac only, where it occurs 15 times, and instead of the predic. acc. 5 times.

See F. Schulthess (*ZNTW* xxi. 221) for denial that לְ predicative is Aramaic. Where it is found in Bibl. Aram. it is לְ resultant and is a Hebraism. So in Syriac it is restricted to OT translation.

1. With γίνεσθαι. Mt 21[42] (LXX), Lk 13[19], Ac 5[36].
   With εἶναι. Mt 19[5] (LXX), Lk 3[5] (LXX).
   With λογισθῆναι. Ac 19[27].
   For predicative acc. Mt 21[46], Ac 7[21] (LXX) 13[47] (LXX) 13[22] (cf. 1 K 13[14] εἰς ἄρχοντα=לְנָגִיד).

2 With γίνεσθαι. Jn 16[20], Rev 8[11] 16[19].
   With εἶναι. 1 Jn 5[8]. (But A. E. Brooke *in loc.* takes it=*are for the one thing, tend in the same direction, exist for the same object.*)

3. With εἶναι. 2 Co 6^{18} (LXX), Eph 5^{31} (LXX). Cf. Ro 5^{18} (εἰς κατάκριμα (sc. ἐγένετο).
With λογισθῆναι Rom 2^{26} 4^{3} (LXX) 9^{8}.

4. With εἶναι Heb 1^{5} (LXX) 8^{10} (LXX).

(*b*) πιστεύειν εἰς c. acc. See Burney, *Aram. Orig.* 34, and *Proleg.* 68, where a table is given showing the distribution of the various constructions with πιστεύειν. Semitic influence is recognised in the literal translation of הֶאֱמִין בְּ by the prepositional phrase, reserving the simple dative for ה״ לְ.

1. Mt 18^{6} (=Mk 9^{42} ABLΘ), Ac 10^{43} 14^{23} 19^{4}.

2. Jn 1^{12} $2^{11.\ 23}$ $3^{16.\ 18.\ 36}$ 4^{39} $6^{29.\ 35.\ 40}$ $7^{5.\ 31.\ 38.\ 39.\ 48}$ 8^{30} $9^{35.\ 36}$ 10^{42} $11^{25.\ 26.\ 45.\ 48}$ $12^{11.\ 36.\ 37.\ 42.\ 44.\ 46}$ $14^{1.\ 12}$ 16^{9} 17^{20}.
1 Jn $5^{10.\ 13}$.

3. Rom 10^{14}, Gal 2^{16}, Phil 1^{29}.

4. 1 Pet 1^{8}.

(*c*) A curious use of εἰς appears in Ac 7^{53} εἰς διαταγὰς ἀγγέλων, where Torrey (*CDA* 33) explains that εἰς = לְ, which sometimes means "according to," "by." לְפִקּוּדֵי מַלְאָכִין "by the ordering of angels." Cf. Ps 119^{91} לְמִשְׁפָּטֶיךָ "according to thy ordinances."

(*d*) The phrase πορεύου (ὕπαγε) εἰς εἰρήνην (Mk 5^{34}, Lk 7^{50} 8^{48}) must be due to the LXX, where it often represents the Hebrew לֵךְ לְשָׁלוֹם. See *OHL*, p. 516, for similar examples of this adverbial use of לְ with abstract nouns.

(*e*) For εἰς ἀπάντησιν = לִקְרַאת see *Proleg.* 14 n.[4]. [Med. Gr.—R. McK.]

Ἐν.

(*a*) For the instrumental use of ἐν see *Proleg.* 12, 61, 104, and above p. 23; also Kuhring 43 f., Rossberg 28. [Med. Gr.—R. McK.]

(*b*) The causal use of ἐν has some support from the papyri: see Kuhring 43, Rossberg 29, *Vocab.* 210. H. A. A. Kennedy (*Exp T* xxviii. 323), however, gives a list of passages in which the LXX rendering of בְּ has probably left its influence, with the meaning *because of, by reason of, for the sake of.*

1. Mt 6^{7}, Ac 7^{29} (LXX). Add Ac 24^{16}.

2. Jn 16^{30}.

3. Rom $1^{21.\ 24}$ 5^{3}, 1 Co 4^{6} 7^{14}, 2 Co $12^{5.\ 9}$, Ph 1^{13}. Add Rom 9^{7} (LXX).

4. Add Heb 10^{10} 11^{18} (LXX).

(*c*) Dr. Moulton acknowledged a Semitism in ὁμολογεῖν ἐν (*Prol.* 104), and observes Nestle's warning that the construction with בְּ is Aramaic rather than Hebrew (*Einl.* 169). Lagrange *S. Matthieu*, p. civ, "En aram. ידא à *Pa.* ou plutôt *Aph.* Le *syr sin* met le ב même à Jo 12^{42}."

Moulton also accepted G. G. Findlay's suggestion that ὀμνῦναι ἐν and εἰς (LXX, but not in Pent.) are Hebraistic, occurring in religious formulae, and only in Mt and Rev.

1. Mt 5³⁵·³⁶ 23¹⁶⁽ᵇⁱˢ⁾ ¹⁸⁽ᵇⁱˢ⁾ ²⁰⁽ᵇⁱˢ⁾ ²¹⁽ᵇⁱˢ⁾ ²²⁽ᵇⁱˢ⁾.
2. Rev 10⁶ (LXX).

Lagrange (*l.c.* p. civ) " En grec on emploie l'accus. ou κατά, ou le dat. La construction avec ἐν est donc sûrement sémitique ; en aram. שבע à l'Itpe. et ב."

The πιστεύειν ἐν of Mk 1¹⁵ Moulton afterwards accepted as translation Greek (*contra*, *Proleg.* 67) under the influence of Dr. Burkitt, who compared Jer 12⁶ μὴ πιστεύσῃς ἐν αὐτοῖς ὅτι λαλοῦσιν πρὸς σὲ καλά.[1]

" Then εὐδοκεῖν ἔν τινι (once in Polyb.) would be encouraged by the same tendency, in place of regular simple dative (see Milligan *Thess.* p. 106)—the acc. also is used " (J. H. M.).

To the same class belongs σκανδαλίζεσθαι ἐν.

1. Mt 11⁶ 13⁵⁷ 26³¹·³³, Mk 6³, Lk 7²³.

Lagrange *S. Matthieu*, p. cviii, " Le prép. ἐν est un reflet du sémitique . . . . L'araméen est probablement תקל à *Itpa.* Les verss. syrr. ont repris כשל comme l'héb."

In addition to these verbal constructions with ἐν, *W*¹ 32 ²24 claims ἔρχεσθαι ἐν=" to come with," " to bring."

1. Mt 21³² ἦλθεν . . . ἐν ὁδῷ δικαιοσύνης=*brought the method of righteousness.*
   16²⁸ ἐρχόμενον ἐν τῇ βασ. αὐτοῦ=*bringing his kingdom.*
   Lk 23⁴² ὅταν ἔλθῃς ἐν τῇ βασ. σου (BL εἰς=ἐν acc. to Wellh. Note that D reads ἐν τ. ἡμέρᾳ τ. ἐλεύσεώς σου).

This interpretation seems gratuitous in every instance.

Other uses of this preposition mentioned by Wellh. may be simply instances of the intrusive ἐν so common in the Κοινή (Kuhring 12), *e.g.* ἐν ποίᾳ ἐξουσίᾳ (Mk 11²⁸), ἐν δυνάμει (Mk 9¹), ἐν δόλῳ (Mk 14¹). Add to these Mt 7² ἐν ᾧ μέτρῳ, 7⁶ ἐν τοῖς ποσὶν αὐτῶν, 22¹⁶ ἐν ἀληθείᾳ (contr. Mk 12¹⁴=Lk 20²¹ ἐπ' ἀληθείας).

1. Lk 16²⁶ ἐν πᾶσι τούτοις (ℵBL) is corrected to ἐπί in AD; cf. σὺν πᾶσιν τούτοις (24²¹). Possibly both represent בְּ.
   Mk 1²³ 5² ἐν πνεύματι ἀκαθάρτῳ is a Semitism of thought which naturally employs this possible construction in Greek.

(*d*) ἐν τῷ c. infin. with *temporal* force. See pp. 25, 450 f. A distinctive feature of Luke. Hebraic, not Aramaic construction.

---

[1] F C. B. to J. H. M. (letter, 30/8/10), " οὐκ ἐπιστεύσατε αὐτῷ (Mk 11³¹ =Mt 21²⁵) is trd. by the Old Syriac, ' believed not in him ' : in the Peshiṭta is ' believed not him.' The Peshiṭta is literal : the Old Syriac gives the Aramaic idiom."

῎Εμπροσθεν, ἔναντι, ἐναντίον, ἐνώπιον. (See above, § 130.)

Radermacher (*Gr.*[2] 145) speaks of the first and last of these, together with πρὸ προσώπου and ἀπὸ προσώπου, as Semitising substitutes in the province of πρό.

῎Εμπροσθεν 84 times in LXX for לִפְנֵי. **᾿Ενώπιον** hundreds of times in LXX, for either לִפְנֵי or לְעֵינֵי, **ἔναντι** and **ἐναντίον** both very common in LXX, generally for בְּעֵינֵי. Burney remarks (*Aram. Orig.* 15) that Hebrew distinguishes between לע" *in the* (*physical*) *sight of*, and בע" *in the* (*mental*) *sight of*, and finds a corresponding distinction in the NT use of ἐνώπιον and ἐναντίον.

For the three Hebrew expressions, Aramaic uses קֳדָם.

῎Εμπροσθεν is good Greek, surviving in MGr as ἐμπρός, μπροστά. The two following uses, however, are undeniably Semitic.

1. Mt 11[26]=Lk 10[21] *οὕτως εὐδοκία ἐγένετο ἔμπροσθέν σου.*

Hebrew רָצוֹן מִלְּפָנֶי, Aram. רַעֲוָא קֳדָם = *thy good pleasure, thy will.*

Mt 18[14] οὕτως οὐκ ἔστιν θέλημα ἔμπροσθεν τοῦ πατρὸς ὑμῶν.

Mt 23[13] ὅτι κλείετε τὴν βασιλείαν τ. οὐρ. ἔμπροσθεν τῶν ἀνθρώπων, may be due to wrong translation of קֳדָם which serves also for ἐναντίον

῎Εναντι. For Κοινή use see Wackernagel *Hellenistica* 1 ff. and *Vocab. s.v.*

Lk 1[8], Ac 7[10] (LXX) 8[21] אABD (LXX).

᾿Εναντίον. *Before, in the presence of.* For use in this sense in papp. see *Vocab. s.v.*

Lk 1[6] 20[26] 24[19], Ac 7[10] ABCD (LXX) 8[32] (LXX).

᾿Ενώπιον. See above, p. 15, and *Vocab. s.v.* Survives in the καθαρεύουσα, not in MGr vernacular. [Med. Gr.—R. McK.]

1. Lk 22 times, Ac 13 times.
2. Jn 20[30], 1 Jn 3[22], 3 Jn [6], Rev 34 times.
3. Rom (3), 1 Co (1), 2 Co (3), Gal (1), 1 Ti (6), 2 Ti (2): 4 of which from LXX.
4. Heb (2), Ja (1), 1 Pet (1)

Κατέναντι. *Opposite, over against*, Mt 21[2], Mk 11[2] 12[41] 13[3].
In the presence of, Mt 27[24] (BD).
Rom 4[17], 2 Co 2[17] 12[19].
For the former meaning in Κοινή, see *Vocab. s.v.* Very common in LXX.

Κατενώπιον. *In the presence of*, Eph 1[4], Col 1[22], Jude [24].
LXX 7 times (+Dan Θ, 1). See *Vocab. s.v.*

᾿Απέναντι. *Over against*, Mt 27[61]; *against*, Ac 17[7].
In the presence of, Mt 27[24] (אAL), Ac 3[16] Rom 3[18] (LXX).

Here we may conveniently take the prepositional phrases with *πρόσωπον*.

Ἀπὸ προσώπου = מִפְּנֵי.

1. Ac 3[20] 5[41] 7[45].
2. Rev 6[16] (? LXX) 12[14] 20[11] (LXX).
3. 2 Th 1[9] (LXX).

Ἐπὶ πρόσωπον = עַל פְּנֵי.

1. Lk 21[35].

Ἐπὶ προσώπου.

1. Ac 17[26] (cf. Jer 32[12] [LXX = 25[26] Heb.]).

Πρὸ προσώπου = לִפְנֵי.

1. Mk 1[2] = Mt 11[10] = Lk 7[27] (LXX).
   Lk 1[76] (LXX), 9[52] 10[1], Ac 13[24].

In all these passages the influence of the Greek of the LXX is unmistakable.

Κατὰ πρόσωπον used adverbially, as in Ac 25[16], 2 Co 10[1], Gal 2[11], is certainly not Semitic, but its prepositional use in Lk 2[31], Ac 3[13], though not uncommon in Greek (cf. Xen. *Cyr.* VI. iii. 35, *τὴν κατὰ πρόσωπον τῆς ἀντίας φάλαγγος τάξιν*, "the post immediately in front of the enemy's phalanx"), is suggested by the OT idiom.

Radermacher (*Gr.*[2] 143) observes that while some of the improper prepositions and prepositional substitutes so common in NT are good enough Greek (*e.g.* *ἄτερ, ἔναντι, κατέναντι, ἀπέναντι*), as a general rule this wealth of substitutes (esp. periphrastic substitutes as *ἀπὸ προσώπου, πρὸ προσώπου*) is due to Semitic influence, from which those papyri are not free which exhibit corresponding usages (*e.g.* *ἐνώπιόν τινος*).

Μετά.

(*a*) **Ποιεῖν** (*ἔλεος*) **μετά** *τινος* corresponding to עָשָׂה חֶסֶד עִם (as often in LXX, *e.g.* Gen 26[29]).

1. Lk 1[72] 10[37] : 1[58] (*μεγαλύνειν ἔλεος μετά*).
   Ac 14[27] 15[4] (*ὅσα ἐποίησεν ὁ θεὸς μετ' αὐτῶν*).
   Cf. Tob 12[6] *περὶ ὧν ἐποίησεν μεθ' ὑμῶν.*
   1 Mac 10[27] *καὶ ἀνταποδώσομεν ὑμῖν ἀγαθὰ ἀνθ' ὧν ποιεῖτε μεθ' ἡμῶν.*
   Herm. *Sim.* v. 1[1] *περὶ πάντων ὧν ἐποίησε μετ' ἐμοῦ.*

See *Proleg.*[3] 246 and *Vocab.* 401*a*, where, on the strength of Kuhring's citation from a Byzantine pap., this "solitary Hebraism left to *μετά*" was said to be demolished. But J. H. M. afterwards was inclined to withdraw this statement and recognise translation Greek (note by W. F. H., 1914). For Hebr. and Aram. idiom see Torrey *CDA* 38).

(*b*) **Πολεμεῖν μετά** *τινος.*

2. Rev 2^{16} 12^{7} 13^{4} 17^{14} (also *ποιῆσαι πόλεμον μετά*, Rev 11^{7} 12^{17} 13^{7} 19^{19}).

See *Proleg.*[3] 106, 246, *Vocab.* 401*a* for use in papp. and MGr (for which see Thumb *Hellen.* 125, *Handb.* 103). But in view of Charles's treatment of Rev 12^{7} (*ICC* i. 322, 356: see above, pp. 448 f.), we should probably allow for the influence of the LXX in all these passages.

Μεταξύ.

The idiom in Mt 18^{15} *μεταξὺ σοῦ καὶ αὐτοῦ μόνου*=*privately* is Aramaic (*W*[1] 32, [2]26, " unter vier augen," Nöldeke, *Syr. Gr.* 189 n.[1]: " Even the Greek text has the Aramaising idiom "). This is literally rendered by syr[vet], which gives the same idiom for *κατ' ἰδίαν* in 17^{19} 20^{17}, Mk 9^{28} (see *W*[1] 32, [2]26 also McNeile *Comm. Matthew*, 266).

Παρά.

Παρά c. acc. to mark comparison after a positive adj. or a noun, or a verb. Semitic acc. to *W*[1] 28, [2]21 (=מִן).

1. Lk $13^{2.\,4}$ 18^{14} (אBL).

The use of *παρά* after a comparative is very common in Hellenistic, merely extending a classical usage. There are many exx. in NT, esp. in Hebrews. But the instances given above conform to the very frequent construction in LXX, where Thackeray (*Gr.* 23) recognises influence of Hebr. גָּדוֹל מִן, but notices that in MGr *μεγαλύτερος ἀπό* has become a normal phrase (see Thumb *Handb.* 102).

Πρός.

Πρός c. acc.=*with* has been claimed as due to Aram. לְוָת (=*apud*, *παρά*, or *ad*, *πρός*) by J. R. Harris (*OPJ* 7 ff.), Burney (*Aram. Orig.* 28 f.).

1. Mk 6^{3} (=Mt 13^{56}) 9^{19} (=Lk 9^{41}) 14^{49}.
2. Jn 1^{1}, 1 Jn 1^{2}.
3. 1 Th 3^{4}, 2 Th 2^{5} 3^{10}, 1 Co $16^{6.\,7}$, 2 Co 5^{8} 11^{9}, Gal 1^{18} 2^{5} $4^{18.\,20}$, Ph 1^{26}, Philem [13].
4. Heb 4^{13}.

Mr. G. R. Driver (*Orig. Lang.* 2*a*) denies Aramaism in any strict sense, regarding this as " an extension of many classical usages, particularly in such phrases as *ἐνθυμεῖσθαι πρὸς αὐτόν*." He cft. *πρός με παῖσαι* " to play with me," quoted by Stephanus (*Thes.* iii. 573).

Hellenistic usage may be seen in *Syll.*[3] 1109^{41} (A.D. 178) *διδόντες ἡμιφόριον μέχρις ὅτου πρὸς γυναῖκας ὦσιν.* D. S. Sharp cites Epict. iv. 9. 13, *πρὸς ὃν ἐστί σου πιθανώτερος.* With Heb 4^{13} cf. the formula *ὡς πρὸς σὲ τοῦ λόγου ἐσόμενου*, " Knowing that you will be held accountable," P Hib 53^{0} (B.C. 246), P Oxy ix. 1188^{17}. [Med. Gr.—R. McK. See also Jannaris *Gr.* § 1658 (*c*).]

9. Conjunctions and Particles.

Ἀλλά.—The Aramaic אֶלָּא combines exceptive and adversative meanings. Hence it has been claimed that ἀλλά and εἰ μή are sometimes confused in the NT (*W.*[1] 24, [2]16). We must note, however, that in LXX ἀλλά translates בִּלְתִּי in Gen 21[26].

Ἀλλά *for* εἰ μή (or ἐὰν μή).

The clearest cases are:

Mk 4[22] οὐ γάρ ἔστιν τι κρυπτόν, ἐὰν μὴ ἵνα φανερωθῇ· οὐδὲ ἐγένετο ἀπόκρυφον, ἀλλ' ἵνα ἔλθῃ εἰς φανερόν

where ἀλλά and ἐὰν μή are parallel;

9[8] οὐκέτι οὐδένα εἶδον ἀλλὰ τὸν Ἰησοῦν μόνον μεθ' ἑαυτῶν (ACLWΘ. εἰ μὴ ℵBD 33=Mt 17[8] εἰ μή *sine var.*)

where the alternative texts are equivalent.

For Mk 10[40] (=Mt 20[23]) see *Proleg.* 241. In *Einl.* 269 n.[1], Moulton cft. Soph. OT 1331, but adds, "Of course I have nothing against the recognition of an Aramaic idiom as the reason for the choice of a similar Greek usage to render an Aramaic locution."

Εἰ μή (or ἐὰν μή) for ἀλλά.

1. Mt 12[4] ὃ οὐκ ἐξὸν ἦν αὐτῷ φαγεῖν . . . εἰ μὴ τοῖς ἱερεῦσιν μόνοις.
   Lk 4[26] καὶ πρὸς οὐδεμίαν αὐτῶν ἐπέμφθη Ἠλείας εἰ μὴ εἰς Σάρεπτα. . . .
2. Rev 21[27] καὶ οὐ μὴ εἰσέλθῃ εἰς αὐτὴν πᾶν κοινὸν καὶ ὁ ποιῶν βδέλυγμα καὶ ψεῦδος, εἰ μὴ οἱ γεγραμμένοι ἐν τῷ βιβλίῳ τῆς ζωῆς τοῦ Ἀρνίου.
3. Gal 2[16] οὐ δικαιοῦται ἄνθρωπος ἐξ ἔργων νόμου ἐὰν μὴ διὰ πίστεως Χ. Ἰ.

Hort (*Comm. James*, p. xvi) denies identification in Gal 1[19]: "For the very late exchange of εἰ μή and ἀλλά in NT there is no probability whatever. In three other books of NT in less good Greek (Mt, Lk, Rev), the meaning *looks like* this, but fallaciously."

We may quote for classical usage Xen. *Hellen.* II. ii. 10, ἐνόμιζον δὲ οὐδεμίαν εἶναι σωτηρίαν εἰ μὴ παθεῖν upon which G. M. Edwards observes, "'They had no safety except to suffer' may be equivalent for 'they had no safety, but must suffer.' Cf. Mt 26[42] and Shaks. *Kg John* IV. i. 91." ("Is there no remedy? None but to lose your eyes.") For ἐὰν μή= "but only" Mr. E. E. Genner cft. Andocides *de Myst.* § 89: μηδ' ἐπ' ἀνδρὶ νόμον τιθέναι ἐὰν μὴ τὸν αὐτὸν ἐπὶ πᾶσιν Ἀθηναίοις.

Εἰ.

In solemn asseverations εἰ *negandi* corresponds to Hebrew אִם. (1 Sam 14[45] חַי יהוה אִם יִפֹּל ζῇ Κύριος εἰ πεσεῖται, cf. 2 Sam 11[11].)

1. Mk 8[12] ἀμὴν λέγω ὑμῖν, εἰ δοθήσεται τῇ γενεᾷ ταύτῃ σημεῖον.

   (*N.B.*—In parallels Mt 16[4] 12[39], Lk 11[29], καὶ σημεῖον οὐ δοθήσεται.)

4. Heb 3[11] 4[3. 5] (LXX).

A Hebrew idiom. "Aramaic has nothing like it, except in the Targums. Probably a reminiscence of LXX; Gen 14[23] etc." Lagrange, *S. Marc*, p. lxxxi.

Καί.

The use of καί in contrasted statements is a characteristic of the Fourth Gospel. Burney (p. 66) treats this as a literal rendering of ו adversative, which is common to Hebrew and Aramaic. This use of καί "but" is a slight extension of καί "and yet," discussed under *A*, 4 (*f*) (β), and can be found in class. Gr., both with and without οὐ. (See K-G ii. 248.) The best examples in the Gospel are Jn 1[5] 17[11]. Cf. also 1[10. 11] 3[11. 19. 32] 4[20] 5[39. 40. 43. 44] 6[70] 7[4. 19. 30] 8[20. 52] 9[30] 12[34] 16[5] 20[29] 21[11]. [Med. and MGr.—R. McK.]

For other uses of καί see under *A*, 4 above (Parataxis).

Ὅτι.

(*a*) Ὅτι *recitativum* is of course well established in Greek, (Goodwin *MT* 285 f). Guillemard observes that in Gen 28[16] 44[28] [*v.l.*] it is used to translate אַךְ or אָכֵן "verily," and is often used for כִּי, which is sometimes (*e.g.* Gen 29[33], Jos 2[24], Jer 22[22]) strongly asseverative. He claims that in many NT passages (*e.g.* Mt 7[23] 10[7] 14[26] 19[8] 26[65. 72. 74] 27[43]) that is the force of ὅτι.

Archd. Allen (*Exp T* xiii. 330, *Comm. Mark* 48) attributes frequency in Mark to influence of Aramaic דְּ. For use of ὅτι *recitativum* in papp. see *Vocab. s.v.* [Med. and MGr.—R. McK.]

(*b*) Ὅτι for relative pronoun. See above *B*, 1 (*e*) (β).

(*c*) Ὅτι for temporal particle. Burney (*Aram. Orig.* 78) detects confusion of דְּ = ὅτι and דְּ = ὅτε in two passages:

Jn 9[8] *οἱ θεωροῦντες αὐτὸν τὸ πρότερον ὅτι προσαίτης ἦν.*
12[41] *ταῦτα εἶπεν Ἠσαίας ὅτι εἶδεν τὴν δόξαν αὐτοῦ.*

In the latter this explanation is unnecessary, whilst in the former Mr. G. R. Driver (*ut supra*) cft. 4[35], also Ps-Nicod. I. B. i. 3 εἶδον τοὺς Ἑβραίους ὅτι ἐστρώννυον ἐν τῇ ὁδῷ τὰ ἱμάτια αὐτῶν, where the ὅτι clause, according to the late Greek use, plainly means "strewing their garments in the way."

Similarly—

Ἵνα.

(*a*) Ἵνα for relative pronoun. See above *B*, 1 (*e*) (pp. 434 ff.).

(*b*) Ἵνα for temporal particle. Burney (*l.c.* 78) accounts for ἵνα as for ὅτι above in the phrase ἔρχεται ὥρα ἵνα c. subj.,—a characteristic of Jn (who however uses ὅτε in 4[21. 23] 5[25] 16[25], and ἐν ᾗ in 5[28]).

2. Jn 12^{23} 13^{1} $16^{2.\,32}$ [1]
   [Rev 2^{21}, but here ἵνα μετανοήσῃ is clearly final.]

Mr. G. R. Driver cites several instances from late Greek of καιρὸς ἔρχεται (ἐστιν) ἵνα, whilst MGr εἶνε καιρὸς νὰ ἔλθῃς is the regular idiom for "it is time for you to come." To this we may add, ἦρθεν ἡ ὥρα νὰ πεθάνῃ, "the hour came to die" (Thumb *Hdb.* 187). This usage is therefore at most a secondary Semitism, and can quite as easily be explained by the writer's strong partiality for this particle, which had already gained great flexibility in the Κοινή.

Ἵνα μή.

Burney (*Aram. Orig.* 100) finds very cogent proof of translation from Aramaic in

Jn 12^{40}, where ἵνα μή represents the Aram. דְּלָא, though the Hebr. פֶּן is rendered μήποτε in LXX, which is retained when the same citation (Is 6^{10}) is given in Mt 13^{15} and Mk 4^{12}. Moreover, the Pesh. translates *dᵉlâ*. But ἵνα μή is perfectly good Greek (see K-G ii. 378 f., Goodwin *MT* § 315), and its general use in the Ptolemaic papyri is clear from Mayser *Gr.* ii. 240 ff. When Burney says that μήποτε never occurs in Jn, though found in Mt 8 times, Mk 2, Lk 6, he does not add that ἵνα μή is found in every book of the NT except 2 Th, 2 Tim, 1 Pet, 3 Jn, often with the meaning "lest." It is equally significant that μήποτε does not occur in Rev, though ἵνα μή is found there 11 times. Yet Dr. Charles claims that Hebr. not Aram. is the background of the Apocalypse.

Dr. McKinlay observes that in the Modern Version of the NT διὰ νὰ μή is used in every passage in Jn where ἵνα μή occurs. Pallis generally has γιὰ νὰ μή, but sometimes μήπως.

C. MISTRANSLATION OF SEMITIC WORDS OR PHRASES.

The following instances are amongst those that have been offered:

1. Mk 2^{4} ἀπεστέγασαν τὴν στέγην καὶ ἐξορύξαντες χαλῶσι. Wellhausen, because of the reversed order and the redundancy, retranslates the first clause שַׁקְלוּהִי לְגַּרָא which might also mean "they brought him to the roof" (*W*[1] 37). Schulthess (*ZNTW* xxi, 220) protests that this Aramaic phrase would mean "to uncover the roof," but not "to bring him to the roof," for which אַפִּיק would be the right word.

[1] C. J. Ball *Exp T* xxi. 91 so takes it in 8^{56}, reading אפי for יומי "rejoiced when he saw my face." For a different explanation see under *C*, below (p. 475). But see *Vocab. s.v.* ἵνα (5).

Mk 7[31] *ἐξελθὼν ἐκ τ. ὁρίων Τύρου ἦλθεν διὰ Σιδῶνος εἰς τ. θάλασσαν τ. Γαλ.* Wellh. (*ib.* 37) suspects *διὰ Σιδῶνος*=בְּצַיְדָן, which should have been rendered *πρὸς Βησσαϊδάν* (so 6[45] D). But this geographical correction is unnecessary.

See also Archd. W. C. Allen, *Comm. Mark*, 50 f.

Mt 23[25] *καθαρίζετε τὸ ἔξωθεν τοῦ ποτηρίου κ. τῆς παροψίδος, ἔσωθεν δὲ γέμουσιν ἐξ ἁρπαγῆς κ. ἀκρασίας.* Luke 11[39], rightly, *τὸ δὲ ἔσωθεν ὑμῶν γέμει.* The sense in Mt requires *γέμετε* for *γέμουσιν*. In Aram., participle in both clauses. (*W*[1] 36, [2]27.)

28[1] *ὀψὲ δὲ σαββάτων, τῇ ἐπιφωσκούσῃ εἰς μίαν σαββάτων.* Torrey (*C. H. Toy Studies*, 300) postulates an Aram. בַּאֲפּוּקֵי שַׁבְּתָא נָגְהֵי חַד בְּשַׁבָּא, "after the Sabbath, in the night introducing the first day of the week." This is not a case of mistranslation, but of a painfully close rendering of an Aramaic phrase. We are asked to believe that Mt adds this Aram. clause to the sentence in the Greek Mk, which he is following pretty closely, and then translates it into Greek!

Lk 1[39] *εἰς πόλιν Ἰούδα.* Torrey (*l.c.* 290 ff.) solves this palpable difficulty by supposing Hebr. אֶל מְדִינַת יהוּדָה (better than Aram. לִיהוּד מְדִינְתָא), which should have been translated *εἰς τ. χώραν τῆς Ἰουδαίας.* During the first century A.D. the meaning "city" supplanted the earlier "province" as the force of מְדִינָה.

2[1] *ἀπογράφεσθαι πᾶσαν τὴν οἰκουμένην.* Torrey (*l.c.* 293) conjectures כָּל־הָאָרֶץ, *i.e.* "all the land" (*γῆν*), not "all the world."

11[41] *τὰ ἐνόντα δότε ἐλεημοσύνην, καὶ ἰδοὺ πάντα καθαρὰ ὑμῖν ἐστι.*

For the first clause Mt 23[36] has *καθάρισον πρῶτον τὸ ἐντός*, which alone gives the right sense. Wellh. (*W*[1] 36, [2]27) attributed the variants to a confusion between דַּכִּי "cleanse," and זַכִּי "give alms." Torrey (*l.c.* 312) doubts such a use of זַכִּי in the time of the evangelists, but had independently conjectured an Aram. original הִיא דִלְגוֹ עֲבִדוּ צַדִּקָא "that which is within make righteousness." Here עֲבִדוּ צִדְקָא is the regular idiom for "give alms," and exactly represents *δικαιοσύνην ποιεῖν*, which has that meaning in Mt 6[1-4]. On the other hand, Burney (*Aram. Orig.* 9) gives evidence that in New Hebr. and Aram. זַכֵּי means both "to purify" (as well as the normal דַּכֵּי) and also "to give alms."

11[47. 48] *οὐαὶ ὑμῖν, ὅτι οἰκοδομεῖτε τὰ μνημεῖα τ. προφητῶν, οἱ δὲ πατέρες ὑμῶν ἀπέκτειναν αὐτούς. Ἄρα μάρτυρές ἐστε καὶ συνευδοκεῖτε τοῖς ἔργοις τῶν πατέρων ὑμῶν· ὅτι αὐτοὶ μὲν ἀπέκτειναν αὐτούς, ὑμεῖς δὲ οἰκοδομεῖτε.*

Torrey (*l.c.* 313) shows that *ὑμεῖς δὲ οἰκοδομεῖτε* should be as Mt 23[31] *υἱοί ἐστε* (*αὐτῶν*). The Aram. וְאַתּוּן בְּנִין לְהוֹן "and ye are children of theirs," was misread, the noun בְּנִין being easily confused with the participle בָּנַיִן which had come in the previous verse, and the word לְהוֹן, now taken as the direct object, was omitted from the Greek as unnecessary.

Lk 12[46] *καὶ διχοτομήσει αὐτὸν καὶ τὸ μέρος αὐτοῦ μετὰ τῶν ἀπίστων θήσει* (=Mt 24[51], where *ὑποκριτῶν* for *ἀπίστων*). Torrey (*l.c.* 314 f.) suspects Aram. original וִיפַלְּגִנֵּהּ מְנָתֵהּ עִם שַׁקָּרַיָּא "and will divide him his portion with the unfaithful," assuming that ו was inserted before מְנָתֵהּ through mistaking the indirect object of the first suffix for a direct object. The verb יְשִׂים would then be added to the sentence to complete the sense, and the whole now ran וִיפַלְּגִנֵּהּ וּמְנָתֵהּ עִם שַׁקָּרַיָּא יְשִׂים.

On the other hand, the commentators point to the barbarous methods of punishing oriental slaves. Plummer cites Herodotus for *διατέμνω*, and Suetonius *Calig.* xxvii: *multos honesti ordinis . . . medios serra dissecuit.* Moulton, *Exp T* xiv. 430, *Vocab.* 165, quotes from a sepulchral inscr. (iii/iv A.D.) *διχοτομέω* in a figurative sense.

In any case Q seems to have been followed by both Mt and Lk without question.

12[49] *καὶ τί θέλω εἰ ἤδη ἀνήφθη;* The required meaning, "How I wish that it were already kindled," can hardly be got from the Greek, but appears at once if the two Hebraisms are recognised. (*a*) מָה not only=*τί* "what?" but is used in exclamations="how," for exx. see G-K § 148. (*b*) Θέλω εἰ found twice in LXX (unfortunately the underlying Hebr. is not available in either passage), "to wish that": Is 9[5] *καὶ θελήσουσιν εἰ ἐγενήθησαν πυρίκαυστοι* "and they shall wish that they had been burned with fire" (see Ottley *Isaiah* i. p. 97); Sir 23[14] *καὶ θελήσεις εἰ μὴ ἐγεννήθης* "so shalt thou wish that thou hadst not been born."

The exclamatory use of *τί* is found in MGr, *τί καλά* "how fine!" (Thumb *Handb.* 181).

Torrey (*l.c.* 315) finds that literal translation into Aramaic gives the regular idiom for the meaning required וּמָה צָבֵא אֲנָא אִלּוּ מִן כַּדּוּ דְלֵקַת.

24[32] *οὐχὶ ἡ καρδία ἡμῶν καιομένη ἦν;* Variants for *καιομένη* in D and oldest verss. (syr. lat[vet]) testify to difficulty felt from beginning. Torrey (*l.c.* 316) suggests יָקָר "heavy," "slow to understand" for יָקֵד "burning" (*καρδία* = לֵב = intelligence).

Ac 2^{47} *ὁ δὲ κύριος προσετίθει τοὺς σωζομένους καθ' ἡμέραν ἐπὶ τὸ αὐτό.*

Torrey (*CDA* 10 f.) rejects the ordinary meaning of *ἐπὶ τὸ αὐτό* which is the LXX equivalent for יַחְדָּו, pointing out that the Aram. word for this is לַחֲדָא "together," "into one," and is indeed used in the Pal. Syr. in Jn 17^{23}, and by the Syr. verss. in Jn 11^{52}, to translate *εἰς ἕν*. But in the Judæan dialects of Aramaic this word means "greatly," and is used regularly in the Onkelos Targum for the Heb. מְאֹד. The original Aramaic is thus reconstructed: וּמָרְיָא מוֹסֵף הֲוָא לְדִי חַיִּין כָּל יוֹם לַחֲדָא. The translator is then supposed to have misread לְדִי as a direct object (*vide supra, ap.* Lk 12^{46}), and to have taken the last word as = *ἐπὶ τὸ αὐτό* instead of *σφόδρα*: "And the Lord added greatly day by day to the saved."

The main objections to this conjecture are: (*a*) Such a blunder is not likely on the part of one who could give the right rendering in 6^{7}: *καὶ ἐπληθύνετο ὁ ἀριθμὸς τῶν μαθητῶν ἐν Ἰερουσαλὴμ σφόδρα.* (*b*) A comparison of 1 Co 11^{18} *συνερχομένων ὑμῶν ἐν ἐκκλησίᾳ ἀκούω σχίσματα ἐν ὑμῖν ὑπάρχειν*, with *v.*^{20} *συνερχομένων οὖν ὑμῶν ἐπὶ τὸ αὐτὸ οὐκ ἔστιν κυριακὸν δεῖπνον φαγεῖν*, shows clearly that *ἐπὶ τὸ αὐτό* and *ἐν ἐκκλησίᾳ* are synonymous terms. Indeed, we are inclined to account for the juxtaposition of the two phrases in Ac 2^{47} D *ἐπὶ τὸ αὐτὸ ἐν τῇ ἐκκλησίᾳ* as a marginal gloss by a scribe who recognised their equivalence. Mr. A. A. Vazakas (*JBL* xxxvii. 106 ff.) shows that the phrase under discussion is an ordinary Greek expression very common in the LXX, but in the NT (Ac 1^{15} $2^{1.\,47}$, 1 Co $11^{18.\,20}$ 14^{23}) and the Apostolic Fathers (Barn 4^{10}, Ignat. *Eph.* 13^{1}, *Magn.* 7^{1}, *Philad.* 6^{2} 10^{1}, Clem. *ad Cor.* 34^{7}) it has a technical meaning, signifying the union of the Christian body. It might generally be translated "in church." Professor Burkitt (*JTS* xx. 321 ff.) repudiates Dr. Torrey's Aramaic explanation and translates "The Lord was joining such as He had foreordained to be saved daily together."

J. de Zwaan (*Beginnings of Christianity*, I. ii. 55) accepts this "splendid observation of Torrey." Dr. Foakes-Jackson (*HTR* x. 358) is forced to the conclusion that "an Aramaic original is at the back of this and other strange expressions." Dr. H. J. Cadbury (*AJT* xxiv. 454), while not granting that the intensive explanation of *ἐπὶ τὸ αὐτό* is really necessary, shows cause for thinking that, if it does seem required, "an original Hebr. or even an extensive use of the Greek phrase, like that familiar to Luke from its abundant use in the LXX, would cover the case fully as well."

3^{16} *καὶ ἐπὶ τῇ πίστει τοῦ ὀνόματος αὐτοῦ τοῦτον ὃν θεωρεῖτε καὶ οἴδατε ἐστερέωσεν τὸ ὄνομα αὐτοῦ καὶ ἡ πίστις ἡ δι' αὐτοῦ ἔδωκεν αὐτῷ τὴν ὁλοκληρίαν ταύτην ἀπέναντι πάντων ὑμῶν.*

Torrey (*l.c.* 14 ff.) remarks that "the ugly repetition of *τὸ ὄνομα αὐτοῦ* obscures the sense and spoils the sound." A literal rendering into Aramaic is given.

וּבְהֵימָנוּתָא דִּי שְׁמֵהּ לְהָדֵן דִּי חָזַיִן אַנְתּוּן וְיָדְעִין אַנְתּוּן תקף שמה
וְהֵימָנוּתָא דִּי בֵהּ יַהֲבַת לֵהּ חֲלִימוּתָא דָא קֳדָם כָּלְכוֹן׃

By pointing תַּקֵּף שְׁמֵהּ (=*ἐστερέωσε τὸ ὄνομα αὐτοῦ*) as תַּקִּף שָׁמֵהּ (=*ὑγιῆ ἐποίησεν αὐτόν*) the sentence now reads: "And by faith in His name He hath made strong this one whom ye see and know; yea, the faith which is through Him hath given him this soundness before you all."

Dr. Burkitt, however, secures excellent sense, as well as "characteristically Lucan rhetoric," by placing a colon before *τοῦτον* and omitting *ἐπί* with א*B. The passage now runs: "Ye killed the Prince of Life, whom God raised from the dead, whereof we are witnesses, even to the faith in His name: this man whom ye see and know His name hath made strong, and the faith which is through Him hath given Him this perfect soundness before you all."

Ac 4[25] *ὁ τοῦ πατρὸς ἡμῶν διὰ πνεύματος ἁγίου στόματος Δαυεὶδ παιδός σου εἰπών.*

Torrey (*l.c.* 16 f.) offers an Aramaic rendering

הוּא דִּי אֲבוּנָא לְפוּם רוּחָא דִּי קוּדְשָׁא דָּוִיד עַבְדָּךְ אָמַר׃

and shows that the common confusion between היא and הוא has obscured the true meaning, "that which our father David, Thy servant, said by the mouth (command) of the Holy Spirit." The feminine היא must be so rendered, but the masc. הוא gave rise to the first clause in the Greek text.

11[28] Here, as in Lk 2[1], Torrey would remove the rhetorical exaggeration by supposing that an original אַרְעָא has been rendered by *οἰκουμένη* instead of by *γῆ*. In neither case is the explanation convincing. The remaining instances given by Professor Torrey are less impressive (Ac 8[10] 13[1] 15[7]). See *CDA* 18 ff., and discussions by Burkitt, Vazakas, and de Zwaan already referred to.

2. Burney (*Aram. Orig.* 103 ff.), in addition to the many examples of mistranslated דְּ, thinks that mistranslation is to be traced in the following passages: Jn 1[15. 29] 2[22] 6[63] 7[37. 38] 8[56] 9[25] 20[2. 18]. But since so eager a supporter of his thesis as Professor Torrey confesses that he is "unable to follow Burney in any one of these instances" (*HTR* xvi. 329), it will be enough to take the two most important.

Jn 7[37. 38] Dr. Rendel Harris (*Expos* VIII. xx. 196) followed some Old Latin and Western texts (*e.g.* D) in redivision of verses, which Burney, it seems (*l.c.* pp. 385 ff.), had already adopted for Semitic parallelism. Thus the passage reads:

'Εάν τις διψᾷ ἐρχέσθω πρός με
καὶ πινέτω ὁ πιστεύων εἰς ἐμέ,
καθὼς εἶπεν ἡ γραφή, Ποταμοὶ ἐκ τῆς κοιλίας αὐτοῦ
ῥεύσουσιν ὕδατος ζῶντος.

Burney's solution of this "scripture" allusion is gained by a blending of Joel 3[18] (4[18] Hebr.) and Zech 14[8], together with an identification of מַעְיָן, the word for "fountain" in Joel (also found in the Targum of Ps 104[10], Pr 5[16] 8[28]) and מְעִין (Hebr. מֵעִים) used of "belly" (Dn 2[32]).

Mr. G. R. Driver (*Orig. Lang.* 6 n.) quotes G. B. Gray's criticism, that this explanation ignores the pronoun *αὐτοῦ*, whilst מֵיעוֹהִי and מַעְיָנֵיהּ would not easily be confused either by eye or ear.

Dr. Rendel Harris's explanation is drawn from the very slight difference between the Syriac words for "belly" *Karsâ*, and for "throne" *Kurseyâ*. His theory is that in an early Aramaic Book of Testimonies a composite quotation from Zech 14[8], "Living water shall go out of Jerusalem," and Jer 3[17], "They shall call Jerusalem the Lord's throne" occurred, which may also be traced in Rev 22[1. 17]. It is to be noted that *ὁ θέλων* in the last passage corresponds closely to *ὁ πιστεύων* in Jn 7[38]. Under this treatment the words *καθὼς εἶπεν . . . ζῶντος* are a comment by the evangelist.

For explanations dispensing with any emendation of the Greek text, see W. E. Barnes *JTS* xxiii. 421, H. St. J. Thackeray, *The Septuagint and Jewish Worship*, 66 f.

8[56] *'Αβραὰμ ὁ πατὴρ ὑμῶν ἠγαλλιάσατο ἵνα ἴδῃ τὴν ἡμέραν τὴν ἐμήν, καὶ εἶδεν καὶ ἐχάρη.*

Burney, observing that "rejoiced to see" does not give a satisfactory meaning, suggests that "longed to see" is what we should expect. This he finds in the Syriac *sewaḥ*, used in the Pesh. for this verb. The ordinary meaning of *sewaḥ* is "long for," but in Mt 12[18] "delights in," "rejoices," where in the quotation from Is 42[1] it represents the Hebr. רָצָה.

He acknowledges that the verb is not known to occur in W. Aramaic.

Torrey (*HTR* xvi. 340) improves on this by showing that in the Targums בָּע (בּוּעַ) is the regular equivalent of the Hebr. גִּיל and the Gr. *ἀγαλλιᾶσθαι*, whilst the most common Aramaic verb for "seek," "pray," is בְּעָא. It is easy to see how the final א might be dropped by haplography, בְּעָא אברהם

"Abraham prayed that he might see," thus becoming בָּע אברהם "Abraham exulted to see." Lagrange seems to doubt whether the form בָּע is found. In any case Burney's suspicion of an Aramaism in the ἵνα clause is needless.

Dr. McKinlay quotes ἀγιαλλοῦται ἡ ψυχὴ νὰ μάθῃ διὰ τὴν κόρην from a mediaeval romance, and cft. MGr *χαίρομαι νά σε θωρῶ*, "I'm glad to see you."

It should be added that Torrey proposes (*l.c.* 338 ff.) emendations of the text by working back to an Aramaic original at 7$^{3.37}$ 11$^{33.38}$ 14$^{2.31}$ 20^{17}.

Archdeacon Charles has shown with abundance of illustration throughout his Commentary on the *Revelation of John* that the successful resolution of difficulties in the text lies often in retranslation into Hebrew. The following examples are the most impressive:

Rev 10^{1} *καὶ οἱ πόδες αὐτοῦ ὡς στῦλοι πυρός.*

Hebr. רֶגֶל, which normally = "foot," also means "leg" (so rendered by LXX in 1 Sam 17^{6}, Dt 28^{57}), whilst *πόδες* also translates כְּרָעַיִם = "legs," "thighs," Ex 29^{17}, and other passages.

This is obviously the meaning here. (See Charles *Studies* 97 ff., *ICC* i. 259.) [So often in Med. and MGr.—R. McK.]

13^{3} *καὶ ἐθαυμάσθη ὅλη ἡ γῆ ὀπίσω τοῦ θηρίου.*

That is וַתִּתְמַהּ כָּל־הָאָרֶץ מֵאַחֲרֵי הַחַיָּה, where מֵאַחֲרֵי is corrupt for מֵרְאוֹת = *βλέπουσα*. Cf. 17^{8} *καὶ θαυμασθήσονται οἱ κατοικοῦντες ἐπὶ τῆς γῆς, ὧν οὐ γέγραπται τὸ ὄνομα ἐπὶ τὸ βιβλίον τῆς ζωῆς ἀπὸ καταβολῆς κόσμου βλεπόντων τὸ θηρίον.* Also 17^{6} *ἐθαύμασα ἰδὼν αὐτήν.* (See *ICC* i. 351.)

13^{11} *καὶ ἐλάλει ὡς δράκων* = וַתְּדַבֵּר כַּתַּנִּין probably for וַתְּאַבֵּד כַּתַּנִּין = *καὶ ἀπώλλυε* or *καὶ ἦν ἀπολλύων*. This very confusion occurs in 2 Chr 22^{10} וַתָּקָם וַתְּדַבֵּר אֶת־כָּל־זֶרַע הַמַּמְלָכָה (LXX *ἀπώλεσε*, Vulg. *interfecit*, scribal error for וַתְּאַבֵּד 2 Ki 11^{1}. *Oxf. Hebr. Lex.* 181*b*). Cf. Rev 9^{11} *ὄνομα αὐτῷ Ἑβραιστί Ἀβαδδών, καὶ ἐν τῇ Ἑλληνικῃ ὄνομα ἔχει Ἀπολλύων.* (See Charles *Studies* 100 f., *ICC* i. p. cli.)

15^{5} *(ἠνοίγη) ὁ ναὸς τῆς σκηνῆς τοῦ μαρτυρίου ἐν τῷ οὐρανῷ.*

This very difficult phrase = הֵיכַל אֹהֶל מוֹעֵד בַּשָּׁמַיִם which may be a corruption of הֵיכַל אֱלֹהִים שֶׁבַּשָּׁמַיִם = *ὁ ναὸς τοῦ θεοῦ ὁ ἐν τῷ οὐρανῷ*. (Cf. 11^{19} where this very sentence occurs, *ἠνοίγη ὁ ναὸς τ. θεοῦ ὁ ἐν τ. οὐρ.*)

15^{6} *ενδεδυμένοι λίθον καθαρὸν λαμπρόν.*

Λίθον AC (defended as original text against *λίνον* by WH *App.*[2] 139) is extremely difficult. Charles (*ICC* ii. 38) shows that ἐνδεδυμένοι λίθον = לְבוּשִׁים שֵׁשׁ. But שֵׁשׁ = βύσσινος in Gen 41[42], Ex 28[35], whilst it seems to mean λίθος in Esth 1[6], and the phrase which is there rendered στῦλοι λίθινοι (עַמּוּדֵי שֵׁשׁ) is given as στῦλοι μαρμάρινοι in Cant 5[15]. For the same mistranslation as here in Ep Jer [72] see Dr C. J. Ball's note *OA*. i. p. 610.

(2[22] ἰδοὺ βάλλω αὐτὴν εἰς κλίνην = הִנְנִי מַפִּיל אֹתָהּ לְמִשְׁכָּב, where βάλλω represents the causative of πίπτω and נָפַל לְמִשְׁכָּב = "fall ill." See Charles *Studies* 99, *ICC* i. 71. Here retroversion does not remove a mistranslation, but explains an obscure idiom.) [But the pass. of βάλλω = "to be laid up" occurs in Aesop *Fab*. cclvii (cited Field *Notes* 70 n.[3]); πίπτω in Med. Gr. = "to fall ill," and in MGr πέφτω = "to go to bed," "fall asleep."—R. McK.]

D. GENERAL SUMMARY.

1. Classification of Semitisms.

In the Introduction to this volume (pp. 14 ff.) Semitism has been defined as " a deviation from genuine Greek idiom to a too literal rendering of the language of a Semitic original." The term secondary Semitism marks a possible but unidiomatic Greek construction, which strains ordinary Greek usage to conform to a normal Semitic construction. Dr. J. de Zwaan[1] has analysed the possibilities very carefully by distinguishing between (*a*) a " Greek," *i.e.* a writer with a perfect knowledge of Greek, and (*b*) a " Semite," *i.e.* one who writes Greek with an imperfect knowledge of the language. He then shows that either (*a*) or (*b*) may attempt four things: translation from a Semitic dialect into (1) idiomatic, or (2) Semiticising Greek; original composition in (3) idiomatic, or (4) Semiticising Greek. Primary Semitisms are said to be those which a " Semite " commits in attempting (1) and (3), though his imperfect knowledge of natural Greek may betray him in (2) and (4). Secondary Semitisms are said to be those deviations which a " Greek " may let pass in cases (1), (2) and (4) " through such factors as the exigencies of his readers or of the documents he is translating." Another factor is the degree of familiarity which this " Greek " translator has with the Semitic idiom of the source which he is using. This subjective aspect is important, but in many of the points in dispute we cannot say whether the author, or the translator of the source which he is following, is properly to be designated (*a*) or (*b*). We start from the objective data and consider them in their double relationship to Semitic usage, and to the tendencies that appear in the later stages of the development of the Greek language. When all allowance has been made for the coincidence of many Semitic constructions with those found in Hellenistic, the presence of a large number of apparent Semitisms in any writing

[1] *Beginnings of Christianity*, I. ii. 53 ff.

will justify the application of de Zwaan's term "Semiticising Greek." But what criteria will enable us to determine whether this "Semiticising Greek" is due to literal translation, or has found its way into original composition in Greek through inadvertence, or habit, or design? Professor Torrey[1] mentions three methods by which the fact of translation can be demonstrated in a document which resembles an original composition. (1) The precarious evidence of the feeling that certain phrases and constructions "sound Semitic rather than Greek." (2) Mistranslation, *i.e.* the removal of a grave difficulty in the Greek text by the restoration of the Semitic original, which was thus evidently misunderstood or misread by a translator. (3) The cumulative argument based on "the continual presence, in texts of considerable extent, of a Semitic idiom underlying the Greek." But obviously the first and third of these tests will not enable us to distinguish between (2) and (4) in de Zwaan's classification, whether the writer be a "Semite" or a "Greek." Even a translator may by force of habit introduce Semitisms into his Greek when the Hebrew original is quite different, as many examples from the LXX would show. But when once the LXX had become a standard of sacred speech for Hellenistic Jews and proselytes, its idioms would easily find their way into free composition. Dr. H. J. Cadbury[2] very aptly uses the analogy of extempore prayer in public worship, and the use of Biblical language by Bunyan and Lincoln. Torrey writes of the second test, that it is "immensely valuable in the rare cases where it is convincing: there is no other internal proof of translation which is so immediately cogent." Certainly it is a method to be applied with caution, for even Dr. Torrey confesses that "it happens in nine cases out of ten that renewed study of the 'mistranslations' which we have discovered shows us that there was no translation at all, or else that it was quite correct."[3] A striking example of this difficulty is furnished by the *Acts of Thomas*. This work survives in both a Greek and a Syriac text. Here there can be no question that one of these is a translation of the other. But even with the two texts available for comparison, Professor Burkitt finds most of the more obvious lines of argument "double-edged," and points to the "ambiguous nature of much that might have been expected to produce results." "The only way by which we can prove the Greek to be taken from the Syriac is to find instances where the Greek translator has actually mistranslated a Syriac idiom, or has followed a reading which rests upon a palæographical corruption in the Syriac."[4]

It is for this reason that so much importance attaches to such instances of possible mistranslation as are collected in *C* above. Even here, however, we must observe that the Semitists themselves are not in agreement. Dr. Burney, in face of Wellhausen's well-marshalled evidence, declares with regard to Mark, "What is needed to substantiate the theory

---

[1] *C. H. Toy Studies*, 283 ff.

[2] *AJT* xxiv. 453. An instructive contrast can be drawn between the simple Biblical English of John Wesley's published sermons (see p. 9) and the crisp conversational English of his Letters and Journals.

[3] *C. H. Toy Studies*, 284. [4] *JTS* i. 282.

of an Aramaic original is some cogent evidence of mistranslation; and this has not yet been advanced." [1] In the same way Dr. Torrey, who promises to produce such evidence of mistranslation in Mark as Wellhausen failed to give, thinks that the case for John is weaker. "Burney's argument, for all its learning and acumen, weakens at the crucial point. Among those who are inclined to demand in John what Burney demands in Mark, I think the verdict is likely to be 'Not proven.'" [2]

Even when there is the strongest reason to suspect a translator's error, we are often left in doubt whether this is due to a corruption in the original document, to a mistranslation of the original text, or to a linguistic confusion in the writer's mind with no documentary cause at all. Thus in the notorious example referred to by Mr. G. R. Driver, did the translator of Mommsen faithfully reproduce a printer's blunder *Feuerwerk* for *Feuerwehr*, or did he, by some inexplicable confusion, translate *Feuerwehr* by *fireworks*? We know that the book is a translation, and that the context requires *fire-brigade*. Only a reference to the original German edition can settle the point.[3] But such errors occur when there is no documentary explanation. I once heard so perfect a bilinguist as Mr. Hilaire Belloc in a lecture on the French Revolution speak of the "sermon in the tennis court." Though the speaker instantly corrected himself, the audience could recognise at once the confusion between *serment* (oath) and the other French word indistinguishable in sound. There is no more brilliant conjecture in Wellhausen's work on the Gospels than his solution of the difficult *τὰ ἐνόντα δότε ἐλεημοσύνην* (Lk 11^{41}). The sense requires *καθάρισον*, which is actually found in the Matthaean parallel (Mt 23^{26}), and, as we have seen above (p. 471), Wellhausen makes this a moral certainty by restoring the Aramaic. But what inference are we to draw? There are three alternatives. (*a*) Mt and Lk may both have translated from a common Aramaic original, one correctly, the other incorrectly; (*b*) Mt and Lk may have had the same Greek translation, but whilst Mt knew enough Aramaic to correct the mistranslation, Lk faithfully retained it; (*c*) Mt and Lk may have used different editions of a Greek translation of Q. Similarly, if we are convinced that some of the idioms in the Fourth Gospel presuppose Aramaic, we have still the further point to settle, whether there ever was an Aramaic Fourth Gospel, elsewhere than in the mind of the author who wrote directly in Greek. In other words, granted that "John" was a "Semite," to which of de Zwaan's four classes does the Greek Gospel belong?

2. The Semitic Stamp in Translation Greek.

We have seen that Professor Torrey emphasises the importance as also the precariousness of his first test. It is the starting-point in any investigation. Nor is it entirely subjective, for it can be applied, especially where Hebraisms are concerned, by watching the tendencies of

---

[1] *Aram. Orig.* 19. [2] *HTR* xvi. 332.

[3] I have failed to discover the passage.

translators when we know Hebrew originals to underlie the Greek. The comparative study of the LXX with the Hebrew text is invaluable for this purpose, and helps to furnish the list of suspected Semitisms provided by the Oxford Apocrypha in the critical introductions to several of the books. Still more valuable is the evidence which Canon Box gives in his edition of the Ezra-Apocalypse to show that the Latin text preserves a number of Hebrew constructions mediated through a lost Greek text. But if the presence of many such constructions in any one book raises a presumption of translation (or else suggests a deliberate adoption of Semiticising Greek), the absence of such constructions will tell against translation. The Semitic mind of the writer may, however, sometimes betray itself by the repetition of a solitary Semitism,[1] such as the adverbial use of προστίθημι in Josephus (see p. 445). Generally speaking, the presence of numerous Hebraisms will suggest the influence of the LXX, whereas numerous Aramaisms or idioms common to Hebrew and Aramaic will point to a background of Aramaic. With the exception of parts of the Apocalypse and the first two chapters of Luke, it seems hardly likely that Hebrew sources were translated by any of the NT writers.

3. Conditions under which the Gospel Tradition became Fixed.

The four Gospels record events which happened on the soil of Palestine, and preserve the sayings of One whose mother tongue was Aramaic. The primitive Christian tradition was inevitably formulated and transmitted with an Aramaic colouring. The second stage of the Christian movement had Antioch as its headquarters, a bilingual city where this tradition passed over into its Greek form. It was only after evangelists and teachers had carried the Christian message into the world of Hellenism that the *paradosis* was stereotyped in documents. It is hardly open to question that our first and third evangelists drew material from documentary sources, and it is almost certain that these were written in Greek. A factor often overlooked in discussions of the Semitic tinge of the Gospels is the linguistic *milieu* in which the authoritative tradition grew up. Its pre-documentary history lies in a region and a community where there would be a tendency to fit the idioms of the Κοινή as closely as possible to the Aramaic tradition.[2] This was a community in which the OT was not only studied in its authoritative Greek translation, but widely used in the form of *Testimonia*, compiled first in Aramaic, then translated into Greek.[3] The leaders in those formative years when the Church was acquiring a Christian vocabulary and phraseology were men whose habits of thought were Jewish. It is thus not surprising that we

---

[1] I recall a German friend who spent all his boyhood in London, and speaks perfect English but for the German idiom, "I should like to go with" (*Ich möchte gern mitgehen*, omitting the unaccented pronoun "you").

[2] See Schulthess *Das Problem*, pp. 43, 56.

[3] J. Rendel Harris *Testimonies*, i. 125.

find "Semitisms of Vocabulary"[1] in the Pauline letters and in *Hebrews*, where grammatical Semitisms are very rare and purely "secondary."

4. The Several Books.

1. Synoptic Gospels and Acts.

Mark is the most Aramaic of the Gospels. The very few Hebraisms may be attributed to the use of the LXX in the Gentile mission, but they are echoes few and faint. Burney's misgivings have already increased the doubtfulness of Archdeacon Allen's claim that the earliest of our Gospels was originally written in Aramaic. When Dr. Torrey's promised list of mistranslations appears, a good case may be made out for the partial use of Aramaic memoranda. But so far we remain of the opinion so well expressed by Père Lagrange, "His Greek is always Greek, yet translation Greek; not that he translates an Aramaic writing, but because he reproduces an Aramaic κατήχησις."

When we turn to *Matthew* it is perplexing to find these two eminent Aramaists in reverse disagreement, for while Dr. Allen bases his belief, with most scholars, on the demonstrable use of a Greek Mk by the author of the first Gospel, the French commentator argues that our Mt is a translation from an Aramaic original. This is perhaps largely due to the great stress which the Roman Catholic scholar puts upon early Church tradition. But his masterly array of the linguistic data is not convincing, especially when one observes how many of the Aramaisms are found in the teaching of Jesus. It is just in this part of the Gospel that we should look for the Aramaic idiom to emerge, however free the author's Greek elsewhere. There is one point, however, on which the present writer thinks that fresh evidence may modify the judgment passed by Dr. Moulton.[2] Dr. Burney's remarkable study of the parallelism of the sayings of Jesus gives weighty support to Harnack's preference for the Matthaean as the more faithful record of the discourses.[3] Though this is a matter of poetic structure rather than of syntax, it may well be urged that the author of the first Gospel was familiar with Aramaic, and recognised the Semitic form behind the Greek rendering that lay before him.

On two points only is it needful to add anything to what has been written above (pp. 18 ff.), regarding the Lucan books;[4] for the Infancy narratives, and more especially the hymns in Lk 1–2, constitute a special problem, and the theory that we have a translation of an Aramaic docu-

---

[1] See *Proleg.* 11 f., also p. 26 above.

[2] See pp. 10 and 20 above. But in view of Burney's argument it is the more important to re-read Moulton's two *Expositor* articles referred to on p. 10 n.[2].

[3] See *The Poetry of our Lord*, 7.

[4] As a footnote to Moulton's judgment from the Hellenistic side that Luke probably did not speak Aramaic, we add the opinion of a distinguished Aramaist, "Il n'était pas juif de naissance ni d'éducation, et s'il était Syrien d'origine, rien ne prouve que l'araméen ait été sa langue maternelle" (Lagrange *S. Luc* xcvi).

ment throughout Ac 1–15 has entered on a new phase since Dr. Moulton's *Introduction* was left unfinished in 1915.

It may be well to refer to Harnack's thorough investigation of the linguistic phenomena in Lk 1–2,[1] and to quote his emphatic judgment: "The vocabulary and style characteristic of Lk 1–2 are so absolutely Lucan that, in spite of all conjectures that have been made, the hypothesis of a Greek source is impossible, for there is almost nothing left for it. Two things only are possible: either Luke has here translated an Aramaic source, or he was dependent for his subject-matter upon no written source at all, but has followed oral tradition, with which he has dealt quite freely, so far as form is concerned. At all events the two great psalms of Lk 1–2 were not handed down to the author (either in Greek or Aramaic), but were composed by himself." "It is possible that for the narrative an Aramaic source has been used, but this hypothesis is not probable. On closer view the Magnificat and the Benedictus present the form of a single complicated, correctly constructed Greek period that does all honour to the author of the prologue. This period is simply forced into its Hebrew dress. The hands are Esau's hands, but the voice is that of Jacob. But if this is so, then it is plain that Luke in composing these canticles has *purposely* kept to the language of the Psalms and prophets (LXX). The Hebraisms, whether adopted or inserted from the Old Testament, are *intentional*; the whole style is artificial, and is intended to produce an impression of antiquity." Now Professor Torrey[2] will not hear of such deliberate imitation of the language of the LXX, "for the motive for such a grotesque performance on his part is by no means apparent." But he is as convinced as is Harnack that "the Gospel of the Infancy" is by every consideration of vocabulary and style the language of Luke himself. In his judgment the only satisfactory theory is "that the author of the Third Gospel himself translated the Narrative of the Infancy from Hebrew into Greek." The strongest argument for translation from Hebrew, either by Luke or by the translator of his source, is the use of a phrase which does not occur in the LXX and is yet a "translation of the painfully literal kind." The example given by Dr. Torrey is Lk 1^{51}, ἐποίησε κράτος ἐν βραχίονι αὐτοῦ, obviously a rendering of עָשָׂה חַיִל בִּזְרוֹעוֹ "or (less probably) its Aramaic equivalent." But if we examine this verse with care its diction can easily be paralleled from the LXX. Thus, Lk 1^{51}:

ἐποίησεν κράτος ἐν βραχίονι αὐτοῦ,
διεσκόρπισεν ὑπερηφάνους διανοίᾳ καρδίας αὐτῶν.

Cf. Ps 88^{10}:

σὺ ἐταπείνωσας ὡς τραυματίαν ὑπερήφανον,
καὶ ἐν τῷ βραχίονι τῆς δυνάμεώς σου διεσκόρπισας τοὺς ἐχθρούς σου,

and 117^{15}:

δεξιὰ Κυρίου ἐποίησεν δύναμιν.

---

[1] *Luke the Physician*, 96–105, 199–218.

[2] See *C. H. Toy Studies*, 286, 295.

The Hebraic phraseology is beyond question, but there is nothing that lies beyond the range of composition by one who was steeped in the diction of the Greek version of the Psalter.[1]

The theory that the first fifteen chapters of *Acts* are Luke's literal translation of an Aramaic document has been urged with a mass of detailed illustration by Professor Torrey, who claims that his argument is cumulative. We have already considered some of his strongest instances of possible mistranslation, and can only mention here one or two reasons for the failure of this great Semitist to win general consent to his conclusions. Several of the alleged Aramaisms can be paralleled from Paul's letters and other writings in free Greek. Others are found in the second part of Acts, where they are attributed to the influence of the LXX on the writer's style. Others can be paralleled in Luke's Gospel, but not from Mt and Mk, which are declared by Dr. Torrey to be translated directly from the Aramaic. Finally, instances are given of mistranslation although in the same part of the book the correct phrase is found, thus proving that ignorance of the true meaning of the idiom must not be imputed to the author.[2]

2. The Johannine Writings.

The case for an Aramaic original of our *Fourth Gospel* has been greatly strengthened since the editor wrote the sentences on this subject in the Introduction to this volume (p. 32). It was but natural to rely upon the great authority of Wellhausen, as Dr. Torrey[3] has generously allowed. But Dr. Burney's masterly work has proved convincingly the Semitic cast of mind of the author. His attempt to prove that the Gospel was written in Aramaic by one man, and translated into Greek by another, has not carried the same conviction. The decisive factor in the establishment of such a theory is a few instances of almost certain mistranslation. Now, as we have seen above (p. 474), Dr. Burney has furnished us with several plausible examples, but it is significant that such highly competent Semitists as Père Lagrange and Mr. G. R. Driver recognise that even the most difficult passage can be understood without recourse to this kind of treatment. Moreover, the most impressive evidence which is offered for the confusion of the particles ἵνα and ὅτι with the relative loses much of its force when this same tendency is found to be increasingly prevalent in the later stages of the Greek language. The weakness of Dr. Burney's case is that he has not allowed for the coincidence of many of the Aramaic constructions found in the Greek of the Fourth Gospel with usages that were equally common in the colloquial Greek of that period. It is only to be expected that one whose

[1] A striking feature of the Third Gospel is, to use a phrase of Lagrange's, the "nests of Semitisms" which we meet with here and there in Lk.

[2] All these statements are exemplified in Dr. H. J. Cadbury's searching examination of Professor Torrey's contention: see *Luke: Translator or Author?* (*AJT* xxiv. 436–455).

[3] *HTR* xvi. 324.

native tongue was Aramaic would tend to fall into those forms of speech when writing Greek which most closely resembled his own idiom. Again, when we notice how many of the Aramaisms are found in passages that profess to record the actual words of Jesus, we may well suppose that John "was mentally translating, as he wrote, *logia* handed down by tradition and current in Christian circles in Aramaic, from that language into the Greek in which he was actually composing his Gospel."[1] Finally, it is only right to point out that Dr. Torrey, who is entirely with Burney in his main contention, disagrees with all his attempts at the recovery of a mistranslated original. The same might almost be said of Dalman's verdict.[2] A written Aramaic original is therefore by no means established.

The Hebraic style of many passages in *Revelation* was made clear by Archdeacon Charles in his *Studies in the Apocalypse* (see p. 33 above). Since the closing page of the Introduction to the present volume was written nine years ago, Dr. Charles's incomparable edition of the Apocalypse has appeared, with a wealth of material for those who study the grammar of this book.

The solution of the tangled problem of the language of the Apocalypse is said to be this: (*a*) The author writes in Greek, but thinks in Hebrew; (*b*) he has taken over some Greek sources already translated from the Hebrew; (*c*) he has himself translated and adapted some Hebrew sources. The instances of mistranslation corrected by retroversion which have been given above go some way to proving the third statement, though they might still better come under the second heading. One ventures to wonder whether the first assertion has been made good. The writer's familiarity with Hebrew seems to lie beyond question, but why should not Aramaic be his mother-tongue, the language in which his thoughts would first frame themselves? Many of the peculiarities of idiom, such as the use of the resumptive pronoun after a relative, the co-ordination of a participle with a finite verb, the *casus pendens*, might betray an Aramaic cast of sentence. It is also noteworthy that several of the instances of the very free use of *ἵνα* in the Fourth Gospel can be paralleled in Revelation. All of these come within the range of late Greek usage, and show that the writer was more familiar with the vernacular than with literary models, and naturally adopted such locutions as he found most in accord with his Semitic habit of speech. But we are convinced that more importance should be allowed to the influence of the LXX. One instance must suffice. We have already referred to Dr. Charles's acute perception of the Hebraic idiom behind the crux in 12⁷. But why should ל c. inf. in Hebr. be rendered by *τοῦ* c. inf. by one who has to give a desperately literal transla-

[1] G. R. Driver *The Original Language of the Fourth Gospel*, 1 n. (This reprint from *The Jewish Guardian* is the most complete and competent criticism of Dr. Burney's thesis that has yet appeared.)

[2] *ThLZ*, xlviii. 8. "Die angenommenen Uebersetzungsfehler, von denen oben nur eine Auswahl mitgeteilt wurde, sind nicht zwingender Natur."

tion? He might have used εἰς τό c. inf. Dr. Charles himself shows that at Hos 9^{13} the LXX translates the same idiom in precisely the same way.[1] Is it not likely that one who was trying to write in Greek, a language with which he was not perfectly familiar, would prepare himself for the sacred task of declaring his heavenly message by studying the revelation of bygone seers, not only in the sacred tongue of the Hebrews, but also in the version which was hallowed as the Bible of the Greek-speaking Dispersion and of the Gentile Christian Church? We therefore think that the material supplied in Dr. Charles's great commentary would justify us in finding a solution of the linguistic problem in a combination of factors: (*a*) a mind that thought in Aramaic and found in the vernacular Greek of his world many idioms sufficiently close to his mother-tongue for his purpose; (*b*) sources in translated Greek and in Hebrew, which he worked into his book in Hebraic Greek; (*c*) a knowledge of the LXX and of various apocalypses already current in a Greek form, which supplied him with a vocabulary and often suggested an idiom.[2]

Of the remaining books of the New Testament there is little to add to what has already been said in the Introduction. Those who think that Paul's amanuensis or colleague, who was allowed a freer hand in the composition of *Ephesians* than of any other letter, was deeply under the Hebraic influence of the LXX, will find a few additions to the data offered on p. 22. Secondary Hebraisms may be discovered in Eph 1^{3} εὐλογήσας ἐν πάσῃ εὐλογίᾳ. Apart from the use of ἐν, we are reminded of the group of pleonasms in this Epistle to which Dr. Rendel Harris has called attention (p. 419). An unidiomatic use of the genitive of definition may perhaps be termed the Hebraic genitive in 1^{14} τῷ πνεύματι τῆς ἐπαγγελίας ("the promised Spirit") and 4^{22} τὰς ἐπιθυμίας τῆς ἀπάτης ("deceitful lusts"). The breathless sentence which spans the second half of chapter 1 is built after no Hebrew model, yet a keen eye may possibly detect Dr. Charles's construction (see pp. 34 and 429) in 1^{22} ἐγείρας αὐτὸν . . . καὶ καθίσας . . . καὶ πάντα ὑπέταξεν. The next line shows us ἔδωκεν (clearly נָתַן, cf. 4^{11}). Yet another secondary Hebraism may lurk in the phrase (6^{19}) ἐν ἀνοίξει τοῦ στόματός μου (בְּ c. infin. "when I open . . ."). We have already seen (p. 453) that exegesis is against treating the participle as otiose in 2^{17} ἐλθὼν εὐηγγελίσατο. Nor does there seem good reason for agreeing with Guillemard that μαρτύρομαι ἐν Κυρίῳ (4^{17}) is the familiar הִשְׁבַּע בְּ. Rather is it analogous to Paul's παρακαλοῦμεν ἐν κυρίῳ Ἰησοῦ (1 Th 4^{1}) and to the words in Rom 16^{22}, with which another Tertius would now bring his pious duty to a close, ἀσπάζομαι ὑμᾶς ἐγὼ Τέρτιος ὁ γράψας τὴν ἐπιστολὴν ἐν Κυρίῳ.

---

[1] For further exx. of τοῦ c. inf. as common LXX equivalent for לְ c. inf. in Hebr., see p. 449 above.

[2] For a rather different explanation of the language of the Apocalypse, see Lohmeyer's recent commentary, *HNT* IV. iv. 193 ff.

I. INDEX TO QUOTATIONS.

(*a*) New Testament.

LUKE—*continued*

LUKE—*continued*

LUKE—*continued*

(b) Old Testament.

N.B.—The numbering of the chapters is according to the English Bible; where the LXX differs, the numbers are added in brackets. So with titles of Books.

(*c*) Apocrypha and Pseudepigrapha of Old Testament.

(*d*) Early Christian Writings.

Clement of Rome (i/A.D.)

Ignatius (ii/A.D.)

Didache (ii/A.D.)

(*e*) Inscriptions and Ostraca.

Cagnat

Inscriptiones Graecae ad Res Romanas pertinentes, ed. R. Cagnat (Paris 1911–).

	PAGE		PAGE		PAGE
i. p. 26 (no. 41)	79	iii. p. 75 (no. 159)	437	iii. p. 427 (no. 1145)	70

GDI

Sammlung der griechischen Dialektinschriften, ed. H. Collitz and F. Bechtel, (Göttingen, 1884–).

2561 D47 . . 277

IG

Inscriptiones Graecae, ed. cons. et auct. Acad. Regiae Borussicae (Berlin, 1873–).

IGSI (=**IG** vol. xiv.)

Inscriptiones Graecae Siciliae et Italiae, ed. G. Kaibel (Berlin, 1890).

no. 966 . . 79 | no. 1671 . . 349

IMAe (=**IG** vol. xii.)

i. 406	106	iii. 248	127	v. 653	86
iii. 168	178	iii. 525, 526	124		

JHS

Journal of Hellenic Studies (Hellenic Society).

iv. 385 . . 126

Kaibel

Epigrammata Graeca ex lapidibus conlecta, ed. G. Kaibel (Berlin, 1878).

no. 426 . . 140

Larfield

Handbuch der Epigraphik, W. Larfeld (Leipzig, i. 1907, ii. 1902).

i. 16 . . . 174

Letr.

Recueil des inscriptions grecques et latines de l'Égypte, ed. M. Letronne (Paris, i. 1842, ii. 1848).

i. 12 . . . 91 | i. 525 . . 189

Magn.

Die Inschriften von Magnesia am Maeander, ed. O. Kern (Berlin, 1900).

no. 17 . . 195 | no. 47 . . 195

OGIS

Orientis Graeci Inscriptiones Selectae, ed. W. Dittenberger (Leipzig, 1903–5).

no. 193	66	no. 201	202, 380, 425	no. 214	200
194	90				

Perg.

Die Inschriften von Pergamon (in *Altertümer von Pergamon*, viii.), ed. M. Fränkel (Berlin, 1900).

no. 248 . . 72

Preisigke, Sammelbuch

Sammelbuch griechischer Urkunden aus Ägypten, ed. F. Preisigke (Strassburg, 1915–).

	PAGE		PAGE		PAGE
no. 1323	264	no. 1540	154		

PAS

Papers of American School of Classical Studies at Athens (Boston).

iii. 204 . . . 177

Ramsay, C. and B.

Cities and Bishoprics of Phrygia, by W. M. Ramsay, 2 vols. (Oxford, 1895, 1897).

ii. p. 662 (no. 627) 272 | ii. p. 565 (no. 466) 460

REGr.

Revue des Études grecques (Paris, 1888 ff.).

xviii. 205 . . . 127

Syll.

Sylloge Inscriptionum Graecarum, ed. W. Dittenberger (Leipzig, ed. 2, 1898–1901, ed. 3, 1915–1924).

ed.[2]	(=ed.[3])		ed.[2]	(=ed.[3])		ed.[2]	(ed.[3])	
177	344	66, 200	596	1011	178	737	1109	101, 467
493	722	178	598	1012	178	757	1125	154
583	996	73, 307	615	1024	299	803	1169	83
588	om.	328	641	1044	386	805	1171	132
594	1009	178				901	1251	108

Viereck SG

Sermo Graecus quo Senatus Populusque Romanus . . . usi sunt, by P. Viereck (Göttingen, 1888).

p. 16 . . . 199

Meyer Ostr.

Ostraka der Sammlung Deissmann, ed. P. M. Meyer in *Griechische Texte aus Ägypten* (Berlin, 1916).

no. 57 . . . 380

Preisigke Ostr.

Die Prinz-Joachim-Ostraka, edd. F. Preisigke and W. Spielenberg (Strassburg, 1914).

no. 15 . . . 114

Wilcken Ostr.

Griechische Ostraka, ed. U. Wilcken (2 vols. Leipzig, 1899).

i. 190	306	i. 493	339	ii. 1089	73
i. 255	339	ii. 1084	73		

Mélanges Nicole

Recueil de Mémoires de Philologie, Classique et d'Archéologie offerts à Jules Nicole (Geneva, 1905).

p. 184 . . . 102 | p. 185 . . . 210

(*f*) Papyri.

N.B.—For the references given in brackets, see pp. 511 f. of this Index. Wilcken and Mitteis's *Chrestomathie* is cited by volume and page.

P Amh

The Amherst Papyri, i. ii., ed. B. P. Grenfell and A. S. Hunt (London, 1900–1).

Archiv (see under (*e*) above)

BGU

Ägyptische Urkunden aus den königlichen (staatlichen) Museen zu Berlin: Griechische Urkunden i.–vii. (Berlin, 1895–1926) Vol. i. nos. 1–361 (1895).

Vol. ii. nos. 362–696 (1898).

Vol. iii. nos. 697–1012 (1903).

Vol. iv. nos. 1013–1209 (1912).

P Catt

P. Cattoui, ed. G. Botti in *Revista Egiziana*, vi. 529 ff. See *Chr.* ii. 420 ff.

CP Herm

Corpus Papyrorum Hermopolitanorum, i., ed. C. Wessely (Leipzig, 1905).

P Par

Paris Papyri, in *Notices et Extraits*, xviii. part 2, ed. Brunet de Presle (1865).

P Par 574

The Paris Magical Papyrus, ed. C. Wessely, in *Denkschriften der philosophisch-historischen Classe der kaiserlichen Academie der Wissenschaften zu Wien*, xxxvi. (1888), pp. 75 ff. (= Wessely, *Zauberpap.*).

ii. *Hellenistic.*

(*h*) Latin.

II. INDEX OF WORDS AND FORMS.

(*a*) Greek.

(b) Modern Greek.

(c) Hebrew and Aramaic.

[See pp. 143 ff., 152 ff., for Greek spelling and inflexion of Semitic words, also pp. 470–477 for retroversion of difficult readings into Aramaic or Hebrew.]

III. INDEX OF SUBJECTS.